BEFORE THE LAW

BEFORE THE LAW

An Introduction to the Legal Process

SECOND EDITION

John J. Bonsignore

Ethan Katsh

Peter d'Errico

Ronald M. Pipkin

Stephen Arons

Janet Rifkin

Legal Studies Program
The University of Massachusetts at Amherst

Houghton Mifflin Company · Boston
Dallas · Geneva, Ill. · Hopewell, N.J. · Palo Alto · London

To the students and teachers of legal studies and to Col. Claude Shepard, Jr., whose tremendous personal effort and energy are so essential to making our work possible.

Printed in the U.S.A.

Library of Congress Catalog Card Number: 78-69606

ISBN: 0-395-27514-8

CONTENTS

The Prisons, etching by Giovanni B. Piranesi, courtesy Museum of Fine Arts, Boston.

PREFACE

Before the Law stands a doorkeeper. To this door-keeper there comes a man from the country who begs for admittance to the Law. But the doorkeeper says that he cannot admit the man at the moment. The man, on reflection, asks if he will be allowed, then, to enter later. "It is possible," answers the door-keeper, "but not at the moment." Since the door leading into the Law stands open as usual and the doorkeeper steps to one side, the man bends down to peer through the entrance. When the doorkeeper sees that, he laughs and says: "If you are so strongly tempted, try to get in without my permission. But note that I am powerful. And I am only the lowest doorkeeper. From hall to hall, keepers stand at every door, one more powerful than the other. And the sight of the third man is already more than even I can stand." These are difficulties which the man from the country has not expected to meet. The Law, he thinks, should be accessible to every man and at all times, but when he looks more closely at the doorkeeper in his furred robe, with his huge pointed nose and long thin Tartar beard, he decides that he had better wait until he gets permission to enter. The doorkeeper gives him a stool and lets him sit down at the side of the door. There he sits wait-ing for days and years. He makes many attempts to be allowed in and wearies the doorkeeper with his importunity. The doorkeeper often engages him in brief conversation, asking him about his home and about other matters, but the questions are put quite impersonally, as great men put questions, and always conclude with the statement that the man cannot be allowed to enter yet. The man, who has equipped himself with many things for his journey, parts with all he has, however valuable, in the hope of bribing the doorkeeper. The doorkeeper accepts it all, say-ing, however, as he takes each gift: "I take this only to keep you from feeling that you have left something undone." During all these long years the man watches the doorkeeper almost incessantly. He forgets about the other doorkeepers, and this one seems to him the only barrier between himself and the Law. In the

first years he curses his evil fate aloud; later, as he grows old, he only mutters to himself. He grows childish, and since in his prolonged study of the doorkeeper he has learned to know even the fleas in his fur collar, he begs the very fleas to help him and to persuade the doorkeeper to change his mind. Fi-nally his eyes grow dim and he does not know whether the world is really darkening around him or whether his eyes are only deceiving him. But in the darkness he can now perceive a radiance that streams inextinguishably from the door of the Law. Now his life is drawing to a close. Before he dies, all that he has experienced during the whole time of his sojourn condenses in his mind into one question, which he has never yet put to the doorkeeper. He beckons the doorkeeper, since he can no longer raise his stiffening body. The doorkeeper has to bend far down to hear him, for the difference in size between them has increased very much to the man's dis-advantage. "What do you want to know now?" asks the doorkeeper, "you are insatiable." "Everyone strives to attain the Law," answers the man, "how does it come about, then, that in all these years no one has come seeking admittance but me?" The doorkeeper perceives that the man is nearing his end and his hearing is failing, so he bellows in his ear: "No one but you could gain admittance through this door, since this door was intended for you. I am now going to shut it."

Franz Kafka, *The Trial* *

Kafka's parable, like other great literature, speaks to all that is fundamental in human life —one's feeble understanding of oneself, one's relationship to others, and one's place in the Universe. Taking only one thread of this intense existential message, the relationship of people to law, what does the parable tell us?

The man from the country is a believer in law. He expects a system that is designed for his benefit, but he is thwarted when he invokes what he believes to be his right; he finds law inaccessible, befuddling, and outright cruel. Had he known better, would he have abandoned his efforts as fruitless? Probably not. Was he forceful enough in seeking admittance to the law? Did he fail to enter because of his own guilt or fear? Perhaps. He seeks justice but it seems to transcend him. His relationships with others are his hope, but his interactions with others also produce his grief. The quest for justice spawns the institution of law, but law, in its operation, undermines the very purpose for which it is created.

These contradictions in life and the tensions between individuals and institutions are ever present in contemporary society.

Like Kafka's hero, all people stand in some relationship to the institution of law. The complexity of this relationship is a fundamental theme of this book. All people yearn for a system of law that is "accessible to every man and at all times." Yet, all people also know that law can be an impenetrable thicket to be avoided if at all possible and wonder, with Swift, "how it should come to pass, that the law which was intended for every man's preservation, should be any man's ruin."

What is law? Nearly every person has thought of at least a one- or two-line statement of the nature and functions of law. Examples of such statements would include the following:

1. Law consists of rules and regulations of the state for the governance of society.

2. Law protects what is of value in society.

3. Law is a means to make society run more smoothly through the recognition and securing of rights.

4. Law is whatever the people want it to be.

5. Law is a means of oppression—it is designed to preserve the economic, political, and social position of the haves at the expense of the have-nots.

6. It's who you know—let's face it, the law is what judges, lawyers, and police say it is.

Despite the rich possibilities for critical inquiry that these sketches might inspire, law study until comparatively recently has been almost exclusively concerned with professional training. Now, fortunately, there has been an awakening to the idea that in a democratic society study about law and legal process is just as fundamental as study about economics, history, or physics.

The upswing of interest in law by students from every department of the university has made development of new materials for study mandatory. It is not enough to demonstrate what would-be business people, writers, engineers, or hotel-keepers need to know to use law. What is needed is to answer the first questions all persons have about law and to explore the fundamental significance of law in society.

There is no one correct way to approach this awesome challenge, but we believe that most first thoughts about law concern actors in the legal system—judges, police, lawyers, jurors, jailers, and so on. There is also a recognition that law has a central importance in shaping values, hence, the high sentiment from people of all political persuasions about such issues as law and order, drugs, sexual preference, abortion, environmental pollution, and so on.

We have tried to preserve the best of the first edition while making some logical extensions —a new Chapter 5 on prisons and an extensive Chapter 6 on law in a variety of social contexts. Some thirty percent of the material is new and introduces emerging issues in bioethics and contemporary penology. The transdisciplinary orientation of the first edition has been deepened, while materials normally found in introductory law texts, such as cases, have been expanded. We hope that a variety of scholar-teachers who might be at the edge of their own disciplines will see law as a useful vehicle for the study of contemporary society.

The chapters can be taken in various order. Some teachers may choose to start with the broad issues raised by the material in the last chapter; others may prefer to provide their own framework for organizing the material. We share the sentiment of C. S. Lewis who said about books:

> It is impossible that we should ever know the whole meaning of our own works. And the meaning we never intended may be the best and truest one. Writing a book is much less like creation than it is like planting a garden or begetting a child; in all three cases we are only entering as one cause into a causal stream which works, so to speak, in its own way.

It may come as no surprise that the six authors of this book have never used it identically. Doris Lessing, speaking in the same vein as C. S. Lewis provides an out: "(T)he book is alive and potent and fructifying and able to promote thought and discussion only when its plan and intention are not understood, because that moment of seeing the shape and plan and intention is also the moment when there isn't any more to be got out of it." To the extent that textbooks approach this literary goal, they have some chance of becoming a more engaging genre.

We have some fresh acknowledgments for help especially associated with this edition. We had very thoughtful internal reviews of the first edition from James Gibson of the University of Wisconsin-Milwaukee, Stephen Halpern of the State University of New York at Buffalo, William Vanderpool of Appalachian State University, and Arthur Wolfe of Michigan State University.

We also want to acknowledge the help of Judi Gleit and Claude Shepard who are on our staff at the University of Massachusetts Legal Studies Program.

Needless to say, we would not have made it to a second edition without the response of teachers and students of legal studies who used our materials and suggested new possibilities for this edition.

J.J.B.
E.K.
P.d'E.
R.M.P.
S.A.
J.R.

The University of Massachusetts
  at Amherst

BEFORE THE LAW

A Scholar in His Study Watching a Magic Disk, etching by Rembrandt van Ryn; National Gallery of Art, Washington, D.C., gift of R. Horace Gallatin.

They tell you out at the Law School that the law is a wonderful science—the perfection of reason. 'Tis in fact a hodge-podge of Roman law, Bible texts, canon law, superstitions, scraps of feudalism, crazy fictions, and long dead statutes. Your professors try to bring order out of chaos and make sense where the devil himself couldn't find any.

Ephraim Tutt, *Yankee Lawyer*, 1944

Political philosophies are intellectual and moral creations; they contain high ideals, easy slogans, dubious facts, crude propaganda, sophisticated theories. Their adherents select some facts and ignore others, urge the acceptance of ideals, the inevitability of events, argue with this theory and debunk that one.

C. Wright Mills

All logical systems, East-West, scientific-religious, cyclic or linear, originate in an analysis of the way reality is structured.

J. Pearce

chapter one

A Theoretical Overview

Definitions of law are statements of belief akin to political philosophies, articles of faith in religion, or intuition in science. The person who defines has a flash of genius, and all of the legal universe falls momentarily into place. Once a definition is reached, events are shaped to fit the definition, and what is at first only a psychic reality becomes a reality "out there" as well. It is this phenomenon that makes definitions so important and yet so dangerous;

3

they provide concentrated explanations of the legal world but also foreclose possibilities that are disruptive of the definition.

Law as a system of thought is only one of many possible structures of reality. As with other systems of thought, model precedes rather than follows data—map often both precedes and supersedes territory itself. Put a different way, conventional wisdom says that we see what exists. Unconventional wisdom says that we see what we are taught to see, or that we see what we instruct ourselves to see, or that we see what we let ourselves instruct ourselves to see.

One of the purposes of an introductory law text is to enrich the ways that people view law. To accomplish this, it is desirable to demonstrate at the start that there are alternative ways of looking at law, that people can teach themselves to see alternatives to the existing legal order, and that the act of teaching and learning will involve breaking down stereotypical thinking and will also offer constructive possibilities.

What is needed, therefore, at the outset is a reading that shows how models of thinking affect perception. Incoming students, while they say that they know nothing about law and that the lack of knowledge of law is the very reason for their taking an introductory law course, in fact have models of law and expectations that can be traced to television, newspapers, personal experiences, family history, and other sources. This incoming knowledge both interferes with and facilitates new learning.

If one of the central problems in law study lies with the arrangement of personal knowledge and the way that our culture structures the acquisition of knowledge, we need a case in point to bring this idea home—"Assembly Line."

Assembly Line *B. Traven*

Mr. E. L. Winthrop of New York was on vacation in the Republic of Mexico. It wasn't long before he realized that this strange and really wild country had not yet been fully and satisfactorily explored by Rotarians and Lions, who are forever conscious of their glorious mission on earth. Therefore, he considered it his duty as a good American citizen to do his part in correcting this oversight.

In search for opportunities to indulge in his new avocation, he left the beaten track and ventured into regions not especially mentioned, and hence not recommended, by travel agents to foreign tourists. So it happened that one day he found himself in a little, quaint Indian village somewhere in the State of Oaxaca.

Walking along the dusty main street of this pueblecito, which knew nothing of pavements, drainage, plumbing, or of any means of artificial light save candles or pine splinters, he met with an Indian squatting on the earthen-floor front porch of a palm hut, a so-called jacalito.

The Indian was busy making little baskets from bast and from all kinds of fibers gathered by him in the immense tropical bush which surrounded the village on all sides. The material used had not only been well prepared for its purpose but was also richly colored with dyes that the basket-maker himself extracted from various native plants, barks, roots and from certain insects by a process known only to him and the members of his family.

His principal business, however, was not producing baskets. He was a peasant who lived on what the small property he possessed—less than fifteen acres of not too fertile soil—would yield, after much sweat and labor and after constantly worrying over the most wanted and best suited distribution of rain, sunshine, and wind and the changing balance of birds and insects beneficial or harmful to his crops. Baskets he made when there was nothing else for him to do in the fields, because he was unable to dawdle. After all, the sale of his baskets, though to a rather limited degree only, added to the small income he received from his little farm.

In spite of being by profession just a plain peasant, it was clearly seen from the small baskets he made that at heart he was an artist, a true and accomplished artist. Each basket looked as if covered all over with the most beautiful sometimes fantastic ornaments, flowers, butterflies, birds, squirrels, antelope, tigers, and a score of other animals of the wilds. Yet, the most amazing thing was that these decorations, all of them symphonies of color, were not painted on the baskets but were instead actually part of the baskets themselves. Bast and fibers dyed in dozens of different colors were so cleverly—one must actually say intrinsically—interwoven that those attractive designs appeared on the inner part of the basket as well as on the outside. Not by painting but by weaving were those highly artistic effects achieved. This performance he accomplished without ever looking at any sketch or pattern. While working on a basket these designs came to light as if by magic, and as long as a basket was not entirely finished one could not perceive what in this case or that the decoration would be like.

People in the market town who bought these baskets would use them for sewing baskets or to decorate tables with or window sills, or to hold little things to keep them from lying around. Women put their jewelry in them or flowers or little dolls. There were in fact a hundred and two ways they might serve certain purposes in a household or in a lady's own room.

Whenever the Indian had finished about twenty of the baskets he took them to town on market day. Sometimes he would already be on his way shortly after midnight because he owned only a burro to ride on, and if the burro had gone astray the day before, as happened frequently, he would have to walk the whole way to town and back again.

At the market he had to pay twenty centavos in taxes to sell his wares. Each basket cost him between twenty and thirty hours of constant work, not counting the time spent gathering bast and fibers, preparing them, making dyes and coloring the bast. All this meant extra time and work. The price he asked for each basket was fifty centavos, the equivalent of about four cents. It seldom happened, however, that a buyer paid outright the full fifty centavos asked—or four reales as the Indian called that money. The prospective buyer started bargaining, telling the Indian that he ought to be ashamed to ask such a sinful price. "Why, the whole dirty thing is nothing but ordinary petate straw which you find in heaps wherever you may look for it; the jungle is packed full of it," the buyer would argue. "Such a little basket, what's it good for anyhow? If I paid you, you thief, ten centavitos for it you should be grateful and kiss my hand. Well, it's your lucky day, I'll be generous this time, I'll pay you twenty, yet not one green centavo more. Take it or run along."

So he sold finally for twenty-five centavos, but then the buyer would say, "Now, what do you think of that? I've got only twenty centavos change on me. What can we do about that? If you can change me a twenty-peso bill, all right, you shall have your twenty-five fierros." Of course, the Indian could not change a twenty-peso bill and so the basket went for twenty centavos.

He had little if any knowledge of the outside world or he would have known that what happened to him was happening every hour of every day to every artist all over the world. That knowledge would perhaps have made him very proud, because he would have realized that he belonged to the little army which is the salt of the earth and which keeps culture, urbanity and beauty for their own sake from passing away.

Often it was not possible for him to sell all the baskets he had brought to market, for people here as elsewhere in the world preferred things made by the millions and each so much like the other that you were unable, even with the help of a magnifying glass, to tell which was which and where was the difference between two of the same kind.

Yet he, this craftsman, had in his life made several hundreds of those exquisite baskets, but so far no two of them had he ever turned out alike in design. Each was an individual piece of art and as different from the other as was a Murillo from a Velásquez.

Naturally he did not want to take those baskets which he could not sell at the market place home with him again if he could help it. In such a case he went peddling his products from door to door where he was treated partly as a beggar and partly as a vagrant apparently looking for an opportunity to steal, and he frequently had to swallow all sorts of insults and nasty remarks.

Then, after a long run, perhaps a woman would finally stop him, take one of the baskets and offer him ten centavos, which price through talks and talks would perhaps go up to fifteen or even to twenty. Nevertheless, in many instances he would actually get no more than just ten centavos, and the buyer, usually a woman, would grasp that little marvel and right before his eyes throw it carelessly upon the nearest table as if to say, "Well, I take that piece of nonsense only for charity's sake. I know my money is wasted. But then, after all, I'm a Christian and I can't see a poor Indian die of hunger since he has come such a long way from his village." This would remind her of something better and she would hold him and say, "Where are you at home anyway, Indito? What's your pueblo? So, from Huehuetonoc? Now, listen here, Indito, can't you bring me next Saturday two or three turkeys from Huehuetonoc? But they must be heavy and fat and very, very cheap or I won't even touch them. If I wish to pay the regular price I don't need you to bring them. Understand? Hop along, now, Indito."

The Indian squatted on the earthen floor in the portico of his hut, attended to his work and showed no special interest in the curiosity of Mr. Winthrop watching him. He acted almost as if he ignored the presence of the American altogether.

"How much that little basket, friend?" Mr. Winthrop asked when he felt that he at least had to say something as not to appear idiotic.

"Fifty centavitos, patroncito, my good little lordy, four reales," the Indian answered politely.

"All right, sold," Mr. Winthrop blurted out in a tone and with a wide gesture as if he had bought a whole railroad. And examining his buy he added, "I know already who I'll give that pretty little thing to. She'll kiss me for it, sure. Wonder what she'll use it for?"

He had expected to hear a price of three or even four pesos. The moment he realized that he had judged the value six times too high, he saw right away what great business possibilities this miserable Indian village might offer to a dynamic promoter like himself. Without further delay he started exploring those possibilities. "Suppose, my good friend, I buy ten of these little baskets of yours which, as I might as well admit right here and now, have practically no real use whatsoever. Well, as I was saying, if I buy ten, how much would you then charge me apiece?"

The Indian hesitated for a few seconds as if making calculations. Finally he said, "If you buy ten I can let you have them for forty-five centavos each, señorito gentleman."

"All right, amigo. And now, let's suppose I buy from you straight away one hundred of these absolutely useless baskets, how much will cost me each?"

The Indian, never fully looking up to the American standing before him, and hardly taking his eyes off his work, said politely and without the slightest trace of enthusiasm in his voice, "In such a case I might not be quite unwilling to sell each for forty centavitos."

Mr. Winthrop bought sixteen baskets, which was all the Indian had in stock.

After three weeks' stay in the Republic, Mr. Winthrop was convinced that he knew this country perfectly, that he had seen everything and knew all about the inhabitants, their character and their way of life, and that there was nothing left for him to explore. So he returned to good old Nooyorg and felt happy to be once more in a civilized country, as he expressed it to himself.

One day going out for lunch he passed a confectioner's and, looking at the display in the window, he suddenly remembered the little baskets he had bought in that faraway Indian village.

He hurried home and took all the baskets he still had left to one of the best-known candy-makers in the city.

"I can offer you here," Mr. Winthrop said to the confectioner, "one of the most artistic and at the same time the most original of boxes, if you wish to call them that. These little baskets would be just right for the most expensive chocolates meant for elegant and high-priced gifts. Just have a good look at them, sir, and let me listen."

The confectioner examined the baskets and found them extraordinarily well suited for a certain line in his business. Never before had there been anything like them for originality, prettiness and good taste. He, however, avoided most carefully showing any sign of enthusiasm, for which there would be time enough once he knew the price and whether he could get a whole load exclusively.

He shrugged his shoulders and said, "Well, I don't know. If you asked me I'd say it isn't quite what I'm after. However, we might give it a try. It depends, of course, on the price. In our business the package mustn't cost more than what's in it."

"Do I hear an offer?" Mr. Winthrop asked.

"Why don't you tell me in round figures how much you want for them? I'm not good in guessing."

"Well, I'll tell you, Mr. Kemple: since I'm the smart guy who discovered these baskets and since I'm the only Jack who knows where to lay his hands on more, I'm selling to the highest bidder, on an exclusive basis, of course. I'm positive you can see it my way, Mr. Kemple."

"Quite so, and may the best man win," the confectioner said. "I'll talk the matter over with my partners. See me tomorrow same time, please, and I'll let you know how far we might be willing to go."

Next day when both gentlemen met again Mr. Kemple said: "Now, to be frank with you, I know art on seeing it, no getting around that. And these baskets are little works of art, they surely are. However, we are no art dealers, you realize that of course. We've no other use for these pretty little things except as fancy packing

for our French pralines made by us. We can't pay for them what we might pay considering them pieces of art. After all to us they're only wrappings. Fine wrappings, perhaps, but nevertheless wrappings. You'll see it our way I hope, Mr.——oh yes, Mr. Winthrop. So, here is our offer, take it or leave it: a dollar and a quarter apiece and not one cent more."

Mr. Winthrop made a gesture as if he had been struck over the head.

The confectioner, misunderstanding this involuntary gesture of Mr. Winthrop, added quickly, "All right, all right, no reason to get excited, no reason at all. Perhaps we can do a trifle better. Let's say one-fifty."

"Make it one-seventy-five," Mr. Winthrop snapped, swallowing his breath while wiping his forehead.

"Sold. One-seventy-five apiece free at port of New York. We pay the customs and you pay the shipping. Right?"

"Sold," Mr. Winthrop said also and the deal was closed.

"There is, of course, one condition," the confectioner explained just when Mr. Winthrop was to leave. "One or two hundred won't do for us. It wouldn't pay the trouble and the advertising. I won't consider less than ten thousand, or one thousand dozens if that sounds better in your ears. And they must come in no less than twelve different patterns well assorted. How about that?"

"I can make it sixty different patterns or designs."

"So much the better. And you're sure you can deliver ten thousand let's say early October?"

"Absolutely," Mr. Winthrop avowed and signed the contract.

Practically all the way back to Mexico, Mr. Winthrop had a notebook in his left hand and a pencil in his right and he was writing figures, long rows of them, to find out exactly how much richer he would be when this business had been put through.

"Now, let's sum up the whole goddamn thing," he muttered to himself. "Damn it, where is that cursed pencil again? I had it right between my fingers. Ah, there it is. Ten thousand he ordered. Well, well, there we got a clean-cut profit of fifteen thousand four hundred and forty genuine dollars. Sweet smackers. Fifteen grand right into papa's pocket. Come to think of it, that Republic isn't so backward after all."

"Buenas tardes, mi amigo, how are you?" he greeted the Indian whom he found squatting in the porch of his jacalito as if he had never moved from his place since Mr. Winthrop had left for New York.

The Indian rose, took off his hat, bowed politely and said in his soft voice, "Be welcome, patroncito. Thank you, I feel fine, thank you. Muy buenas tardes. This house and all I have is at your kind disposal." He bowed once more, moved his right hand in a gesture of greeting and sat down again. But he excused himself for doing so by saying, "Perdoneme, patroncito, I have to take advantage of the daylight, soon it will be night."

"I've got big business for you, my friend," Mr. Winthrop began.

"Good to hear that, señor."

Mr. Winthrop said to himself, "Now, he'll jump up and go wild when he learns what I've got for him." And aloud he said: "Do you think you can make me one thousand of these little baskets?"

"Why not, patroncito? If I can make sixteen, I can make one thousand also."

"That's right, my good man. Can you also make five thousand?"

"Of course, señor. I can make five thousand if I can make one thousand."

"Good. Now, if I should ask you to make me ten thousand, what would you say? And what would be the price of each? You can make ten thousand, can't you?"

"Of course, I can, señor. I can make as many as you wish. You see, I am an expert in this sort of work. No one else in the whole state can make them the way I do."

"That's what I thought and that's exactly why I came to you."

"Thank you for the honor, patroncito."

"Suppose I order you to make me ten thousand of these baskets, how much time do you think you would need to deliver them?"

The Indian, without interrupting his work,

cocked his head to one side and then to the other as if he were counting the days or weeks it would cost him to make all these baskets.

After a few minutes he said in a slow voice, "It will take a good long time to make so many baskets, patroncito. You see, the bast and the fibers must be very dry before they can be used properly. Then all during the time they are slowly drying, they must be worked and handled in a very special way so that while drying they won't lose their softness and their flexibility and their natural brilliance. Even when dry they must look fresh. They must never lose their natural properties or they will look just as lifeless and dull as straw. Then while they are drying up I got to get the plants and roots and barks and insects from which I brew the dyes. That takes much time also, believe me. The plants must be gathered when the moon is just right or they won't give the right color. The insects I pick from the plants must also be gathered at the right time and under the right conditions or else they produce no rich colors and are just like dust. But, of course, jefecito, I can make as many of these canastitas as you wish, even as many as three dozens if you want them. Only give me time."

"Three dozens? Three dozens?" Mr. Winthrop yelled, and threw up both arms in desperation. "Three dozens!" he repeated as if he had to say it many times in his own voice so as to understand the real meaning of it, because for a while he thought that he was dreaming. He had expected the Indian to go crazy on hearing that he was to sell ten thousand of his baskets without having to peddle them from door to door and be treated like a dog with a skin disease.

So the American took up the question of price again, by which he hoped to activate the Indian's ambition. "You told me that if I take one hundred baskets you will let me have them for forty centavos apiece. Is that right, my friend?"

"Quite right, jefecito."

"Now," Mr. Winthrop took a deep breath, "now, then, if I ask you to make me one thousand, that is, ten times one hundred baskets, how much will they cost me, each basket?"

That figure was too high for the Indian to grasp. He became slightly confused and for the first time since Mr. Winthrop had arrived he interrupted his work and tried to think it out. Several times he shook his head and looked vaguely around as if for help. Finally he said, "Excuse me, jefecito, little chief, that is by far too much for me to count. Tomorrow, if you will do me the honor, come and see me again and I think I shall have my answer ready for you, patroncito."

When on the next morning Mr. Winthrop came to the hut he found the Indian as usual squatting on the floor under the overhanging palm roof working at his baskets.

"Have you got the price for ten thousand?" he asked the Indian the very moment he saw him, without taking the trouble to say "Good Morning!"

"Si, patroncito, I have the price ready. You may believe me when I say it has cost me much labor and worry to find out the exact price, because, you see, I do not wish to cheat you out of your honest money."

"Skip that, amigo. Come out with the salad. What's the price?" Mr. Winthrop asked nervously.

"The price is well calculated now without any mistake on my side. If I got to make one thousand canastitas each will be three pesos. If I must make five thousand, each will cost nine pesos. And if I have to make ten thousand, in such a case I can't make them for less than fifteen pesos each." Immediately he returned to his work as if he were afraid of losing too much time with such idle talk.

Mr. Winthrop thought that perhaps it was his faulty knowledge of this foreign language that had played a trick on him.

"Did I hear you say fifteen pesos each if I eventually would buy ten thousand?"

"That's exactly and without any mistake what I've said, patroncito," the Indian answered in his soft courteous voice.

"But now, see here, my good man, you can't do this to me. I'm your friend and I want to help you get on your feet."

"Yes, patroncito, I know this and I don't doubt any of your words."

"Now, let's be patient and talk this over quietly as man to man. Didn't you tell me that if I would buy one hundred you would sell each for forty centavos?"

"Si, jefecito, that's what I said. If you buy one hundred you can have them for forty centavos apiece, provided that I have one hundred, which I don't."

"Yes, yes, I see that." Mr. Winthrop felt as if he would go insane any minute now. "Yes, so you said. Only what I can't comprehend is why you cannot sell at the same price if you make me ten thousand. I certainly don't wish to chisel on the price. I am not that kind. Only, well, let's see now, if you can sell for forty centavos at all, be it for twenty or fifty or a hundred, I can't quite get the idea why the price has to jump that high if I buy more than a hundred."

"Bueno, patroncito, what is there so difficult to understand? It's all very simple. One thousand canastitas cost me a hundred times more work than a dozen. Ten thousand cost me so much time and labor that I could never finish them, not even in a hundred years. For a thousand canastitas I need more bast than for a hundred, and I need more little red beetles and more plants and roots and bark for the dyes. It isn't that you just can walk into the bush and pick all the things you need at your heart's desire. One root with the true violet blue may cost me four or five days until I can find one in the jungle. And have you thought how much time it costs and how much hard work to prepare the bast and fibers? What is more, if I must make so many baskets, who then will look after my corn and my beans and my goats and chase for me occasionally a rabbit for meat on Sunday? If I have no corn, then I have no tortillas to eat, and if I grow no beans, where do I get my frijoles from?"

"But since you'll get so much money from me for your baskets you can buy all the corn and beans in the world and more than you need."

"That's what you think, señorito, little lordy. But you see, it is only the corn I grow myself that I am sure of. Of the corn which others may or may not grow, I cannot be sure to feast upon."

"Haven't you got some relatives here in this village who might help you to make baskets for me?" Mr. Winthrop asked hopefully.

"Practically the whole village is related to me

somehow or other. Fact is, I got lots of close relatives in this here place."

"Why then can't they cultivate your fields and look after your goats while you make baskets for me? Not only this, they might gather for you the fibers and the colors in the bush and lend you a hand here and there in preparing the material you need for the baskets."

"They might, patroncito, yes, they might. Possible. But then you see who would take care of their fields and cattle if they work for me? And if they help me with the baskets it turns out the same. No one would any longer work his fields properly. In such a case corn and beans would get up so high in price that none of us could buy any and we all would starve to death. Besides, as the price of everything would rise and rise higher still how could I make baskets at forty centavos apiece? A pinch of salt or one green chili would set me back more than I'd collect for one single basket. Now you'll understand, highly estimated caballero and jefecito, why I can't make the baskets any cheaper than fifteen pesos each if I got to make that many."

Mr. Winthrop was hard-boiled, no wonder considering the city he came from. He refused to give up the more than fifteen thousand dollars which at that moment seemed to slip through his fingers like nothing. Being really desperate now, he talked and bargained with the Indian for almost two full hours, trying to make him understand how rich he, the Indian, would become if he would take this greatest opportunity of his life.

The Indian never ceased working on his baskets while he explained his points of view.

"You know, my good man," Mr. Winthrop said, "such a wonderful chance might never again knock on your door, do you realize that? Let me explain to you in ice-cold figures what fortune you might miss if you leave me flat on this deal."

He tore out leaf after leaf from his notebook, covered each with figures and still more figures, and while doing so told the peasant he would be the richest man in the whole district.

The Indian without answering watched with a genuine expression of awe as Mr. Winthrop wrote down these long figures, executing complicated multiplications and divisions and subtrac-

tions so rapidly that it seemed to him the greatest miracle he had ever seen.

The American, noting this growing interest in the Indian, misjudged the real significance of it. "There you are, my friend," he said. "That's exactly how rich you're going to be. You'll have a bankroll of exactly four thousand pesos. And to show you that I'm a real friend of yours, I'll throw in a bonus. I'll make it a round five thousand pesos, and all in silver."

The Indian, however, had not for one moment thought of four thousand pesos. Such an amount of money had no meaning to him. He had been interested solely in Mr. Winthrop's ability to write figures so rapidly.

"So, what do you say now? Is it a deal or is it? Say yes and you'll get your advance this very minute."

"As I have explained before, patroncito, the price is fifteen pesos each."

"But, my good man," Mr. Winthrop shouted at the poor Indian in utter despair, "where have you been all this time? On the moon or where? You are still at the same price as before."

"Yes, I know that, jefecito, my little chief," the Indian answered, entirely unconcerned. "It must be the same price because I cannot make any other one. Besides, señor, there's still another thing which perhaps you don't know. You see, my good lordy and caballero, I've to make these canastitas my own way and with my song in them and with bits of my soul woven into them. If I were to make them in great numbers there would no longer be my soul in each, or my songs. Each would look like the other with no difference whatever and such a thing would slowly eat up my heart. Each has to be another song which I hear in the morning when the sun rises and when the birds begin to chirp and the butterflies come and sit down on my baskets so that I may see a new beauty, because, you see, the butterflies like my baskets and the pretty colors on them, that's why they come and sit down, and I can make my canastitas after them. And now, señor jefecito, if you will kindly excuse me, I have wasted much time already, although it was a pleasure and a great honor to hear the talk of such a distinguished caballero like you. But I'm afraid I've to attend to my work now, for day after tomorrow is market day in town and I got to take my baskets there. Thank you, señor, for your visit. Adiós."

And in this way it happened that American garbage cans escaped the fate of being turned into receptacles for empty, torn, and crumpled little multicolored canastitas into which an Indian of Mexico had woven dreams of his soul, throbs of his heart: his unsung poems.

Questions

1. a. Winthrop seems to leave his encounter with the Indian with the same understanding that he had when he arrived. What prevents him from learning from his experience?
   b. How does question *a* relate to the comment in the introductory note above, "model precedes rather than follows data—map often both precedes and supersedes the territory itself"?
   c. What ideas do you already have about legal order? Where do your ideas come from?

2. If the Indian were to be a guest lecturer in a modern economics class, how would his instruction be received?

3. Both Winthrop and the Indian define life, the world, interpersonal relationships, and economic relationships differently. Can law be a useful institution in such instances of value conflict? Should one reality be adopted and enforced by law?

4. We want to identify with the Indian rather than Winthrop, who is trying to subvert the values and lifestyle of the Indian.
   a. What aspects in the lives of each do we find compelling or repulsive?
   b. Have our own interpersonal and institutional encounters been helpful or destructive of what we consider important?

5. The story has been called "unrealistic" as it speaks to people today. What makes the story "unrealistic"? What is contemporary realism? Compare the notion of realism with the desire to identify with the Indian. Also compare the following:

   > By the end of the Seventeenth Century, mysticism has lost its old significance...and is more than half dead. "Well, what of it," may be asked. "Why shouldn't it die? What use is it when it's alive?"—The answer to these questions is that where there is no vision, the people perish; and that, if those who are the salt of the earth lose their savour, there is nothing to keep that earth disinfected, nothing to prevent it from falling into complete decay. The mystics are channels through which a little knowledge of reality filters down into our human universe of ignorance and illusion. A totally unmystical world would be a world totally blind and insane.*

6. It might be said that the Indian is "happy." What elements of suffering do you see in his life? What are the sources of his suffering? What is the relationship between suffering and personal development?

* A. Huxley, *Grey Eminence* (1943), p. 98 (quoted in C. G. Jung, *Mysterium Coniunctionis*).

Traven's story, if engaging, nevertheless leaves us with a critical question: What has all this to do with law? The answer is everything or nothing, depending upon the level at which you are studying the idea of law. If you are interested in the unique ways that culture and disciplined training create a structure of perception, then the story has everything to do with law. If you wish to know about a given system at a given time, about courts, judges, and the like, then the example looks far-fetched.

We gain more critical insight by looking across a range of definitions about law. Each definition includes the flash of genius of its proponent; each, the element of limited vision caused by exclusion of the unexplainable. When law is defined as a system of rules and regulations, a forum for value inquiry, a regime for the resolution of conflict, a reflection of popular will, a power play of elites, or a cover for the whimsy of officials, we have a set of partial explanations, promising leads for study. Thinking across this field of explanations promotes clearer insight, since competing ideas create tensions and provide a dynamic in law. These tensions create similar conflicts within students of law who might be inclined to settle on *the one best way* to explain law; yet it is these tensions that make law study a unique educational experience.

In the sections that follow some major theoretical explanations of law and process are successively explored. Because no conversation can proceed for long without the discussion of rules, the first section concerns what judges and lawyers do with rules. Value dilemmas in selecting one rule over another are introduced in Section 2. Section 3 discusses the function of courts in adjudicating competing claims, and Section 4 the relationship between popular will and legal action. Section 5 develops the antagonistic thesis that law is nothing more than a means for the preservation of the economic, political, and social position of elites. Since legal officials, including judges, lawyers, and police, are often the final arbiters of the competing philosophies of law, Section 6 is devoted to an overview of the decisional process.

The case of *People* v. *Collins* which follows offers an immediate opportunity to consider law in theory as well as practice. Most of the short explanations of law set out above can be tested in a preliminary way through this case, and most of the chapters that follow are also partially anticipated in the case.

People v. Collins   *66 Cal. Rptr. 497, 438 P. 2d 33 (S. Ct., 1968)*

Sullivan, Justice.

We deal here with the novel question whether evidence of mathematical probability has been properly introduced and used by the prosecution in a criminal case. While we discern no inherent incompatibility between the disciplines of law and mathematics and intend no general disapproval or disparagement of the latter as an auxiliary in the fact-finding processes of the former, we cannot uphold the technique employed in the instant case. As we explain in detail *infra,* the testimony as to mathematical probability infected the case with fatal error and distorted the jury's traditional

role of determining guilt or innocence according to long-settled rules. Mathematics, a veritable sorcerer in our computerized society, while assisting the trier of fact in the search for truth, must not cast a spell over him. We conclude that on the record before us defendant should not have had his guilt determined by the odds and that he is entitled to a new trial. We reverse the judgment.

A jury found defendant Malcolm Ricardo Collins and his wife defendant Janet Louise Collins guilty of second degree robbery (Pen.Code, §§ 211, 211a, 1157). Malcolm appeals from the judgment of conviction. Janet has not appealed.

On June 18, 1964, about 11:30 A.M. Mrs. Juanita Brooks, who had been shopping, was walking

---

(Some footnotes omitted, others renumbered.)

home along an alley in the San Pedro area of the City of Los Angeles. She was pulling behind her a wicker basket carryall containing groceries and had her purse on top of the packages. She was using a cane. As she stooped down to pick up an empty carton, she was suddenly pushed to the ground by a person whom she neither saw nor heard approach. She was stunned by the fall and felt some pain. She managed to look up and saw a young woman running from the scene. According to Mrs. Brooks the latter appeared to weigh about 145 pounds, was wearing "something dark," and had hair "between a dark blonde and a light blonde," but lighter than the color of defendant Janet Collins' hair as it appeared at trial. Immediately after the incident, Mrs. Brooks discovered that her purse, containing between $35 and $40, was missing.

About the same time as the robbery, John Bass, who lived on the street at the end of the alley, was in front of his house watering his lawn. His attention was attracted by "a lot of crying and screaming" coming from the alley. As he looked in that direction, he saw a woman run out of the alley and enter a yellow automobile parked across the street from him. He was unable to give the make of the car. The car started off immediately and pulled wide around another parked vehicle so that in the narrow street it passed within six feet of Bass. The latter then saw that it was being driven by a male Negro, wearing a mustache and beard. At the trial Bass identified defendant as the driver of the yellow automobile. However, an attempt was made to impeach his identification by his admission that at the preliminary hearing he testified to an uncertain identification at the police lineup shortly after the attack on Mrs. Brooks, when defendant was beardless.

In his testimony Bass described the woman who ran from the alley as a Caucasian, slightly over five feet tall, of ordinary build, with her hair in a dark blond ponytail, and wearing dark clothing. He further testified that her ponytail was "just like" one which Janet had in a police photograph taken on June 22, 1964.

On the day of the robbery, Janet was employed as a housemaid in San Pedro. Her employer tes-tified that she had arrived for work at 8:50 A.M. and that defendant had picked her up in a light yellow car[1] about 11:30 A.M. On that day, according to the witness, Janet was wearing her hair in a blonde ponytail but lighter in color than it appeared at trial.[2]

There was evidence from which it could be inferred that defendants had ample time to drive from Janet's place of employment and participate in the robbery. Defendants testified, however, that they went directly from her employer's house to the home of friends, where they remained for several hours.

In the morning of June 22, Los Angeles Police Officer Kinsey, who was investigating the robbery, went to defendants' home. He saw a yellow Lincoln automobile with an off-white top in front of the house. He talked with defendants. Janet, whose hair appeared to be a dark blonde, was wearing it in a ponytail. Malcolm did not have a beard. The officer explained to them that he was investigating a robbery specifying the time and place; that the victim had been knocked down and her purse snatched; and that the person responsible was a female Caucasian with blonde hair in a ponytail, who had left the scene in a yellow car driven by a male Negro. He requested that defendants accompany him to the police station at San Pedro and they did so. There, in response to police inquiries as to defendants' activities at the time of the robbery, Janet stated, according to Officer Kinsey, that her husband had picked her up at her place of employment at 1 P.M. and that they had then visited at the home of friends in Los Angeles. Malcolm confirmed this. Defendants were detained for an hour or two, were photographed but not booked,

---

[1] Other witnesses variously described the car as yellow, as yellow with an off-white top, and yellow with an eggshell white top. The car was also described as being medium to large in size. Defendant drove a car at or near the times in question which was a Lincoln with a yellow body and a white top.

[2] There are inferences which may be drawn from the evidence that Janet attempted to alter the appearance of her hair after June 18. Janet denies that she cut, colored or bleached her hair at any time after June 18, and a number of witnesses supported her testimony.

and were eventually released and driven home by the police.

Late in the afternoon of the same day, Officer Kinsey, while driving home from work in his own car, saw defendants riding in their yellow Lincoln. Although the transcript fails to disclose what prompted such action, Kinsey proceeded to place them under surveillance and eventually followed them home. He called for assistance and arranged to meet other police officers in the vicinity of defendants' home. Kinsey took a position in the rear of the premises. The other officers, who were in uniform and had arrived in a marked police car, approached defendants' front door. As they did so, Kinsey saw defendant Malcolm Collins run out the back door toward a rear fence and disappear behind a tree. Meanwhile the other officers emerged with Janet Collins whom they had placed under arrest. A search was made for Malcolm who was found in a closet of a neighboring home and also arrested. Defendants were again taken to the police station, were kept in custody for 48 hours, and were again released without any charges being made against them.

Officer Kinsey interrogated defendants separately on June 23 while they were in custody and testified to their statements over defense counsel's objections based on the decision in *Escobedo* and our first decision in *Dorado*. According to the officer, Malcolm stated that he sometimes wore a beard but that he did not wear a beard on June 18 (the day of the robbery), having shaved it off on June 2, 1964.[3] He also explained two receipts for traffic fines totalling $35 paid on June 19, which receipts had been found on his person, by saying that he used funds won in a gambling game at a labor hall. Janet, on the other hand, said that the $35 used to pay the fines had come from her earnings.[4]

On July 9, 1964, defendants were again arrested and were booked for the first time. While they were in custody and awaiting the preliminary hearing, Janet requested to talk with Officer Kinsey. There followed a lengthy conversation during the first part of which Malcolm was not present. During this time Janet expressed concern about defendant and inquired as to what the outcome would be *if* it appeared that she committed the crime and Malcolm knew nothing about it. In general she indicated a wish that defendant be released from any charges because of his prior criminal record and that if someone must be held responsible, she alone would bear the guilt. The officer told her that no assurances could be given, that if she wanted to admit responsibility disposition of the matter would be in the hands of the court and that if she committed the crime and defendant knew nothing about it the only way she could help him would be by telling the truth. Defendant was then brought into the room and participated in the rest of the conversation. The officer asked to hear defendant's version of the matter, saying that he believed defendant was at the scene. However, neither Janet nor defendant confessed or expressly made damaging admissions although constantly urged by the investigating officer to make truthful statements. On several occasions defendant denied that he knew what had gone on in the alley. On the other hand, the whole tone of the conversation evidenced a strong consciousness of guilt on the part of both defendants who appeared to be seeking the most advantageous way out. Over defense counsel's same objections based on *Escobedo* and *Dorado,* some parts of the foregoing conversation were testified to by Officer Kinsey and in addition a tape recording of the entire conversation was introduced in evidence and played to the jury.[5]

---

[3] Evidence as to defendant's beard and mustache is conflicting. Defense witnesses appeared to support defendant's claims that he had shaved his beard on June 2. There was testimony that on June 19 when defendant appeared in court to pay fines on another matter he was bearded. By June 22 the beard had been removed.

[4] The source of the $35, being essentially the same amount as the $35 to $40 reported by the victim as having been in her purse when taken from her the day before the fines

were paid, was a significant factor in the prosecution's case. Other evidence disclosed that defendant and Janet were married on June 2, 1964, at which time they had only $12, a portion of which was spent on a trip to Tiajuana. Since the marriage defendant had not worked, and Janet's earnings were not more than $12 a week, if that much.

[5] Included in the conversation are the following excerpts from Janet's statements:

"If I told you that he didn't know anything about it

At the seven-day trial the prosecution experienced some difficulty in establishing the identities of the perpetrators of the crime. The victim could not identify Janet and had never seen defendant. The identification by the witness Bass, who observed the girl run out of the alley and get into the automobile, was incomplete as to Janet and may have been weakened as to defendant. There was also evidence, introduced by the defense, that Janet had worn light-colored clothing on the day in question, but both the victim and Bass testified that the girl they observed had worn dark clothing.

In an apparent attempt to bolster the identifications, the prosecutor called an instructor of mathematics at a state college. Through this witness he sought to establish that, assuming the robbery was committed by a Caucasian woman with a blond ponytail who left the scene accompanied by a Negro with a beard and mustache, there was an overwhelming probability that the crime was committed by any couple answering such distinctive characteristics. The witness testified, in substance, to the "product rule," which states that the probability of the joint occurrence of a number of *mutually independent* events is equal to the product of the individual probabilities that each of the events will occur. *Without presenting any statistical evidence whatsoever in support of the probabilities for the factors selected,* the prosecutor then proceeded to have the

and I did it, would you cut him loose?"

"I just want him out, that's all, because I ain't never been in no trouble. I won't have to do too much [time], but he will."

"What's the most time I can do?"

"Would it be easier if I went ahead and said, if I was going to say anything, say it now instead of waiting till court time?"

Defendant indicated that he should "go and have trust in [the officer], but maybe I'd be wrong. I mean, this is a little delicate on my behalf."

At another point defendant stated: "I'm leaving it up to her."

Defendant expressed concern during the conversation that any statement by Janet would not necessarily relieve him because he admittedly had been with her all that day since 11:30 A.M. The conversation closed when defendants indicated that they wished more time to think it over.

witness *assume* probability factors for the various characteristics which he deemed to be shared by the guilty couple and all other couples answering to such distinctive characteristics.[6]

Applying the product rule to his own factors the prosecutor arrived at a probability that there was but one chance in 12 million that any couple possessed the distinctive characteristics of the defendants. Accordingly, under this theory, it was to be inferred that there could be but one chance in 12 million that defendants were innocent and that another equally distinctive couple actually committed the robbery. Expanding on what he had thus purported to suggest as a hypothesis, the prosecutor offered the completely unfounded and improper testimonial assertion that, in his opinion, the factors he had assigned were "conservative estimates" and that, in reality, "the chances of anyone else besides these defendants being there,...having every similarity,...is somewhat like one in a billion."

Objections were timely made to the mathematician's testimony on the grounds that it was im-

[6] Although the prosecutor insisted that the factors he used were only for illustrative purposes—to demonstrate how the probability of the occurrence of mutually independent factors affected the probability that they would occur together—he nevertheless attempted to use factors which he personally related to the distinctive characteristics of defendants. In his argument to the jury he invited the jurors to apply their own factors, and asked defense counsel to suggest what the latter would deem as reasonable. The prosecutor himself proposed the individual probabilities set out in the table below. Although the transcript of the examination of the mathematics instructor and the information volunteered by the prosecutor at that time create some uncertainty as to precisely which of the characteristics the prosecutor assigned to the individual probabilities, he restated in his argument to the jury that they should be as follows:

Characteristic	Individual probability
A. Partly yellow automobile	1/10
B. Man with mustache	1/4
C. Girl with ponytail	1/10
D. Girl with blonde hair	1/3
E. Negro man with beard	1/10
F. Interracial couple in car	1/1000

In his brief on appeal defendant agrees that the foregoing appeared on a table presented in the trial court.

material, that it invaded the province of the jury, and that it was based on unfounded assumptions. The objections were "temporarily overruled" and the evidence admitted subject to a motion to strike. When that motion was made at the conclusion of the direct examination, the court denied it, stating that the testimony had been received only for the "purpose of illustrating the mathematical probabilities of various matters, the possibilities for [their] occurring or re-occurring."

Both defendants took the stand in their own behalf. They denied any knowledge of or participation in the crime and stated that after Malcolm called for Janet at her employer's house they went directly to a friend's house in Los Angeles where they remained for some time. According to this testimony defendants were not near the scene of the robbery when it occurred. Defendants' friend testified to a visit by them "in the middle of June" although she could not recall the precise date. Janet further testified that certain inducements were held out to her during the July 9 interrogation on condition that she confess her participation.

Defendant makes two basic contentions before us: First, that the admission in evidence of the statements made by defendants while in custody on June 23 and July 9, 1964, constitutes reversible error under the rules announced in the *Escobedo* and *Dorado* decisions; and second, that the introduction of evidence pertaining to the mathematical theory of probability and the use of the same by the prosecution during the trial was error prejudicial to defendant. We consider the latter claim first.

As we shall explain, the prosecution's introduction and use of mathematical probability statistics injected two fundamental prejudicial errors into the case: (1) The testimony itself lacked an adequate foundation both in evidence and in statistical theory; and (2) the testimony and the manner in which the prosecution used it distracted the jury from its proper and requisite function of weighing the evidence on the issue of guilt, encouraged the jurors to rely upon an engaging but logically irrelevant expert demonstration, foreclosed the possibility of an effective defense by an attorney apparently unschooled in

mathematical refinements, and placed the jurors and defense counsel at a disadvantage in sifting relevant fact from inapplicable theory.

We initially consider the defects in the testimony itself. As we have indicated, the specific technique presented through the mathematician's testimony and advanced by the prosecutor to measure the probabilities in question suffered from two basic and pervasive defects—an inadequate evidentiary foundation and an inadequate proof of statistical independence. First, as to the foundation requirement, we find the record devoid of any evidence relating to any of the six individual probability factors used by the prosecutor and ascribed by him to the six characteristics as we have set them out in footnote 6, *ante*. To put it another way, the prosecution produced no evidence whatsoever showing, or from which it could be in any way inferred, that only one out of every ten cars which might have been at the scene of the robbery was partly yellow, that only one out of every four men who might have been there wore a mustache, that only one out of every ten girls who might have been there wore a ponytail, or that any of the other individual probability factors listed were even roughly accurate.

The bare, inescapable fact is that the prosecution made no attempt to offer any such evidence. Instead, through leading questions having perfunctorily elicited from the witness the response that the latter could not assign a probability factor for the characteristics involved,[7] the prosecutor himself suggested what the various probabilities should be and these became the basis of the witness' testimony (see fn. 6, ante). It is a curious circumstance of this adventure in proof that the prosecutor not only made his own assertions of these factors in the hope that they were "conservative" but also in later argument to the jury

---

[7] The prosecutor asked the mathematics instructor: "Now, let me see if you can be of some help to us with some independent factors, and you have some paper you may use. Your specialty does not equip you, I suppose, to give us some probability of such things as a yellow car as contrasted with any other kind of car, does it? . . . I appreciate the fact that you can't assign a probability for a car being yellow as contrasted to some other car, can you? A. No, I couldn't."

invited the jurors to substitute their "estimates" should they wish to do so. We can hardly conceive of a more fatal gap in the prosecution's scheme of proof. A foundation for the admissibility of the witness' testimony was never even attempted to be laid, let alone established. His testimony was neither made to rest on his own testimonial knowledge nor presented by proper hypothetical questions based upon valid data in the record. (See generally: 2 Wigmore on Evidence (3d ed. 1940) §§ 478, 650–652, 657, 659, 672–684; Witkin, Cal. Evidence (2d ed. 1966) § 771; McCormick on Evidence pp. 19–20; Evidence: Admission of Mathematical Probability Statistics Held Erroneous for Want of Demonstration of Validity (1967) Duke L.J. 665, 675–678, citing *People* v. *Risley* (1915) 214 N.Y. 75, 85, 108 N.E. 200; *State* v. *Sneed* (1966) 76 N.M. 349, 414 P.2d 858.) In the *Sneed* case, the court reversed a conviction based on probabilistic evidence, stating: "We hold that mathematical odds are not admissible as evidence to identify a defendant in a criminal proceeding *so long as the odds are based on estimates, the validity of which have [sic] not been demonstrated."* (Italics added.) (414 P.2d at p. 862.)

But, as we have indicated, there was another glaring defect in the prosecution's technique, namely an inadequate proof of the statistical independence of the six factors. No proof was presented that the characteristics selected were mutually independent even though the witness himself acknowledged that such condition was essential to the proper application of the "product rule" or "multiplication rule." (See Note, *supra*, Duke L.J. 665, 669–670, fn. 25.) To the extent that the traits or characteristics were not mutually independent (e. g. Negroes with beards and men with mustaches obviously represent overlapping categories), the "product rule" would inevitably yield a wholly erroneous and exaggerated result even if all of the individual components had been determined with precision. (Siegel, Nonparametric Statistics for the Behavioral Sciences [1956] 19; see generally Harmon, Modern Factor Analysis [1960.])

In the instant case, therefore, because of the aforementioned two defects—the inadequate evidentiary foundation and the inadequate proof of statistical independence—the technique employed by the prosecutor could only lead to wild conjecture without demonstrated relevancy to the issues presented. It acquired no redeeming quality from the prosecutor's statement that it was being used only "for illustrative purposes" since, as we shall point out, the prosecutor's subsequent utilization of the mathematical testimony was not confined within such limits.

We now turn to the second fundamental error caused by the probability testimony. Quite apart from our foregoing objections to the specific technique employed by the prosecution to estimate the probability in question, we think that the entire enterprise upon which the prosecution embarked, and which was directed to the objective of measuring the likelihood of a random couple possessing the characteristics allegedly distinguishing the robbers, was gravely misguided. At best, it might yield an estimate as to how infrequently bearded Negroes drive yellow cars in the company of blonde females with ponytails.

The prosecution's approach, however, could furnish the jury with absolutely no guidance on the crucial issue: *Of the admittedly few such couples, which one, if any, was guilty of committing this robbery?* Probability theory necessarily remains silent on that question, since no mathematical equation can prove beyond a reasonable doubt (1) that the guilty couple *in fact* possessed the characteristics described by the People's witnesses, or even (2) that only *one* couple possessing those distinctive characteristics could be found in the entire Los Angeles area.

As to the first inherent failing we observe that the prosecution's theory of probability rested on the assumption that the witnesses called by the People had conclusively established that the guilty couple possessed the precise characteristics relied upon by the prosecution. But no mathematical formula could ever establish beyond a reasonable doubt that the prosecution's witnesses correctly observed and accurately described the distinctive features which were employed to link defendants to the crime. Conceivably, for example, the guilty couple might have included a light-skinned Negress with bleached hair rather than a Caucasian blonde; or the driver of the car might have been wearing a false beard as a disguise; or the prosecution's witnesses might simply have been unreliable.

The foregoing risks of error permeate the prosecution's circumstantial case. Traditionally, the jury weighs such risks in evaluating the credibility and probative value of trial testimony, but the likelihood of human error or of falsification obviously cannot be quantified; that likelihood must therefore be excluded from any effort to assign a *number* to the probability of guilt or innocence. Confronted with an equation which purports to yield a numerical index of probable guilt, few juries could resist the temptation to accord disproportionate weight to that index; only an exceptional juror, and indeed only a defense attorney schooled in mathematics, could successfully keep in mind the fact that the probability computed by the prosecution can represent, *at best,* the likelihood that a random couple would share the characteristics testified to by the People's witnesses—*not necessarily the characteristics of the actually guilty couple.*

As to the second inherent failing in the prosecution's approach, even assuming that the first failing could be discounted, the most a mathematical computation could *ever* yield would be a measure of the probability that a random couple would possess the distinctive features in question. In the present case, for example, the prosecution attempted to compute the probability that a random couple would include a bearded Negro, a blonde girl with a ponytail, and a partly yellow car; the prosecution urged that this probability was no more than one in 12 million. Even accepting this conclusion as arithmetically accurate, however, one still could not conclude that the Collinses were probably *the* guilty couple. On the contrary, . . . the prosecution's figures actually imply a likelihood of over 40 percent that the Collinses could be "duplicated" by at least *one other couple who might equally have committed the San Pedro robbery.* Urging that the Collinses be convicted on the basis of evidence which logically establishes no more than this seems as indefensible as arguing for the conviction of X on

the ground that a witness saw either X or X's twin commit the crime.

Again, few defense attorneys, and certainly few jurors, could be expected to comprehend this basic flaw in the prosecution's analysis. Conceivably even the prosecutor erroneously believed that his equation established a high probability that *no* other bearded Negro in the Los Angeles area drove a yellow car accompanied by a ponytailed blonde. In any event, although his technique could demonstrate no such thing, he solemnly told the jury that he had supplied mathematical proof of guilt.

Sensing the novelty of that notion, the prosecutor told the jurors that the traditional idea of proof beyond a reasonable doubt represented "the most hackneyed, stereotyped, trite, misunderstood concept in criminal law." He sought to reconcile the jury to the risk that, under his "new math" approach to criminal jurisprudence, "on some rare occasion . . . an innocent person may be convicted." "Without taking that risk," the prosecution continued, "life would be intolerable . . . because . . . there would be immunity for the Collinses, for people who chose not to be employed to go down and push old ladies down and take their money and be immune because how could we ever be sure they are the ones who did it?"

In essence this argument of the prosecutor was calculated to persuade the jury to convict defendants whether or not they were convinced of their guilt to a moral certainty and beyond a reasonable doubt. (Pen.Code, § 1096.) Undoubtedly the jurors were unduly impressed by the mystique of the mathematical demonstration but were unable to assess its relevancy or value. Although we make no appraisal of the proper applications of mathematical techniques in the proof of facts (see *People* v. *Jordan* (1955) 45 Cal.2d 697, 707, 290 P.2d 484; *People* v. *Trujillo* (1948) 32 Cal.2d 105, 109, 194 P.2d 681; in a slightly differing context see *Whitus* v. *State of Georgia* (1967) 385 U.S. 545, 552, fn. 2, 87 S.Ct. 643, 17 L.Ed.2d 599; Finkelstein, The Application of Statistical Decision Theory to the Jury Discrimination Cases (1966) 80 Harv.L.Rev. 338, 338–340), we have strong feelings that such applications, particularly in a criminal case, must be critically examined in view of the substantial unfairness to a defendant which may result from ill conceived techniques with which the trier of fact is not technically equipped to cope. (See *State* v. *Sneed,* supra, 414 P.2d 858; Note, supra, Duke L.J. 665.) We feel that the technique employed in the case before us falls into the latter category.

We conclude that the court erred in admitting over defendant's objection the evidence pertaining to the mathematical theory of probability and in denying defendant's motion to strike such evidence. The case was apparently a close one. The jury began its deliberations at 2:46 P.M. on November 24, 1964, and retired for the night at 7:46 P.M.; the parties stipulated that a juror could be excused for illness and that a verdict could be reached by the remaining 11 jurors; the jury resumed deliberations the next morning at 8:40 A.M. and returned verdicts at 11:58 A.M. after five ballots had been taken. In the light of the closeness of the case, which as we have said was a circumstantial one, there is a reasonable likelihood that the result would have been more favorable to defendant if the prosecution had not urged the jury to render a probabilistic verdict. In any event, we think that under the circumstances the "trial by mathematics" so distorted the role of the jury and so disadvantaged counsel for the defense, as to constitute in itself a miscarriage of justice. After an examination of the entire cause, including the evidence, we are of the opinion that it is reasonably probable that a result more favorable to defendant would have been reached in the absence of the above error. (*People* v. *Watson* [1956] 46 Cal.2d 818, 836; 299 P.2d 243.) The judgment against defendant must therefore be reversed.

In view of the foregoing conclusion, we deem it unnecessary to consider whether the admission of defendants' extrajudicial statements constitutes error under the rules announced in *Escobedo* and *Dorado.* Upon retrial, the admissibility of these or any other extrajudicial statements sought to be introduced by the prosecution must be determined in the light of the rules set forth in *Miranda* v. *State of Arizona* (1966) 384 U.S. 436, 86 S.Ct. 1602, 16 L.E.2d 694. (*People* v. *Doherty* [1967]

67 A.C. 1, 4, 9–13, 59 Cal.Rptr. 857, 429 P.2d 177.) As we have pointed out, the trial herein took place between our first and second *Dorado* decisions (see fn. 4, ante). Although defense counsel was commendably alert in basing objections to the admission of the statements upon the decisions in *Escobedo* and *Dorado,* he of course did not have the benefit of our numerous decisions beginning with the second *Dorado* decision expounding various facets of the exclusionary rule. In the event any extrajudicial statements made by defendant are offered in evidence on retrial, the parties will have an opportunity to make a record on pertinent issues subject to prior determination by the court in the light of *Miranda* rules before such statements are received in evidence. It would be fruitless for us to essay such a task at this point when such record does not yet exist.

The judgment is reversed.

TRAYNOR, C. J., and PETERS, TOBRINER, MOSK and BURKE, JJ., concur.

McCOMB, Justice.

I dissent. I would affirm the judgment in its entirety.

Questions

1. The *Escobedo* and *Dorado* cases referred to in the opinion rule that when the investigation of the police begins to focus and become accusatory, legal counsel must be provided. If counsel is absent, evidence procured at the police station is inadmissible. Would not such evidence be highly relevant? What is the purpose of making it inadmissible?

2. What is the rule in the *Collins* case? Does the judge say that statistics may never be used or that statistics may be used, if used appropriately?

3. Although there is a reluctance to accept statistics as a feature of criminal cases, several expressions in criminal cases parallel the language of statistics. For example, jurors are asked to find guilt "beyond a reasonable doubt," and statistics involves formulations about doubt and the risk of error. Like statisticians, jurors might be saying, "Chances are that facts exist or don't exist." Given these

parallel features, why is there resistance to more extensive use of statistics or scientific method in legal process?

4. Return to the thumbnail definitions of law that are given in the text preceding the case. Which definition best captures the *Collins* case?

5. What does the *Collins* case tell you about police, trial judging, appellate judging, prosecuting and defense attorneys, and the jury?

6. Did the opinion of the court deal with all of the questions that you thought pertinent to the case? Is there a difference between your sense of what is important and the court's sense of what is important? Do difficulties suggest lay versus professional structuring of reality?

7. a. Some of the opinion is not in ordinary language. Is the use of specialized language necessary or is it contrived to prevent you from following what is going on? Can the opinion be rewritten in a page or so of plain English that would include all that the court said with legal language?

   b. Compare your first encounter with a legal case and the encounter between Winthrop and the Indian in *Assembly Line*.

1 Legal Reasoning

What great king, is the Jewel of the Analytical Powers proclaimed by the Exalted one? Four in number, great king, are the Analytical Powers: Understanding of the Meaning of Words, Understanding of the Doctrine, Grammar and Exegesis, and Readiness in Speaking. Adorned, great king with these Four Analytical Powers, a monk, no matter what manner of assemblage he approaches, whether it be an assemblage of Warriors or an assemblage of Brahmans or an assemblage of householders or an assemblage of religious, approaches confidently, approaches that assemblage untroubled, unafraid, unalarmed, untrembling with no bristling of the hair of the body.

A Buddhist parable

How does a lawyer determine whether a client has a good or a bad case? Typically, lawyers begin with facts told them by clients and, after other investigation, "apply" the law to the facts and predict a result. Lawyers assume that judges will decide like cases in like manner; that is, when cases involve comparable facts, prior results will be repeated. Two sources of ambiguity arise in conventional legal work: factual ambiguity (What happened?) and legal ambiguity (What law might apply to what

happened?). Putting aside for a moment factual ambiguity, how do lawyers know what the law is? Oliver Wendell Holmes, Jr. (1841–1935), the famous American jurist, observed:

> Take the fundamental question, what constitutes the law? You will find some text writers telling you that it is something different from what is decided by the courts of Massachusetts or England, that it is a system of reason, that it is a deduction from principles or ethics or admitted axioms ... which may or may not coincide with decisions. But if we take the view of our friend the bad man we shall find that he does not care two straws for the axioms or deductions, but that he does want to know what the Massachusetts or English courts are likely to do in fact. I am much of his mind. The prophecies of what the courts will do in fact, and nothing more pretentious are what I mean by the law.*

Prophecies about law rest in part upon a comparison between cases in question and

* O. W. Holmes, "The Path of the Law," *Harvard Law Review* 10 (1897): 457.

prior cases that have been decided. Skill in finding similarities and differences among cases therefore becomes a fundamental part of professional law study. In this section the writ- ing of Karl Llewellyn (1893–1962) and a line of cases from North Carolina demonstrate what judges and lawyers do with cases.

The Bramble Bush *Karl N. Llewellyn*

First, what is precedent? In the large, disregarding for the moment peculiarities of our law and of legal doctrine—in the large, precedent consists in an official doing over again under similar circumstances substantially what has been done by him or his predecessor before. The foundation, then, of precedent is the official analogue of what, in society at large, we know as folkways, or as institutions, and of what, in the individual, we know as habit. And the things which make for precedent in this broad sense are the same which make for habit and for institutions. It takes time and effort to solve problems. Once you have solved one it seems foolish to reopen it. Indeed, you are likely to be quite impatient with the notion of reopening it. Both inertia and convenience speak for building further on what you have already built; for incorporating the decision once made, *the solution once worked out,* into your operating technique *without reexamination* of what *earlier went into* reaching your solution. From this side you will observe that the urge to precedent will be present in the action of any official, irrespective of whether he wants it, or not; irrespective likewise of whether he thinks it is there, or not. From this angle precedent is but a somewhat dignified name for the *practice* of the officer or of the office. And it should be clear that unless there were such practices it would be hard to know there was an office or an officer. It is further clear that with the institution of written records the background range of the practice of officers is likely to be considerably extended; and

even more so is the possible outward range, the possibility of outside imitation. Finally, it is clear that if the written records both exist and are somewhat carefully and continuously consulted, the possibility of change creeping into the practices unannounced is greatly lessened. At this place on the law side the institution of the bar rises into significance. For whereas the courts might make records and keep them, but yet pay small attention to them; or might pay desultory attention; or might even deliberately neglect an inconvenient record if they should later change their minds about that type of case, the lawyer searches the records for convenient cases to support his point, presses upon the court what it has already done before, capitalizes the human drive toward repetition by finding, by making explicit, by urging, the prior cases...

To continue past practices is to provide a new official in his inexperience with the accumulated experience of his predecessors. If he is ignorant, he can learn from them and profit by the knowledge of those who have gone before him. If he is idle he can have their action brought to his attention and profit by their industry. If he is foolish he can profit by their wisdom. If he is biased or corrupt the existence of past practices to compare his action with gives a public check upon his biases and his corruption, limits the frame in which he can indulge them unchallenged. Finally, even though his predecessors may themselves, as they set up the practice, have been idle, ignorant, foolish and biased, yet the knowledge that he will continue what they have done gives a basis from which men may predict the action of the courts; a basis to which they can adjust their expectations and their affairs in advance. To know the law is

From Karl N. Llewellyn, *The Bramble Bush* (Oceana Press Publication, 1951), pp. 64–69. Reprinted by permission.

helpful, even when the law is bad. Hence it is readily understandable that in our system there has grown up first the habit of following precedent, and then the legal norm that precedent is to be followed. The main form that this principle takes we have seen. It is essentially the canon that each case must be decided as one instance under a general rule. This much is common to almost all systems of law. The other canons are to be regarded rather as subsidiary canons that have been built to facilitate working with and reasoning from our past decisions.

Questions

1. The doctrine of *stare decisis* means that courts will decide like cases in like manner, or that past decisions will be followed. Is there a theory of justice implicit in this doctrine? What are the sources of injustice in such a system?

2. Compare with Llewellyn the following excerpts from Robert Ornstein, *The Psychology of Consciousness* and A. Huxley, *The Doors of Perception*:

> The sense organs discard most of the important information reaching us. The brain further limits input, by selectively inhibiting the sensory activity, sending down efferent signals which can modify stimulation even in the receptor itself. Our senses and central nervous system select by responding primarily to changes. We quickly learn to "habituate" to the constancies of the world. Further, we sort the input into categories that depend on transitory needs, language, our past history, our expectations and our cultural biases.*

To make biological survival possible, Mind at

* Robert Ornstein, *The Psychology of Consciousness* (San Francisco: Freeman, 1972), p. 43.

Large has to be funneled through the reducing valve of the brain and nervous system.... To formulate and express the contents of this reduced awareness man has invented and endlessly elaborated those symbol-systems and implicit philosophies that we call languages Every individual is at once the beneficiary and the victim of the linguistic tradition into which [s]he has been born—the beneficiary inasmuch as language gives access to the accumulated records of other people's experience, the victim insofar as it confirms...the belief that reduced awareness is the only awareness, and as it bedevils [the] sense of reality, so that [s]he is all too apt to take... concepts for data,...words for actual things. That which, in the language of religion, is called "this world" is the universe of reduced awareness expressed and, as it were, petrified by language.†

3. Return to the story "Assembly Line" in the Introduction. Can the theories of Llewellyn, Ornstein, and Huxley explain why Winthrop cannot learn from the Indian?

4. Llewellyn says that it is helpful to know the law even when the law is bad. How is it helpful?

5. Precedent in law becomes more possible by having written records, and so when we think of a precedent system as a general reference to "the past" we should remember that we are most often referring to a *written record* of the past. Is there a difference? What is the written record of your life? Does the record adequately encompass your past?

6. Do you use a precedent system in making personal decisions? Does a precedent system operate in your home, in the various classes you attend, at work, in social groups, and so on?

† Aldous Huxley, *The Doors of Perception* (New York: Harper & Row, 1954), pp. 22–23.

All the cases that follow in this section are drawn from reports of the North Carolina Supreme Court. They are designed to illustrate the doctrine of *stare decisis*.

State v. Pendergrass   *2 Dev. & B., N.C. 365 (1837)*

INDICTMENT for assault and battery. The offense consisted of a whipping with a switch, inflicted by defendant, a schoolmistress, upon one of her younger pupils. The switching left marks upon the body of the child, upon which were also found marks apparently made by some blunter instrument than a switch. All of these marks, however, disappeared in a few days. The nature of the charge to the jury appears from the opinion. Verdict was against defendant, who thereupon appealed....

GASTON, J. It is not easy to state with precision, the power which the law grants to schoolmasters and teachers, with respect to the correction of their pupils. It is analogous to that which belongs to parents, and the authority of the teacher is regarded as a delegation of parental authority. One of the most sacred duties of parents, is to train up and qualify their children, for becoming useful and virtuous members of society; this duty can not be effectually performed without the ability to command obedience, to control stubbornness, to quicken diligence, and to reform bad habits; and to enable him to exercise this salutary sway, he is armed with the power to administer moderate correction, when he shall believe it to be just and necessary. The teacher is the substitute of the parent; is charged in part with the performance of his duties, and in the exercise of these delegated duties, is invested with his power.

The law has not undertaken to prescribe stated punishments for particular offenses, but has contented itself with the general grant of the power of moderate correction, and has confided the graduation of punishments, within the limits of this grant, to the discretion of the teacher. The line which separates moderate correction from immoderate punishment, can only be ascertained by reference to general principles. The welfare of the child is the main purpose for which pain is permitted to be inflicted. Any punishment, therefore, which may seriously endanger life, limbs, or health, or shall disfigure the child, or cause any other permanent injury, may be pronounced in itself immoderate, as not only being unnecessary for, but inconsistent with, the purpose for which correction is authorized. But any correction, however severe, which produces temporary pain only, and no permanent ill, can not be so pronounced, since it may have been necessary for the reformation of the child, and does not injuriously affect its future welfare. We hold, therefore, that it may be laid down as a general rule, that teachers exceed the limits of their authority when they cause lasting mischief; but act within the limits of it, when they inflict temporary pain.

When the correction administered, is not in itself immoderate, and therefore beyond the authority of the teacher, its legality or illegality must depend entirely, we think, on the *qui animo* with which it was administered. Within the sphere of his authority, the master is the judge when correction is required, and of the degree of correction necessary; and like all others intrusted with a discretion, he can not be made penally responsible for error of judgment, but only for wickedness of purpose. The best and the wisest of mortals are weak and erring creatures, and in the exercise of functions in which their judgment is to be the guide, can not be rightfully required to engage for more than honesty of purpose, and diligence of exertion. His judgment must be presumed correct, because he is the judge, and also because of the difficulty of proving the offense, or accumulation of offenses, that called for correction; of showing the peculiar temperament, disposition, and habits, of the individual corrected; and of exhibiting the various milder means, that may have been ineffectually used, before correction was resorted to.

But the master may be punishable when he does not transcend the powers granted, if he grossly abuse them. If he use his authority as a cover for malice, and under pretense of administering correction, gratify his own bad passions, the mask of the judge shall be taken off, and he will stand amenable to justice, as an individual not invested with judicial power.

We believe that these are the rules applicable to the decision of the case before us. If they be, there was error in the instruction given to the jury, that if the child was whipped by the defendant so as to occasion the marks described by the prosecutor, the defendant had exceeded her authority, and was guilty as charged. The marks were all temporary, and in a short time all disappeared. No permanent injury was done to the child. The only appearances that could warrant the belief or suspicion that the correction threatened permanent injury, were the bruises on the neck and the arms; and these, to say the least, were too equivocal to justify the court in assuming that they did threaten such mischief. We think that the instruction on this point should have been, that unless the jury could clearly infer from the evidence, that the correction inflicted had produced, or was in its nature calculated to produce, lasting injury to the child, it did not exceed the limits of the power which had been granted to the defendant. We think also, that the jury should have been further instructed, that however severe the pain inflicted, and however in their judgment it might seem disproportionate to the alleged negligence or offense of so young and tender a child, yet if it did not produce nor threaten lasting mischief, it was their duty to acquit the defendant; unless the facts testified induced a conviction in their minds, that the defendant did not act honestly in the performance of duty, according to her sense of right, but under the pretext of duty, was gratifying malice.

We think that rules less liberal towards teachers, can not be laid down without breaking in upon the authority necessary for preserving discipline, and commanding respect; and that although these rules leave it in their power to commit acts of indiscreet severity, with legal impunity, these indiscretions will probably find their check and correction, in parental affection, and in public opinion; and if they should not, that they must be tolerated as a part of those imperfections and inconveniences, which no human laws can wholly remove or redress.

By Court.

Judgment reversed.

Notes and Questions

1. The *Pendergrass* case follows the pattern of all judicial opinions: Facts are discussed, legal questions are raised, and a rule or rules are applied. Usually courts give some explanation justifying the application of rules to convince readers that the result reached in the case is appropriate. The analysis of cases for facts, issues, rules, and reasons is a central feature in lawyer training. With modest practice, anyone can master this technique and see the strengths and weaknesses of the case method.

2. The court acknowledges that no human law can "wholly remove or redress" certain "imperfections and inconveniences." This is said in support of the delegation of power to teachers, parents, and others given control over the day-to-day lives of children. Do you agree with the court's reluctance to intervene?

3. How effective as a limitation on teacher power is parental influence or public opinion? If the court had chosen to intervene here, would it have dulled parental activism or community outrage?

4. If you were a teacher or a student interested in knowing the law of corporal punishment as of the time of the *Pendergrass* case, would the case tell you where you stand? If you were a lawyer rendering advice based on the case, would you find the case useful as a predictive device?

5. The principal reason for the court's decision seems to be the protection of established authority or the maintenance of hierarchical relationships. Is nonhierarchical education thinkable? A powerless teacher? Can law require nonhierarchy? Is law itself inherently hierarchical? If school and the legal order are hierarchical, what are the institutions for training in democratic governance?

Joyner v. Joyner   *59 N.C. 322 (1862)*

Petition for divorce. Appeal from an interlocutory order allowing alimony *pendente lite* [during the lawsuit]. The petitioner alleged her marriage with the defendant; that she herself was well-bred and of respectable family, and that her husband was not less than a fair match for her; that her husband had struck her with a horse-whip on one occasion, and with a switch on another, leaving several bruises on her person; and that on several occasions, he had used abusive and insulting language towards her. The petition concluded as set forth in the opinion of the court.

By Court, PEARSON, C. J. The legislature has deemed it expedient to enlarge the grounds upon which divorces may be obtained; but as a check or restraint on applications for divorces, and to guard against abuses, it is provided that the cause or ground on which the divorce is asked for shall be set forth in the petition "particularly and specially...."

By the rules of pleading in actions at the common law, every allegation of fact must be accompanied by an allegation of "time and place." This rule was adopted in order to insure proper certainty in pleading, but a variance in the *allegata* and *probata,* that is, a failure to prove the precise time and place, as alleged in the pleading, was held not to be fatal, unless time or place entered into the essence, and made a material part of the fact relied on, in the pleading.

There is nothing on the face of this petition to show us that time was material, or a part of the essence of the alleged cause of divorce, that is, that the blows were inflicted at a time when the wife was in a state of pregnancy, with an intent to cause a miscarriage, and put her life in danger; and there is nothing to show us that the place was a part of the essence of the cause of divorce, that is, that the blows were inflicted in a public place, with an intent to disgrace her, and make her life insupportable—so we are inclined to the opinion that it was not absolutely necessary to state the time and place, or if stated, that a variance in the proof, in respect to time and place, would not be held fatal.

But we are of opinion that it was necessary to state the circumstances under which the blow with the horse-whip, and the blows with the switch, were given; for instance, what was the conduct of the petitioner; what had she done, or said, to induce such violence on the part of the husband? We are informed by the petitioner that she was a woman, "well-bred, and of respectable family, and that her husband was not less than a fair match for her." There is no allegation that he was drunk, nor was there any imputation of unfaithfulness on either side (which is the most common ingredient of applications for divorce), so there was an obvious necessity for some explanation, and the cause of divorce could not be set forth, "particularly and specially," without stating the circumstances which gave rise to the alleged grievances.

It was said on the argument that the fact that a husband on one occasion "struck his wife with a horse-whip, and on another occasion with a switch, leaving several bruises on her person," is of itself a sufficient cause of divorce, and consequently the circumstances which attended the infliction of these injuries are immaterial, and need not be set forth. This presents the question in the case.

The wife must be subject to the husband. Every man must govern his household, and if by reason of an unruly temper, or an unbridled tongue, the wife persistently treats her husband with disrespect, and he submits to it, he not only loses all sense of self-respect, but loses the respect of the other members of his family, without which he cannot expect to govern them, and forfeits the respect of his neighbors. Such have been the incidents of the marriage relation from the beginning of the human race. Unto the woman it is said: "Thy desire shall be to thy husband, and he shall rule over thee": Gen. iii. 16. It follows that the law gives the husband power to use such a degree of force as is necessary to make the wife behave herself and know her place. Why is it, that by the principles of the common law, if a wife slanders or assaults and beats a neighbor, the husband is made to pay for it? Or if the wife commits a criminal offense, less than felony, in the presence of her husband, she is not held responsible? Why is it that the wife cannot make a will disposing of her land, and cannot sell her land without a privy examination, "separate and apart from her husband," in order to see that she did so voluntarily, and without compulsion on the part of her husband? It is for the reason that the law gives this power to the husband over the person of the wife, and has adopted proper safeguards to prevent an abuse of it.

We will not pursue the discussion further. It is not an agreeable subject, and we are not inclined unnecessarily to draw upon ourselves the charge of a want of proper respect for the weaker sex. It is sufficient for our purpose to state that there may be circumstances which will mitigate, excuse, and so far justify the husband in striking the wife "with a horse-whip on one occasion and with a switch on another, leaving several bruises on the person," so as not to give her a right to abandon him, and claim to be divorced. For instance, suppose a husband comes home, and his wife abuses him in the strongest terms—calls him a scoundrel, and repeatedly expresses a wish that he was dead and in torment; and being thus provoked in the

furor brevis, he strikes her with the horse-whip, which he happens to have in his hands, but is afterwards willing to apologize, and expresses regret for having struck her; or suppose a man and his wife get into a discussion and have a difference of opinion as to a matter of fact, she becomes furious and gives way to her temper, so far as to tell him he lies, and upon being admonished not to repeat the word, nevertheless does so, and the husband taking up a switch, tells her if she repeats it again he will strike her, and after this notice she again repeats the insulting words, and he thereupon strikes her several blows,—these are cases in which, in our opinion, the circumstances attending the act, and giving rise to it, so far justify the conduct of the husband as to take from the wife any ground of divorce for that cause, and authorize the court to dismiss her petition, with the admonition, "If you will amend your manners, you may expect better treatment": See Shelford on Divorce. So that there are circumstances under which a husband may strike his wife with a horse-whip, or may strike her several times with a switch, so hard as to leave marks on her person, and these acts do not furnish sufficient ground for a divorce. It follows that when such acts are alleged as the causes for a divorce, it is necessary in order to comply with the provisions of the statute to state the circumstances attending the acts, and which gave rise to them....

State v. Black   *60 N.C. 262 (1864)*

By Court, Pearson, C. J. A husband is responsible for the acts of his wife, and he is required to govern his household, and for that purpose the law permits him to use towards his wife such a degree of force as is necessary to control an unruly temper and make her behave herself; and unless some permanent injury be inflicted, or there be an excess of violence, or such a degree of cruelty as shows that it is inflicted to gratify his own bad passions, the law will not invade the domestic forum or go behind the curtain. It prefers to leave the parties to themselves, as the best mode of inducing them to make the matter up

and live together as man and wife should.

Certainly the exposure of a scene like that set out in this case can do no good. In respect to the parties, a public exhibition in the court-house of such quarrels and fights between man and wife widens the breach, makes a reconciliation almost impossible, and encourages insubordination; and in respect to the public, it has a pernicious tendency; so, *pro bono publico,* such matters are excluded from the courts, unless there is a permanent injury or excessive violence or cruelty indicating malignity and vindictiveness.

In this case, the wife commenced the quarrel.

The husband, in a passion provoked by excessive abuse, pulled her upon the floor by the hair, but restrained himself, did not strike a blow, and she admits he did not choke her, and she continued to abuse him after she got up. Upon this state of facts the jury ought to have been charged in favor of the defendant: *State* v. *Pendergrass,* 2 Dev. & B. 365 [31 Am. Dec. 416]; *Joyner* v. *Joyner,* 6 Jones Eq. 325.

It was insisted by Mr. Winston that, admitting such to be the law when the husband and wife lived together, it did not apply when, as in this case, they were living apart. That may be so when there is a divorce from bed and board, because the law then recognizes and allows the separation, but it can take no notice of a private agreement to live separate. The husband is still responsible for her acts, and the marriage relation and its incidents remain unaffected.

Questions

1. The court cites the *Pendergrass* and *Joyner* cases as precedent. What are the similarities between those cases and the facts of the *Black* case? The differences?

2. How clear were the prior cases as a guide in the *Black* case? Was the result in *Black* preordained by the earlier cases?

3. In the *Joyner* case there was no evidence as to who started the fight, whereas in the *Black* case there was evidence that the wife started it. Is this case, therefore, easier for the court to decide than the *Joyner* case? If so, is this a stronger case or a weaker case establishing a husband's right to beat his wife?

4. In the *Pendergrass* case, the court said that intervention in the school situation would be dependent upon the *qui animo,* or motive, of the teacher in punishing. Only for wickedness of purpose would the court find an assault. In the *Black* case, the court spoke of cruelty or the use of force "to gratify his own bad passions." How can these interior states of teachers or husbands be proved?

5. The court indicates in the *Black* case that if the parties make a private agreement to live apart it need not be recognized. Why is the preservation of this agreement less compelling as a public good than the preservation of the privacy of the "domestic forum"?

6. In reading these cases we have difficulty in moving beyond the questions of whether it is a good idea for teachers to beat students or for husbands to beat their wives. The court does not stay on the larger questions, but instead moves to questions of how, when, and where the beating may take place. The latter questions are more manageable than the larger ones and can be handled with "less emotion."

What does this tell about legal analysis? About rules of law? Can a profession, such as law, be based on emotion? What would emotional rules of law look like?

State v. Rhodes   *61 N.C. 453 (1868)*

Assault and battery, in which it appeared that the husband struck the wife three blows with a switch about the size of one of his fingers. The other facts are stated in the opinion.

By Court, Reade, J. The violence complained of would, without question, have constituted a battery, if the subject of it had not been the defendant's wife. The question is, how far that fact affects the case.

The courts have been loth to take cognizance of trivial complaints arising out of the domestic relations—such as master and apprentice, teacher and pupil, parent and child, husband and wife. Not because those relations are not subject to the law, but because the evil of publicity would be greater than the evil involved in the trifles complained of, and because they ought to be left to family government. On the civil side of this court, under our divorce laws, such cases have been unavoidable and not infrequent. On the criminal side, there are but two cases reported. In one, the question was whether the wife was a competent witness to prove a battery by the husband upon her, which inflicted no great or permanent injury. It was decided that she was not. In discussing the subject, the court said that the abstract question of the husband's right to whip his wife did not arise: *State* v. *Hussy,* Busb. 123. The other case was one of a slight battery by the husband upon the wife after gross provocation. He was held not to be punishable. In that case, the court said that unless some permanent injury be inflicted, or there be an excess of violence, or such a degree of cruelty as shows that it is inflicted to gratify his own bad passions, the law will not invade the domestic forum, or go behind the curtain: *State* v. *Black,* 1 Winst. 266. Neither of those cases is like the one before us. The first case turned upon the competency of the wife as a witness, and in the second there was a slight battery upon a strong provocation.

In this case no provocation worth the name was proved. The fact found was, that it was "without any provocation except some words which were not recollected by the witness." The words must have been of the slightest import to have made no impression on the memory. We must therefore consider the violence as unprovoked. The question is therefore plainly presented whether the court will allow a conviction of the husband for moderate correction of the wife without provocation.

Our divorce laws do not compel a separation of husband and wife, unless the conduct of the husband be so cruel as to render the wife's condition intolerable or her life burdensome. What sort of conduct on the part of the husband would be allowed to have that effect has been repeatedly considered. And it has not been found easy to lay down any iron rule upon the subject. In some cases it has been held that actual and repeated violence to the person was not sufficient; in others, that insults, indignities, and neglect, without any actual violence, were quite sufficient;— so much does each case depend upon its peculiar surroundings.

We have sought the aid of the experience and wisdom of other times and of other countries. Blackstone says: "That the husband, by the old law, might give the wife moderate correction; for

as he was to answer for her misbehavior, he ought to have the power to control her; but that in the polite reign of Charles the Second this power of correction began to be doubted": 1 Bla. Com. 444. Wharton says that by the ancient common law, the husband possessed the power to chastise his wife; but that the tendency of criminal courts in the present day is to regard the marital relation as no defense to a battery: Crim. Law, secs. 1259, 1260. Chancellor Walworth says of such correction that it is not authorized by the law of any civilized country; not, indeed, meaning that England is not civilized, but referring to the anomalous relics of barbarism which cleave to her jurisprudence: Bishop on Marriage and Divorce, 446, note. The old law of moderate correction has been questioned even in England, and has been repudiated in Ireland and Scotland. The old rule is approved in Mississippi, but it has met with but little favor elsewhere in the United States: Id. 485. In looking into the discussions of the other states, we find but little uniformity.

From what has been said, it will be seen how much the subject is at sea. And probably it will ever be so; for it will always be influenced by the habits, manners, and condition of every community. Yet it is necessary that we should lay down something as precise and practical as the nature of the subject will admit of for the guidance of our courts.

Our conclusion is, that family government is recognized by law as being as complete in itself as the state government is in itself, and yet subordinate to it; and that we will not interfere with or attempt to control it in favor of either husband or wife, unless in cases where permanent or malicious injury is inflicted or threatened, or the condition of the party is intolerable. For however great are the evils of ill temper, quarrels, and even personal conflicts inflicting only temporary pain, they are not comparable with the evils which would result from raising the curtain and exposing to public curiosity and criticism the nursery and the bed-chamber. Every household has and must have a government of its own, modeled to suit the temper, disposition, and condition of its inmates. Mere ebullitions of passion, impulsive violence, and temporary pain, affection will soon forget and forgive; and each member will find excuse for the other in his own frailties. But when trifles are taken hold of by the public, and the parties are exposed and disgraced, and each endeavors to justify himself or herself by criminating the other, that which ought to be forgotten in a day will be remembered for life.

It is urged in this case that as there was no provocation the violence was of course excessive and malicious; that every one, in whatever relation of life, should be able to purchase immunity from pain by obedience to authority and faithfulness in duty. And it is insisted that in *State* v. *Pendergrass,* 2 Dev. & B. 365 [31 Am. Dec. 416], which was the case of a school-mistress whipping a child, that doctrine is laid down. It is true that it is there said that the master may be punishable even when he does not transcend the powers granted; i.e., when he does not inflict permanent injury, if he grossly abuse his powers, and use them as a cover for his malice. But observe, the language is if he grossly abuse his powers. So that every one would say at once there was no cause for it, and it was purely malicious and cruel. If this be not the rule, then every violence which would amount to an assault upon a stranger would have to be investigated to see whether there was any provocation. And that would contravene what we have said, that we will punish no case of trifling importance. If in every such case we are to hunt for the provocation, how will the proof be supplied? Take the case before us. The witness said there was no provocation except some slight words. But then, who can tell what significance the trifling words may have had to the husband? Who can tell what had happened an hour before, and every hour for a week? To him they may have been sharper than a sword. And so in every case it might be impossible for the court to appreciate what might be offered as an excuse, or no excuse might appear at all, when a complete justification exists. Or suppose the provocation could in every case be known, and the court should undertake to weigh the provocation in every trifling family broil, what would be the standard? Suppose a case coming up to us from a hovel, where neither delicacy of sentiment nor refinement of manners

is appreciated or known. The parties themselves would be amazed if they were to be held responsible for rudeness or trifling violence. What do they care for insults and indignities? In such cases, what end would be gained by investigation or punishment? Take a case from the middle class, where modesty and purity have their abode, but nevertheless have not immunity from the frailties of nature, and are sometimes moved by the mysteries of passion. What could be more harassing to them or injurious to society than to draw a crowd around their seclusion? Or take a case from the higher ranks, where education and culture have so refined nature that a look cuts like a knife, and a word strikes like a hammer; where the most delicate attention gives pleasure, and the slightest neglect pain; where an indignity is disgrace, and exposure is ruin. Bring all these cases into court side by side, with the same offense charged and the same proof made, and what conceivable charge of the court to the jury would be alike appropriate to all the cases, except that they all have domestic government, which they have formed for themselves, suited to their own peculiar conditions, and that those governments are supreme, and from them there is no appeal, except in cases of great importance requiring the strong arm of the law, and that to those governments they must submit themselves?

It will be observed that the ground upon which we have put this decision is not that the husband has the right to whip his wife much or little, but that we will not interfere with family government in trifling cases. We will no more interfere where the husband whips the wife than where the wife whips the husband, and yet we would hardly be supposed to hold that a wife has a right to whip her husband. We will not inflict upon society the greater evil of raising the curtain upon domestic privacy to punish the lesser evil of trifling violence. Two boys under fourteen years of age fight upon the play-ground, and yet the courts will take no notice of it, not for the reason that boys have the right to fight, but because the interests of society require that they should be left to the more appropriate discipline of the school-room and of home. It is not true that boys have a right to fight; nor is it true that a husband has a right to whip his wife. And if he had, it is not easily seen how the thumb is the standard of size for the instrument which he may use, as some of the old authorities have said, and in deference to which was his honor's charge. A light blow, or many light blows, with a stick larger than the thumb might produce no injury; but a switch half the size might be so used as to produce death. The standard is the effect produced, and not the manner of producing it, or the instrument used.

Because our opinion is not in unison with the decisions of some of the sister states, or with the philosophy of some very respectable law-writers, and could not be in unison with all because of their contrariety, a decent respect for the opinions of others has induced us to be very full in stating the reasons for our conclusion. There is no error.

Questions

1. In light of the prior cases, is it fair for the court to say that the subject at issue is "at sea"?

2. Has the court here rejected the common law rule that a husband may chastise his wife?

3. If the courts will not involve themselves in family quarrels below a certain threshold and it is likely that husbands will be the aggressors in family assaults, has not the court, through a promise of inaction, acknowledged the right of the husband to chastise up to the threshold?

4. If a family is a government, what kind of government is it? What is the relationship between the government of the family and the government of the state? Does the analogy of the family to a government help the court to reach a resolution of the questions before it?

5. What is the status of the "rule of thumb" after this case?

6. Why does the court cite examples from other countries and other states which seem to differ from its decision? Do these references strengthen or weaken the case as precedent on the right of chastisement?

State v. Mabrey   *64 N.C. 592 (1870)*

ASSAULT, tried before *Walls, J.,* at Spring Term, 1870, of HALIFAX.

The jury found, by a special verdict, that on 7 June, 1869, at the house of the defendant, etc., the latter and his wife had some words and he threatened to leave her; after some very improper language by him, she started off, when he caught her by the left arm and said he would kill her, and drew his knife and struck at her with it, but did not strike her; that he drew back as if to strike again, and his arm was caught by a bystander, whereupon the wife got away and ran about fifteen steps; that the defendant did not pursue her, but told her not to return, if she did he would kill her; that he did not strike her or inflict any personal injury, and that he was a man of violent character, etc., etc.

His Honor thereupon being of opinion that the defendant was not guilty, there was a verdict

and judgment accordingly; and the Solicitor for the State appealed.

READE, J. The facts present a case of savage and dangerous outrage, not to be tolerated in a country of laws and Christianity. We rigidly adhere to the doctrine, in (593) *State* v. *Rhodes,* 61 N.C., 453, and precedent cases in our reports, that the courts will not invade the domestic forum, to take cognizance of trifling cases of violence in family government; but there is no relation which can shield a party who is guilty of malicious outrage or dangerous violence committed or threatened. In *State* v. *Rhodes* the jury had been charged that "the husband had the right to whip his wife with a switch no larger than his thumb." In combating that error the Court said: "A light blow, or many light blows with a stick larger than the thumb, might produce no injury; but a switch half the size might be so used as to produce death. The standard is the *effect produced,* and not the manner of producing it, or the instrument used." Those words were used as applicable to the facts in that case. But on the argument at the bar in this case they were perverted to mean that in any case, no matter what weapon was used or from what motive or intent, unless permanent injury were inflicted, the Court would not interfere; therefore, *here,* although death was threatened and a deadly knife used, yet as it was averted by a bystander, the Court will not interfere. We repudiate any such construction of *State* v. *Rhodes.*

Upon the special verdict there ought to have been judgment against the defendant.

PER CURIAM.

Error.

Questions

1. Judge Reade wrote the opinion in the *Rhodes* case and writes the opinion here. Are there any words that he wished he had not written in the earlier opinion? Are there any he might have wished he included?

2. What is the combined effect of the *Rhodes* and *Mabrey* cases?

Keep the foregoing cases in mind as you read additional material on precedent from Llewellyn.

The Bramble Bush   *Karl N. Llewellyn*

We turn first to what I may call the orthodox doctrine of precedent, with which, in its essence, you are already familiar. Every case lays down a rule, the rule of the case. The express ratio decidendi is prima facie the rule of the case, since it is the ground upon which the court chose to rest its decision. But a later court can reexamine the case and can invoke the canon that no judge has power to decide what is not before him, can, through examination of the facts or of the procedural issue, narrow the picture of what was actually before the court and can hold that the ruling made requires to be understood as thus restricted. In the extreme form this results in what is known as expressly "confining the case to its particular facts." This rule holds only of redheaded Walpoles in pale magenta Buick cars. And when you find this said of a past case you know that in effect it has been overruled. Only a convention, a somewhat absurd convention, prevents flat overruling in such instances. It seems to be felt as definitely improper to state that the

From Karl N. Llewellyn, *The Bramble Bush* (Oceana Press Publication, 1951), pp. 66–69. Reprinted by permission.

court in a prior case was wrong, peculiarly so if that case was in the same court which is speaking now. It seems to be felt that this would undermine the dogma of the infallibility of courts. So lip service is done to that dogma, while the rule which the prior court laid down is disembowelled. The execution proceeds with due respect, with mandarin courtesy.

Now this orthodox view of the authority of precedent—which I shall call the *strict* view—is but *one of two views* which seem to me wholly contradictory to each other. It is in practice the dogma which is applied to *unwelcome* precedents. It is the recognized, legitimate, honorable technique for whittling precedents away, for making the lawyer, in his argument, and the court, in its decision, free of them. It is a surgeon's knife....

...when you turn to the actual operations of the courts, or, indeed, to the arguments of lawyers, you will find a totally different view of precedent at work beside this first one. That I shall call, to give it a name, the *loose view* of precedent. That is the view that a court has decided, and decided authoritatively, *any* point or all points on which it chose to rest a case, or on which it chose, after due argument, to pass. No matter how broad the statement, no matter how unnecessary on the facts or the procedural issues, if that was the rule the court laid down, then that the court has held. Indeed, this view carries over often into dicta, and even into dicta which are grandly obiter. In its extreme form this results in thinking and arguing exclusively from *language* that is found in past opinions, and in citing and working with that language wholly without reference to the facts of the case which called the language forth.

Now it is obvious that this is a device not for cutting past opinions away from judges' feet, but for using them as a springboard when they are found convenient. This is a device for *capitalizing welcome precedents*. And both the lawyers and the judges use it so. And judged by the *practice* of the most respected courts, as of the courts of ordinary stature, this doctrine of precedent is like the other, recognized, legitimate, honorable.

What I wish to sink deep into your minds about the doctrine of precedent, therefore, is that it is two-headed. It is Janus-faced. That it is not one doctrine, nor one line of doctrine, but two, and two which, *applied at the same time to the same precedent, are contradictory of each other.* That there is one doctrine for getting rid of precedents deemed troublesome and one doctrine for making use of precedents that seem helpful. That these two doctrines exist side by side. That the same lawyer in the same brief, the same judge in the same opinion, may be using the one doctrine, the technically strict one, to cut down half the older cases that he deals with, and using the other doctrine, the loose one, for building with the other half. Until you realize this you do not see how it is possible for law to change and to develop, and yet to stand on the past....

...The strict view—that view that cuts the past away—is *hard* to use. An ignorant, an unskilful judge will find it hard to use: the past will bind him. But the skilful judge—he whom we would make free—*is* thus made free. He has the knife in hand; and he can free himself.

Nor, until you see this double aspect of the doctrine-in-action, do you appreciate how little, in detail, you can predict *out of the rules alone;*

how much you must turn, for purposes of prediction, to the reactions of the judges to the facts and to the life around them....

...The first question is, how much can this case fairly be made to stand for by a later court to whom the precedent is welcome? ... The second question is, how much is there in this case that cannot be got around, even by a later court that wishes to avoid it?

You have now the tools for arguing from that case as counsel on *either* side of a new case. You turn then to the problem of prediction. Which view will this same court, on a later case on slightly different facts, take: will it choose the narrow or the loose? Which use will be made of this case by one of the other courts whose opinions are before you? Here you will call to your aid the matter of attitude that I have been discussing. Here you will use all that you know of individual judges, or of the trends in specific courts, or, indeed, of the trend in the line of business, or in the situation, or in the times at large —in anything which you may expect to become apparent and important to the court in later cases. But always and always, you will bear in mind that each precedent has not one value, but two, and that the two are wide apart, and that whichever value a later court assigns to it, such assignment will be respectable, traditionally sound, dogmatically correct. Above all, as you turn this information to your own training you will, I hope, come to see that in most doubtful cases the precedents *must* speak ambiguously until the court has made up its mind whether each one of them is welcome or unwelcome. And that the job of persuasion which falls upon you will call, therefore, not only for providing a technical ladder to reach on authority the result that you contend for, but even more, if you are to have *your* use of the precedents made as *you* propose it, the job calls for you, on the facts, to persuade the court your case is sound.

People—and they are curiously many—who think that precedent produces or ever did produce a certainty that did not involve matters of judgment and of persuasion, or who think that what I have described involves improper equivocation by the courts or departure from the court-ways of some golden age—such people simply do not know our system of precedent in which they live.

Questions

1. What are the two views of precedent given by Llewellyn?

2. To the lawyer representing Mabrey before the Supreme Court of North Carolina, are the prior cases of *Pendergrass, Joyner, Black,* and *Rhodes* welcome or unwelcome precedents? In part welcome, in part unwelcome? How would the lawyer have presented the rules and facts of those cases to the court? Compare the way the opposition would have viewed the cases and explained the prior cases to the court.

3. Could the judge in *Mabrey* have decided in favor of Mabrey using the precedents available?

4. The judge in fact decided against Mabrey. Does the opinion make a fair application of precedent?

5. Return to the case of *People* v. *Collins* in the Introduction.
   a. Assume that in a later criminal case the prosecution desires to use statistical evidence. How would *Collins* be read by them? How would obstacles presented by the *Collins* case be overcome and helpful features of the case highlighted? Compare to Llewellyn.
   b. How would defense counsel interested in opposing the introduction of statistics use the same method of case analysis?

6. Does any of the foregoing material on what judges and lawyers do with cases smack of dishonesty?

7. In 1873 a man in North Carolina came home intoxicated one morning. After complaining to his wife about the food that was around for him to eat, he went out in the yard, cut some switches, and struck her several times with them, leaving bruises that lasted two weeks, but not disabling her from her work. She went to the prosecutor and asked what could be done about it. What would he have advised her in light of the foregoing cases?

State v. Oliver   *70 N.C. 60 (1874)*

INDICTMENT for an assault and battery, tried before *Mitchell, Judge,* at Fall Term, 1873, ALEXANDER Superior Court.

On the trial the jury found the following facts:

Defendant came home intoxicated one morning after breakfast was over; got some raw bacon, said it had skippers on it, and told his wife she [*sic*] would not clean it. He (61) sat down and ate a little, when he threw the coffee cup and pot into the corner of the room and went out; while out he cut two switches, brought them in, and, throwing them on the floor, told his wife that if he whipped her she would leave; that he was going to whip her, for she and her d—d mother had aggravated him near to death. He then struck her five licks with the two switches, which were about four feet long, with the branches on them about half way and some leaves. One of the switches was about half as large as a man's little finger; the other not so large. He had them in both hands, and inflicted bruises on her arm which remained for two weeks, but did not disable her from work.

One of the witnesses swore he struck as hard as he could. Others were present, and after defendant had struck four licks told him to desist. Defendant stopped, saying if they had not been there he would have worn her out.

Upon these facts the Court found defendant guilty and fined him $10. Defendant appealed.

Armfield, for defendant.

Attorney General Hargrove, for the State, called the attention of the Court to the cases of *State* v. *Black,* 60 N.C., 262; *State* v. *Mabrey,* 64 N.C., 592; *State* v. *Rhodes,* 61 N.C., 453; *State* v. *Hussey,* 44 N.C., 123, and *State* v. *Pendergrass,* 19 N.C., 365.

SETTLE, J. We may assume that the old doctrine that a husband had a right to whip his wife, provided he used a switch no larger than his thumb, is not law in North Carolina. Indeed, the Courts have advanced from that barbarism until they have reached the position that the husband has no right to chastise his wife under any circumstances.

But from motives of public policy, and in order to preserve the sanctity of the domestic circle, the Courts will not listen to trivial complaints.

If no permanent injury has been inflicted, nor malice, cruelty nor dangerous violence shown by the husband, it is better to draw the curtain, shut out the public gaze, and leave the parties to forget and forgive.

No general rule can be applied, but each case must depend upon the circumstances surrounding it.

Without adverting in detail to the facts established by the special verdict in this case, we think that they show both malice and cruelty.

In fact it is difficult to conceive how a man who has promised upon the altar to love, comfort, honor and keep a woman can lay rude and violent hands upon her without having malice and cruelty in his heart.

Let it be certified that the judgment of the Supreme Court is affirmed.

PER CURIAM.

Judgment affirmed.

Notes and Questions

1. The court had several cases called to its attention, but cited none of them in the opinion. How can this be explained?

2. Could the outcome reached here have been predicted in light of the earlier cases?

3. If Oliver had seen his lawyer shortly after the events complained of and asked bluntly, "What are my chances?", how might the lawyer have responded?

4. Is an injustice done to Oliver here? Could he say that he had planned his affairs in reliance upon the state of the prior law?

5. Has the court at last solved the problem of family quarreling? Are future cases predictable?

6. It might be helpful to consider the following presentation of time perspectives of a decision maker:

Past (Historical or precedent [general sense] oriented)
What are the past decisions where the same or equivalent facts, issues, and so forth, have been involved?

Present (Existential)
To what extent does this case (transaction, event) present dimensions that are unanswerable by reference to the past? To what extent is "the answer" of the past inadequate to meet the "felt needs" of the present?

Future (Impact orientation)
Will a result contribute to or detract from purposes that the law is designed to serve? Will a result lead to improvement? To a better society?

One or another of these orientations emerges in the various North Carolina cases. After relatively smooth sailing with the right of chastisement rule gaining strength and scope, Mabrey uplifts his knife and thereby imposes a need to reconsider carefully the prior law. The impact of a pro-Mabrey result does not look promising; knife play with or without dire effects runs counter to the peace-keeping purposes of law. The pressures of the present and the future on the past forces a reconsideration of the prior law.

What is particularly noteworthy about these cases is that the court makes practically a complete turnabout, without even acknowledging it. In thinking about this odd way in which change is made with all pretenses of stability, one is reminded of the story of the ax that had been in the family for hundreds of years—with two new heads and six new handles.

7. After having studied these cases from North Carolina, how is your understanding of precedent and legal reasoning different from someone who has not studied them?

8. What do you now see to be the essential strengths and weaknesses in legal reasoning? When is legal reasoning preferable to nonlegal reasoning? If thinking like a lawyer involves careful reading of cases and legal reasoning, do you want to think like one?

9. We are still left with the question of the applicability of the idea of precedent in out-of-court settings, such as the home, among family members, or at school. Are precedents used in your situations? Do strict and loose interpretations of

precedents operate? Who gets to "set" precedents in such groups?

(When questions like the foregoing can be addressed, at least tentatively answered, and acted upon, students will have discovered a highly useful aspect of law study and an effective link between law study and other forms of social study.)

10. There is currently much being written about battered women, both here and in Great Britain. For consideration of battered women in one city, see "The Silent Victims: Denver's Battered Women"—A Report on the Colorado Advisory Committee to the United States Commission on Civil Rights (1977).

2 Law and Values

My intention was to write it in a cool and detached manner but it came to naught; indignation and pity kept seeping in. This is perhaps just as well, for capital punishment is not merely a problem of statistics and expediency, but also of morality and feeling.

A. Koestler, *Reflections on Hanging*, 1956

Each person always thinks that [s]he is right, but ... such a claim is the equivalent of an iron filing proclaiming that it is the total magnetic field. ...

This field condition of values thus presents us with a relativism in the context of a universal absolute. If we stand furiously in our personalities in the theater of conflict of history, our actions can only be tragic or comic, appropriate or inappropriate. If we stand in our daimonic consciousness outside of history, we become full of truth because we can hold onto no thing. But man lives at the place where time and eternity meet, and that is a place of crucifixion where the opposites cross. In the human world of conflict, every action creates its equal and opposite reaction, and so static values can only be mocked by the very dynamic process of history itself.

W. I. Thompson, *At the Edge of History*

Even a fairy story—a single fairy story—can call up a normative generalization about the right behavior of mice and pumpkins, and of fairy godmothers and princes. ...

K. N. Llewellyn, "The Normative, the Legal and the Law Jobs"

The study of the relationship of values to any subject matter, including law, is generally out of favor. Scholars who are in fledgling disciplines are reluctant to delve into such matters lest their colleagues in the established hard sciences consider them "prescientific" or just plain soft-headed. This drive for respectability leads to a selection of questions for teaching and research that are "manageable."

Part of the reluctance to consider values is traceable to relativism, which takes both crude and sophisticated forms. Relativism—crude form—is captured in such conversation stoppers as, "Well, that depends upon your point of view." At times, the refusal to discuss competing points of view takes on similarities to the small-town diplomat who piously proclaims: "There are two topics I never discuss —politics and religion." Underlying these contentions may be a deep fear of exposing oneself to the psychic risks attendant to the exploration of values.

Sophisticated relativism is typified in the academician's contention that all values are situational, that is, dependent on time and place. Having concluded thus, instead of relentlessly pursuing a detailed inquiry into the various situations, times, and places and the moralities pertinent to them, some academicians drop inquiry altogether, thereby eliminating wide areas of thought. In addition, it is commonly asserted that research (good research) is (ought to be) value-free. Apart from the non-recognition that this assertion is itself value-laden—as the parenthetical material indicates—the tenet leads "scholars" to put little psychic investment into their work and aggravates the already excessive antiethical bias that characterizes most schoolwork.

Lawyers are not immune from the pressures of relativism and value freedom. Law students are schooled in the mixed doctrines of precedent and are taught that any side of a case has merit and can be argued with vigor. If they forget that technical arguments are not necessarily *good* arguments, they do not prepare themselves to meet the public demand for improvement of law. As practitioners their readiness to argue any cause at any time for a fee will at times be of great social benefit, but at its worst will produce a neglect of the value dimensions of law practice. By default, lawyers as a group often simply adopt the values of their clients.

In judicial process when technique and mere craftsmanship predominate, *legalism* results to the chagrin of all those who must encounter the results. Jacques Ellul, a French jurist, observes:

> The judicial element (which becomes principally organization) is no longer charged with pursuing justice or creating law in any way whatsoever. It is charged with applying the laws. This role can be perfectly mechanical. It does not call for a philosopher or a man with a sense of justice. What is needed is a good technician, who understands the principles of the technique, the rules of interpretation, the legal terminology, and the ways of deducing consequences and finding solutions.*

Ellul explains, "Justice is not a thing to be grasped or fixed. If one pursues genuine justice...one never knows where one will end. A law created as a function of justice has something unpredictable in it which embarrasses the jurist." † And yet, as he later adds, "Men of law have certain scruples and are unable to eliminate justice from the law completely without the twinges of conscience." ‡

Because most contested cases are situational and brim over with questions of value, relativism and value freedom are misplaced maxims with respect to them. Values must be explained, demonstrated where possible or otherwise fully debated if law and legal process are to transcend mere technique. As the dialectic over values unfolds, a socially desirable tension arises between rules and values, pressuring decision makers to integrate the present with the past in anticipation of the future. Llewellyn poignantly describes the dimensions of a contested case:

> The case of trouble...is the case of doubt, or is that in which discipline has failed, or is that in which unruly personality is breaking through into new paths of action or of leadership, or is that which an ancient institution is being tried against emergent forces. It is the case of trouble which makes, breaks, twists, or flatly establishes a rule, an institution, an authority. Not all such cases do so. There are also petty rows, the routine of law-stuff which exists among primitives as well as among moderns. For all that, if there be a portion of a society's life in which tensions of the culture come to expression, in which the play of variant urges can be felt and seen, in which emergent power-patterns, ancient security-drives, religion, politics, personality,

---

* Jacques Ellul, *The Technological Society* (New York: Random House, 1964), p. 294.

† *Ibid.*, p. 292.
‡ *Ibid.*, p. 295.

and cross-purposes views of justice tangle in the open, that portion of the life will concentrate in the case of trouble or disturbance. Not only the making of new law and the effect of old, but the hold and the thrust of all other vital aspects of the culture, shine clear in the crucible of conflict.§

§ From *The Cheyenne Way,* by Karl N. Llewellyn and E. Adamson Hoebel, p. 29. Copyright 1941 by the University of Oklahoma Press. Reprinted by permission.

The Queen v. Dudley and Stephens *L.R. 14 Q.B.D. 273 (1884)*

INDICTMENT for the murder of Richard Parker on the high seas within the jurisdiction of the Admiralty.

At the trial before Huddleston, B., at the Devon and Cornwall Winter Assizes, November 7, 1884, the jury, at the suggestion of the learned judge, found the facts of the case in a special verdict, which stated "that on July 5, 1884, the prisoners, Thomas Dudley and Edward Stephens, with one Brooks, all able-bodied English seamen, and the deceased also an English boy, between seventeen and eighteen years of age, the crew of an English yacht, a registered English vessel, were cast away in a storm on the high seas 1600 miles from the Cape of Good Hope, and were compelled to put into an open boat belonging to the said yacht. That in this boat they had no supply of water and no supply of food, except two 1 lb. tins of turnips, and for three days they had nothing else to subsist upon. That on the fourth day they caught a small turtle, upon which they subsisted for a few days, and this was the only food they had up to the twentieth day when the act now in question was committed. That on the twelfth day the remains of the turtle were entirely consumed, and for the next eight days they had nothing to eat. That they had no fresh water, except such rain as they from time to time caught in their oilskin capes. That the boat was drifting on the ocean, and was probably more than 1000 miles away from land. That on the eighteenth day, when they had been seven days without food and five without water, the prisoners spoke to Brooks as to what should be done if no succour came, and suggested that some one should be sacrificed to save the rest, but Brooks dissented, and the boy, to whom they were understood to refer, was not consulted. That on the

24th of July, the day before the act now in question, the prisoner Dudley proposed to Stephens and Brooks that lots should be cast who should be put to death to save the rest, but Brooks refused to consent, and it was not put to the boy, and in point of fact there was no drawing of lots. That on that day the prisoners spoke of their having families, and suggested it would be better to kill the boy that their lives should be saved, and Dudley proposed that if there was no vessel in sight by the morrow morning the boy should be killed. That next day, the 25th of July, no vessel appearing, Dudley told Brooks that he had better go and have a sleep, and made signs to Stephens and Brooks that the boy had better be killed. The prisoner Stephens agreed to the act, but Brooks dissented from it. That the boy was then lying at the bottom of the boat quite helpless, and extremely weakened by famine and by drinking sea water, and unable to make any resistance, nor did he ever assent to his being killed. The prisoner Dudley offered a prayer asking forgiveness for them all if either of them should be tempted to commit a rash act, and that their souls might be saved. That Dudley, with the assent of Stephens, went to the boy, and telling him that his time was come, put a knife into his throat and killed him then and there; that the three men fed upon the body and blood of the boy for four days; that on the fourth day after the act had been committed the boat was picked up by a passing vessel, and the prisoners were rescued, still alive, but in the lowest state of prostration. That they were carried to the port of Falmouth, and committed for trial at Exeter. That if the men had not fed upon the body of the boy they would probably not have survived to be picked up and rescued, but would within the four days have died of famine. That the boy, being in a much weaker condition, was likely to have died before them. That at the time of the act in question there was no sail in sight, nor any reasonable prospect of relief. That under these circumstances there appeared to the prisoners every probability that unless they then fed or very soon fed upon the boy or one of themselves they would die of starvation. That there was no appreciable chance of saving life except by killing some one for the others to eat. That assuming any necessity to kill anybody, there was no greater necessity for killing the boy than any of the other three men." But whether upon the whole matter by the jurors found the killing of Richard Parker by Dudley and Stephens be felony and murder the jurors are ignorant, and pray the advice of the Court thereupon, and if upon the whole matter the Court shall be of opinion that the killing of Richard Parker be felony and murder, then the jurors say that Dudley and Stephens were each guilty of felony and murder as alleged in the indictment. . . .

LORD COLERIDGE, C.J.

. . . It was further objected that, according to the decision of the majority of the judges in the *Franconia Case,* there was no jurisdiction in the Court at Exeter to try these prisoners. But in that case the prisoner was a German, who had committed the alleged offence as captain of a German ship; these prisoners were English seamen, the crew of an English yacht, cast away in a storm on the high seas, and escaping from her in an open boat; the opinion of the minority in the *Franconia Case* has been since not only enacted but declared by Parliament to have been always the law; and 17 & 18 Vict. c. 104, s. 267, is absolutely fatal to this objection. By that section it is enacted as follows:—"All offences against property or person committed in or at any place either ashore or afloat, out of her Majesty's dominions by any master seaman or apprentice who at the time when the offence is committed is or within three months previously has been employed in any British ship, shall be deemed to be offences of the same nature respec-

tively, and be inquired of, heard, tried, determined, and adjudged in the same manner and by the same courts and in the same places as if such offences had been committed within the jurisdiction of the Admiralty of England." We are all therefore of opinion that this objection . . . must be overruled.

There remains to be considered the real question in the case—whether killing under the circumstances set forth in the verdict be or be not murder. The contention that it could be anything else was, to the minds of us all, both new and strange, and we stopped the Attorney General in his negative argument in order that we might hear what could be said in support of a proposition which appeared to us to be at once dangerous, immoral, and opposed to all legal principle and analogy. All, no doubt, that can be said has been urged before us, and we are now to consider and determine what it amounts to. First it is said that it follows from various definitions of murder in books of authority, which definitions imply, if they do not state, the doctrine, that in order to save your own life you may lawfully take away the life of another, when that other is neither attempting nor threatening yours, nor is guilty of any illegal act whatever towards you or any one else. But if these definitions be looked at they will not be found to sustain this contention. The earliest in point of date is the passage cited to us from Bracton, who lived in the reign of Henry III. It was at one time the fashion to discredit Bracton, as Mr. Reeve tells us, because he was supposed to mingle too much of the canonist and civilian with the common lawyer. There is now no such feeling, but the passage upon homicide, on which reliance is placed, is a remarkable example of the kind of writing which may explain it. Sin and crime are spoken of as apparently equally illegal, and the crime of murder, it is expressly declared, may be committed "linguâ vel facto"; so that a man, like Hero "done to death by slanderous tongues," would, it seems, in the opinion of Bracton, be a person in respect of whom might be grounded a legal indictment for murder. But in the very passage as to necessity, on which reliance has been placed, it is clear that Bracton is speaking of necessity in the ordinary sense—the repelling by violence, violence justified so far as it was necessary for the object, any illegal violence used towards oneself. If, says Bracton, the necessity be "evitabilis, et evadere posset absque occisione, tunc erit reus homicidii"—words which shew clearly that he is thinking of physical danger from which *escape* may be possible, and that the "inevitabilis necessitas" of which he speaks as justifying homicide is a necessity of the same nature.

It is, if possible, yet clearer that the doctrine contended for receives no support from the great authority of Lord Hale. It is plain that in his view the necessity which justified homicide is that only which has always been and is now considered a justification. "In all these cases of homicide by necessity," says he, "as in pursuit of a felon, in killing him that assaults to rob, or comes to burn or break a house, or the like, which are in themselves no felony" (1 Hale's Pleas of the Crown, p. 491). Again, he says that "the necessity which justifies homicide is of two kinds: (1) the necessity which is of a private nature; (2) the necessity which relates to the public justice and safety. The former is that necessity which obligeth a man to his own defence and safeguard, and this takes in these inquiries:—What may be done for the safeguard of a man's own life;" and then follow three other heads not necessary to pursue. Then Lord Hale proceeds:—"As touching the first of these—viz., homicide in defence of a man's own life, which is usually styled se defendendo." It is not possible to use words more clear to shew that Lord Hale regarded the private necessity which justified, and alone justified, the taking the life of another for the safeguard of one's own to be what is commonly called "self-defence." (Hale's Pleas of the Crown, i. 478.)

But if this could be even doubtful upon Lord Hale's words, Lord Hale himself has made it clear. For in the chapter in which he deals with the exemption created by compulsion or necessity he thus expresses himself:—"If a man be desperately assaulted and in peril of death, and cannot otherwise escape unless, to satisfy his assailant's fury, he will kill an innocent person then present, the fear and actual force will not acquit him of the crime and punishment of murder, if he commit the fact, for he ought rather to die himself than kill an innocent; but if he cannot otherwise save his own life the law permits him in his own defence to kill the assailant, for by the violence of the assault, and the offence committed upon him by the assailant himself, the law of nature, and necessity, hath made him his own protector cum debito moderamine inculpatæ tutelæ." (Hale's Pleas of the Crown, vol. i. 51.)

But, further still, Lord Hale in the following chapter deals with the position asserted by the casuists, and sanctioned, as he says, by Grotius and Puffendorf, that in a case of extreme necessity, either of hunger or clothing; "theft is no theft, or at least not punishable as theft, as some even of our own lawyers have asserted the same." "But," says Lord Hale, "I take it that here in England, that rule, at least by the laws of England, is false; and therefore, if a person, being under necessity for want of victuals or clothes, shall upon that account clandestinely and animo furandi steal another man's goods, it is felony, and a crime by the laws of England punishable with death." (Hale, Pleas of the Crown, i. 54.) If, therefore, Lord Hale is clear—as he is—that extreme necessity of hunger does not justify larceny, what would he have said to the doctrine that it justified murder?

It is satisfactory to find that another great authority, second, probably, only to Lord Hale, speaks with the same unhesitating clearness on this matter. Sir Michael Foster, in the 3rd chapter of his Discourse on Homicide, deals with the subject of "homicide founded in necessity"; and the whole chapter implies, and is insensible unless it does imply, that in the view of Sir Michael Foster "necessity and self-defence" (which he defines as "opposing force to force even to the death") are convertible terms. There is no hint, no trace, of the doctrine now contended for; the whole reasoning of the chapter is entirely inconsistent with it.

In East's Pleas of the Crown (i. 271) the whole chapter on homicide by necessity is taken up with an elaborate discussion of the limits within which necessity in Sir Michael Foster's sense (given above) of self-defence is a justification of or excuse for homicide. There is a short section at the end very generally and very doubtfully expressed, in which the only instance discussed is the well-known one of two shipwrecked men on a plank able to sustain only one of them, and the conclusion is left by Sir Edward East entirely undetermined.

What is true of Sir Edward East is true also of Mr. Serjeant Hawkins. The whole of his chapter on justifiable homicide assumes that the only justifiable homicide of a private nature is the defence against force of a man's person, house, or goods. In the 26th section we find again the case of the two shipwrecked men and the single plank, with the significant expression from a careful writer, "*It is said* to be justifiable." So, too, Dalton c. 150, clearly considers necessity and self-defence in Sir Michael Foster's sense of that expression, to be convertible terms, though he prints without comment Lord Bacon's instance of the two men on one plank as a quotation from Lord Bacon, adding nothing whatever to it of his own. And there is a remarkable passage at page 339, in which he says that even in the case of a murderous assault upon a man, yet before he may take the life of the man who assaults him even in self-defence, "cuncta prius tentanda."

The passage in Staundforde, on which almost the whole of the dicta we have been considering are built, when it comes to be examined, does not warrant the conclusion which has been derived from it. The necessity to justify homicide must be, he says, inevitable, and the example which he gives to illustrate his meaning is the very same which has just been cited from Dalton, shewing that the necessity he was speaking of was a physical necessity, and the self-defence a defence against physical violence. Russell merely repeats the language of the old text-books, and adds no new authority, nor any fresh considerations.

Is there, then, any authority for the proposition which has been presented to us? Decided cases there are none. The case of the seven English sailors referred to by the commentator on Grotius and by Puffendorf has been discovered by a gentleman of the Bar, who communicated with my Brother Huddleston, to convey the authority (if it conveys so much) of a single judge of the is-

land of St. Kitts, when that island was possessed partly by France and partly by this country, somewhere about the year 1641. It is mentioned in a medical treatise published at Amsterdam, and is altogether, as authority in an English court, as unsatisfactory as possible. The American case cited by my Brother Stephen in his Digest, from Wharton on Homicide, in which it was decided, correctly indeed, that sailors had no right to throw passengers overboard to save themselves, but on the somewhat strange ground that the proper mode of determining who was to be sacrificed was to vote upon the subject by ballot, can hardly, as my Brother Stephen says, be an authority satisfactory to a court in this country. The observations of Lord Mansfield in the case of *Rex* v. *Stratton and Others,* striking and excellent as they are, were delivered in a political trial, where the question was whether a political necessity had arisen for deposing a Governor of Madras. But they have little application to the case before us, which must be decided on very different considerations.

The one real authority of former time is Lord Bacon, who, in his commentary on the maxim, "necessitas inducit privilegium quoad jura privata," lays down the law as follows:—"Necessity carrieth a privilege in itself. Necessity is of three sorts—necessity of conservation of life, necessity of obedience, and necessity of the act of God or of a stranger. First of conservation of life; if a man steal viands to satisfy his present hunger, this is no felony nor larceny. So if divers be in danger of drowning by the casting away of some boat or barge, and one of them get to some plank, or on the boat's side to keep himself above water, and another to save his life thrust him from it, whereby he is drowned, this is neither se defendendo nor by misadventure, but justifiable." On this it is to be observed that Lord Bacon's proposition that stealing to satisfy hunger is no larceny is hardly supported by Staundforde, whom he cites for it, and is expressly contradicted by Lord Hale in the passage already cited. And for the proposition as to the plank or boat, it is said to be derived from the canonists. At any rate he cites no authority for it, and it must stand upon his own. Lord Bacon was great even as a lawyer; but it is permissible to much smaller men, relying upon principle and on the authority of others, the equals and even the superiors of Lord Bacon as lawyers, to question the soundness of his dictum. There are many conceivable states of things in which it might possibly be true, but if Lord Bacon meant to lay down the broad proposition that a man may save his life by killing, if necessary, an innocent and unoffending neighbour, it certainly is not law at the present day.

There remains the authority of my Brother Stephen, who, both in his Digest and in his History of the Criminal Law, uses language perhaps wide enough to cover this case. The language is somewhat vague in both places, but it does not in either place cover this case of necessity, and we have the best authority for saying that it was not meant to cover it. If it had been necessary, we must with true deference have differed from him, but it is satisfactory to know that we have, probably at least, arrived at no conclusion in which if he had been a member of the Court he would have been unable to agree. Neither are we in conflict with any opinion expressed upon the subject by the learned persons who formed the commission for preparing the Criminal Code. They say on this subject:—

"We are certainly not prepared to suggest that necessity should in every case be a justification. We are equally unprepared to suggest that necessity should in no case be a defence; we judge it better to leave such questions to be dealt with when, if ever, they arise in practice by applying the principles of law to the circumstances of the particular case."

It would have been satisfactory to us if these eminent persons could have told us whether the received definitions of legal necessity were in their judgment correct and exhaustive, and if not, in what way they should be amended, but as it is we have, as they say, "to apply the principles of law to the circumstances of this particular case."

Now, except for the purpose of testing how far the conservation of a man's own life is in all cases and under all circumstances, an absolute, unqualified, and paramount duty, we exclude from our consideration all the incidents of war. We are dealing with a case of private homicide, not one imposed upon men in the service of their Sovereign and in the defence of their country. Now it is admitted that the deliberate killing of this unoffending and unresisting boy was clearly murder, unless the killing can be justified by some well-recognized excuse admitted by the law. It is further admitted that there was in this case no such excuse, unless the killing was justified by what has been called "necessity." But the temptation to the act which existed here was not what the law has ever called necessity. Nor is this to be regretted. Though law and morality are not the same, and many things may be immoral which are not necessarily illegal, yet the absolute divorce of law from morality would be of fatal consequence; and such divorce would follow if the temptation to murder in this case were to be held by law an absolute defence of it. It is not so. To preserve one's life is generally speaking a duty, but it may be the plainest and the highest duty to sacrifice it. War is full of instances in which it is a man's duty not to live, but to die. The duty, in case of shipwreck, of a captain to his crew, of the crew to the passengers, of soldiers to women and children, as in the noble case of the *Birkenhead;* these duties impose on men the moral necessity, not of the preservation, but of the sacrifice of their lives for others, from which in no country, least of all, it is to be hoped, in England, will men ever shrink, as indeed, they have not shrunk. It is not correct, therefore, to say that there is any absolute or unqualified necessity to preserve one's life. "Necesse est ut eam, non ut vivam," as a saying of a Roman officer quoted by Lord Bacon himself with high eulogy in the very chapter on necessity to which so much reference has been made. It would be a very easy and cheap display of commonplace learning to quote from Greek and Latin authors, from Horace, from Juvenal, from Cicero, from Euripides, passage after passage, in which the duty of dying for others has been laid down in glowing and emphatic language as resulting from the principles of heathen ethics; it is enough in a Christian country to remind ourselves of the Great Example whom we profess to follow. It is not needful to point out the awful danger of admitting the principle which has been contended for. Who is to be the judge of this sort of necessity? By what measure is the comparative value of lives to be measured? Is it to be strength, or intellect, or what? It is plain that the principle leaves to him who is to profit by it to determine the necessity which will justify him in deliberately taking another's life to save his own. In this case the weakest, the youngest, the most unresisting, was chosen. Was it more necessary to kill him than one of the grown men? The answer must be "No"—

> So spake the Fiend, and with necessity,
> The tyrant's plea, excused his devilish deeds.

It is not suggested that in this particular case the deeds were "devilish," but it is quite plain that such a principle once admitted might be made the legal cloak for unbridled passion and atrocious crime. There is no safe path for judges to tread but to ascertain the law to the best of their ability and to declare it according to their judgment; and if in any case the law appears to be too severe on individuals, to leave it to the Sovereign to exercise that prerogative of mercy which the Constitution has intrusted to the hands fittest to dispense it.

It must not be supposed that in refusing to admit temptation to be an excuse for crime it is forgotten how terrible the temptation was; how awful the suffering; how hard in such trials to keep the judgment straight and the conduct pure. We are often compelled to set up standards we cannot reach ourselves, and to lay down rules which we could not ourselves satisfy. But a man has no right to declare temptation to be an excuse, though he might himself have yielded to it, nor allow compassion for the criminal to change or weaken in any manner the legal definition of the crime. It is therefore our duty to declare that the prisoners' act in this case was wilful murder, that the facts as stated in the verdict are no legal justification of the homicide; and to say that in our unanimous opinion the prisoners are upon this special verdict guilty of murder.[1]

THE COURT then proceeded to pass sentence of death upon the prisoners.[2]

Notes and Questions

1. Did Coleridge do justice here? How does one judge the quality of judgments? What values are at stake in this case? What good is accomplished by the decision? What harm?

2. Many students, upon reading the case, agree with the decision of Coleridge *and* the decision of the queen to commute the sentence to six months. Can one consistently agree with both?

3. What impels Coleridge to rule against the men while at the same time almost inviting the queen to commute the sentence?

4. Coleridge seems afraid—"It is not needful to point out the awful danger of admitting the principle which has been contended for." Is justice done if the basis for a decision is not so much the case at hand but some future case that might come up?

5. How does a judge's sense of values affect the treatment of prior cases or other authority? What were the prior materials available to Coleridge? Could he have written a persuasive contrary opinion based on available authority?

6. Judge Coleridge states: "We are often compelled to set standards we cannot reach ourselves and to lay down rules which we could not ourselves satisfy." Compare the following statement of O. W. Holmes:

   > It may be the destiny of man that the social instincts shall grow to control his actions absolutely, even in antisocial situations. But they have not done so, and as the rules of law are or should be based on a morality that is generally accepted, no rule of law founded on a theory of absolute unselfishness can be laid down without a breach between law and working beliefs.*

   Which contention should be the predominant value in law?

---

[1] My brother Grove furnished me with the following suggestion, too late to be embodied in the judgment but well worth preserving: "If the two accused men were justified in killing Parker, then if not rescued in time, two of the three survivors would be justified in killing the third, and of the two who remained the stronger would be justified in killing the weaker, so that three men might be justifiably killed to give the fourth a chance of surviving."—C.

[2] This sentence was afterwards commuted by the Crown to six months' imprisonment.

* Oliver Wendell Holmes, *The Common Law* (Boston: Little, Brown, 1886), p. 44.

7. Should the attorneys representing either Dudley and Stephens or the Crown be expected to believe in their cases, or is it enough for them to do a craftsmanlike job?

8. Return to Note 6 on page 34. Can the classification of time perspectives presented there be applied to the *Dudley and Stephens* case?

9. Return to the North Carolina cases on school discipline and wife beating. What values are at stake in them? Are they adequately considered by the courts? Compare the results reached in the cases with the quotation from O. W. Holmes in question 6 above.

10. Evaluate, in view of your experiences in the course to date, the contention that law is or ought to be value-free.

11. a. Suppose that the people in the boat had cast lots to see who would be killed to save the rest and who would do the killing. Would you consider the killing in those events justifiable?
    b. According to law, consent to be killed cannot be made. Compare the law about consent with your answer to part *a*.

12. It is sometimes said that procedure is the heart of the law, that is, the *way* that a decision is made is more important than *what* is decided. Evaluate in light of the *Dudley and Stephens* case.

13. Consider the following statements about the relationship between law and morality:*

    Law shapes the values and, therefore, the ethical tone of the community. The kinds of legal procedure the society develops shape the goals and indeed the whole character and ethos of a society. (C. Silberman)

    The law must be a study of society in the moral sense of ought and should. (C. Reich)

    In the Athenian state, law was not only the "king," but the school of citizenship. Indeed, law was the highest teacher of every citizen; for law is the most universal and final expression of current moral standards. (Jaeger)

    But compare the following from Ivan Illich:

    ...institutionalization of values inevitably leads to physical pollution, social polarization, and psychological impotence; three dimensions in a process of global degradation and modernized misery.†

14. Consider the following from an opinion of Justice Brennan of the United States Supreme Court in a case involving the question of whether the death penalty violates the constitutional provision against cruel and unusual punishment.

    The basic concept underlying the [Eighth Amendment] is nothing less than the dignity of man. While the state has the power to punish, the Clause stands to assure that this power be exercised within the limits of civilized standards.

    Death is truly an awesome punishment. The calculated killing of a human being by the State involves, by its very nature, a denial of the executed person's humanity.... When a man is hung, there is an end of our relationship with him. His execution is a way of saying, You are not fit for this world. Take your chances elsewhere.‡

15. Consider the following from Justice Blackmun of the United States Supreme Court in the famous case of *Roe* v. *Wade* on abortion:

    We forthwith acknowledge our awareness of the sensitive and emotional nature of the abortion controversy, of the vigorous opposing views even among physicians, and of the deep and seemingly absolute convictions that the subject inspires. One's philosophy, one's experiences, one's exposure to the raw edges of human existence, one's religious training, one's attitudes toward life and family and their values, and the moral standards one establishes and seeks to observe, are all likely to influence and to color one's thinking and conclusions about abortion.

    In addition, population growth, pollution, poverty, and racial overtones tend to complicate and not to simplify the problem.

    Our task, of course, is to resolve the issue by constitutional measurement, free of emotion and predilection.*

    Is it possible to consider the abortion question "free of emotion and predilection"? What is constitutional measurement?

* These quotes are found in C. Silberman, *Crisis in the Classroom* (New York: Vintage, 1970), p. 42.

† Ivan Illich, *Deschooling Society* (New York: Harper & Row, 1971), p. 1.
‡ *Furman v. Georgia*, 92 S. Ct. 272 (1972).
* *Roe* v. *Wade*, 93 S. Ct. 756.

When Coleridge stated his fears about allowing the defense of necessity, he did not, of course, have the dilemmas of twentieth-century science in mind. But his observations speak to many contemporary dilemmas being encountered in the sustenance and care of the malformed, the infirmed, the senile aged, or the gravely ill:

> Who is to be the judge of this sort of necessity? By what measure is the comparative value of lives to be measured? Is it to be strength, intellect or what? It is plain that the principle leaves to him who is to profit by it to determine the necessity which will justify him in deliberately taking another's life to save his own. In this case the weakest, the youngest, the most unresisting was chosen.

Since 1969, the Hastings Center has been examining the ethical problems of contemporary science: human experimentation, death and dying, behavior control, genetics, and other areas of the life sciences. To promote discussions, Hastings uses hypothetical cases such as the following one on fetal research.

The Human Fetus as Useful Research Material   *Case No. 138*

The ———— government's Committee on Biological Research Review examines all research proposals submitted for funding by government grants and contracts. This day's meeting was devoted to examining one specific proposal. It came from the world famous Institute of Embryology at the country's most prestigious university teaching hospital. No one on the Biological Research Review Committee doubted the scientific merit of the proposed research or the ability of the research team who would jointly undertake this major study. Their doubts were fundamentally ethical.

The Institute of Embryology had long been concerned with the plight of women who were prone to spontaneous abortions. They had pioneered in the development of acute care facilities for premature newborns. Now they were eager to develop techniques which would permit the salvaging of pre-viable and marginally-viable fetuses in the 300 to 1200 gram range. The research proposed for review and funding was for the development of an artificial placenta. Fetuses would be obtained from those aborted voluntarily by hysterotomy under the country's uniform abortion statute which permits abortion up to the twenty-fourth week of gestation. They would be transferred to the Institute's research facilities. The technique would involve cannulation of the internal iliac vessels offering total perfusion of the fetus/infant. It was recognized that success would be limited for the early stages of the research. The research team anticipated maintenance of vital signs for periods of no more than minutes or hours. It was hoped, however, that especially with fetuses in the 1000 gram range, survival time would increase gradually as the technique was perfected. It was decided for the purposes of this phase of the research that during the critical period of transfer of the fetus to the artificial placenta no fetus would be maintained for more than a two-week period because of possible damage. Fetuses would be obtained from the obstetrical services of six hospitals in the immediate vicinity. Adequate compensation would be made to the hospitals to cover expenses including supplies and staff time necessary for maintenance of the fetus prior to the time it was delivered to the embryology clinic.

[Should the grant be made? Before proceeding further, answer the question.——Ed.]

Questions

1. Record, with as much detail as possible, the way you personally arrived at a decision in the preceding fetal research case. How does your method compare with the description of the use of precedent in Section 1 of this chapter?

2. What do your deliberations and discussions of the case tell you about the sources and content of your values?

3. At what point in your encounter with the fetal research case did you know how you would decide?

4. What does class discussion of the case yield? Does each person start with and retain his or her own point of view throughout? Do such discussions inevitably depend upon points of view? (What does point of view mean?) Does a consensus emerge from discussion?

5. a. If you had *power* to decide, would matters become clearer? How does *power* affect "point of view"?
   b. It might be somewhat difficult for you to imagine yourself in power. How does being out of power affect "point of view"?

6. Officials, by virtue of preappointment credentialing or experience, are expected to have better judgment in difficult cases than do nonofficials. Is this expectation reasonable? Would you and your classmates do as well in deciding difficult questions as scientists, doctors, philosophers, lawyers, and so on?

7. The decision of the "Biological Research Review Board" is not, strictly speaking, a *legal* decision. But what differences are there between such decisions and decisions in a court of law or a legislature? Is it useful to consider the general idea of *decision*, rather than whether a decision is customarily regarded as legal or nonlegal?

3 Law and Conflicting Interests

It is the best expedient that can be devised in any government, to secure a steady, upright, and impartial administration of the laws.

The Federalist, LXXVIII

In Greek mythology, Themis is the blindfolded, impartial goddess of justice who carries scales to weigh competing contentions and a sword to enforce her decrees. This powerful metaphor is most extensively developed in the jurisprudence of Roscoe Pound (1870–1964), who observed:

[W]e all want the earth. We all have a multiplicity of desires and demands which we seek to satisfy. There are very many of us but there is only one earth. The desires of each continually conflict with or overlap those of his neighbors. So there is, as one might say, a great task of social engineering. There is a task of making the goods of existence, the means of satisfying the demands and desires of men living together in a politically organized society, if they cannot satisfy all the claims that men make upon them, at least go round as far as possible. This is what we mean when we say that the end of law is justice. We do not mean justice as an individual virtue. We do not mean justice as the ideal relation among men. We mean a regime. We mean such an adjustment of relations and ordering of conduct as will make the goods of existence the means of satisfying human claims to have things and do things, go round as far as possible with the least friction and waste.*

According to Pound legal systems are designed to determine which of the competing claims to material wealth and lifespace are to be recognized and secured and which are to be denied.

How does a legal system provide for the evaluation of claims? Pound suggests that the first way is pragmatic; results that have worked or are likely to work are utilized. He states, "In the whole development of modern law, courts and lawmakers and law teachers, very likely with no clear theory of what they were doing but guided by a clear instinct of practical purpose, have been at work finding practical adjustments and reconcilings and, if nothing more was possible, practical compromises of conflicting and overlapping interests."† Prior dispositions of trouble provide a start, but fresh conflict may indicate inadequacies in prior solutions.

A second method of evaluation is by reference to what Pound termed *jural postulates,* the common underlying assumptions of men in society:

1. In civilized society men must be able to assume that others will commit no intentional aggressions upon them.

2. In civilized society men must be able to assume that they may control for beneficial purposes what they have discovered and appropriated to their own use, what they have created by their own labor, and what they have acquired under the existing social and economic order.

3. In civilized society men must be able to assume that those with whom they deal in the general intercourse of society will act in good faith and hence

(a) will make good reasonable expectations which their promises or other conduct reasonably create;

(b) will carry out their undertakings according to the expectations which the moral sentiment of the community attaches thereto;

(c) will restore specifically or by equivalent what comes to them by mistake or unanticipated or not fully intended situation whereby they receive at another's expense what they could not reasonably have expected to receive under the circumstances.

4. In civilized society men must be able to assume that those who are engaged in some course of conduct will act with due care not to cast an unreasonable risk of injury upon others.

5. In civilized society men must be able to assume that those who maintain things likely to get out of hand or to escape and do damage will restrain them or keep them within their proper bounds.‡

A third way that he considered is more diffuse; he suggested that a legal system reflects the overall ethos, directions, and goals of the society in which it functions. In Pound's time American society was in transition from individualistic-agrarian values to collective, urban-industrial values, and this trend could be noted in legal outcomes. Were he alive today, he might be interested in the way that such social pressures as the drive for racial equality, equitable distribution of wealth, ecology, suburbanization, ruralization, and decentralization will intrude upon legal consciousness and determine legal results.

Pound's assumptions about society and the resulting legal order are presented diagrammatically in Figure 1.

Pound thus provided a theory of justice—the reduction of waste; a theory of the source of conflict—scarcity; an explanation of the

* From Roscoe Pound, *Social Control Through Law* (New Haven: Yale University Press, 1968), pp. 64–65. Reprinted by permission.
† *Ibid.*, p. 111.
‡ *Ibid.*, pp. 113–115.

Figure 1 *Pound's Model of Conflict and the Role of Legal Systems*

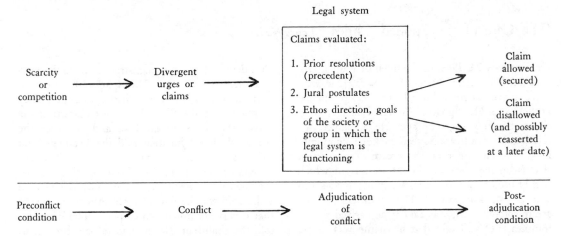

function of legal systems—the adjudication of competing claims and interests; a theory of change—the reassertion of previously unrecognized claims; and a theory as to the way claims are evaluated—through experience, the jural postulates, and what officials in the legal system perceive as the overall value orientations of the society in which they function.

Questions

1. The pervasive underlying assumption in Pound's jurisprudence is that law and legal systems have an exclusively beneficial effect. Given scarcity, competing claims, and so on, people who do legal work try to resolve conflict with a minimum of waste. But compare the following commentary from Laura Nader, a contemporary anthropologist:

   [S]carcity or perceived scarcity has an effect on how people behave. In terms of law, scarcity of land and other property crucial to subsistence leads people to use forums and procedures that will allow them to win, regardless of what it does to relationships. However, if there is a desire to continue relationships, there is a strong likelihood that compromise will be preferred to a winner-take-all solution. It also appears that the use of penalty or retribution, or at least noncompromise resolu-

   tions, is likely to increase where relationships are not important.*

   In light of the foregoing, is the resorting to the legal order the sign of a beginning of conflict resolution, or is it the sign of a serious breakdown in human relationships?

   If the use of law is the signal of breakdown, how can it be said that law minimizes friction and waste?

2. According to Pound the jural postulates are the aspirations of all peoples at all times. Do you think this is true, or are the jural postulates highly ethnocentric to the West—a unique set of goals rather than cultural universals?

   Are Pound's ideas of contract, property, competition, and aggression aspects of human nature or are they learned responses in Western culture?

   Could the postulates be rewritten to reflect revolutionary consciousness?

3. In Pound's schema, as partially noted above, courts, judges, and other legal professionals are not part of the problem, but are solely part of the solution to problems. Does this theory make law, the legal order, and functionaries within it look better than they really are? (As tangible reference points use *People* v. *Collins*, the North Carolina cases, and the case of *Queen* v. *Dudley and Stephens*.)

   * Laura Nader, "Forums for Justice," 31 *J. Soc. Issues*, 152.

The Case of the Spoiled Chiles   *Laura Nader*

On February 24, 1964, in the town of Ralu'a, District of Villa Alta, State of Oaxaca [Mexico], there arrived at nine thirty before this municipal authority a Mr. Ignacio Andres Zoalage, merchant, fifty-five years of age. He explained the following: "I am coming to make a complaint about the chauffeur of the cream-colored truck that is on the platform, in the middle of which is a bruised basket of chiles weighing forty-seven and a half kilograms." The chauffeur of the cream-colored truck was called; he arrived fifteen minutes later and said that his name was Mario Valdez Herrero, chauffeur of the truck. The Court President asked him whether it was true that he had bruised the basket of chiles, and he answered: "Actually, I bruised it, but this happened because I don't have anyone to advise me. It is also the truck owner's fault because he ought to let me have a helper. Also, I could not see because the driver's compartment is high. Besides, it is the senor's fault—they put the things they have for sale on the ground, knowing that there is truck traffic."

The Municipal Court President asked Mr. Ignacio Andres: "Why did you put your merchandise down, knowing that the truck would go by?" Mr. Andres answered that there was room for the truck to pass. The chauffeur then said that this was not true, as the space there was at an angle. Mr. Andres said: "Look, Mr. President, the truck came this way, then this way and that way." The Municipal Court President said that it would be most convenient in this case if the chauffeur paid for the damage he had caused, and that the basket of chiles should be brought in, so that an estimate could be made of how much of it had been spoiled.

The plaintiff left and the Municipal Court President ordered the magistrate to have the merchandise brought in. The magistrate returned with the owner, carrying a basket of chiles. They emptied it on the floor. The court magistrate observed the chiles on the floor and put aside the damaged chiles; he then told the President that the quantity ruined was about one and a half kilograms. The Municipal Court President asked the owner of the basket how much he wanted to be paid for the damage. Mr. Andres answered that it was not much—three pesos. The President told the chauffeur that he had to pay three pesos for the damage. Upon this the chauffeur said: "All right, I will go right now for the three pesos." Meanwhile the Municipal Court President reminded the plaintiff to be more careful on the next occasion and to watch where he put his booth—not to put it just anywhere and especially not in front of a truck. Thus this case was closed and the owner walked out with his load of chiles, leaving the damaged merchandise with the municipal authority.

Questions

1. What is the function of the court in this case?

2. How can the ideas of Pound be applied here?

3. It appears that the court has no interest in the matter beyond getting the dispute settled to the satisfaction of the parties. Is this always the case, or must courts take into account interests that transcend the particular case? Does this case become part of the borderland between truckers and merchants?

4. Do courts sometimes have interests of their own to foster, e.g., rendering consistent results, preserving respect for law, the court, and so forth? In case of a conflict between the interests of the parties and systemic interest, which should yield?

5. Contemporary Americans might marvel at the directness, understandability, and simple justice of the folk court in the *Chiles* case. However, Sylvia

---

* Laura Nader, "Styles of Court Procedure," in *Law in Culture and Society* (Chicago: Aldine, 1969), p. 74. Reprinted by permission.

Forman, in her field work in Ecuador, found that people will behave differently depending on what is in dispute. She found people were most reluctant to compromise in cases when important property, prestige, or access to community power and influence were at stake. Zero-sum strategies are

pursued in such instances regardless of the effect of the conflict on social relationships.*

* S. H. Forman, "Law and Conflict in Rural Highland Ecuador" (Unpub. diss., University of California, Berkeley, 1972).

The *Spoiled Chiles* case suggests the involvement of a court in a petty dispute. In the cases that follow on the early judicial response to air pollution, richer dimensions emerge.

Susquehanna Fertilizer Co. v. Malone   *20 A. 900 73 Md. 268 (1890)*

ROBINSON, J. This is an action for a nuisance, and the questions to be considered are questions of more than ordinary interest and importance. At the same time, it does not seem to us that there can be any great difficulty as to the principles by which they are governed. The plaintiff is the owner of five dwelling-houses on Eighth avenue, in Canton, one of the suburbs of Baltimore city. The corner house is occupied and kept by the plaintiff as a kind of hotel or public house, and the other houses are occupied by tenants. On the adjoining lot is a large fertilizer factory, owned and operated by the defendant, from which the plaintiff alleges noxious gases escape, which not only cause great physical discomfort to himself and his tenants, but also cause material injury to the property itself. The evidence on the part of the plaintiff shows that this factory is used by the defendant for the manufacture of sulphuric acid and commercial fertilizers; that noxious gases escape therefrom, and are driven by the wind upon the premises of the plaintiff, and of his tenants; that they are so offensive and noxious as to affect the health of the plaintiff's family, and at times to oblige them to leave the table, and even to abandon the house. It further shows that these gases injure, materially, his property, discolor and injure clothing hung out to dry, slime the glass in the windows, and even corrode the tin spouting on the houses. The evidence on the part of the defendant is in direct conflict with the evidence offered by the plaintiff; but still, assuming the facts testified to by plaintiff's witnesses to

be true,—and this was a question for the jury,— an actionable injury was done to the plaintiff, for which he was entitled to recover.* No principle is better settled than that where a trade or business is carried on in such a manner as to interfere with the reasonable and comfortable enjoyment by another of his property, or which occasion material injury to the property itself, a wrong is done to the neighboring owner for which an action will lie; and this, too, without regard to the locality where such business is carried on; and this, too, although the business may be a lawful business, and one useful to the public, and although the best and most approved appliances and methods may be used in the conduct and management of the business. . . .

. . . As far back as *Poynton* v. *Gill,* 2 Rolle, Abr. 140, an action, it was held, would lie for melting lead so near the plaintiff's house as to cause actual injury to his property, even though the business was a lawful one, and one needful to the public, "for the defendant," say the court, "ought to carry on his business in waste places and great commons remote from inclosures so that no damage may happen to the owner of adjoining property." And the doctrine thus laid down has been, to this day, the doctrine of every case in which a similar question has arisen.

We cannot agree with the appellant that the court ought to have directed the jury to find whether the place where this factory was located was a convenient and proper place for the carry-

* [In this case, money damages.——ED.]

ing on of the appellant's business, and whether such a use of his property was a reasonable use, and if they should so find the verdict must be for the defendant. It may be convenient to the defendant, and it may be convenient to the public, but, in the eye of the law, no place can be convenient for the carrying on of a business which is a nuisance, and which causes substantial injury to the property of another. Nor can any use of one's own land be said to be a reasonable use, which deprives an adjoining owner of the lawful use and enjoyment of his property. . . .

. . . So we take the law to be well settled that, in actions of this kind, the question whether the place where the trade or business is carried on is a proper and convenient place for the purpose, or whether the use by the defendant of his own land is, under the circumstances, a reasonable use, are questions which ought not to be submitted to the finding of the jury. We fully agree that, in actions of this kind, the law does not regard trifling inconveniences; that everything must be looked at from a reasonable point of view; that, in determining the question of nuisance in such cases, the locality and all the surrounding circumstances should be taken into consideration; and that, where expensive works have been erected and carried on, which are useful and needful to the public, persons must not stand on extreme rights, and bring actions in respect of every trifling annoyance, otherwise, business could not be carried on in such places. But still, if the result of the trade or business thus carried on is such as to interfere with the physical comfort, by another, of his property, or such as to occasion substantial injury to the property itself, there is wrong to the neighboring owner for which an action will lie. . . .

But then it is said there was a fertilizer factory on the lot on which the appellant's works are now erected, and that this factory was used for the manufacture of sulphuric acid and fertilizers several years before the plaintiff built his house, and that the plaintiff has no right to complain, because he "came to the nuisance." But this constitutes no defense in this action. If the appellant had acquired a prescriptive right, that is to say, a user of the place for 20 years, that would present a different question. But no such right is claimed

in this case; and, that being so, the appellant had no right to erect works which would be a nuisance to the adjoining land owned by the plaintiff, and thus measurably control the uses to which the plaintiff's land may in the future be subject. It could not, by the use of its own land, deprive the plaintiff of the lawful use of his property. The question of coming to a nuisance was fully considered in *Bliss* v. *Hall,* 4 Bing. N. C. 183, where, in an action for a nuisance arising from carrying on the business of making candles, the defendant pleaded that he had carried on his business at the same place, in the same manner, and to the same extent, three years before the plaintiff became possessed of his messuage. In sustaining the demurrer to this plea, TINDAL, C.J., says: "That is no answer to the complaint in the declaration, for the plaintiff came to the house he now occupies with all the rights which the common law affords, and one of them is a right to wholesome air. Unless the defendant shows a prescriptive right to carry on his business, the plaintiff is entitled to judgment." . . .

It does not seem to us, therefore, that the defendant has any reason to complain of the several instructions granted by the court. . . . Now, as to the evidence offered in the first exception, it does not seem to us that the fact that $500,000 had been invested in other fertilizer factories in the neighborhood could have any bearing upon the issues before the jury. The defendant had already proved that there was a number of fertilizer factories in the neighborhood, and had offered evidence tending to prove that the nuisance complained of was caused by these factories. Such evidence as this was admissible and proper evidence. But the fact that $500,000 had been invested in other works in the neighborhood could not in any manner affect the plaintiff's right to recover. The only effect of such evidence, it seems to us, would be to show what loss or injury the owners of these factories might sustain if the business carried on by them should be found to be a nuisance. But that was not a question for the consideration of the jury. The law, in cases of this kind, will not undertake to balance the conveniences, or estimate the difference between the injury sustained by the plaintiff and the loss that may result to the defendant from having its trade and business, as now carried on, found to be a nuisance. No one has a right to erect works which are a nuisance to a neighboring owner, and then say he has expended large sums of money in the erection of his works, while the neighboring property is comparatively of little value. The neighboring owner is entitled to the reasonable and comfortable enjoyment of his property, and,

if his rights in this respect are invaded, he is entitled to the protection of the law, let the consequences be what they may.

Judgment affirmed.

Question

1. Compare this opinion with the theory of Pound discussed on pages 45 ff.

Madison v. Ducktown Sulphur, Copper & Iron Co. *83 S.W. 658 (113 Tenn. 331, 1904)*

NEIL, J. These three cases were instituted separately in the court below, but tried together here. They embrace, in the main, the same facts and the same questions of law, and will be disposed of in a single opinion.

The bills are all based on the ground of nuisance, in that the two companies, in the operation of their plants at and near Ducktown, in Polk county, in the course of reducing copper ore, cause large volumes of smoke to issue from their roast piles, which smoke descends upon the surrounding lands, and injures trees and crops, and renders the homes of complainants less comfortable and their lands less profitable than before. The purpose of all the bills is to enjoin the further operation of these plants; the first bill having been filed against the first-named company, the last bill against the second company, and the intermediate bill against both companies.

The following general facts are applicable to all of the cases:

Prior to 1870 one Rhat began the operation of a copper mine at Ducktown, and worked it for several years. Subsequently it was owned by the Union Consolidated Mining Company, Mr. Rhat's successor. These operations were continued until the year 1879, and were then suspended until 1891. During the latter year the Ducktown Sulphur, Copper & Iron Company commenced operating the properties formerly owned and operated by the Union Consolidated Mining Company, and has continued to operate them ever since. The Pittsburgh & Tennessee Copper Company began

operations at Ducktown about the year 1881, and continued until about 1899, when it sold out to the defendant Tennessee Copper Company. The latter began its operations in 1900, and commenced roasting ores in May, 1901. It has continued its works ever since.

Ducktown is in a basin of the mountains of Polk county, in this state, not far from the state line of the states of Georgia and North Carolina. This basin is six or eight miles wide. The complainants are the owners of small farms situated in the mountains around Ducktown.

The method used by the defendants in reducing their copper ores is to place the green ore, broken up, on layers of wood, making large open-air piles, called "roast piles," and these roast piles are ignited for the purpose of expelling from the ore certain foreign matters called "sulphurets." In burning, these roast piles emit large volumes of smoke. This smoke, rising in the air, is carried off by air currents around and over adjoining land.

The lands of the complainants in the first bill, Carter, W. M. Madison and Margaret A. Madison, Verner, and Ballew, lie from two to four miles from the works. The land of Farner, complainant in the last bill, lies six or eight miles away. The distance of McGhee's land is not shown. . . .

These lands are all thin mountain lands, of little agricultural value. Carter's land consists of 80 acres, assessed at $80; Verner's, 89 acres, at $110; Ballew's, 40 acres, at $66; Madison and wife,

43 acres, at $83; W. M. Madison, about 100 acres, at $180; Isaac Farner, 100 acres, at $180. Avery McGhee has 75 acres. W. M. Madison has a tract across the Georgia line, and Mrs. Madison also one of 100 acres there. The assessed value of these last three tracts does not appear. All of these lands, however, lie in the same general section of country, and we assume their value to average about the same, in proportion to acreage.

All of the complainants have owned their several tracts since a time anterior to the resumption of the copper industry at Ducktown in 1891....

The general effect produced by the smoke upon the possessions and families of the complainants is as follows, viz.:

Their timber and crop interests have been badly injured, and they have been annoyed and discommoded by the smoke so that the complainants are prevented from using and enjoying their farms and homes as they did prior to the inauguration of these enterprises. The smoke makes it impossible for the owners of farms within the area of the smoke zone to subsist their families thereon with the degree of comfort they enjoyed before. They cannot raise and harvest their customary crops, and their timber is largely destroyed....

There is no finding in either of the cases that the output of smoke by the Ducktown Sulphur, Copper & Iron Company has increased to any extent since 1891, when the business of mining and reducing copper ore was resumed at Ducktown. There is likewise no finding as to this matter in respect of the Tennessee Copper Company since it began roasting ores in May, 1901.

There is a finding that the Ducktown Sulphur, Copper & Iron Company acquired its plant in 1891, and that it has spent several hundred thousand dollars since that time in improving and enlarging the plant.

The Court of Chancery Appeals find that the defendants are conducting and have been conducting their business in a lawful way, without any purpose or desire to injure any of the complainants; that they have been and are pursuing the only known method by which these plants can be operated and their business successfully carried on; that the open-air roast heap is the only method known to the business or to science by

means of which copper ore of the character mined by the defendants can be reduced; that the defendants have made every effort to get rid of the smoke and noxious vapors, one of the defendants having spent $200,000 in experiments to this end, but without result.

It is to be inferred from the description of the locality that there is no place more remote to which the operations referred to could be transferred.

It is found, in substance, that, if the injunctive relief sought be granted, the defendants will be compelled to stop operations, and their property will become practically worthless, the immense business conducted by them will cease, and they will be compelled to withdraw from the state. It is a necessary deduction from the foregoing that a great and increasing industry in the state will be destroyed, and all of the valuable copper properties of the state become worthless.

The following facts were also found, viz.:

That the total tax aggregate of Polk county for the year 1903 was $2,585,931.43, of which total the assessments of the defendants amounted to $1,279,533. It is also found that prior to the operations of these companies there lived in the district where these works are located only 200 people, whereas there are now living in this district, almost wholly dependent upon these copper industries, about 12,000 people.

It is also found that one of the defendants, the Tennessee Copper Company, employs upon its pay roll 1,300 men, and that the average pay roll is about $40,000 per month, nearly all of which employes have been drawn from the population of Polk and neighboring counties.

It is further found that one of the defendants, the Tennessee Copper Company, consumes approximately 3,000 tons of coke, 2,800 tons of coal, and 1,000 cords of wood per month, and that it purchases and uses 2,110 car loads of coal, coke, wood, etc., per annum. In the year 1901 it purchased and used approximately 1,100 car loads of cord wood, cross-ties, lumber, and quartz. It was also found that 80 per cent of these supplies were purchased from, and delivered by, the citizens of Polk county. The aggregate paid out for supplies is not stated in the findings of the Court of Chancery Appeals, and cannot be here stated accurately, but certainly the amount is very large; and it seems from the figures stated that one of the defendants alone, the Tennessee Copper Company, pays out annually in wages in Polk county nearly a half million of dollars. The Court of Chancery Appeals finds that the other company employs between 1,100 and 1,200 people, and from this it may be inferred that the company pays out in wages and for supplies annually nearly as much as the Tennessee Copper Company.

It is quite apparent that the two companies pay out annually vast sums of money, which are necessarily of great benefit to the people of the county, and that they are conducting and maintaining an industry upon which a laboring population of from ten to twelve thousand people are practically dependent; and it is found, in substance, by the Court of Chancery Appeals, that, if these industries be suppressed, these thousands of people will have to wander forth to other localities to find shelter and work....

We shall now state the principles which, as we conceive, should control the merits of the controversy involved in the several cases before the court:

While there can be no doubt that the facts stated make out a case of nuisance, for which the complainants in actions at law would be entitled to recover damages, yet the remedy in equity is not a matter of course. Not only must the bill state a proper case, but the right must be clear and the injury must be clearly established, as in doubtful cases the party will be turned over to his legal remedy; and, if there is a reasonable doubt as to the cause of the injury, the benefit of the doubt will be given to the defendant, if his trade is a lawful one, and the injury is not the necessary and natural consequence of the act; and, if the injury can be adequately compensated at law by a judgment for damages, equity will not interfere.

And the equitable remedy by injunction must be applied for with reasonable promptness....

In addition to the principles already announced, the following general propositions seem to be established by the authorities: If the case made out

by the pleadings and evidence show with sufficient clearness and certainty grounds for equitable relief it will not be denied because the persons proceeded against are engaged in a lawful business, *Susquehanna Fertilizer Co.* v. *Malone,* 73 Md. 268, 282, 20 Atl. 900, or because the works complained of are located in a convenient place, if that place be one wherein an actionable injury is done to another (*Susquehanna Fertilizer Co.* v. *Malone* ... and ... cases cited); nor will the existence of another nuisance of a similar character at the same place furnish a ground for denying relief if it appears that the defendant has sensibly contributed to the injury complained of.... Nor is it a question of care and skill, but purely one of results.

But there is one other principle which is of controlling influence in this department of the law, and in the light of which the foregoing principle must be weighed and applied. This is that the granting of an injunction is not a matter of absolute right, but rests in the sound discretion of the court, to be determined on a consideration of all of the special circumstances of each case, and the situation and surroundings of the parties, with a view to effect the ends of justice.

A judgment for damages in this class of cases is a matter of absolute right, where injury is shown. A decree for an injunction is a matter of sound legal discretion, to be granted or withheld as that discretion shall dictate, after a full and careful consideration of every element appertaining to the injury.

These propositions will be found to be substantially confirmed and enforced in the following authorities:

In *Powell* v. *Bentley & Gerwig Furniture Co.* (W. Va.) it is said:

"Although a court of equity in such cases follows precedent and goes by rule, as far as it can, yet it follows its own rules, and among them is the one that to abate or restrain in case of nuisance is not a matter of strict right, but of orderly and reasonable discretion, according to the right of the particular case, and hence will refuse relief, and send the party to a court of law, when damages would be a fairer approximation to common justice, because to silence a useful and costly factory is often a matter of serious moment to the state and town as well as to the owner."

In *Clifton Iron Co.* v. *Dye* it is said:

"Counsel have pressed the proposition that mere convenience in the use of its property by the company does not entitle it to pour down upon the appellee's land, and into the stream on his land, the débris from the washers erected by it, and we think the contention is reasonable. But it is not every case of nuisance or continuing trespass which a court of equity will restrain by injunction. In determining this question the court should weigh the injury that may accrue to the one or the other party, and also to the public, by granting or refusing the injunction.

"The court will take notice of the fact that in the development of the mineral interests of this state, recently made, very large sums of money have been invested. The utilization of these ores, which must be washed before using, necessitates in some measure the placing of sediment where it may flow into streams which constitute the natural drainage of the section where the ore banks are situated. This must cause a deposit of sediment on the lands below, and, while this invasion of the rights of the lower riparian owner may produce injury, entitling him to redress, the great public interests and benefits to flow from the conversion of these ores into pig metal should not be lost sight of. As said by the vice chancellor in *Wood* v. *Sutcliffe,* supra: 'Whenever a court of equity is asked for an injunction in cases of such nature as this [a bill to enjoin the pollution of a stream], it must have regard not only to the dry, strict rights of the plaintiff and defendant, but also to the surrounding circumstances.' " 87 Ala. 471, 6 S. 192.

A recent statute passed in this state (Acts 1901, p. 246, c. 139) gives legislative expression to the same considerations of duty and public policy which are contained in the foregoing citations....

The act referred to reads as follows:

An act to amend section 3403 of the Code of Tennessee, 1858 [Shannon's Code, § 5158], and to authorize courts to determine in assessing damages for injuries to real estate, whether the nuisance complained of is a work of public utility and to give to said courts discretionary powers in respect to the abatement of such nuisance.

Section 1. Be it enacted by the General Assembly of the State of Tennessee, that section 3403 of the Code of Tennessee, 1858 [Shannon's Code, § 5158], be so amended as to read as follows: In all suits brought for the recovery of damages resulting from any nuisance and the finding that the matter complained of is a nuisance, the court exercising a sound discretion may immediately upon petition of plaintiff, order or decline to order the nuisance to be abated.

Sec. 2. Be it further enacted, that on the trial of any action for the recovery of damages as above said, either party may show by proof the extent if any of the injury or injuries complained of, and how the alleged nuisance is caused or originates....

It cannot be doubted, therefore, that although the amending acts above copied purport, in terms, to apply only to suits brought for the recovery of damages resulting from nuisances, the purpose was to declare the legislative will in respect of the use of the injunctive power in nuisance cases, when sought to be used in effecting final relief, and to ordain that in administering this relief the court should exercise a sound discretion, and either "order or decline to order the nuisance to be abated," as such sound discretion should dictate. This act must be regarded as declaring the policy of the state upon the subject referred to. It is perceived from the caption that the Legislature had in view the public utility of enterprises attacked on the ground of nuisance, and authorized the court to grant or withhold the injunction as a wise discretion might suggest or warn.

The question now to be considered is, what is the proper exercise of discretion, under the facts appearing in the present case? Shall the complainants be granted, in the way of damages, the full measure of relief to which their injuries entitle them, or shall we go further, and grant their request to blot out two great mining and manufacturing enterprises, destroy half of the taxable values of a county, and drive more than 10,000 people from their homes? We think there can be no doubt as to what the true answer to this question should be.

In order to protect by injunction several small tracts of land, aggregating in value less than $1,000, we are asked to destroy other property worth nearly $2,000,000, and wreck two great mining and manufacturing enterprises, that are engaged in work of very great importance, not only to their owners, but to the state, and to the whole country as well, to depopulate a large town, and deprive thousands of working people of their homes and livelihood, and scatter them broadcast. The result would be practically a confiscation of the property of the defendants—an appropriation without compensation. The defendants cannot reduce their ores in a manner different from that they are now employing, and there is no more remote place to which they can remove. The decree asked for would deprive them of all of their rights. We appreciate the argument based on the fact that the homes of the complainants who live on the small tracts of land referred to are not so comfortable and useful to their owners as they were before they were affected by the smoke complained of, and we are deeply sensible of the truth of the proposition that no man is entitled to any more rights than another on the ground that he has or owns more property than that other. But in a case of conflicting rights, where neither party can enjoy his own without in some measure restricting the liberty of the other in the use of property, the law must make the best arrangement it can between the contending parties, with a view to preserving to each one the largest measure of liberty possible under the circumstances. We see no escape from the conclusion in the present case that the only proper decree is to allow the complainants a reference for the ascertainment of damages, and that the injunction must be denied to them....

Questions

1. Compare the decision reached here with the decision in *Susquehanna, supra.* Looking back to Llewellyn's theory of welcome and unwelcome precedent, would the court in *Ducktown* find *Susquehanna* helpful or not in reaching a pro-company result? The court cites *Susquehanna* as precedent; is this a fair reading of the case?

2. How are the competing interests defined and compared in each of the cases?

3. Are there different views of what is a good society implicit in each decision?

4. How do inequalities of political, social, and economic status and class affect the weighing of competing interests? Consider the following:

> In practice, legal mythology is primarily directed at obscuring the bitter struggle between social classes, and at articulating in consciousness the view that law is unaligned with any given interest; that it does not arise out of society but is a force superimposed on it to mediate and reconcile its conflicts. In fact, the degree of revolutionary consciousness of a people can often be measured by the degree to which the myth of impartiality of state power is accepted.*

5. How does the *Ducktown* case look in contemporary perspective? What does this say about the process of evaluation of competing claims? What was the "public interest" then? What is the "public interest" today? Who should determine what the public interest is—the private parties to a lawsuit, the court, a state or federal agency, the state legislature, the Congress?

* K. Cloke, "Law Is Illegal," p. 27. Reprinted from *Radical Lawyers,* edited by Jonathan Black, by arrangement with Avon Books. Copyright © 1971 by Avon Books.

Georgia v. Tennessee Copper Co. *206 U.S. 236 (1906)*

MR. JUSTICE HOLMES ...

This is a bill in equity filed in this court by the State of Georgia, in pursuance of a resolution of the legislature and by direction of the Governor of the State, to enjoin the Defendant Copper Companies from discharging noxious gas from their works in Tennessee over the plaintiff's territory.

It alleges that in consequence of such a discharge a wholesale destruction of forests, orchards and crops is going on, and other injuries are done and threatened in five counties of the State. It alleges also a vain application to the State of Tennessee for relief. A preliminary injunction was denied, but, as there was ground to fear that great and irreparable damage might be done, an early day was fixed for the final hearing and the parties were given leave, if so minded, to try the case on affidavits. This has been done without objection, and, although the method would be unsatisfactory if our decision turned on any nice question of fact, in the view that we take we think it unlikely that either party has suffered harm.

The case has been argued largely as if it were one between two private parties; but it is not. The very elements that would be relied upon in a suit between fellow-citizens as a ground for equitable relief are wanting here. The State owns very little of the territory alleged to be affected, and the damage to it capable of estimate in money, possibly, at least, is small. This is a suit by a State for an injury to it in its capacity of *quasi*-sovereign. In that capacity the State has an interest independent of and behind the titles of its citizens, in all the earth and air within its domain. It has the last word as to whether its mountains shall be stripped of their forests and its inhabitants shall breathe pure air. It might have to pay individuals before it could utter that word, but with it remains the final power. The alleged damage to the State as a private owner is merely a makeweight, and we may lay on one side the dispute as to whether the destruction of forests has led to the gullying of its roads.

... When the States by their union made the forcible abatement of outside nuisances impossible to each, they did not thereby agree to submit to whatever might be done. They did not renounce the possibility of making reasonable demands on the ground of their still remaining *quasi*-sovereign interests. ...

Some peculiarities necessarily mark a suit of this kind. If the State has a case at all, it is somewhat more certainly entitled to specific relief than a private party might be. It is not lightly to be required to give up *quasi*-sovereign rights for pay; and, apart from the difficulty of valuing such rights in money, if that be its choice it may insist that an infraction of them shall be stopped. The States by entering the Union did not sink to the position of private owners subject to one system of private law. This court has not quite the same freedom to balance the harm that will be done by an injunction against that of which the plaintiff complains, that it would have in deciding between two subjects of a single political power. Without excluding the considerations that equity always takes into account, we cannot give the weight that was given them in argument to a comparison between the damage threatened to the plaintiff and the calamity of a possible stop to the defendants' business, the question of health, the character of the forests as a first or second growth, the commercial possibility or impossibility of reducing the fumes to sulphuric acid, the special adaptation of the business to the place.

It is a fair and reasonable demand on the part of a sovereign that the air over its territory should not be polluted on a great scale by sulphurous acid gas, that the forests on its mountains, be they better or worse, and whatever domestic destruction they have suffered, should not be further destroyed or threatened by the act of persons beyond its control, that the crops and orchards on its hills should not be endangered from the same source. If any such demand is to be enforced this must be, notwithstanding the hesitation that we might feel if the suit were between private parties, and the doubt whether for the injuries which they might be suffering to their property they should not be left to an action at law.

The proof requires but a few words. It is not denied that the defendants generate in their works near the Georgia line large quantities of sulphur dioxide which becomes sulphurous acid by its mixture with the air. It hardly is denied and cannot be denied with success that this gas often is carried by the wind great distances and over great tracts of Georgia land. On the evidence the pollution of the air and the magnitude of that pollution are not open to dispute. Without any attempt to go into details immaterial to the suit,

it is proper to add that we are satisfied by a preponderance of evidence that the sulphurous fumes
cause and threaten damage on so considerable a
scale to the forests and vegetable life, if not to
health, within the plaintiff State as to make out
a case within the requirements of *Missouri* v.
Illinois, 200 U.S. 496. Whether Georgia by insisting upon this claim is doing more harm than
good to her own citizens is for her to determine.
The possible disaster to those outside the State
must be accepted as a consequence of her standing upon her extreme rights. . . .

If the State of Georgia adheres to its determination, there is no alternative to issuing an injunction, after allowing a reasonable time to the
defendants to complete the structures that they
now are building, and the efforts that they are
making, to stop the fumes. The plaintiff may
submit a form of decree on the coming in of this
court in October next.

Injunction to issue.

MR. JUSTICE HARLAN, concurring.

The State of Georgia is, in my opinion, entitled
to the general relief sought by its bill, and, therefore, I concur in the result. With some things,
however, contained in the opinion, or to be implied from its language, I do not concur. When
the Constitution gave this court original jurisdiction in cases "in which a State shall be a party,"
it was not intended, I think, to authorize the
court to apply in its behalf, any principle or rule
of equity that would not be applied, under the
same facts, in suits wholly between private parties. If this was a suit between private parties,
and if under the evidence, a court of equity
would not give the plaintiff an injunction, then
it ought not to grant relief, under like circumstances, to the plaintiff, because it happens to be
a State possessing some powers of sovereignty.
Georgia is entitled to the relief sought, not because it is a State, but because it is a *party* which
has established its right to such relief by proof.
The opinion, if I do not mistake its scope, proceeds largely upon the ground that this court, sitting in this case as a court of equity, owes some
special duty to Georgia as a State, although it is

a party, while under the same facts, it would not
owe any such duty to the plaintiff, if an individual.

Notes and Questions

1. In *Diamond* v. *General Motors,* 20 Cal. App. 3d
   374, 97 Cal. Rptr. 639 (1971), a class action was
   brought on behalf of all the residents of Los
   Angeles County against 293 corporations engaged
   in automobile manufacture, refining and distribut-
   ing oil products, generating energy, transportation for damages, and injunctive relief for air
   pollution. Their suit was dismissed and they appealed. In their brief on appeal the plaintiffs argued:

   This lawsuit was prompted by the steady deterioration of the air supply of Los Angeles
   County, and the lack of any significant response by the executive and legislative
   branches of various levels of government.
   Legislative tinkering with ineffective laws,
   illusory, periodic bureaucratic reorganizations,
   and industry controlled administrators have
   led to drastic increases in discomfort, disease,
   and death. More and more, legal scholars
   have concluded that judicial intervention is
   necessary and proper.

   Later they contended:

   The defendants who ask this Court to defer
   to the legislative and executive branches of
   the government are the same persons who
   continue to corrupt the system with their
   lobbying, influence peddling, and campaign
   contributions. Defendants do not come into
   court with clean hands. This honorable Court
   is the only institution which they cannot contaminate. If there is to be a solution to this
   environmental tragedy, it will have to come
   from the judiciary.

   The court upheld the dismissal stating:

   Once it is acknowledged that a superior court
   cannot, by decree, abolish air pollution, it is
   appropriate to face some demonstrable realities of the problem which plaintiff is asking
   the court to solve. We do not deal with a
   simple dispute between those who breathe the
   air and those who contaminate it. The need
   for controls is not in question. The issue is
   not "shall we," but "what kind, how much,
   how soon."

Both the United States Congress and the California Legislature have decided that the discharge of air contaminants must be controlled. Legislative enactments have provided for administrative machinery at the federal, state and local levels. These agencies conduct research, hold public hearings, and, upon the knowledge thereby acquired, set and revise the allowable limits for the discharge of the various kinds of contaminants. The statutory systems provide means for enforcement of the standards through license revocation, civil injunctions and criminal prosecution.

Plaintiff's brief makes it clear that his case is not based upon violation of any existing air pollution control law or regulation. His position is that the present system of statutes and administrative rules is inadequate, and that the enforcement machinery is ineffective. Plaintiff is simply asking the court to do what the elected representatives of the people have not done: adopt stricter standards over the discharge of air contaminants in this country, and enforce them with the contempt power of the court.

It is indisputable that there exists, within the community, a substantial difference of opinion as to what changes in industrial processes should be required and how soon, what new technology is feasible, what reduction in the volume of goods and services should result and what increase in production costs for the sake of cleaner air will be acceptable. These issues are debated in the political arena and are being resolved by the action of those elected to serve in the legislative and executive branches of government.

We assume, for the purposes of this decision, that notwithstanding the existing administrative machinery, anyone claiming to have sustained personal injury or property damage caused by an unreasonable discharge of contaminants into the atmosphere by one or more of the defendants could state a cause of action for his damages and for injunctive relief. But the class action attempted by plaintiff, as the purported representative of every resident of the county, is a wholly different kind of suit. The objective, which plaintiff envisions to justify his class action, is judicial regulation of the processes, products and volume of business of the major industries of the county.

It was entirely reasonable for the trial court to conclude from the face of the pleading that such an undertaking was beyond its effective capability.

How does the court anticipate that the varying interests in environmental questions will be accommodated? Is this expectation reasonable? Desirable?

2. For a discussion of the contemporary difficulties in moving against intransigent polluting corporations see A. D. Wolfe and F. J. Naffziger, *Legal Perspectives of American Business Associations* (Columbus: Grid, 1977), pp. 650ff. The case involved efforts by environmental groups, the states of Minnesota, Michigan, and Wisconsin and the United States government to stop the dumping into Lake Superior of tailings from taconite mining operations by the Reserve Mining Company, a wholly owned subsidiary of Armco Steel and Republic Steel.

4 Law and Popular Will

The Chief Magistrate derives all of his authority from the people.

A. Lincoln, *First Inaugural Address*

... that this nation, under God, shall have a new birth of freedom—and that government of the people, by the people and for the people, shall not perish from the earth.

A. Lincoln, *Gettysburg Address*

The People, united, can never be defeated.

Kent State Protest, 1977

In a period when alienation from virtually all social institutions proceeds swiftly, it may seem a little absurd to advance the idea that law is an expression of the will of the people. The influence of voters who cast periodic ballots is, at best, diffuse, and they are not likely to believe that they are sovereign, directing the activities of public servants.

When the relationship of law to popular will was refined in the nineteenth century, scholarly interest centered on the origins of law and the evolution of legal institutions. Legal development was thought to be a sequence of events: First, practices and sentiments occur in a group of people, without their being conscious that certain activities are the "right" ones or the "only" ones. After a time, particularly on occasions of deviance from prior practice, a way of acting or believing becomes *the* way of acting or believing; custom becomes law.

Readers of the early literature are left with the idea that there is an organic connection between law and custom: Law grows out of custom; or, in other words, custom is embryonic law, practice on its way to being made perfect—as soon as an appropriate level of consciousness is reached. The materials on the law-government system of the Cheyenne, which appear in this section, suggest that the organic connection between law and custom is not wholly inaccurate, as does the case of the *Spoiled Chiles* in Section 3.

As society grows larger and more specialized, people certainly feel less correspondence between their understanding and the institutions around them. Thus, whereas a Cheyenne came to know intimately much of the law of the tribe, it is highly unlikely that in modern America citizens will know, let alone concur with, much of the law that could touch their lives. Understandably, the expression "Can *they* do that?" displaces "This is how *we* handle situations like that"; bewilderment and alienation replace effortless unity.

Perhaps Stanley Diamond, a contemporary anthropologist, more aptly describes the modern condition:

> [E]fforts to legislate conscience by an external political power are the antithesis of custom; customary behavior comprises precisely those aspects of social behavior which are traditional, moral and religious, which are, in short, conventional and nonlegal. Put another way, custom is social morality. The relationship between custom and law is basically one of contradiction, not continuity.[*]

So if for the earlier writers the connection between law and custom was felicitous, for Diamond the rule of law is a sign of social breakdown. Under law, life is less livable.

There are numerous difficulties in making contemporary applications of either theory. Who are *the* people whose will is expressed or frustrated by law? *The people* may mean a numerical majority, an influential elite, the poor, the middle class, blacks, women, white Anglo-Saxon male Protestants, the young, the aged, and so on. Although popular sentiment may be similar across virtually all subsets of the whole, on many issues sentiments will differ.

By what means do popular sentiments get expressed? By voting? Street protests? Boycotts? "Public interest groups"? Fancy lobbyists? What is the link between belief and legal action and outcomes? Is popular activism designed to get law made or unmade?

Then there is the additional problem of timing the relationship between popular belief and legal action. At what point does the buildup of practice make a reflection of those beliefs

[*] Stanley Diamond, "The Rule of Law Versus the Order of Custom" in Stanley Diamond, *In Search of the Primitive* (New Brunswick, N.J.: Transaction, 1974), p. 257.

in law inevitable? How many marijuana violations make the marijuana laws unenforceable? And when law adequately reflects popular sentiments of one period, what happens in subsequent periods when beliefs have changed but the law has not? Divorce laws may once have been consistent with the wishes of the people, but are not in an era when many marriages end in divorce.

The difficulties in relating popular will to law may tempt one to scrap the whole enterprise, or to limit such an inquiry to "simple" societies. There are enough occasions, however, when legal outcomes are best explained in terms of public sentiment, to warrant some additional study of the notion. In *People* v. *Collins* community attitudes about interracial marriages may have been the prime determinant of police and prosecution zeal. In the North Carolina wife-beating cases, the courts might have been groping for the right fit between law and working beliefs—however horrendous the groping looks in contemporary terms. And in the *Ducktown Sulphur* case the court was no doubt aware that an order closing the plants would have caused a local furor.

Although the ability of people to effect changes in the legal order have been sporadic, there have been numerous instances of popular activism. In the nineteenth century, populism took the form of advocating soft money to ease the payment of debt, opposing railroad power, and pressing for the legal recognition of labor unions; not surprisingly, most people who have sought substantial changes—from blacks to farmers to Wobblies to Suffragettes to immigrants—have found themselves on the wrong side of the law.

More currently, popular opposition to law-government power has been apparent in civil rights activism, Vietnam War resistance, anti-nuclear energy protest, farmer strikes for parity, women's and minority group pressure for equality, the gay rights movement, and others. These groups have historical cousins dating back to the American Revolution.

In criminal law and practice, community pressure sometimes becomes especially important. The *Benge* case presented in this section provides one example of this phenomenon. As an example of formal law running counter to community practice, see *Cox* v. *Cox and the J. I. Case Company,* a New Mexico case involving an on-the-job accident.

The Cheyenne Way   *Karl N. Llewellyn and E. Adamson Hoebel*

The Tribal Ostracism and Reinstatement of Sticks Everything Under His Belt

Once, at a time when all the Cheyenne tribe was gathered together, Sticks Everything Under His Belt went out hunting buffalo alone. "I am hunting for myself," he told the people. He was implying that the rules against individual hunting

From *The Cheyenne Way*, by Karl N. Llewellyn and E. Adamson Hoebel. Copyright 1941 by the University of Oklahoma Press, pp. 9–15. Reprinted by permission. (Footnotes omitted.)

did not apply to him because he was declaring himself out of the tribe—a man on his own.

All the soldier chiefs and all the tribal chiefs met in a big lodge to decide what to do in this case, since such a thing had never happened before. This was the ruling they made: no one could help Sticks Everything Under His Belt in any way, no one could give him smoke, no one could talk to him. They were cutting him off from the tribe. The chiefs declared that if anyone helped him in any way that person would have to give a Sun Dance.

When the camp moved, Sticks Everything Under His Belt moved with it, but the people would not recognize him. He was left alone and it went to his heart, so he took one of his horses (he had many) and rode out to the hilltops to mourn.

His sister's husband was a chief in the camp. This brother-in-law felt sorry for him out there mourning, with no more friends. At last he took pity on his poor brother-in-law; at last he spoke to his wife, "I feel sorry for your poor brother out there and now I am going to do something for him. Cook up all those tongues we have! Prepare a good feast!"

Then he invited the chiefs to his lodge and sent for his brother-in-law to come in. This was after several years had passed, not months.

When the chiefs had assembled, the brother-in-law spoke. "Several years ago you passed a ruling that no one could help this man. Whoever should do so you said would have to give a Sun Dance. Now is the time to take pity on him. I am going to give a Sun Dance to bring him back in. I beg you to let him come back to the tribe, for he has suffered long enough. This Sun Dance will be a great one. I declare that every chief and all the soldiers must join in. Now I put it up to you. Shall we let my brother-in-law smoke before we eat, or after?"

The chiefs all answered in accord, "Ha-ho, ha-ho [thank you, thank you]. We are very glad you are going to bring back this man. However, let him remember that he will be bound by whatever rules the soldiers lay down for the tribe. He may not say he is outside of them. He has been out of the tribe for a long time. If he remembers these things, he may come back."

Then they asked Sticks Everything Under His Belt whether he wanted to smoke before or after they had eaten. Without hesitation he replied, "Before," because he had craved tobacco so badly that he had split his pipe stem to suck the brown gum inside of it.

The lodge was not big enough to hold all the chiefs who had come to decide this thing, so they threw open the door, and those who could not get in sat in a circle outside. Then they filled a big pipe and when it was lighted they gave it to Sticks Everything Under His Belt. It was so

long since he had had tobacco that he gulped in the smoke and fell over in a faint. As he lay there the smoke came out of his anus, he was so empty. The chiefs waited silently for him to come to again and then the pipe·was passed around the circle.

When all had smoked, Sticks Everything Under His Belt talked. "From now on I am going to run with the tribe. Everything the people say, I shall stay right by it. My brother-in-law has done a great thing. He is going to punish himself in the Sun Dance to bring me back. He won't do it alone, for I am going in, too."

After a while the people were getting ready for the Sun Dance. One of the soldiers began to get worried because he had an ugly growth on his body which he did not want to reveal to the people. He was a good-looking young man named Black Horse. Black Horse went to the head chiefs asking them to let him sacrifice himself alone on the hilltops as long as the Sun Dance was in progress.

"We have nothing to say to that," they told him. "Go to the pledger. This is his Sun Dance."

Black Horse went to the brother-in-law of Sticks Everything Under His Belt, who was a brother-in-law to him as well. "Brother-in-law," he begged, "I want to be excused from going into the lodge. Can't you let me go into the hills to sacrifice myself as long as you are in there, to make my own bed?"

"No," he was rebuffed, "you know my rule is that all must be there."

"Well, brother-in-law, won't it be all right if I set up a pole on the hill and hang myself to it through my breasts? I shall hang there for the duration of the dance."

This brother-in-law of his answered him in these words, "Why didn't you take that up when all the chiefs were in the lodge? I have agreed with them that everyone must be in the lodge. I don't want to change the rule. I won't give you permission to go outside."

Then Black Horse replied, "You will not make the rules my way. Now I am going to put in a rule for everybody. Everyone in there has to swing from the pole as I do."

"No," countered the brother-in-law. "That was

not mentioned in the meeting. If you want to swing from the pole, that is all right, but no one else has to unless he wishes to."

When they had the Sun Dance everyone had a good time. Black Horse was the only one on the pole, and there were so many in the lodge that there was not room enough for all to dance. Some just had to sit around inside the lodge. Though they did not dance, they starved themselves for four days. This dance took place near Sheridan, Wyoming, seven years before Custer. I was only a year old at that time, but what I have said here I was told by Elk River and others. We call this place "Where The Chiefs Starved Themselves."

Cries Yia Eya Banished for the Murder of Chief Eagle

Cries Yia Eya had been gone from the camp for three years because he had killed Chief Eagle in a whiskey brawl. The chiefs had ordered him away for his murder, so we did not see anything of him for that time. Then one day he came back, leading a horse packed with bundles of old-time tobacco. He stopped outside the camp and sent a messenger in with the horse and tobacco who was to say to the chiefs for him, "I am begging to come home."

The chiefs all got together for a meeting, and the soldier societies were told to convene, for there was an important matter to be considered. The tobacco was divided up and chiefs' messengers were sent out to invite the soldier chiefs to come to the lodge of the tribal council, for the big chiefs wanted to talk to them. "Here is the tobacco that that man sent in," they told the soldier chiefs. "Now we want you soldiers to decide if you think we should accept his request. If you decide that we should let him return, then it is up to you to convince his family that it is all right." (The relatives of Chief Eagle had told everybody that they would kill Cries Yia Eya on sight if they ever found him. "If we set eyes on him, he'll never make another track," they had vowed.) The soldier chiefs took the tobacco and went out to gather their troops. Each society met in its own separate lodge to talk among them-

selves, but the society servants kept passing back and forth between their different lodges to report on the trend of the discussion in the different companies.

At last one man said, "I think it is all right. I believe the stink has blown from him. Let him return!" This view was passed around, and this is the view that won out among the soldiers. Then the father of Chief Eagle was sent for and asked whether he would accept the decision. "Soldiers," he replied, "I shall listen to you. Let him return! But if that man comes back, I want never to hear his voice raised against another person. If he does, we come together. As far as that stuff of his is concerned, I want nothing that belonged to him. Take this share you have set aside for me and give it to someone else."

Cries Yia Eya had always been a mean man, disliked by everyone, but he had been a fierce fighter against the enemies. After he came back to the camp, however, he was always good to the people.

When Walking Rabbit Raised a Problem

A war party was organizing. Walking Rabbit approached the leader with a question. "Is it true that you have declared we must all go afoot? If so, I would like to be able to lead a horse to pack my moccasins and possibles." The leader gave him an answer. "There is a reason for my ruling. I want no horses, that it may be easier for us to conceal our movements. However, you may bring one horse." Then Walking Rabbit asked for instructions concerning the location of the first and second nights' camps, for he would start late and overtake the party.

Walking Rabbit's sweetheart had been married only recently to another. "My husband is not the man I thought he was," she told her former suitor. So Walking Rabbit took her to join the war party. [The Cheyennes have a phrase for the single man who marries a one-time married woman—"putting on the old moccasin."] In this way, it turned out that the "moccasin" he was packing was a big woman.

When they saw this woman there, the warriors got excited. The party turned into the hills and stopped. The leader opened his pipe. The leader's pipe was always filled before they left the camp, but it was not smoked until the enemy was seen or their tracks reported. Now the leader spoke. "When we take a woman with us it is usually known in the camp. Here is a man who has sneaked off with another's wife. Now what is going to happen?" That is what they were talking about.

The leader declared, "The only thing this man can do is return and make a settlement with the husband. Then he may follow us up."

One warrior was for aiding Walking Rabbit. "Why can't we let him stay?" was his proposal. "If we take any horses, we can give them to her husband." That was rejected.

The decision was that he had to go back. "If you had told us you wanted her so badly, we might have waited for you to settle for her. Then we could have taken her the right way. If you really want to go to war with us, you will be able to overtake us. We are afoot."

Then three or four warriors spoke up, each promising Walking Rabbit a horse to send to the husband. Everyone gave one or two arrows to be sent as well.

In the meantime Walking Rabbit's father had fixed it up with the aggrieved husband. Since he and his wife were incompatible, he was willing to release her. When Walking Rabbit came in and told his father the story of the soldiers' action, the father said, "Just let that stand. The thing is fixed. When those fighters come back they may want to give to the girl's parents. You go back after your party." But Walking Rabbit preferred to stay at home.

When Walking Rabbit did not go out, his closest relatives raised a big tipi. When they heard of the approach of the returning war party, everything was in readiness.

The warriors came charging in, shooting; they had taken many horses. The first coup-counters were in the van. Walking Rabbit's father had a right to harangue; he was a crier. "Don't go to your homes! Don't go to your own lodges! Come here to the lodge of Walking Rabbit, your friend!"

When they were all in this lodge the old man entered and told them his story. "I had this thing all settled before my son returned. You have sent arrows and promised horses. Now I have kept this girl here pending your return. I shall send her back to her parents with presents. I have waited to see what you are going to do."

The leader replied for his followers. "Yes, we will help you. We promised to help your son. When you send her back, we'll send presents with her." The men who had promised horses went out to get them. Others gave captured horses.

Sending her back with these presents was giving wedding gifts. Her relatives got them all. They gathered up their goods to send back. The war party was called together once more; to them this stuff was given. It was a great thing for the people to talk about. It was the first and last time a woman was sent home on enemy horses the day they came in.

Questions

1. What was the law in these cases?

2. What was the relationship between the law and the popular sentiments of the Cheyenne?

3. Was there a precedent system operating here?

4. What values were at stake in the cases?

5. How were the varying positions or interests delineated, recognized, and secured?

6. Did the Cheyenne equivalent of the person on the street have anything to complain about regarding the way trouble was handled or the outcomes reached?

On June 9, 1865, a serious railway accident occurred at Staplehurst, England. The *London Times* carried full coverage of the event and the resulting injuries and deaths. The wreck was the most dramatic in a series of railway accidents which had already produced sharp public criticism of the safety standards on English railroads.

Henry Benge, the defendant in the following case, while by all admissions a man of upright character, came to personify the demand that something be done about the tragic events. After misreading a timetable it was he who had ordered that tracks be taken up at the Staplehurst bridge for repair. The train, proceeding as if the tracks were intact, had plunged at virtually full speed into the breach. The public indignation over the accident is captured in portions of a letter to the *Times:*

> It is impossible to believe that any man in the employ of the railway directors *could,* of malice aforethought, do a deed so diabolical; but it is almost equally unintelligible that a reasoning being, who was not utterly reckless of the lives and sufferings of his fellow creatures, knowing that an express train was at that moment due, should permit that train to rush on to a certain destruction, when the commonest precaution would have averted so horrible a catastrophe.

Regina v. Benge and Another   *4 F. & F. 504. Kent Summer Assizes, 1865*

The prisoners,* Benge and Gallimore, were indicted for that on the 9th of June last they did feloniously kill and slay one Hannah Condliff. There were many other counts, each charging the manslaughter of another person on the same day.

The prosecution arose out of a fatal railway accident, which occurred on the South Eastern Railway at a place called Staplehurst, where there was a bridge, about two miles in the direction towards London from a station called Headcorn. The tidal trains of that day would be due at Staplehurst at 3.15 P.M., on Friday, the 9th of June. The prisoner Benge was foreman of a gang of plate-layers, who had been employed to repair the rails within a certain distance, including the portion of the line at Staplehurst, and for that purpose it would be necessary to take up and replace the rails. There were eight or nine men employed under the prisoner to do this work, and the other prisoner, Gallimore, was inspector of the line for the distance of 36 miles, comprising the Staplehurst part of the line. The time at which the work was done at any part of the line was

* [In Britain, persons held for trial are called prisoners.——Ed.]

left to the direction of the prisoner Benge, as the foreman of the gang. And he was furnished with a time book, in which the precise time of the arrival of the various trains on each day was marked for each week, in columns headed by the name of the day of the week. This book was clear in its arrangement, and printed in good, large, legible type, so that with the least care in its perusal, no mistake would be possible. The hour of arrival of the tidal train varied of course with the tide, and was different on each day. And on the day in question the prisoner Benge had looked at the column for Saturday—the next day—instead of Friday, the 9th. The time of arrival on the Saturday would be 5.20 P.M.; whereas the time for Friday, the day in question, would be 3.15. Thinking that the time would be 5.20, the prisoner Benge, when the last of the trains before the tidal train had passed, which was at 2.50 P.M., directed his gang to take up the rails at Staplehurst bridge, and they were accordingly taken up. There was, it will be seen, barely half an hour between the time at which the 2.50 train passed, and the time—3.15—at which the tidal train would arrive, and half an hour as it turned out, and as indeed was well known would be far too short a time to allow of the rails taken up being replaced! If the prisoner had read the time of arrival of the tidal train rightly, he would not have thought of taking up the rails, but he did not expect it until 5.20, which would have allowed nearly three hours, and the job would be completed in about an hour. He had no particular directions from the other prisoner, Gallimore, the inspector of the line; nor any particular instructions from any one. Nor was any notice sent on to the next station, Headcorn, from which the tidal trains would arrive. Neither did it appear that it was usual to send such notice, or to give notice to the driver of the trains which were to pass. It was usual, however, to send on one of the gang as a signal man with a flag in his hand, who was to go on at least 1000 yards in the direction in which the expected train was to come, and when he had got that distance he was to stand and raise a flag when it appeared, which would be seen at a distance of above 500 yards, and thus would give a distance of 1500 yards, or nearly a mile, between the train and the spot at which the rails were up, so as to allow of ample time to stop the train. Books of printed rules were in the hands of the foreman of plate-layers, and among others, of the prisoner; and these rules expressly provided that rails should not be taken up without these precautions. On the occasion in question one of the men of the prisoner's gang, named Wills, was sent forward as signal man, but without (as it appeared) any particular directions from the prisoner Benge, and instead of going 1000 yards he went, as he said, only 540 yards; and there he stood till he saw the advancing train, and moved his flag. He was observed, but not until the train was too near to be stopped. The engine-driver was not paying a very sharp lookout, and though so soon as he saw the signal man he gave the signal to stop, and the steam was shut off, and the breaks [*sic*] put on, it was too late to stop the train, which was going at the rate of 50 miles an hour, and it came on to the bridge, and then running off the line at the spot where the rails were up, it dashed on to the bridge, and the catastrophe ensued in which many lives were lost.

There was evidence that at the distance of 1000 yards, the train could easily have been stopped, at any rate of speed.

Ballantine, Serjt., admitted that there was no case against Gallimore, who only was arraigned on the coroner's indictment inquisition, the grand jury having thrown out the bill. The case proceeded only against Benge.

Ribton, for the prisoner, submitted that there was no evidence of any criminal act or default on his part which had caused the death. It appeared that the accident could not have happened, notwithstanding the mistake which the prisoner had undoubtedly committed, if other servants of the company had done their duty; if, for instance, the flagman had gone far enough with the signal, or if the engine-driver had kept a sufficient look-out, and had seen the signal, as then he must have seen it earlier than he did, and in time enough to stop the train.

PIGOTT, B., said, that assuming culpable negligence on the part of the prisoner which materially contributed to the accident, it would not be material that others also by their negligence contributed to cause it. Therefore he must leave it to the jury whether there was negligence of the prisoner which had been the substantial cause of the accident. In summing up the case to the jury, he said, their verdict must depend upon whether the death was mainly caused by the culpable negligence of the prisoner. Was the accident mainly caused by the taking up of the rails at a time when an express train was about to arrive, was that the act of the prisoner, and was it owing to culpable negligence on his part? His counsel had urged that it was not so, because the flagman and engine-driver had been guilty of negligence, which had contributed to cause the catastrophe; but they, in their turn, might make the same excuse, and so, if it was valid, no one could be criminally responsible at all. This would be an absurd and unreasonable conclusion, and showed that the contention of the prisoner's counsel could not be sound. Such was not the right view of the law—that of [*sic*] the negligence of several persons at different times and places contributed to cause an accident, any one of them could set up that his was not the sole cause of it. It was enough against any one of them that his negligence was the substantial cause of it. Now, here the primary cause was certainly the taking up of the rails at a time when the train was about to arrive, and when it would be impossible to replace them in time to avoid the accident. And this the prisoner admitted was owing to his own mistake. Was that mistake culpable negligence, and did it mainly or substantially cause the accident? The book was clearly and plainly printed, and must have been read carelessly to admit of such a mistake. Was it not the duty of the prisoner who knew the fearful consequences of a mistake to take reasonable care to be correct? And had he taken such care? Then as to its being the main cause of the accident, it was true that the company had provided other precautions to avoid any impending catastrophe, and that these were not observed upon this occasion; but was it not owing to the prisoner's culpable negligence that the accident was impending, and, if so, did his negligence the less cause it, because if other persons had not been negligent it might possibly have been avoided?

Verdict—Guilty.

Notes and Questions

1. When a disaster occurs, are people likely to demand a result like that reached in the *Benge* case? Does a good legal system accommodate this popular drive or resist it?

2. If the people demand a result and the legal system refuses the result, are there any undesirable consequences?

3. Did the court draw the network of responsibility too narrowly, or should it have extended it to higher officials of the railroad company?

4. How did the treatment of Benge compare with the treatment of Cheyennes who offended?

5. The evolution of the laws pertaining to divorce provide an interesting example of the relationship of law to popular practices.
   a. At the time of the printing of the first edition of this text, Massachusetts had the following statute on the grounds for divorce:
      A divorce from the bond of matrimony may be decreed for adultery, impotency, utter desertion continued for two consecutive years next prior to the filing of the libel, gross and confirmed habits of intoxication caused by the voluntary and excessive use of intoxicating liquor, opium or other drugs, cruel and abusive treatment or, on the libel of the wife, if the husband, being of sufficient ability, grossly or wantonly and cruelly refuses or neglects to provide suitable maintenance for her. As amended St.1967, c. 585, §1. (Mass. General Laws, Ch. 208, §1.)
      But shortly afterward the law was amended to allow divorce for "irretrievable breakdown of the marriage." However, the state did not move completely to "no fault" divorce because the waiting period for the more liberal ground was longer than for the grounds spelled out in the above provision. Lawyers practicing under the older law had stretched the idea of cruel and abusive treatment so that divorce had become more easily available, and so whether the new ground will be used is problematical.
   b. More "advanced" states like Oregon have had "no fault" divorce for a number of years:
      (1) The doctrines of fault and of *in pari delicto** are abolished in suits for the annulment and dissolution of marriage.
      (2) The court shall not receive evidence of specific acts of misconduct, excepting where child custody is an issue and such evidence is relevant to that issue, or excepting at a hearing when the court finds such evidence necessary to prove irreconcilable differences.
      (3) In dividing, awarding and distributing the real and personal property (or both) of the parties . . . and in fixing the amount and duration of the contribution one party is to make to the support of another, the court shall not consider the fault, if any, of either of the parties in causing grounds for the annulment or dissolution of the marriage. (Oregon Revised Statutes.)

6. Marijuana is probably the best example since Prohibition of the futility of using the threat of criminal sanction to counter common practice. A 1972 report by the federal government states that as of 1971, 42 per cent of college students had used marijuana. In the population over the age of eleven, the estimate of the total number of people

* [The doctrine providing that where both parties were shown to be at fault in divorce proceedings, neither party could get a divorce.——Ed.]

who had used marijuana ranged up to almost 25 million.

The retreat of law from marijuana has been slow, but predictable. While under some state laws, being "in the presence of marijuana" is enough for a conviction, the law on the books and in practice has made such offenses increasingly rare. Simple possession and use have become distinguishable from "dealing." The practices in each state and locality will differ as to the severity of treatment of each of these acts, but the overall trend of abandonment of efforts to "stop" marijuana usage is unmistakable.

Sometimes officials proudly proclaim that the loosening of the law has resulted from their interest in "giving kids a break." In fact, the reason lies in expediency—there are simply too many occasions when the law is violated. The law folds in on itself when the president of the high school class gets busted for grass.

For additional material on marijuana, consult: *Marihuana: First Report,* House Report 91–978, 91st Cong. 2d sess. (1970); *Marihuana and Health,* Report of Sec. of Health, Educ. & Welfare, 92d Cong., 2nd sess. (1972); *Marihuana: A Signal of Misunderstanding* (Washington, D.C.: Government Printing Office, 1972).

It seems safe to predict that the next decade will see the legalization of the personal use of marijuana.

Cox v. Cox v. J. I. Case Company   *555 P. 2d 378 (N.M. 1976)*

Hendley, Judge.

Plaintiff appeals a summary judgment entered in defendant's favor.... We affirm.

Plaintiff has worked for defendant all of his adult life. He has operated a cotton stripper for at least twenty years. He had been using the stripper for several days before the accident happened. On the front part of the stripper is a nonmoving lifter approximately 16 inches long. This is where the clogging occurs. Behind the lifter are stripper bars and elevating augers—both are turning. When working in short cotton the lifter has a tendency to clog. When unclogging the machine it is sometimes stopped and other times left running. If the machine is stopped it takes longer to get it unclogged. It presents no danger when stopped. A kicker is sometimes used in order to prevent clogging. It is a homemade device similar to a 5 or 6 blade walking wheel. It does not always prevent clogging. The kicker has no safety aspect.

On the day of the accident plaintiff was working in short cotton. He did not have the kicker mounted because defendant told him to go ahead and try to finish without the kicker. In the process the left lifter became clogged. This was not the first time it became clogged that day. In attempting to unclog the lifter, plaintiff got off, left the

(Citations omitted.)

machine running, and was attempting to kick the clog loose with his foot. Plaintiff cannot remember what happened, that is whether he slipped or fell, but his foot got caught in the left auger of the left unit. He was able to shut off the stripper. A cutting torch had to be used to free plaintiff's foot. As a result of the accident plaintiff's right foot was severed.

For the purpose of our discussion we will assume there is a factual issue as to defendant's negligence. The issue is then whether plaintiff was contributorily negligent as a matter of law....

The question of contributory negligence becomes one of law only when reasonable minds cannot differ on the question and readily reach the conclusion that plaintiff's conduct falls below the standard to which he should have conformed for his own protection and that it was plaintiff's negligent conduct which proximately contributed to cause the injury of which he complains....

Plaintiff asserts that there are factual issues relating to whether his "... conduct involved a reasonable risk of injury to himself under those circumstances...." We disagree. Given the foregoing facts we believe that plaintiff was contributorily negligent as a matter of law. The fact that plaintiff subjectively did not consider his actions dangerous is not the issue.... The issue is would a reasonable prudent person anticipate the danger of using his foot to dislodge a clog in an area where there were moving parts of the machine which could cause serious injury.

Plaintiff also asserts that there was an issue of fact as to whether his employer's instructions "...not to use the kicker affected the issue of proximate cause of the plaintiff's injury...." We disagree. It is undisputed that the kicker does not always prevent clogging nor does it add a safety dimension to the machine. Plaintiff attempts to relate this with a failure to provide a safe place to work is misplaced.... Here it is undisputed that the danger was obvious. He also knew of other similar type accidents. Further, for the purpose of this opinion we have already assumed that the defendant was negligent.

Lastly, plaintiff asserts that there was an issue of fact as to "[w]hat effect the custom of the community had on the standard of care when all the witnesses testified it was the common custom in the community to do what plaintiff did." Several witnesses testified by deposition that it was customary in the community to use one's foot to kick loose and unstop the machine when it became clogged.

As stated in *Wills v. Paul,* ... :

> ...In determining whether the particular acts of a plaintiff constitute negligence, the test is not the frequency with which other men commit such acts but whether the plaintiff at the time of the occurrence, used that degree of care which an ordinarily careful person would have used for his own safety under like circumstances....

"We find it difficult to accept a philosophy which asserts that negligent and careless conduct by frequent repetition in a community converts it into a non-negligent conduct...." .... Custom in and of itself is not conclusive. It must meet the standard of ordinary care....

Affirmed.

Questions

1. A summary judgment is given only when there is no factual dispute and the case can be resolved without trial by court or jury. Do you think that the injured party would have fared better if the case had been submitted to a jury? Is the jury the better barometer of community practice?

2. Contributory negligence, which was said to prevent recovery of damages by the injured workman, is defined as the want of ordinary care by the person injured. If people in the community generally operated the machinery in the way that the injured worker did, how can it be said that he had taken less than ordinary care for his own safety?

3. The court states that there is a difference between the community definition of substandard behavior and substandard behavior as "a matter of law." What is the factual basis for conclusions that are a matter of law?

4. Should the manufacturers of agricultural equipment anticipate that there will be pressure on workers to take shortcuts? Must they design their machines so that pressured workers will not be injured in getting out production?

5. Cox was said to have known of similar accidents that should have made him more careful. Is the manufacturer of the machinery held to a knowledge of those instances when their machines have caused injury? If both are at fault for not taking knowledge into account, how should the case be decided?

6. The manufacturer of the equipment is not part of the community where the accident happened. Would it make a difference in the way the dispute were handled if the manufacturer and the injured party were in the same community? If the manufacturer were a person rather than a corporation?

5 Law, Status, Wealth, and Power

When leaving his surgery on the morning of April 16 Dr. Bernard Rieux felt something soft under his foot. It was a dead rat lying in the middle of the landing. On the spur of the moment he kicked it to one side and without giving it further thought, continued on his way downstairs. Only when he stepped forth into the street did it occur to him that a dead rat had no business to be on his landing.

A. Camus, *The Plague*

The preservation of power is a vital necessity for the powerful, since it is their power which provides their sustenance; but they have to preserve it both against their rivals and against their inferiors, and these latter cannot do otherwise than try to rid themselves of dangerous masters; for, through a vicious circle, the master produces fear in the slave by the very fact that he is afraid of him, and vice versa; and the same is true as between rival powers.

Simone Weil, *Oppression and Liberty*

Control the coinage and the courts—let the rabble have the rest.

Frank Herbert, *Dune*

If you're strong, you don't have to say thank you.

Fenna Lee Bonsignore, age four

Max Weber, German lawyer and sociologist, defined law as a *coercive* order, an order that has the potential backing of the full force of the state. He thus distinguished law from other norms such as custom, ethics, or religion that have different sanctions. Elsewhere, he observed that a society has two basic ways of providing rewards to its membership—honor (status) and economic return (wealth, class). A troublesome question arises when law and social rewards are considered together: Is the legal system used to perpetuate prevailing patterns in the allocation of status and wealth?

This is an unpleasant question in American law since our society is said to be classless and each citizen is deemed equal before the law. Notable jurists like Holmes, Llewellyn, and Pound rarely develop the power dimension in law perhaps because it is almost unthinkable that law and legal process may do no more than reinforce social and economic positionings; it is more comfortable to think of law as impartial than as a means to accomplish the wishes of a few well-placed elites.

And yet there are a number of concrete instances that can be explained in no other way. There are rules of law that inhibit the raising of large questions that cut to the quick of the social, political, and economic order. Despite the furor over the fighting of an undeclared war in Vietnam, the courts refused to consider the legality of the war on the ground that a political rather than a legal question was involved. For this reason the courts refused for many years to consider the legality of legislative districting, although historical districts were obviously biased in favor of rural areas at the expense of urban areas. In addition, disputes involving housing, welfare, employment, and other areas that have wide impact are channeled into discrete confines so that contesting parties do not see themselves as representatives of a large group of similarly situated persons who have an interest in redressing larger grievances than those that are apparent on the surface.

Beyond the dampening of threats to the status quo by rules inhibiting legal action, the powerful spend large sums of money and devote substantial energy to keep the law in a favorable configuration. Most notable is the growth of lobbying and other forms of influence peddling at the state and national levels, but also significant are the resources devoted to win contested cases that threaten. Most of the law of contracts and property has been shaped to perpetuate the status quo. Not surprisingly, fine print which is virtually always inimical to the interests of the poor and low-income wage earners—to say nothing of people in small businesses or the consuming public generally—becomes the legal currency of the powerful. It is they who furnish the documentation for transactions, and it is they who benefit from the documents. Insurance policies, promissory notes, mortgages, conditional sales contracts, leases, and other papers are as often instruments of domination as they are evidence of an evenly bargained deal; courts typically will not look beyond the documentation to uncover the realities of a transaction.

Other examples can readily be found. For decades it has been known that laws "governing" corporations have been shaped to meet managerial interests rather than those of shareholders or the general public. Taxation at all levels of government is shot through with preferential rules for the wealthy. And administrative law, covering utility rates, communication, transportation, and other vital services proceeds silently under the sure guidance of those who stand to benefit most from favorable action.

In the making and enforcement of criminal law comparable skewings appear. Gentlemanly offenses like tax evasion, abusing expense accounts, antitrust violations, and embezzlement are treated differently from poor people's offenses such as theft, burglary, or purse-snatching. It is expected that discretion will be exercized by police and prosecutors so that people who are not "criminals" will be saved from the opprobrium that accompanies arrest, criminal process, probation, jail, or prison. Watergate was an unusual and distinctly small exception to this rule, and even there President Nixon got away to write memoirs and do television specials and his aides served token sentences.

The following material examines the impact of status, wealth, class, and power in the civil and criminal law.

Streich v. General Motors Corp. *126 N.E. 2d 389 S. Ill. App. 2d 485 (1955)*

McCormick, J. . . .

. . . The complaint was filed in an action for damages occasioned by the defendant's alleged wrongful cancellation of a contract. . . .

A motion to dismiss the complaint was filed by the defendant, in which, among other things, it was alleged that purchase order No. 11925 shows on its face that the plaintiff need not make or deliver, and that the defendant need not buy, any air magnet valves as therein identified, except when and as specified in written releases issued by the defendant. . . .

The trial court . . . dismissed the suit. . . .

There were three exhibits attached to the complaint. Purchase Order No. 11925 provided that it was a purchase order for air magnet valves, drawing 8024271 Rev. A, at a price of $13.50 net each. On the face of the purchase order it was provided:

This Purchase Order is issued to cover shipments of this part, to be received by us from September 1, 1948, to August 31, 1949, as released and scheduled on our series 48 "Purchase Order release and Shipping Schedule" No. 478412 attached and all subsequent Purchase Order releases.

The total quantity covered by this Purchase Order will always be included in the amount shown under "Total Released" on the latest "Purchase Order Release and Shipping Schedule."

This order was dated April 19, 1948. It provided that the order, including the terms and conditions on the face and reverse side, constitute "the complete and final agreement between Buyer and Seller and no other agreement in any way modifying any of said terms and conditions will be binding upon Buyer unless made in writing and signed by Buyer's authorized representative."

On the reverse side are twenty-three provisions, among which are the following:

The contract resulting from the acceptance of this order is to be construed according to the laws of the state.... This contract is nonassignable by Seller.

Deliveries are to be made both in quantities and at times specified in schedules furnished by Buyer. Buyer will have no liability for payment for material or items delivered to Buyer which are in excess of quantities specified in the delivery schedules. Buyer may from time to time change delivery schedules or direct temporary suspension of scheduled shipments.

Buyer reserves the right to cancel all or any of the undelivered portion of this order if Seller does not make deliveries as specified in the schedules, or if Seller breaches any of the terms hereof including the warranties of Seller.

Unless otherwise herein agreed, Seller at its own expense shall furnish, keep in good condition and replace when necessary all dies, tools, gauges, fixtures and patterns necessary for the production of the material ordered.... Buyer has the option, however, to take possession of and title to any dies, tools, gauges, fixtures and patterns that are special for the production of the material covered by this order and shall pay to Seller the unamortized cost thereof; provided, however, that this option shall not apply if the material hereby ordered is the standard product of Seller or if a substantial quantity of like material is being sold by Seller to others....

It is the contention of the plaintiff, Frank Streich, hereafter referred to as "seller," that the defendant, General Motors Corporation, hereafter referred to as the "buyer," had entered into a binding contract to purchase all the requirements of the buyer from September 1, 1948, through August 31, 1949, from the seller, and that, while the amount of the requirements was not specified, parol evidence [oral agreements] might be properly introduced to show what the requirements were....

... The promise of the seller to furnish identified items at a stated price is merely an offer and cannot become a contract until the buyer issues a release or order for a designated number of items. Until this action is taken the buyer has made no promise to do anything, and either party may withdraw. The promise is illusory, and the chimerical contract vanishes. "An agreement to sell to another such of the seller's goods, wares, and merchandise as the other might from time to time desire to purchase is lacking in mutuality because it does not bind the buyer to purchase any of the goods of the seller, as such matter is left wholly at the option or pleasure of the buyer." ...

... The agreement in question is an adaptation of what was termed an "open end contract," which was used extensively by the federal government during the late war. However, it was used only in cases where the commodities dealt with were staples and either in the possession of or easily accessible to the seller. In this case the use of the contract is shifted and extended to cover commodities which must be manufactured before they are available for sale. According to the admitted statements in the complaint, special tools had to be manufactured in order to produce the item herein involved. The seller here, misled by the many and detailed provisions contained in purchase order No. 11925 and ordinarily applicable to an enforceable bilateral contract, undoubtedly, as he alleged in his complaint, did go to considerable expense in providing tools and machines, only to find that by the accepted agreement the buyer had promised to do absolutely nothing. A statement of expectation creates no duty. Courts are not clothed with the power to make contracts for parties, nor can they, under the guise of interpretation, supply provisions actually lacking or impose obligations not actually assumed.

... The seller also argues the fact that he has alleged in his complaint he was advised by the defendant it would release approximately 1,600 units for shipment under the said purchase order. The written purchase order 11925 contains a provision that the terms and conditions thereof are the complete and final agreement between the buyer and the seller....

> In *Sterling-Midland Coal Co.* v. *Great Lakes Coal [& Coke] Co.,* 334 Ill. 281, at page 290, 165 N.E. 793, at page 797, wherein the Supreme Court in passing upon a contract similar to this one, said: "If a written contract purports on its face to be a complete expression of the whole agreement, it is to be presumed that the parties introduced into it every material item and term, and parol evidence is not admissible to add another term to the agreement about which the contract is silent.... In the instant case, any such rights, duties, or liabilities which would arise by implication of law are specifically negatived by the provisions which each contract contains, 'there are no understandings or agreements relative to this contract or its subject matter that are not fully expressed herein.' ... The clause of the contract just quoted not only negatives the fact that there are any contemporaneous parol understandings or agreements existing between the parties relative to the contract, but also expressly negatives the fact that there are any understandings, whether arising by implication of law or otherwise, between the parties, as to the subject-matter of the contract—i. e., as to the coal itself which is the subject-matter of the contract. This clause of the contract is just as binding upon the parties as any other clause, and the municipal and Appellate Courts had no right to disregard it."

In the instant case the seller argues that the suit should not be dismissed because if the case were tried he should be permitted to introduce parol evidence for the purpose of showing an agreement on the part of the buyer to purchase approximately 1,600 valves. The formal agreement contained in purchase order 11925 purports to be a final and complete agreement. A provision therein contained so recites. Parol evidence of this character would vary and contradict the terms of the agreement, and such evidence is inadmissible.

Professor Fuller, discussing insurance and correspondence school contracts, says:

> One often has the impression of a kind of running battle between draftsmen and the courts, with much shifting of ground on the part of both.
>
> Back of this development lies a problem that touches the basic philosophy of contract law. The law of contracts is founded generally on the principle that it is the business of the courts to interpret and enforce the agreements that the parties have negotiated. This theory confronts the social reality that in many cases no real negotiations take place, and the terms of the contract are in fact set by the will of one party alone. This situation may arise where one party is indifferent or ignorant, or it may result from a superiority of bargaining power on one side. In such situations, there seems to be emerging a principle of law not yet frankly acknowledged which might be phrased something as follows: where one party to a contract has the power to dictate its terms, the terms of the contract are subject to judicial review, and may be modified by the court if they are unduly harsh. [Fuller, Basic Contract Law, p. 260.]

The courts have many times passed on cases involving insurance contracts, which in many respects are similar to the agreement in this case. Concerning such cases it has been said:

> The history of the cases is, very largely, the history of a struggle between the insurance companies and the courts.... The courts, endeavoring to compel fair play, but trammelled and often thwarted by the stringent terms of the contracts, have devised doctrines and asserted principles which are sometimes more creditable to the ingenuity and subtlety of the judges than easily harmonized with decisions rendered, under less violent bias, in other departments of the law.

The agreement contained in purchase order No. 11925 was artfully prepared. It contains, in print so fine as to be scarcely legible, more than twenty-three clauses, most of which are applicable to bilateral contracts. It has all the indicia of a binding and enforceable contract, but it was not a binding and enforceable contract because the promise was defective. Behind the glittering facade is a void. This agreement was made in the higher echelons of business, overshadowed by the aura of business ethics. To say the least, the agreement was deceptive. In a more subterranean atmosphere and between persons of lower ethical standards it might, without any strain on the language, be denominated by a less deterged appellation.

Nevertheless, as the law is today, on the pleadings in the instant case, the trial court could do nothing but sustain the motion to dismiss the complaint. The judgment of the Circuit Court is affirmed.

Judgment affirmed.

Notes and Questions

1. The judge seems to be saying at the end of his opinion that the result is legally correct, but ethically wrong. What rules of law impeded his reaching a contrary result? What interests stand to benefit most from such rules of law?

2. Some of the provisions of the purchase order are set out in the opinion. Who drew them up? Who stands to benefit from them? Why would a person disadvantaged under a proposed agreement sign? What does that person's signature indicate?

3. Which interests in society stand to benefit most from rules of law that require strict interpretation of contracts and limit the court from going beyond the documentation?

4. The court states that the parties here had an agreement, but no contract. What is the difference? Would most people think that there is a difference?

5. Sometimes agreements are compared to private governments set up to accomplish a result. What kind of government was established by the parties here?

6. In the 1972 issue of Martindale Hubbell, a directory of lawyers, Robert J. Gorman, counsel to Streich, is shown to be a solo practitioner. Pope and Ballard, attorneys for General Motors, is a firm with forty-eight lawyers in Chicago and eleven in Washington, D.C. While it must be conceded that a legal David can slay a Goliath with a well-placed stone, the figures demonstrate that there can be gross differences in the availability of legal talent and resources in contested cases. Under American practice, parties must pay for their own lawyers whether they win or lose (unless a contrary provision is written into the agreement!).

7. At the most General Motors stood to pay $23,600 to Streich. Why all the commotion and high-priced legal talent?

8. Streich is regarded as having his own personal lawsuit against General Motors. Suppose that he could find other suppliers to General Motors who were similarly situated to him. Would it be appropriate for them to gather their claims and other grievances in one lawsuit? Lacking this, should a party to a particular lawsuit be able to demonstrate General Motors' contracting and cancellation practices through a number of contracts?

The State *V. I. Lenin*

In primitive society, when people lived in small family groups and were still at the lowest stages of development, in a condition approximating to savagery—an epoch from which modern, civilized human society is separated by several thousands of years—there were yet no signs of the existence of a state. We find the predominance of custom, authority, respect, the power enjoyed by the elders of the clan; we find this power sometimes

V. I. Lenin, *The State* (Peking: Foreign Languages Press, 1965).

accorded to women—the position of women then was not like the downtrodden and oppressed condition of women today—but nowhere do we find a special *category* of people who are set apart to rule others and, for the sake and purpose of rule, systematically and permanently to wield a certain apparatus of coercion, an apparatus of violence, such as is represented at the present time, as you all realize, by the armed detachments of troops, the prisons and the other means of subjugating the will of others by force—all that which constitutes the essence of the state.

If we abstract ourselves from the so-called religious teachings, subtleties, philosophical arguments and the various opinions advanced by bourgeois scholars, if we abstract ourselves from these and try to get at the real essence of the matter, we shall find that the state really does amount to such an apparatus of rule separated out from human society. When there appears such a special group of men who are occupied with ruling and nothing else, and who in order to rule need a special apparatus of coercion and of subjugating the will of others by force—prisons, special detachments of men, armies, etc.—then there appears the state.

But there was a time when there was no state, when general ties, society itself, discipline and the ordering of work were maintained by force of custom and tradition, or by the authority or the respect enjoyed by the elders of the clan or by women—who in those times not only frequently enjoyed equal status with men, but not infrequently enjoyed even a higher status—and when there was no special category of persons, specialists in ruling. History shows that the state as a special apparatus for coercing people arose only wherever and whenever there appeared a division of society into classes, that is, a division into groups of people some of whom are permanently in a position to appropriate the labour of others, where some people exploit others.

And this division of society into classes must always be clearly borne in mind as a fundamental fact of history. The development of all human societies for thousands of years, in all countries without exception, reveals a general conformity to law, a regularity and consistency in this development; so that at first we had a society without classes—the original patriarchal, primitive society, in which there were no aristocrats; then we had a society based on slavery—a slaveowning society. The whole of modern civilized Europe has passed through this stage—slavery ruled supreme two thousand years ago. The vast majority of peoples of the other parts of the world also passed through this stage. Among the less developed peoples traces of slavery survive to this day; you will find the institution of slavery in Africa, for example, at the present time. Slaveowners and slaves were the first important class divisions. The former group not only owned all the means of production—the land and the implements, however primitive they may have been in those times—but also owned people. This group was known as slaveowners, while those who laboured and supplied labour for others were known as slaves.

This form was followed in history by another—feudalism. In the great majority of countries slavery in the course of its development evolved into serfdom. The fundamental division of society was now into feudal landlords and peasant serfs. The form of relations between people changed. The slaveowners had regarded the slaves as their property; the law had confirmed this view and regarded the slave as a chattel completely owned by the slaveowner. As far as the peasant serf was concerned, class oppression and dependence remained, but it was not considered that the feudal landlord owned the peasants as chattels, but that he was only entitled to their labour and to compel them to perform certain services. In practice, as you know, serfdom, especially in Russia, where it survived longest of all and assumed the grossest forms, in no way differed from slavery.

Further, with the development of trade, the appearance of the world market and the development of money circulation, a new class arose within feudal society—the capitalist class. From the commodity, the exchange of commodities and the rise of the power of money, there arose the power of capital. During the eighteenth century—or rather, from the end of the eighteenth century and during the nineteenth century—revolutions took place all over the world. Feudalism was eliminated in all the countries of Western Europe. This took place latest of all in Russia. In 1861 a radical change took place in Russia as well, as a consequence of which one form of society was replaced by another—feudalism was replaced by capitalism, under which division into classes remained, as well as various traces and relics of serfdom, but in which the division into classes fundamentally assumed a new form.

The owners of capital, the owners of the land, the owners of the mills and factories in all capitalist countries constituted and still constitute an insignificant minority of the population who have complete command of the labour of the whole people, and, consequently, command, oppress and exploit the whole mass of labourers, the majority of whom are proletarians, wage workers, that procure their livelihood in the process of production only by the sale of their own workers' hands, their labour power. With the transition to capitalism, the peasants, who were already disunited and downtrodden in feudal times, were converted partly (the majority) into proletarians, and partly (the minority) into wealthy peasants who themselves hired workers and who constituted a rural bourgeoisie.

This fundamental fact—the transition of society from primitive forms of slavery to serfdom and finally to capitalism—you must always bear in mind, for only by remembering this fundamental fact, only by inserting all political doctrines into this fundamental framework will you be able properly to appraise these doctrines and understand what they refer to; for each of these great periods in the history of mankind—slave-owning, feudal and capitalist—embraces scores and hundreds of centuries and presents such a mass of political forms, such a variety of political doctrines, opinions and revolutions, that this extreme diversity and immense variety can be understood—especially in connection with the political, philosophical and other doctrines of bourgeois scholars and politicians—only by firmly holding, as to a guiding thread, to this division of society into classes, this change in the forms of class rule, and from this standpoint examining all social questions—economic, political, spiritual, religious, etc.

...People are divided into ruled, and into specialists in ruling, those who rise above society and are called rulers, representatives of the state. This apparatus, this group of people who rule others, always takes possession of a certain apparatus of coercion, of physical force, irrespective of whether this violence over people is expressed in the primitive club, or, in the epoch of slavery, in more perfected types of weapons, or in the firearms which appeared in the Middle Ages, or, finally, in modern weapons, which in the twentieth century are marvels of technique and are entirely based on the latest achievements of modern technology. The methods of violence changed, but whenever there was a state there existed in every society a group of persons who ruled, who commanded, who dominated and who in order to maintain their power possessed an apparatus of physical coercion, an apparatus of violence, with those weapons which corresponded to the technical level of the given epoch. And by examining these general phenomena, by asking ourselves why no state existed when there were no classes, when there were no exploiters and exploited, and why it arose when classes arose—only in this way shall we find a definite answer to the question of the essence of the state and its significance.

Questions

1. How would the case of *Streich* v. *General Motors* be explained by reference to the theory advanced by Lenin?

2. How well does Lenin explain the present? Is the full and complete domination of the individual by the state an endpoint in the political-legal evolution of humans?

Theory of Law and Marxism   *E. B. Pashukanis*

The criminal law is...the sphere where juridic intercourse attains its maximum intensity. The

Reprinted by permission of the publishers from John N. Hazard, ed., and Hugh W. Babb, tr., *Soviet Legal Philosophy*, pp. 206–207 and 211–213, Cambridge, Mass.: Harvard University Press. Copyright, 1951, by the President and Fellows of Harvard College.

juridic element is here disassociated from the life element surpassingly and most clearly and acquires complete independence. In court proceedings, the perversion of the actions of the specific man into the actions of a party—that is to say, of a juridic subject—comes out with particular distinctness. In order to emphasize the distinction between the actions of everyday living and the manifestations of will on the one hand and juridic manifestations of will on the other, the ancient law employed special solemn formulae and rituals. The drama of court proceedings graphically created a peculiar juridic existence side by side with the world of facts.

Of all the species of law, it is the criminal law which possesses the capacity of coming into the most direct and rough contact with the individual personality. Accordingly, it always evokes the most burning—as well as a practical—interest. A statute and the punishment for its breach are in general closely associated with each other and the criminal law thus takes upon itself, as it were, the role of the representative of law in general: it is the part which replaces the whole. . . .

[Pashukanis here reviews criminal law in primitive times, identifying its origin in blood vengeance and tracing the control of blood vengeance by the payment of money to victims or their clan. Later, payments were taken by public authorities to assure social discipline or class dominance, as well as to provide a source of revenue. ——Ed.]

The position of affairs changes as the partitions between the classes and between the feudal orders develop and become firmly established. The appearance of a hierarchy—spiritual and temporal—puts into first place the safeguarding of its privileges and the struggle with the lower and oppressed classes of the population. The disintegration of natural economy and the consequent expansion of peasant exploitation, the development of trade and the organization of a state based on feudal orders, poses new tasks before criminal justice. During this epoch criminal justice becomes not so much a means of amplifying income as of dealing severely and without pity with "bad people"—that is to say, in the first instance, with peasants who have fled from the intolerable exploitation of squires and a squire state, with a pauperized population, with vagrants, beggars, and so forth. The police and the machinery for investigation begin to play the principal part. Punishments become a means either of physical extermination or of inspiring fear. This is the epoch of tortures, corporal punishments, and cruel means of carrying out capital punishment.

Thus the complex amalgam which makes up the criminal law of the present day was gradually made ready. The historical strata of which it was composed are easily discernible. In essence—that is to say, from the purely sociological viewpoint—bourgeois society supports its class dominance by its system of criminal law and thereby holds the exploited classes in obedience. In this regard, its courts and its private "voluntary" organizations of strike-breakers pursue the same objective. If the matter is looked at from this point of view, the criminal court is merely an appendage of the machinery made up of the police and the department of investigation. . . .

The criminal jurisdiction of the bourgeois state is organized class terror, differing only in degree from the so-called extraordinary measures applied to the elements of civil war. As long ago as Herbert Spencer, the complete analogy—and even the identity—between the defensive reaction directed against an attack from without (war) and the reaction directed against those who violate internal order (legal or court defense) was pointed out. The circumstance that measures of the former sort—that is to say, measures of the criminal punishment—are applied *principally* against the degenerate elements of society, while measures of the second class are applied *principally* against the most active champions of the new class which is rising to power, makes no essential change in the matter in respect of principle and the same is true as to the greater or less correctness and complexity of the procedure applied. The true meaning of the punitive action of the class state can be understood only if we start from its antagonistic nature. So-called theories of criminal law which deduce the principles of punitive policy from the interests of society as a whole are engaged—consciously or unconsciously—in a perversion of reality. "Society as a whole" exists only in the imagination of these jurists: actually we have before us classes possessed of contradictory and clashing interests. Every system of punitive policy furnished by history bears the imprint of the class interests of the class which carried it into effect. The feudal lord punished peasants and citizens who were disobedient, who rebelled against his authority. The united cities hanged the robber-knights and razed castles. During the Middle Ages, one who wished to engage in handcraft without becoming a member of a guild was considered a lawbreaker. The capitalist bourgeoisie—which had scarcely succeeded in coming into being—declared that the aspiration of workers to be united into associations was criminal.

Class interest thus places the imprint of historical concreteness upon each given system of punitive policy.

Questions

1. If Pashukanis is correct, what features would one look for in American criminal law and procedure? What frailties in Pashukanis's explanation are disclosed by a study of the American system of criminal law?

2. Compare the following with Pashukanis:

Inasmuch as crime is an offense against the state, an understanding of the class relations which are the basis of state power make crime more understandable. As Eugene Debs once remarked, it is often true that more can be told about a society by the kind of criminals in its prisons and lunatics in its mental institutions than by those on the outside. It is likewise true that there is a high correlation between crime and social contradiction. If the commandment "Thou shalt not steal" appears in a society, it means that private property in movable objects has appeared, and that society has created a need on a mass scale to steal.*

* K. Cloke, "Law Is Illegal," p. 39. Reprinted from *Radical Lawyers* edited by Jonathan Black, by arrangement with Avon Books. Copyright © 1971 by Avon Books.

The following material is drawn from the proceedings of the California Sentencing Institute, an annual conference where the various trial court judges of California met to discuss problems in sentencing persons who had been convicted of crime.

Criteria Suggesting Straight Probation According to the Personal Characteristics and Background of Offender   *1965 California Sentencing Institute, 45 Cal. Rptr. (Appendix)*

The type of offender who should be seriously considered for straight probation is one who possesses favorable characteristics listed in the following categories:

Criminal History

1. If he had a prior criminal history, it was minor and infrequent. Its nature and frequency have markedly improved. There has been a substantial time lapse since defendant's last offense. In addition, community social services, such as half-way houses, family counselling, psychiatric clinics, and A.A. have aided defendant.

2. Defendant's past activities show no aggressive, assaultive tendencies, or excessive contempt for property rights.

3. He has had no prior state prison or C.Y.A. experience.

4. Past criminal experiences have not embittered defendant against society or his family.

5. He has not been given any real opportunity previously to utilize probation.

6. His activities, while out on bail for the present offense, are commendable. A contrary example is the defendant, on bail for bad checks, who passes more of them.

7. He has not perjured himself, or had others

perjure themselves, on this or past offenses. He has not threatened witnesses or caused their absence at his trial.

Mental and Emotional Factors

A. *Intelligence*

1. He is reasonably intelligent, with the capacity to reform.

2. He desires, and sees, the wisdom of reforming.

3. He understands the implications of his crime, what motivated it, and firmly believes that he has conquered such motivation and will not be impelled by it into future crime.

4. He accurately evaluates his own capabilities and limitations, and accepts and can adjust to them.

5. His intelligence affords him many available job opportunities.

6. His educational background is good and suggests good rehabilitation potential.

B. *Attitudes*

1. He is ashamed of his crimes, past life and associates, sincerely wants to live a law-abiding life, and the prospects are good that he will.

2. He genuinely accepts, rather than resists, probationary controls over his actions—not from preferring it to imprisonment, but because he realizes it will benefit him.

3. He has no desire for gain at whatever cost to society, and is, generally, considerate of the feelings and property rights of others.

4. He is loyal to family, friends, and employer, and they to him.

5. He is not gullible, nor unduly suspicious of others' motives and actions.

6. If in previous trouble, his attitude toward the treatment he received is good, and he and society benefited.

7. He has been cooperative with the authorities, and has cleared up offenses of others.

8. He has pleaded guilty and given truthful testimony for the prosecution.

C. *Psychological Considerations*

1. His general pattern of behavior is predictable, stable, and mature.

2. He does not, typically, go to pieces and act impulsively under stress, but accepts frustrations as part of life and seeks to solve them rationally.

3. He has basically good values, and realistic goals he can achieve.

4. He has an inferiority complex which triggered his desire for recognition, through crime. He now realizes this, and the probation officer is convinced he can overcome his weakness.

5. The mental aberration which caused the crime has been removed by medical treatment.

6. He has obtained, or can obtain, treatment for an alcoholic, narcotic, senile, psychotic, or personality disturbance condition, through nonpenal facilities, and the prognosis is good.

7. He has no unusual mental quirks, deficiencies, or abnormalities.

8. His total personality strength overcomes the partial personality weakness which precipitated the crime.

Physical Health

1. He is healthy.

2. If he has physical defects that were factors in his crime, he now recognizes this, and dental, medical and surgical care will cure them in a reasonable time.

3. His physical infirmities will not permit imprisonment, but probationary restrictions will protect society.

Social Influences

A. *Family Status*

1. Defendant's family respects and conforms to law and order. It is eager to help him.

2. Parents have given, or will give, reasonable and consistent discipline.

3. Family is highly respected and defendant is proud of this reputation, social position and standing.

4. Defendant's return to the family won't affect it adversely.

5. He is loyal to his family, and it to him.

6. The family does things together, and generates a healthy environment.

B. *School Background*

1. His adjustment to school authorities and students was good. He was interested in and did well in his studies.

2. His attendance was steady and he fully participated in all phases of school activities.

C. *Church Record*

1. He attended regularly and participated in church functions, individually, and with his family.

2. He is benefiting from church counseling, support, and spiritual and moral guidance.

D. *Military Experience*

1. The fact of military service is not as revealing as defendant's adjustments to its disciplines. If his record in the military and the type of discharge he received were good, and he showed progress and accomplishments, his probationary prognosis is good.

E. *Work History*

1. He has a steady and dependable employment history, is respected as an able craftsman, and liked by employers and fellow workers.

2. He is well trained and in demand. If jailing has stopped his work, his job awaits him.

3. He follows orders readily and participates in wholesome after-work activities with fellow workers.

F. *Marital Status*

1. Defendant is married, and marriage has been a good influence.

2. The marriage is desired by, and its continuance has deep meaning to defendant, as distinguished from the mere fact of its existence.

3. The marital relationship is close, affectionate, and satisfying, and he supports his family, which is loyal, and wants to help him.

G. *Environment*

1. Neighborhood, family setting, and working environment are crime free.

2. Associates are law-abiding.

3. There are ample and excellent treatment and recreational facilities.

4. The environment did not help cause the instant crime.

5. It is non-nomadic and stable.

H. *Participation in Community Life*

1. He is community and socially conscious, and is actively engaged in civic improvement organizations.

I. *Debt Status*

1. He lives within his means, which shows self discipline. (Typical defendants in court often have pressing financial problems, which precipitate many crimes.)

Age

1. The young defendant is showing promising signs of normal maturity, and the flexibility of youth promises reform.

2. More significant than age itself is the time the criminal behavior first began. A middle-aged, or older man, whose first crime is recent, is more likely to succeed on probation than a young man whose crimes started early in life, and have been continuous.

3. The defendant's advanced age does not suggest future involvement in crimes he committed in his younger days. Because of advanced age, imprisonment would entail extreme hardship on defendant and have little benefit to society.

Habits

1. Defendant has had bad habits for only a brief time.

2. He has no alcoholic or gambling problems.

3. If he is a follower rather than a leader, he won't follow into wrongdoing just to be following.

4. He keeps reasonable hours, at proper places.

Community Attitudes

1. If the kind of crime, and its impact and surrounding circumstances, don't upset the community; the background of the offender does not offend it; the volume of criminality is reasonable; its atmosphere or security, or its fears and prej-

udices are not disturbed; and its local history and tradition do not suggest cause for alarm; then straight probation is feasible.

2. The offender will be accepted upon his return to the community.

3. Community-centered treatment facilities for supervision and reclamation are good, and available, and a favorable attitude is indicated toward defendant. There is assistance from public and private welfare agencies, church groups, physical and mental health services, and fraternal and service groups; Alcoholics and Gamblers Anonymous; and Synanon.

4. There is no need for making an example of defendant because of any policy embodied in the statute violated.

JUDGE LOUIS B. DeMATTEIS: . . .

I wish I could outline definite formulas, equations and guides for the determination of the proper and wise sentence to be pronounced on each offender who appears before you. But determining and pronouncing judgment in a criminal case is not an exact science. The sentence in each case must be hand-tailored to the individual offender before the court based on all the surrounding circumstances of the crime of which he has been convicted and with due consideration to the welfare, composition and temperament of the community involved.

It has been well said by an eminent jurist, Justice Henry Alford McCardie, that, "Trying a man is easy, as easy as falling off a log, compared with deciding what to do with him when he has been found guilty."

As our program appropriately suggests, there are three general categories in which we may classify criminal sentences:

At one end of the spectrum is probation, without a term in the county jail, for the first offender involved in a relatively minor crime who has a good background and holds great promise of rehabilitation. At the other extreme is the commitment to a state correctional institution for the hardened recidivist or the offender who has clearly shown a disinclination in previous offenses and conduct, to adjust himself to become a law-abiding citizen. I shall endeavor to express a few thoughts concerning the great mass of "in-between cases" which, in my opinion, present the most difficult problems for a judge.

In this group of cases the social, criminal and psychological factors involved are generally quite complex, difficult of evaluation, and many times suggest conflicting answers. In imposing judgment in such cases, as, of course, in all cases, our objective is to deter the commission of future crime by the offender and others and, if at all possible, to rehabilitate the offender. Society wants its offenders punished, but it also wants them rehabilitated. To attain that end requires great wisdom, foresight, patience, understanding of human nature and often a willingness to take a calculated gamble on the future conduct of the subject offender.

The incarceration of an offender in the county jail, honor farm, or road camp as a condition of probation, offers a means of attaining this objective and permits great elasticity and adaptation to the individual case. If wisely and appropriately used, it can be a very effective tool in the hands of a conscientious judge. It permits a judge to "individualize" a sentence to fit the needs of the particular offender and to make it proportionate to the offender and the offense. I have found it very helpful in getting many an offender to realize that the court means business, yet sparing him a prison sentence, with a resultant change in his subsequent behavior. Such dispositions have also received favorable reactions from law enforcement agencies and the general public.

In the exercise of our discretion in this area, we first of all must be thoroughly familiar with the type of local detention facilities we have available in our county; the therapeutic and work program that is provided at such facilities; the degree of success attained with certain types of offenders as well as the limitations of the staff and program. It makes a great difference if confinement in a county jail or other local facility means merely sitting in a cell or whether it means engaging in some type of physical activity, constructive work and helpful counseling. . . .

Secondly, we must have available the services of

a competent, well-trained probation staff experienced in obtaining and presenting reliable information upon which we can base our judgment, and supervising the offender during the probationary period.

We are all quite familiar with the many complex factors which must be considered in determining a disposition which is fair both to the offender and to society. In trying to reach a proper decision three factors are commonly recognized as those which should be considered, namely: (1) The nature of the crime and circumstances surrounding its commission; (2) The defendant, his physical and mental capacities, and moral attitude, and (3) The community, its attitude toward crime, its reaction to the particular crime and its need for protection against such crimes.

Questions

1. Do the criteria suggesting probation according to the personal characteristics and background of the offender discriminate against lower-class persons?

2. If lower-class persons are really less likely to stay out of trouble on probation, would discrimination against them in the criteria be justified?

3. If the criteria which indicate probable success on probation are the same factors which indicate probable success in society, it would seem that those persons *least* likely to get into trouble with the law in the first place are *most* likely to be put on probation if they do get into trouble. Does such a system make sense? Is there any other way to grant probation?

4. The criteria for probation are written in terms of "he." Would the criteria be appropriate for women?

At the 1968 California Sentencing Institute the following hypothetical case was prepared for discussion by conference participants.

A Forgery Case   1968 California Sentencing Institute, 77 Cal. Rptr. (Appendix)

OFFENSE: FORGERY Defendant cashed a forged check amounting to $145 at a department store. The blank check was taken from the company by which he was formerly employed. There were other checks involved but they were uncharged. Defendant pleaded guilty.

PRIOR CRIMINAL HISTORY

11/60	Arizona	Auto theft and burglary second	Committed to boys' school
10/65	County X	Drunk driving	One year probation
12/66	County X	Burglary	Six months county jail, one year probation
4/68	County X	PRESENT OFFENSE	

CASE HISTORY INFORMATION: This is a 24-year-old man, the third of five children of a Mexican-American working-class family. The father died when defendant was six years of age and thereafter the family was supported by public assistance. He claims he got along well with his mother and the members of his family. However, he asserts they regard him as a "black sheep" because of his difficulties as a youth and as an adult.

Probation officer in Arizona indicates that defendant suffered from rheumatic fever as a child and was overindulged by his mother. He has withdrawn from his family.

Defendant claims high school graduation but verification shows he only completed the ninth grade. His employment record has also been quite spotty. He worked for one year as a warehouse helper and quit because creditors attached his wages. He also has worked as a bus boy.

For the past year and a half subject has been married and one child was born of that union. Wife indicates that marriage has been satisfactory although defendant has difficulty managing finances and friction developed. They have also been plagued by large bills as a result of time payments for furniture and other household goods. Wife had been employed until the time baby was born three months ago.

Subject has a drinking problem which has caused him some difficulty and it has gotten progressively worse in recent years.

CASE EVALUATION: This is a 24-year-old immature man of average intelligence. He gives the appearance of being friendly and likeable but obviously has been unable to accept responsibility. There are a total of eight checks outstanding, amounting to approximately $1,000 worth of purchases in various types of business establishments. He said he would like to have probation so that he could make restitution. His adjustment on probation for the burglary has been marginal and he was placed in a special caseload where the probation officer could furnish intensive supervision. His wife says this simply worried the defendant and may have contributed to his present offense. He appears to have support from his wife, who assumes major responsibility for family stability. The recent birth of his child has created more anxiety for the defendant and he says that this has affected his relationship with his wife.

Notes and Questions

1. The foregoing information is comparable to that which a sentencing judge would receive. On the basis of this report, would you grant probation? Probation with conditions? County jail time? A state prison sentence? Prepare one page giving your decision and the reasons for it.

2. Now proceed with the opinions of California judges who also considered the case and compare.

JUDGE SCHOENIG: I would place this man on three years' probation on the condition that he take treatment at DeWitt State Hospital for both alcoholism and emotional problems. Upon his release from the hospital he would be placed under the intensive supervision unit of the probation department and the family would be outpatients at the mental health clinic or Family Service Agency. Work could be secured for him in the food processing plants and deductions would be made from his checks for restitution.

There are other alternatives, of course, which embody the thoughts behind this sentence and that would be first a work furlough program if one was available in the county of sentencing. The same supervision and payroll deduction could be made through the Sheriff's office, but added to the work furlough program would be a continuing period of time under the probation department for proper supervision and outpatient care.

Also to be considered would be the right of the defendant to refuse probation. Since probation has bothered this defendant in the past, he might indicate to the court that the terms of probation are too onerous and refuse same. If such is the case, I would then impose a state prison sentence.

My reasons for the sentence are as follows: In reviewing the case of this 24-year-old Mexican-American, it appears that he does not have a lengthy arrest record and there is no history of violence. His first offense for burglary 2nd degree occurred when he was 16 years of age and he was committed to a boys' school. I assume this was not a State Correctional Institution. Six years later, he was again arrested for burglary and given 6 months in county jail and 1 year probation. His present offense occurred when he was not under probation.

As of this time, this young man is not a confirmed "paper hanger," but merely used this offense as a means to make certain purchases which were evidently for his family. These checks were given as payment in full for various articles that he bought. Inasmuch as we know he has a drinking problem, this undoubtedly is a factor in lowering his will power so that he breaches the rules and regulations set up by society.

His case history indicates that he is an inadequate individual, which has affected his employment and ability to manage his finances. It is also noted that his wife has a certain amount of awareness of his problems. However, I am not in agreement with her statement relative to probation. Her husband's present arrest occurred after he completed his probationary period. The wife is the dominant figure in this family because it appears the husband has refused to face or accept responsibility. I would consider this a further reason for psychiatric help and further, from all indications, this defendant is amenable to such counsel. It would appear that this defendant again needs the intensive supervision of the probation department for the purpose of obtaining professional help for his drinking problem and counselling for him and his wife.

If he were given a straight county jail sentence or committed to state prison, that would defer the treatment that must be implemented to help this man adjust to society and with his family.

I am aware that his previous adjustment on probation was marginal but I am not averse to taking this risk with the defendant when there is some definite goal in mind. If this defendant resided in my jurisdiction, employment could be obtained for him in food processing for the year round with one of the corporate farms in that area. This type of employment would prevent the defendant from handling any money other than his paycheck. Also, the defendant, through the probation department, would be helped in managing his financial obligations, inasmuch as I would order restitution payments on his outstanding checks.

I would recommend outpatient treatment at the mental health facility because of the history of rejection of this defendant by his family and his inability to face problems.

JUDGE COAKLEY: I've had several bad check cases and this is always the type of person you find. What do you do with a fellow who is repeatedly this kind of a customer and yet doesn't have too bad a record otherwise? Well, in any event it's open now for discussion.

JUDGE ROSS A. CARKEET (Tuolumne County): I voted for prison but after doing that I've been thinking that this might be a good case for a Penal Code Sec. 1168 commitment. This guy needs a real good scare. It might do him good to send him to prison and put a recall on him, and see if you want to take him back.

JUDGE D. STERRY FAGAN (Los Angeles County): I gave this man a straight jail sentence. My feeling was that he had a shot at probation and didn't do well. The only reason I would think of probation is that he could make some restitution. His background as presented here is marginal so I feel that it's touch and go between a prison sentence or a county jail sentence. I choose the county jail because of the nonviolence of his criminal activity. I note that in 1966 his crime was burglary and everybody says that now he's changed to a "paper hanger." I also note that the check that was used on this occasion and possibly the other one came from his former employer and I presume that he took them while he was employed there, or he went back and burglarized the place to get the checks after he was terminated. It is highly inferable that he committed a burglary to get the checks and had some knowledge of how they would be passed and what signatures were necessary to pass them.

JUDGE LEONARD M. GINSBURG (Tulare County): I would have sentenced the man to prison on the basis that he's been around the track. He's been in everything from boys' school to apparently ordinary probation on the drunk driving charge, county jail and intensive probation on the burglary. To me, he's reached the point where there's nothing left to do with him and it would be largely on that basis that I believe the protection of society as well as possible rehabilitation of the individual requires this prison sentence.

JUDGE COAKLEY: Dr. Olivier, have you any comments?

DR. OLIVIER: ...I feel this is a man who hasn't been violent and for whom psychiatry hasn't been tried. I also feel that he's a rather inadequate, dependent guy and...I think this fellow would develop a relationship rather easily with a psychotherapist. I don't think prison would do anything at all for him. I think it would increase his dependency and his inadequacy and I think this man would be easily led and if he were to stay in prison very long he would form more identification with the anti-social element. I think he has a lot of problems around his sexual identification and his being a man and if he could stay employed and make restitution, this would be the most ego-enhancing thing that he could do. I think it would well be worth probation on the condition that he obtain psychiatric treatment.

JUDGE HAYDEN: How much treatment do you think would be likely to be developed? Assume he had a service such as yours, how often and how long would you be seeing this man?

DR. OLIVIER: Well, we don't have any kind of a standard for length of treatment. If we feel that someone needs a lot of treatment initially to get into a treatment contract then we often recommend our day treatment program where the person can come in eight hours a day, five days a week, for somewhere between two to six weeks. Then, we follow them up with a once a week basis in the out-patient clinic. For a man like this who has been nonviolent and whose latest offense has to do with check forgery, I would think it would be reasonable to start on a once a week basis and I would predict reasonably good results within a matter of six months to a year.

JUDGE GARDINER: I recognize the different kinds of treatment that are available, but I don't see how you come to the conclusion that this fellow hasn't had any treatment. What do you think these other things have been?

DR. OLIVIER: Well, I'm making a distinction between probation where he sees a probation officer periodically and seeing a psychotherapist for a half hour to an hour each and every week with great regularity.

JUDGE GARDINER: There is obviously a tremendous quality difference between the different kinds of people, but must we not recognize the fact that probation officers are giving something which is not unlike psychiatric treatment? Isn't this their objective?

DR. OLIVIER: Well, most of them are not professionally trained. Certainly they can do a great deal of good in a warm human relationship with an individual. That's the vehicle for any professional treatment, but what I'm saying is that this person has not had any kind of intensive psychiatric treatment and I think that we can do more to help him alter his maladapted patterns of life than a probation officer can. But I think the probation officer would play a vital role in helping him to see that he got to sessions and utilized them.

JUDGE J. KELLY STEELE (Kern County): You mentioned several times that this party is nonviolent. Of course, writing checks is a nonviolent offense and he could write them every day and still be considered not violent. On the other hand, you mentioned that it represents an inadequate personality and, of course, an inadequate personality could be shown by crimes of violence as well as crimes of nonviolence. My question is what difference does it make whether he's violent or nonviolent? He might stick a gun in your chest and take the shirt off your back or he might steal your bank account; what difference does it make?

DR. OLIVIER: Well, in the sense that I'm using an inadequate personality, I mean the kind of a guy that isn't very aggressive at all and tends to be passive and, I feel, unlikely to commit violent, aggressive acts. I think that this is the kind of man I would be willing to take a chance on. He hasn't forged checks every day. He had one little spree here and hasn't had a chronic, repetitive pattern at this point and we hope that it wouldn't become one if he had treatment.

JUDGE STEELE: Would you treat a single act of violence differently because of the fact that it is violent?

Dr. Olivier: Yes, I think society needs more protection from someone who is likely to be violent.

Judge Schauer: I agree with you, Doctor. I'm not quite ready to give up on this man. He needs one more chance anyway, although I think I'd give him a long term in custody as a condition of probation, such as county jail. I probably would impose a felony on him by suspending an execution of a state prison sentence, but I think I would try probationary supervision with a condition of probation, possibly that he attend Alcoholics Anonymous. I smell in his background here the odor of alcohol and I just wonder what your opinion is in connection with AA as opposed to psychiatric treatment with respect to alcoholism problems.

Dr. Olivier: Well, I think that could be a very useful adjunct to the program. I think a lot of people that join AA switch a lot of their dependency on alcohol to a dependency on the AA group. It helps them to structure their time in a useful way, they have places to go in the evening but I don't think the goals are exactly the same. I don't see this person as a hard core chronic alcoholic, but nevertheless, I think AA could be a useful adjunct and I don't see it as replacing psychiatric treatment. I think it's interesting that when I recently participated in a Municipal & Justice Court Judges Institute in San Diego one of the judges pointed out that when there were crimes against property, judges tended to be more punitive than in cases of aggression against individuals. Someone who had stolen 50¢ worth of meat from a super market would get a more severe sentence than someone who had threatened his girl friend with a knife, or even injured her and had been assaultive before. I think it's kind of an interesting sidelight of the way society views crimes against property.

Judge Hayden: You may have gotten a distorted sample, and I would respond to Judge Steele's remarks by saying that I would much rather have a guy hang a thousand dollar bad

check on me than take $10 out of my pocket with a gun. I have a different hierarchy of values there.

Mr. Shain: I want to comment on the discussion at the Institute for Municipal & Justice Court Judges that Dr. Olivier mentioned. The reference that Dr. Olivier had involved discussion of a case in which there was a husband and wife conflict. I think all of us would agree that the violence that emerges from a husband and wife conflict is a far different cry from violence in the more commonly accepted term of assaulting somebody that you don't know. That's the mitigating circumstance in those cases.

Dr. Olivier: Yes, that is an important point that I had forgotten.

Judge Dell: I just don't think it's our function to lock up everybody who is a hazard to property. Now in this case, I would have imposed a felony sentence and as a condition of probation have given the man a maximum period in the county jail with work furlough which we have in Los Angeles County. There are certain crimes that you just have a price tag for. I'd be very reluctant to send a person who is a "paper hanger" to the state prison. I don't think it accomplishes a great deal except to fill up the state prison with people who don't belong there and who learn new crimes. I am concerned about the aspect that Judge Fagan raised, namely, that this is not just a "paper hanger"—this is a burglary and an embezzlement besides which resulted in it. But generally speaking, I don't think a property crime where there is no "bunco" scheme and where it is not very carefully planned to victimize an individual or an institution, should carry a state prison sentence. On the other hand I think that a violent crime is another matter and there we are talking about protecting life and person. I think that's a great deal more important than simply the protection of property.

Judge Edward P. Fogg (San Bernardino County): I think we've overlooked one fact in this case history that's important to me, at least. This man's employment record had been quite spotty. His record obviously shows that he has had no real occupational training. He isn't fitted to make a good living for his family. Wouldn't state prison and his commitment to the Department of Corrections give the Department an opportunity to offer this man vocational training of some type that would eventually assist in his rehabilitation?

JUDGE SCHOENIG: I thought about that. What bothered me with that is you're giving him a felony rap and saying you're rehabilitating him so that he can get a job. When he comes out he's got a felony rap sheet and who's going to hire him, a Mexican-American with a felony rap? These are all things we have to consider. And I thought about all the other things we were kicking around today. So that bothered me, too. We are a biased society and we might as well face it.

JUDGE HAYDEN: If you have an adequate probation office in your county, which we do not, you should be able to get in much more satisfactory vocational training on probation than he would ever get in a state prison. I think you can ex-

amine the history of the state prison's vocational services. Their record is extremely spotty. They, in very few cases, lead to successful continued use of the training received in state prison and there is at least a chance that if you put him on probation and as a condition of probation, make him get a trade, you might make it stick.

JUDGE COAKLEY: Cy, will you come up and give us the results of the poll?

MR. SHAIN: Here is the vote for this case: ⅔ would have committed him to jail with probation; a little more than ¼ would have sent him to prison, about 1 out of 14 would have just given him jail without probation and about 3 percent would have granted him probation using the time that he had already served in jail as fulfilling his incarceration term.

Question

1. Analyze the deliberations of the judges using the criteria for probation set out earlier in this section and the theories of Lenin and Pashukanis.

Cook v. State   *495 P. 2d 768 (Or. 1972)*

FOLEY, Judge.

This is an appeal from an order of the circuit court which affirmed an order of the State Board of Social Protection after trial... in the circuit court.

On May 21, 1971, the State Board of Social Protection entered an order for plaintiff's sterilization based on findings:

(2) ... That in the judgment of a majority of the Board the condition of the examinee is such that procreation by the examinee would produce a child or children: ... (b) who would become neglected or dependent children as a result of the parent's inability by reason of mental illness or mental retardation to provide adequate care.

(3) That in the judgment of the majority of the Board there is no probability that the condition of the examinee investigated and examined will improve to such an extent as to avoid the indicated consequences as set forth in paragraph (2) hereof. ...

Plaintiff contends that the trial court erred in denying her motion that the state elect between mental retardation and mental illness as the basis for sterilization and that the trial court erred in affirming the Board's order. The remaining assignment of error alleges that ORS 436.070(1) (b) is unconstitutional because it discriminates against indigents in violation of the equal protection provisions of the state and federal constitutions. ORS 436.070 provides:

(1) The investigation, findings and orders of the board ... shall be made with the purpose in view of avoiding the procreation of children:

... (b) Who would become neglected or dependent children as a result of the parent's inability by reason of mental illness or mental retardation to provide adequate care. ...

Plaintiff is a 17-year-old girl with a history of severe emotional disturbance. At age 13 she was declared a ward of the court and was taken out of her home under circumstances which indicate that she had been physically and sexually abused by her family for some period of time. During the last four years she has been placed in two foster homes, juvenile detention home, F. W. Dammasch State Hospital and Hillcrest School of Oregon. The longest period in any one place was one and one-half years at Dammasch. Her behavior has vacillated between periods of stability that lasted up to three months and aggressive hostility expressed in verbal or physical threats towards others, self-inflicted injury and running away. A petition was filed with the Board of Social Protection* after appellant engaged in a series of indiscriminate and impulsive sexual involvements while she was in the hospital.

A psychiatrist who specializes in child guidance has followed plaintiff's care since she became a ward of the court. His uncontradicted testimony was that she would never be able to provide the parental guidance and judgment which a child requires even though she might be able to master the skills necessary to take physical care of herself and a child. He based this conclusion on the girl's lack of emotional control, her consistent low scores in areas of judgment on psychological tests, and the likelihood that she would abuse a child. He said the prognosis is poor because the presence of brain damage makes her condition inherently unstable despite continuous medication. He testified further

---

* ORS 436.025 provides:

"Any two persons or any person licensed to practice medicine and surgery by the State Board of Medical Examiners may file a petition with the State Board of Social Protection alleging that any other person within the state is within the jurisdiction of the board as provided in subsection (1) of ORS 436.070."

that both mental illness and mental retardation are contributing factors and are interrelated.

Because of their interrelated nature, plaintiff's condition could not be intelligently considered without reference to both mental illness and mental retardation. The statute provides for, and the plaintiff was accorded, counsel at public expense, adequate notice and opportunity to be heard. The statute thus satisfies the due process clause. The trial court's denial of the motion to elect was proper. ...

It is now necessary to determine whether the statute denies plaintiff equal protection of the laws.

In *Buck* v. *Bell* ... (1927), the United States Supreme Court upheld a Virginia sterilization law. Sterilization was considered beneficial to the patient and to society because it allowed people to be discharged from state institutions, to return to the community, and to become self-supporting.

The only other case involving sterilization laws to come before the United States Supreme Court was *Skinner* v. *Oklahoma* ... (1942). The purpose of the Oklahoma law was to prevent criminal traits from being inherited by ordering the sterilization of those who had been thrice-convicted of various specified felonies. The law was held unconstitutional as a violation of equal protection because there was no rational basis for distinguishing those felonies which would result in sterilization (one of petitioner's convictions was for chicken stealing) from other felonies which were exempt (embezzlement, for example). The premise that state sterilization laws are constitutional when validly drawn was not disturbed.

The statute with which we are concerned does not discriminate on its face between rich and poor. Plaintiff contends that the statute actually applies only to the poor because a mentally ill or mentally retarded person with money would be able to hire others to care for his child and would never allow the child to become neglected or dependent.†

---

† The statute denies the fundamental right of procreation to those who come within its terms. The usual deference

The words "neglected or dependent" are not defined in ORS ch. 436. Plaintiff urges us to interpret both as dependent on state support and to adopt the reasoning in *Smith* v. *Wayne Probate Judge,* cit.... (1925). The purpose of the statute in that case was to protect the state from public charges:

> "That he would not be able to support and care for his children, if any, and such children would probably become public charges by reason of his own mental defectiveness."...

The Oregon law specifies that the potential offspring would become dependent or neglected as a result of the parent's inability to provide adequate care and is not concerned with the parent's financial status.*

The state's concern for the welfare of its citizenry extends to future generations and when there is overwhelming evidence, as there is here, that a potential parent will be unable to provide a proper environment for a child because of his own mental illness or mental retardation, the state has sufficient interest to order sterilization.

Affirmed.

---

given to the judgment of state legislatures does not apply to laws affecting fundamental human rights....

"...[S]trict scrutiny of the classification which a State makes in a sterilization law is essential, lest unwittingly or otherwise invidious discriminations are made against groups or types of individuals in violation of the constitutional guaranty of just and equal laws...." Skinner v. Oklahoma, supra, 316 U.S. at 541, 62 S.Ct. at 1113.

* Plaintiff has referred us to the minutes of the House Judiciary Committee, May 17, 1967, and the testimony of one of the principal witnesses who replied, when asked if the legislation was for the welfare of child or parent:

> "...Many of these girls can be trained for ordinary housework or simple skills in a community, but if they had the added stress and strain of the responsibility of infants are then unable to function properly. Furthermore, the children become public charges...."

The same witness stated that the children become neglected and "have all sorts of problems." Hearing, Senate Judiciary Committee, May 2, 1967.

Questions

1. The court states that due process has been provided under the statute allowing sterilization. Due process generally means that the state must go about what it does in a prescribed manner. For example, in the famous case of *in re Gault,* a case involving juvenile proceedings, the United States Supreme Court said that due process includes the right to be informed about the nature of charges pending against the juvenile, the right to counsel, the right to confront and cross-examine witnesses, the privilege against self-incrimination, the right to a transcript of proceedings, and a right to appellate review.

   Given these "protections," does the woman in the *Cook* case have anything to fear?

   How can the idea of due process be related to the central ideas of this section—status, power, and wealth?

2. In reading the case, one is struck by at least two areas of vagueness. A first is the language of the statute itself—"the *condition* of the examinee," "adequate care," no probability of improvement, and so on. A second concerns the group that stands to benefit from the sterilization. The board bears the name "Board for Social Protection." Elsewhere the court says that the sterilization will be beneficial to *society,* or that *the state* has a concern that children be raised in a "proper environment." Is it clear enough who is to benefit and what evil is being eradicated? In cases of doubt, should ambiguity be resolved in favor of individual integrity or the interests of "the state" or "society"?

3. The court says that the statute *on its face* does not discriminate between rich and poor, which probably means that the statute as written is potentially applicable to all people within the state of Oregon.

   Ought there to be additional tests to determine whether laws are discriminatory?

4. Is a person who inherits one million dollars at birth self-supporting?

6 Law and Official Discretion

A crow can pass for a peacock or a nightingale when there is no rivalry and nobody knows the difference.
                                          B. Traven, *Government*, 1971

If a Hollywood studio were casting for the role of judge in a movie or television series, what would it be likely to look for? A man, fiftyish, flowing gray hair—or at least hair graying at the temples—horn-rimmed glasses, mildly imperious but not totally devoid of compassion, sober, thoughtful, remote, and so on. These images have been perpetuated for so long in popular culture that they take on a life of their own which may mask the realities of the judging process. Popular myths become highly useful to professionals in law: For example, rather than make a frontal assault on a judge's wisdom and authority, lawyers often explain that a judge was "forced" to rule in a certain way. One of the memorable features of the Chicago conspiracy case in 1969 is that the sacrosanctity of the judge and his role in

legal process was so thoroughly questioned there.

Jerome Frank (1889–1957), a teacher, lawyer, and later judge, began to expose the realities of judicial process in *Law and the Modern Mind*, which stands as perhaps the finest book ever written about American law. There, he uncovered the dominant popular and professional myths about law and process, probed their psychoanalytic sources and recommended changes that he thought would be helpful. Since judges, police, prosecutors, and other decision makers filter all the competing notions of law, justice, and process, and control the day-to-day outcomes in law, Frank's writing adds a vital link between law in theory and in practice. Frank continually recommended that legal study focus on law making at the "lowest levels"; this lead is followed in this section with an additional case from the California Sentencing Institute, as well as in the subsequent chapters of this book.

The Judging Process and the Judge's Personality   *Jerome Frank*

As the word indicates, the judge in reaching a decision is making a judgment. And if we would understand what goes into the creating of that judgment, we must observe how ordinary

Selections from *Law and the Modern Mind* by Jerome Frank, pp. 108–126, copyright 1930, 1933, 1949 by Coward McCann, Inc., copyright 1930 by Brentano's Inc., are from Anchor Books Edition, 1963. Copyright renewed in 1958 by Florence K. Frank. Reprinted by arrangement with the estate of Barbara Frank Kristein. (Some footnotes omitted.)

men dealing with ordinary affairs arrive at their judgments.

The process of judging, so the psychologists tell us, seldom begins with a premise from which a conclusion is subsequently worked out. Judging begins rather the other way around—with a conclusion more or less vaguely formed; a man ordinarily starts with such a conclusion and afterwards tries to find premises which will substantiate it.[1] If he cannot, to his satisfaction, find

[1] A convenient analogy is the technique of the author of a detective story.

proper arguments to link up his conclusion with premises which he finds acceptable, he will, unless he is arbitrary or mad, reject the conclusion and seek another.

In the case of the lawyer who is to present a case to a court, the dominance in his thinking of the conclusion over the premises is moderately obvious. He is a partisan working on behalf of his client. The conclusion is, therefore, not a matter of choice except within narrow limits. He must, that is if he is to be successful, begin with a conclusion which will insure his client's winning the lawsuit. He then assembles the facts in such a fashion that he can work back from this result he desires to some major premise which he thinks the court will be willing to accept. The precedents, rules, principles and standards to which he will call the court's attention constitute this premise.

While "the dominance of the conclusion" in the case of the lawyer is clear, it is less so in the case of the judge. For the respectable and traditional descriptions of the judicial judging process admit no such backward-working explanation. In theory, the judge begins with some rule or principle of law as his premise, applies this premise to the facts, and thus arrives at his decision.

Now, since the judge is a human being and since no human being in his normal thinking processes arrives at decisions (except in dealing with a limited number of simple situations) by the route of any such syllogistic reasoning, it is fair to assume that the judge, merely by putting on the judicial ermine, will not acquire so artificial a method of reasoning. Judicial judgments, like other judgments, doubtless, in most cases, are worked out backward from conclusions tentatively formulated.

As Jastrow says, "In spite of the fact that the answer in the book happens to be wrong, a considerable portion of the class succeeds in reaching it.... The young mathematician will manage to obtain the answer which the book requires, even at the cost of a resort to very unmathematical processes." Courts, in their reasoning, are often singularly like Jastrow's young mathematician. Professor Tulin has made a study which prettily illustrates that fact. While driving at a reckless rate

of speed, a man runs over another, causing severe injuries. The driver of the car is drunk at the time. He is indicted for the statutory crime of "assault with intent to kill." The question arises whether his act constitutes that crime or merely the lesser statutory crime of "reckless driving." The courts of several states have held one way, and the courts of several other states have held the other.

The first group maintain that a conviction for assault with intent to kill cannot be sustained in the absence of proof of an actual purpose to inflict death. In the second group of states the courts have said that it was sufficient to constitute such a crime if there was a reckless disregard of the lives of others, such recklessness being said to be the equivalent of actual intent.

With what, then, appears to be the same facts before them, these two groups of courts seem to have sharply divided in their reasoning and in the conclusions at which they have arrived. But upon closer examination it has been revealed by Tulin that, in actual effect, the results arrived at in all these states have been more or less the same. In Georgia, which may be taken as representative of the second group of states, the penalty provided by the statute for reckless driving is far less than that provided, for instance, in Iowa, which is in the first group of states. If, then, a man is indicted in Georgia for reckless driving while drunk, the courts can impose on him only a mild penalty; whereas in Iowa the judge, under an identically worded indictment, can give a stiff sentence. In order to make it possible for the Georgia courts to give a reckless driver virtually the same punishment for the same offense as can be given by an Iowa judge, it is necessary in Georgia to construe the statutory crime of assault with intent to kill so that it will include reckless driving while drunk. If, and only if, the Georgia court so construes the statute can it impose the same penalty under the same facts as could the Iowa courts under the reckless driving statute. On the other hand, if the Iowa court were to construe the Iowa statute as the Georgia court construes the George statute, the punishment of the reckless driver in Iowa would be too severe.

In other words, the courts in these cases began

with the results they desired to accomplish: they wanted to give what they considered to be adequate punishment to drunken drivers: their conclusions determined their reasoning.

But the conception that judges work back from conclusions to principles is so heretical that it seldom finds expression.[2] Daily, judges, in connection with their decisions, deliver so-called opinions in which they purport to set forth the bases of their conclusions. Yet you will study these opinions in vain to discover anything remotely resembling a statement of the actual judging process. They are written in conformity with the time-honored theory. They picture the judge applying rules and principles to the facts, that is, taking some rule or principle (usually derived from opinions in earlier cases) as his major premise, employing the facts of the case as the minor premise, and then coming to his judgment by processes of pure reasoning.

Now and again some judge, more clear-witted and outspoken than his fellows, describes (when off the bench) his methods in more homely terms. Recently Judge Hutcheson essayed such an honest report of the judicial process. He tells us that after canvassing all the available material at his command and duly cogitating on it, he gives his imagination play,

> and brooding over the cause, waits for the feeling, the hunch—that intuitive flash of understanding that makes the jumpspark connection between question and decision and at the point where the path is darkest for the judicial feet, sets its light along the way.... In feeling or 'hunching' out his decisions, the judge acts not differently from but precisely as the lawyers do in working on their cases, with only this exception, that the lawyer, in having a predetermined destination in view,—to win the lawsuit for his client—looks for and regards only

[2] Years ago the writer, just after being admitted to the bar, was shocked when advised by S. S. Gregory, an ex-president of the American Bar Association—a man more than ordinarily aware of legal realities—that "the way to win a case is to make the judge want to decide in your favor and then, and then only, to cite precedents which will justify such a determination. You will almost always find plenty of cases to cite in your favor." All successful lawyers are more or less consciously aware of this technique. But they seldom avow it—even to themselves.

those hunches which keep him in the path that he has chosen, while the judge, being merely on his way with a roving commission to find the just solution, will follow his hunch wherever it leads him....

And Judge Hutcheson adds:

> I must premise that I speak now of the judgment or decision, the solution itself, as opposed to the apologia for that decision; the decree, as opposed to the logomachy, the effusion of the judge by which that decree is explained or excused.... The judge really decides by feeling and not by judgment, by hunching and not by ratiocination, such ratiocination appearing only in the opinion. The vital motivating impulse for the decision is an intuitive sense of what is right or wrong in the particular case; and the astute judge, having so decided, enlists his every faculty and belabors his laggard mind, not only to justify that intuition to himself, but to make it pass muster with his critics. Accordingly, he passes in review all of the rules, principles, legal categories, and concepts which he may find useful, directly or by an analogy so as to select from them those which in his opinion will justify his desired result.

We may accept this as an approximately correct description[3] of how all judges do their thinking. But see the consequences. If the law consists of the decisions of the judges and if those decisions are based on the judge's hunches, then the way in which the judge gets his hunches is the key to the judicial process. Whatever produces the judge's hunches makes the law.

What, then, are the hunch-producers? What are the stimuli which make a judge feel that he should try to justify one conclusion rather than another?

The rules and principles of law are one class of

[3] ...A century ago a great American judge, Chancellor Kent, in a personal letter explained his method of arriving at a decision. He first made himself "master of the facts." Then (he wrote) "I saw where justice lay, and the moral sense decided the court half the time; I then sat down to search the authorities.... I might once in a while be embarrassed by a technical rule, *but I almost always found principles suited to my view of the case.*" ...

such stimuli.[4] But there are many others, concealed or unrevealed, not frequently considered in discussions of the character or nature of law. To the infrequent extent that these other stimuli have been considered at all, they have been usually referred to as "the political, economic and moral prejudices" of the judge.[5] A moment's reflection would, indeed, induce any open-minded person to admit that factors of such character must be operating in the mind of the judge.

But are not those categories—political, economic and moral biases—too gross, too crude, too

[4] If Hutcheson were to be taken with complete literalness, it would seem that such legal rules, principles and the like are merely for show, materials for window dressing, implements to aid in rationalization. They are that indeed. But although impatience with the orthodox excessive emphasis on the importance of such devices might incline one at times to deny such formulations any real value, it is necessary—and this even Hutcheson would surely admit—to concede them more importance. In part, they help the judge to check up on the propriety of the hunches. They also suggest hunches....

[5] Most of the suggestions that law is a function of the undisclosed attitudes of judges stress the judges' "education," "race," "class," "economic, political and social influences" which "make up a complex environment" of which the judges are not wholly aware but which affect their decisions by influencing their views of "public policy," or "social advantage" or their "economic and social philosophies" or "their notions of fair play or what is right and just."

It is to the economic determinists and to the members of the school of "sociological jurisprudence" that we owe much of the recognition of the influence of the economic and political background of judges upon decisions. For this much thanks. But their work has perhaps been done too well. Interested as were these writers in problems of labor law and "public policy" questions, they over-stressed a few of the multitude of unconscious factors and over-simplified the problem.

Much the same is to be said of the views of the "historical school" with respect to the effect of custom on judicial decisions. "Whether a custom will or will not be ratified by the courts depends after all on the courts themselves," says Dickinson.... "Whatever forces can be said to influence the growth of the law, they exert that influence only by influencing the judges.... Current *mores*... are things about which there is room for considerable difference of opinion and ... when it is a question of their writing themselves into law, the opinion which prevails is the judges' opinion." See Cardozo, "The Nature of the Judicial Process," 174. "In every court there are likely to be as many estimates of the Zeitgeist as there are judges on its bench."

wide? Since judges are not a distinct race and since their judging processes must be substantially of like kind with those of other men, an analysis of the way in which judges reach their conclusions will be aided by answering the question, What are the hidden factors in the inferences and opinions of ordinary men? The answer surely is that those factors are multitudinous and complicated, depending often on peculiarly individual traits of the persons whose inferences and opinions are to be explained. These uniquely individual factors often are more important causes of judgments than anything which could be described as political, economic, or moral biases.

In the first place, all other biases express themselves in connection with, and as modified by, these idiosyncratic biases. A man's political or economic prejudices are frequently cut across by his affection for or animosity to some particular individual or group, due to some unique experience he has had; or a racial antagonism which he entertains may be deflected in a particular case by a desire to be admired by someone who is devoid of such antagonism.

Second (and in the case of the judge more important), is the consideration that in learning the facts with reference to which one forms an opinion, and often long before the time when a hunch arises with reference to the situation as a whole, these more minute and distinctly personal biases are operating constantly. So the judge's sympathies and antipathies are likely to be active with respect to the persons of the witness, the attorneys and the parties to the suit. His own past may have created plus or minus reactions to women, or blonde women, or men with beards, or Southerners, or Italians, or Englishmen, or plumbers, or ministers, or college graduates, or Democrats. A certain twang or cough or gesture may start up memories painful or pleasant in the main. Those memories of the judge, while he is listening to a witness with such a twang or cough or gesture, may affect the judge's initial hearing of, or subsequent recollection of, what the witness said, or the weight or credibility which the judge will attach to the witness's testimony.

That the testimony of witnesses is affected by their experiences and temperaments has been often observed....

Men are prone to see what they want to see.

"It must be admitted that at the present day the testimony of even a truthful witness is much over-rated."

No doubt the eyes of some witnesses are livelier than those of others and the sense of sight may be quickened or diminished by the interest or bias of him who possesses it.

Even where witnesses are upright or honest, their belief is apt to be more or less warped by their partiality or prejudice for or against the parties. It is easy to reason ourselves into a belief in the existence of that which we desire to be true, whereas the facts testified to, and from which the witness deduces his conclusions, might produce a very different impression on the minds of others.

It frequently happens that a person, by long dwelling on a subject, thinks that a thing may have happened, and he at last comes to believe that it actually did occur.

The courts have been alive to these grave possibilities of error and have therefore repeatedly declared that it is one of the most important functions of the trial judge, in determining the value and weight of the evidence, to consider the demeanor of the witness.

They have called attention, as of the gravest importance, to such facts as the tone of voice in which a witness's statement is made, the hesitation or readiness with which his answers are given, the look of the witness, his carriage, his evidences of surprise, his gesture, his zeal, his bearing, his expression, his yawns, the use of his eyes, his furtive or meaning glances, or his shrugs, the pitch of his voice, his self-possession or embarrassment, his air of candor or of seeming levity. It is because these circumstances can be manifest only to one who actually hears and sees the witnesses that upper courts have frequently stated that they are hesitant to overturn the decision of the trial judge in a case where the evidence has been based upon oral testimony; for the upper courts have recognized that they have before them only a stenographic or printed report of the testimony, and that such a black and white report cannot reproduce anything but the cold words of the witness. "The tongue of the witness," it has been said, "is not the only organ

for conveying testimony." Yet it is only the words that can be transmitted to the reviewing court, while the story that is told by the manner, by the tone, by the eyes, must be lost to all but him who observes the witness on the stand.

It is, then, a legal commonplace that a witness cannot mechanically reproduce the facts, but is reporting his judgment of the facts and may err in the making of this judgment.

Strangely enough, it has been little observed that, while the witness is in this sense a judge, *the judge, in a like sense, is a witness*. He is a witness of what is occurring in his courtroom. He must determine what are the facts of the case from what he sees and hears; that is, from the words and gestures and other conduct of the witnesses. And like those who are testifying before him, the judge's determination of the facts is no mechanical act. If the witnesses are subject to lapses of memory or imaginative reconstruction of events, in the same manner the judge is subject to defects in his apprehension of the testimony, so that long before he has come to the point in the case where he must decide what is right or wrong, just or unjust, with reference to the facts of the case as a whole, the trial judge has been engaged in making numerous judgments or inferences as the testimony dribbles in. His beliefs as to what was said by the witnesses and with what truthfulness the witnesses said it, will determine what he believes to be the "facts of the case." If his final decision is based upon a hunch and that hunch is a function of the "facts," then of course what, as a fallible witness of what went on in his courtroom, he believes to be the "facts," will often be of controlling importance. So that the judge's innumerable unique traits, dispositions and habits often get in their work in shaping his decisions not only in his determination of what he thinks fair or just with reference to a given set of facts, but in the very processes by which he becomes convinced what those facts are.

The peculiar traits, disposition, biases and habits of the particular judge will, then, often determine what he decides to be the law. In this respect judges do not differ from other mortals: "In every case of actual thinking," says F. C. S. Schiller, "the whole of a man's personality enters into and colors it in every part." To know the judge's hunch-producers which make the law we must know thoroughly that complicated congeries we loosely call the judge's personality....

...The following is from the reminiscences of a man who has served both as prosecuting attorney and as judge:

> The jockeying for a judge is sometimes almost humorous. Lawyers recognize the peculiarities, previous opinions, leanings, strength and weakness, and likes or dislikes of a particular judge in a particular case. Some years ago one of the bright lawyers of Chicago conferred with me as an assistant state's attorney, to agree on a judge for the trial of a series of cases. We proceeded to go over the list. For the state's attorney, I objected to but one judge of all the twenty-eight Cook County judges, and as I went through the list I would ask him about one or another, "How about this one?" As to the first one I named he said, "No, he decided a case a couple of weeks ago in a way that I didn't like, and I don't want him to use my client as a means to get back to a state of virtue." As to another, he said, "No, he is not very clear-headed; he is likely to read an editorial by the man who put him on the ticket, and get confused on the law." Of another he said, "No, he might sneer at my witnesses, and I can't get the sneer in the record." To another he objected that "If my clients were found guilty this judge would give them the limit." To still another he said, "No, you can't get him to make a ruling in a case without creating a disturbance in the court room, he is so careful of the Supreme Court." Again he replied to one, "No, if the state's attorney should happen to sit in the court room I won't get a favorable ruling in the entire case." And so we went along.

One bit of statistical evidence as to the differences between judges is available: A survey was made of the disposition of thousands of minor criminal cases by the several judges of the City Magistrate's Court in New York City during the years 1914 to 1916 with the express purpose of finding to what extent the "personal equation" entered into the administration of justice. It was disclosed that "the magistrates did differ to an amazing degree in their treatment of similar classes of cases." Thus of 546 persons charged with intoxication brought before one judge, he discharged only one and found the others (about 97%) guilty, whereas of the 673 arraigned before another judge, he found 531 (or 79%) not guilty. In disorderly conduct cases, one judge discharged only 18% and another discharged 54%. "In other words, one coming before Magistrate Simons had only 2 chances in 10 of getting off. If he had come before Judge Walsh he would have had more than 5 chances in 10 of getting off." In vagrancy cases, the percentage of discharges varied from 4.5% to 79%. When it came to sentences, the same variations existed. One judge imposed fines on 84% of the persons he found guilty and gave suspended sentences to 7%, while one of his fellows fined 34% and gave suspended sentences to 59%. Everson concludes that these figures show to what a remarkable degree the individuality of the magistrates is mirrored in their disposition of cases. "Justice," he says, "is a very personal thing, reflecting the temperament, the personality, the education, environment and personal traits of the magistrate."

But if we determine that the personality of the judge has much to do with law-making, have we done enough? Can we rest content with this mere recognition? Can we stop with the blanket statement that our judicial process at its best will be based upon "the trained intuition of the judges," on the hunches of experienced men? Perhaps it will be found that we must stop there, but who can tell? When only a small fraction of the bench and bar as yet admit, and then timidly, that concrete human beings and not abstract rules make the law, it is too early to decide that a new technique of wise and discriminating judging cannot be developed. That those jungles of the mind which we are just beginning to discover will soon be reduced to a high state of civilized order is not likely, but that they must ever remain in their present chaotic state is equally far from certain.

Just what form a new technique of judging will take, it is too soon to guess. And the same may be said of conjectures as to how long it will be before such a technique can become effective. It would not be wise to be over-optimistic. Schroeder, one of the few lawyers who has thought deeply and courageously about this problem, has fallen into the error of assuming that a blending of law and psychology will promptly produce remarkable results. He anticipates that, with the insight that modern psychology affords, we shall quickly be able to ascertain, from the language employed by a judge in his opinions, the hidden predispositions and impulses which brought about his decision. He believes that "every choice of conclusion, argument, precedent, phrase or word," in a judge's opinion, "is expressive of an unconscious, a dominant personal motive in the judge. Every such choice is a fragment of autobiography because it reveals not only the present conscious motive, but also the still potent, past and immature experimental causes, which determined the unconscious impulses submerged in, but controlling the avowed motive.... So we may read the life of the judge backwards. Every opinion thus amounts to a confession."

If Schroeder were right, the discovery of the hidden causes of decisions would be fairly simple. But the job is not so easy. The directing impulses of judges will not so readily appear from analyses of their rationalizing words. We shall not learn how judges think until the judges are able and ready to engage in ventures of self-discovery....

... What we may hope some day to get from our judges are detailed autobiographies containing the sort of material that is recounted in the autobiographical novel; or opinions annotated, by the judge who writes them, with elaborate explorations of the background factors in his personal experience which swayed him in reaching his conclusions. For in the last push, a judge's decisions are the outcome of his entire life-history. Judges can take to heart the counsel Anatole France gave to the judges of literature:

All those who deceive themselves into the belief that they put anything but their own personalities into their work are dupes of the most fallacious of illusions. The truth is that we can never get outside ourselves.... We are shut up in our own personality as if in a perpetual prison. The best thing for us, it seems to me, is to admit this frightful condition with a good grace, and to confess that we speak of ourselves every time we have not strength enough to remain silent....

Everson, in his report on the statistics of the decisions by the judges of the City Magistrate's Court, expressed the belief that the publication of these records would cause a better understanding by the judges of their own work and lead them to

a viewpoint somewhat tempered by the knowledge of what the other judges are doing and with a broader viewpoint of the problems before them. Each magistrate will come to recognize his own personal peculiarities and seek to correct any that cannot be justified in the light of the records of his associates.

But a different result ensued. The disclosures "were so startling and so disconcerting that it seemed advisable to discontinue the comparative tables of the records of the justices." The bench and bar did not want to have called to their attention the extent to which judging is affected by the temperament, training, biases and predilections of the respective judges.

No one can know in advance what a judge will believe to be the "facts" of a case. It follows that a lawyer's opinion as to the law relating to a given set of facts is a guess as to (1) what a judge thereafter will guess were the facts and (2) what that judge will consider to be the proper decision on the basis of that judge's guess as to the facts. Even that is too artificial a statement. The judge, in arriving at his hunch, does not nicely separate his belief as to the "facts" from his conclusion as to the "law"; his general hunch is more integral and composite, and affects his report—both to himself and to the public—concerning the facts. Only a superficial thinker will assume that the facts as they occurred and as they later appear to the judge (and as he reports them) will invariably—or indeed often—correspond. The judge's decision is determined by a hunch arrived at long after the event on the basis of his reaction to fallible testimony. It is, in every sense of the word, *ex post facto*. It is fantastic, then, to say that usually men can warrantably act in reliance upon "established law." Their inability to do so may be deplorable. But mature persons must face the truth, however unpleasant.

Why such resistance to the truth? Why has there been little investigation of the actualities of the judging process? If we are right in assuming that the very subject matter of the law activates childish emotional attitudes, we can perhaps find an answer to these questions.

It is a marked characteristic of the young child, writes Piaget, that he does very little thinking about his thinking. He encounters extreme difficulty if asked to give an account of the "how" of his mental processes. He cannot reflect on his own reasoning. If you ask him to state how he reached a conclusion, he is unable to recover his own reasoning processes, but instead invents an artificial account which will somehow seem to lead to the result. He cannot correctly explain what he did to find this result. "Instead of giving a retrospect he starts from the result he has obtained as though he had known it in advance and then gives a more or less elaborate method for finding it again.... He starts from his conclusion and argues towards the premises as though he had known from the first whither those premises would lead him."

Once more these difficulties find their explanation in the child's relative unawareness of his self, of his incapacity for dealing with his own thoughts as subjective. For this obtuseness produces in the child an overconfidence in his own ideas, a lack of skepticism as to the subjectivity of his own beliefs. As a consequence, the child is singularly nonintrospective. He has, according to Piaget, no curiosity about the motives that guide his thinking. His whole attitude towards his own thinking is the antithesis of any introspective habit of watching himself think, of alertness in detecting the motives which push him in the direction of any given conclusion. The child, that is, does not take his own motives into account. They are ignored and never considered as a constituent of thinking.

...One recalls a dictum of Piaget in talking of the child:

> The less a mind is given to introspection the more it is the victim of the illusion that it knows itself thoroughly.

Questions

1. How do you reach decisions? Do you get a "hunch" and rationalize it later, or do you assemble all the pros and cons and only then reach a conclusion?

2. By what criteria do the people whom you routinely encounter make decisions? Does actual decision making match the officially prescribed ways that decisions are to be made? Would the decision process be different if all people were to be called judges? How does your teacher determine your grade? How are decisions made in your family or in other groups in which you find yourself?

3. Judge Hutcheson, quoted in Frank, talks about feeling and hunching as helpful aspects of decision making. What role should intuition play in decisions? If others ask you how you make your decisions, are you likely to acknowledge that intuition and feelings play a part?

   In published legal opinions, there is no acknowledgment of intuition. What gives intuition such a bad name?

   Can intuition be cultivated or improved, or is the only safe course of action to root out intuition and make decisions "objective"?

   In light of Frank, is there any such thing as an objective decision?

4. Are judges ordinary people or are they different by virtue of their legal training, because they must act in public, with lawyers present, in the presence of antagonists in dispute, and with announced results? Do these ingredients become "steadying factors" that prevent a judge from being wildly idiosyncratic?

5. How does the material from Frank complement the material in Section 1 on Legal Reasoning? What leads does he furnish for additional study of other sections of the chapter?

6. Frank focuses on the psychoanalytic bases for decisions whereas Section 5 suggests that the determinants for decisions are socioeconomic and political. Can the thesis of Section 5 be integrated with the thesis of Frank?

7. Frank's theory focuses on the judge. Does his theory apply equally well to other decision makers, such as police, lawyers, jurors, or jailors? To decisional processes generally?

8. Return to the judges' decisions in the check forgery case in Section 5. Does Frank's theory help you sort out the personal characteristics of the judges? Which judges would you want if accused of a crime? If you represented an accused? If you were a prosecutor?

A Case of Robbery and Rape

1968 California Sentencing Institute, 77 Cal. Rptr. (Appendix)

OFFENSE: ROBBERY AND RAPE Defendant offered a ride to a young coed, waiting for a bus, and carrying a heavy bag of freshly washed laundry. She got into the car and upon reaching her residence, he pulled out a gun and ordered her to lie down in the back of the car. He then proceeded to drive to a remote park where he ordered her to hand over her wallet, removing $18, and then ordered her to remove all her clothing. Frightened, she complied, and then defendant proceeded to rape her. She struggled, and defendant choked and beat her severely. He also ordered her to commit an unnatural sex act. After she managed to escape, she reported the offense and defendant's license number to the police. Upon apprehension, defendant admitted offense, and was contrite, blaming recent unemployment for creating feelings of tension and unrest.

PRIOR CRIMINAL RECORD
4/67 County X Petty theft 6 months probation
5/68 County X PRESENT OFFENSE

CASE HISTORY INFORMATION This 23-year-old adult male was the second of four children from a broken home. He was raised by his mother and stepfather, who subsequently divorced. He said his stepfather was quite harsh. He ran away quite often, as a result of which the Illinois juvenile court placed him in a succession of foster homes where he remained from the ages of 11 to 17, at which time he joined the armed forces.

He is a high school graduate, receiving his diploma through correspondence courses while serving in the armed forces. He later attended junior college for a semester but left to work.

He has been married for the past year and his wife is expecting their first child. He asserts that she understands his problem and that she plans to stick by him. His wife indicated that he has had periodic fits of depression, especially during times of unemployment, and also displayed a violent temper, and has beaten her up several times. She indicates that he agreed to see a psychiatrist but they could never afford such treatment. She also feels that her husband harbors considerable inferiority feelings. Defendant had been employed as a production worker in a local plant and prior employers indicate that his work was satisfactory.

He was arrested and convicted of petty theft last year, stealing items from a department store, and placed on probation. He claims it was an impulsive act for which he was sorry.

MILITARY HISTORY Subject served three years in the armed service and received a general discharge (under honorable conditions), brought about following his apprehension for "peeping" in nurses' quarters windows while stationed overseas.

CASE EVALUATION This is a fairly polite, articulate young man, the product of an unsettled background featuring a hostile stepfather and various foster home placements. He has not been able to maintain steady employment and seems to be easily discouraged and lacking in self-confidence. In interview, he reveals a lengthy history of voyeurism. He is aware that he has a serious disorder and was quite eager to discuss his sex problems. Three psychiatrists have interviewed him and disagree regarding his disposition. One would send him to Atascadero,* another would order institutional treatment in a state correctional facility because of the assaultive behavior in the offense and the third would grant him probation under close supervision with psychiatric treatment.

Question

1. What should be done?

* [A California institution for "mentally disordered sexual offenders."——ED.]

Conclusion

The purpose of this chapter has been to introduce some of the major explanations of law. Most of the themes will recur in later chapters, and there will be numerous opportunities to measure the worth of the various explanations in a variety of settings. Each orientation—rules, values, competing interests, popular sentiments, power, discretion—tends to be imperialistic, to drive competing contenders from the field. But law is a *field* of forces, and no one theory encompasses the whole.

Rule lovers drive toward certainty, only to be upended by difficulties in interpretation and vagaries of fact. Those who probe for values become philosopher-kings without territory and usually settle for a running dialogue with people in power. Lawyers who see themselves as neutral arbiters of competing claims fail to see that involvement is never neutral. Neopopulists seek a demise of elitism and a return to institutional intimacy, but sometimes overlook the dark side of popular will and the reasons why old institutions failed. Power theorists drive toward revolutionary change but rarely get beyond current pathology. Students of discretion emphasize choice, while neglecting social and institutional constraints that narrow the range of choice.

After such investigation one should be left open and perplexed rather than closed and dogmatic. This confusion differs in quality from unalloyed relativism since it is an aspect of growth rather than a retreat from the complexities of legal life. The confusion should not lead to inactivity or deference to experts. After all, if *so-called* experts were *complete* experts, they would be as confused as the rest of us. Instead, we should act with strength and humility, and with an appreciation for the richness and complexity of both life and law.

Suggested Additional Readings

Introduction to Law

Auerbach, Carl et al. *The Legal Process.* San Francisco: Chandler, 1961.

Berman, Harold, and Greiner, William. *The Nature and Functions of Law.* Mineola, N.Y.: Foundation, 1966.

Frankel, Lionel. *Law, Power and Personal Freedom.* St. Paul, Minn.: West, 1975.

Karlen, Delmar, *The Citizen in Court.* New York: Holt, Rinehart and Winston, 1964.

Schur, Edwin. *Law and Society.* New York: Random House, 1968.

Legal Reasoning

Cardozo, Benjamin. *The Nature of the Judicial Process.* New Haven: Yale University Press, 1921.

Levi, Edward. *An Introduction to Legal Reasoning.* Chicago: University of Chicago Press, 1949.

Llewellyn, Karl. *The Bramble Bush.* New York: Oceana Publications, 1930.

Zelermyer, William. *The Process of Legal Reasoning.* Englewood Cliffs, N.J.: Prentice-Hall, 1963.

Law and Values

Cahn, Edmond. *The Moral Decision*. Bloomington, Ind.: Indiana University Press, 1955.
———. *The Sense of Injustice*. Bloomington, Ind.: Indiana University Press, 1964.
Cohen, Morris. *Reason and Law*. New York: The Free Press, 1950.
Ellul, Jacques. *The Technological Society*. New York: Random House, 1964.
Fuller, Lon. *The Morality of Law*. New Haven: Yale University Press, 1964.
Hart, H. L. A. *The Concept of Law*. Oxford: Clarendon, 1961.
Piaget, Jean. *The Moral Judgement of the Child*. New York: The Free Press, 1965.
Rawls, John. *A Theory of Justice*. Cambridge: Harvard University Press, 1971.
Shklar, Judith. *Legalism*. Cambridge: Harvard University Press, 1964.
Thompson, William. *At the Edge of History*. New York: Harper & Row, 1971.

Law and Conflicting Interests

Coser, Lewis. *The Functions of Social Conflict*. New York: The Free Press, 1956.
Ehrlich, Eugen. *Fundamental Principles of the Sociology of Law*. Translated by W. Moll. New York: Russell & Russell, 1962.
Hartzler, H. Richard, and Allan, Harry. *An Introduction to Law*. Glenview, Ill.: Scott, Foresman, 1969.
Pound, Roscoe. *Social Control Through Law*. New Haven: Yale University Press, 1942.
Summers, Robert. *Law: Its Nature, Functions and Limits*. Englewood Cliffs, N.J.: Prentice-Hall, 1972.

Law and Popular Will

Bohannan, Paul, ed. *Law and Warfare*. Garden City, N.Y.: Natural History Press, 1967.
Llewellyn, Karl, and Hoebel, E. Adamson. *The Cheyenne Way*. Norman, Okla.: University of Oklahoma Press, 1941.
Maine, Henry. *Ancient Law*. London: Oxford University Press, 1931.
Nader, Laura, ed. *Law in Culture and Society*. Chicago: Aldine, 1969.

Savigny, Fredrick. *Of the Vocation of Our Age for Legislation and Jurisprudence*. Translated by A. Hayward, London: Littlewood, 1831.
Tönnies, Ferdinand. *Community and Society*. Edited and translated by Charles P. Loomis. New York: Harper & Row, 1963.

Law, Status, Wealth, and Power

Babb, Hugh, trans. *Soviet Legal Philosophy*. Cambridge: Harvard University Press, 1951.
Balbus, Isaac. *The Dialectics of Legal Repression*. New Brunswick, N.J.: Transaction, 1973.
Bankowski, Zenon, and Mungham, Geoff. *Images of Law*. London: Routledge and Kegan Paul, 1976.
Black, Jonathan, ed. *Radical Lawyers*. New York: Avon Books, 1971.
Chambliss, William, and Seidman, Robert. *Law, Order and Power*. Reading, Mass.: Addison-Wesley, 1971.
Kirchheimer, Otto. *Political Justice*. Princeton, N.J.: Princeton University Press, 1961.
Lefcourt, Robert. *Law Against the People*. New York: Random House, 1971.
Mills, C. Wright. *The Power Elite*. New York: Oxford University Press, 1957.
Quinney, Richard. *Class, State & Crime*. New York: McKay, 1977.
tenBroek, ed. *The Law of the Poor*. Berkeley: California Law Review, 1966.
Weber, Max. *On Law in Economy and Society*. Translated with introduction by Max Rheinstein et al. Cambridge: Harvard University Press, 1954.

Law and Official Discretion

Arnold, Thurman. *The Symbols of Government*. New Haven: Yale University Press, 1935.
Frank, Jerome. *Courts on Trial*. Princeton, N.J.: Princeton University Press, 1949.
———. *Law and the Modern Mind*. New York: Anchor Books, 1930.
Llewellyn, Karl. *The Common Law Tradition: Deciding Appeals*. Boston: Little, Brown, 1962.
Noonan, John. *Persons and Masks of the Law*. New York: Farrar, Straus & Giroux, 1976.

Photograph by Charles Gatewood.

It was the first time I had ever been called on by the police. There was a short middle-aged man in a soft hat with a rough but kindly face and a broken nose and the tall good-looking young man in uniform. "Mr. Pulling?" the detective asked.

"Yes."

"May we come in for a few moments?"

"Have you a warrant?" I asked.

"Oh no, no, it hasn't come to that. We just want to have a word or two with you." I wanted to say something about the Gestapo, but I thought it wiser not. I led them into the dining-room, but I didn't ask them to sit down. The detective showed me an identity card and I read on it that he was Detective-Sergeant Sparrow, John.

"You know a man called Wordsworth, Mr. Pulling?"

"Yes, he's a friend of my aunt's."

"Did you receive a package from him in the street yesterday?"

"I certainly did."

"Would you have any objection to our examining the package, Mr. Pulling?"

"I most certainly would."

"You know, sir, we could easily have obtained a search warrant, but we want to do things delicately...."

Graham Greene, *Travels With My Aunt* (1969)

chapter two

The Police

In the stereotyped frontier town the sheriff, not Gilbert and Sullivan's judge, would have sung "I am the law." Indeed, he was even referred to as the "lawman." To many persons, it is still the police officer who not only symbolizes the law, but *is* the law. As the above excerpt illustrates, in many instances a person may feel that the law is not what a judge says it is, but rather what the police officer says it is.

One source of such feelings is the power

101

that the police have. Other parts of this book discuss the discretionary powers of district attorneys, judges, and even juries. As an integral part of the same system, it should not be surprising to find the police holding a great deal of the same power. The articles in this chapter raise many of the same issues that may have occurred to you when reading the short excerpt above. For example, how do the police affect the law, and how does the law affect them? What controls are there over police discretion? Should police have any discretion about when to act? What are the functions of the police?

What should they be doing? What do they do?

The following story is by George Orwell, a brilliant essayist and journalist most widely known as the author of *1984* and *Animal Farm*. The story is about Orwell's service as a policeman in Burma under British rule, and presents an intriguing first-person account about the use of power and authority and how, in any context, decisions are made and carried out. One might consider, too, how Orwell's experience in Burma influenced his thinking on the themes of freedom and totalitarian rule which are explored in his famous novels.

Shooting an Elephant   *George Orwell*

In Moulmein, in Lower Burma, I was hated by large numbers of people—the only time in my life that I have been important enough for this to happen to me. I was sub-divisional police officer of the town, and in an aimless, petty kind of way anti-European feeling was very bitter. No one had the guts to raise a riot, but if a European woman went through the bazaars alone somebody would probably spit betel juice over her dress. As a police officer I was an obvious target and was baited whenever it seemed safe to do so. When a nimble Burman tripped me up on the football field and the referee (another Burman) looked the other way, the crowd yelled with hideous laughter. This happened more than once. In the end the sneering yellow faces of young men that met me everywhere, the insults hooted after me when I was at a safe distance, got badly on my nerves. The young Buddhist priests were the worst of all. There were several thousands of them in the town and none of them

seemed to have anything to do except stand on street corners and jeer at Europeans.

All this was perplexing and upsetting. For at that time I had already made up my mind that imperialism was an evil thing and the sooner I chucked up my job and got out of it the better. Theoretically—and secretly, of course—I was all for the Burmese and all against their oppressors, the British. As for the job I was doing, I hated it more bitterly than I can perhaps make clear. In a job like that you see the dirty work of Empire at close quarters. The wretched prisoners huddling in the stinking cages of the lock-ups, the grey, cowed faces of the long-term convicts, the scarred buttocks of the men who had been flogged with bamboos—all these oppressed me with an intolerable sense of guilt. But I could get nothing into perspective. I was young and ill-educated and I had had to think out my problems in the utter silence that is imposed on every Englishman in the East. I did not even know that the British Empire is dying, still less did I know that it is a great deal better than the younger empires that are going to supplant it. All I knew was that I was stuck between my hatred of the empire I served and my rage against the evil-spirited little beasts who tried to make my job impossible. With one part of my mind I thought of the British Raj as an unbreakable tyranny, as something clamped down, in *saecula saeculorum,* upon the will of prostrate peoples; with another part I thought that the greatest joy in the world would be to drive a bayonet into a Buddhist priest's guts. Feelings like these are the normal by-products of imperialism; ask any Anglo-Indian official, if you can catch him off duty.

One day something happened which in a roundabout way was enlightening. It was a tiny incident in itself, but it gave me a better glimpse than I had had before of the real nature of imperialism—the real motives for which despotic governments act. Early one morning the sub-inspector at a police station the other end of the town rang me up on the 'phone and said that an elephant was ravaging the bazaar. Would I please come and do something about it? I did not know what I could do, but I wanted to see what was happening and I got on to a pony and started out. I took my rifle, an old .44 Winchester and much too small to kill an elephant, but I thought the noise might be useful *in terrorem.* Various Burmans stopped me on the way and told me about the elephant's doings. It was not, of course, a wild elephant, but a tame one which had gone "must." It had been chained up, as tame elephants always are when their attack of "must" is due, but on the previous night it had broken its chain and escaped. Its mahout, the only person who could manage it when it was in that state, had set out in pursuit, but had taken the wrong direction and was now twelve hours' journey away, and in the morning the elephant had suddenly reappeared in the town. The Burmese population had no weapons and were quite helpless against it. It had already destroyed somebody's bamboo hut, killed a cow and raided some fruit-stalls and devoured the stock; also it had met the municipal rubbish van and, when the driver jumped out and took to his heels, had turned the van over and inflicted violences upon it.

The Burmese sub-inspector and some Indian constables were waiting for me in the quarter where the elephant had been seen. It was a very poor quarter, a labyrinth of squalid bamboo huts, thatched with palm-leaf, winding all over a steep hillside. I remember that it was a cloudy, stuffy morning at the beginning of the rains. We began questioning the people as to where the elephant had gone and, as usual, failed to get any definite information. That is invariably the case in the East; a story always sounds clear enough at a distance, but the nearer you get to the scene of events the vaguer it becomes. Some of the people said that the elephant had gone in one direction, some said that he had gone in another, some professed not even to have heard of any elephant. I had almost made up my mind that the whole story was a pack of lies, when we heard yells a little distance away. There was a loud, scandalized cry of "Go away, child! Go away this instant!" and an old woman with a switch in her hand came round the corner of a hut, violently shooing away a crowd of naked children. Some more women followed, clicking their tongues and exclaiming; evidently there was something that the children ought not to have seen. I rounded the hut and saw a man's dead body sprawling in the mud. He was an Indian, a black Dravidian coolie, almost naked, and he could not have been dead many minutes. The people said that the elephant had come suddenly upon him round the corner of the hut, caught him with its trunk, put its foot on his back and ground him into the earth. This was the rainy season and the ground was soft, and his face had scored a trench a foot deep and a couple of yards long. He was lying on his belly with arms crucified and head sharply twisted to one side. His face was coated with mud, the eyes wide open, the teeth bared and grinning with an expression of unendurable agony. (Never tell me, by the way, that the dead look peaceful. Most of the corpses I have seen looked devilish.) The friction of the great beast's foot had stripped the skin from his back as neatly as one skins a rabbit. As soon as I saw the dead man I sent an orderly to a friend's house nearby to borrow an elephant rifle. I had already sent back the pony, not wanting it to go mad with fright and throw me if it smelt the elephant.

The orderly came back in a few minutes with

a rifle and five cartridges, and meanwhile some Burmans had arrived and told us that the elephant was in the paddy fields below, only a few hundred yards away. As I started forward practically the whole population of the quarter flocked out of the houses and followed me. They had seen the rifle and were all shouting excitedly that I was going to shoot the elephant. They had not shown much interest in the elephant when he was merely ravaging their homes, but it was different now that he was going to be shot. It was a bit of fun to them, as it would be to an English crowd; besides they wanted the meat. It made me vaguely uneasy. I had no intention of shooting the elephant—I had merely sent for the rifle to defend myself if necessary—and it is always unnerving to have a crowd following you. I marched down the hill, looking and feeling a fool, with the rifle over my shoulder and an ever-growing army of people jostling at my heels. At the bottom, when you got away from the huts, there was a metalled road and beyond that a miry waste of paddy fields a thousand yards across, not yet ploughed but soggy from the first rains and dotted with coarse grass. The elephant was standing eight yards from the road, his left side towards us. He took not the slightest notice of the crowd's approach. He was tearing up bunches of grass, beating them against his knees to clean them and stuffing them into his mouth.

I had halted on the road. As soon as I saw the elephant I knew with perfect certainty that I ought not to shoot him. It is a serious matter to shoot a working elephant—it is comparable to destroying a huge and costly piece of machinery—and obviously one ought not to do it if it can possibly be avoided. And at that distance, peacefully eating, the elephant looked no more dangerous than a cow. I thought then and I think now that his attack of "must" was already passing off; in which case he would merely wander harmlessly about until the mahout came back and caught him. Moreover, I did not in the least want to shoot him. I decided that I would watch him for a little while to make sure that he did not turn savage again, and then go home.

But at that moment I glanced round at the crowd that had followed me. It was an immense crowd, two thousand at the least and growing every minute. It blocked the road for a long distance on either side. I looked at the sea of yellow faces above the garish clothes—faces all happy and excited over this bit of fun, all certain that the elephant was going to be shot. They were watching me as they would watch a conjurer about to perform a trick. They did not like me, but with the magical rifle in my hands I was momentarily worth watching. And suddenly I realized that I should have to shoot the elephant after all. The people expected it of me and I had got to do it; I could feel their two thousand wills pressing me forward, irresistibly. And it was at this moment, as I stood there with the rifle in my hands, that I first grasped the hollowness, the futility of the white man's dominion in the East. Here was I, the white man with his gun, standing in front of the unarmed native crowd—seemingly the leading actor of the piece; but in reality I was only an absurd puppet pushed to and fro by the will of those yellow faces behind. I perceived in this moment that when the white man turns tyrant it is his own freedom that he destroys. He becomes a sort of hollow, posing dummy, the conventionalized figure of a sahib. For it is the condition of his rule that he shall spend his life in trying to impress the "natives," and so in every crisis he has got to do what the "natives" expect of him. He wears a mask, and his face grows to fit it. I had got to shoot the elephant. I had committed myself to doing it when I sent for the rifle. A sahib has got to act like a sahib; he has got to appear resolute, to know his own mind and do definite things. To come all that way, rifle in hand, with two thousand people marching at my heels, and then to trail feebly away, having done nothing—no, that was impossible. The crowd would laugh at me. And my whole life, every white man's life in the East, was one long struggle not to be laughed at.

But I did not want to shoot the elephant. I watched him beating his bunch of grass against his knees, with that preoccupied grandmotherly air that elephants have. It seemed to me that it would be murder to shoot him. At that age I was not squeamish about killing animals, but I had never shot an elephant and never wanted to. (Somehow it always seems worse to kill a *large* animal.) Besides, there was the beast's owner to be considered. Alive, the elephant was worth at least a hundred pounds; dead, he would only be worth the value of his tusks, five pounds, possibly. But I had got to act quickly. I turned to some experienced-looking Burmans who had been there when we arrived, and asked them how the elephant had been behaving. They all said the same thing: he took no notice of you if you left him alone, but he might charge if you went too close to him.

It was perfectly clear to me what I ought to do. I ought to walk up to within, say, twenty-five yards of the elephant and test his behavior. If he charged, I could shoot; if he took no notice of me, it would be safe to leave him until the mahout came back. But also I knew that I was going to do no such thing. I was a poor shot with a rifle and the ground was soft mud into which one would sink at every step. If the elephant charged and I missed him, I should have about as much chance as a toad under a steamroller. But even then I was not thinking particularly of my own skin, only of the watchful yellow faces behind. For at that moment, with the crowd watching me, I was not afraid in the ordinary sense, as I would have been if I had been alone. A white man mustn't be frightened in front of "natives"; and so, in general, he isn't frightened. The sole thought in my mind was that if anything went wrong those two thousand Burmans would see me pursued, caught, trampled on and reduced to a grinning corpse like that Indian up the hill. And if that happened it was quite probable that some of them would laugh. That would never do. There was only one alternative. I shoved the cartridges into the magazine and lay down on the road to get a better aim.

The crowd grew very still, and a deep, low, happy sigh, as of people who see the theatre curtain go up at last, breathed from innumerable throats. They were going to have their bit of fun after all. The rifle was a beautiful German thing with cross-hair sights. I did not then know that in shooting an elephant one would shoot to cut an imaginary bar running from ear-hole to ear-hole. I ought, therefore, as the elephant was sideways on, to have aimed straight at his ear-hole; actually I aimed several inches in front of this, thinking the brain would be further forward.

When I pulled the trigger I did not hear the bang or feel the kick—one never does when a shot goes home—but I heard the devilish roar of glee that went up from the crowd. In that instant, in too short a time, one would have thought, even for the bullet to get there, a mysterious terrible change had come over the elephant. He neither stirred nor fell, but every line of his body had altered. He looked suddenly stricken, shrunken, immensely old, as though the frightful impact of the bullet had paralysed him without knocking him down. At last, after what seemed a long time—it might have been five seconds, I dare say—he sagged flabbily to his knees. His mouth slobbered. An enormous senility seemed to have settled upon him. One could have imagined him thousands of years old. I fired again into the same spot. At the second shot he did not collapse but climbed with desperate slowness to his feet and stood weakly upright, with legs sagging and head drooping. I fired a third time. That was the shot that did for him. You could see the agony of it jolt his whole body and knock the last remnant of strength from his legs. But in falling he seemed for a moment to rise, for as his hind legs collapsed beneath him he seemed to tower upward like a huge rock toppling, his trunk reaching skywards like a tree. He trumpeted, for the first and only time. And then down he came, his belly towards me, with a crash that seemed to shake the ground even where I lay.

I got up. The Burmans were already racing past me across the mud. It was obvious that the elephant would never rise again, but he was not dead. He was breathing very rhythmically with long rattling gasps, his great mound of a side painfully rising and falling. His mouth was wide open—I could see far down into caverns of pale pink throat. I waited a long time for him to die, but his breathing did not weaken. Finally I fired my two remaining shots into the spot where I thought his heart must be. The thick blood welled out of him like red velvet, but still he did not die. His body did not even jerk when the shots hit him, the tortured breathing continued without a pause. He was dying, very slowly and in great agony, but in some world remote from me where not even a bullet could damage him further. I felt that I had got to put an end to that dreadful noise. It seemed dreadful to see the great beast lying there, powerless to move and yet powerless to die, and not even to be able to finish him. I sent back for my small rifle and poured shot after shot into his heart and down his throat. They seemed to make no impression. The tortured gasps continued as steadily as the ticking of a clock.

In the end I could not stand it any longer and went away. I heard later that it took him half an hour to die. Burmans were bringing dahs and baskets even before I left, and I was told they had stripped his body almost to the bones by the afternoon.

Afterwards, of course, there were endless discussions about the shooting of the elephant. The owner was furious, but he was only an Indian and could do nothing. Besides, legally I had done the right thing, for a mad elephant has to be killed, like a mad dog, if its owner fails to control it. Among the Europeans opinion was divided. The older men said I was right, the younger men said it was a damn shame to shoot an elephant for killing a coolie, because an elephant was worth more than any damn Coringhee coolie. And afterwards I was very glad that the coolie had been killed; it put me legally in the right and it gave me a sufficient pretext for shooting the elephant. I often wondered whether any of the others grasped that I had done it solely to avoid looking a fool.

Orwell's description of a police officer's decision, although it occurs in a remote time and place, suggests many important themes of contemporary significance and is an appropriate introduction for this chapter. The enforcement of law, it can be seen, is not an automatic process. The police officer is not part of a mechanistic system in which the law is always clear and can be easily and predictably applied. Rather, the police officer, like the law itself as described in Chapter One, is influenced by a variety of social, economic, and political factors. Although the blue uniform of police officers may often mask their individuality and humanity (or inhumanity), a close examination will reveal the police officer to be at the center of a maelstrom of interacting forces.

Orwell's essay illustrates the paradox of police power. To the Burmese citizen, it is obvious that the police officer, carrying an elephant gun and representing the might of the colonial power, has much power. Yet, Orwell the policeman feels almost powerless, pushed by the crowd in undesired directions. This perceptual difference of police power continues to exist as a source of police-citizen misunderstanding and antagonism.

In the following section, Charles Reich, a former law professor at the Yale Law School, graphically describes his feelings about his own confrontations with the police. He also clarifies some elements of the police role in society and gives one view on how to find an acceptable balance between the need for social order and predictable rules, and the competing need for flexibility and individual freedom. Subsequent articles and cases in this chapter explore other perspectives on this issue, on what the role of the Supreme Court is in controlling police power, and on what alternatives there are to the present structure and composition of police forces.

1 A Citizen's Perspective

If law is not made more than a policeman's night-stick, American society will be destroyed.

Arthur J. Goldberg

Police Questioning of Law Abiding Citizens   *Charles A. Reich*

For a member of one of the most staid occupations, I have had a disturbing number of encounters with the police. I can count nine or ten times that I have been stopped and questioned in the past few years—almost enough to qualify me as an adjunct member of the Mafia. Most recently, when the officer told me he had the right to stop anyone any place any time—and for no reason—I decided I had better write an article. Let me describe some of my adventures.

My problem is that I like to walk. In Chevy Chase, Maryland, a tree-lined suburb that smells of honeysuckle on spring nights, a police car swooped down on me about eleven at night. The officer wanted me to identify myself: where did I live, where was I going. He was not looking for anyone in particular; just on patrol. In Santa Barbara, California, where I had gone to give a paper on conservation, I was stopped on Main Street, about ten blocks from where I was staying. I was looking for a restaurant, a search which I was allowed to continue after giving a satisfactory explanation of my presence. In Belmont, Massachusetts, I was halted two blocks from my brother's house. I admit that it was *very* early morning. But my small niece had been up. In New Haven, about eleven at night, I was stopped a half mile from my own residence. Since this was home territory, and since the officers had summoned me

off the sidewalk without even getting out of their patrol car, I protested. This was the only time that the police implied they were actually looking for someone—a prowler, they said. Two more patrol cars and a sergeant arrived as I continued to stand my ground on the sidewalk. Aften ten minutes' discussion we all dispersed. In Long Lake, New York, an Adirondack vacation town, a state policeman stopped me on the main street about ten at night. I was walking on the sidewalk. He demanded I tell my age, occupation, and reason for being out on the street, and that I produce some identification. When I told him I had none, he was ready to arrest me—for walking on the wrong side of the street, or for vagrancy, he said. I pointed out that my family has owned a house at Long Lake for sixty years—and that there was no sidewalk on the other side of the street.

I should add that I have been stopped many times without cause while driving a car. It has happened in New York State, in Massachusetts, and as far away as Oregon; always in broad daylight; each time I asked why I had been flagged down with siren and flashing light; each time at first no answer was given; only when I was dismissed did the officer say "just checking." In each case the officer wanted not only to see my license, but also to know where I was going, where I was coming from, and my business. In all of my experiences, I have never been arrested, never told that I was committing an offense, and never told that I answered a particular description.

Reprinted by permission of The Yale Law Journal Company and Fred B. Rothman & Company from *The Yale Law Journal*, Vol. 75, pp. 1161–1172.

These circumstances define the problem that I wish to discuss. In this article, I am not concerned with police investigations after a crime has been reported, or with circumstances which suggest that the individual who has been stopped may be doing something illegal. My problem is this: no crime has been reported, no suspect has been described, there is no visible sign of an offense, there is nothing whatever to direct police attention to this particular individual. I am concerned with what is called *preventive* police work.

Although the experiences I have had are in themselves trivial, the increasing preventive activities of the police present an issue of first importance. What happens when the person stopped is a Negro, or poor, or frightened? What intrusions upon privacy, what affronts to dignity, occur? How much discretion do the police have to invent an offense for anyone who objects to being questioned? May the police establish a regular routine of requiring pedestrians to carry identification and explain their presence, or of requiring motorists to stop and tell where they are going? I do not have answers, but I have some questions. Let us focus on the moment of contact between the citizen and the police.

The first issue that troubles me is whether the police have any power at all to stop a law abiding person on a public street. Of course any individual has a right to approach any other individual—to ask him the time, to ask him how to find the Yale Divinity School, or to ask his opinion about foreign policy. But it is not quite the same when the police stop someone. There is authority in the approach of the police, and command in their tone. I can ignore the ordinary person, but can I ignore the police? Police officers tell me that they have a *right* to stop anyone in a public place, without having a reason. I think I have a *right* not to be stopped. So far as I know, reported court decisions do not supply us with an answer.

The next issue is what questions the police may ask. Name? Address? Occupation? Age? Marital status? Explanation of presence and destination? Documentary proof of identity? Many people might have no objection to giving out any or all of these facts about themselves. But I have a strong sense that however innocuous the facts may be, some things are nobody's business. I do not particularly like to be probed, and I like it much less when the probing is official. I certainly do not think that every police officer has a roving commission to satisfy his curiosity about anyone he sees on the street.

Closely related to questioning is the issue of the individual's replies. May he refuse to answer? May he demand to know the identity of the officer? May he demand to know why he is being stopped? May he lie to the officer about his age, or why he is out on the street? May he turn and go on his way? I submit that very few people know what their rights are under such circumstances. I do not even know how to find out.

The next issue is what *actions* the officer may take if the individual attempts to claim some rights. May the officer detain him? Frisk him? Search him? Take him to the police station? Hold him there for questioning? Here the law does supply an answer in general terms, for we know that arrests and searches can be made only upon probable cause. But concrete answers really depend upon what we conclude about the right to stop and to ask questions.

The last issue is what remedies are available to the citizen to test out the law in the circumstances I have described. There is always the right to defend against any criminal charge that may result. There is always a tort action for false arrest. Perhaps in some extreme circumstances there might be grounds for an action under one of the civil rights statutes, or for an injunction against a continuing police practice. But these remedies are often costly, time-consuming, and ultimately unsuccessful. No one effectively "polices the police."

The questions that I have raised are difficult, but they should be faced. Let me suggest some of the fundamental issues that are at stake in these small encounters.

1. Tone On one occasion when a patrol car flagged me down for a "routine check" on Route 2 near Boston, the officer, after ascertaining my name by looking at my driver's license, said

"What were you doing in Boston, Charlie?" And he continued quite deliberately to address me in that fashion. The incident happened a couple of years ago, so that I do not think he mistook me for a teenager. On several of the other occasions I have mentioned, I was either called by my first name or addressed in a way that was intentionally familiar. Nor am I unique in having such experiences. My brother, a psychiatrist, his wife, and a lady friend, also a psychiatrist, were driving through Keene, New Hampshire early on a Sunday evening after a weekend in Vermont. A policeman stopped them—for no reason. He made all of them get out of the car and stand in the rain. He called my brother by his first name. After looking at identification papers belonging to their friend, he said, in a tone that carried insult, "What kind of a doctor are you, Ellie?"

I have read that when Negroes complain of "police brutality" in areas like the Watts section of Los Angeles, they are as much concerned with verbal tone as with physical violence. And this is understandable; incidents like those described cause a sense of injury to the person in a direct, visceral sense. Members of a minority group are likely to be especially sensitive to such address. There is something deeply offensive in familiarity which is deliberately used by a person in authority for the purpose of causing humiliation.

The crucial importance of tone may be demonstrated by a simple test: Imagine that in any of the ten incidents I have related the officer said "Mr." or "Sir" or "excuse me" as I would do when addressing a stranger. The average person's response would be quite different; perhaps I would not even be writing this article. I am not so unrealistic as to suppose that every encounter with the police can leave the ego unbruised, nor do I suggest that the police should practice obsequious manners. But we are dealing with the chief point of personal contact between the individual citizen and the law, and what is at stake is the respect and dignity due to each individual from his government. It is no small matter.

2. Discrimination Although I have based much of what I have said so far on personal experience,

it is not for myself that I write. For what is but a rare occurrence in my life may be a much more significant part of the lives of minority groups and of the poor. I suspect that the police are far more likely to stop a Negro than a white man; far more likely to question a shabbily dressed man than one in an expensive suit. I imagine that the tone of the questioning is different. I can get away with asking a policeman what right he has to stop me; could a Negro safely do this? Of course the crime statistics show that the crime rate is higher among Negroes and among the poor, but that is just what worries me—that statistics and appearances will be held against individuals, and that the police in their contacts with the populace will treat some group differently from others. It is a form of discrimination which is particularly baleful because it is so hard to prove and so hard to correct. And it is a form of discrimination which must deeply affect the attitudes of minority groups toward the police and government. It is the raw material of alienation and rebellion.

There is one minority group that deserves special mention in connection with police questioning—youth; in particular, teenagers. This is a group easily identified and easily harassed. It is a group with a special need for privacy in public, since they have insufficient privacy at home. It is a group acutely conscious of its dignity and resentful of authority. The boy humiliated by a police officer in front of others must surely feel his whole self threatened.

I recall one story told by a college freshman in California: police officers stopped a whole group of college boys and girls on their way by car to a picnic. The officers questioned everyone with an infuriating slowness, insisting that the boys call them "sir" and finally making everyone sit and wait for a long time. No charges of any kind were made, and finally the group was granted permission to go on its way.

Youth present a problem in every community, and many adults are ready to wish their responsibilities on the police. If the police are not scrupulous in their contacts with youth, the effect may be to aggravate just the cynicism, alienation and resentment which are already the sources of trouble. Here the use of authority to stop and question is likely to inflict direct harm to society in terms of a lasting disrespect for law.

3. Discretionary Laws Discrimination and tone in questioning are important problems only because the questioner has authority. It seems to be customary in the retail automobile business to call everyone by his first name; if a buyer finds it annoying, he can lower his offer for the car. If the questioner is a government man but not a policeman, we are still in the realm of annoyance rather than a great issue; one can always talk back, or lodge a complaint. It is the police officer's power to *arrest* that makes his mode of address a matter of concern. That power raises the important question of discretionary laws.

The police officer who stopped me in Long Lake, New York told me that he could arrest me on any of three or four charges if he chose to. He mentioned vagrancy and walking on the wrong side of the road; he might also have mentioned disorderly conduct, refusal to obey an order, loitering and perhaps the catchall notion of "suspicion" used in some jurisdictions. Laws on the subject of vagrancy and disorderly conduct are so broad and so vague that a policeman has almost unlimited discretion; walking down the street might indeed come within the literal definition of vagrancy. It is small comfort that the person arrested for vagrancy might eventually be found innocent by a court. The source of an officer's power is not so much the possibility that he can subject a person to arrest, delay, a night in jail, frantic calls to relatives and lawyers, the expense and trouble of a trial, and the undeniable uncertainty about whether a local magistrate's court might, in fact, convict. No one who refuses to "cooperate" with the police can be certain that the policeman will not arrest him. The motorist is still more vulnerable; he can always be charged with having faulty equipment or an obstructed window, or with careless driving, and his license can be revoked in some states even if he is not convicted of any charge. For either the pedestrian or the motorist, arrest, no matter how unjustified, can have lasting consequences. Many application,

employment, and security forms ask whether the "subject" has ever been *arrested*. And for most people, custody and jail can be a severe and disturbing shock.

My present concern is not with these discretionary laws as such. They present a separate issue which should be of major concern to lawyers. My point here is that this virtually unlimited sanction lurks behind the policeman's questions and the citizen's answers; it makes me think twice before I tell a policeman that my reason for going for a walk is none of his business.

4. Institutionalizing the Questioning Process So long as police questioning remains genuinely casual and occasional, the problems it presents are comparatively limited. But when such a practice becomes accepted in theory, it tends to be made part of regular routine. We now have a number of police practices which are essentially institutionalizations of, or extrapolations from, the questioning process.

Most of these practices have grown up around the automobile. In Connecticut, the state police set up roadblocks and stop whole lines of cars in order to check drivers' licenses and registrations. Connecticut also uses roadblocks on holidays to check all drivers for signs of drinking. And near the New York border, Connecticut police have regularly placed roadblocks to stop teenage drivers to see if they have been drinking in New York State, where the minimum age is lower. Some states also use roadblocks to check for equipment such as faulty brakes and worn tires. Several years ago, I discovered that at toll booths on the Connecticut Turnpike and the New York State Thruway cameras were used to take photographs of vehicles passing through. The Acting Counsel of the New York State Thruway Authority wrote me that such photographic records were used to determine "if vehicles are being properly classified by our toll collectors." "With respect to the question of authority for making such records, if thereby you mean statutory authority, we need none...."

5. Unchecked Authority Police questioning carries with it the inherent danger of any unchecked, unreviewable authority. What safeguards exist to prevent authority from being used as the instrument of malice, revenge, or even crime? Is it safe to incur a policeman's anger? In one case that reached the federal courts, a motorist in Colorado was stopped at a police roadblock for a "routine check of his car and driver's license." He exchanged "rather harsh words" with one patrolman. On a later date, this patrolman spotted the motorist, followed him for six miles, and then stopped him, accusing him of failing to dim his lights. The man had misplaced his driver's license and had tried earlier that day to get a duplicate, but the office was closed. The patrolman said he was going to arrest the motorist. After further words, the patrolman wrenched the motorist's arm, hit the unresisting man on the head, shoulders, hands and wrists with a blackjack, handcuffed him, and took him to jail. His clothing and other belongings were taken from him, and he was offered no medical attention for his injuries until late that evening. After spending the night in jail, the motorist found he now was charged with drunken driving, and bail was set at $1,000. He was sent back to jail and told he must stay there unless he pleaded guilty. He said he would lose his job if he did not get out of jail by Monday, but the justice insisted that he plead guilty. Finally he did, and the justice allowed the patrolman to tell his version of the incident but refused to hear the motorist's version. The man was fined $355, given a 90-day suspended jail sentence, and lost his driver's license for one year. Prior to the arraignment, the justice of the peace and the patrolman conferred, and the justice was heard to say if the motorist pleaded innocent "he would make it rough enough on him for him to change his plea." The man was 40 years old, married with five children, had been arrested only once before in his life, had worked as a miner in Leadville for the same company for 14 years, had contracted silicosis during that time, and had he lost his job he would have been unable to secure employment with another company. He paid a lawyer $661 in an effort to appeal his case, lost one day's earnings, and had to pay a fee to get his car back. The federal court eventually held that he was entitled to damages under the Civil Rights statutes for arbitrary misuse of official power. *Stringer* v. *Dilger,* 313 F.2d 536 (10th Cir. 1963).

I cite this case as an officially reported instance of what *can* happen. Police are human, and there is a very real possibility that a person who stands on his rights one day may find the same officer "out to get him" another day. Moreover, we have all too much evidence that talking back to a police officer can produce violence and perhaps serious injury to the individual, particularly if he is a Negro or an outcast. And as was previously noted, an ensuing arrest can set off a chain reaction of disasters, very rarely compensated by a successful damage suit....

6. *Constitutional Rights and Privacy* In the encounter between citizen and police officer, certain major constitutional principles are at stake. Among these are rights deriving from the Fourth Amendment's protection against unreasonable searches and seizures, and the Fifth Amendment's guarantee of due process of law. I shall not attempt a definition of these rights here, but will point out how in a general sense these values are threatened.

There is a very real danger of erosion of rights through failure to challenge possible invasions. If the average person is intimidated by an encounter with the police, if remedies for abuses are relatively unusable, it is likely that the constitutionality of police practices will go untested. Thus there are few cases on the validity of police roadblocks, although the practice is common. There are even fewer cases on the questioning of pedestrians who are not suspected of crime. With the constitutionality of these practices unsettled and a matter of debate and uncertainty among lawyers, the community, worried about crime, may readily accept whatever the police say is necessary. After all, what is "reasonable" in a constitutional sense rests to some degree on what is thought "necessary." Thus constitutional protections are likely to be abandoned by default. The First Amendment remains healthy because possible invasions of it can usually be challenged in a civilized, scholarly way in a dignified appellate court. Constitutional rights that must be defended, if at all, on a lonely street, on a highway at night, in a police station or before a justice of the peace are always in trouble.

In addition to the values specifically protected by the constitution, there is the more general right of privacy, recently recognized by the Supreme Court, but yet only gradually emerging as an accepted legal principle. In our society privacy and anonymity are increasingly hard pressed. Many police officers seem to think that everyone should carry identification papers to be produced on demand, a requirement which is common in Europe. Such requirements are at war with the notion that one should be able to go out, for an hour or for a month, and merge into the anonymity of a new street or a new city.

How shall we begin to develop guidelines for encounters between the police and the law abiding citizen? The primary sources of standards are the Constitution and the courts. I expect to see the constitutional right of privacy, recently enunciated by the Supreme Court in the Connecticut Birth Control case, expand to form a protective shield for the individual against an increasingly intrusive world. I also expect that the constitutional right to be free of arbitrary searches, seizures and arrests will grow, and that the Supreme Court will gradually limit any official right to question a person except in the presence of counsel. But although I strongly favor a judicial philosophy which constantly strives to keep the Constitution meaningful in terms of contemporary problems and needs, I do not think that the courts should be the first line of approach in regulating police work. Policing is not imposed from above; it is a service to the community, and the community can take the initiative in seeing that police service is what we want it to be. Legislatively or administratively, it is possible for a community to establish guidelines for police and citizens as well.

The broad outline of a set of rules for the police can be suggested briefly.

(1) The police should not be allowed to stop anyone unless something particular about him, as distinguished from the mass of people, gives cause to believe that he has committed a crime.

(2) When a person is stopped, the officer should identify himself, and explain, with particularity, his reasons for stopping the person.

(3) The person may be questioned, but the person cannot be required to answer. He may be asked, but not required, to produce identification.

(4) The officer must conduct himself in a manner that would be proper in ordinary business relationships between equals.

(5) The officer may search a person only if he reasonably believes that he (the officer) is in danger, or if he has probable cause in the constitutional sense.

(6) If the person stopped desires to continue on his way, the officer may not detain him unless he has probable cause to arrest him for a crime.

These guidelines are a beginning: there is much room for working out details, but almost any rules will have the virtue of some certainty in an area where unlimited uncertainty now exists. Perhaps such instructions might be effectively enforced by a civilian police review board which could provide the sort of sanctions and remedies that the courts are unable to provide.

Perhaps this article sounds as if I have something against police officers—as if I do not appreciate the difficulties and dangers they face, the impossible demands upon them, and how well most of them perform their duty. But this is not my meaning. My meaning is that everyone, including the police, must live under rules. All organizations, and all officials, get out of hand if they do not have rules to guide them, if they do not do their work within limits.

I should add that while I believe that prevention is a far more desirable way of controlling crime than apprehension and punishment, I do not think that prevention is primarily a job for the police. Highway safety is more a function of better engineering of cars and roads, and better training of those who drive. Neighborhood safety is to a large extent a function of social conditions. Just as I do not believe that any amount of harsh punishment will significantly diminish crime, so I do not believe that any amount of surveillance will succeed.

We live in a society that is increasingly concerned with safety, but we give little thought to the price of safety. Suppose we had electric eyes and computers which could catch *every* traffic violation, *every* miscalculation of income tax, *every* instance of shoplifting. Would this really be the good society? Let me quote a letter to the New York Times on the subject of lifeguarding at public swimming places. The letter-writer protests that bathers, even good swimmers, are shepherded into small areas. "By such tactics the guards convert the great ocean into a wading pool and treat all bathers like children." The writer continues that at Cape May, he found that in a perfectly calm ocean bathers were rarely allowed beyond their depth, and were not even allowed to swim parallel to the shore beyond the lifeguard's station; the lifeguards mostly devoted themselves "to the castigation of bathers recalcitrant in obeying the whistle's orders." The letter ends, "I think, however, that in a free society I should be allowed to face my own dangers and challenges as long as I do not directly endanger others."

Overemphasis on safety also masks a great deal of hypocrisy and avoidance of responsibility. I think particularly of the attempts to put a stop to teenage drinking—an effort to make teenagers conform to standards adults do not themselves observe and an effort to secure a surface appearance of the rightness of things to cover up the profound wrongness within. Some of the most extreme examples of police surveillance are likely to be found in just those neat suburban communities which push all turmoil down into some invisible place, where it is left to fester unseen.

But I have a larger point to make. I fully recognize that safety is important and that safety requires measures. But other qualities also require measures: I mean independence, boldness, creativity, high spirits. In a society that presses toward sameness and safeness these all too perishable qualities must be given some help—they must be fostered and nourished. Otherwise their seed will fall upon asphalt and concrete, and die. The good society must have its hiding places—its protected crannies for the soul. Under the pitiless eye of safety the soul will wither. If I choose to get in my car and drive somewhere, it seems to me that where I am coming from, and where I am going, are nobody's business; I know of no law that requires me to have either a purpose or a destination. If I choose to take an evening walk to see if Andromeda has come up on schedule, I think I am entitled to look for the distant light of Almach and Mirach without finding myself staring into the blinding beam of a police flashlight.

Notes and Questions

1. What functions of the police is Reich describing? Are they legitimate functions?

2. What values does Reich cherish most highly?

3. What is Reich willing to sacrifice in order to achieve a more secure society? What isn't he willing to sacrifice? What liberties are you willing to give up?

4. Would you mind being one of many cars being stopped at a roadblock? Would you feel any different if you were the only one who is stopped and questioned? If there is a difference, how would you account for it?

5. What would you take into account if you had to decide whether or not the police should be allowed to demand identification from persons?

6. Did Reich ever benefit from police discretion?

7. Is Reich arguing that police should have no discretion? Is such a system possible?

8. What does Reich mean by "preventive" police work? The meaning of this phrase may be confusing because in many instances the goal of "preventive" police work is not simply to prevent crimes before they occur. Rather, it is often designed to catch law violators whose criminal actions have not been reported to the police. For example, the police may know that statistically a certain percentage of cars on an interstate highway will be stolen vehicles even though no particular stolen car has been described to them to look for. Preventive police work at present may consist of stopping every car and asking for proof of purchase.

Such practices conflict with the general rule that individuals should be free to go where they desire and do what they want unless there is something special about them that would lead a police officer to believe that they have committed a crime. In legal terms, the police must normally have "probable cause" to believe that an individual has done some illegal act before the citizen may be stopped. The policy behind the law, therefore, is to protect a person's freedom, liberty, and privacy unless there is a good reason to believe that that person has infringed upon someone else's rights. Understanding this, do you believe that Reich is being unreasonable? Are we demanding too high a price from nightwalkers? To answer this question, it is necessary to determine what the price is to the individual who is stopped. Is it simply inconvenience? Or is it an invasion of privacy, the "right to be let alone," a fundamental freedom? Is losing one's privacy too high a price to pay for additional security? Should we be more reluctant to invade people's privacy than to cause them inconvenience?

These are not easy questions and the answers are made even more difficult by the fact that the same act may invade someone's privacy as well as cause inconvenience. For example, having one's briefcase searched at the library exit or at the airplane boarding ramp are both inconveniences and invasions of privacy. Although some people have threatened to contest the constitutionality of airport searches, most people do not find the practice repugnant. Do you think this is because the fear of hijackings is high, or because we have simply become accustomed to the practice? Could we become more accepting of street searches if it became "safer" to walk the streets? This question is particularly relevant today because technology is available which would reduce some crime, make the streets safer, cause us little inconvenience, and the only price to be paid would be loss of privacy and anonymity. Consider the following item which appeared in the *New York Times,* March 21, 1973:

TV to Spot Crime on Boardwalk

A closed-circuit television surveillance system will be installed on a two-mile stretch of the Atlantic City Boardwalk by June to help cut crime.

Mrs. Claire Ordile, the city's Deputy Commissioner of Public Safety, said yesterday that cable for the $50,000-to-$60,000 municipally operated system already had been laid. The system, she said, will include $6,000 pan-and-tilt cameras with ranges up to 400 feet. The cameras will be mounted on poles.

A public-address system, especially valuable for communicating information to visitors and other boardwalk strollers, is being in-

stalled at the same time, Mrs. Ordile said. The hookup will extend from the Steel Pier to a block south of Convention Hall.*

Is this any different from the replacement of bank guards with television cameras? Does it make a difference whether the camera is on the street or inside a building? Whether it is the state or a private corporation that installs the camera? Why should privacy be protected?

9. In an excellent book on the threat to privacy from computers and technology, Prof. Arthur R. Miller raised another crime prevention possibility which will soon be feasible:

The ultimate step in mechanical snooping may be the implantation of sensing devices in the human body. These devices might be able to transmit data relating to physiological and chemical changes resulting from various bodily processes to a computer that is programmed to record the data. It might then transmit a response or a command to the sensor, or sound an alarm when specified chemical or biological events occur that indicate the individual is becoming too "aggressive" or is about to do something criminal. To be sure, monitoring systems of this type are adaptable to many beneficial and humanitarian purposes. But telemetry also could be involuntarily imposed on a so-called "antisocial" or "aberrational" individual in order to reveal whether the concentration of personality-altering chemicals in his bloodstream was at a "stable" level, or to administer electronically stimulated rewards and punishments by remote control when sensors reveal that the subject has engaged in certain kinds of behavior.†

What is it that is objectionable in such a procedure? Would any of the Amendments to the Constitution be violated by this practice?

10. Television cameras, radar guns, and helicopters are the most visible part of the law enforcement effort. In the long run, however, the technological development that will be most important is the computer. In reading the following, consider whether Professor Reich's concept of privacy can exist in a computer-dominated society.

* © 1973 by The New York Times Company. Reprinted by permission.
† Arthur R. Miller, *The Assault on Privacy* (Ann Arbor, Mich.: University of Michigan Press, 1971), pp. 60–61.

The computerization of police information is rapidly on its way to completion. In 1968, only 10 states had automated state-level criminal justice information systems. By 1972, computerization existed in 47 states with the main centralized intelligence files being held by the F.B.I.'s National Crime Information Center (NCIC) in Washington, D.C. The Federal Government's Law Enforcement Assistance Administration has made this development possible by providing nearly $90 million to over 100 computerized information systems.

The computer is used for rationalizing various aspects of the criminal justice system, but its primary function will be to develop a fast and efficient intelligence-retrieval network on people (criminal histories) and events (crimes, identification of stolen autos, weapons, etc.).

The computerized intelligence systems will allow the police and other agencies quicker access to more information. Previous examples of political fugitives eluding detection and identification because of delays in receiving F.B.I. reports will occur less frequently with the new systems. Also, police intelligence agents will use the network in their attempt to penetrate and disrupt progressive political work.... A significant result of the computer technology will be a lessening of inter-agency and regional rivalry within law enforcement, which previously has caused much inefficiency. With the computerized systems, requests for information will be directed to machines instead of personnel.

The use of computerized information systems has generated intense debate concerning invasion of privacy. In February, 1974, the Justice Department and Senator Sam Ervin, Jr. (D-N.C.), both presented privacy bills to Congress which would regulate the kinds of information that police can collect and disseminate. While these bills will control some of the more blatant police tactics, they will not prevent the police from routinely using the computerized systems to enforce the status quo.

The largest computerized intelligence system is the F.B.I.'s National Crime Information Center (NCIC). NCIC was established in 1967 as a national index of wanted persons, stolen autos, and stolen property, consisting of less than 500,000 entries that could be retrieved by only 15 computer terminals throughout the country. By 1974 there were links to ninety-four law enforcement agencies plus all 55 F.B.I. field offices. The system contains 400,000 computerized criminal histories, 4.9 total entries, and handles about 130,000 transactions daily. In many cases, NCIC is linked to state and regional terminals which are entire systems in themselves. For example, in Michigan, NCIC links with the Law Enforcement Intelligence Network (LEIN) which holds 150,000 entries and links to 225 terminals, including the Michigan Secretary of State's files.

Federal agencies which contribute and receive information with NCIC include the Secret Service, the Internal Revenue Service, Alcohol and Tax Division of the Treasury Department, Customs Service, Immigration and Naturalization Service, U.S. Courts, Attorneys and Marshals, and the Bureau of Prisons.

The NCIC system is an outgrowth of an earlier LEAA computer information project— SEARCH (System for Electronic Analysis and Retrieval of Criminal Histories), initiated in 1969 out of Sacramento, California. Starting with the same concept of state-held files and a central index, SEARCH brought together information from Arizona, Connecticut, Florida, Michigan, Minnesota, New York, Texas, the District of Columbia, and the F.B.I. onto its computer network, and began to expand the index to contain the histories of individuals on the system. From July 1969 to December 1970, a test run of the system was carried out in which Michigan acted as the central index with 2.5 million records. The states participating plus five "observer" states accounted for 75 percent of the crime in the United States. Prior to this test, SEARCH was considering some of the following points: standardizing data input, updating records in the central file, accessibility by persons whose records were in the system, accessibility by commercial and other non-law enforcement agencies, and further computer development to enable the transmission of fingerprints. Evaluation of the 18-month test raised additional questions: (1) location of the central file, (2) type of controls and responsibilities to be imposed on the system, and (3) procedures for maintaining short retrieval time when the file becomes extremely large.

However, by the end of 1970 the primary issue became who would control the system. In November, the security and privacy committee of SEARCH recommended that individuals should be allowed to review their files. The F.B.I. disagreed and in December, only ten days after money had been budgeted by LEAA to continue SEARCH, Attorney General John Mitchell transferred authority to develop the system to the F.B.I., with the NCIC acting as the centralized file.

Since the take-over, the F.B.I. and LEAA money have encouraged more states and their local law enforcement agencies to join the system by feeding their files into the NCIC computer. At present, Massachusetts is the only state to openly refuse to enter the system, claiming that the NCIC's massive invasion of privacy results in misleading and incorrect information on individuals being indiscriminately circulated by the federal government. NCIC's potential role in large-scale repressive control is clear when a Presidential Commission on Law estimates that at the present rate 50 million Americans will have criminal arrest records by the end of the decade.*

* Center for Research on Criminal Justice, *The Iron Fist and the Velvet Glove* (Oakland, Calif., 1975), pp. 40–41. Reprinted by permission.

2   Police Perspectives

A policeman's lot is not a happy one.
Gilbert and Sullivan,
The Pirates of Penzance

"Most cops I know will walk into the mouth of a cannon. But they're terrified of words. Don't forget, most cops don't have any education, they're inarticulate. In a way, I think, the police feel much more challenged by the words of Columbia students than by any threat there may have actually been."

"You must consider that many cops have just bought houses in Farmington, L.I., that many are in the process of escaping from boyhoods in white slums and that this tends to make them super middle class. They really become outraged and confused when they hear some kid question the guts of those fighting in Vietnam or hear some Barnard girl shouting dirty words. Their idea of a woman is a nice, quiet young Catholic girl from Queens."

Two policemen talking about the New York policemen who beat up Columbia University students. Burnham, "Police Violence: A Changing Pattern," *New York Times,* July 7, 1968

Professor Reich confronts us with a frequently heard complaint about the police. Why, the citizen asks, should the police stop me if I am doing no wrong? The police officer, on the other hand, may be asking why a law-abiding citizen would object to answering a few simple questions? We might ask several additional questions, namely, why would a police officer want to stop Professor Reich or any other person with unusual habits? What values and fears do police officers have that lead them to have a different perspective from that of many citizens? This section explores the background, conflicts, and values prevalent among police, and the ways in which these factors relate to the job our society has assigned to them. Such an analysis will, it is hoped, enable us to determine whether the problems are caused by the structure of the system, by the kind of people employed in the system, or by some combination of the two.

From Professor to Patrolman:
A Fresh Perspective on the Police   *George L. Kirkham*

Persons such as myself—members of the academic community—have traditionally been quick to find fault with the police. From isolated incidents reported in the various news media we have fashioned for ourselves a stereotyped image of the police officer which conveniently conforms to our notions of what he is. We see the brutal cop, the racist cop, the grafting cop, the discourteous cop. What we do not see, however, is the image of thousands of dedicated men and women struggling against almost impossible odds to preserve our society and everything in it which we cherish.

For some years, first as a student and later as a professor of criminology, I found myself troubled by the fact that most of us who have written books and articles about the police have never served as policemen. I began to be increasingly bothered by the attitude of many of my students who were former policemen. Time and again they would respond to my frequently critical lectures on the police with the argument that I could not possibly understand what a police officer has to endure in modern society until I had been one myself. Under the weight of this frustration, and my personal conviction that knowledge has an applied as well as a theoretical dimension, I decided to take up this challenge. I would become a policeman myself as a means of establishing once and for all the accuracy of what we criminologists had been saying about the police for so long.

My announced intention to become a uniformed patrolman was at first met with fairly widespread disbelief on the part of family, friends, and colleagues alike. At 31, with a family and an estab-

Reprinted by permission of *Journal of Police Science and Administration*, Volume II, No. 2, June, 1974, pp. 127–137. © 1974 by Northwestern University School of Law. Reprinted by permission.

lished career as a criminologist, I was surely an unlikely candidate for the position of police recruit. The very idea, it was suggested to me, was outrageous and absurd. I was told that no police administrator in his right mind would allow a representative of the academic world to enter his organization. It had never been done and could not be done.

Fortunately, many of my students who either had been or were then policemen sounded a far more optimistic and enthusiastic note. Police administrators and officers alike, they said, would welcome the opportunity to expose members of the academic community to the problems of their occupation. If one of us was really willing to see and feel the policeman's world from behind a badge and blue uniform, instead of from the safe and comfortable vantage point of a classroom or university office, police officers themselves would do everything in their power to make the opportunity available. Despite these assurances from my policeman-students, I remained skeptical about my chances of being allowed to do such an unorthodox thing.

This skepticism was, however, soon to be overcome. One of my better criminology students at the time was a young police officer on educational leave from the Jacksonville, Florida, Sheriff's Office. Upon learning of my desire to become a police officer in order to better understand the problems of the police, he urged me to contact Sheriff Dale Carson and Undersheriff D. K. Brown of his department with my proposal. I had earlier heard other police officers describe the consolidated 800-man force of Jacksonville-Duval County as one of the most progressive departments in the country. I learned that Sheriff Carson and Undersheriff Brown, two former FBI agents, had won considerable respect in the law enforcement profession as enlightened and innovative administrators.

The size and composition of Jacksonville, as well as its nearness to my university and home, made it appear to be an ideal location for what I wished to do. Numbering just over one-half million residents, Jacksonville impressed me as being the kind of large and rapidly growing American city which inevitably experiences the major social problems of our time: crime and delinquency, racial unrest, poverty and mental illness. A seaport and industrial center, Jacksonville offered a diversity of urban, suburban, and even rural populations in its vast land area. I took particular note of the fact that it contained a fairly typical inner-city slum section and black ghetto, both of which were in the process of being transformed through a massive program of urban redevelopment. This latter feature was especially important to me insofar as I wanted to experience personally the stresses and strains of today's city policeman. It is, after all, he who has traditionally been the subject of such intense interest and criticism on the part of social scientists such as myself.

Much to my surprise, both Sheriff Carson and Undersheriff Brown were not only supportive of my proposal but enthusiastic as well. I made it clear to them at the onset that I did not wish to function as an observer or reserve officer. I wanted to become a sworn and full-time member of their department for a period of between four and six months. I further stated that I hoped to spend most of this period working as a uniformed patrolman in those inner-city beats most characterized by violence, poverty, social unrest and high crime rates. They agreed to this, with the understanding that I would first have to meet the same requirements as any other police candidate. It would be necessary, for example, to submit to a thorough character investigation, a physical examination, and to meet the same requirements as any other police candidate, including the training standards required of all Florida police officers. Since I was to be unpaid, I would be exempted, however, from departmental civil service requirements. Both Carson and Brown set about overcoming various administrative and insurance problems which had to be dealt with in advance

of my becoming a police officer. Suppose, for example, I should be injured or killed in the line of duty, or should injure or kill someone else; what of the department and city's liability? These and other issues were gradually resolved with considerable effort on their part. The only stipulation set forth by both administrators was one with which I strongly agreed: for the sake of morale and confidence in the department, every officer must know in advance exactly who I was and what I was doing. Other than being in the unusual position of a "patrolman-professor," I would be indistinguishable from other officers in every respect, from the standard-issue .38 Smith and Wesson revolver I would carry to the badge and uniform I would wear.

The biggest and final obstacle which I faced was the necessity that I comply fully with a 1967 Florida Police Standards law, which requires that every police officer and deputy sheriff in the state complete a minimum of 280 hours of law enforcement training prior to being sworn in and assigned to regular duty. Since I had a full-time university job nearly 200 miles from Jacksonville, this meant that I would be unable to attend the regular Sheriff's Academy. I would have to attend a certified academy in my own area, something which I arranged to do with Sheriff Carson's sponsorship.

For four months, for four hours each evening, and five nights a week, I attended the Tallahassee Area Police Academy, along with 35 younger classmates. As a balding intellectual, I stood out at first as an oddity in the class of young men destined to become local law enforcement officers. With the passage of time, however, they came to accept me, and I them. We joked, drank coffee, and struggled through various examinations and lessons together. At first known only as "the professor," the men later nick-named me "Doc," over my good natured protests.

As the days stretched into weeks and the weeks into months, I took lengthy notes on interviewing witnesses at crime scenes, investigated imaginary traffic accidents, and lifted fingerprints. Some nights I went home after hours of physical defense training, designed for my uniformly younger and stronger peers, with tired muscles, bruises, and the feeling that I should have my head examined for undertaking such a rugged project.

As someone who had never fired a handgun, I quickly grew accustomed to the noise of 35 revolvers firing at the cardboard silhouettes which we transformed into real assailants at the sound of the range whistle. I learned how to make car stops properly, approach a front door or a darkened building, question suspects, and a thousand other things that every modern police officer must know. After what seemed an eternity, graduation from the academy finally came, and with it what was to become the most difficult but rewarding educational experience of my life: I became a policeman.

I will never forget standing in front of the Jacksonville police station on that first day. I felt incredibly awkward and conspicuous in the new blue uniform and creaking leather. Whatever confidence in my ability to "do the job" I had gained during the academy seemed to evaporate as I stood there watching other blue figures hurrying in the evening rain toward assembly. After some minutes, I summoned the courage to walk into the station and into my new career as a core city patrolman.

That first day seems long ago now. As I write this, I have completed over 100 tours of duty as a patrolman. Although still a rookie officer, so much happened in the short space of six months that I will never again be either the same man or the same scientist who stood in front of the station on that first day. While it is hard even to begin to describe in a brief article the many changes which have occurred within me during this time, I would like to share with fellow policemen and colleagues in the academic community a few of what I regard as the more important of my "street lessons."

I had always personally been of the opinion that police officers greatly exaggerate the amount of verbal disrespect and physical abuse to which they are subjected in the line of duty. During my first few hours as a street officer, I lived blissfully in a magic bubble which was soon to burst. As a college professor, I had grown accustomed to being treated with respect and deference by those I encountered. I somehow naively assumed that this same quality of respect would carry over into my new role as a policeman. I was, after all, a representative of the law, identifiable to all by the badge and uniform I wore as someone dedicated to the protection of society. Surely that fact would entitle me to a measure of respect and cooperation —or so I thought. I quickly found that my badge and uniform, rather than serving to shield me from such things as disrespect and violence, only acted as a magnet which drew me toward many individuals who hated what I represented.

I had discounted on my first evening the warning of a veteran sergeant who, after hearing that I was about to begin work as a patrolman, shook his head and cautioned, "You'd better watch yourself out there, Professor! It gets pretty rough sometimes!" I was soon to find out what he meant.

Several hours into my first evening on the streets, my partner and I were dispatched to a bar in the downtown area to handle a disturbance complaint. Inside, we encountered a large and boisterous drunk who was arguing with the bartender and loudly refusing to leave. As someone with considerable experience as a correctional counselor and mental health worker, I hastened to take charge of the situation. "Excuse me, sir," I smiled pleasantly at the drunk, "but I wonder if I could ask you to step outside and talk with me for just a minute?" The man stared at me through bloodshot eyes in disbelief for a second, raising one hand to scratch the stubble of several days growth of beard. Then suddenly, without warning, it happened. He swung at me, luckily missing my face and striking me on the right shoulder. I couldn't believe it. What on earth had I done to provoke such a reaction? Before I could recover from my startled condition, he swung again—this time tearing my whistle chain from a shoulder epaulet. After a brief struggle, we had the still shouting, cursing man locked in the back of our cruiser. I stood there, breathing heavily with my hair in my eyes as I surveyed the damage to my new uniform and looked in bewilderment at my partner, who only smiled and clapped me affectionately on the back.

Something was very wrong, I remember thinking to myself in the front seat as we headed for the jail. I had used the same kind of gentle, rapport-building approach with countless offenders in prison and probation settings. It had always worked so well there. What was so different about being a policeman? In the days and weeks which followed, I was to learn the answer to this question the hard way. As a university professor, I had always sought to convey to students the idea that it is a mistake to exercise authority, to make decisions for other people, or rely upon orders and commands to accomplish something. As a police officer myself, I was forced time and again to do just that. For the first time in my life, I encountered individuals who interpreted kindness as weakness, as an invitation to disrespect or violence. I encountered men, women, and children who, in fear, desperation, or excitement, looked to the person behind my blue uniform and shield for guidance, control and direction. As someone who had always condemned the exercise of authority, the acceptance of myself as an unavoidable symbol of authority came as a bitter lesson.

I found that there was a world of difference between encountering individuals, as I had, in mental health or correctional settings, and facing them as the patrolman must: when they are violent, hysterical, desperate. When I put the uniform of a police officer on, I lost the luxury of sitting in an air-conditioned office with my pipe and books, calmly discussing with a rapist or armed robber the past problems which had led him into trouble with the law. Such offenders had seemed so innocent, so harmless in the sterile setting of prison. The often terrible crimes which they had committed were long since past, reduced like their victims to so many printed words on a page.

Now, as a police officer, I began to encounter the offender for the first time as a very real menace to my personal safety and the security of our society. The felon was no longer a harmless figure sitting in blue denims across my prison desk, a "victim" of society, to be treated with compassion and leniency. He became an armed robber fleeing from the scene of a crime; a crazed maniac threatening his family with a gun; someone who

might become my killer crouched behind the wheel of a car on a dark street.

Like crime itself, fear quickly ceased to be an impersonal and abstract thing. It became something which I regularly experienced. It was a tightness in my stomach as I approached a warehouse where something had tripped a silent alarm. I could taste it as a dryness in my mouth as we raced with blue lights and siren toward the site of a "Signal Zero" (armed and dangerous) call. For the first time in my life, I came to know—as every policeman knows—the true meaning of fear. Through shift after shift it stalked me, making my palms cold and sweaty and pumping the adrenalin through my veins.

I recall particularly a dramatic lesson in the meaning of fear which took place shortly after I joined the force. My partner and I were on routine patrol one Saturday evening in a deteriorated area of cheap bars and pool halls when we observed a young black male double-parked in the middle of the street. I pulled alongside and asked him in a civil manner to either park or drive on, whereupon he began loudly cursing us and shouting that we couldn't make him go anywhere. An angry crowd began to gather as we got out of our patrol car and approached the man, who was by this time shouting that we were harassing him and calling to bystanders for assistance.

As a criminology professor, some months earlier I would have urged that the police officer who was now myself simply leave the car double-parked and move on rather than risk an incident. As a policeman, however, I had come to realize that an officer can never back down from his responsibility to enforce the law. Whatever the risk to himself, every police officer understands that his ability to back up the lawful authority which he represents is the only thing which stands between civilization and the jungle of lawlessness.

The man continued to curse us and adamantly refused to move his car. As we placed him under arrest and attempted to move him to our cruiser, an unidentified male and female rushed from the crowd, which was steadily enlarging, and sought to free him. In the ensuing struggle, a hysterical female unsnapped and tried to grab my service revolver, and the now-angry mob began to converge on us.

Suddenly, I was no longer an "ivory-tower" scholar watching typical police "overreaction" to a street incident: I was part of it, fighting to remain alive and uninjured. I remember the sickening sensation of cold terror which filled my insides as I struggled to reach our car radio. I simultaneously put out a distress call and pressed the hidden electric release button on our shotgun rack as my partner sought to maintain his grip on the prisoner and hold the crowd at bay with his revolver.

How harshly I would have judged the officer who now grabbed the shotgun only a few months before. I rounded the rear of our cruiser with the weapon and shouted at the mob to move back. The memory flashed through my mind that I had always argued that policemen should not be allowed to carry shotguns because of their "offensive" character and the potential damage to community relations as a result of their display. How readily as a criminology professor I would have condemned the officer—now myself, trembling with fear and menacing an unarmed assembly with a shotgun. The new circumstances in which I now found myself suddenly changed my perspective. The tables were turned on me. Now it was *my* life and safety that were in jeopardy; it was *my* pregnant wife who in a few seconds might be a widow, and *my* child who might never see his father again. I was no longer sitting comfortably in my study with a morning cup of coffee reading an impersonal newspaper account of some patrolman who had been seriously injured or killed trying to uphold the law.

For all the things that were to happen to me as a rookie patrolman, this particular incident represented a major turning point in my perspective as a professor of criminology. It marked the beginning of what was to become the most profoundly important of all my street lessons—a depressing and at times personally crushing awareness that the toughest adversary a street cop must confront each day is not the armed robber or enraged mob, not the addict, the burglar or the mugger. Rather it is, ironically, the very law which he must struggle against increasingly difficult odds to enforce. It is the smugness and complacency of courts and legislatures, which spin out a hopelessly entangling web of procedural restraints upon men who are charged with the awesome responsibility of protecting our society. This was a bitter discovery, one which the liberal scientist within me had long refused to accept.

I remember feeling a sense of imminent justice as I wrote "resisting arrest with violence" on the booking forms of the couple who had sought to free the prisoner in the previously described double-parking case incident. True, we had narrowly escaped injury in our attempts to enforce the law, but I derived some comfort from the expectation that persons like that would soon learn in court the meaning of attacking a police officer—or so I naively thought! Peering over my shoulder at the arrest reports, my partner shook his head. "Hell, Doc. They'll get off. Just wait and see!" The next evening I recognized the same couple standing on a street corner, laughing and jeering at us, confident in the experience-based belief that the felony charge of resisting arrest with violence would soon be bargained down to a bare misdemeanor. I will never forget the feeling of bitterness and despair which filled me a few days later when I learned that both of our assailants had been allowed to plead guilty to "breach of peace." "Breach of peace!" I raged in disbelief to my partner. Only a lucky grasp had prevented me from being shot with my own service revolver; now our assailants were being let off with a mild slap on the wrist, a charge which contained the implicit legal view that what had happened to us that night was no more serious in the eyes of the courts than spitting on the sidewalk or uttering a public obscenity.

As a policeman myself, I learned that there is something terribly wrong in the relationship between our police and those who make and administer the law. As a university professor, I had hailed the spate of restrictive Supreme Court decisions which have been levied on the police in recent years. *Mapp! Escobedo! Miranda!* All were victories for individual liberty, steps essential to prevent abuses of power in American police officers. It never crossed my mind that such decisions might represent personal triumphs for law violators, and that they might diminish the ability of the police to protect society.

Like the average judge, juror, or legislator, who seldom views the law as anything more than an abstract phenomenon, I was really unconcerned in my life as a university professor with the practical consequences of piling an even larger burden of restrictive legislation upon the American police. Until I put on the uniform myself and stepped into the role, I could not realize the profoundly negative consequences of such action upon both the policeman and the society he strives to protect.

As a policeman myself, I had to struggle on a daily basis through a maze of incredibly and incomprehensibly complex restrictions on how the game of enforcing the law is to be played. And a game I discovered it was indeed, with the odds stacked heavily against the police and society and decidedly in favor of the criminal. I well remember one evening drawing my "*Miranda* warning" card from my wallet and reading it slowly and carefully to a known narcotics pusher whom we had just arrested with a large quantity of heroin in his possession, fearful that a recitation of it from memory might cause me to omit some word or syllable which might later be transformed by a skilled attorney into a violation of the suspect's "rights." "Lay it on me, baby!" he said as he convulsed with laughter halfway through my reading of his rights. Still amused with the degrading spectacle of forcing me to read a statement which I knew by heart from previous arrests, he joined in a word for word recall of his "rights" as I methodically read them off to him. Experiences such as this, which I encountered time and again, led me to the inescapable conclusion that we often allow the law to be turned into a mockery of justice, a tool to be used against society by law violators who are its enemies.

Like every police officer today, I was often overcome with a sense of being forced to walk through a legal minefield in my attempts to protect the community, being distracted from my primary mission on calls by the haunting fear that I might be violating some obscure element of an offender's rights. One night my partner and I responded to a call of several suspects sniping with firearms from an apartment building. As two other units covered the rear and sides of the building, my partner and I approached the front door with guns drawn. One suspect appeared at the door, started to step out, then abruptly jumped back into the apartment. As I ran after him and put my hand on the doorknob, a virtual blast of legal considerations hit my mind; it was dark and I had not actually *seen* a gun in his hands. Should I enter? What if there were no visible weapons in the room or on the suspects? Dare we search the rest of the house? I submit that it is patently absurd—cruel, even monstrous—for a police officer, palms sweating at the prospect of being shot down in such a situation, to have to deal with such considerations. Yet, as we entered the house, I could imagine myself having to provide to superiors and a defense attorney a detailed recollection of our every move, with the virtual certainty that a single wrong move would quickly cast us in the role of law violators.

Given the drift of legislation and the decisions of the Supreme Court under Chief Justice Warren during the decade 1960–70, it is little wonder to me that police officers often despair of their mission, and shirk enforcement responsibilities. I recall a rather typical illustration of the pessimism which assails every policeman today. My partner and I pulled up abruptly one evening on a "junkie" who stood trembling for a fix at curbside. As he watched us approach, he quickly, and in our plain view, removed several objects from a bag he was holding and furtively dropped them behind him on the ground. We quickly discovered that the objects in question were pieces of a narcotics kit, and we placed the individual under arrest. On the way to jail my partner sighed heavily and suggested with an air of resignation, "Well, we didn't find any drugs. Hell, Doc, not much point in charging him with possession of narcotics paraphernalia. They [the courts] won't do anything. Let's just destroy the kit and book him on P.I. [public intoxication]."

Today's police officer is inexorably pushed toward viewing the entire judicial process as his enemy. He senses that it represents a great and impenetrable barrier which stands between him and his goal of protecting society. It is not that he values individual liberty any less than those who make and administer our system of laws, but as one who must live with the law in action, he simply cannot understand why the preservation of our democracy should require crippling the efficiency of law enforcement.

As someone who has always been greatly concerned with the rights of offenders, I have begun to consider for the first time the rights of police officers and the law-abiding public they serve. It is wrong that the safety and security of both should be menaced by the instrumentality of the law. As a policeman myself, I have many times felt that this is precisely so. As with other patrolmen, I have grown weary of trying to do my job in the face of frustrating—sometimes impossible—legal restrictions, while thugs and hoodlums consistently twist the law to their own advantage. Each time I put on my uniform and step into the streets, I have the distinct feeling that my personal safety is diminished and my task as a law enforcement officer is made more difficult by our society's great solicitude for the law violator's rights, and its ostensible indifference to mine. As an educated man, I find myself unable to answer the questions of fellow police officers as to why our society manifests so little concern for their physical safety.

The policeman's inner conviction that the law often menaces his very life was brought home to me recently on a very personal level. One night my patrol car was hailed by a passing motorist. As I approached the darkened driver's side of the man's car, he began to shout hysterically and sob: "I've just killed a man. I've got a gun!" My first concern *should* have been for my personal safety and that of anyone else in the area. Instead, like so many police officers who have been killed or injured because of hesitation, the first thing to rush into my mind was a jumble of legalistic considerations: "A confession? Rights . . . no, wait, it's a spontaneous confession. Okay, admissible!" If I had been shot to death because of the split-second delay caused by anxiety over following procedural technicalities, where would the moral responsibility for my death lie? Clearly, a measure

of it would reside with a society which consciously jeopardizes the safety of its police officers by requiring them to function within a maze of unwarranted legal considerations.

As a corrections worker, and as someone raised in a comfortable middle-class home, I had always been insulated from the kind of human misery and tragedy which become part of the policeman's everyday life. Now, however, the often terrible sights, sounds, and smells of my job began to haunt me hours after I had taken off the blue uniform and badge. Some nights I would lie in bed unable to sleep, trying desperately to forget the things I had seen during a particular tour of duty: the rat-infested shacks that served as homes to those less fortunate than I; a teen-age boy dying in my arms after being struck by a car; small children, clad in rags, with stomachs bloated from hunger, playing in urine-spattered halls; the victim of a robbery, senselessly beaten and murdered.

In my new role as a police officer, I found that the victims of crime ceased to be impersonal statistics. As a corrections worker and criminology professor, I had never given much thought to those who are victimized by criminals in our society. Now the sight of so many lives ruthlessly damaged and destroyed by the perpetrators of crime left me preoccupied with the question of society's responsibility to protect the men, women and children who are victimized daily.

Of all the tragic victims of crime I have seen during my first six months as a police officer, one case stands out above all. There was an elderly man who lived with his dog in my apartment building downtown. He was a retired bus driver and his wife was long since deceased. As time went by, I became friends with the old man and his dog. I could usually count on finding both of them standing at the corner as I was on my way to work. I would engage in casual conversation with the old man, and sometimes he and his dog would walk several blocks toward the station with me. They were both as predictable as a clock: each evening around 7 o'clock, the old man would walk to the same small restaurant several blocks away, where he would eat his evening meal while the dog waited dutifully outside. One evening my partner and I received a call to a street shooting near my apartment building. My heart sank as we pulled up. I saw the old man's mutt in a crowd of people gathered on the sidewalk. The old man was lying on his back in a large pool of blood, half trying to brace himself on an elbow. He clutched a bullet wound in his chest and gasped to me that three young men had stopped him and demanded his money. After taking his wallet and seeing how little he had, they shot him and left him on the street. As a police officer, I became enraged, as I was to become enraged time and again, at the cruelty and senselessness of acts such as this—at the arrogance of the brazen thugs who prey with impunity on innocent citizens, confident in the belief that the likelihood of their being brought to justice and punished has steadily diminished in recent years.

The same kinds of daily stresses which affected my fellow officers soon began to take their toll on me. I became sick and tired of being reviled and attacked by criminals who could usually find a most sympathetic audience in judges and jurors eager to understand their side of things and provide them with "another chance." I grew tired of living under the ax of news media and community pressure groups, eager to seize upon the slightest mistake made by me or by a fellow police officer. As a criminology professor, I had always enjoyed the luxury of having great amounts of time in which to make difficult decisions. As a police officer, however, I found myself forced to make the most critical choices in a time frame of seconds, rather than days: to shoot or not to shoot, to arrest or not to arrest, to give chase or let go— always with the nagging certainty that others, those with great amounts of time in which to analyze and think, stood ready to judge and condemn me for whatever action I might take or fail to take. I found myself not only forced to live a life consisting of seconds and adrenalin, but also forced to deal with human problems which were infinitely more difficult than anything I had ever confronted in a correctional or mental health setting. Family fights, mental illness, potentially explosive crowd situations, dangerous individuals—I found myself progressively awed by the complexity of tasks faced by men whose work I once thought was fairly simple and straightforward.

Indeed, I would like to take the average clinical psychologist or psychiatrist and invite him to function for just a day in the world of the policeman, to confront people whose problems are both serious and in need of immediate solution. I would invite him to walk, as I have, into a smoke-filled pool room where five or six angry men are swinging cues at one another. I would like the prison counselor and parole officer to see their client—not calm and composed in an office setting, but as the street cop sees him: beating his small child with a heavy belt buckle, or kicking his pregnant wife. I wish that they, and every judge and juror in our country, could see the ravages of crime as the cop on the beat does— innocent people cut, shot, beaten, raped, robbed, and murdered. It would give him, I feel certain, a different perspective on crime and criminals, just as it did to me.

For all the human misery and suffering which police officers must witness in their work, I found myself amazed at the incredible humanity and compassion which seems to characterize most of them. My own stereotypes of the brutal, sadistic cop were time and again shattered by the sight of humanitarian kindness on the part of the thin blue line: a young patrolman giving mouth-to-mouth resuscitation to a filthy derelict: a grizzled old veteran embarrassed when I discovered the bags of jelly beans which he carried in the trunk of his car for impoverished ghetto kids, to whom he was the closest thing to an Easter Bunny they would ever know; an officer giving money out of his own pocket to a hungry and stranded family he would probably never see again; and another one taking the trouble to drop by on his own time in order to give worried parents information about their problem son or daughter.

As a police officer, I found myself repeatedly surprised at the ability of my fellow patrolmen to withstand the enormous daily pressures of their work: long hours, frustration, danger, and anxiety—all seemingly taken in stride as just part of the business of being a cop. I eventually went through the humbling discovery that I, like the men in blue with whom I worked, was simply a human being with definite limits to the amount of stress I could endure in a given period of time.

I recall, in particular, one evening when this point was dramatized to me. My tour of duty had been a long, hard one—one that had ended with a high-speed chase of a stolen car in which we narrowly escaped serious injury when another vehicle pulled in front of our patrol car. As we checked off duty, I was vaguely aware of feeling tired and tense. My partner and I were headed for a restaurant and a bite of breakfast when we both heard the unmistakable sound of breaking glass coming from a church, and we spotted two long-haired, teenaged boys running from the area. We confronted them and I asked one for identification, displaying my own police identification. He sneered at me, cursed, turned, and started to walk away. The next thing I knew I had grabbed the youth by his shirt and spun him around, shouting, "I'm talking to you, punk!" I felt my partner's arm on my shoulder and heard his reassuring voice behind me, "Take it easy, Doc!" I released my grip on the adolescent and stood silently for several seconds, unable to accept the inescapable reality that I had "lost my cool." My mind flashed back to a lecture during which I had told my students, "Any man who is not able to maintain absolute control of his emotions at all times has no business being a police officer." I was at the time of this incident director of a human relations project designed to teach policemen "emotional control" skills. Now here I was, an "emotional control" expert, being told by a patrolman to "calm down!"

As someone who had always regarded policemen as a "paranoid" lot, I discovered that, in the daily round of violence which became a part of my life, chronic suspiciousness is something which a good cop cultivates in the interest of being able to go home to his family after each tour of duty. As with so many other officers, my daily exposure to street crime soon had me carrying an off-duty weapon virtually everywhere I went. I began to become watchful of who and what was around me. Things began to acquire a new meaning: an open door, someone loitering on a dark corner, a rear license plate covered with dirt. According to my family, friends, and colleagues, my personality slowly began to change as my career as a policeman progressed. Once quick to drop critical barbs about policemen to intellectual friends, I now became extremely sensitive about such remarks—and several times became engaged in heated arguments over them.

As a police officer myself, I found that society demands too much of its policemen. Not only are they expected to enforce the law, they must also be curbside psychiatrists, marriage counselors, social workers—even ministers and doctors. I found that a good street officer combines in his daily work splinters of each one of these complex professions, and many more. It is unreasonable, of course, to ask so much of the men in blue; nevertheless, there is no one else to whom a person can turn for help in the kind of crises and problems with which policemen must deal. No one else wants to counsel a family with problems at 3 a.m. on Sunday morning! No one else wants to enter a darkened building after a burglar! No one else wants to stare poverty, mental illness, and human tragedy in the face, day after day, or to pick up the pieces of shattered lives.

As a policeman, I have often asked myself "Why does a man become a cop? What makes him stay with it?" Surely it is not the disrespect, or the legal restrictions which make the job increasingly rough, or the long hours and low pay, or the risk of being killed or injured trying to protect people who often do not seem to care. The only answer I can offer to this question is the one based upon my own limited experience as a policeman. As I came home from work and took off the badge and blue uniform I experienced a sense of satisfaction over a contribution to society—something that I have never known in any other job. Somehow that feeling seemed to make everything worthwhile, despite the disrespect, the danger, and the boredom so often associated with police responsibility.

For all too long, America's colleges and universities have conveyed to young men and women the subtle message that there is, somehow, something wrong with "being a cop." It's time for that to stop! And that point was forcibly brought home to me one evening not long ago. I had just completed a day shift and had to rush back to the university with no chance to change out of uniform for a late afternoon class. As I rushed into my office to pick up my lecture notes, my secretary's jaw dropped at the sight of the uniform. "Why, Dr. Kirkham, you're not going to class looking like *that,* are you?" I felt momentarily embarrassed. And then I was struck by the realization that I would not feel the need to apologize if I appeared before my students with long hair or a beard. After all, free love advocates and revolutionaries do not apologize for their group memberships, so why should someone whose appearance symbolizes a commitment to serve and protect society? "Why not?" I replied with a slight smile. "I'm proud to be a cop!" I picked up my notes and went on to class.

Let me conclude by saying that I hope that other educators might take the trouble to observe firsthand some of the policeman's problems be-

fore being so quick to condemn and pass judgment on him. We are all familiar with the old expression which urges us to refrain from judging the worth of another man's actions until we have walked at least a mile in his shoes. To be sure, I have not walked that mile as a rookie patrolman, but at least I have tried the shoes on, and I have taken a few difficult steps in them. Those few steps, however, have given me a profoundly new understanding and appreciation of our police. They left me with the humbling realization that possession of even a top-flight college degree does not give a person a corner on knowledge, or place him in the lofty position where he cannot take lessons from those with considerably less education.

Professor Kirkham writes passionately about police concerns and fears. The following selection is also by a police officer but presents a very different attitude about police work and court decisions. What do you think accounts for the difference?

A Black Policeman's Perspective on Law Enforcement　*Theodore Kirkland*

It has been fifteen years since I donned the blue uniform representing the Buffalo Police Department. Buffalo is an industrial, multi-ethnic, predominantly Catholic city located in the western section of the state of New York. Within its boundaries more than 450,000 people reside, including approximately 150,000 persons of Afro-American heritage living mainly in the core area of the city. The periphery of the city is reserved mainly for whites, with a few scattered blacks. Economic necessity and job security were the reasons I applied for the position, not because of any strong patriotic desire. Police officers were not popular in my community.

In addition to his service on the police force, Mr. Kirkland is founder and past president of the Afro-American Police Association of Buffalo, New York, and a member of the Executive Boards of the Buffalo branch of the NAACP and of the American Civil Liberties Union. Reprinted by permission of the author.

I, a black, entered the police department at age twenty-eight, having previously completed four years of military service as an Air Police Officer in the United States Air Force. Entering the police department, I was full of optimism, fear, and appreciation. After all, I had passed a competitive civil service examination which most blacks are said to be unable to do. Blacks in America, like women, have been conditioned mentally and intellectually to feel elated when they enter a vocation which has excluded or limited them in numbers, a field that consists primarily of white males. There were twenty-eight blacks on the force then and fifteen women. Now, fifteen years later, there are thirty-five blacks and seventeen women out of a total force of 1,275 members.

For fifteen years police work has been my occupation, my means of providing food for my family, my means of legitimacy; and for several of those earlier years, police work was my image, my hero maker, my status among the powerless.

My police career began in the police academy. There were twenty-four others in training with me. Training consisted mostly of classroom orientation on the state penal code and its procedures. Defensive tactics and marksmanship with a variety of weapons were the highlight of the training. There seemed among the trainees to be an inherent desire to fire and possess weapons, as if it were certain proof of masculinity. This love for guns was also common among the police officials. It was police policy to give a day off with pay each month for the top marksman in the police department.

When we were halfway through our training, we were allowed to carry our weapons. Up to that point our weapons had been kept in the police academy. Suddenly, with .38s strapped to their belts, grown men forgot how to walk. Vicariously, they were back in the wild West, swaggering with their gun arm away from their body ready to draw. Many hours were spent on the technique of quick drawing a weapon. Recruits were told to practice constantly on drawing, using a mirror at home. Repeatedly, we were told that our lives might depend on the speed with which we could pull and fire our weapon. Recruits could be seen practicing with each other, presumably with empty weapons. We practiced vigorously with our weapons, determined to be the best shooters and the fastest on the draw in the Buffalo Police Department.

The remainder of our training consisted of courses in human relations and first aid. Police officials tacitly transmitted to the recruits, however, that human relations was worthless and, therefore, little attention was given to these particular courses. Human relations as presented by the police instructors and others was the course which was supposed to sensitize police officers to minority problems and views. This sensitivity training was a mockery to the trainees and was resented by the police officers because of its social ramifications. It was impressed upon the trainees that human relations was social work of the type handled by the welfare department, whereas police work meant handling criminals by any means necessary. We were told repeatedly that

respect was at the other end of a baton. Violence was glorified by instructors and recommended where communications and understanding were lacking on the part of the police.

I did not appreciate the dimensions of racism and exploitation until I became a police officer. Racism was such a dominant factor of training that it made racists out of persons previously considered incapable of such feelings. Even among black recruits, fear was instilled, a fear of the neighborhood in which we lived, a fear of the people with whom we lived, a fear of dark alleys, the same alleys in which we had played and walked nightly; we now feared those alleys.

This indoctrination of racism and fear, subtly at first, intensified as training progressed. Instructors (all white) continuously, with the aid of training films, slides, and previous criminal cases, placed a disproportionate number of Afro-Americans in the role of the evil doers, while placing Caucasians in the heroic or positive position. When violence and youth gang activity were discussed, blacks were characterized as the perpetrators while whites were described as the innocent hard-working victims. To increase the emotion (euphemism for racism) among the white trainees, victims of rape were described as pretty white females, the rapists as grotesque black males. After these sessions, black-white relations in class were usually very strained. I felt as if I were under suspicion; after all, we were being conditioned to suspect all blacks. I was to learn later that the quickest way to get a police officer was to call in a report that a white woman was being attacked by a black male. White police officers in radio patrol cars would race to the scene with heroism and violence on their minds. Some of the most thorough investigations are those involving the alleged rape of white women by black men; the reverse merits little or no attention.

In training, the one other black and I were treated as invisible species. Our comments were taken as meaningless. We were constantly reminded of our ethnicity as it related to the criminal element. Because we had passed the civil service examination for patrolman, we were told that we were better than other blacks and that we had to "prove" ourselves to the white officers, a phrase I was to hear repeated on numerous occasions.

Most of those in my class were from suburbia or predominantly white communities far removed from the black ghetto. They lacked knowledge of inner city problems, including the ability to communicate with nonwhites. Minorities were neither their neighbors nor their schoolmates. Neither integration of schools nor total integration of neighborhoods had reached Buffalo. My classmates' knowledge of nonwhites came primarily from the police instructors who were also limited in their knowledge of ethnicity and urban problems. Blacks are viewed by most whites as physical characters: mentally they are considered irrelevant.

At the conclusion of our training, mandatory academic, physical tactics, and marksmanship examinations were given. One of the trainees who was well-liked by the higher-ups received the answers to the written examination in advance. He was Irish-American like all of the top officials. He offered the answers to me and when I refused, he explained that he would purposely miss two answers, since he was afraid that someone might challenge him if he received a perfect score. Receiving a mark of 98 he was awarded the academic achievement award for being the outstanding police officer in our class. This same officer has on several occasions been accused of criminal activity, only to be protected by his superiors. He has often been described as a good police officer.

After graduation from the police academy, I was assigned to precinct duty where I walked the beat. My beat was in the black section of the precinct. Blacks were not allowed to ride in police cars in that precinct. The precinct captain would have parked police cars himself before he would have allowed a black to ride in one. Car patrol was considered superior to walking a beat, so their tactic placed blacks at a psychological disadvantage. In terms of their image, those who patrol in police cars are considered the real police, whereas those on the beat are labeled *door shakers*. Car patrol personnel are erroneously depicted as being intellectually superior to the beat patrol.

The truth is that those who patrol in cars are more mobile and have an opportunity to gain experience in handling a wider variety of cases. They are also prone to meet more people, including media personnel who may focus positive attention upon them for their participation in certain criminal cases to which they are dispatched. They are, therefore, more likely to be better promotional candidates. Blacks being relegated to the beat too often succumb to a psychological inferiority complex, failing to recognize the economic, political, and racist purposes of the system.

Reflecting back, neither the Buffalo Police Department's ideology nor its personnel has changed; the training period has increased, but not its quality. The police officers are still the racist occupiers they were when I first started, but I now understand the role of the police in an urban society. When we graduated from the Police Academy, I did not consciously realize that we had been psychologically conditioned to be contemporary cowboys. Our purpose—to protect by any means necessary the property and its owners from the propertyless and to maintain the status quo. Because of the highly disproportionate numbers of Afro-Americans who are propertyless and indigent, and many who wish to be nonsubservient, they are identified as the modern day Indians to be patrolled and controlled by the modern day cowboys—the police.

In this cowboy role, the police ride through the ghetto in pairs or groups, many of them carrying two guns. They are usually white, of working-class background, conservative in nature, and traditionally authoritarian. Their police sirens, which are commonly heard in the black community, have taken the place of the hooting and hollering on horseback. Masculinity, American style, must be proven at all times, for it is through this barbaric activity that police officers of poor immigrant backgrounds gain their sense of worth. Their powers are bestowed upon them by the controlling class, which depicts heroes as being those who possess violent traits and who utilize this violence, any kind of violence, to maintain the status quo. It is this violence and its maintenance procedures which contribute to the high percentage of police assaults upon citizens. Violence is the status symbol of the police. To be accepted, one is expected to show masculinity by his toughness. To be contrary is unacceptable, and one is ridiculed, harassed, and possibly forced out.

Assaults on citizens by police, especially against black Americans, have persisted in the Buffalo Police Department. It reached epidemic proportions in 1974 and the Afro-American Police Association of Buffalo, a black police organization created in 1969 to fight racism and discriminatory hiring in the Buffalo Police Department, sent telegrams to the governor of the state of New York and to the president of the United States requesting their assistance and intervention. These telegrams were to no avail and assaults against black people continued. Numerous white police officers have been charged by black citizens with assault only to be found not guilty due to the insensitivity of police officials, judges, and juries.

Within the Buffalo Police Department racism is so common that black officers either succumb to it or find themselves in a constant state of rage which keeps them at odds with their so-called coworkers. Numerous fights between black and white officers have broken out in precinct stations. Derogatory ethnic remarks are heard over the police radio. Black police officers have been known to be investigated merely for protecting the constitutional rights of themselves, blacks, and others.

It has been the police officer's function to maintain peace, not to promote equality. Thus law enforcement officers should not expect those who suffer from inequality to do so gladly. The police role is to preserve the equality of those who have it, from those who lack it. Those without equality are usually identified as the poor and minority persons and groups who have been deprived economically, politically, and socially.

This deprivation is a conspiratorial act which brings industry, government, and political forces together in their exploitation of the poor. Merchants are allowed to sell inferior goods to the indigent, and government agencies are allowed to render inferior services, such as education and fire protection, and providing no protection against slum landlords, while the political system consistently perpetuates discriminatory employ-

ment practices against blacks. The police are beholden to these institutions and accept their unequal treatment of the indigent. In my official capacity on numerous occasions, I have had to use aggressive measures to impress upon established institutions the importance of equal treatment to minorities.

One case of interest occurred at the County Hospital in the mental ward. My patrol partner and I were dispatched to assist other officers in the removal of an outpatient. Four police officers and two hospital security personnel were on the scene; a huge shirtless black male acting irrationally was in the corridor. The officers were holding batons and guardedly watching this man who was positioned in a fighting stance.

The man was screaming that he was not leaving. I then questioned him as to what he wanted. He responded by saying that he wanted to be readmitted to the hospital before he hurt someone (he had previously killed his wife). I questioned a doctor who was standing nearby regarding this patient's request. He informed us that the man was an outpatient from the State Hospital, and upon his request "State" had refused him.

During our conversation the patient ceased his irrational behavior and standing adjacent to me sensed a glint of recognition toward me in his eyes. I told him that I would get him admitted into the hospital if that was his request. I then proceeded to contact the State Hospital by phone; they still refused to readmit him claiming there was no room available. They suggested that I arrest and incarcerate him. I disagreed replying that he was a sick man and not a criminal. I then obtained the name of the hospital personnel with whom I had spoken informing them that criminal and civil charges would be filed against them and the hospital for placing us (including the outpatient) in an injurious position. My assertiveness forced them to reconsider, and they gave the patient readmittance permission. I accompanied the patient in the ambulance without any disturbance.

Over the years I have had confrontations with members of the departments of education, welfare, public transportation, and even the police department in their manner of treating blacks and other minority members. Most police officers feel beholden to these institutions and support them in their oppression of poor people.

Obvious partiality is shown between white and black arrestees. Whites are usually allowed an appearance ticket for which they promise to appear in court at a later date, whereas most blacks are locked up with an unaffordable bail. The rationale is that most blacks are without roots in the community and cannot be trusted.

Black people are placed at the mercy of alien white police officials who too often use minorities as statistics to obtain federal funds under the pretense of crime control. These funds are used for purchasing weaponry, police cars, computers, and lately to curtail layoffs in the police department. For the police, therefore, crime in the black community is very profitable. As another example, police officers are able to subsidize their salaries by attending court after they make an arrest. The more arrests one makes, the more he attends court and the larger his paycheck becomes (many officers brag about being able to pay their mortgages from court subsidies). To transfer an officer from the black community is often seen as punishment, thus decreasing his income. Many who are transferred find their way back, usually by political connections.

Too often our zealous white police officers are supported in their improprieties toward minorities by the white media, which persuades the public that the officers' actions were proper. This type of action is thus reinforced because of public sanction—"public" meaning the white public. Police officers who are constantly in the news because of altercations in the black community are in essence mentally incompetent, but they are often rewarded for their seemingly heroic conduct by being promoted, given citations, and by being protected from any minority onslaught precipitated by those inhuman actions. There also seems to be a correlation between those officers who are consistently involved in altercations and those officers who earn large amounts in court pay.

The Buffalo police psyche consists of two societies: one white in which they belong, the other black and considered the enemy. Progressive

change has not reached this urban police department. Archaic procedures initiated by antiquated officials are dominant. Brute force still takes precedence over progressive knowledge, which places learned personnel at a disadvantage.

Throughout urban America, black police organizations are attempting to eliminate racism and discriminatory hiring practices within urban police departments by charging them with violating the Civil Rights Act of 1964. With the aid of the United States Justice Department, black people are asking that all federal funds be discontinued in accused departments until practices have been eradicated. Seventy million dollars was withheld from the Chicago police department following a complaint by the Afro-American Patrolmens League of Chicago. Buffalo is presently involved in federal court litigation which also includes discrimination against women. Women are basically denied equal employment opportunity in urban police departments because the controlling mentality of the police profession believes that women are not physically conditioned to perform brute force; they focus not at all on their intellectual capacity.

Communication between the police and different groups in society is one of the major problems confronting urban police agencies today. This problem is made more severe by racist police administrators who refuse to utilize the true expertise of knowledgeable blacks in the field of urban problems. Police administrators, often because of inherent racism, view blacks as too inferior to know anything different from what is known by white police officers. This mental blockage by police superiors perpetuates one perspective within police departments which provokes problems instead of respect between the races. It is totally degrading for white officials to believe that they are more knowledgeable in communicating with minorities than are representatives of the oppressed minority group. This disrespect of minority group representatives within police departments is transmitted to the larger segment; after all, they are a part of the whole. It is usually the case that when police departments utilize blacks they are often those blacks who have been totally indoctrinated by the white police world which makes them duplicators instead of innovators. Like their counterparts, they are usually far removed from the black community and its problems; they are also aware that it is not advantageous to associate with the enemy. They are not found to be involved in the intricacies of the community. Those who are, are usually harassed, kept under surveillance, and denied meaningful promotions. This treatment toward blacks who actively participate in community affairs is used as an example to others; therefore, few minorities will openly expose themselves to this consequence. This is ironic, because being a resident of the community in which I work, and understanding its language, history, and politics is my greatest asset to law enforcement.

Notes and Questions

1. In his book, *Police in Trouble,* James Ahern, formerly Chief of Police in New Haven, Conn., vividly described some of the conflicts policemen feel after joining the force. He writes:

> No one outside the policeman's closed fraternity knows the cop. Shrewdness and mistrust separate him from the people in the houses his speeding car passes. He does not mix with them. They do not seek him out. Yet national problems and local problems all focus on him in the end. The cop in the squad car who is underqualified or undereducated or undertrained, who is subject to all the warping influences that society brings to bear on him, is the basic unit of police service. He is the person who interacts with the public, and he is the person who personifies police service....
>
> The day the new recruit steps through the doors of a police academy, he leaves society behind to enter a "profession" that does more than give him a job; it defines who he is. For all the years that he remains, closed into the sphere of its rituals and its absurdities in the town where he began, until he takes the ransom money of his pension and retires, he will be a cop.
>
> Few if any jobs claim a man so completely, and there are few other jobs whose moments of glamour have held more fascination for the public. The moments of glamour *are there.* At times they rival the perfections of fiction. Yet the public that buys murder mysteries in bookstores and watches cop shows on television is ignorant of what a policeman's job really is and of what kind of person it makes him....
>
> Before joining the police force, the policeman has probably had a circle of friends with whom he has been more or less close for years. As soon as he joins the force, it begins to shrink. The cop's strange hours make him difficult to reach. But more important, his identity as a police officer makes him a social liability, even when he is off duty. Wherever he goes he is recognized by bartenders, bookies, newspaper sellers, and waitresses, who want to talk shop with him. And even if these people are not around, others who realize that he is a policeman stop him to harangue him about the inadequacies of police service. In this way the cop's "professional" situation is similar to that of the doctor, who cannot go out without hearing about half a dozen appendectomies, but it is hardly as enviable.
>
> So the cop tends to socialize with other cops. When he gets off duty on the swing shift, there is little to do but go drinking and few people to do it with but other cops. He finds himself going bowling with them, going fishing, helping them paint their houses or fix their cars. His family gets to know their families, and a kind of mutual protection society develops which turns out to be the only group in which the policeman is automatically entitled to respect.
>
> This shrinking of his circle of friends, which usually continues until only one or two very close friends are left, invariably makes the policeman dull. His life becomes routine. And even as it does, the pettinesses of police politics become more real....
>
> The cop soon learns that on the whole the public is not to be trusted. He finds that many people who call police want to manipulate them for their own purposes. This recognition closes him more completely into the brotherhood of his fellow officers.
>
> The cop learns that many people who have grudges against others want to use the police to take care of them. And after he has been asked to write a number of theft reports, he realizes that many reports that he writes in

good faith are phony ones and that people are using him to defraud insurance companies.

The cop eventually reaches a point where he trusts no one. At this point the notorious secretiveness of the police profession becomes a part of his way of life. . . .

As his years in the squad car wear on, the endless cycle of shifts takes its toll, and the cop's frustration increases as he sees that he is running hard but getting nowhere. He arrests drunks and sees them thrown into jail, where the causes of their alcoholism are compounded. He knows he will arrest them again. He refers juveniles to juvenile courts and sees them on the streets again with the same lack of support and direction that led to their delinquency. He knows he will arrest them again too, when they have grown, through neglect, into full-fledged criminals. He sees everyone on the take and no one giving. He tires of being trapped between his superiors and the courts, between prosecutors and the public. He tires of making instantaneous judgments on the street that are meticulously analyzed *ex post facto* by people who have no idea what the street as he sees it is like. He becomes exhausted with climbing endless flights of stairs and knocking on the same doors, with finding himself in the middle of fights and brawls, with treating endless problems for which there is —for him—no solution.*

2. Consider the following suggestions† by a police expert, on who should be selected for a field interrogation:
   A. Be suspicious. This is a healthy police attitude, but it should be controlled and not too obvious.
   B. Look for the unusual.
      1. Persons who do not "belong" where they are observed.
      2. Automobiles which do not "look right."
      3. Businesses opened at odd hours, or not according to routine or custom.

* From *Police in Trouble* by James F. Ahern. Copyright © 1972 by James F. Ahern. By permission of Hawthorn Books, Inc.

† From Thomas F. Adams, "Field Interrogation," *Police,* March–April, 1963, p. 28.

C. Subjects who should be subjected to field interrogations.
   1. Suspicious persons known to the officer from previous arrests, field interrogations, and observations.
   2. Emaciated appearing alcoholics and narcotics users who invariably turn to crime to pay for cost of habit.
   3. Person who fits description of wanted suspect as described by radio, teletype, daily bulletins.
   4. Any person observed in the immediate vicinity of a crime very recently committed or reported as "in progress."
   5. Known trouble-makers near large gatherings.
   6. Persons who attempt to avoid or evade the officer.
   7. Exaggerated unconcern over contact with the officer.
   8. Visibly "rattled" when near the policeman.
   9. Unescorted women or young girls in public places, particularly at night in such places as cafes, bars, bus and train depots, or street corners.
   10. "Lovers" in an industrial area (make good lookouts).
   11. Persons who loiter about places where children play.
   12. Solicitors or peddlers in a residential neighborhood.
   13. Loiterers around public rest rooms.
   14. Lone male sitting in car adjacent to schoolground with newspaper or book in his lap. . . .
   16. Hitchhikers.
   17. Person wearing coat on hot days.
   18. Car with mismatched hub caps, or dirty car with clean license plate (or vice versa).
   19. Uniformed "deliverymen" with no merchandise or truck.
   20. Many others. How about your own personal experiences?

What do these criteria suggest to the policeman about the value of respecting an individual's freedom except where "probable cause" exists?

3. Consider also the following conflicts faced by policemen:
   . . . The police in democratic society are required to maintain order and to do so under

the rule of law. As functionaries charged with maintaining order, they are part of the bureaucracy. The ideology of democratic bureaucracy emphasizes initiative rather than disciplined adherence to rules and regulations. By contrast, the rule of law emphasizes the rights of individual citizens and constraints upon the initiative of legal officials. This tension between the operational consequences of ideas of order, efficiency, and initiative, on the one hand, and legality, on the other, constitutes the principal problem of police as a democratic legal organization.*

Police officers occupy a unique role in the system of criminal justice. In their relations with citizens, whereby inputs are introduced into the system, they occupy the role of interrogator, and command authority; but when they generate outputs, they are themselves subject to interrogation, submitting to another's authority.†

For legislators and judges the police are a godsend, because all the acts of oppression that must be performed in this society to keep it running smoothly are pushed upon the police. The police get the blame, and the officials stay free of the stigma of approving their highhanded acts. The police have become the repository of all the illiberal impulses in this liberal society; they are under heavy fire because most of us no longer admit so readily to our illiberal impulses as we once did.‡

The primary goals of the police organization are intangible, ambiguous, and contradictory. This ambiguity is to a great extent an integral part of a policed society that espouses democratic norms. On the one hand, society asks the police to maintain peace and order, but, on the other, the Rule of Law requires that obstacles be established lest this job be done too efficiently. There is thus an important and inherent conflict between efficiency and restraint. Because these two concepts are themselves intangible and difficult to measure,

society itself has great difficulty in determining acceptable police behavior.§

4. In 1968, the Police Commissioner of the City of Baltimore refused to appoint a practicing nudist to the police force, even though he had received the highest test scores of more than 200 applicants. A Federal District Court ordered the man's appointment, ruling that the exclusion of all nudists was arbitrary. The Court, however, also stated that, "A police officer holds a position of public trust, and in that respect, his conduct must be of a higher moral character than that of the ordinary citizen." *Bruns* v. *Pomerleau,* 319 F. Supp. 58, 65 (D. Md., 1970). Is this necessarily true? Is it desirable? What value is there to having nudists on a police force? What problems does the evaluation of moral character cause?

5. Would a police officer agree with the California Sentencing Institute (see Chapter 1, page 77) considerations for probation?

6. Implicit in both Professor Kirkham's and Mr. Ahern's descriptions is the police officers' beliefs that their role and job are misunderstood. To a large extent this is true. The function of the police, most people would probably say, is to catch criminals and protect the public. Many people therefore also believe that the rising crime rate is a consequence of the police officers' failure to do their jobs properly. Some police officers, accepting this job description, displace their aggression by blaming Supreme Court rulings which restrict the way in which the police may gather evidence. In turn, the federal government has responded to this, and the public cry for law and order, by spending large amounts of money on new police cars, helicopters, radios, and more advanced equipment, and by making an attempt to slowly negate the effect of the Supreme Court rulings.

These developments and the process of reasoning just described are based on several misconceptions. Among the most prominent is that the basic function of the police is to catch criminals. Although it is this image that initially attracts many police recruits and gives the police officer power and authority, it is not what most police officers spend their time doing. One scholar defined the problem this way:

---

* Jerome Skolnick, *Justice Without Trial: Law Enforcement in a Democratic Society* (New York: John Wiley, 1966), p. 6.

† Albert Reiss, *The Police and the Public* (New Haven: Yale University Press, 1971), p. 134.

‡ Paul Chevigny, *Police Power: Police Abuses in New York City* (New York: Vintage Books, 1969), p. 280.

§ N. A. Milner, "Supreme Court Effectiveness and the Police Organization," *Law and Contemporary Problems* 36 (1971): 467, 469.

Basing their opinions, perhaps, on the Western, the detective story, and the "cops and robbers" saga, Americans tend to see police officers as spending most of their time in investigating felons and arresting them, often after a gun battle. In fact, most officers can serve for years without using their guns, except for practice, and their arrests of felons, or even serious misdemeanants, are not very frequent. Except for detectives, who usually constitute only a small proportion of an urban police department, most officers do not even spend a substantial portion of their time in investigation.

Most officers spend their time doing routine patrol. This patrol is interrupted frequently or occasionally, depending on the character of the area, by events requiring their presence. These events are likely to consist of a fight, which may include use of a knife or other weapon, between spouses, relatives, or friends; a party which is noisy and disturbing the neighborhood; a group of youngsters congregating on a street corner and bothering passers-by; a drunk lying on the sidewalk; or a person who is lost.

These situations require delicate judgments about how the officer should handle the situation. He has a variety of possible methods from which to choose. For example, after a fight, the officer can often make an arrest for assault as a felony or misdemeanor—the line between the two is extremely imprecise; order one or both persons to leave the scene on threat of being arrested; refer one or both persons to a social agency for help; or himself attempt to settle the matter. Similarly, a group of youngsters who are congregating can be arrested for loitering or another minor crime; warned to move on upon threat of arrest; or influenced to leave or behave themselves by friendly advice from an officer who has previously earned their respect.

The point is that the situations in which police officers most frequently find themselves do not require the expert aim of a marksman, the cunningness of a private eye, or the toughness of a stereotyped Irish policeman. Instead, they demand knowledge of human beings and the personal, as opposed to official, authority to influence people without the use or even threat of force.

These characteristics are not commonly found in police officers because police departments do not consider these values as paramount. As a result, persons with these abilities are not attracted to police work nor rewarded by promotion or other incentive if they happen to enter a department.

The image of police officers must be radically changed to consider them as a part of the broad category of occupations which deal with people who are sometimes difficult to handle. Others with similar problems include teachers, gang workers, recreation workers, and parole, probation, and correctional officers. If police work were seen in this light, individuals who were more sympathetic to human beings, and less prejudiced on racial and other grounds, would enter police work because they wanted to help human beings, instead of young men who are looking for excitement and the opportunity to exercise authority. However, just as gang work generally requires persons with above-average physical abilities in order to deal with delinquents, so police officers must have the physical bearing needed to deal with delinquents and other hostile persons without constantly using force.*

Professor James Q. Wilson has described these two broad police functions as "order maintenance" and "law enforcement." The first category would include helping public drunks, responding to family quarrels, dealing with noisy teenagers, keeping traffic moving around accidents, etc. The latter category would include responding to reports of burglaries and the like. The difference, he points out,

> ... between order maintenance and law enforcement is not simply the difference between "little stuff" and "real crime" or between misdemeanors and felonies. The distinction is fundamental to the police role, for the two functions involve quite dissimilar police actions and judgments. Order maintenance arises out of a dispute among citizens who accuse each other of being at fault; law enforcement

* Reprinted from "The Role of the Police" by Bruce J. Terris in volume no. 374 of *The Annals* of The American Academy of Political and Social Science, © 1967, by The American Academy of Political and Social Science. All rights reserved, pp. 67–68.

arises out of the victimization of an innocent party by a person whose guilt must be proved. Handling a disorderly situation requires the officer to make a judgment about what constitutes an appropriate standard of behavior; law enforcement requires him only to compare a person's behavior with a clear legal standard. Murder or theft is defined, unambiguously, by statutes; public peace is not. Order maintenance rarely leads to an arrest; law enforcement (if the suspect can be found) typically does.†

Thus, police discretion results not simply from the inadequate resources of police departments or the need to consider the circumstances of individual cases. Discretion also occurs because the order maintenance function requires some police response other than arrest. Wilson goes on to say,

> Because an arrest cannot be made in most disorderly cases, the officer is expected to handle the situation by other means and on the spot, but the law gives him almost no guidance on how he is to do this; indeed, the law often denies him the right to do anything at all *other* than make an arrest. No judge will ever see the case, and thus no judge can decide the case for the officer. Alone, unsupervised, with no policies to guide him and little sympathy from onlookers to support him, the officer must "administer justice" on the curbstone.‡

7. Professor Kirkham mentions the police officer's badge and uniform. What functions does the uniform serve? Do you think a police uniform is necessary?

8. How do you account for the differences in attitude toward Supreme Court decisions between Of-

† James Q. Wilson, "What Makes a Better Policeman," *The Atlantic Monthly* (March 1969), p. 131.
‡ *Ibid.*

ficer Kirkland and Professor Kirkham? Why do you think Officer Kirkland does not view the Supreme Court as his enemy?

9. How appropriate do you think the following analogy is?

> A clue to the understanding of the dynamics of this curious amalgam of conforming and aggressive behavior can be gotten by studying the school monitor. A teacher selects a child who is usually a conforming, obedient child to be her surrogate concerning discipline when she is out of the room. This child in his desire to keep the approval and conditional love of the teacher will carry out her commands both direct and implied about law and order. In his eagerness to please the teacher he may become officious, tyrannical, even aggressive in the performance of his duties. As long as the teacher commends him, he will perform eagerly and willingly the surrogate functions of her discipline and authority. That he becomes alienated from his peer group seems less important than that of losing adult approval. He appears to be more vulnerable to authorities' disapproval than peer rejection.*

10. Do you think that Orwell would empathize with Professor Kirkham's complaints?

11. For one view of the ghetto police officer, see the statement by James Baldwin on p. 173.

12. Professor Kirkham describes the "major social problems of our time" as "crime and delinquency, racial unrest, poverty, and mental illness." Officer Kirkland focuses on racism and exploitation as the central issues. Which perspective is more accurate? What is the difference between describing the problem as "racial unrest" or categorizing it as "racism"?

* Martin Symonds, "Policemen and Policework: A Psychodynamic Understanding," *The American Journal of Psychoanalysis* 32:163 (1972).

Professor Kirkham argues that one cause of the crime problem has been Supreme Court decisions which have "handcuffed" the police. As Professor Reich's article illustrated, and as most citizens know very well themselves, it is generally advisable to be polite and courteous, if not obsequious, when dealing with the police. The reason, quite simply, is that the police have a great deal of power. What, we might ask, has the Supreme Court done to limit this power? What could it do? What do the "handcuffs" consist of?

The following two cases raise many questions regarding the relationship between Supreme Court rulings and police behavior. In the majority opinion in the first case, *Terry* v. *State of Ohio,* former Chief Justice Warren explicitly acknowledges the problem. The opinion also shows us what some judges perceive the police officer's perspective to be. The second case, *Pennsylvania* v. *Mimms,* was decided ten years after *Terry.* It again confronts the problem of regulating police-citizen encounters and reveals how a choice is made between the police and citizen perspectives.

Terry v. State of Ohio   *392 U.S. 1 (1968)*

Mr. Chief Justice Warren delivered the opinion of the Court.

This case presents serious questions concerning the role of the Fourth Amendment in the confrontation on the street between the citizen and the policeman investigating suspicious circumstances.

Petitioner Terry was convicted of carrying a concealed weapon and sentenced to the statutorily prescribed term of one to three years in the penitentiary. Following the denial of a pretrial motion to suppress, the prosecution introduced in evidence two revolvers and a number of bullets seized from Terry and a codefendant, Richard Chilton, by Cleveland Police Detective Martin McFadden. At the hearing on the motion to suppress this evidence, Officer McFadden testified that while he was patrolling in plain clothes in downtown Cleveland at approximately 2:30 in the afternoon of October 31, 1963, his attention was attracted by two men, Chilton and Terry, standing on the corner of Huron Road and Euclid Avenue. He had never seen the two men before, and he was unable to say precisely what first drew his eye to them. However, he testified that he had been a policeman for 39 years and a detective for 35 and that he had been assigned to patrol this vicinity of downtown Cleveland for shop-

lifters and pickpockets for 30 years. He explained that he had developed routine habits of observation over the years and that he would "stand and watch people or walk and watch people at many intervals of the day." He added: "Now, in this case when I looked over they didn't look right to me at the time."

His interest aroused, Officer McFadden took up a post of observation in the entrance to a store 300 to 400 feet away from the two men. "I get more purpose to watch them when I seen their movements," he testified. He saw one of the men leave the other one and walk southwest on Huron Road, past some stores. The man paused for a moment and looked in a store window, then walked on a short distance, turned around and walked back toward the corner, pausing once again to look in the same store window. He rejoined his companion at the corner, and the two conferred briefly. Then the second man went through the same series of motions, strolling down Huron Road, looking in the same window, walking on a short distance, turning back, peering in the store window again, and returning to confer with the first man at the corner. The two men repeated this ritual alternately between five and six times apiece—in all, roughly a dozen trips. At one point, while the two were standing together on the corner, a third man approached them and engaged them briefly in conversation. This man then left the two others and walked

---

(Footnotes and some case citations have been omitted.)

west on Euclid Avenue. Chilton and Terry resumed their measured pacing, peering and conferring. After this had gone on for 10 to 12 minutes, the two men walked off together, heading west on Euclid Avenue, following the path taken earlier by the third man.

By this time Officer McFadden had become thoroughly suspicious. He testified that after observing their elaborately casual and oft-repeated reconnaissance of the store window on Huron Road, he suspected the two men of "casing a job, a stick-up," and that he considered it his duty as a police officer to investigate further. He added that he feared "they may have a gun." Thus, Officer McFadden followed Chilton and Terry and saw them stop in front of Zucker's store to talk to the same man who had conferred with them earlier on the street corner. Deciding that the situation was ripe for direct action, Officer McFadden approached the three men, identified himself as a police officer and asked for their names. At this point his knowledge was confined to what he had observed. He was not acquainted with any of the three men by name or by sight, and he had received no information concerning them from any other source. When the men "mumbled something" in response to his inquiries, Officer McFadden grabbed petitioner Terry, spun him around so that they were facing the other two, with Terry between McFadden and the others, and patted down the outside of his clothing. In the left breast pocket of Terry's overcoat Officer McFadden felt a pistol. He reached inside the overcoat pocket, but was unable to remove the gun. At this point, keeping Terry between himself and the others, the officer ordered all three men to enter Zucker's store. As they went in, he removed Terry's overcoat completely, removed a .38-caliber revolver from the pocket and ordered all three men to face the wall with their hands raised. Officer McFadden proceeded to pat down the outer clothing of Chilton and the third man, Katz. He discovered another revolver in the outer pocket of Chilton's overcoat, but no weapons were found on Katz. The officer testified that he only patted the men down to see whether they had weapons, and that he did not put his hands beneath the outer garments of

either Terry or Chilton until he felt their guns. So far as appears from the record, he never placed his hands beneath Katz' outer garments. Officer McFadden seized Chilton's gun, asked the proprietor of the store to call a police wagon, and took all three men to the station, where Chilton and Terry were formally charged with carrying concealed weapons.

On the motion to suppress the guns the prosecution took the position that they had been seized following a search incident to a lawful arrest. The trial court rejected this theory, stating that it "would be stretching the facts beyond reasonable comprehension" to find that Officer McFadden had had probable cause to arrest the men before he patted them down for weapons. However, the court denied the defendants' motion on the ground that Officer McFadden, on the basis of his experience, "had reasonable cause to believe ... that the defendants were conducting themselves suspiciously, and some interrogation should be made of their action." Purely for his own protection, the court held, the officer had the right to pat down the outer clothing of these men, who he had reasonable cause to believe might be armed. The court distinguished between an investigatory "stop" and an arrest, and between a "frisk" of the outer clothing for weapons and a full-blown search for evidence of crime. The frisk, it held, was essential to the proper performance of the officer's investigatory duties, for without it "the answer to the police officer may be a bullet, and a loaded pistol discovered during the frisk is admissible."

After the court denied their motion to suppress, Chilton and Terry waived jury trial and pleaded not guilty. The court adjudged them guilty, and the Court of Appeals for the Eighth Judicial District, Cuyahoga County, affirmed. *State* v. *Terry,* 5 Ohio App.2d 122, 214 N.E.2d 114 (1966). The Supreme Court of Ohio dismissed their appeal on the ground that no "substantial constitutional question" was involved. We granted certiorari, 387 U.S. 929, 87 S.Ct. 2050, 18 L.Ed.2d 989 (1967), to determine whether the admission of the revolvers in evidence violated petitioner's rights under the Fourth Amendment, made applicable to the States by the Fourteenth. *Mapp* v.

Ohio, 367 U.S. 643, 81 S.Ct. 1684, 6 L.Ed.2d 1081 (1961). We affirm the conviction.

The Fourth Amendment provides that "the right of the people to be secure in their persons, houses, papers, and effects, against unreasonable searches and seizures, shall not be violated...." We have recently held that "the Fourth Amendment protects people, not places," *Katz* v. *United States,* 389 U.S. 347, 351, 88 S.Ct. 507, 511, 19 L.Ed.2d 576 (1967), and wherever an individual may harbor a reasonable "expectation of privacy," id., at 361, 88 S.Ct. at 507 (Mr. Justice Harlan, concurring), he is entitled to be free from unreasonable governmental intrusion.... Unquestionably petitioner was entitled to the protection of the Fourth Amendment as he walked down the street in Cleveland. The question is whether in all the circumstances of this on-the-street encounter, his right to personal security was violated by an unreasonable search and seizure....

On the one hand, it is frequently argued that in dealing with the rapidly unfolding and often dangerous situations on city streets the police are in need of an escalating set of flexible responses, graduated in relation to the amount of information they possess. For this purpose it is urged that distinctions should be made between a "stop" and an "arrest" (or a "seizure" of a person), and between a "frisk" and a "search." Thus, it is argued, the police should be allowed to "stop" a person and detain him briefly for questioning upon suspicion that he may be connected with criminal activity. Upon suspicion that the person may be armed, the police should have the power to "frisk" him for weapons. If the "stop" and the "frisk" give rise to probable cause to believe that the suspect has committed a crime, then the police should be empowered to make a formal "arrest," and a full incident "search" of the person. This scheme is justified in part upon the notion that a "stop" and a "frisk" amount to a mere "minor inconvenience and petty indignity," which can properly be imposed upon the citizen in the interest of effective law enforcement on the basis of a police officer's suspicion.

On the other side the argument is made that the authority of the police must be strictly circumscribed by the law of arrest and search as it has developed to date in the traditional jurisprudence of the Fourth Amendment. . . . The heart of the Fourth Amendment, the argument runs, is a severe requirement of specific justification for any intrusion upon protected personal security, coupled with a highly developed system of judicial controls to enforce upon the agents of the State the commands of the Constitution. Acquiescence by the courts in the compulsion inherent in the field interrogation practices at issue here, it is urged, would constitute an abdication of judicial control over, and indeed an encouragement of, substantial interference with liberty and personal security by police officers whose judgment is necessarily colored by their primary involvement in "the often competitive enterprise of ferreting out crime." *Johnson* v. *United States,* 333 U.S. 10, 14, 68 S.Ct. 367, 369, 92 L.Ed. 436 (1948). This, it is argued, can only serve to exacerbate police-community tensions in the crowded centers of our Nation's cities.

. . . The State has characterized the issue here as "the right of a police officer . . . to make an on-the-street stop, interrogate and pat down for weapons (known in street vernacular as 'stop and frisk')." But this is only partly accurate. For the issue is not the abstract propriety of the police conduct, but the admissibility against petitioner of the evidence uncovered by the search and seizure. Ever since its inception, the rule excluding evidence seized in violation of the Fourth Amendment has been recognized as a principal mode of discouraging lawless police conduct. Thus its major thrust is a deterrent one, and experience has taught that it is the only effective deterrent to police misconduct in the criminal context, and that without it the constitutional guarantee against unreasonable searches and seizures would be a mere "form of words." The rule also serves another vital function—"the imperative of judicial integrity...."

The exclusionary rule has its limitations, however, as a tool of judicial control.... In some contexts the rule is ineffective as a deterrent. Street encounters between citizens and police officers are incredibly rich in diversity. They range from wholly friendly exchanges of pleasantries or mutually useful information to hostile confrontations of armed men involving arrests, or injuries, or loss of life. Moreover, hostile confrontations are not all of a piece. Some of them begin in a friendly enough manner, only to take a different turn upon the injection of some unexpected element into the conversation. Encounters are initiated by the police for a wide variety of purposes, some of which are wholly unrelated to a desire to prosecute for crime. Doubtless some police "field interrogation" conduct violates the Fourth Amendment. But a stern refusal by this Court to condone such activity does not necessarily render it responsive to the exclusionary rule. Regardless of how effective the rule may be where obtaining convictions is an important objective of the police, it is powerless to deter invasions of constitutionally guaranteed rights where the police either have no interest in prosecuting or are willing to forgo successful prosecution in the interest of serving some other goal.

Proper adjudication of cases in which the exclusionary rule is invoked demands a constant awareness of these limitations. The wholesale harassment by certain elements of the police community, of which minority groups, particularly Negroes, frequently complain, will not be stopped by the exclusion of any evidence from any criminal trial. Yet a rigid and unthinking application of the exclusionary rule, in futile protest against practices which it can never be used effectively to control, may exact a high toll in human injury and frustration of efforts to prevent crime. No judicial opinion can comprehend the protean variety of the street encounter, and we can only judge the facts of the case before us. Nothing we say today is to be taken as indicating approval of police conduct outside the legitimate investigative sphere. Under our decision, courts still retain their traditional responsibility to guard against police conduct which is overbearing or harassing, or which trenches upon personal security without the objective evidentiary justification which the Constitution requires. When such conduct is identified, it must be condemned by the judiciary and its fruits must be excluded from evidence in criminal trials. . . .

Having thus roughly sketched the perimeters of the constitutional debate over the limits on police investigative conduct in general and the background against which this case presents itself, we turn our attention to the quite narrow question posed by the facts before us: whether it is always unreasonable for a policeman to seize a person and subject him to a limited search for weapons unless there is probable cause for an arrest. Given the narrowness of this question, we have no occasion to canvass in detail the constitutional limitations upon the scope of a policeman's power when he confronts a citizen without probable cause to arrest him. . . .

. . . In order to assess the reasonableness of Officer McFadden's conduct as a general proposition, it is necessary "first to focus upon the governmental interest which allegedly justifies official intrusion upon the constitutionally protected interests of the private citizen," for there is "no ready test for determining reasonableness other than by balancing the need to search [or seize] against the invasion which the search [or seizure] entails." And in justifying the particular intrusion the police officer must be able to point to specific and articulable facts which, taken together with rational inferences from those facts, reasonably warrant that intrusion. The scheme of the Fourth Amendment becomes meaningful only when it is assured that at some point the conduct of those charged with enforcing the laws can be subjected to the more detached, neutral scrutiny of a judge who must evaluate the reasonableness of a particular search or seizure in light of the particular circumstances. And in making that assessment it is imperative that the facts be judged against an objective standard: would the facts available to the officer at the moment of the seizure or the search "warrant a man of reasonable caution in the belief" that the action taken was appropriate? *Cf. Carroll* v. *United States,* 267 U.S. 132, 45 S.Ct. 280, 69 L.Ed. 543 (1925); *Beck* v. *State of Ohio,* 379 U.S. 89, 96–97, 85 S.Ct. 223, 229, 13 L.Ed.2d 142 (1964). Anything less would invite intrusions upon constitutionally guaranteed rights based on nothing more substantial than inarticulate hunches, a result this Court has consistently refused to sanction. And simple " 'good faith on the part of the arresting officer is not enough. . . .' If subjective good faith alone were the test, the protections of the Fourth Amendment would evaporate, and the people would be 'secure in their persons, houses, papers and effects,' only in the discretion of the police."

Applying these principles to this case, we consider first the nature and extent of the governmental interests involved. One general interest is of course that of effective crime prevention and detection; it is this interest which underlies the recognition that a police officer may in appropriate circumstances and in an appropriate manner approach a person for purposes of investigating possibly criminal behavior even though there is no probable cause to make an arrest. It was this legitimate investigative function Officer McFadden was discharging when he decided to approach petitioner and his companions. He had observed Terry, Chilton, and Katz go through a series of acts, each of them perhaps innocent in itself, but which taken together warranted further investigation. There is nothing unusual in two men standing together on a street corner, perhaps waiting for someone. Nor is there anything suspicious about people in such circumstances strolling up and down the street, singly or in pairs. Store windows, moreover, are made to be looked in. But the story is quite different where, as here, two men hover about a street corner for an extended period of time, at the end of which it becomes apparent that they are not waiting for anyone or anything; where these men pace alternately along an identical route, pausing to stare in the same store window roughly 24 times; where each completion of this route is followed immediately by a conference between the two men on the corner; where they are joined in one of these conferences by a third man who leaves swiftly; and where the two men finally follow the third and rejoin him a couple of blocks away. It would have been poor police work indeed for an officer of 30 years' experience in the detection of thievery from stores in this same neighborhood to have failed to investigate this behavior further.

The crux of this case, however, is not the propriety of Officer McFadden's taking steps to investigate petitioner's suspicious behavior, but rather, whether there was justification for McFadden's invasion of Terry's personal security by searching him for weapons in the course of that investigation. We are now concerned with more than the governmental interest in investigating crime; in addition, there is the more immediate interest of the police officer in taking steps to assure himself that the person with whom he is dealing is not armed with a weapon that could unexpectedly and fatally be used against him. Certainly it would be unreasonable to require that police officers take unnecessary risks in the performance of their duties. American criminals have a long tradition of armed violence, and every year in this country many law enforcement officers are killed in the line of duty, and thousands more are wounded. Virtually all of these deaths and a substantial portion of the injuries are inflicted with guns and knives.

In view of these facts, we cannot blind ourselves to the need for law enforcement officers to protect themselves and other prospective victims of violence in situations where they may lack probable cause for an arrest. When an officer is justified in believing that the individual whose suspicious behavior he is investigating at close range is armed and presently dangerous to the officer or to others, it would appear to be clearly unreasonable to deny the officer the power to take necessary measures to determine whether the person is in fact carrying a weapon and to neutralize the threat of physical harm.

We must still consider, however, the nature and quality of the intrusion on individual rights which must be accepted if police officers are to be conceded the right to search for weapons in situations where probable cause to arrest for crime is lacking. Even a limited search of the outer clothing for weapons constitutes a severe, though brief, intrusion upon cherished personal security, and it must surely be an annoying, frightening, and perhaps humiliating experience. Petitioner contends that such an intrusion is permissible only incident to a lawful arrest, either for a crime involving the possession of weapons or for a crime the commission of which led the officer to investigate in the first place. However, this argument must be closely examined.

Petitioner does not argue that a police officer

should refrain from making any investigation of suspicious circumstances until such time as he has probable cause to make an arrest; nor does he deny that police officers in properly discharging their investigative function may find themselves confronting persons who might well be armed and dangerous. Moreover, he does not say that an officer is always unjustified in searching a suspect to discover weapons. Rather, he says it is unreasonable for the policeman to take that step until such time as the situation evolves to a point where there is probable cause to make an arrest. When that point has been reached, petitioner would concede the officer's right to conduct a search of the suspect for weapons, fruits or instrumentalities of the crime, or "mere" evidence, incident to the arrest.

There are two weaknesses in this line of reasoning however. First, it fails to take account of traditional limitations upon the scope of searches, and thus recognizes no distinction in purpose, character, and extent between a search incident to an arrest and a limited search for weapons. The former, although justified in part by the acknowledged necessity to protect the arresting officer from assault with a concealed weapon, is also justified on other grounds and can therefore involve a relatively extensive exploration of the person. A search for weapons in the absence of probable cause to arrest, however, must, like any other search, be strictly circumscribed by the exigencies which justify its initiation. Thus it must be limited to that which is necessary for the discovery of weapons which might be used to harm the officer or others nearby, and may realistically be characterized as something less than a "full" search, even though it remains a serious intrusion.

A second, and related, objection to petitioner's argument is that it assumes that the law of arrest has already worked out the balance between the particular interests involved here—the neutralization of danger to the policeman in the investigative circumstance and the sanctity of the individual. But this is not so. An arrest is a wholly different kind of intrusion upon individual freedom from a limited search for weapons, and the interests each is designed to serve are likewise quite different. An arrest is the initial stage of a criminal prosecution. It is intended to vindicate society's interest in having its laws obeyed, and it is inevitably accompanied by future interference with the individual's freedom of movement, whether or not trial or conviction ultimately follows. The protective search for weapons, on the other hand, constitutes a brief, though far from inconsiderable, intrusion upon the sanctity of the person. It does not follow that because an officer may lawfully arrest a person only when he is apprised of facts sufficient to warrant a belief that the person has committed or is committing a crime, the officer is equally unjustified, absent that kind of evidence, in making any intrusions short of an arrest. Moreover, a perfectly reasonable apprehension of danger may arise long before the officer is possessed of adequate information to justify taking a person into custody for the purpose of prosecuting him for a crime. Petitioner's reliance on cases which have worked out standards of reasonableness with regard to "seizures" constituting arrests and searches incident thereto is thus misplaced. It assumes that the interests sought to be vindicated and the invasions of personal security may be equated in the two cases, and thereby ignores a vital aspect of the analysis of the reasonableness of particular types of conduct under the Fourth Amendment.

Our evaluation of the proper balance that has to be struck in this type of case leads us to conclude that there must be a narrowly drawn authority to permit a reasonable search for weapons for the protection of the police officer, where he has reason to believe that he is dealing with an armed and dangerous individual, regardless of whether he has probable cause to arrest the individual for a crime. The officer need not be absolutely certain that the individual is armed; the issue is whether a reasonably prudent man in the circumstances would be warranted in the belief that his safety or that of others was in danger. And in determining whether the officer acted reasonably in such circumstances, due weight must be given, not to his inchoate and unparticularized suspicion or "hunch," but to the specific reasonable inferences which he is entitled to draw from the facts in light of his experience.

We must now examine the conduct of Officer

McFadden in this case to determine whether his search and seizure of petitioner were reasonable, both at their inception and as conducted. He had observed Terry, together with Chilton and another man, acting in a manner he took to be preface to a "stick-up." We think on the facts and circumstances Officer McFadden detailed before the trial judge a reasonably prudent man would have been warranted in believing petitioner was armed and thus presented a threat to the officer's safety while he was investigating his suspicious behavior. The actions of Terry and Chilton were consistent with McFadden's hypothesis that these men were contemplating a daylight robbery—which, it is reasonable to assume, would be likely to involve the use of weapons—and nothing in their conduct from the time he first noticed them until the time he confronted them and identified himself as a police officer gave him sufficient reason to negate that hypothesis. Although the trio had departed the original scene, there was nothing to indicate abandonment of an intent to commit a robbery at some point. Thus, when Officer McFadden approached the three men gathered before the display window at Zucker's store he had observed enough to make it quite reasonable to fear that they were armed; and nothing in their response to his hailing them, identifying himself as a police officer, and asking their names served to dispel that reasonable belief. We cannot say his decision at that point to seize Terry and pat his clothing for weapons was the product of a volatile or inventive imagination, or was undertaken simply as an act of harassment; the record evidences the tempered act of a policeman who in the course of an investigation had to make a quick decision as to how to protect himself and others from possible danger, and took limited steps to do so.

The manner in which the seizure and search were conducted is, of course, as vital a part of the inquiry as whether they were warranted at all. The Fourth Amendment proceeds as much by limitations upon the scope of governmental action as by imposing preconditions upon its initiation. The entire deterrent purpose of the rule excluding evidence seized in violation of the Fourth Amend-

ment rests on the assumption that "limitations upon the fruit to be gathered tend to limit the quest itself." Thus, evidence may not be introduced if it was discovered by means of a seizure and search which were not reasonably related in scope to the justification for their initiation.

We need not develop at length in this case, however, the limitations which the Fourth Amendment places upon a protective seizure and search for weapons. These limitations will have to be developed in the concrete factual circumstances of individual cases. Suffice it to note that such a search, unlike a search without a warrant incident to a lawful arrest, is not justified by any need to prevent the disappearance or destruction of evidence of crime. The sole justification of the search in the present situation is the protection of the police officer and others nearby, and it must therefore be confined in scope to an intrusion reasonably designed to discover guns, knives, clubs, or other hidden instruments for the assault of the police officer. The scope of the search in this case presents no serious problem in light of these standards. Officer McFadden patted down the outer clothing of petitioner and his two companions. He did not place his hands in their pockets or under the outer surface of their garments until he had felt weapons, and then he merely reached for and removed the guns. He never did invade Katz' person beyond the outer surfaces of his clothes, since he discovered nothing in his pat-down which might have been a weapon. Officer McFadden confined his search strictly to what was minimally necessary to learn whether the men were armed and to disarm them once he discovered the weapons. He did not conduct a general exploratory search for whatever evidence of criminal activity he might find.

We conclude that the revolver seized from Terry was properly admitted in evidence against him. At the time he seized petitioner and searched him for weapons, Officer McFadden had reasonable grounds to believe that petitioner was armed and dangerous, and it was necessary for the protection of himself and others to take swift measures to discover the true facts and neutralize the threat of harm if it materialized. The policeman carefully restricted his search to what was appropriate to the discovery of the particular items which he sought. Each case of this sort will, of course, have to be decided on its own facts. We merely hold today that where a police officer observes unusual conduct which leads him reasonably to conclude in light of his experience that criminal activity may be afoot and that the persons with whom he is dealing may be armed and presently dangerous, where in the course of investigating this behavior he identifies himself as a policeman and makes reasonable inquiries, and where nothing in the initial stages of the encounter serves to dispel his reasonable fear for his own or others' safety, he is entitled for the protection of himself and others in the area to conduct a carefully limited search of the outer clothing of such persons in an attempt to discover weapons which might be used to assault him. Such a search is a reasonable search under the Fourth Amendment and any weapons seized may properly be introduced in evidence against the person from whom they were taken.

Affirmed.

[Concurring opinion of Mr. Justice HARLAN has been omitted.——ED.]

Mr. Justice DOUGLAS, dissenting.

I agree that petitioner was "seized" within the meaning of the Fourth Amendment. I also agree that frisking petitioner and his companions for guns was a "search." But it is a mystery how that "search" and that "seizure" can be constitutional by Fourth Amendment standards, unless there was "probable cause" to believe that (1) a crime had been committed or (2) a crime was in the process of being committed or (3) a crime was about to be committed.

The opinion of the Court disclaims the existence of "probable cause." If loitering were in issue and that was the offense charged, there would be "probable cause" shown. But the crime here is carrying concealed weapons; and there is no basis for concluding that the officer had "probable cause" for believing that that crime was being committed. Had a warrant been sought, a magistrate would, therefore, have been unauthorized to issue one, for he can act only if there is a showing of "probable cause." We hold today that the police have greater authority to make a "seizure" and conduct a "search" than a judge has to authorize such action. We have said precisely the opposite over and over again.

In other words, police officers up to today have been permitted to effect arrests or searches without warrants only when the facts within their personal knowledge would satisfy the constitutional standard of *probable cause*. At the time of their "seizure" without a warrant they must possess facts concerning the person arrested that would have satisfied a magistrate that "probable cause" was indeed present. The term "probable cause" rings a bell of certainty that is not sounded by phrases such as "reasonable suspicion." Moreover, the meaning of "probable cause" is deeply imbedded in our constitutional history. As we stated in *Henry* v. *United States,* 361 U.S. 98, 100–102, 80 S.Ct. 168, 170:

> The requirement of probable cause has roots that are deep in our history. The general warrant, in which the name of the person to be arrested was left blank, and the writs of assistance, against which James Otis inveighed, both perpetuated the oppressive practice of allowing the police to arrest and search on suspicion. Police control took the place of judicial control, since no showing of "probable cause" before a magistrate was required....
>
> That philosophy [rebelling against these practices] later was reflected in the Fourth Amendment. And as the early American decisions both before and immediately after its adoption show, common rumor or report, suspicion, or even "strong reason to suspect" was not adequate to support a warrant for arrest. And that principle has survived to this day....
>
> ...To give the police greater power than a magistrate is to take a long step down the totalitarian path. Perhaps such a step is desirable to cope with modern forms of lawlessness. But if it is taken, it should be the deliberate choice of the people through a constitutional amendment....

There have been powerful hydraulic pressures throughout our history that bear heavily on the

Court to water down constitutional guarantees and give the police the upper hand. That hydraulic pressure has probably never been greater than it is today.

Yet if the individual is no longer to be sovereign, if the police can pick him up whenever they do not like the cut of his jib, if they can "seize" and "search" him in their discretion, we enter a new regime. The decision to enter it should be made only after a full debate by the people of this country.

Commonwealth of Pennsylvania v. Harry Mimms   *98 S.Ct. 330 (1977)*

PER CURIAM.

Petitioner Commonwealth seeks review of a judgment of the Supreme Court of Pennsylvania reversing petitioner's conviction for carrying a concealed deadly weapon and a firearm without a license. That court reversed the conviction because it held that respondent's "revolver was seized in a manner which violated the Fourth Amendment to the Constitution of the United States." Because we disagree with this conclusion, we grant the Commonwealth's petition for certiorari and reverse the judgment of the Supreme Court of Pennsylvania.

The facts are not in dispute. While on routine patrol, two Philadelphia police officers observed respondent Harry Mimms driving an automobile with an expired license plate. The officers stopped the vehicle for the purpose of issuing a traffic summons. One of the officers approached and asked respondent to step out of the car and produce his owner's card and operator's license. Respondent alighted, whereupon the officer noticed a large bulge under respondent's sports jacket. Fearing that the bulge might be a weapon, the officer frisked respondent and discovered in his waistband a .38-caliber revolver loaded with five rounds of ammunition. The other occupant of the car was also carrying a .32-caliber revolver. Respondent was immediately arrested and subsequently indicted for carrying a concealed deadly weapon and for unlawfully carrying a firearm without a license. His motion to suppress the revolver was denied, and after a trial at which the revolver was introduced into evidence respondent was convicted on both counts.

The Supreme Court of Pennsylvania reversed respondent's conviction, however, holding that the revolver should have been suppressed because it was seized contrary to the guarantees contained in the Fourth and Fourteenth Amendments to the United States Constitution.[1] The Pennsylvania court did not doubt that the officers acted reasonably in stopping the car. It was also willing to assume, *arguendo,* that the limited search for weapons was proper once the officer observed the bulge under respondent's coat. But the court nonetheless thought the search constitutionally infirm because the officer's order to respondent to get out of the car was an impermissible "seizure." This was so because the officer could not point to "objective observable facts to support a suspicion that criminal activity was afoot or that the occupants of the vehicle posed a threat to police safety." Since this unconstitutional intrusion led directly to observance of the bulge and to the subsequent "pat down," the revolver was the fruit of an unconstitutional search, and, in the view of the Supreme Court of Pennsylvania, should have been suppressed.

We do not agree with this conclusion. The touchstone of our analysis under the Fourth Amendment is always "the reasonableness in all the circumstances of the particular governmental invasion of a citizen's personal security." *Terry* v. *Ohio,* 392 U.S. 1, 19, 88 S.Ct. 1868, 1878, 20 L.Ed.2d 889 (1968). Reasonableness, of course, depends "on a balance between the public interest, and the individual's right to personal security free from arbitrary interference by law officers."

(Some footnotes have been omitted.)

[1] Commonwealth v. Mimms, 471 Pa. 546, 548, 370 A.2d 1157, 1158 (1977). Three judges dissented on the federal constitutional issue.

United States v. *Brignoni-Ponce,* 422 U.S. 873, 878, 95 S.Ct. 2574, 45 L.Ed.2d 607 (1975).

In this case, unlike *Terry* v. *Ohio,* there is no question about the propriety of the initial restrictions on respondent's freedom of movement. Respondent was driving an automobile with expired license tags in violation of the Pennsylvania Motor Vehicle Code. Deferring for a moment the legality of the "frisk" once the bulge had been observed, we need presently deal only with the narrow question of whether the order to get out of the car, issued after the driver was lawfully detained, was reasonable and thus permissible under the Fourth Amendment. This inquiry must therefore focus not on the intrusion resulting from the request to stop the vehicle or from the later "patdown," but on the incremental intrusion resulting from the request to get out of the car once the vehicle was lawfully stopped.

Placing the question in this narrowed frame, we look first to that side of the balance which bears the officer's interest in taking the action that he did. The State freely concedes the officer had no reason to suspect foul play from the particular driver at the time of the stop, there having been nothing unusual or suspicious about his behavior. It was apparently his practice to order all drivers out of their vehicles as a matter of course whenever they had been stopped for a traffic violation. The State argues that this practice was adopted as a precautionary measure to afford a degree of protection to the officer and that it may be justified on that ground. Establishing a face-to-face confrontation diminishes the possibility, otherwise substantial, that the driver can make unobserved movements; this, in turn, reduces the likelihood that the officer will be the victim of an assault.[2]

We think it too plain for argument that the State's proffered justification—the safety of the officer—is both legitimate and weighty. "Certainly it would be unreasonable to require that police officers take unnecessary risks in the performance of their duties." *Terry* v. *Ohio,* supra. 392 U.S. at 23, 88 S.Ct. at 1881. And we have specifically recognized the inordinate risk confronting an officer as he approaches a person seated in an automobile. " 'According to one study, approximately 30% of police shootings occurred when a police officer approached a suspect seated in an automobile.' Bristow, "Police Officer Shootings—A Tactical Evaluation," 54 Crim.L.C. & P.S. 93 (1963).—" *Adams* v. *Williams,* 407 U.S. 143, 148 n. 3, 92 S.Ct. 1921, 1924, 32 L.Ed.2d 612 (1972). We are aware that not all these assaults occur when issuing traffic summons, but we have before expressly declined to accept the argument that traffic violations necessarily involve less danger to officers than other types of confrontations. *United States* v. *Robinson,* 414 U.S. 218, 234, 94 S.Ct. 467, 38 L.Ed.2d 427 (1973). Indeed, it appears "that a significant percentage of murders of police officers occurs when the officers are making traffic stops." *Id.,* at 234, n. 5, 94 S.Ct. at 476.

The hazard of accidental injury from passing traffic to an officer standing on the driver's side of the vehicle may also be appreciable in some situations. Rather than conversing while standing exposed to moving traffic, the officer prudently may prefer to ask the driver of the vehicle to step out of the car and off onto the shoulder of the road where the inquiry may be pursued with greater safety to both.

Against this important interest we are asked to weigh the intrusion into the driver's personal liberty occasioned not by the initial stop of the vehicle, which was admittedly justified, but by the order to get out of the car. We think this additional intrusion can only be described as *de minimis.* The driver is being asked to expose to view very little more of his person than is already exposed. The police have already lawfully decided that the driver shall be briefly detained; the only question is whether he shall spend that period sitting in the driver's seat of his car or standing alongside it. Not only is the insistence of the police on the latter choice not a "serious intrusion upon the sanctity of the person," but it hardly

[2] The State does not, and need not, go so far as to suggest that an officer may frisk the occupants of any car stopped for a traffic violation. Rather, it only argues that it is permissible to order the driver out of the car. In this particular case, argues the State, once the driver alighted, the officer had independent reason to suspect criminal activity and present danger and it was upon this basis, and not the mere fact that respondent had committed a traffic violation, that he conducted the search.

rises to the level of a " 'petty indignity.' " *Terry v. Ohio,* supra, 392 U.S. at 17, 88 S.Ct. at 1877. What is at most a mere inconvenience cannot prevail when balanced against legitimate concerns for the officer's safety.[3]

There remains the second question of the propriety of the search once the bulge in the jacket was observed. We have as little doubt on this point as on the first; the answer is controlled by *Terry* v. *Ohio,* supra. In that case we thought the officer justified in conducting a limited search for weapons once he had reasonably concluded that the person whom he had legitimately stopped might be armed and presently dangerous. Under the standard enunciated in that case—whether "the facts available to the officer at the moment of the seizure or the search 'warrant a man of reasonable caution in the belief' that the action taken was appropriate"[4]—there is little question the officer was justified. The bulge in the jacket permitted the officer to conclude that Mimms was armed and thus posed a serious and present danger to the safety of the officer. In these circumstances, any man of "reasonable caution" would likely have conducted the "pat-down."

MR. JUSTICE MARSHALL, dissenting.

I join my Brother STEVENS' dissenting opinion, but I write separately to emphasize the extent to which the Court today departs from the teachings of *Terry* v. *Ohio,* 392 U.S. 1, 88 S.Ct. 1868, 20 L.Ed.2d 889 (1968).

In *Terry* the policeman who detained and "frisked" the petitioner had for 30 years been patrolling the area in downtown Cleveland where the incident occurred. His experience led him to watch petitioner and a companion carefully, for a long period of time, as they individually and

[3] Contrary to the suggestion in the dissent of our Brother STEVENS, *post,* p. 149, we do not hold today "that whenever an officer has an occasion to speak with the driver of a vehicle, he may also order the driver out of the car." We hold only that once a motor vehicle has been lawfully detained for a traffic violation the police officers may order the driver to get out of the vehicle without violating the Fourth Amendment's proscription of unreasonable searches and seizures.

[4] *Terry* v. *Ohio,* 392 U.S. 1, 21–22, 88 S.Ct. 1868, 1880, 20 L.Ed.2d 889 (1963).

repeatedly looked in a store window and then conferred together. Suspecting that the two men might be " 'casing' " the store for a " 'stick-up' " and that they might have guns, the officer followed them as they walked away and joined a third man with whom they had earlier conferred. At this point the officer approached the men and asked for their names. When they " 'mumbled something' " in response, the officer grabbed petitioner, spun him around to face the other two, and "patted down" his clothing. This frisk led to discovery of a pistol and to petitioner's subsequent weapons conviction. *Id.,* at 5–7, 88 S.Ct., at 1871–1872.

The "stop and frisk" in *Terry* was thus justified by the probability, not only that a crime was about to be committed, but also that the crime "would be likely to involve the use of weapons." *Id.,* at 28, 88 S.Ct., at 1883. The Court confined its holding to situations in which the officer believes "that the persons with whom he is dealing may be armed and presently dangerous" and "fear[s] for his own or others' safety." *Id.,* at 30, 88 S.Ct., at 1884. Such a situation was held to be present in *Adams* v. *Williams,* 407 U.S. 143, 92 S.Ct. 1921, 32 L.Ed.2d 612 (1972), which involved a person who "was reported to be carrying ...a concealed weapon." *Id.,* at 147, 92 S.Ct., at 1924; see *id.,* at 146, 148, 92 S.Ct., at 1923, 1924.

In the instant case, the officer did not have even the slightest hint, prior to ordering respondent out of the car, that respondent might have a gun. As the Court notes, "the officer had no reason to suspect foul play." The car was stopped for the most routine of police procedures, the issuance of a summons for an expired license plate. Yet the Court holds that, once the officer had made this routine stop, he was justified in imposing the additional intrusion of ordering respondent out of the car, regardless of whether there was any individualized reason to fear respondent.

Such a result cannot be explained by *Terry,* which limited the nature of the intrusion by reference to the reason for the stop. The Court held that "the officer's action [must be] reasonably related in scope to the circumstances which justified the interference in the first place." 392 U.S., at 20, 88 S.Ct., at 1879. In *Terry* there was an obvious connection, emphasized by the Court, *id.,* at 28–30, 88 S.Ct., at 1883–1884, between the officer's suspicion that an armed robbery was being planned and his frisk for weapons. In the instant case "the circumstances which justified the interference in the first place" was an expired license plate. There is simply no relation at all between that circumstance and the order to step out of the car....

MR. JUSTICE STEVENS, with whom MR. JUSTICE BRENNAN and MR. JUSTICE MARSHALL join, dissenting.

Ten years ago in *Terry* v. *Ohio,* 392 U.S. 1, 88 S.Ct. 1868, 20 L.Ed.2d 889, the Court held that "probable cause" was not required to justify every seizure of the person by a police officer. That case was decided after six months of deliberation following full argument and unusually elaborate briefing. The approval in *Terry* of a lesser standard for certain limited situations represented a major development in Fourth Amendment jurisprudence.

Today, without argument, the Court adopts still another—and even lesser—standard of justification for a major category of police seizures. More important, it appears to abandon "the central teaching of this Court's Fourth Amendment jurisprudence"—which has ordinarily required individualized inquiry into the particular facts justifying every police intrusion—in favor of a general rule covering countless situations. But what is most disturbing is the fact that this important innovation is announced almost casually, in the course of explaining the summary reversal of a decision the Court should not even bother to review.

Since Mimms has already served his sentence, the importance of reinstating his conviction is minimal at best. Even if the Pennsylvania Supreme Court has afforded him greater protection than is required by the Federal Constitution, the conviction may be invalid under state law. Moreover, the Pennsylvania Supreme Court may still construe its own constitution to prohibit what it described as the "indiscriminate procedure" of ordering all traffic offenders out of their vehicles. *Id.,* 370 A.2d at 1161. In all events, whatever error

the state court has committed affects only the Commonwealth of Pennsylvania. Its decision creates no conflict requiring resolution by this Court on a national level. In most cases, these considerations would cause us to deny certiorari.

No doubt it is a legitimate concern about the safety of police officers throughout the Nation that prompts the Court to give this case such expeditious treatment. I share that concern and am acutely aware that almost every decision of this Court holding that an individual's Fourth Amendment rights have been invaded makes law enforcement somewhat more difficult and hazardous. That, however, is not a sufficient reason for this Court to reach out to decide every new Fourth Amendment issue as promptly as possible. In this area of constitutional adjudication, as in all others, it is of paramount importance that the Court have the benefit of differing judicial evaluations of an issue before it is finally resolved on a nationwide basis.

This case illustrates two ways in which haste can introduce a new element of confusion into an already complex set of rules. First, the Court has based its legal ruling on a factual assumption about police safety that is dubious at best; second, the Court has created an entirely new legal standard of justification for intrusions on the liberty of the citizen.

Without any attempt to differentiate among the multitude of varying situations in which an officer may approach a person seated in an automobile, the Court characterizes the officer's risk as "inordinate" on the basis of this statement:

> According to one study, approximately 30% of police shootings occurred when a police officer approached a suspect seated in an automobile. Bristow, "Police Officer Shootings—A Tactical Evaluation," 54 Crim.L.C. & P.S. 93 (1963).— *Adams v. Williams,* 407 U.S. 143, 148 n. 3, 92 S.Ct. 1921, 1924, 32 L.Ed.2d 612 (1972). *Ante,* at 333.

That statement does not fairly characterize the study to which it refers. Moreover, the study does not indicate that police officers can minimize the risk of being shot by ordering drivers stopped for routine traffic violations out of their cars. The study reviewed 110 selected police shootings that occurred in 1959, 1960, and 1961. In 35 of those cases, "officers were attempting to investigate, control, or pursue suspects who were in automobiles."[5] Within the group of 35 cases, there were examples of officers who "were shot through the windshield or car body while their vehicle was moving"; examples in which "the officer was shot while dismounting from his vehicle or while approaching the suspect's vehicle"; and, apparently, instances in which the officer was shot by a passenger in the vehicle. *Ibid.*

In only 28 of the 35 cases was the location of the suspect who shot the officer verified. In 12 of those cases the suspect was seated behind the wheel of the car, but that figure seems to include cases in which the shooting occurred before the officer had an opportunity to order the suspect to get out. In nine cases the suspect was outside the car talking to the officer when the shooting occurred.

These figures tell us very little about the risk associated with the routine traffic stop;[6] and they lend no support to the Court's assumption that ordering the routine traffic offender out of his car significantly enhances the officer's safety. Arguably, such an order could actually aggravate the officer's danger because the fear of a search might cause a serious offender to take desperate action that would be unnecessary if he remained in the vehicle while being ticketed. Whatever the reason, it is significant that some experts in this area of human behavior strongly recommend that the po-

lice officer "never allow the violator to get out of the car. . . ."

Obviously, it is not my purpose to express an opinion on the safest procedure to be followed in making traffic arrests or to imply that the arresting officer faces no significant hazard, even in the apparently routine situation. I do submit, however, that no matter how hard we try we cannot totally eliminate the danger associated with law enforcement, and that, before adopting a nationwide rule, we should give further consideration to the infinite variety of situations in which today's holding may be applied.

The Court cannot seriously believe that the risk to the arresting officer is so universal that his safety is *always* a reasonable justification for ordering a driver out of his car. The commuter on his way home to dinner, the parent driving children to school, the tourist circling the Capitol, or the family on a Sunday afternoon outing hardly pose the same threat as a driver curbed after a high speed chase through a high-crime area late at night. Nor is it universally true that the driver's interest in remaining in the car is negligible. A woman stopped at night may fear for her own safety; a person in poor health may object to standing in the cold or rain; another who left home in haste to drive children or spouse to school or train may not be fully dressed; an elderly driver who presents no possible threat of violence may regard the police command as nothing more than an arrogant and unnecessary display of authority. Whether viewed from the standpoint of the officer's interest in his own safety, or of the citizen's interest in not being required to obey an arbitrary command, it is perfectly obvious that the millions of traffic stops that occur every year are not fungible.

Until today the law applicable to seizures of a person has required individualized inquiry into the reason for each intrusion, or some comparable guarantee against arbitrary harassment. A factual demonstration of probable cause is required to justify an arrest; an articulable reason to suspect criminal activity and possible violence is needed to justify a stop and frisk. But to eliminate any requirement that an officer be able to explain the

---

[5] *Ibid.* Since 35 is 32% of 110, presumably this is the basis for the "30%" figure used in the Court's statement. As the text indicates, however, not all of these cases involved police officers approaching a parked vehicle. Whether any of the incidents involved routine traffic offenses, such as driving with an expired license tag, is not indicated in the study.

[6] Over the past 10 years, more than 1,000 police officers have been murdered. Federal Bureau of Investigations, Uniform Crime Reports 289 (1977). Approximately 10% of those killings, or about 11 each year, occurred during "traffic pursuits and stops," but it is not clear how many of those pursuits and stops involved offenses such as reckless or high speed driving, rather than offenses such as driving on an expired license, or how often the shootings could have been avoided by ordering the driver to dismount.

reasons for his actions signals an abandonment of effective judicial supervision of this kind of seizure and leaves police discretion utterly without limits. Some citizens will be subjected to this minor indignity while others—perhaps those with more expensive cars, or different bumper stickers, or different-colored skin—may escape it entirely.

The Court holds today that "third-class" seizures may be imposed without reason; how large this class of seizures may be or become we cannot yet know. Most narrowly, the Court has simply held that whenever an officer has an occasion to speak with the driver of a vehicle, he may also order the driver out of the car. Because the balance of convenience and danger is no different for passengers in stopped cars, the Court's logic necessarily encompasses the passenger. This is true even though the passenger has committed no traffic offense. If the rule were limited to situations in which individualized inquiry identified a basis for concern in particular cases, then the character of the violation might justify different treatment of the driver and the passenger. But when the justification rests on nothing more than an assumption about the danger associated with every stop—no matter how trivial the offense—the new rule must apply to the passenger as well as to the driver.

If this new rule is truly predicated on a safety rationale—rather than a desire to permit pretextual searches—it should also justify a frisk for weapons, or at least an order directing the driver to lean on the hood of the car with legs and arms spread out. For unless such precautionary measures are also taken, the added safety—if any—in having the driver out of the car is of no value when a truly dangerous offender happens to be caught.

I am not yet persuaded that the interest in police safety requires the adoption of a standard any more lenient than that permitted by *Terry* v. *Ohio.* In this case the offense might well have gone undetected if respondent had not been ordered out of his car, but there is no reason to assume that he otherwise would have shot the officer. Indeed, there has been no showing of which I am aware that the *Terry* standard will not provide the police with a sufficient basis to take appropriate protective measures whenever there is any real basis for concern. When that concern does exist, they should be able to frisk a violator, but I question the need to eliminate the requirement of an articulable justification in each case and to authorize the indiscriminate invasion of the liberty of every citizen stopped for a traffic violation, no matter how petty.

Notes and Questions

1. Why did Chief Justice Warren say that the exclusionary rule is not very effective in regulating police actions in which arrest is not the police officer's aim?

2. For an excellent analysis of the effect of the controversial police-related Supreme Court decisions of the 1960s, see Amsterdam, "The Rights of Suspects," in N. Dorsen, ed., *The Rights of Americans* (New York: Random House, 1970). Consider the following statement by Professor Amsterdam:

   > Certain police practices (for example, the "booking" and "mugging" of suspects and the assorted minor and major indignities that attend station-house detention, ranging from the taking of a suspect's belt and shoelaces to vicious beatings) will virtually never become the subject of judicial scrutiny, because they virtually never produce evidence against the suspect. Since there can arise no exclusionary-rule challenges to these practices, there have been no significant judicial decisions concerning them; and since . . . judicial decisions are almost the only source of legal rights of suspects, suspects do not now have legal rights against or in connection with such practices.[*]

   The famous decisions of the Warren court concerning policemen [e.g., *Miranda* v. *Arizona,* 384 U.S. 436 (1966), *Escobedo* v. *Illinois,* 378 U.S. 478 (1964), *Mapp* v. *Ohio,* 367 U.S. 643 (1961)] all involved cases in which the defendant had been convicted after trial. What role can the Supreme Court play in the vast majority of cases in which defendants plead guilty and do not have a trial?

[*] Anthony Amsterdam, "The Rights of Suspects," in N. Dorsen, ed., *The Rights of Americans* (New York: Random House, 1970), p. 404.

3. The Burger court's most predictable decisions are probably those relating to police searches and almost all of these decisions have permitted questionable searches that revealed criminal conduct. From 1972 to 1977, there were twenty-five cases decided by the court involving the legality of police searches. In twenty-two of these cases, the court sustained the search as valid. One indicator of the radical change in Fourth Amendment law which occurred in these cases is that in twenty of the cases, the court reversed lower court rulings that the searches had been unconstitutional.

In another four cases decided between 1972 and 1977, the court severely limited the right of persons who were searched to invoke the exclusionary rule, which prohibits illegally seized evidence from being introduced at a hearing. Because of these rulings, evidence seized illegally may be used against a defendant in a civil case or a grand jury proceeding, although it still may not be admitted into evidence in a criminal trial. In three of these four cases, the court reversed lower court decisions which had allowed the citizen to invoke the exclusionary rule in noncriminal trial situations.

4. Chapter 41, Sec. 98 of the Massachusetts General Laws provides, in part:

[The chief and other police officers] may examine all persons abroad whom they have reason to suspect of unlawful design and may demand of them their business abroad and whither they are going. . . .

If a police officer stops a person for questioning pursuant to this section and reasonably suspects that he is in danger of life or limb, he may search such person for a dangerous weapon. If he finds such weapon or any other thing the possession of which may constitute a crime, he may take and keep it until the completion of the questioning, at which time he shall return it if lawfully possessed, or he shall arrest such person.

In such situations, the police are not required to warn individuals of their right to remain silent. Under the rule required by *Miranda* v. *Arizona,* 384 U.S. 436 (1966), the police must give this warning only when the person is in custody or freedom of action is limited. Even though the police do not explicitly inform you of your right to refuse to answer their questions, however, the right is yours regardless. You may remain silent, even if doing so may appear rude or discourteous.

Consider, however, the following from the 1972 Massachusetts Law Enforcement Officers Handbook:

If the subject refuses to cooperate, you may not compel him to answer. His refusal to cooperate may serve as an element creating probable cause. But courts will be unwilling to consider this factor alone as very important. There must be sufficient reasons in addition to such failure or refusal to answer, to justify an arrest.[*]

Would Professor Reich have been wise to refuse to answer the policeman's questions?

Should Professor Reich have been warned of his right to remain silent?

In the brief excerpt from Graham Greene's *Travels With My Aunt* at the beginning of this chapter, did the police (assuming they were American police) act properly?

5. Do you think that Officer McFadden acted properly?

6. If you had been in Officer McFadden's place, what would you have done?

7. Was his fear that Terry and Chilton had guns justifiable?

8. How much do you think Officer McFadden's fear of violence motivated his behavior?

9. If police officers are more afraid of attack than are other citizens, how can the judge, when determining the reasonableness of the officer's perception, evaluate the "specific reasonable inferences which he is entitled to draw from the facts in light of his experience"? (page 141) Under this test, would it be permissible for police officers to stop and frisk blacks more often than whites? Youths more often than the elderly? Men more often than women?

10. Why does Douglas believe that "probable cause" is a more meaningful concept than "reasonable suspicion"?

11. Would it have been lawful, after the decision of *Terry* v. *Ohio,* to interrupt Professor Reich's nighttime walks and frisk him?

12. How often is your behavior suspicious?

13. What do these decisions tell police who find a gun on someone they search about what they

---

[*] 1972 Massachusetts Law Enforcement Officers Handbook, p. 36.

should say in court? For an excellent analysis of why and when police lie in court, see Irving Younger, "The Perjury Routine," *The Nation,* 8 May 1967, p. 596.

14. What effect might the decision of *Terry* v. *Ohio* have on the Fifth Amendment right to remain silent?

15. Which of the "suspicious" persons described on page 132 might justifiably be searched for a gun?

16. Should the police have the right to carry out routine weapon checks of the general public as a protection against the danger of concealed weapons?

17. The majority opinion in the *Mimms* case describes the intrusion into a driver's liberty by the order to get out of the car as *de minimis*. How do you think Professor Reich would describe it?

3 The Media Perspective

The squad was a shock. It was absurd. Really. It was like a raft in the middle of a tidal wave, and people trying to bail. The *mobs* of complainants, thinking something could be done to help them. You know, expecting television detectives who'll run out and find the attacker and bring him to justice. Man, I saw complainants get *educated*. Burglary victims. They all wanted to know why the detectives weren't over at their apartments dusting for prints. "He came in the door. He came in the window. There must be fingerprints. Get the fingerprints." They didn't believe it when you told them you needed all ten for identification. And that anyway the burglar was probably some junkie with no address. They looked at you like you were contradicting twenty years of television.

James Mills, *Report To The Commissioner,* 1972

Throughout history, once a ruling class has established its rule, the primary function of its cultural media has been the legitimization and maintenance of its authority. Folk tales and other traditional dramatic teaching stories have always reinforced established authority, teaching that when society's rules are broken, retribution is visited upon the violators. The importance of the existing social order is always implicit in such stories.

George Gerbner and Larry Gross, "The Scary World of TV's Heavy Viewer," *Psychology Today* (April 1976)

For most people, information about the police comes not from personal experiences but from

television and newspapers. The question of whether one can obtain an accurate vision of reality and of law from the mass media is not new. Thomas Jefferson, for example, once wrote of his concern for "his fellow citizens, who reading newspapers, live and die in the belief, that they have known something of what has been passing in the world in their time." * But the introduction and popularity of television makes this issue much more important than it has ever been. In a relatively short period of time, television has become a major educational and social force in the United States. The introduction of television has caused "the most rapid change in popular communications and culture the human race has ever experienced." † The typical adult spends more time watching television than doing anything else, except for working and sleeping. ‡ By the time of high school graduation, a person will have spent an average of 15,000 hours in front of the television set, com-

* The Writings of Thomas Jefferson 73 (P.L. Ford ed. 1892–1899), cited in Harry Kranz, "The Presidency v. The Press—Who Is Right?" *Human Rights* 2, no. 1 (March 1972).

† B. Bagdikian, *The Information Machines* 182 (1971).

‡ T. Schwartz, *The Responsive Chord* 52 (1973).

pared with 12,000 hours spent in school. § For most people, television is the primary source of information. The number of television sets in the United States is nearly twice the total daily circulation of newspapers. ||

Among the most popular television dramas have been those involving the police. Each of

§ D. Cater, "The Intellectual in Videoland," *Saturday Review*, May 31, 1975.
|| *Ibid.*

these programs is watched by approximately twenty-five million people. Millions more watch these programs overseas, dubbed into other languages, where they are among the most popular programs. Epitomized by violent beginnings, car chases, violent middles, more chases, and violent endings, the shows may also be a major source of information about law.

A Television Cop in King Richard's Court   *Stephen Arons and Ethan Katsh*

In TV crime shows, the real star is the action: high-speed, twisting car chases; rooftop shootouts; and scenes in which supercops crash through locked doors and slap suspects around before finally making the collar.

The trouble with this passion for "action" is that it has a way of doing violence to the very law and order the police are sworn to uphold. Here, for instance, is TV detective Bert d'Angelo:

D'ANGELO: "What do I know about the law? I'm not a lawyer, I'm a cop."
INSPECTOR KELLER: "It's your job to enforce it."
D'ANGELO: "It's my job to protect people from the mugger, the rapist, the armed robber, and the killer. People like Joey, like my partner Mickey, did the law help them? Did the law stop that killer? All the laws in the world won't stop one man with a gun. It's going to take me or somebody like me. And you know what? I'll do it any way I can."
INSPECTOR KELLER: "You're a dangerous man, Bert."
D'ANGELO: "That's right. You'd better be damn glad I'm on your side."

Today, *Bert d'Angelo* is off the air. It would be encouraging if we could report that the series

Originally published in *Saturday Review*'s March 19, 1977 issue under the title of "How TV Cops Flout the Law."

was scratched because the average TV buff was fed up with having his 26 hours of weekly viewing time dominated by attitudes like D'Angelo's. But one look at the hard-nosed, antilaw crime series that are still running convinces us that public revulsion against lawlessness had nothing to do with the show's demise. Take, as a case in point, this scene from *Kojak*:

The police laboratory reports that particles of tin and lead with traces of red paint were found on the soles of a murdered person's shoes. Kojak theorizes that the murdered person had stepped on a red tin soldier in a collection owned by a doctor of whom Kojak is suspicious, but the detective has insufficient evidence to arrest or search. The following discussion then takes place in Kojak's office:
CAPTAIN McNEIL: "Theo, could you get your hands on one of those broken soldiers to send it to the lab?"
KOJAK: [*To another detective.*] "C'mon, Crocker, I'll do the talking and you swipe the soldier."

No doubt scenes like this can be viewed as nothing more than good, slambang entertainment. But there is more here than meets the casual eye. The image of police on television has been changing, and the change has political significance.

During the Vietnam War years, the police

earned themselves a bad image. Newscasts regularly showed helmeted riot police clubbing student protesters or gassing antiwar demonstrators. The effect was one of public disapproval. Today even the most blatantly illegal and unconstitutional behavior of police officers is glorified by an endless stream of television police dramas. The result, we believe, is that what started off as merely fictional entertainment has now begun to have the political effect of "softening up" public opinion and making it more accepting of such police conduct.

All of this very much includes our courts. Over the past few years, for example, the Supreme Court—with its conservative Nixon appointees—has been moving steadily to the right on police and civil liberties issues. The Court has been legalizing outrageous police conduct, enacting into law principles much like those projected in the TV crime shows. Those principles include the notions that the end justifies the means, that the state is always right, and that violence is perfectly acceptable when resorted to by the right people.

We are not suggesting here a one-to-one causal relationship between TV crime shows and Supreme Court decisions. And yet, one wonders. In a recent Supreme Court brief by the state of Iowa, in which the state attempted to undercut a defendant's access to his attorney during police questioning, the following statement appeared: "What is really wrong with tricking a man into telling the truth? That is one of the goals of a good Perry Mason-type cross-examination." In any case, we would say that these crime shows and the recent decisions of the Supreme Court are both modifying and responding to a body of public opinion that is increasingly permissive about the flouting of our laws by law enforcers themselves.

These dark conclusions of ours are not based on guesswork. They arise from our decision, several years ago, to monitor TV police shows and analyze them from the point of view of constitutional law. We undertook this study because we'd read an article in *The Wall Street Journal* that extolled TV police thrillers as morality plays that "encourage belief in moral values, in law, in government institutions." This encomium didn't seem to square at all with what we'd been seeing on the tube, so we decided to check the matter for ourselves....

During a one-and-a-half-year period, from the fall of 1974 to the spring of 1976, we videotaped the various TV police shows, viewing and reviewing them as if they were hypothetical court cases. We were looking for the image of law projected by the shows occupying so much of prime time, looking to see whether the behavior legitimized by television drama is the same as that required by the Constitution that the man on the beat is sworn to uphold and protect. We were thinking seriously about these essentially foolish shows because their incessantly repeated episodes are the average person's main contact with police work, and his or her primary exposure to the conflict between individual privacy and police logic. If television had indeed joined the courts, schools, and political institutions as a teacher of values, we wanted to know what was being taught.

The following typical scenes are gleaned from a statistically random sample of television police dramas screened during the course of the study. In reading these passages, one might keep in mind these words from the Bill of Rights:

> The right of the people to be secure in their persons, houses, papers, and effects, against unreasonable searches and seizures, shall not be violated....
>
> —U.S. Constitution, Amendment IV

Bumper Morgan, the "Blue Knight," is on the trail of jewelry store thieves and has been told that one of the persons he is looking for is in Room 330 of the Riverside Hotel. As the next scene opens, Morgan is at the hotel desk looking through the guest register:

CLERK: "I assume you have a warrant for that, Morgan."

MORGAN: "Yes, size 13EEE.... Give me the key."

CLERK: "I'm going to testify that it was an illegal entry."

MORGAN: "You do that."

POLICE LT.: [*Later, at the police station.*]

"Well, I've got to hand it to you, Bumper. That was damn good work."

Sergeant Friday [Jack Webb in a "Dragnet" rerun] has just taken a suspect's photograph from her roommate, Sara, and is continuing his search for information about the absent girl:
FRIDAY: "Do you have any samples of her handwriting?"
SARA: "Yes, the book by the phone. That's her address book."
FRIDAY: "We'll have to take this along with us, too. It'll be returned."
SARA: "But what do I tell Mary if she notices her picture and address book are gone?"
FRIDAY: "What time do you expect her today?"
SARA: "Right after work, about five."
FRIDAY: "All right. These'll be back by four P.M. Now, we'd appreciate it if you wouldn't say anything about it until we've completed our investigation."
SARA: "Oh, don't worry. I don't want to make things any worse than they are. I just know Mary isn't guilty. She's too nice."
FRIDAY: "Well, if she's that nice, she *isn't* guilty, and if she's guilty, she's not that nice."

These scenes are typical of the nonchalance with which some constitutional rights are obliterated on TV. We found the same fate in store for the right to counsel and the right against self-incrimination. In 15 randomly selected prime-time police programs televised during one week in March 1976, we found 43 separate scenes in which serious questions could be raised about the propriety of the police action. They stacked up as follows:

Clear constitutional violations	Omissions of constitutional rights	Police brutality and harassment
21	7	15

... The 21 "clear constitutional violations" occurred during scenes in which people were interrogated without being informed of their rights; in which evidence was taken without a warrant; or in which another form of illegal search was conducted. In the "omissions" scenes, we were unable to judge from the context whether a person's rights were being violated or whether he had waived his rights. (For example, there were scenes in which a person was being interrogated in a police station without a lawyer being present. The arrest, however, had never been shown. Therefore, what appeared to be an invasion of the suspect's rights might have resulted from a decision by the suspect to answer questions in spite of his right to remain silent.) The "police brutality and harassment" category consisted of a variety of improper, but perhaps not unconstitutional, police actions. Police officers trying to get information from various people on the street frequently obtained it by force. For example, Bumper Morgan, the Blue Knight, is by no means as chivalrous as some of his legendary namesakes:

MORGAN: [*Standing across the street from a shoeshine stand.*] "Hey, Tully, come here a minute."
TULLY: "You got something to say, come over here, my man." [*Morgan crosses the street, throws Tully against the wall, and grabs him by his shirt lapels.*]
TULLY: "Hey, man, wait a minute, what's going on here?"
MORGAN: "Let me fill you out on a couple of things, my man. First of all, I ain't your man and secondly, when you see this badge, you'll call me officer and you'll do it nice and polite. You got that?"
TULLY: [*Shaken again by Morgan.*] "Sure, sure."
MORGAN: "Now where's the stuff?"
TULLY: "What are you talking about? What stuff?"
MORGAN: [*Shakes Tully again.*] "The stones from Harry's."
TULLY: "I ain't been to Harry's, man."
MORGAN: [*Shakes Tully again.*] "Listen. You know what you are doing now? You are insulting my intelligence."

TULLY: "I haven't done anything. Who said I did something?"
MORGAN: "I said it was you. You calling me a liar? That's called contempt of cop. Now you're really making me mad." [*Morgan angrily shakes him again.*]
TULLY: "All right...all right...all right. Hey, it was this chick. She's a hooker. Her name is Linda. Now let me go and I'll find her for you."
MORGAN: "Linda, huh, yeah. I know her." [*Morgan's demeanor changes and, exuding friend-liness, he straightens out Tully's shirt, pats him, and walks away.*]
TULLY: [*Angrily.*] "I'm making a complaint on this, too."
MORGAN: "What? I just asked you a question."

Such TV abuses of constitutional rights and basic political values are not new, but they do seem to have increased dramatically shortly after the election of Richard Nixon on a hard-line, law-and-order platform. Albert Tedesco, a researcher on the communications faculty of Drexel University in Philadelphia, found that the number of law enforcement characters on television increased from 80 in 1969 to 168 in 1971. At the same time, the number of characters who were lawyers or other legal professionals decreased from 25 to 18. More significant are Tedesco's findings on illegal searches and the absence of counsel for suspects. In an average week's viewing during the period from 1969 to 1971, the number of instances in which police failed to secure search warrants, when that would have been appropriate, rose from 21 to 62. During the same period, the number of times per week that police failed to advise suspects of their right to counsel upon arrest rose from 13 to 32. Tedesco is still analyzing much of his data, but he claims to see an emerging correlation between television content and the political values of the early Nixon reign.

Beyond the statistics lie the qualitative impressions we gained from our immersion in the shows we covered in our own study. The overall image the shows project is clearly one that is alien to the Constitution. The facts would horrify the average judge if they were brought into court as real cases. Hardly a single viewing hour passes without an illegal search, or a confession obtained by coercion, or the failure to provide counsel. Warrants are not sought or issued, and hardly any mention is made of notifying suspects of their right against self-incrimination. Scores of citizens uninvolved in the crime under investigation are roughed up, shaken down, or harassed—by police. Homes, offices, and cars are broken into regularly—by police. With a sixth sense that only scriptwriters can generate, every such invasion of personal privacy turns up the real, and usually demented, criminal, or is justified because the victim was probably guilty of some crime anyway. Honest, law-abiding citizens are miraculously never hurt by these methods. There are no trials, no plea bargains, no defense, no argument about illegal police conduct affecting the guilty, the innocent, or the society as a whole....

There is an ironic inconsistency in this fast-action fairyland. The Television Broadcasters Code, a sanitized version of middle-American morality that is supposed to fend off congressional regulation of artistic expression on the tube, states that "the treatment of criminal activities should always convey their social and human effects." Crime is not supposed to pay, and on television, at least, we can be sure that it won't. But what about all the crimes committed by our video police in the process of catching their criminal counterparts? The television producers' answer is that people with badges shouldn't be treated the same way as everyone else. You can tell by the color of their hats or their horses that these people have only the noblest of aims; and they never miss. Besides, as Bert d'Angelo knew, law can't stop crime; and as TV producers know, handcuffing the police with the Bill of Rights would make for dull viewing.

One television screenwriter, discussing his own experiences, sees the same images inside the TV industry as viewers see from the outside: "The message we're getting is that authority is never wrong. The desired image is of a paternalistic 'great society' in which all law enforcement agents are properly motivated and their opponents are hippies, crazies, and un-American weirdos. It is clearly not good to criticize the institutions of the country."

This authoritarian attitude—possibly the product of a fear that only repression can prevent the world order from crumbling—comes from all corners: from producers, studios, and network executives. Like the television signal itself, the message that the status quo must be protected at all costs seems simply to be "in the air." David Rintels, president of the Writers Guild of America West, says there are no written rules and rarely any clear commands from those who own and operate commercial television, but that the prevailing values are clear to everyone in the industry. The world's most effective salesman of laundry detergent and hemorrhoid ointment is selling political ideology, too. And on television, by Rintels's lights, "make-believe makes belief."

We have asked ourselves whether the repeated images in which illegal police conduct is ignored or pays off on television are softening up the public about individual freedom. As we have discovered in showing videotape clips from our study to university students, many people are unaware of the police violations they see on the screen until after considerable discussion. It may not be a very great leap from this dim awareness of constitutional rights to the failure to recognize or react to constitutional violations perpetrated by police in everyday life. If the examples of police conduct we see on TV fail to make us more aware of the clash between civil liberties and police logic, and if crime-show violations of the Constitution always turn out to be a good thing, then these TV morality plays may amount to nothing more than reactionary propaganda.

There is a clear contradiction between what common sense and the Constitution permit flesh-and-blood police to do and what scriptwriters let TV cops get away with. This contradiction seems destined to be resolved before too long. Most of the illegal TV police activities we discovered in our study are still, a year later, violations of the Constitution. But over the past few years the Supreme Court has been moving so steadily to the right on police and civil liberties issues that

the gaps between the Court and the television may be all but erased by the next TV season.

Many of the personal freedoms that the police lobby views as "technicalities," and that the producers think would make such dull television viewing, seem lately to have escaped the consciousness of both the broadcasters and the judiciary. A single, uncontradictory image of acceptable police behavior is being fashioned by both institutions; and the Constitution and the public's welfare are having little effect on it. If we follow some of these recent decisions of the Supreme Court, we can imagine what the television cop shows of the future may be like—shows in which all the police behavior will be legal and neither the courts nor the citizenry will be offended. Herewith, several of these decisions, in each case followed by the sort of TV crime show that the decision might logically inspire:

CASE ONE: In 1974, the Supreme Court ruled in *Gustafson* v. *Florida* [and *United States* v. *Robinson*——ED.] that a police officer making even a minor custodial arrest was not violating a citizen's privacy by conducting a complete search of the citizen's person, even though the officer lacked either a warrant or probable cause to make the search.

TV SHOW ONE: A bank robbery has reportedly been committed by two men with long hair. After a frustrating search for other clues, the police decide simply to search everywhere for the money. Since searches without probable cause are generally unacceptable to the courts, but since almost everyone spends some time in his car daily and has a broken taillight or commits some minor traffic offense, over the next three days the police make traffic arrests of every long-haired male in town. Lots of contraband is turned up, personal grudges are acted out, and the town is generally "cleaned up," but no money is found. Under the pressure of prosecution for drug possession, however, one person reveals information leading to the bank robbers. The dragnet idea is commended as being generally useful.

CASE TWO: In 1976, the Supreme Court ruled in *Hampton* v. *U.S.* that police setting up a defendant are not guilty of entrapping him, nor have they conducted themselves so outrageously as to violate his due process rights, as long as the defendant "was predisposed to commit the crime." The police in this case supplied narcotics to the defendant and also bought the narcotics from him.

TV SHOW TWO: Several police on the city force discover that searches of citizens (such as those in *Show One*) have yielded narcotics that do not have to be turned in as evidence if no charges are filed against the defendant. This leaves several officers with large stores of heroin, which they begin peddling on the sly (in plain clothes and disguises) to supplement their meager incomes. One street pusher with a grudge catches on to the scam and tries to contact federal agents to expose the city police. Before he can do this, the police get wind of it and set him up, selling him one pound of heroin as usual, but buying it from him in small packages a few hours later as undercover agents. The buyer is then arrested by the police and charged with selling narcotics. Claims that the police were running an illegal dope ring are met with statements that this was a ruse to catch pushers and that the defendant was a known pusher. The defendant is convicted and the police go on with their business.

CASE THREE: In 1976, the Supreme Court ruled in *Paul* v. *Davis* that the police did not violate a citizen's privacy or his due process rights when they publicly circulated a flyer with his name and picture under the title "Active Shoplifters." The citizen had never been convicted of shoplifting, but had been detained as a shoplifter by a store detective two years earlier. No charges had ever been placed against him. While the majority opinion condoned this police tactic, Justice Brennan dissented: "The Court today holds that police officials acting in their official capacities as law enforcers may on their own initiative, and without trial, constitutionally condemn innocent individuals as criminals and thereby brand them

with one of the most stigmatizing and debilitating labels in our society."

TV SHOW THREE: At this point, the Court's steady progress in strengthening the forces of law and order by legalizing crimes by police officers overtakes television police dramas. As television values and judicial values merge, the definitions of crime and freedom are reversed, and a brave new fiction emerges in the public mind: More freedom for police reduces crime. *Show Three* may appear on the networks, in the courts, or on the street.

One may wonder whether the Court shares with television the blindness to individual liberty that is the easy byproduct of a single-minded devotion to stopping crime. One may wonder, too, whether the public consciousness is pushed in unhealthy directions by either of these great norm-molding institutions, or whether in court and on television we simply get what we want, as the market researchers would say.

The line between television logic, police logic, and judicial logic is becoming all but indiscernible. The ideological tension between security and liberty seems to have diminished, very much to the disadvantage of liberty. For television, the challenge is how to give sane, constitutional values access to the TV crime scene. Meanwhile, sad to say, our study of television police dramas indicates that a very dubious type of police logic is in clear control of the airwaves.

Notes and Questions

1. Police programs misrepresent the nature of police work as well as the nature of constitutional rights. Consider the following:

> The society which TV police shows imply is possible has the police as our primary protectors and saviors from criminals. This image actually does a disservice to both citizens and the real police. Citizens come to expect the police to reduce the crime rate. They hold the police primarily responsible if the crime rate goes up. Policemen, who then become the object of criticism, respond by attacking

the "handcuffs" placed on them by the Supreme Court. The TV image which increases the status of police thus creates an impossible task and leads to unwarranted criticism of or insensitivity to the very values which protect innocent persons from police-state activities.

There is an interesting experiment one can do when watching a television police show. Concentrate on the information the police officer has. Disregard the information communicated to the viewer which the police officer does not know. The errorless identification of criminals by TV police will then be seen to be both miraculous and illegal. We cannot and should not expect the same from local police officers. As an antidote to the message communicated by these programs, consider the following facts:

1. The best estimates are that at least half the crimes committed are never reported to the police. Even Kojak could not solve these crimes. He would not know whom or what to begin looking for.

2. Persons who are caught by the police rarely are convicted of the main crime they are arrested for. Plea bargaining usually results in a reduction of charges. In New York City, for example, 80% of the persons arrested for felonies in 1974 pleaded guilty to misdemeanors.

3. The recidivism rate for persons who are released from prison is so high that even if the police could catch everyone who committed a crime, a serious problem would remain. A major part of the problem is the criminal justice system itself.

The point to be understood is that crime is caused by many complex and interrelated factors. Police shows end happily with arrest but in real life this is only the starting point in what one judge has called "America's only working railroad." *

2. The uniform message presented by police programs seems to be systematically created and not merely the result of coincidence. A 1971 survey of the Writers Guild of America revealed that of those who responded:

Eighty-six (86) percent have found, from personal experience, that censorship exists in television. Many state, further, that they have never written a script, no matter how innocent, that has not been censored.

Eighty-one (81) percent believe that television is presenting a distorted picture of what is happening in this country today—politically, economically, and racially.

Only eight (8) percent believe that current television programming is "in the public interest, convenience and necessity," as required by The Federal Communications Act of 1934, Title 47, U.S. Code, Secs. 307a, 307d.*

The kind of content control exercised over scriptwriters for police programs was graphically illustrated by David Rintels, president of the Writers Guild of America-West, in testimony before the Senate Subcommittee on Constitutional Rights several years ago. Mr. Rintels stated that:

I was asked to write another episode of "The FBI" on a subject of my choice, at about the time, five or six years ago, when the four little black girls were killed by the bomb in the Birmingham Church. It had been announced that the FBI was involving itself in the case and I told the producer I wanted to write a fictional account of it. He checked with the sponsor, the Ford Motor Company, and with the FBI—every proposed show is cleared sequentially through the producing company, Quinn Martin; the Federal Bureau of Investigation; the network, ABC; and the sponsor, Ford; and any of the four can veto any show for any reason, which it need not disclose—and reported back that they would be delighted to have me write about a Church bombing subject only to these stipulations: The Church must be in the North, there could be no Negroes involved, and the bombing could have nothing at all to do with civil rights. After I said I wouldn't write that program, I asked if I could do a show on police brutality, also in the news at that time; certainly, the answer came back, as long as the charge was trumped up, the policeman vindicated, and the man who brought the specious charge prosecuted.†

---

* Ethan Katsh and Stephen Arons, "Television, the Law, and the Police," *Wall Street Journal*, July 22, 1975, p. 16. © 1975 Dow Jones & Company, Inc. All Rights Reserved.

* *Hearings on Freedom of the Press Before the Subcommittee on Constitutional Rights of the Senate Committee on the Judiciary*, 92nd Cong. 1st and 2nd sessions, at 522 (1972).

† *Ibid.*, at 525.

4 Discretionary Justice

The police—with limited formal training and minimal qualification requirements—are granted more latitude and discretion in dealing with the lives and welfare of people than any other professional group.

> Abraham S. Blumberg and Arthur Niederhoffer, "The Police in Social and Historical Perspective," in Blumberg and Niederhoffer, *The Ambivalent Force: Perspectives on the Police* (1970)

The exercise of discretionary power by all participants in the legal process is a central theme of this book. Many citizens, however, find it difficult to accept the fact that judges, prosecutors, jurors, and police, have discretion. They cling, in Judge Jerome Frank's words, to the "myth of certainty," and to the belief that law is predictable and certain. They see the mere existence of discretion as being a negation of law. The excerpt that follows analyzes why discretion is an inevitable component of the system.

Once this is recognized, the most important question becomes when and how discretion should be exercised so as to lead to the most equitable result. As Karl Davis wrote in his book *Discretionary Justice,*

> Engraved in stone on the Department of Justice Building in Washington, on the Pennsylvania Avenue side where swarms of bureaucrats and others pass by, are these five words: "Where law ends tyranny begins."
>
> I think that in our system of government, where law ends tyranny need not begin. Where law ends, discretion begins, and the exercise of discretion may mean either beneficence or tyranny, either justice or injustice, either reasonableness or arbitrariness.*

* Karl Davis, *Discretionary Justice* (Baton Rouge: Louisiana State University Press, 1969), p. 3.

Arrest: The Decision to Take a Suspect into Custody   *Wayne R. LaFave*

It is obvious that in practice some discretion must be employed somewhere in the existing criminal justice system. The exercise of discretion in interpreting the legislative mandate is necessary because no legislature has succeeded in formulating a substantive criminal code which clearly encompasses all conduct intended to be made criminal and which clearly excludes all other conduct. Poor draftsmanship and a failure to revise the criminal

From Wayne R. LaFave, *Arrest: The Decision to Take a Suspect into Custody* (Boston: Little, Brown and Company, 1965), pp. 69–72, 76–78. (Some footnotes omitted.) Reprinted by permission.

law to eliminate obsolete provisions have contributed to existing ambiguities. However, even where care has been taken, it has not been possible to draft substantive provisions which are entirely free from ambiguity. This is a result not only of limitations upon the effectiveness of language but also of the inability of a legislature to envisage all of the day-to-day law enforcement problems which may arise.

Even more important is the fact that not enough financial resources are allocated to make possible enforcement of all the laws against all offenders. The legislative body responsible for granting appropriations makes a general decision as to how much it is willing to pay for law enforcement, but usually provides no guidance as to how this sum is to be expended. Allocation of resources to enforcement agencies is ordinarily decided by a municipal legislative body, while the criminal law is defined by the state legislature, which often leaves the administrator subject to conflicting legislative mandates. The same conflict occurs when the state legislature appropriates money to a state police unit, since the crime-defining and budget decisions are essentially unrelated even within the same unit of government. Because of the obvious dilemma created by limited resources and lack of established priorities for enforcement, the necessity of discretionary enforcement on this basis has received some recognition. Yet there are no suggested principles to guide the exercise of such discretion.[1]

Finally, the exercise of discretion seems necessary in the current criminal justice system for reasons unrelated to either the interpretation of criminal statutes or the allocation of available enforcement resources. This is because of the special circumstances of the individual case, particularly the characteristics of the individual offender which "differentiate him from other offenders in personality, character, sociocultural background, the mo-

[1] Police materials are usually devoted to *how* to make an arrest and *when* to arrest in terms of probability of guilt, with the allocation of resources problem completely ignored. An exception is California State Department of Education, California Police Officers' Training Bulletin No. 71, Police Supervisory Control 26–27 (1957): "Finally, note must be made of one insurmountable obstacle to supervisory control which confronts every chief of police: the fact that it is absolutely impossible to enforce all laws. One illustration will suffice.

"A study of traffic violations at Rose and Grove Streets, Berkeley, California, revealed that if conditions at other intersections were similar, three million violations of traffic regulations were occurring daily in Berkeley and that it would take more than fourteen thousand traffic officers to enforce the traffic laws in that city. With hundreds of thousands of federal, state and municipal laws to be enforced, it becomes obvious that considerable discretion must be exercised in the direction of the enforcement policy.

"It is at this point that the difficulty is met. The general enforcement policy of a police department is partly the result of traditional practices, partly the general orders of the chief modifying or amplifying these unwritten laws, and partly the character that the intelligent and honest official puts into his work."

tivations of his crime, and his particular potentialities for reform or recidivism." The infinite variety of individual circumstances complicates administration by mere application of rules. Justice Charles D. Breitel, who has had extensive administrative, legislative, and judicial experience, stresses this point:

> If every policeman, every prosecutor, every court, and every post-sentence agency performed his or its responsibility in strict accordance with rules of law, precisely and narrowly laid down, the criminal law would be ordered but intolerable.

Individualized treatment of an offender, based upon the circumstances of the particular case, is well recognized at the sentencing stage, where discretion is provided. These same circumstances may be apparent at the arrest stage and may seem to the police to dictate that the criminal process not be invoked against a particular offender. While sentence discretion is widely recognized, arrest discretion is not. This may reflect an assumption that, while individual circumstances may justify mitigation, the individualization of criminal justice should never go so far as to result in the complete exoneration of a particular offender. The contrary view is that the individual circumstances sometimes make conviction and even arrest excessive, so that proper administration requires the exercise of discretion at the early as well as at subsequent stages in the process. . . .

. . . Almost every state has some legislation relevant to police discretion. However, there is a distinct lack of originality in the statutes defining the powers and duties of the police agencies. It is obvious that the question of police discretion has not received careful legislative attention. Most of the statutes have existed for many years, usually without the benefit of judicial interpretation. Therefore, while a good case can be made for the proposition that the state legislatures have generally denied the police authority to exercise discretion a review of all the applicable laws leaves the matter in some doubt.

The most convincing evidence that the police have been denied discretion is found in statutes which set forth the duties of various police agencies. Some impose a duty upon sheriffs or city police to arrest "all" violators of the criminal law. Others employ more limited terms, declaring it the officer's responsibility to arrest "all felons" or "all persons committing an offense in his presence." A lesser number state a duty to enforce "all" the criminal laws. Seldom are the statutes phrased in permissive terms.

Statutes frequently impose a duty of full enforcement in a particular, sensitive area of the criminal law such as gambling, prostitution, narcotics, or liquor violations. While these provisions do seem to demonstrate a special legislative desire for full enforcement in these areas, it is questionable whether one can properly infer from them a recognition that discretion does exist in regard to crimes not specifically mentioned. In practice, police do tend to conform to specific commands for full enforcement while at the same time exercising considerable discretion in other enforcement areas.

Over two-thirds of the states have passed general arrest statutes prescribing the circumstances under which police can make an arrest without warrant. A great majority are in permissive terms, usually indicating that the police "may" arrest upon a given quantum of evidence. By comparison, only a few states have declared that police "shall" arrest when such evidence exists. Occasionally courts have suggested that even the permissive language must be read as imposing a duty to arrest when the officer obtains the necessary evidence.

Questions

1. How can we assure that discretionary powers will not be used unjustly?

2. What other actions might Officer McFadden in *Terry* v. *Ohio* have taken?

3. What is the difference between discretion and unchecked power?

4. How can we determine whether in a particular instance a police officer is exercising discretion or unchecked power?

5. What does the phrase "law and order" mean to you? Is discretionary power compatible with "law and order"?

6. In what ways are a police officer's duties similar to a judge's?

7. What discretion does your teacher have? Does she or he have too much discretion? What limits, if any, are there on his or her powers? Are there comparable limitations on police discretion?

8. Consider the following findings of a recent study:
   Our observations...show that officers decided not to make arrests of one or more suspects for 43 percent of all felonies and 52 percent of all misdemeanors judged by observers as situations where an arrest could have been made on probable cause. Something other than probable cause is required, then, for the officer to make an arrest.

   For the police, that something else is a *moral belief* that the law should be enforced and the violation sanctioned by the criminal justice system. The line officer usually reaches that decision by conducting an investigation to establish probable cause and by conducting a "trial" to determine who is guilty. His decision, therefore, is in an important sense judicial. This judicial determination will be influenced, as it is in the courts, by the deference and demeanor of the suspect, argument as to mitigating circumstances, complainant preferences for justice, and the willingness of the complainant to participate in seeing that it is done. All in all, an officer not only satisfies probable cause but also concludes after his careful evaluation that the suspect is guilty and an arrest is therefore just.*

9. Does requiring police officers to justify their actions before a civilian review board take away the officers' discretion?

10. In an earlier article, Professor George Kirkham wrote that "an officer can never back down from his responsibility to enforce the law." What do you think he meant by this statement?

* Albert Reiss, *The Police and the Public* (New Haven: Yale University Press, 1971), p. 134.

5 A Societal Perspective

It is a startling *déjà vu* experience for someone immersed in contemporary police problems to search early English history for the roots of our modern police system. The feeling grows as the record of the centuries is rolled back to the Magna Carta. Between the lines of the law can be deciphered the same problems and complaints about the police: abuse of power, false arrest, oppression, apathy, and their ignorance of and contempt for the law. For example, the Magna Carta of June 15, 1215, is replete with restrictions upon the police of those days, the sheriffs, bailiffs, and constables. It is a fair and reasonable assumption that since the following chapters were part of that epochal document, they were meant to correct abuses that were widespread.

> 28. No constable or other bailiff of ours shall take anyone's grain or other chattels without immediately paying for them in money....
> 29. No constable shall require any knight to give money in place of his ward of a castle....
> 30. No sheriff or bailiff of ours or any one else shall take horses or wagons of any free man for carrying purposes except on the permission of that free man....
> 38. No bailiff for the future shall place any one to his law on his simple affirmation without credible witnesses brought for this purpose.

And the remedies of that ancient time were no different from those proposed today: recruit better policemen, stiffen the penalties for malfeasance, create a civilian review board as an external control upon the police. King John agreed that

> 45. We will not make justiciars, constables, sheriffs, or bailiffs except of such as know the law of the realm and are well inclined to observe it.

The barons opposing King John wanted more than mere promises and forced the king to consent to the supervision of a civilian review board of twenty-five barons with power to enforce compliance with the law.

Abraham S. Blumberg and Arthur Niederhoffer, "The Police in Social and Historical Perspective," in Blumberg and Niederhoffer, *The Ambivalent Force: Perspectives on the Police* (1970)

Both in England and America, the emergence of full-time, uniformed police forces is traceable to industrialization, the growth of cities, and resultant social disorders. Prior to the formation of organized police forces in the mid-1800s, a night watch system existed in most of the towns in the United States. These watchmen alarmed the people in case of fire, prevented destruction by stray animals, and, in general, fulfilled some of the order maintenance functions performed by the police today. Solving crimes was not an official function of these early police forces. Indeed, responsibility for catching criminals rested primarily on the victim of the crime, who could, once a suspect was found, hire a constable to take the suspect into custody.

Riots and gang wars in the early 1800s made it apparent that such a system was inadequate. As one historian has written,

> New York City was alleged to be the most crime-ridden city in the world, with Philadelphia, Baltimore and Cincinnati not far behind.... Gangs of youthful rowdies in the larger cities ... threatened to destroy the American reputation for respect for law. ... Before their boisterous demonstrations the crude police forces of the day were often helpless.*

In 1838, therefore,

> Boston created a day police force to supple-

* Arthur Charles Cole, "The Irrepressible Conflict, 1859–1865," *A History of American Life* in 12 volumes, vol. VIII, Arthur M. Schlesinger, Sr. and Dixon Ryan Fox, eds. (New York: Macmillan, 1934), pp. 154–155.

ment the nightwatch, and other cities soon followed its lead. Crime, cities were finding, was no respecter of daylight. There were certain inherent difficulties, however, in these early two-shift police systems. Keen rivalries existed between the day and night shifts, and separate administrations supervised each shift. Recognizing the evils of separate police forces, the New York Legislature passed a law in 1844 that authorized creating the first unified day and night police, thus abolishing its nightwatch system. Ten years later Boston consolidated its nightwatch with the day police.

Following the New York model, other cities developed their own unified police forces during the next decade. By the 1870s the Nation's largest cities had full-time police forces. And by the early 1900s there were few cities of consequence without such unified forces. These forces gradually came under the control of a chief or commissioner, often appointed by the mayor, sometimes with the consent of the city council and sometimes elected by the people †

† Task Force Report: *The Police,* Report to the President's Commission on Law Enforcement and the Administration of Justice (1967), p. 5.

The following articles contain several additional perspectives on how the police reflect the nature of a society and how they can affect it. In the first article, Bernard Garmire suggests that the redefinition of police responsibilities and the reorganization of the police into more efficient units would restore public confidence in the police. The second selection presents a much more radical analysis of the role the police play in contemporary American society, arguing that they reflect the values and needs of the economic system. The final article describes the Japanese police, a force that operates very differently from any police force in the United States.

It will quickly become evident to the reader that these three selections present very different, and often contradictory, views on the role that the police should play in society. They share, however, an important message: any discussion of the police should consider the nature of the society in which it is located.

The Police Role in an Urban Society *Bernard L. Garmire*

If we are to restore any semblance of faith in the police by the public—and the police themselves—we must begin first by defining the police role very carefully so that it does not distort reality. The historical definition of the police role eventually achieved this regrettable result by fostering the belief that police, because they were present and visible twenty-four hours a day, could function as a gigantic surrogate service agency to the community handling all the needs of the people all of the time.

From Bernard L. Garmire, "The Police Role in an Urban Society," in Robert F. Steadman, ed., *The Police and the Community* (Baltimore: The Johns Hopkins University Press, 1972), pp. 3–7. Copyright by The Committee for Economic Development. Reprinted by permission.

To establish credibility or faith in the police service requires that the police role be delineated so that there are reasonable expectations about what the police should do and can do. Once we know what the police are to do, then we can address the three critical problems of police recruitment, training, and leadership. As matters stand now, we do not know what we are recruiting men for, what kind of training and education they ought to be developing—because we don't know where we want to lead them in the first place.

The result of this failure is that the police perform two conflicting basic roles that cannot be integrated administratively in any single agency. Yet operationally, individual police officers are assigned those very same conflicting roles and are expected to master them psychologically so that, in the street, they can perform each with proficiency as the occasion demands. These two roles are community service and law enforcement.

I define the community-service role as one in which the police provide essentially a social service to the community; i.e., intervening in domestic quarrels, handling those who are under the influence of alcohol or drugs, working with dependent and neglected children, rendering emergency medical or rescue services and generally acting as a social agency of last resort—particularly after 5:00 P.M. and on weekends—for the impoverished, the sick, the old, and the lower socioeconomic classes.

An example of the community-service role is the family fight. What is needed here are the skills and resources of a marriage counselor, a psychiatrist, or a social worker. It does not serve the interests of either the state or the man and the wife to make an arrest. Nor does it serve the interests of the state or the family simply to suppress the noise level of the quarrel or to prevent an assault by invoking the threat of arrest and jail.

I define the law-enforcement role as one in which the police enforce criminal laws. This is the role for the crime fighter and the thief catcher. In this role, the primary tasks are criminal investigation, collection of evidence, interrogation of suspects, arrests of suspects, maintenance of order and safety, combatting organized crime, suppression of disturbances and riots, and, generally, the hard core enforcement of criminal laws.

The commission of a robbery in which the victim was brutally assaulted clearly falls within the law-enforcement role. In this case, law-enforcement and criminal-investigation skills are required to identify the suspect and to bring him before the court.

Police agencies and police officers are attempting to fill both roles, and I submit that they are not properly trained, equipped, or capable of performing *either* role with any degree of success, let alone both of them. Even if the numbers of policemen were vastly increased, even if their train-

ing were improved, and even if their resources were expanded, I still submit that they could not perform both roles—so sharply do they conflict and so different are the skills required. One person simply cannot reasonably be expected to master both roles intellectually and jump psychologically from one to another in an instant's notice. Furthermore, the law-enforcement role of police is so strongly perceived by some citizens that they totally reject the idea that police could or should fill a community-service role even if they were capable of doing so.

Here is the kind of thing that we expect of today's police officer:

At 9:00 P.M. he responds to a robbery in progress and upon arrival exchanges gunshots with a suspect.

At 10:00 P.M., after he has made a report of the incident, he receives a call of a violent family brawl. He is white, they are black, and the suspect with whom he just exchanged gunfire an hour earlier was black. The officer is expected to handle their marital problems effectively and dispassionately, but he also has to return to radio service quickly because it is Saturday night and two other calls are waiting for him. Need more be said? Do we really believe that one man can do this night after night, month in and month out? Granted, the officer is not fired upon or assaulted every night. But the potential is there and he knows it: witness the frequent news reports concerning the ambushes, sniping, and other offenses directed against police. Is it not time that we took notice of the realities of policing and admit that one man or one group of men cannot intellectually and psychologically do all this?

In order to consider this question, the Miami police department collaborated with the Psychiatric Institute Foundation to study police response to stress. This study was financed by the Law Enforcement Assistance Administration (LEAA). The results of this study...suggest that the multiplicity of roles that officers must fill contributes significantly to police fatigue and stress. My own personal experience of thirty-three years in the police service in all ranks strongly affirms this finding.

Such studies must be regarded only as a beginning; we must explore much more fully the possibilities of developing a psychiatric set of standards for police work, which in turn poses this basic question: What are the roles police perform and what are the criteria and measurement methods to identify those applicants who are best suited to perform each role or a combination of roles? We must examine the hypothesis that there is a constellation of psychological factors that makes some persons better suited for one kind of police role than another. We must determine what makes a good community-service worker, a good crime fighter, and a good administrator; we must discover, if possible, ways of finding persons who can perform adequately in two or more different roles.

Two Agencies Under Civilian Control

What is implicit in the foregoing analysis is a drastic reorganization of the administration of the police function.... The police service must be reorganized both structurally and functionally so that it conforms in a rational way to the realities of the roles to be performed. I will outline here one organizational scheme for accomplishing this.

The contemporary police organization should be divided into two agencies under one department, one concerned with the law-enforcement function, the other with the community-service function. The community-service agency would operate on a twenty-four-hour basis and would be staffed by people who are psychologically best suited for this function as well as specifically educated and trained to perform it. There would be no need for them to operate in uniform, and, depending on the locality generally, no need for them to be armed. They may or may not have full powers of arrest.

The law-enforcement agency would function as criminal investigators, thief catchers, and so forth, and it likewise would be composed of people psychologically attuned to the law-enforcement role and for it. In essence, they would be performing the police functions of patrol and investigation; they would, of course, be armed and possess full police powers.

Administering both agencies at the departmental level would be a professional staff composed of public administrators directly responsible to the elected or appointed head of government. The public administrators would not necessarily be policemen. Indeed, they should be chosen for their administrative expertise—not just for their law-enforcement or community-service expertise. The overhead or staff agencies should be predominantly staffed by civilians possessing required skills in such areas as planning, budgeting, personnel administration, and systems analysis. I wish to emphasize the importance of developing and maintaining civilian control over both the law-enforcement and community-service agencies.

The highest career professional in each agency would be a director, who reports to the public administrator. The director would have only a small administrative staff because the bulk of the staff services would be provided and controlled at the departmental level, further strengthening the concept of civilian control. In short, the law-enforcement and community-service agencies would be strictly line or operating agencies.

Additionally, a citizen advisory board should be established composed of persons appointed and elected to that board. The members should represent and be drawn from all elements of the community. This would be a board charged not with investigating civilian complaints against the police, but with the far more important responsibility of advising the department on problems, means, and goals. The board should deliberately seek to provide policy input and feedback.

Questions

1. Why doesn't Garmire believe that professionalism and better training are the best solutions?

2. Why should the community service role be part of the police department? Why should these workers be called police officers?

3. What benefits might there be to a police officer engaging in both law enforcement and community service activities?

4. Would Garmire's proposal increase or decrease the power of the police? Would there be more or less civilian control over the police?

The Iron Fist and the Velvet Glove　*Center for Research on Criminal Justice*

During the past ten years, the police have taken on an unprecedented importance in the U.S. In the past, the police forces in this country were, for the most part, fragmented and scattered in many different levels and jurisdictions, uncoordinated with each other, without central planning or comprehensive strategies. Relatively little money was spent on strengthening local police forces and little attention was given to developing new concepts and techniques of police practice. In the 1960's all this began to change.

First, there has been a rapid growth in the sheer number of police in this country and in the amount of funds generated to support them. According to one estimate, the total number of Federal, State, and local police officers increased from 339,000 in 1967 to about 445,000 in 1974. In some areas, the increase has been even more dramatic. For example, in California the number of authorized police personnel has been increasing at a rate of 5–6 percent annually, while the overall population is increasing at about 2.5 percent a year. In California in 1960, there were about 22,000 police officers; in 1972, there were almost 52,000, and it has been estimated that there will be 180,000 by the year 2,000. Government spending on the police, too, has been rising significantly. The rate of spending on criminal justice *generally* has been increasing for about twenty years, and increasing more rapidly in the last decade. In 1955, government spending on the criminal justice system amounted to about one-half of one percent of the U.S. Gross National Product (GNP); in 1965 the rate had risen to two-thirds of one percent. By 1971, government spending on criminal justice was about one percent of GNP, and the rate of increase since 1966 was about five times as great as it was in the previous decade.

Center for Research on Criminal Justice, *The Iron Fist and the Velvet Glove* (Oakland, Calif., 1975), pp. 7–12. Reprinted by permission. [Footnotes omitted.]

Over \$10.5 billion was spent on criminal justice, at all levels of government, in 1971. In 1974, the figure reached over \$14 billion, over \$8 billion of which went for the police alone.

Even more significant than this increase in the size and fiscal importance of the police is the growing sophistication and increasing centralization of the U.S. police system over the last ten years. For the first time, the Federal government has become deeply involved in the police system, mainly through the creation of the massive Federal Law Enforcement Assistance Administration (LEAA), devoted primarily to standardizing and centralizing the police and other criminal justice agencies, and to funding the development of new and increasingly sophisticated police strategies. At the same time, the 1960's saw the rise of a whole "police-industrial complex," a rapidly growing industry that took technical developments originally created for overseas warfare or for the space program and, backed by government funds, applied them to the problems of domestic "order" in the United States.

In addition to the rise of new, sophisticated technologies, another striking development in the U.S. police apparatus during the sixties was the growth of new strategies of community penetration and "citizen participation" that sought to integrate people in the process of policing and to secure the legitimacy of the police system itself. Along with this has been a dramatic increase in the money and attention given to various kinds of "police education" programs and other efforts designed to give a new "professional" look to the police. The federal government in the early 1970's began spending about \$20 million annually on police education in the universities, colleges, and even high schools, and today over 750 colleges and universities offer degrees or courses in "police science" or "criminal justice." On the other side of the coin, the police have developed a variety of new "tough" specialized units—special antiriot and tactical patrol forces, "special weapons" teams, and highly sophisticated intelligence units. And the growth and spread of the U.S. police apparatus has not stopped at the national boundaries; since the sixties, the United States has been actively exporting its police concepts, technologies, and personnel to the far corners of the American empire. Finally, the government effort to beef up and streamline the police system has been matched by an equally dramatic increase in the number of private police, security guards, and private corporations engaged in producing and selling all kinds of complicated security hardware and services.

The new emphasis on the police is also reflected in popular culture in the United States. Today there are so many television shows dealing with the police that it is hard to keep up with them, and movies with some kind of police theme dominate the neighborhood theaters.

What happened to cause this sudden growth in the size and significance of the police? Most importantly, the 1960's and early '70's have been a time of great crisis for American capitalism—not the first crisis the U.S. capitalist system has undergone, but one of the most severe. The crisis has had many different aspects, economic, social, and political, but in terms of the growth of the police, the most important is the erosion of the popular acceptance of the corporate system and of the political power that supports it, both at home and abroad. During the last ten years, this crisis in legitimacy has been manifested in many ways—not only in the widespread resistance and rebellion in the Third World, student, and White working-class communities, but in the rapidly and steadily rising rates of street crime. The combined rates of the seven "serious" crimes as defined by the F.B.I. (murder, rape, robbery, burglary, aggravated assault, larceny, and auto theft) rose by 158 percent between 1960 and 1971. Crime became a central preoccupation and fear for many people during this period, and emerged as a crucial political issue of the sixties. It became especially critical in the "inner cities," where by the early seventies one person in every five was being victimized by some form of serious crime each year.

The new emphasis on strengthening and streamlining the police is one of the most important responses of the American government to the widespread challenge to its legitimacy. It goes along with other, similar attempts to refurbish the "correctional" system, to harness the public schools more tightly to corporate values and interests, and to rationalize the "mental health" and welfare systems in the face of the growing disintegration of the "consensus" that was supposed to exist in the U.S. in the 1940's and '50's. How successful the state is in developing such means of integration and repression will depend on how effectively we are able to resist that development.

The Role of the Police

Why are we so concerned about the growth of the police in the first place? Why don't we welcome it as a step toward a safer and more decent society?

The answer lies in our basic view of the functions that the police perform in the U.S. today, and have performed throughout U.S. history. Although the actual role of the police at any given time—like the role of the state in general or advanced capitalist societies—is complex and should not be oversimplified, it is clear that the police have *primarily* served to enforce the class, racial, sexual, and cultural oppression that has been an integral part of the development of capitalism in the U.S. As long as this function remains, any strengthening of the powers of the police, any movement toward greater efficiency or sophistication in their methods, must be seen as inherently contrary to the interests and needs of the majority of people in this country, and in other countries where the U.S. police system penetrates.

Our position is very different from that of most people who write about the police. Whether "liberal" or "conservative," most commentators on the police share a common assumption: they all take the existence of the police for granted. They assume that any modern society necessarily has to have a large and ever-present body of people whose purpose is to use coercion and force on other people. "Conservatives" usually point to such things as the decline in respect for authority, the breakdown of traditional values or of family discipline, as the source of the need for the police, who are seen as a "thin blue line" holding back the forces of evil and destruction that lurk just beneath the surface of civilization. This view is often found within police departments (and was promoted for decades by the F.B.I. under J. Edgar Hoover) and in many popular movie and T.V. portrayals of the police. A more "liberal" approach—increasingly evident among academic and professional police reformers—sees the need for police in the growing complexity and diversity of modern urban society. Liberal commentators often point to social and economic conditions—especially poverty and unemployment—as factors underlying the crime and social disorder that make the police necessary. But these conditions are usually accepted, in the liberal view, as either inevitable or as problems that can only be solved in the "long run." In the meantime, we have to accept the basic role of the police for the indefinite future, although we can do something about correcting police abuses and inefficiency. A classic example of this kind of thinking can be found in the (1967) Report of the President's Crime Commission, a standard source for modern liberal platitudes about the police. The Commission recognized that "the police did not create and cannot resolve the social conditions that stimulate crime" and went so far as to acknowledge that "the economy is not geared to provide (criminals) with jobs." But the Commission did not go on to examine in detail the particular conditions that cause crime, or how these conditions are related to the most basic structures of the U.S. economy. It did not ask, for example, why the economy has not been able to provide enough jobs throughout the entire twentieth century. The larger social and economic issues were raised, but then conveniently dropped, and the rest of the Report deals with ways of improving the functional capacity of the criminal justice system.

To accept the basic role of the police in this way is to accept the system of social, political, and economic relations that role supports. Behind both the liberal and conservative views of the police there is a basic pessimism about the possibilities for human liberation and cooperation, a pessimism that we do not share. We believe that a society that must be held together by constant force or the threat of force is an oppressive society, and we do not believe that oppression is inevitable. Around us there are examples of societies that have done much to eliminate the sources of exploitation and suffering that generate crime. A main premise of our approach to the police, then, is that we believe things *can* be different; that we can build a society without grinding poverty, ill-health, mutual exploitation and fear—and, therefore, without a vast, repressive police apparatus.

How do the present police enforce the oppressive social and personal relations of capitalist society? There are two different, but related, ways in which this is accomplished.

(1) The laws that define what is and what is not "crime"—and thus what is or is not a concern of the police—have been primarily defined in U.S. history by and for the people who benefit most from the capitalist system;

(2) Even within the inherently one-sided system of laws the police have been used *selectively,* enforcing *some* of the laws against *some* kinds of people, while allowing other laws to fall into disuse and letting other kinds of law-breakers go free, or nearly free.

(1) THE DEFINITION OF CRIME The most violent and socially harmful acts in the history of the U.S. have been carried out by the government and the wealthy rulers of the corporate economy. Whether measured in human lives or dollars, these acts constitute the most severe crimes of all, though they are not labelled as such in the criminal codes. The overwhelming number of killings in the 1960's were committed by the U.S. armed forces in Southeast Asia. The largest thefts in U.S. history were carried out by the U.S. government against the lands of Mexicans and the various Native American tribes. The most brutal kidnapping since Blacks were forced into slavery was carried out by the U.S. government, against the Japanese-Americans in the 1940's, when they were stripped of their belongings and held in camps during World War II. Perhaps most importantly, the process of getting rich off the labor of other people, far from being considered a crime, is the basis of normal economic life in the

U.S., and people who do it successfully have great prestige and power.

Historically, the *main* function of the police has been to protect the property and well-being of those who benefit most from an economy based on the extraction of private profit. The police were created primarily in response to rioting and disorder directed against oppressive working and living conditions in the emerging industrial cities. . . . They were used consistently to put down striking workers in the industrial conflicts of the late 19th and early 20th centuries. The police did not shoot or beat the corporate executives of Carnegie Steel, the Pullman Company, or the Pennsylvania Railroad who subjected their workers to long hours, physical danger, and low pay; instead, they shot and beat the workers who protested against that exploitation. In the 1960's, the police did not arrest the men who planned and directed the U.S. aggression in Southeast Asia; they arrested the people who protested against that aggression. And in the ghetto revolts of Harlem, Watts, and Newark, the police did not use tear gas and shotguns on slumlords or on merchants who sold shoddy and overpriced goods; they used them on the Black people who rebelled against that victimization.

All of this is often conveniently forgotten in discussions of the police. It adds up to the simple fact that the police were not created to serve "society" or "the people," but to serve *some* parts of society and *some* people at the expense of others. Sometimes, this means that things like racism, sexism, economic exploitation, or military aggression are defined as worthy rather than criminal. In other cases, something more subtle happens. Many of the most socially and personally damaging acts that *are* forbidden in U.S. law are handled as "civil" rather than "criminal" issues. This is often true, for example, for such things as denying people jobs on the grounds of sex or race, or violating safety or anti-pollution regulations. Generally, the executives of corporations and other institutions that violate these laws are not visited by armed police, handcuffed and thrown in patrol wagons, and taken to jail. Instead, a long, drawn out, and expensive process of litigation takes place, during which "business as usual" goes on as before. This distinction, like the basic definition of crime, is not natural or inevitable, but reflects the social priorities and sources of political power in a society built on private profit.

(2) SELECTIVE ENFORCEMENT Even when the actions of the wealthy and powerful are defined as criminal and detected, the penalties they face are usually relatively mild and rarely applied in practice. Offenses such as embezzlement, fraud, tax fraud, and forgery resulted in a loss of $1.73 billion in 1965. In the same year, robbery, burglary, auto theft, and larceny resulted in a loss of $690 million—less than half as much. Although the "crime in the suites" represented much more stolen wealth, it was much less severely punished. Less than 20 percent of those convicted of tax fraud in 1969 (which averaged $190,000) served prison terms, and these terms averaged only 9 months. At the same time, over 90 percent of those convicted of robbery were sentenced to prison, where they served an average of 52 months.

Alongside this systematic leniency toward white-collar or corporate offenders, there is considerable evidence showing that underneath the formal structure of the criminal law there is an unofficial but systematic pattern of selective use of the police to coerce and intimidate oppressed people. Studies of police street practices consistently show that the police use their discretion to arrest more often against working-class people than others. For example, middle-class youth are much more likely to be let off with a reprimand for many kinds of crimes, while working-class youth are far more likely to be formally arrested and charged, for the same kinds of offenses. More dramatically, it has been shown that the police systematically use their ultimate weapon, deadly force, much more often against Black people than against Whites. A recent study found that between 1960 and 1968, 51 percent of the people killed by police were Black in a country where Blacks make up something over 10 percent of the population. The police response to the crime of rape is another example of this pattern, for although rape—unlike most expressions of sexism—is considered in law as a serious crime, it is typically dealt with in ways that serve to degrade and further victimize women and to enforce oppressive and stereo-typical conceptions of women's role. In these and other ways too numerous to mention here, the routine operation of the police creates an informal system of criminal law that, even more than the formal one, is designed to support the fundamentally oppressive social relations of capitalism. It should be emphasized that this is not just a question of easily correctible police "abuses." The selective use of the police has been a systematic and constant feature of the whole pattern of "social control" in the U.S., and its consistency shows how tightly it is tied in to the repressive needs of the system as a whole.

Dealing with Crime

Even though we believe that the most dangerous criminals sit in corporate and government offices, we recognize that the more conventional kinds of crime—"street" crimes—are a real problem which must be confronted. In the U.S., people are faced every day with the danger of theft or personal violence. This is especially true of poor people. Most street crimes are committed by the poor against the poor—particularly against poor Third World people. Blacks are four times as likely to be robbed as Whites; Black women are four times as likely to be raped as White women. In general, people who live in inner cities are three times more likely to be victimized by major crime than those who live in the suburbs. The fear of crime is a demoralizing and oppressive fact of life for many people. Because of this, many people believe that the police should be encouraged and supported, since they at least provide *some* protection against this type of crime. We understand this attitude, but we believe it is fundamentally mistaken.

The reasons why there is so much street crime in the U.S. are complex, but they are rooted in the material deprivations and personal alienation and misery that capitalism produces. No "war on crime" can provide a truly enduring solution to the problem of crime unless it directly attacks the sources of that misery and alienation. Strengthening the existing police does not do this; but only helps to strengthen the system that generates crime in the first place. This isn't to say that

beefing up the police might not reduce some kinds of crime; obviously, flooding the society with more and better-equipped police—putting a cop on every corner—could have some effect on rates of crime. But this kind of "solution" would not touch the underlying roots of crime, and could only be done at a tremendous cost in social and personal values.

To deal with crime by strengthening the police is to accept the inevitability of crime and the permanence of the oppressive social system that breeds it. We believe that real solutions to the problem of crime must begin by challenging that system itself: by moving toward programs that take power away from that system and its rulers, and transfer it to the people it now oppresses. Alternative approaches to crime must be of a kind that increase the consciousness of oppressed people and extend their ability to control their own lives. They must be linked to the broader movement to totally transform the economic and political institutions of U.S. society—the movement to build socialism in this country. In this way, the fight against crime and for a safer and more decent life can be joined with the larger struggle against the real crimes of racism, sexism, and exploitation at home and abroad.

Some Cautions

It's important to emphasize that although we believe that crime is deeply bound up with the nature of capitalist society, we are not suggesting that capitalism is responsible for *all* crime or that crime will necessarily magically disappear when capitalism does. The picture is a little more complicated than that. From what we know about crime in socialist societies, for example, it's clear that crime has not altogether disappeared in them; but it's also clear that many kinds of crime—including theft, drug use, and crimes of personal violence—have strikingly decreased, and are likely to decrease even more in the future, as the traces of earlier, oppressive relationships are gradually obliterated. It is also obvious that crime appears differently in different capitalist societies. The U.S. has much higher rates of crime than most other "developed" capitalist countries, for example Sweden, Switzerland, or England. This means that it isn't really possible to predict exactly how much or what kinds of crime will be present in a society simply by knowing that it is capitalist. To understand the specific extent and pattern of crime in any actual capitalist system, it has to be seen as a historically unique society with its own special conditions and traditions. In the U.S., for example, the historical patterns of racism and the internal colonization of Third World people are crucially connected to the types and amount of crime in this country, and have to be considered equally with the capitalist nature of the system in understanding them. Because capitalist development in the U.S. has depended heavily on the special exploitation of Third World people both here and overseas, the special op-pression of Third World people is a fact of life of American capitalism, and it contributes strongly to the especially high rates of crime (as well as of disease, infant mortality, and other symptoms of oppression) in the U.S. as opposed to some other capitalist countries. Recognizing this, though, does not mean that it is any less true that we must end capitalism in order to end crime; it simply means that ending capitalism must also mean ending racism (and all other forms of human exploitation and domination) as well. In other words, the understanding that capitalism creates conditions that are likely to lead to crime is just the *beginning* of an analysis of crime and the police in the U.S., not the end of it.

Jammed Tokyo's Crime Rate Is Far Below New York's   *Sydney H. Schanberg*

People in Tokyo rarely cross the street against a red light. They do not scrawl graffiti on subway walls. And they do not commit many murders either.

Indeed, the world's most populous city—11.6 million people—has the lowest crime rate. Tokyo had 196 murders last year; New York, with a population of almost eight million, had 1,680—nearly nine times as many.

That Japan's capital is the least crime-troubled of any big city in the world is in itself not news. Tourist brochures regularly make the same point: "Even on dark, lonely streets in the dead of night, you need not be afraid of lurking shadows."

But seldom does anyone here try to explain why, for law and order is a condition of life the Japanese have come to take for granted.

Though the "why" is not some Oriental mystery, neither is it simple to explain, for it involves a mixture of social and legal factors that go to the heart of the national character.

Consider a few of them: The gun-control and drug laws are severe, and they are enforced by an efficient police force. Public respect for law and authority is traditionally strong. Arrest is a deep disgrace both for oneself and for one's family.

The level of education is high. Unemployment is low. The country is ethnically and culturally homogeneous, with virtually no racial strains.

Finally, the Japanese, living close together on an isolated and densely populated island group, have developed an ability to deal with stresses and an adaptability to others, as well as a sense of obligation not to trespass on the lives of their neighbors.

"In Japan most people agree on what is right and what is wrong," said a young businessman who had just returned from several years in the United States. "In America different groups have different ideas about right and wrong."

Not surprisingly, the people proudest about Tokyo's low crime rate are the metropolitan police. "We sent two men to New York last year to study crime there," said Inspector Junzo Hirooka, chief of the crime prevention section. "They found crime so high that even they were afraid of walking around at night."

The Tokyo police are especially fond of contrasting their crime level with that of New York, where murderers and muggers lead a more active life. Other things being equal, New York—which, in fact, is not the most crime-ridden of American cities—ought to have less crime. But as the statistics demonstrate—and the 42,420 Tokyo policemen are as proud of their statistical accuracy as they are of their crime rate—other things are clearly not equal.

New York, with a 31,000-man police force, had 72,750 reported robberies last year; Tokyo had 361. New York had 3,735 reported rapes, Tokyo 426. New York had 38,148 reported assaults, Tokyo 17,171. New York had 82,731 reported auto thefts, Tokyo 3,550. New York reported 22,843 drug crimes, Tokyo 1,283. And so on.

In brief, while cities in Europe and the United States have seen their crime rates double and more over the last decade, crime in Tokyo has not increased. In the category of major crimes the rate has actually dropped despite steady population growth.

Are the Japanese less criminally inclined than other urbanized people, or are the Japanese police simply more effective in controlling and preventing crime?

Probably some of both—although the police are more visible and easier to explain than the intricacies of Japanese psychology. They are also one of the few vehicles through which an outsider can get a glimpse of that psychology at work.

The Tokyo police are recruited from all over the country in a search for the best men—which gives them added prestige in a nation where prestige is important. Here, the neighborhood policeman is known respectfully as O-Mawari-San—Mr. Walkaround.

He earns about $6,000 a year after three years' service, compared with the $16,000 of a New York policeman with the same experience. And he does walk around, for there are many more foot patrolmen here than in New York. Sprinkled every few blocks throughout the city are koban, or police booths, manned by one to a dozen or so men, who patrol their neighborhoods constantly. There are 1,242 such booths, which vary in size depending on population and crime rate.

Every koban policeman has responsibility, on the average, for about 150 households, each of which he is required to visit at least twice a year. Moreover, he must provide his headquarters with data on the occupants of each household and what they do for a living.

There is also a voluntary civilian crime-prevention organization, set up under police aegis, with

an unpaid block captain for every 30 households; the purpose is to encourage cooperation with the police and the speedy reporting of crimes and traffic accidents by use of the police emergency telephone number, 110.

In these ways—and through patrol cars and a modern communications system, with a computerized control room at headquarters—the police cover virtually every square foot of territory and usually know as much about each resident as any nosy neighbor in a small American town.

This helps explain the high arrest rate. It also provides occasional surprises for residents. The other day an American businessman living here received a call from his O-Mawari-San, who reminded him that his dog was due for its rabies shot.

The police are unusual in other ways. Their restraint impressed an American reporter who spent a night on the streets with them in Kabuki-cho, the neighborhood in the bustling Shinjuku district with the worst crime rate in the city. A district of garish and often sleazy bars, cabarets, coffee shops and amusement parlors, it used to be thick with organized criminal gangs, but has been somewhat cleaned up.

As the policemen walked through the neon-bathed alleys in pairs—in most other areas they patrol alone—drunken revelers would occasionally toss wisecracks at them. The policemen never gave them a glance.

They approached a man who had parked illegally on a sidewalk and asked for his license and registration. His tone was rude and arrogant. They asked why he had parked illegally. He retorted that he did not know the traffic regulations "because I have been in jail for two years and just got out."

Unfazed by his disrespectful attitude, the policemen simply called back to the koban on their walkie-talkie to check his papers. Once they had established his identity, his previous record and the validity of his present address, they returned the papers and sent him on his way.

Policemen get no bonus, financial or otherwise, for making a lot of arrests for minor offenses. There also seems to be no adversary relationship between the average citizen and the policeman—he is not the enemy.

Police energies seem directed mainly at winning the neighborhood's confidence and checking serious crime. Drunks, for example, are not treated as criminals. Even if one is abusive and in falling-down condition, the police will merely carry him to the koban, put him in a corner where he can sleep it off and send him home in the morning—giving him careful directions in case he is lost.

Policemen rarely draw their pistols; the rules on firearms are rigid and strictly circumscribed. Force of any kind is to be used only when absolutely necessary.

So strict is the precept that when the special riot policemen, who do not carry arms, become too vigorous in pushing against demonstrators with their metal shields, their chief, behind them, will rap them on their plastic riot helmets with his baton—a command to get hold of themselves and show more restraint.

"Our policemen have self-control—they do not get carried away by emotion," said Takashi Miyatami, a sergeant at the Kabukicho police booth, who has a long scar from the bridge of his nose to his chin—a legacy from a student's rock in a riot in Yokosuka eight years ago.

He said he bore no grudge against students for injuring him. "It is simply my professional duty to deal with left-wing students and restrict them," he added blandly.

The man in the police booth affords a close-up of how the force works. At the other end of the elaborate communications network is the central control room at headquarters, which is one of the best places to monitor Tokyo crime. There, television sets, computers, tape decks, radiophoto machines, alarm buzzers, telephones and flashing lights are awesomely arrayed against the criminal.

The officer in charge reels off for the visitor more of the department's ever-handy statistics. There have been 823 calls from citizens and policemen since last midnight. There were 140,757 calls about traffic accidents last year. The average response time between a citizen's call and the arrival of a police car is 3 minutes 40 seconds.

The alarm buzzer rings. A citizen is calling to report that a neighbor is waving a long knife; no one has been injured yet. A radio car is dispatched.

The officer goes back to ticking off more statistics, but the buzzer goes again. This time it is a report of two missing teen-agers quickly followed by a report that some demonstrating workers have shifted the route of their protest march.

There is only one thing that does not quite fit in this gargantuan room dedicated to transistor technology—everyone has to wear slippers. Maybe it's a venerated tradition, the visitor thinks, a touching contrast. Just the opposite: It's more worship of the machine. The officer in charge explains that shoes bring in dust and dust is bad for the machines.

Notes and Questions

1. Consider the following description by James Baldwin of the ghetto policeman:

> [T]he only way to police a ghetto is to be oppressive. None of the Police Commissioner's men, even with the best will in the world, have any way of understanding the lives led by the people they swagger about in twos and threes controlling. Their very presence is an insult, and it would be, even if they spent their entire day feeding gumdrops to children. They represent the force of the white world, and that world's real intentions are, simply ...to keep the black man corraled up here, in his place.
>
> ... The white policeman standing on a Harlem street corner finds himself at the very center of the revolution now occurring in the world. He is not prepared for it—naturally, nobody is—and, what is possibly much more to the point, he is exposed, as few white people are, to the anguish of the black people around him. Even if he is gifted with the merest mustard grain of imagination, something must seep in. He cannot avoid observing that some of the children, in spite of their color, remind him of children he has known and loved, perhaps even of his own children. He knows that he certainly does not want *his* children living this way. He can retreat from his uneasiness in only one direction: into a callousness which very shortly becomes second nature. He becomes more callous, the popu-

lation becomes more hostile, the situation grows more tense, and the police force is increased.*

Could Garmire's proposal significantly change Baldwin's image of the ghetto police officer?

2. Would Garmire's suggestions satisfy any of the criteria for change suggested in "The Iron Fist and the Velvet Glove"?

3. Why should the Japanese police be called police? Consider the following:

Many kobans post scorecards outside listing yesterday's frightening traffic toll, others post photos or drawings of suspects wanted by police. Inside, it isn't unusual to be greeted by a photo of the revered Mt. Fuji or by a delightful floral display. Despite Tokyo's urban sprawl and heavy pollution, Japanese have a unique appreciation for beauty and aesthetic touches. This is said to reflect the influence of Confucianism. In any event Tokyo police recruits—required to demonstrate skill in judo, kendo, and other martial arts—may be the only policemen in the world whose curriculum includes flower arrangement, mu-

* James Baldwin, *Nobody Knows My Name* (New York: Dell Publishing Company, 1961), pp. 61–63.

sic appreciation and the tea ceremony....

Like the Japanese approach to so much else, the concept of Japanese justice and law are based on conciliation and compromise. Indeed, the oldest written code in Japan, Prince Shotoku's historic 17 maxims established almost 1,400 years ago, begins, "Concord is to be honored." Today, local police stations provide conciliation rooms where elders seek to reconcile warring parties. Laymen participate widely in judicial proceedings to mediate civil and domestic disputes. After an active night in any of Tokyo's 28,000 drinking establishments, which form an integral part of Japan's social and business milieu, obstreperous drunks are made to sleep it off in special foam rubber padded detention centers—and are punished by having to listen to tape recordings of their previous night's ranting and raving.*

4. How do you think Professor Reich would feel about the Japanese police?

* Edwin McDowell, "Tokyo, Where Law Means Order," *Wall Street Journal*, November 29, 1973. Reprinted by permission of the Wall Street Journal © 1973 Dow Jones & Co., Inc. All Rights Reserved.

Suggested Additional Readings

A Civilian Perspective

Gillers, Stephen. *Getting Justice: The Rights of People*. New York: Basic Books, 1971.

Kafka, Franz. *The Trial*. New York: Knopf, 1937.

Malamud, Bernard. *The Fixer*. New York: Farrar Straus & Giroux, 1966.

Packer, Herbert. "Two Models of the Criminal Process." *University of Pennsylvania Law Review* 113 (1964): 1.

Ryland, Walter. "Police Surveillance of Public Toilets." *Washington and Lee Law Review* (1966): 23.

"*Tracking Katz:* Beepers, Privacy and the Fourth Amendment," *Yale Law Journal* 86 (1977): 1461.

Zimbardo, Philip. "The Psychology of Police Confessions." *Psychology Today,* June 1967.

A Police Perspective

Milner, N. A. "Supreme Court Effectiveness and the Police Organization." *Law and Contemporary Problems* 36 (1971): 467.

Reiss, Albert. *The Police and the Public*. New Haven: Yale University Press, 1971.

Rubenstein, Jonathan. *City Police*. New York: Farrar, Straus & Giroux, 1973.

Skolnick, Jerome. *Justice without Trial: Law Enforcement in a Democratic Society*. New York: John Wiley, 1966.

Westley, William A. *Violence and the Police*. Cambridge: The M.I.T. Press, 1971.

Wilson, James Q. *Varieties of Police Behavior.* Cambridge: Harvard University Press, 1968.

Younger, Irving. "The Perjury Routine." *The Nation,* May 8, 1967, p. 596.

The Media Perspective

Arnold, Thurman. *The Symbols of Government.* New Haven: Yale University Press, 1935.

Gerbner, George, and Gross, Larry. "The Scary World of TV's Heavy Viewer." *Psychology Today,* April 1976, p. 89.

Goldsen, Rose. *The Show and Tell Machine.* New York: Dial Press, 1977.

McLuhan, Marshall. *Understanding Media.* New York: McGraw-Hill, 1964.

Mander, Jerry. *Four Arguments for the Elimination of Television.* New York: William Morrow, 1978.

Mankiewicz, Frank, and Swerdlow, Joel. *Remote Control.* New York: Quadrangle, 1978.

Read, William. *America's Mass Media Merchants.* Baltimore: The Johns Hopkins University Press, 1977.

Schwartz, Tony. *The Responsive Chord.* New York: Doubleday, 1973.

Winn, Marie. *The Plug-In Drug.* New York: The Viking Press, 1977.

Zuckerman, Edward. "The Year of the Cop." *Rolling Stone,* April 1, 1977, p. 57.

Discretionary Justice

Davis, Karl. *Discretionary Justice.* Baton Rouge: Louisiana State University Press, 1969.

Frank, Jerome. *Courts On Trial.* Princeton: Princeton University Press, 1949.

Goldstein, Herman. "Police Discretion: The Ideal Versus the Real." *Public Administration Review* 23 (September 1963): 140.

Goldstein, Joseph. "Police Discretion Not to Invoke the Criminal Process: Low Visibility Decisions in the Administration of Justice." *Yale Law Journal 69* (1960): 534.

Nimmer, Raymond. "The Public Drunk: Formalizing the Police Role as a Social Help Agency." *Georgetown Law Journal 58* (1970): 1089.

A Societal Perspective

Bayley, David. *Forces of Order: Police Behavior in Japan and in the United States.* Berkeley: University of California Press, 1976.

———. *The Police and Political Development in India.* Princeton: Princeton University Press, 1961.

Chevigny, Paul. *Police Power: Police Abuses in New York City.* New York: Vintage Books, 1969.

Hall, Livingston and Kamisar, Yale, LaFave, Wayne R., and Israel, Jerold H. *Modern Criminal Procedure,* 3rd ed. St. Paul: West, 1969.

Hersey, John. *The Algiers Motel Incident.* New York: Knopf, 1968.

Manning, Peter. *Police Work: The Social Organization of Policing.* Cambridge: The M.I.T. Press, 1977.

National Commission on the Causes and Prevention of Violence, Staff Report: James S. Campbell, Joseph Sahid, and David P. Stang, *Law and Order Reconsidered.* New York: Bantam Books, 1970.

——— Staff Report: Donald J. Mulvihill and Melvin M. Tumin, with Lynn Curtis, *Crimes of Violence.* Washington, D.C. U.S. Government Printing Office, 1969.

——— Staff Report: Hugh Davis Graham and Ted Robert Gurr, *Violence in America: Historical and Comparative Perspectives.* New York: Bantam Books, 1970.

President's Commission on Law Enforcement and Administration of Justice, Report. *The Challenge of Crime in a Free Society.* Washington, D.C.: U.S. Government Printing Office, 1967.

———. Task Force on the Police, Task Force Report: *The Police.* Washington, D.C.: U.S. Government Printing Office, 1967.

Saunders, Charles. *Upgrading The American Police.* Washington, D.C.: The Brookings Institution, 1970.

Wilson, James. "Can the Police Prevent Crime?" *New York Times Magazine,* October 6, 1974, p. 18.

Grand Stairway of the Palace of Justice, View of Faces, from
Les Gens de Justice by Honoré Daumier, courtesy Boston Public Library.

Woe unto you also, ye lawyers, for ye lade men with burdens grievous to be borne, and ye yourselves touch not the burdens with one of your fingers.

New Testament, *Luke*, XI, 46

The first thing we do, let's kill all the lawyers.

Shakespeare, *Henry VI*, Act I, Sc. 3

The most innocent and irreproachable life cannot guard a lawyer against the hatred of his fellow citizens.

John Quincy Adams, *Writings* (1787)

Could the ambivalence toward law ... be related to the possibility that the lawyer must do things the community regards as necessary—but still disapproves of? Hence is the lawyer something of a scapegoat? Now to be sure this does not distinguish lawyers from prostitutes, politicians, prison wardens, some debtors and many other occupational groups. What does distinguish lawyers in the role is that they are feared and disliked—but needed—because of their matter-of-factness, their sense of relevance, their refusal to be impressed by magical solutions to peoples' problems.

David Riesman, "Toward an Anthropological Science of Law and the Legal Profession," in *Individualism Reconsidered* (1954)

chapter three

The Legal Profession

The legal system is intended to resolve society's conflicts. Law moderates both the relationships among property, wealth, and commerce considered central to the commonweal, as well as the particular concerns about self-aggrandizement, personal mishap, violence, and domestic felicity that are important to individuals. The legal system is imbued with the repressive force of state power and democratically pressed by the popular demand to do justice. In matters of power, justice, property, personal fortune, and crime, sentiments are disparate and conflicting. No wonder that the profession associated with articulating partisan interests in such areas should itself be the object of strong and ambivalent views. Probably no other legitimate occupation has to the same extent been simultaneously subject to the extremes of homage and vilification as have lawyers. They are champions or the most despicable villains.

In this chapter we shall examine that profession: its position in society; its training; its role in the adversary process; and the character of its experiment legally to enfranchise the nation's poor.

The readings in the first section strike several themes that carry through the chapter: the relationship of lawyers to sources of power; their role in the maintenance of democratic institutions and social stability; the openness of the profession to competing claims of justice; the relationship of the profession's structure to the ambitions of its members; and the organization of legal practice as it affects the distribution and price of justice.

The second section deals with an important question raised in the first part: how is it that people of common origin take on the lawyer's habits of mind and social posture that Tocqueville called aristocratic? Specifically, the focus here is on legal education.

Section 3 concerns lawyers in court and in the adversary process. A central question is the nature and meaning of client representation. Who is the client? Is it, as seems most obvious, primarily the individual or group who employs the lawyer's services? Or rather, is the client more generally society through its de-

mands for truth and justice in the resolution of individual disputes? Or is legal representation a facade to mask the lawyer's pursuits in self-interest or to accommodate the needs of law's bureaucracy? Further, what duties are owed by a lawyer to the client? How far should they be pressed?

The fourth set of readings concerns the lawyer's involvement in social reform. Although the specific focus is legal representation for the poor, the issues raised here surround the lawyer's role within the larger panoply of social movements (civil rights, consumer protection, ecology, the rights movements of women, children, aged, students, gays, prisoners, insane, and any other group with self-awareness about institutional repression). What is the lawyer's obligation to the client's political ends? What should be the balance between pressing for fundamental changes in the legal order in the hope of relieving collective grievances and working to ameliorate the suffering of specific persons within the group? What about the intrusion of lawyer's self-interests which may be incompatible with the client's cause?

The legal profession is presently enjoying unprecedented popularity in the aspirations of college students. Very likely many persons reading this book are themselves seriously considering whether they should attempt to become lawyers. This chapter is designed to provide a theoretical understanding of the place of lawyers in society and the legal system, and to raise some issues about the practice of law that are important to discuss; but readers may also use this information and project themselves into the discussion in order to answer more personal questions.

1   The Lawyer in Society

[The lawyer's] profession enables him to *serve the State*. As well as any other, better than any other profession or business or sphere, more directly, more palpably, it enables and commands him to perform certain grand and difficult and indispensable duties of patriotism,—certain grand, difficult and indispensable duties to our endeared and common native land.... [Service to the State raises the profession] from a mere calling by which bread, fame, and social place may be earned, to a function by which the republic may be served. It raises it from a dexterous art and a subtle and flexible science,—from a cunning logic, a gilded rhetoric, and an ambitious learning, wearing the purple robe of the sophists, and letting itself to hire,—to the dignity of almost a department of government,—an instrumentality of the State for the well-being and conservation of the State.

> Rufus Choate, "The Position and Functions of the American Bar, as an Element of Conservatism in the State." Address delivered before the Harvard Law School (1845)

[T]he law is a hustle.

> Florynce Kennedy, "The Whorehouse Theory of Law," in Robert Lefcourt, ed., *Law Against the People* (1971)

Any number of disadvantaged people may believe as fervently as they know God is their friend that the lawyer is an unscrupulous rascal bent on gouging the helpless. Yet these same people could find no greater happiness than for their children to go to school to become—lawyers.

> Jethro K. Lieberman, "How to Avoid Lawyers," in Ralph Nader and Mark Green, eds., *Verdict on Lawyers* (1976)

As Adam Smith pointed out years ago, and as the latest Irish sweepstakes will bear out, people are unduly attracted by a few large prizes. Therefore, even when many lawyers are unemployed, people will flock to law schools in the hope of becoming a

Charles Evans Hughes. Each overestimates his chances.

> Paul A. Samuelson, Lecture given at Columbia Law School (1975)

The tension in American society between lawyers and other social elements is as old as the country itself. In 1640, when the Massachusetts Bay Colony founded its short-lived utopia in the New World, like Plato's Republic, it had no room for lawyers. That men by legal training should defend with equal tenacity the cause of the righteous and the sinner, the aggrieved and those who injure, the interests of society and the evils of its most pernicious elements, was completely unacceptable to the Puritan moral community.

Nor were lawyers welcomed elsewhere in the colonies. In Virginia, the landed aristocracy jealously guarded its governing powers from the intrusion of lawyers by restricting the practice of law to the most petty circumstances. In New York, first under the Dutch and later the English occupation, the practice of law was permitted, but with licensure and fee regulation imposed by the dominant merchant and land-holding class.

For the first seventy years after the settlement of Pennsylvania there were no lawyers in that colony. The hostility of Quakers to the tyranny of English law and their religious antipathy to those preoccupied with conflict and social strife was carried over to their frontier society.

The absence of lawyers did not mean that the colonies were lawless nor did the hostility toward lawyers prevent "law-jobs"—to use Llewellyn's term—from being done. Acting for others as legal advocates, counselors, and advisors were a plethora of clergymen, laymen court clerks and justices, traders and merchants, sheriffs, and a class called pettifoggers, who had the gift of clever penmanship or sharp oratory. In addition, frontier self-sufficiency often included knowing enough law to get by. For the greater part of the seventeenth century the American colonies used a legal system without lawyers.

The demand for a trained bar came with the first stages of urban growth and increasing commercialism at the close of the seventeenth century. Earlier reticence toward the encouragement of a professional lawyer class succumbed to the immediate legal needs of a growing nation.

In the fifty years before the Revolutionary War the bar flourished in the colonies. Many prosperous Southern families sent their sons to England to be trained at the Inns of Court. In the North and New England the more typical path was by apprenticeship to a successful attorney after having attended Harvard, Yale, Dartmouth, or one of the other colleges for gentlemen. By the time of the War the majority of lawyers in the colonies were college educated; the practice of law by laymen at a minimum; the licensure requirements tightly controlled by the legal elite.

Twenty-five of the fifty-two signers of the Declaration of Independence were lawyers. But the War decimated the bar. Many lawyers, including some of the most prominent, consistent with their conservative views, had aligned themselves with the interests of the state and king. Most were forced to flee when the legal government toppled. Massachusetts lost nearly a third of its bar to the Tory cause.

After the War the popular antilawyer sentiment, which had been submerged most of the century, resurfaced when the chief law business became cleaning up the War's legal debris: collecting debts, imprisoning intractable debtors, foreclosing mortgages, assisting the collection of ruinous taxes, and litigating the cases of returning Tories and English creditors. In 1787, Daniel Shays led an army of farmers out of the hills of Massachusetts in the country's first antilawyer riot.

In the early nineteenth century, under the influence of Jeffersonian—later Jacksonian—persuasions, state legislatures began dismantling the restrictive licensure requirements for the practice of law by which the bar had been garrisoned from "the common man." Individual omnicompetence was the prevailing view. That any man could be a lawyer was supported by the national principles of equality and democracy, by the American repudiation of class privileges associated with European societies, and by the demonstrated self-sufficiency of life on the frontier. In most states admission to legal practice became a right of citizenship, not education or social position. The era of easy access to a lawyer's license for socially mobile aspirants began. The bar lost, for a century, its traditional power of self-regulation and its position of gatekeeper to the profession.

Americans of this period were ambivalent as to what should be the place of law and lawyers in society. On the one hand, the United States Supreme Court, constitutionally an equal branch in the governmental triumvirate, was considered too insignificant to merit special space in the Capitol Building built in Washington. From 1801 to 1860, the highest court in the land "was driven, like a poor-paying tenant, from one abode to another: from the marshal's office to the clerks' office, to the Law Library in the basement, to the clerk's home on Pennsylvania Avenue, thence to the North Wing of the Capitol Building, then back to the Law Library, then to the old Senate Chamber, then to the District of Columbia Committee Room, then to the Judiciary Committee Room, and finally back to the Senate Chamber." * The justices were made to ride judicial circuits, spending as much as six months of the year in undignified travel of the muddy backroads of the country.

The legislative loosening of licensure requirements was meant to depreciate the status of the legal profession. However, simultaneously, it was a recognition of the importance of law and the profession for the society. By opening the profession to those who were not well-born, it was assumed that the ranks of lawyers would include representation of interests from all segments of society. Thus, the bar would be democratic; law would be democratic.

* Drew Pearson and Robert S. Allen, *The Nine Old Men* (New York: Doubleday, Doren, and Company, 1937), p. 7.

Into this milieu, in 1831, arrived a young French lawyer, named Alexis de Tocqueville —one of history's most extraordinary perceptive tourists. His official mission was to study American prison reform. His personal mission was to satisfy himself, and report to his countrymen, whether this new experiment in democracy could succeed.

He saw the antagonism between populism and lawyers' elitism, between a fundamental faith in the common man and a claim for the legitimacy of authority, between a "tyranny of the masses" and the restraint required for the maintenance of democratic institutions. He concluded that lawyers have a special role in this democracy. His analysis is not of mere historical interest; it frames the issues still surrounding the legal profession today.

The Temper of the Legal Profession in the United States *Alexis de Tocqueville*

In visiting the Americans and studying their laws, we perceive that the authority they have entrusted to members of the legal profession, and the influence that these individuals exercise in the government, are the most powerful existing security against the excesses of democracy. This effect seems to me to result from a general cause, which it is useful to investigate, as it may be reproduced elsewhere. . . .

Men who have made a special study of the laws derive from this occupation certain habits of order, a taste for formalities, and a kind of instinctive regard for the regular connection of ideas, which naturally render them very hostile to

From *Democracy in America*, Volumes I & II, by Alexis de Tocqueville, translated by Henry Reeve, revised by Francis Bowen, and edited by Phillips Bradley. Copyright 1945 and renewed 1973 by Alfred A. Knopf, Inc. Reprinted by permission of the publisher, Vol. I, pp. 283–290.

the revolutionary spirit and the unreflecting passions of the multitude.

The special information that lawyers derive from their studies ensures them a separate rank in society, and they constitute a sort of privileged body in the scale of intellect. This notion of their superiority perpetually recurs to them in the practice of their profession: they are the masters of a science which is necessary, but which is not very generally known; they serve as arbiters between the citizens; and the habit of directing to their purpose the blind passions of parties in litigation inspires them with a certain contempt for the judgment of the multitude. Add to this that they naturally constitute *a body;* not by any previous understanding, or by an agreement that directs them to a common end; but the analogy of their studies and the uniformity of their methods connect their minds as a common interest might unite their endeavors.

Some of the tastes and the habits of the aristocracy may consequently be discovered in the characters of lawyers. They participate in the same instinctive love of order and formalities; and they entertain the same repugnance to the actions of the multitude, and the same secret contempt of the government of the people. I do not mean to say that the natural propensities of lawyers are sufficiently strong to sway them irresistibly; for they, like most other men, are governed by their private interests, and especially by the interests of the moment.

In a state of society in which the members of the legal profession cannot hold that rank in the political world which they enjoy in private life, we may rest assured that they will be the foremost agents of revolution. . . .

I am in like manner inclined to believe that a monarch will always be able to convert legal practitioners into the most serviceable instruments of his authority. There is a far greater affinity between this class of persons and the executive power than there is between them and the people, though they have often aided to overturn the former; just as there is a greater natural affinity between the nobles and the monarch than between the nobles and the people, although the higher orders of society have often, in concert with the lower classes, resisted the prerogative of the crown.

Lawyers are attached to public order beyond every other consideration, and the best security of public order is authority. It must not be forgotten, also, that if they prize freedom much, they generally value legality still more: they are less afraid of tyranny than of arbitrary power; and, provided the legislature undertakes of itself to deprive men of their independence, they are not dissatisfied.

I am therefore convinced that the prince who, in presence of an encroaching democracy, should endeavor to impair the judicial authority in his dominions, and to diminish the political influence of lawyers, would commit a great mistake: he would let slip the substance of authority to grasp the shadow. He would act more wisely in introducing lawyers into the government; and if he entrusted despotism to them under the form of

violence, perhaps he would find it again in their hands under the external features of justice and law.

The government of democracy is favorable to the political power of lawyers; for when the wealthy, the noble, and the prince are excluded from the government, the lawyers take possession of it, in their own right, as it were, since they are the only men of information and sagacity, beyond the sphere of the people, who can be the object of the popular choice. If, then, they are led by their tastes towards the aristocracy and the prince, they are brought in contact with the people by their interests. They like the government of democracy without participating in its propensities and without imitating its weaknesses; whence they derive a two-fold authority from it and over it. The people in democratic states do not mistrust the members of the legal profession, because it is known that they are interested to serve the popular cause; and the people listen to them without irritation, because they do not attribute to them any sinister designs. The lawyers do not, indeed, wish to overthrow the institutions of democracy, but they constantly endeavor to turn it away from its real direction by means that are foreign to its nature. Lawyers belong to the people by birth and interest, and to the aristocracy by habit and taste; they may be looked upon as the connecting link between the two great classes of society.

The profession of the law is the only aristocratic element that can be amalgamated without violence with the natural elements of democracy and be advantageously and permanently combined with them. I am not ignorant of the defects inherent in the character of this body of men; but without this admixture of lawyer-like sobriety with the democratic principle, I question whether democratic institutions could long be maintained; and I cannot believe that a republic could hope to exist at the present time if the influence of lawyers in public business did not increase in proportion to the power of the people.

This aristocratic character, which I hold to be common to the legal profession, is much more distinctly marked in the United States and in England than in any other country. This proceeds not only from the legal studies of the English and American lawyers, but from the nature of the law and the position which these interpreters of it occupy in the two countries. The English and the Americans have retained the law of precedents; that is to say, they continue to found their legal opinions and the decisions of their courts upon the opinions and decisions of their predecessors. In the mind of an English or American lawyer a taste and a reverence for what is old is almost always united with a love of regular and lawful proceedings.

This predisposition has another effect upon the character of the legal profession and upon the general course of society. The English and American lawyers investigate what has been done; the French advocate inquires what should have been done; the former produce precedents, the latter reasons. A French observer is surprised to hear how often an English or an American lawyer quotes the opinions of others and how little he alludes to his own, while the reverse occurs in France. There the most trifling litigation is never conducted without the introduction of an entire system of ideas peculiar to the counsel employed; and the fundamental principles of law are discussed in order to obtain a rod of land by the decision of the court. This abnegation of his own opinion and this implicit deference to the opinion of his forefathers, which are common to the English and American lawyer, this servitude of thought which he is obliged to profess, necessarily gives him more timid habits and more conservative inclinations in England and America than in France.

The French codes are often difficult to comprehend, but they can be read by everyone; nothing, on the other hand, can be more obscure and strange to the uninitiated than a legislation founded upon precedents. The absolute need of legal aid that is felt in England and the United States, and the high opinion that is entertained of the ability of the legal profession, tend to separate it more and more from the people and to erect it into a distinct class. The French lawyer is simply a man extensively acquainted with the statutes of his country; but the English or American lawyer resembles the hierophants of Egypt, for like them

he is the sole interpreter of an occult science....

In America there are no nobles or literary men, and the people are apt to mistrust the wealthy; lawyers consequently form the highest political class and the most cultivated portion of society. They have therefore nothing to gain by innovation, which adds a conservative interest to their natural taste for public order. If I were asked where I place the American aristocracy, I should reply without hesitation that it is not among the rich, who are united by no common tie, but that it occupies the judicial bench and the bar.

The more we reflect upon all that occurs in the United States, the more we shall be persuaded that the lawyers, as a body, form the most powerful, if not the only, counterpoise to the democratic element. In that country we easily perceive how the legal profession is qualified by its attributes, and even by its faults, to neutralize the vices inherent in popular government. When the American people are intoxicated by passion or carried away by the impetuosity of their ideas, they are checked and stopped by the almost invisible influence of their legal counselors. These secretly oppose their aristocratic propensities to the nation's democratic instincts, their superstitious attachment to what is old to its love of novelty, their narrow views to its immense designs, and their habitual procrastination to its ardent impatience....

The influence of legal habits extends beyond the precise limits I have pointed out. Scarcely any political question arises in the United States that is not resolved, sooner or later, into a judicial question. Hence all parties are obliged to borrow, in their daily controversies, the ideas, and even the language, peculiar to judicial proceedings. As most public men are or have been legal practitioners, they introduce the customs and technicalities of their profession into the management of public affairs. The jury extends this habit to all classes. The language of the law thus becomes, in some measure, a vulgar tongue; the spirit of the law, which is produced in the schools and courts of justice, gradually penetrates beyond their walls into the bosom of society, where it descends to the lowest classes, so that at last the whole people contract the habits and the tastes of the judicial magistrate. The lawyers of the United States form a party which is but little feared and scarcely perceived, which has no badge peculiar to itself, which adapts itself with great flexibility to the exigencies of the time and accommodates itself without resistance to all the movements of the social body. But this party extends over the whole community and penetrates into all the classes which compose it; it acts upon the country imperceptibly, but finally fashions it to suit its own purposes.

Notes and Questions

1. Of the thirty-nine American presidents, twenty-five have been lawyers. In the president's Cabinet (1977), eight of fourteen members are lawyers: secretary of state; secretary of the treasury; secretary of the army; secretary of the navy; the attorney general; secretary of health, education, and welfare; secretary of housing and urban development; and secretary of transportation.

   Lawyers occupied a majority of the seats in the five sessions of Congress between 1967 and 1976. In the first session of the 95th Congress (1977) 68 of 100 Senators and 223 of 435 Representatives were lawyers.

   Lawyers are also commonplace in state governments. Since 1900, about one-fourth of all state legislators have been members of the legal profession. In 1977, twenty-six state governors were lawyers.

   Finally, one out of every ten lawyers is a governmental employee. Is the ubiquity of lawyers in government an example of Tocqueville's observation that lawyers gravitate to loci of power? Are lawyers indispensable to democratic political institutions? If lawyers were somehow categorically excluded from public office, is it likely, as Tocqueville states, that they would become "the foremost agents of revolution"?

2. Legal education has historically been organized to train lawyers to be rule technicians. Tocqueville would have us understand the legal profession in the more politically powerful role of power broker.

   The authors of the following excerpt, Lasswell and McDougal, attempted to reform legal education by accounting for the public policy roles of lawyers. Their analysis has a Tocquevillian ring.

   It should need no emphasis that the lawyer is today, even when not himself a "maker" of policy, the one indispensable advisor of every responsible policy-maker of our society—whether we speak of the head of a government department or agency, of the executive of a corporation or labor union, of the secretary of a trade or other private association, or even of the humble independent enterpriser or professional man. As such an advisor the lawyer, when informing the policy-maker of what he can or cannot *legally* do, is, as policy-makers often complain, in an unassailably strategic position to influence, if not create, policy.*

   What are the political implications of casting lawyers' work in these terms? What should be the education of power brokers?

3. Tocqueville described lawyers as though they were all of a single character: having a taste for formalism, a dislike for arbitrary power, conservative, harboring a contempt for the judgment of the masses, and a natural affinity with sources of power. How do lawyers acquire these singular attributes? In what ways do these qualities contribute to the profession's function in the maintenance of democratic institutions?

4. What is Tocqueville's view of the assumption of individual omnicompetence—that all persons are capable of being lawyers regardless of education or social station? In contemporary times, is there an assumption of omnicompetence for law-trained persons? Note the areas of substantive responsibility assigned to the Cabinet members who are lawyers listed above.

5. Tocqueville states lawyers "are less afraid of tyranny than of arbitrary power," and they can turn despotism into "the external features of justice and law." What does this mean in the context of a democratic society?

6. Tocqueville posits that the legal profession has the trust of the people: "the people in democratic states do not mistrust the members of the legal profession, because it is known that they are interested to serve the popular cause...." But, if the legal profession, by "force of occupational habits," gravitates toward loci of power and the standards

---

* Harold Lasswell and Myres McDougal, "Legal Education and Public Policy," *The Yale Law Journal* 52 (1943): 208–209.

of the status quo, how can it also "serve the popular cause" when that cause calls for social change? How can lawyers maintain the trust of the people while simultaneously thwarting their "intoxicated passions" and "impetuous ideas"?

7. Tocqueville predicted that in the United States law would become a "vulgar tongue" of the people—the language and concepts of law would pervade all institutions and daily interactions in the society. Has the prediction been borne out?

The following essay is included to illustrate some of Tocqueville's themes from a later point in history. While the specific focus is the early development of the concept of legal aid for the poor, much broader questions concerning the role assumed by the legal profession in society should be considered.

Legal aid societies began and first flourished in the late nineteenth, early twentieth centuries. For America, it was a time of extreme social strife. The capitalist system appeared to be faltering, its proponents' faith was shaken. Depression, industrial violence, political corruption, and rampant exploitation of the poor and working classes were rending the very fabric of society. Radical alternatives for the reorganization of society's central institutions were popular among intellectuals and the common working class. Clearly, it was a time of social crisis and "intoxicated passions."

Legal Aid and Elitism in the American Legal Profession *Ronald M. Pipkin*

Reginald Heber Smith's treatise *Justice and the Poor,* first published in 1919, is now a landmark in legal aid literature and the legal aid movement. It was the first major attempt to argue on behalf of the interests of the poor in the legal system of newly industrialized America. It was the first systematic survey of existing efforts to reduce inequities in the administration of justice, meager though these efforts were. It was a reformer's tract which spoke to and influenced not only the bench and the bar but the public as well. Smith, and those who supported his work, intended this

book to mobilize public opinion and the bar on behalf of the nascent legal aid movement.

At the time of Smith's writing, with fifty years of lucrative practice in the "Age of Enterprise" behind it, the bar had no interest in the small man with the small claim, especially the alien immigrant living in the urban slums. Yet lawyers, partly to insure their own indispensability to developing capitalism, had created a legal process so complicated that few laymen, let alone the ignorant and unresourceful, could pursue their own legal remedies. Perhaps more importantly in Smith's view, the indifference of the legal system and the bar to the problems of the poor had not only created an injustice but had directly contributed to the corruption of society itself. The inability of poor persons to enforce the rights afforded them by law had promoted their own exploitation; it had perverted the promise of the American Dream.

This work first appeared in the Patterson Smith Series in Criminology, Law Enforcement and Social Problems, Publication No. 139, as the introductory essay to Reginald Heber Smith, *Justice and the Poor,* third edition (Montclair, N.J., 1972), pp. xi–xxvii. Copyright © 1972 by Patterson Smith Publishing Corp. It is reprinted here with the permission of the publisher. (Abridged, some footnotes omitted, others renumbered.)

Smith stated his case with the fervor of a revolutionist:

> The system not only robs the poor of their only protection, but it places in the hands of their oppressors the most powerful and ruthless weapon ever invented. The law itself becomes the means of extortion. [p. 9]
>
> The poor come to think of American justice as containing only laws that punish and never laws that help. They are against the law because they consider the law against them. A persuasion spreads that there is one law for the rich and another for the poor. [p. 10]

The language was meant to provoke, but Smith was not a radical or revolutionary. He saw no class bias in the law: "The substantive law, with minor exceptions, is eminently fair and impartial" [p. 15]. He did not see the rules of law as reinforcing the unequal distribution of wealth and power in the country or as fostering rather than inhibiting the exploitation of the poor and the working classes.[1] No injustice lay in the doctrine of freedom of contract when applied to the markedly unequal relationship between worker and capitalist employer. No injustice lay in the legal exploitation of tenant by landlord, debtor by creditor, where the laws favored one class over the other, nor in the large-scale violation of personal rights by legal officials. "The existing denial of justice to the poor," said Smith, "is not attributable to any injustice in the heart of the law itself" [p. 15]. The injustice, Smith held, occurred in the misadministration of a basically just system—court delay, complex legal procedures, high court costs, the lack of inexpensive legal counsel. The system needed reforming, but what it needed was procedural reforms—legal aid, small-claims courts, conciliation and arbitration procedures, administrative agencies, etc.—not a substantive reallocation of power.

In Smith's view, the state provided to all citizens, rich and poor alike, all components of justice, except one. The legal system—the state's forum of justice—was unexcelled in its provision of just rules, just procedures, and just judges. But it did not provide lawyers. There a laissez-faire model prevailed. If legal counsel were readily available, no person who felt wronged would need to look outside the law and the state for more radical means of obtaining justice. If the bar were to make legal services accessible to the poor, a denial of justice would not exist. Such accessibility once prevailed, Smith said, but after the commencement of the American industrial revolution (circa 1870) "the largest and best [law] offices gave up general practice and engaged exclusively in business and corporation law. The charity work which had always been a part of the older type of office was discarded under the pressure of the new era" [p. 85]. The elite law firms no longer willingly took on the burden of the poor. The lower-class members of the bar could not be relied on to do it. To Smith the answer was clear: a program of legal aid.

Smith believed that legal aid could avert injustice by merely making lawyers available to the poor. The need for an attorney arose from technical aspects of the law. Once the problems of "pleadings, procedure, and evidence have been eliminated, there is nothing left for the lawyer to do" [p. 72]. But the value of the legal-aid attorney to society went beyond giving legal services to the poor. Clients were not only poor people with legal problems—they were often themselves problems for the legal system and society. A large part of the legal-aid lawyer's role was to adjust clients' expectations to the justice of the American system and, where necessary, to divert their clients' hostilities away from the system itself (a process which has come to be called "cooling out"). Smith wrote approvingly of legal aid societies who placed "their duty to the court before their duty to the client." The poor were "served," but more often society and its dominant interests were the client.

If the reforming programs outlined in *Justice*

---

[1] It is important to realize that in the late nineteenth and early twentieth centuries the poor and the working class were basically the same societal subsection—one which corresponded, furthermore, very largely with the foreign born. See Herman P. Miller, ed. *Poverty American Style* (Belmont, Calif.: Wadsworth Publishing Co., 1968), pp. 6, 18; Don D. Lescohier, "Working Conditions," in John R. Commons, ed., *History of Labor in the United States 1896–1932*, Vol. III (New York: Macmillan, 1935), pp. 41, 62.

and the Poor were widely accepted, Smith believed, then tremendous benefits would accrue to society. Class hostilities would diminish, the turbulent marketplace would return to stability, and the poor's disposition toward righteous conflict would be diverted. Society would be cleansed of its anarchistic elements, and the confidence of poor people in lawyers and the legal system would be re-established. . . .

The enthusiasm generated by the initial publication of Smith's report carried into the 1920 meetings of the American Bar Association. A large audience attended the association's first symposium on legal aid. The principal attraction was Charles Evans Hughes, the previous Republican presidential candidate, former governor of New York, and president of the New York Legal Aid Society. Other members of the panel were Judge Ben B. Lindsey of Denver, a controversial judicial reformer, Ernest L. Tustin, connected with Philadelphia's municipal legal aid program, and Reginald Heber Smith, who was now a partner in the prestigious Boston firm of Hale and Dorr and, since the publication of his popular survey, the association's legal expert on legal aid.

At the conclusion of the panel discussion a "spontaneous" motion was introduced from the floor and approved: that a special committee on legal aid be immediately established to be chaired by the bar's most august figure, Charles Evans Hughes.

The following year, the special committee, by its own recommendation and the unanimous consent of the 1921 convention, became the Standing Committee on Legal Aid of the American Bar Association. With Hughes having resigned to join President Harding's cabinet, Reginald Heber Smith was made chairman, a position he retained for fifteen years. The committee's first appropriation was only $250: but it signified investiture by the national bar of the concept of legal aid, whose previous forty-year existence had been tenuous and parochial.

Origins of Legal Aid

Organized legal aid in the United States began in 1876 with the establishment of the Deutscher Rechtsschutz-Verein (German Legal Protection Society), a specialized spin-off of the German Society. The mother organization, founded in 1784, had become active and influential with the massive German immigration to America of the 1840s. Its manifest purpose was to help confused and ignorant German immigrants adjust to the new country. In some cases this meant merely providing a cultural refuge for German-speaking people in an English-speaking society. In others, it meant protecting immigrants from being cheated by the swindlers who swarmed the docks and from being exploited by petit-bourgeois shopkeepers and employers. In still others, it was to assuage the frustration and anger that inevitably came from disillusionment with the American Dream. But like most early ethnic self-improvement organizations, the German Society and the Rechtsschutz-Verein felt their essential, overall, unstated responsibility to be to the group's elite. The low-status German-American immigrant was to be prevented from jeopardizing in any way the social and economic position of the group's affluent members who had "made it" in the new world.

In 1890, Arthur von Briesen was appointed second president of the Rechtsschutz-Verein. By this time the great German immigration had passed. The German-American elite was relatively secure in American society and no longer feared being displaced. Other ethnic immigrations were bringing in floods of people more threatening to Anglo-Saxon dominance than Germans. The easing of pressures on the German-Americans had left the Rechtsschutz-Verein in bad financial condition. Donations from wealthy German-Americans were sporadic and declining. The men who had appointed von Briesen assumed that he would merely supervise the organization's demise.

But von Briesen knew that the organization would survive if he could convince the elite of the dominant society that they could make use of the service legal aid had performed for the German-American community. He cut off ties with the German Society and went to the capitalists for patronage. What he had realized was that among the Anglo-Saxon elite there was a strong fear that the masses would rise up and seize the wealth which many had gained through ruthless means.

In the nineties, laissez-faire economics was in crisis. The system so passionately supported by the capitalists no longer seemed to work. Society was being shaken by economic chaos and social violence. A financial crisis beginning in 1893 gave way to a double-cycle depression lasting until 1898. The violence of the Haymarket Riot in 1886 had been followed by the bloody Carnegie Homestead Strike in 1892, and the even more extensive and brutal Pullman Strike in 1894. Many of the corporate elite believed a revolution was imminent.

According to one historian of the period, the capitalists became Marxists: "The proponents of the system . . . accepted, on the evidence of their own experience as well as their casual and distorted knowledge of his ideas, the analysis made by Karl Marx, and set about to prevent his prophecy of socialism and communism being fulfilled."[2] It was directly to this phobia and this program that Arthur von Briesen appealed.

His argument was simple. Legal aid is counterrevolutionary. It could help protect the ruling class from Marx's dire predictions. From 1890 to 1900, von Briesen's annual reports of the legal aid society included the following paean:

> The work done by us comes home to every citizen; *it keeps the poor satisfied,* because it establishes and protects their rights; it produces better workingmen and better workingwomen, better house servants; *it antagonizes the tendency toward communism;* it is the best argument against the socialist who cries that the poor have no rights which the rich are bound to respect. *Communism and socialism have, it seems, lost their grip upon our New York population since our Society has done its effective work in behalf of the poor.*[3]

Von Briesen's appeal was successful. The Rechtsschutz-Verein had not been expected to survive much longer but at the end of 1893 it had more cash on hand than the year previous. In 1896 it changed its name to "The Legal Aid Society."

While the society took credit for undercutting the proletariat in the class struggle, on occasion it performed a less abstract service for New York's upper classes. An early historian of the society recounted that:

> One of the Society's long-standing rules is that an applicant to have his case accepted must present a claim sound not merely in the technical sense but also in the moral sense. Many miscellaneous illustrations of this doctrine might be adduced, but its largest and most striking application provides the very best example. It is law, at least in New York, that a person employed for an indefinite period is subject to discharge without notice and, correspondingly, may throw over his position without notice and without forfeiting his right to unpaid compensation for time actually worked. In the field of domestic service this principle may originally have operated favorably for employers, but of late years, with an increasing demand for and a decreasing supply of competent servants, it has had quite the reverse effect. The New York cook not infrequently walked out at six P.M. with a dinner party coming on, the New York coachman or chauffeur sometimes abandoned his box or steering-wheel in the very midst of a shopping trip. And on top of such annoying action the departed servant could and would make a legally enforceable demand for back pay. . . .
>
> The word went forth that, where a domestic servant abandoned his or her employment without reasonable notice, the Society would refuse to further recovery of back wages. New York gasped. Mere men had dared to tackle the servant problem![4]

Most cases brought to the society did not involve relationships between the upper and lower classes. The elite's interests benefited by the society's refusal to assist workers injured in industrial accidents, or defendants charged with crimes, or victims of official violence, or organizations such as unions whose purpose was to organize

---

[2] William Appleton Williams, *The Contours of American History* (Cleveland: World Publishing Co., 1961), p. 351.

[3] John MacArthur Maguire, *The Lance of Justice* (Cambridge: Harvard University Press, 1928), p. 55. Emphasis added.

[4] *Ibid.,* pp. 83–84.

the poor. Nor did it defend those individual liberties we have come to call civil rights.

What the society did do was attempt to rationalize the economic relationships of the urban working class, chiefly by handling wage claims against small employers.[5] By representing workers in disputes with dishonest employers (those who cut their labor costs by refusing to pay wages), a blow was struck against unionism, labor strife, radicalism, and revolution. In many ways this policy paralleled the attempt of big business to rationalize its operations through federal regulation. Gabriel Kolko has persuasively argued that during this period business interests, in order to create their mammoth trusts free from local and state control, promoted the "progressive era" legislation which supposedly was for their own regulation.[6] Legal aid's efforts were obviously on a smaller scale. But it is significant that two men who were closely aligned with the interests and the promotion of the Legal Aid Society were also major figures in the development of a philosophy for "anti-trust" regulation—Elihu Root, the capitalists' legal spokesman, and Theodore Roosevelt, known as the "trust-buster."

Of the latter, the historian Eric Goldman wrote, "Roosevelt had a patrician's disdain for greedy businessmen, a patrician's sense of *noblesse oblige* toward the downtrodden, and a patrician's fear of socialism or some other 'riotous wicked' surge from the bottom groups."[7] "Roosevelt," according to Kolko, "was consciously using government regulation to save the capitalist system, perhaps even from itself, for the greatest friend of socialism was the unscrupulous businessman who did not recognize that moderate regulation could save him from a more drastic fate in the hands of the masses."[8]

In New York City the same Rooseveltian philosophy lay behind Arthur von Briesen's extension of business regulation into the lower reaches of society through legal aid. It was this concept of legal aid that was the prototype for other cities. . . .

Although the legal aid movement's first effort dated from 1876, when Smith began his survey most programs were recent ventures. Only fifteen societies were operating in the country by 1910, eleven of which were less than ten years old. But within six years of that threshold year, the total number of organizations which could be identified as providing legal aid increased to forty-one. Part of the reason was that the provision of a free lawyer had become one aspect of the relief work adopted by many "progressive" charities. However, none of these were particularly large efforts. The typical legal aid society consisted of one full-time lawyer and, if he were fortunate, some secretarial assistance and perhaps the occasional part-time services of another attorney. The legal aid effort was intimately related to the success of the charitable fund-raising abilities of the supporting agencies.

These pre-war years in which legal aid flourished were in terms of labor strife the bloodiest in American history. The violent suppression of unions and strikes intensified and expanded labor-management conflicts. The widespread appeal of domestic socialism and the increasing threats of the nihilistic International Workers of the World began to terrify the business community. Rampant and ruthless political, economic and legal exploitation of the working class provoked bloody reaction. As in the nineties, the country again seemed to be on the brink of chaos. . . .

The legal aid organizations remained outside this mainstream of social strife, quietly doing their work of transforming the collective political and economic grievances of the urban working class into individualized legal categories. Justice for the poor meant fragmenting the nascent class-consciousness of the exploited, the immigrant poor, and those whose impoverished condition might lead them to support radical movements.

In April, 1917, the country went to war. In many cities legal aid work was immediately sus-

---

[5] The wage claim disappeared as a staple of the legal aid diet and as a source of legal fees in the twenties: improper withholding of pay was changed from a civil offense to a crime.

[6] Gabriel Kolko, *The Triumph of Conservatism: A Reinterpretation of American History, 1900–1916* (New York: The Free Press, 1963).

[7] Eric F. Goldman, *Rendezvous with Destiny* (New York: Alfred A. Knopf, 1952), p. 126.

[8] Kolko, *op. cit.*, p. 130.

pended. Contributions had dried up and the country was being drained of young attorneys—the ranks from which legal aid staffs were drawn. Older lawyers were not available for service to take their place. In the best circumstances salaries paid by charities could not compete with those from private practice, and in wartime the private sector was in a scramble for the lucrative practices left behind by the "brothers at the front."

What threatened legal aid as a movement even more than its sudden shortage of funds and staff was the immense vacuum in national leadership created by the resignation, in February, 1916, of von Briesen as president of the New York Legal Aid Society....

Shortly after the war had begun in Europe in 1914, von Briesen, like many prominent German-Americans, had expressed his view that Germany was not solely at fault in the conflict. Though the United States had declared itself neutral, in the sphere of influence of the pro-British New York *Times* such talk was traitorous and labeled as such, even when it was voiced by a veteran of the Union Army. Von Briesen knew he would have to resign from office if his legal aid society were not to lose its benefactors. Rather than see his organization destroyed, he relinquished his presidency in 1916. With active life ended and his loyalty impugned, his health began to fail. He died in 1920, one of the more prominent victims of the anti-German hysteria which plagued the German-American community during the war.

Ironically, the injustice which von Briesen had suffered kept him from the Saratoga Springs conference where the leaders of the legal profession discussed "justice for the poor."... Perhaps the greater irony in the destruction of von Briesen's career, however, was that it was caused by what others, including Smith, have called his greatest achievement—the Americanization of legal aid. In his effort to build a little-known ethnic self-improvement society, the Deutscher Rechtsschutz-Verein, into the New York Legal Aid Society, he had made himself dependent on and vulnerable to the caprice of the dominant classes. Although the society had Carnegie and Rockefeller as its patrons, lesser capitalists as its regular supporters, and Elihu Root and Theodore Roosevelt as directors, none of these influential men defended von Briesen's right to speak.

After America's entry into the war, chauvinism exploded into a national mania, and an open season was declared not only on German-Americans but on labor radicals, the I.W.W., socialists, and civil-libertarians. The flag-waving fervor of a quarter of a million members of the American Protective League (Attorney General Gregory's unofficial "secret service"), the racial hatred of the newly revived Ku Klux Klan, and the nativists' campaign to "Americanize" the foreigner, by violence if necessary, spread throughout the land.[9]

It was during this period of stridency and strife that Smith wrote the tempered pages of a book on justice and the poor. He pleaded for legal aid and court reform to end the *unintentional injustice* which unequal accessibility to the legal system produced. He raised the spector of anarchy should these reforms not be affected. But it was not in Smith's brief to deal with anarchy's root causes or current manifestations: vigilante violence, race riots, private and governmental racial discrimination, exploitive labor contracts, foul working conditions, corrupt courts, and the many forms of lawful injustice inflicted on members of society. In his lawyer's philosophy, the concept of lawful injustice was excluded as self-contradictory....

Effects of Smith's Work

What contributions did Smith and his co-workers make to American society? Although individual persons were certainly aided, the poor as a class seem not to have been much affected, so restricted was the legal aid movement in the range of service it offered its clients and in its efforts in seeking them out. Little was done to broaden the program. In a survey of legal aid conducted in 1947, thirty years after Smith's publication, Emery A. Brownell concluded that legal aid—even

[9] See Joan M. Jensen, *The Price of Vigilance* (Chicago: Rand McNally, 1968); Nathaniel Weyl, *The Battle Against Disloyalty* (New York: Thomas Y. Crowell Co., 1951); and John P. Roche, *The Quest for the Dream* (Chicago: Quadrangle Books, 1963).

on its own terms—had made practically no progress since 1916.[10]

The movement itself was totally unaware of the inadequacy of its effort. In one of his last attempts to cajole the bar into financing legal aid, Smith said in 1951, "The cost of Legal Aid is so modest that there is not the slightest excuse for running hat in hand to Washington." Authorities outside the movement knew differently. The director of the Legal Services Program, operating as part of the federal government's War on Poverty in the 1960s, estimated that $300,000,000 to $500,000,000 would be required to provide adequate civil legal services to the poor. And when the Legal Services Program was introduced, it was immediately smothered in an avalanche of clients—despite the tremendous increase in the number of legal aid lawyers which it provided. The legal aid movement had been operating on such a narrow base during its ninety-year history that the legal profession had failed to anticipate the vast latent demand for legal assistance.

Justice and the Poor, on the other hand, did serve the interests of the elite bar by providing a popular basis on which to formalize a conjunction between legal aid and the bar association. Even token legal aid served to vent anti-elitist pressures directed at the bar's leadership. The profession's concern for the poor could not be doubted if "justice for the poor" were a part of the bar's platform.

Notes and Questions

1. The legal profession was very politically active during the period described in Pipkin's essay. State legislatures and courts were pressed hard by the elite of the bar to restrict access to the profession and to grant it a monopoly on practice and the autonomy of self-regulation. Educational and licensure requirements were to be raised so that the bar could have much greater control over professional preparation—and who should get into the profession. In addition the bar wanted greater control over the definition of legal work by criminalizing as unauthorized practice the competing enterprises of persons lacking a lawyer's license.

Consider this activism and the arguments in Pipkin's essay in light of the following general statement about all professions:

> A profession attains and maintains its position by virtue of the protection and patronage of some elite segment of society which has been persuaded that there is some special value in its work. Its position is thus secured by the political and economic influence of the elite which sponsors it....
>
> If the source of the special position of the profession is granted, then it follows that professions are occupations unique to high civilizations, for there it is common to find not only full-time specialists but also elites with organized control over large populations. Further, the work of the chosen occupation is unlikely to have been singled out if it did not represent or express some of the important beliefs or values of that elite....*

2. Smith's statement that once "pleadings, procedure, and evidence have been eliminated, there is nothing left for the lawyer to do," is a common view of the lawyer as simply a technician. This definition of the lawyer's job is typically given to justify the need for professional competence and the professional monopoly on practice. Is this view consistent with Tocqueville's analysis of what lawyers do? With the then-prevailing ideology of a democratized bar? With the role Pipkin argued that legal aid actually assumed?

3. Consider the implications of Lasswell and McDougal's point that lawyers determine public policy by advising actors concerning the legality of their acts when this view is applied to Smith's or von Briesen's concept of what lawyers should do for the poor.

4. Consider, in light of the following excerpt from the memoirs of a lawyer of that period, Smith's assertion that the provision of an attorney for the poor was in itself the provision of justice.

> I remember one case of the death of a worker in the steel-mill. He had been ordered to repair something at the top of a blast-furnace. Protesting that the place was dangerous, the scaffolding insecure, and the heat unbearable,

[10] Emery A. Brownell, *Legal Aid in the United States* (Rochester: Lawyers Co-operative Publishing Co., 1951), especially pp. 246–248.

* Eliot Freidson, *Profession of Medicine* (New York: Dodd, Mead & Co., 1970), pp. 72–73.

he had been ordered again to do as he was told, and had fallen, in accordance with his own just and terrible prevision, into the mass of blazing iron. The defense was that the man had known the danger and had voluntarily gone into it. He had assumed the risk when he accepted employment. Furthermore, some other employee, and not the corporation, was alleged to be responsible for the defective scaffolding. The workman himself, or one of his fellows, was guilty of the negligence that caused his death.

I still remember the faces of the widow and children, the plaintiffs in the case, who were left penniless. The policy of corporations was to wear out plaintiffs by keeping the cases in the courts. This was cheaper than settlement, and as cases could not be gotten through the Supreme Court inside of three or four years, it meant an all but complete denial of justice. The attitude of corporation lawyers was that claimants for personal injuries were "strikers," and that the lawyers who took their claims on a contingent fee were "ambulance-chasers."

...I never overcame my dislike for the profession and got little enjoyment out of such success as I achieved. Trial work was distasteful to me. In jury cases I was less skilful than rough practitioners for whom I had little respect, and the lack of finality and long delays annoyed me. Cases wore on for years; nothing was ever finished. Personal-injury cases, in which our firm represented corporations sued for death or injury claims arising out of the hazards of employment, I found particularly disagreeable. There were no workmen's compensation laws at that time and corporations were able to avoid responsibility for neglect by pleading the defenses of contributory negligence, the assumption of risk, or the negligence of a fellow employee. These defenses were dug up by judges from mediæval times, when there was no great aggregation of capital, when masters worked close beside their men, when neither steam nor electricity had come into existence. It seemed incredible that a learned profession should countenance the absurdity of applying rules of bygone days to modern industrial conditions.*

What more than a lawyer was needed by the poor client?

* From Frederic C. Howe, *The Confessions of a Reformer* (New York: Quadrangle Books, 1967), pp. 199–200.

In the 1870s lawyers began forming bar associations. At first these groups were largely promoted for the social intercourse of the legal elite. However in time they took on the responsibilities of a guild. In the 1920s bar associations of most states began persuading their respective legislatures to grant closure on the practice of law. Stricter educational and bar admission requirements were imposed by law to replace the earlier permissive ones—the ideology of individual omnicompetence was exhausted. Again the profession became self-defining and self-regulating.

For a century the lawyer had been second only to the captain of industry as the hero of the popular rags-to-riches myths. The profession had been open and had grown. According to best estimates, in 1850 there were about 22,000 lawyers in the country. The bar had increased to 60,000 in 1880, and by 1900 to 114,000 lawyers, the great bulk of whom were sons of merchants and clerks; many were foreign-born or the children of immigrants.

This was a period of change not only in the character of the bar but also in the character of legal practice. The most prestigious and highly paid practices of law moved from the courtroom to the offices of Wall Street. The profession was heterogenous and stratified—a character it retained.

The Impact of Social Backgrounds of Lawyers on Law Practice and the Law *Jack Ladinsky*

This paper reports on a study of family origins, education, and work situations of metropolitan lawyers in two work settings central to the legal profession—individual (solo) and group (medium-to-large firm) law practices. It also tries to bring together the data on early socialization milieux of lawyers and the social agencies through which they move in adult life, with speculations about how these social contexts affect the legal system. From the sociologist's perspective, it is a study in the processes and effects of self-selection and recruitment in the allocation of the lawyer labor supply.

I. A Stratified Urban Bar

Over the past sixty years, a highly stratified bar has evolved in urban America. There are no studies of it, but a few writers have provided rich informal impressions of this lawyers' hierarchy. The following quotation is particularly illuminating:

> In all towns or cities of over 500,000 population, the best law business is in the hands of relatively few people. This inner circle of lawyers handles the work of the local banks, utilities, insurance companies, manufacturing concerns and commercial concerns of any size. In addition, these men represent the large national enterprises whose legal headquarters may be elsewhere....
>
> Outside this inner circle is a fairly narrow fringe of what might be called plaintiff's lawyers who, on the whole, represent interests adverse to those represented by the inner circle. These plaintiff's lawyers are able, hard working, aggressive, respected—and sometimes feared —by the inner circle. On the whole they do quite well financially.
>
> Beyond this narrow fringe lies the realm of outer darkness. It is peopled by a very large number of lawyers who are barely making a living. They haunt the courts in the hope of picking up crumbs from the judicial tables, such as small receiverships, guardianships, and so forth. For the most part they are quite active in the local political clubs, hoping that eventually they will obtain the long-desired plum that will give them a more regular and more substantial income....

The rise of a stratified bar is not unlike the stratification of urban America in general. Around 1890, the lone practitioner still prevailed in America. He could, for the most part, adequately handle the general legal problems required by a predominantly rural and small-town citizenry. But industrialization was swiftly changing all this. With the growth of large-scale corporations, followed gradually by a vast array of laws controlling commercial transactions, it became progressively more difficult for a general practitioner to master the number of specialized services demanded by complex business organizations. Astute city lawyers quickly responded with a new phenomenon—the large law office. In most American cities, the firms rapidly gained pre-eminence in legal affairs. By 1948, there were 284 law firms in the nation with eight or more partners, located in fifty-seven different cities. Today there are offices in New York with over 125 lawyers and total staffs that reach 250 or 300.

But the majority of urban lawyers have con-

This is a reprint of an article that appeared in the *Journal of Legal Education*, Vol. 16, No. 2 (1963), pp. 127–144. Reprinted by permission. (Footnotes omitted.)

tinued to practice alone. In 1958, close to sixty per cent of all working lawyers in cities of 500,000 or above were in individual practice, and the vast majority of these men were undoubtedly general practitioners.

Firm as well as solo lawyers think of themselves as free professionals. They often make invidious comparisons between themselves and "kept counsel" in business or unions. And it is certainly true that neither house counsel nor government lawyers for that matter are in comparable positions to the independent practitioners. Solo and firm lawyers are the hard core of the legal profession because they are *private* practitioners. They are not employed in organizations whose ultimate goals are other than the practice of law. They prevail in numbers, and they dominate today's metropolitan legal world. But they are related to each other hierarchically—as the few on the top and the many on the bottom.

II.   The Data

The analysis is based on a sample of 207 Detroit area lawyers, of which 100 are solo and 107 are medium-to-large firm practitioners, who were interviewed between March and July 1960. Solo lawyers included (1) individual practitioners, (2) "associated" lawyers—those who share office space and secretarial help but maintain their own practices, and (3) two-man family partnerships. No solo lawyers employing other lawyers were included in the sample. Firm lawyers were selected from among the lawyer members of the nineteen law firms in Detroit with ten or more partners and associates. (The largest firm had thirty lawyer-members.) Respondents were selected randomly from a consolidated list of the universe derived from the 1959 *Michigan State Bar Roster* and the 1960 *Martindale-Hubbell Law Directory*.

In order to sift out the specific effects of occupational group and work establishment on leisure style, the design of the larger study applied several controls by selection: Age: 30–55. Race: white. Sex: male. Marital status: married now or in the past. Education: law degree. Family income: more than $8,000 in one of the past five years and fifty per cent or more of their income from law in the previous year. Initial contact was made by telephone to screen in the eligibles. All respondents meeting selection criteria were interviewed in person. The completion rate was ninety per cent.

III.   The Findings

The findings are described below and summarized in Tables 1 to 4.

A.   SOCIAL ORIGINS   Table 1 reveals that the individual practitioners are "minority" lawyers—they more often come from working class and entrepreneurial families of minority religious and ethnic status. While both the solo and firm lawyers come predominantly from homes where fathers held non-manual occupations (seventy and ninety-four per cent, respectively), some thirty per cent of the solo and only seven per cent of the firm lawyers had manually-employed fathers.

In the second part of Table 1, the sample is classified according to whether the family of origin was entrepreneurial or nonentrepreneurial—an indicator of that portion of early socialization most directly relevant to integration into the economy. Seventy-two per cent of the solo but only forty per cent of the firm lawyers come from entrepreneurial families.

Fifty-nine per cent of the solo and only ten per cent of the firm lawyers are themselves first- or second-generation Americans (*i.e.,* immigrants or sons of immigrants). Also, sixty-nine per cent of all the firm lawyers come from Protestant homes, while exactly the same proportion of the solo lawyers come from Catholic and Jewish homes. It is a striking fact that while Protestants, as expected, predominate among the firm lawyers, they are a distinct minority among the solo lawyers (thirty-one per cent). Finally, the solo lawyers come from the Slavic and Mediterranean countries (fifty per cent from East and South Europe), while the firm lawyers are more often of Northwest European origin (seventy-five per cent).

Table 1 *Social Origins of Solo and Firm Lawyers*[a]

	SOLO	FIRM
Father's occupation		
Manual	30%	7%
Nonmanual	70%	94%
Number	(100)	(107)
Entrepreneurial status		
Entrepreneurial	72%	40%
Nonentrepreneurial	28%	60%
Number	(96)	(107)
Generation American (father's side)		
First and second	59%	10%
Third and over	41%	90%
Number	(100)	(104)
Religious origin (mother's preference)		
Protestant	31%	69%
Catholic, Greek Orthodox	34%	26%
Jewish	35%	6%
Number	(100)	(106)
Ethnic origin (father's side)		
Northwest Europe	32%	75%
Central Europe	18%	20%
East and South Europe	50%	6%
Number	(100)	(106)

[a] In this and the following tables, the numbers of cases vary slightly because of "not ascertained" on the comparison variables.

Table 2 *Education of Solo and Firm Lawyers*

	SOLO	FIRM
Undergraduate education		
Has no bachelor's degree	57%	13%
Has bachelor's degree	43%	87%
Number	(100)	(107)
Part-time legal education		
Some or all law training part-time	57%	8%
No part-time training	43%	93%
Number	(100)	(101)
Quality of law school		
National schools	14%	73%
State and local schools	50%	25%
Proprietary schools	36%	2%
Number	(100)	(107)
Law school affiliation		
Private non-Catholic	3%	18%
State university	39%	69%
Catholic	22%	11%
Proprietary	36%	2%
Number	(100)	(107)

B. EDUCATION Table 2 shows that the solo lawyers have quantitatively less and qualitatively inferior educations when compared to the firm lawyers. Eighty-seven per cent of the firm lawyers achieved a bachelor's degree; only forty-three per cent of the solos did. About nine in ten firm lawyers attended law school on a full-time basis, compared with about four in ten of the solo lawyers. The majority of the solo lawyers, fifty-seven per cent, took all or part of their legal training as part-time students. This means, of course, that solo lawyers are more often trained in local Catholic and proprietary law colleges, because most full-time state and national private schools offer neither night classes nor part-time programs. This is reflected in the fact that seventy-three per cent of the firm and fourteen per cent of the solo lawyers attended the top national law schools (Chicago, Columbia, Harvard, Michigan, and Yale). The greatest number of the solo lawyers, fifty per cent, received their legal educations in state universities (other than Michigan) and Catholic law schools (University of Detroit, Duquesne, etc.). More than one-third of the solo and only two per cent of the firm lawyers attended proprietary law colleges (in almost every case, the Detroit College of Law).

When law schools are broken down by affiliation, it can be seen that the firm lawyers more often attended private non-Catholic institutions (eighteen per cent—primarily Chicago, Columbia, Harvard, and Yale) and state universities (sixty-nine per cent—primarily Michigan), whereas the solo lawyers attended state (thirty-nine per cent—primarily Wayne State University in Detroit), Catholic (twenty-two per cent), and proprietary (thirty-six per cent) law schools.

C. WORK HISTORY Table 3 reveals that the solo lawyers have been in the labor force longer than firm lawyers and are more likely to have experi-

Table 3   *Work Histories of Solo and Firm Lawyers*

	SOLO	FIRM
Years in the labor force		
Under twenty years	45%	68%
Twenty years and over	55%	32%
Number	(100)	(107)
Number of jobs		
One to three	56%	64%
Four to six	32%	33%
Seven and over	12%	4%
Number	(100)	(107)
First job after bar examination		
In law work	72%	94%
Marginal or nonlaw work	28%	6%
Number	(100)	(107)
Worklife mobility		
Up-mobility	37%	18%
Stable	50%	7%
Fluctuating and highly fluctuating	13%	8%
Number	(100)	(107)
Orderliness of work history		
Orderly[a]	83%	97%
Partial-orderly and disorderly	17%	3%
Number	(100)	(107)

[a] At least half the worklife in functionally related, hierarchically ordered jobs.

enced marginal law work, upward mobility, and somewhat disorderly work histories.

Fifty-five per cent of the solo and only thirty-two per cent of the firm lawyers have been in the labor force twenty years or more. This result is, in large part, the consequence of selector questions on income used to screen in only the stable lawyers. Thus, it appears that to achieve economic stability (by our criteria, to earn more than $8,000 in one of the last five years and also earn at least fifty per cent of his income from his law practice), the solo lawyer has to be in the labor force a longer time than the firm lawyer.

The solo lawyers show only a slight tendency to have more jobs than the firm lawyers. Twelve per cent of the solo lawyers have had seven or more jobs, and only four per cent of the firm lawyers have had this number; fifty-six per cent of the solo lawyers have had one to three jobs, but sixty-four per cent of the firm lawyers have had this

number. This is a small difference, and one wonders if it derives from the longer period the solo lawyers have been in the labor force. When years in the labor force are held constant (not shown in the table), however, we find that only among those lawyers in the labor force under twenty years do the solo lawyers more often hold a larger number of jobs than the firm lawyers. Somewhere around the twenty-year mark, the firm lawyers must catch up. This would indicate that solo lawyers settle down late in their work lives, whereas firm lawyers settle early and only begin to move about later, perhaps when job status and income ceilings are reached.

For most people, early jobs are significant indicators of later success in the labor market. For the would-be independent practitioner, the first job is an important career contingency because it determines, among other things, entrée to the profession and access to clients. The solo and the firm lawyers were classified according to whether the jobs they held the year after passing the bar examinations were directly in law work or in marginal law-claims adjuster, title or trust examiner, credit manager, broker, etc.—and nonlaw work. The majority of both the solo and the firm lawyers held first jobs in law, but the proportion is far larger among the firm (ninety-four per cent) than among the solo lawyers (seventy-two per cent).

Worklife mobility designates the path in the occupational prestige hierarchy along which a sequence of jobs carries a person—whether up, stable, fluctuating, or down. As would be predicted from previous findings, more solo than firm lawyers experienced up-mobility (thirty-seven per cent as opposed to eighteen per cent), and more firm than solo lawyers were stable (seventy-four per cent and fifty per cent, respectively). Thirteen per cent of the solo and eight per cent of the firm lawyers experienced fluctuating work mobility patterns (*i.e.,* marked rank inconsistency from job to job).

Another perspective from which to view the intricate processes of worklife is orderliness of job pattern, or career. A career is a succession of functionally related jobs arranged in a hierarchy of prestige (within or between broad strata) through which persons move in an ordered (more-or-less predictable) sequence. As anticipated, a rather large proportion, about ninety per cent, of all the lawyers enjoyed the substantial orderliness of job patterns that defines careers. However, seventeen per cent of the solo and only three per cent of the firm lawyers experienced much disorder in their work histories. This means that some fourteen per cent more solo firm lawyers had work histories in which more than one-half of the worklife was spent in jobs that were not functionally related.

D. INCOME   Table 4 shows that the solo lawyers have substantially lower incomes than the firm lawyers and earn a good deal more of their incomes from sources outside of law. The income figures in the first part of table four are total family incomes before taxes in 1959 (only a few cases include wives' incomes). Twenty-one per cent of the solo but only ten per cent of the firm lawyers had incomes under $10,000. On the other extreme, eighteen per cent of the solo and thirty-eight per cent of the firm lawyers had family incomes of $30,000 or more.

The marginal character of solo law practice is manifested by the fact that one-third gain between one-quarter and one-half of their total income from other than the practice of law. Only thirteen per cent of the firm lawyers have comparable amounts of outside income. Fourteen per cent of the solo and three per cent of the firm lawyers claim around fifty per cent of income from law. ("Around fifty per cent" was the minimum level required for sample inclusion).

IV.   Interpretation

Few of the above findings will surprise lawyers who are thoroughly familiar with the metropolitan bar. Much of the value of the analysis lies in the fact that it is systematic and consistent with other research findings.

To explore the possible causal nexus between background characteristics of lawyers and type of law practice, a statistical technique for making causal inferences was applied. Four of the previously considered variables were selected for this

Table 4 *Income of Solo and Firm Lawyers*

	SOLO	FIRM
Family income before taxes, 1959		
Under $10,000	21%	10%
$10,000 to $30,000	61%	52%
$30,000 or more	18%	38%
Number	(95)	(105)
Income from law practice		
About 50%	14%	3%
About 75%	20%	10%
Almost all or all	66%	87%
Number	(100)	(107)

causal analysis: religious origin, father's occupational stratum, father's entrepreneurial status, and quality of law school. Selection of these variables was based on the manner in which the labor supply is distributed among occupational positions. At least two major forces appear to be operating in this social allocation process: (1) *personal self-selection,* which motivates individuals toward certain work positions rather than others; and (2) *organizational recruitment,* which brings about the occupational placement of some and the rejection of others. Personal self-selection (choice) is, socially, the culmination of accumulated early experiences, knowledge, values, and skills cultivated in social groups such as family, friendship group, church, and school. Recruitment criteria are of two classes: general criteria of age, experience, apprenticeship, education, license, etc., which are in varying degrees applied in all occupations; and ascriptive criteria, such as race, religion, ethnicity, and family ancestry, which handicap some would-be acceptable candidates while favoring others. Ascriptive criteria in many instances may partly replace talent, education, and experience. Among lawyers it is commonly held that the conspicuous over-representation of religious and ethnic minorities in solo practice issues in large part from the selective recruitment procedures of businesses, industries, and law firms.

The results of the causal analysis are summarized in the model that appears in Figure 1. (The arrows represent direction of causality.) The model corroborates the existence of direct and

Figure 1 *A Best-Fitting Causal Model Between Background and Present Law Practice*

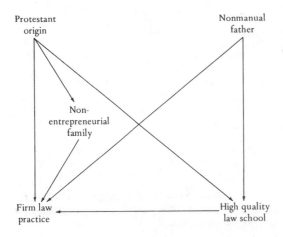

indirect causality from background characteristics to type of law practice. Father's occupational stratum shows a direct and indirect bearing on present work setting, with the indirect influence through quality of law school. Likewise religious origin acts both directly and indirectly upon present work setting. The indirect effect of religion comes through entrepreneurial status of the family, on the one hand, and quality of law school, on the other. Religious origin and father's occupational stratum are not linked causally; neither are father's occupational stratum and entrepreneurial family status, not entrepreneurial status and quality of law school causally linked.

These statistical findings, although inferential, are consistent with the personal self-selection and organizational recruitment processes discussed above. Religion of mother and occupational stratum of father are independent background characteristics that affect the mature, stable lawyer's choice of work setting. Religion acts directly as a career contingency in the form of a tacit recruitment policy to keep Jews and Catholics out of firms. But religion's importance does not cease with discrimination. Religion also acts indirectly, through family entrepreneurial status, as an aspect of early socialization, which shapes later choice of type of law practice. Thus, Jews and

Catholics are not only passed over by law firms, but are often socialized in an entrepreneurial milieu that predisposes them toward individual law practice. Furthermore, interaction undoubtedly takes place between discrimination and socialization. The desire of minority lawyers for lone practice is in part the consequence of avoiding discriminatory situations. Anticipation of firm rejection comes easily to men with protracted experience in dodging the rebuffs of discriminatory practices. "Being your own boss" provides personal security and self-protection. Thus, when firms begin to drop the discriminatory barriers, which appears increasingly to be the case today, few potentially acceptable minority lawyers may take advantage of the opportunity.

Religion also directly influences education. Here it is likely to operate as a psychological motivation determining, for example, self-selection of Catholics into the Catholic law schools, and hearsay discouragement of Catholics and Jews from attempting to enter the national schools.

What part does father's occupational stratum play? The absence of any links to religion and family entrepreneurial status suggests that occupational stratum of father is significant to lawyers primarily for economic reasons. In the pre-work period, father's occupational stratum would be important as a source of financial support for higher education, especially law school. Most manual fathers could not easily support full-time law school for their sons, whereas for most nonmanual fathers, a law school education is not an impossible burden. After education, father's occupational stratum can continue to assist the lawyer in economic ways. Nonmanual fathers have business to bring to their lawyer sons, or to the firms that hire their sons knowing that fathers are potential reservoirs for legal trade. It is probably not uncommon for large firms to favor those young men who can bring family legal business with them. But if fathers cannot offer legal business to their sons then perhaps they can help them financially to establish a practice. It requires a reasonably large investment to set up practice, because there will inevitably be, in addition to office expenses, an extended period during which the new practitioner is building a clientele and, hence has small earnings.

There is a final form of assistance some fathers can offer their sons: contacts. Fathers with the right jobs can help their sons build a clientele or gain admission to a large firm. Manual fathers, it goes without saying, rarely establish these kinds of contacts.

V. Some Implications for Legal Practice and the Law

If the above interpretations of the findings are correct, the social composition of the recruitment base is apt to impose important constraints upon the operation of legal institutions. Family and school background give rise to career contingencies (*i.e.,* they act as social "filters," impinging upon law practice by differentially screening candidates). Social backgrounds seem to prescribe two major career contingencies: level of technical skill, and access to clients.

A. IMPACT ON PRACTICE It is clear that poorly trained men are likely to end up in individual practice. They lack the technical skills provided by high-quality education and specialized work experience; they cannot handle the more complex and demanding kinds of legal problems of modern society. Low-quality education is one major reason why solo lawyers rarely receive invitations to join the big firms. By default, most solo men end up doing the "dirty work" of the bar: personal injury, divorce, criminal work, collections, title-searching, etc.

The kind of work individual lawyers do is further limited by visibility. The average solo lawyer has no contacts with the world of big business. Neighborhood, ethnic group, family, and perhaps organizational contacts are the relations from which he can build a clientele. Firm lawyers, on the other hand, come more often from high-occupational family backgrounds, and are more likely to establish and cultivate relationships that yield business and corporate clienteles. Thus, the "good family" and quality law school candidates look attractive to the large firms.

B. THE ECLIPSE OF SOLO LAW PRACTICE The individual practitioner continues to be in the majority among lawyers in urban America, but he has witnessed a substantial decline in relative rewards over the years. "Centralization of legal talent [in large law offices,]" said C. Wright Mills, "means that many individual practitioners are kept on the fringes." The firms control the field; they do most of the lucrative work. Primarily because of his meagre technical skills and low professional visibility, the solo lawyer experiences a number of unfavorable working conditions.

1. Income The individual lawyer's income is far less than that of firm lawyers. In 1954, the median net income of partners in two-member firms was $9,000; in three-member firms, it rose to $12,500; in four-member firms, to $15,000; in firms of five to eight members, to $20,500; and finally in firms of nine or more members, it was $27,200. In the same year, the median net income of all solo attorneys in the nation was $5,500. Even firm associates, who are not included in the above distribution, earned more than solo lawyers. In 1954, salaried firm lawyers had median incomes of $6,800.

Another set of statistics for 1954 lawyer earnings also points up the differentials in solo and firm lawyers' incomes. Since solo lawyers are more likely to serve individual than corporate clients it is instructive to look at figures on the percentage of gross income for services to individuals. The differences are equally striking. As gross incomes increase, the percentages received from individual clients decrease. Lawyers with seventy-five per cent of their incomes from services to individuals grossed $4,500 in 1954, while those with fifty per cent from individuals grossed $27,300, and those with about one-third of their incomes from individuals grossed $60,000.

In recent years, solo lawyers' earnings have substantially increased. In 1953, nearly two-thirds of all solo practitioners had net incomes of less than $5,000; in 1955, the figure dropped to thirty-six per cent, and in 1957–58, to twenty-seven per cent. Indeed, by 1957–58, seventeen per cent of solo lawyers were clearing over $20,000. But firm earnings have probably increased as rapidly or more rapidly than solo earnings. Large firm lawyers, from the evidence in Detroit, continue to earn a good deal more than individual practitioners.

2. *Client Relations* Because of the restricted fields in which he practices, the big-city solo practitioner's clients tend to be "one-shot" affairs. People who get divorced, hit by automobiles, or run afoul of the law rarely bring more enduring business his way. At best, if he does "a good job" (*i.e.,* wins the case), they will recommend more "one-shot" clients to him. Hence, he rarely enjoys the security and satisfaction of a continuing client-professional relationship. Under these conditions, the solo lawyer is inclined to view his clients as business transactions. And since clients seldom return, he is faced with the recurrent problem of turning up new business without coming into conflict with the organized bar's sanctions against soliciting. Carlin found, for example, that the solo lawyer strategically cultivates persons who are in advantageous positions for channeling legal business his way. These persons act as "brokers" between lawyer and client, and may be another lawyer, an accountant, real estate or insurance broker, doctor, bondsman, or even a policeman, precinct captain, garage mechanic, or undertaker. Firm lawyers do not need outside liaison men. Selective recruiting insures that the successful firm will include a number of men, ultimately prominent senior partners, who bring in the business.

3. *Competition from Laymen* Encroachment upon the lawyer's domain is an old problem in the metropolitan bar. Title and abstract companies began to infringe upon the lawyer's traditional functions as early as the 1890s. This profitable branch of law was lost when clients began to demand title insurance, which lawyers could not supply. Title-guaranty companies sprang up in all important urban areas and prospered at the lawyer's expense. Likewise, credit agencies have reduced the field of collections, and trust companies the field of estates and trust; accountants have taken over a great deal of the tax work; and automobile clubs, insurance and real estate brokers, banks, and savings and loan associations have, each in their way, made inroads upon spheres where lawyers customarily plied their trade. In point of fact, these institutions have seldom eliminated the ultimate need for the lawyer; they have interposed a lay structure between client and attorney. But regardless of the form it has taken, the individual practitioner, not the large law firm, has suffered most severely from this competition. The quantity and complexity of large firm operations, Carlin has noted, do not invite competition from related institutions, and what competition might result from, say, public relations firms or business and management counseling firms is sharply mitigated because the large law firm is in the position to devise some acceptable division of labor that does not violate legal ethics. Individual practitioners have not been able to counteract their lay competition so easily.

4. *Marginal Law Operation* The individual practitioner is often in law, at some stage of his career, only on a part-time basis. Salaried employment or entrepreneurship in nonlegal pursuits are relatively common. Solo lawyers often begin practice part-time, while earning a livelihood in peripheral legal positions with insurance and real estate companies, banks, savings and loan associations, and local government. Many are never able to leave these positions, and thus never able to achieve full law practice. Others are able only to practice law on a full-time basis sporadically, reverting from time to time to salaried status or business ownership. The individual lawyer's practice resembles the small entrepreneur's business. It may fail, forcing him into another line of work until a time more propitious to sustaining an enterprise. This kind of marginality is unique to the individual practitioner; the large firm lawyer reveals no comparable malady. The latter may witness insecurity in the early years, during that trial period that determines his acceptability to partnership status, but once he is a partner, he has the security of both income and a central position in the legal profession.

C. Impact on Legal Institutions How, then, do social backgrounds of lawyers influence legal institutions? By shaping the above career contingencies, social origins seem to leave their mark on the law in the following ways:

1. *Legal talent from quality law schools has flowed heavily into the large firms for many years, and there has been extensive elaboration of legal procedures to handle the problems of corporate enterprises as opposed to those to care for the problems of private citizens.* One result has been a high development of corporation protection, often at the expense of individual citizens. Areas of law unrelated to the operation of corporate enterprises have not, however, had the same level of creativity devoted to them. Developments in public and private welfare, personal injury, divorce, home finance, etc. have been less dramatic than developments in corporate taxation, mergers, stocks and bonds, etc. There are, of course, many historical reasons for this imbalance that have little directly to do with social backgrounds. The important sociological point, however, is that there is no endless store of legal talent to distribute, and "the draining off of best brains into a single channel," as Llewellyn aptly remarked, "has meant that the fitting of law to new conditions has been concentrated on *only one phase* of new conditions: to wit, the furtherance of the business and financing side, *from the angle of the enterpriser and the financier.* It has been focused on organizing their control of others, and on blocking off control of them by others."

2. *There has evolved in metropolitan America what can properly be called an ethnic bar.* It is centered around ethnic legal associations, the local courts, and local politics, and is characterized by many mediocre performers competing for the same bread-and-butter cases. The big firms are insulated from this "intellectual slum," as Riesman has called it, where "a largely ethnic bar carries on the Anglo-Saxon rites of trial by jury and 'contaminates' the legal ideal with the demagogic practice." The majority of firm lawyers, if they litigate at all, rarely venture into the local courts. Their briefs carry them before appellate judges or special federal benches.

The existence of this ethnic bar based on *Gemeinschaftliche* relations has colored the local courts and the administration of justice. Llewellyn, some twenty-five years ago, noted that:

> ...courts are made and shaped more by the character of the bar before them than by any other single factor. Courts, over the long haul, tend in their standards and in their performance to fit the character of the bar with whom they deal.

We do not have studies that would reveal the precise manner in which the ethnic bar has influenced legal institutions. It is an area worthy of research.

3. *Finally, with all the talk about "law factories," it is not the large firm lawyer, but the solo lawyer whose professional position is most vulnerable to bureaucratization.* As noted above, lay organizations in metropolitan areas have successfully taken over many of the spheres where solo practitioners traditionally performed. The result has been that would-be individual practitioners have been driven into salaried positions in these lay organizations. There is irony in this drift toward employment in middle-sized lay bureaucracies. The minority lawyer, inoculated with the ethic of entrepreneurship, goes solo to remain "free," only to discover that freedom to practice the rounded kind of law he desires has eluded him.

These conditions and their relevance for the law have been neglected by sociologists and lawyers alike. The sociology of law sorely needs intensive research into the conditions of law practice, their sources, and their consequences.

Notes and Questions

1. Ladinsky's sample of practitioners excluded both women and minority lawyers. It is appropriate to ask whether the same factors that Ladinsky found to shape aspirations and opportunities in the profession operate for these groups.

   a. *Women* Historically, women have been a statistically minute portion in the legal profession. As late as 1970, women comprised only 2.8 per cent (9,103) of the population of lawyers in the country. However, more recently women have been entering the profession in unprecedented numbers.

Between 1965 and 1976, the student population at accredited law schools nearly doubled (from about 60,000 to over 117,000), but the number of women in law schools increased 1,200 per cent (from about 2,500 to 30,000). The rates in both applications and acceptances of women have been expanding dramatically year by year. Currently, over one-quarter of all law students are women and at some schools women comprise more than half of the entering classes. Clearly, women in the legal profession are becoming more commonplace.

How women are being received by this male-dominated profession has not yet been systematically researched. The only national study on this point, done in 1966, indicated widespread discrimination against women attorneys. The study (James J. White, "Women in the Law," *Michigan Law Review* 65, no. 6: 1051–1122) reported:

> The conclusion is clear: the males make a lot more money than do the females. The differential in present income is approximately $1,500 for those in their first year after graduation, and, with the passage of each year, the males increase their lead over the females until they reach a point at which the differential is represented by a $17,300 to $9,000 lead, and with no substantial appearance of abatement in their rate of gain.

Helene Schwartz wrote the following:

> Throughout my tenure on Wall Street, the men remained suspicious of what they regarded as my unusual double role as woman and lawyer. Their instincts told them that I had no place in the courtroom. They preferred to see me as a super-secretary: carrying files, doing research, writing memos, and generally staying in the office or library.... Many of my women classmates had difficulty getting a job with a law firm. Most of those who did were stuck in the trusts and estates department, where there was little contact with clients, and if there was, the clients were either too young or too old, or dead, to be offended by having their affairs handled by a woman.*

The problem Schwartz describes may abate as women lose their token status in the profession. But as experience in other areas of social life has shown, discrimination has deep roots.

b. Minorities Like women, historically minorities have been extremely underrepresented in the legal profession. In 1970, black attorneys were just slightly over 1 per cent of all lawyers (4,200 of which only 600 were located in the South). (See Gilbert Ware, ed., *From the Black Bar* [New York: G.P. Putnam's Sons, 1976.])

Minority recruitment programs enacted by most law schools in the late sixties have increased the enrollment of minority group students substantially over earlier years, but as of 1977 these groups have still not obtained representation within the law school population anywhere near their percentage of the total population. For academic year 1976–1977, 4.6 per cent of all law students were black Americans (5,503), 0.26 per cent were Native Americans (301), 1.3 per cent were Chicanos (1,488), 0.28 per cent were Puerto Rican (331), 0.47 per cent were other Hispanic Americans (556) and 1.1 per cent were Asian Americans (see Louis B. Schwartz, "The Perils of Racial Handicapping," *Juris Doctor*, vol. 8, number 2 [February 1978] at p. 23).

With regard to the professional status of black lawyers, Marian Goldman, in a study of Chicago's black bar, stated:

> A comparative study of the black and white bars in Chicago would probably show that, on every measure of professional status, most black attorneys fall toward the lower end of the scale. Instead of visualizing a large inclusive status pyramid, it would be more accurate to picture two distinctive, unequal professional status structures. White attorneys maintain their own hierarchy, with partners in the city's largest corporate law firms occupying the highest positions. The most prestigious members of the black bar belong to firms that sustain neither the clientele nor the personnel to compete with the city's largest white law firms. Similar differences in practice situations can be noted in comparisons of black and white attorneys across every level of the two status structures.†

2. Ladinsky noted the eclipse of the solo lawyer. At the time of his study 60 per cent of the practitioners in cities over 500,000 were in solo practice. Now the figure has declined to under 50 per cent. Given the character of legal services provided by

---

* Helene E. Schwartz, *Lawyering* (New York: Farrar, Straus & Giroux, 1976), p. 69.

† Marion S. Goldman, *A Portrait of the Black Attorney in Chicago* (Chicago: American Bar Foundation, 1972), p. 5.

solo practitioners, as described by Ladinsky, what are the implications of this trend?

3. In a recent study of the Chicago bar, Frances K. Zemans found a linear relationship between the status of law schools and the placement of their graduates—suggesting that Ladinsky's distinction between solo and firm lawyers is not sufficiently fine. Graduates of national law schools (for example, Harvard, Yale, Columbia, Chicago, Michigan) comprised 73 per cent of lawyers in the sample who practiced in large firms (fifty lawyers or more), 47 per cent of those in medium firms (nine to forty-nine), 34 per cent in small firms (two to eight), and 22 per cent of solo practitioners.

When the practice specialty was considered, Zemans discovered that many lawyers in smaller firm settings, like those in larger firms, did not practice in the lower status specialties of criminal law, family, poverty, and debtor-creditor law. She concluded, "It is not so much, as Ladinsky says, that solo practitioners do the dirty work of the bar, but that members of large firms do virtually none of it. The extent to which graduation from national law schools predicts practicing in large firms, it also eliminates the possibility of concentrating one's time in lower prestige work." ‡

‡ Frances K. Zemans, "Law School and Law Practice: Credentials for Professional Status," American Bar Foundation, 1977.

4. Ladinsky cites Llewellyn on the point that practitioners get captured by their clients and that their work takes on the client's cast. In the source article, Llewellyn wrote:

Now, any man's interests, any man's outlook, are shaped in greatest part by what he *does*. His perspective is in terms of what he knows. His sympathies and ethical judgments are determined essentially by the things and the people he works on and for and with.... Hence the practice of corporation law not only works for businessmen toward business ends, but develops within itself a business point of view—toward the work to be done, toward the value of the work to the community, indeed, toward the way in which to do the work.§

In *White Collar*, C. Wright Mills wrote: "More than a consultant and counselor to large business, the lawyer is its servant, its champion, its ready apologist, and is full of its sensitivity." ||

If this case can be readily made for business lawyers, what about those working in personal service areas, or what Ladinsky calls "law's dirty work"?

§ Karl N. Llewellyn, "The Bar Specializes—With What Results?" *The Annals*, vol. 167 (1933), p. 177.
|| Mills, *White Collar*, p. 123.

For reasons that are plentiful and diverse, law has recently captured the interest and aspirations of a great number of people—many of whom in an earlier era would have opted for another career. Between 1968 and 1978, enrollment in the nation's law schools doubled to 125,000 students. In 1978 there were 445,000 lawyers in the country, making the ratio of student to practitioner just slightly over 1:3. But among those possibly eligible for admission, in this period of social ferment, economic insecurity, and ecological retrenchment, going to law school became the *zeitgeist*.

In nearly all law schools the ratio of applicants to those admitted has increased several times over what it had been in earlier years. Those academic qualifications which in the sixties would have made an applicant eligible for consideration at the best schools have become barely competitive at lesser schools. The legal profession has sparked an interest in the brightest minds of this generation: law school, through few efforts of its own, is a box-office smash.

Given the stratification in the legal profession, legal education, and the distribution of legal services, the consequences of this bulge for the novice lawyers, the profession, and for society, must be considered. The following article updates Ladinsky's analysis and answers the question of what is likely to happen.

Too Many Lawyers?   *John C. York and Rosemary D. Hale*

The demand for legal services today is mainly a function of institutional economic activity. It is dependent upon the number of corporations in the market, the volume of retail sales, and the number and size of retail and service organizations. Although there are certain forms of demand for legal services which have an obvious relationship to the population—such as personal-injury litigation or will probation—legal services are increasingly demanded by institutions and those who must deal with them. Most of this work is highly specialized and therefore is not a field for the solo practitioner, but rather for partnerships and salaried practitioners both in business and government.

The market comprised of non-institutional clients is less perfect than that made up of business and government. Since lawyers are not permitted either to advertise or to solicit clients, potential clients may have imperfect knowledge of alternatives in cost and service. Individuals and small enterprises often are not even cognizant of their needs for service. On the other hand, a corporation's demand for legal services is continuous and the cost for such service is apt to be an important budgetary item, therefore these buyers are probably better informed and more rational in their decisions about obtaining legal services.

While a large part of the demand for legal services is probably an inelastic one for which there are no substitutes, this is not true for the complete range of legal services—especially those aimed at individuals. Banks and insurance agents offer estate planning. Real estate brokers compete with lawyers in the performance of land-

transaction services. Social scientists have moved into the field of domestic relations and juvenile delinquency. Accountants compete for tax work. Non-lawyers vie for clients before administrative tribunals. And "paralegals" with only a college education are increasingly performing non-research tasks under the supervision of lawyers in larger law firms. Of course, lawyers frequently complain about these laymen practicing law without a license. Meanwhile, the demand for legal service continues to grow.

RELATIONSHIP BETWEEN LAW SCHOOL AND TYPE OF PRACTICE   The caliber of the school attended and, to a lesser extent, one's academic performance at that school determine the type of practice open to each law-school graduate and where that practice will be located.

Among those in private practice "the brightest and most talented lawyers are heavily concentrated in large corporate practices, notably the great private law firms, and this fragment of the profession annually absorbs a high proportion of the top graduates coming out of the law schools." Except for a one- or two-year judicial clerkship in a high-level federal court (some of which are perhaps the most prestigious first jobs for a graduate) the next most desirable employment is as an associate in a prominent firm. The young lawyer, fresh from school, is not a polished practitioner. The five to ten years' apprenticeship as an associate provides the on-the-job training which greatly enhances his legal expertise. He may then be admitted to partnership in his firm or can take this experience to a legal position in industry. Only the large firms in the big cities provide much of an opportunity for such work. This does not mean that top graduates of lesser schools may not have an opportunity to become

This is a reprint of an article that appeared in the *Journal of Legal Education*, vol. 26, no. 1 (1973), pp. 1–31. Reprinted by permission. (Abridged and footnotes omitted.)

associates, but the average graduate probably has little chance. While graduates of "national" law schools are more frequently associates (and later in their careers partners) in law firms consisting of several lawyers, graduates of "municipal" law schools are more apt to be in solo practice. Neither category of school tends to send more of its graduates into government service, although business seems to prefer graduates of the national schools. Thus the law school attended does greatly influence one's employment opportunities.

The law school which a lawyer attends also influences his geographical mobility. Lawyers from "national" law schools (as the very appellation suggests) are the most mobile, being able to find jobs in virtually any city. Graduates of "local" schools may not find a great deal of receptiveness outside the city, state or region which their school serves. The "municipal" schools are mainly located in the large cities, and their graduates are more apt to stay in such cities.

LAWYER'S INCOMES AND THEIR DETERMINANTS
It has long been known that, as measured by dispersion of incomes, law is among the riskiest of professions. Stated alternatively, the financial rewards to lawyers are very uneven. In 1968, the most recent year for which such data is available, the bottom 7 percent or over 5,000 law partners each earned less than $10,000 apiece from their legal endeavors, representing 18 percent of total legal income. The top 5 percent of the partners earned $500,000 or more apiece for an aggregate of 35 percent of total legal income. Income for solo lawyers is more unevenly distributed. In 1968 the bottom 19 percent earned 5 percent of the income, with each lawyer again receiving under $10,000. The top 8 percent earned 25 percent of the income, receiving incomes of more than $100,000 apiece. Although some lawyers in both categories earned over $500,000 from legal work, only 33 solo practitioners were in this category as against 3,390 partners. This wide dispersion makes it difficult for an untutored entrant to project his likely rewards.

Due to the great variation in lawyer's incomes, researchers have attempted to discover relationships between these incomes and other factors which experience indicates would influence incomes. Lawyers differ markedly in earning power among themselves depending upon (1) their type of practice, (2) the nature of their clientele, (3) whether they are specialized, (4) the size of their law firm or business and (5) the quality of the law school which they attended and their record at that school. Also significant are (6) a lawyer's age, the number of years he has been in practice and whether he practices full time, as well as (7) the region, state and size of city in which he practices.

The principal determinant of a lawyer's average income is his type of practice—whether he is a solo private practitioner, a partner or an associate in a private-practice law firm, or a salaried lawyer in government or in business. Partners in private-practice law firms have consistently earned the highest average net incomes of all. Salaried lawyers in business and (salaried) associates in private-practice law firms are closely tied for second place. And of lawyers in business and in private-practice law firms, the larger the enterprise the higher the average net income, as will be discussed later. Salaried lawyers in government earn slightly less across the board. Solo private practitioners have on the average the lowest incomes of all. . . .

A second important determinant of a lawyer's income is the nature of his clientele. With only a few exceptions the smaller the percentage of income received from individual (rather than corporate) clients, the higher is a lawyer's gross income. Large corporate clients are attracted to and are willing to pay premium fees to large law partnerships with their many specialized, top-ranked lawyers. It is not surprising that such lawyers, both as partners and as associates, and in large corporate law departments as well, earn more on the average than do solo lawyers, salaried lawyers in smaller businesses and partners and associates in smaller law firms.

Largeness and specialization are two of the keys to the high incomes received by partners in law firms. Big-firm partners bill clients at up to $125 or more per hour, since the specialist has spent many years in the field and wastes little time supplying the requested guidance. However, from a partner's income must be deducted overhead and associates' salaries; at $100 per hour for a moderate workload of 1500 billable hours a year a partner would take home much less than his $150,000 in earned fees. Yet many partners bill at a lesser rate and many partners also earn more than $100,000 a year. The additional income which bridges the gap is derived from the fact that associates in a large law firm (who often outnumber the partners 2 to 1) bring in about three times in fees what they are paid in salary. The traditional "rule of thirds" states that an associate should bring in at least three times his salary, the other two-thirds going to overhead and to income for the partners, respectively. Associates' time is often billed out at up to $70 per hour although his starting salary will typically be $10–$15 for each billable hour which he produces (e.g., 1,500 hours $\times$ $10 = $15,000 per year).

The relationship between law school attended and the type of practice situation which the graduates of any given school tend to enter was explored earlier.... Knowing the monetary rewards accruing to certain types of practice ... one can predict the expected average financial success as a lawyer of a graduate from a certain law school. The best students from the best law schools usually migrate to the largest, best law firms possessing the most talented and most specialized lawyers, located in the largest cities and attracting the largest, best-paying clients. Associates in such firms are paid the highest relative salaries (with hopes of going on to partnership); partners in these firms earn the highest incomes in the legal profession. While it may be true that the brightest lawyers would probably command higher incomes regardless of the fact that they go to the best schools, graduation from less prestigious schools seems to be a handicap, at least for the average lawyer....

Outlook

EDUCATIONAL PREPARATION In the period from the fall of 1960 to the fall of 1972 the law school population has risen 141 percent. Of this increase, 24 percent was in schools accredited since 1960, 10 percent in the group identified as "least

selective" and 21 percent in "municipal" schools, or a total of 55 percent in schools with only local reputations, while at the other end of the spectrum, the "national" schools enrolled only 4 percent of the increase; the remaining 41 percent of the increase went to schools of medium selectivity and reputation. Thus can one see that schools of differing quality are sharing unequally in the legal-education boom....

A number of different reasons have been given for this burgeoning interest in law. Student idealism and interest in changing societal structure from within is frequently cited. On the other hand, some potential law students—having been led to believe that many national law school graduates are taking public interest jobs—are rushing into law hoping to garner the lucrative jobs which they believe are now going begging. More women see opportunities for a legal career. Minority groups are now being sought by law schools. Conditions of employment in alternate careers are less attractive than formerly, with, for instance, students with scientific or engineering training who see that these fields are over-crowded turning to the law. Returning veterans who either interrupted, deferred or acquired an interest in legal training, provide a one-time increase. These reasons undoubtedly have some merit, but perhaps the most important influence is the large group of persons who are now of law-school age. If this is indeed the most important variable, the increasing numbers requesting admission may continue despite the difficulty of achieving entry.

The phenomenal increase in the demand for approved legal education in the past decade has been met in part by the establishment of new schools but principally by the enlargement of existing programs. Entry by new law schools into the law-school market is not easy, but neither is it prohibitive.... Since new schools have yet to establish a reputation, the profession does not now regard their graduates as equal to those from the better-established schools.

Enrollments have risen in all law schools over the last decade. In the period 1960–72, the "national" schools showed the smallest increase, 36 percent. These schools train 9 percent of the current annual lawyer supply. "Municipals," which train 22 percent of the nation's lawyers, increased their enrollments 118 percent. The "least selective" schools train 8 percent of the lawyers and increased their enrollments 286 percent. Thus it is clear that the less prestigious schools (including newly-established schools) have experienced a rapid growth rate and now train almost half of the nation's annual supply of lawyers. Knowing the traditional career patterns of lawyers from such backgrounds, the implications of this fact become clear....

DEMAND FOR LEGAL SERVICES AND DISTRIBUTION OF LAWYERS The Department of Labor estimates that until 1980 the traditional modes of employment for lawyers will provide jobs for 14,500 new ones annually, or for about half of the estimated annual supply. And law school graduates seem to be sticking to traditional employment.

As discussed earlier... within the profession there has been a trend for law-firm partnerships to increase as users of legal talent both absolutely and relatively. And the partnerships themselves are growing ever-larger. Private industry has hired an increasing number of lawyers. Such demand will continue on the upswing as long as the nation's economy is healthy. While government hiring of lawyers has increased only slightly, there seems to be no prospect that government will play any lesser role in the lives and activities of its citizens. In fact, there is some indication that there will be more governmental regulation, which should increase employment for lawyers both in the public and private sector.

Furthermore, since the supply of lawyers is increasing, lawyers would not seem likely to leave voids which in the past have been filled by non-lawyers. New fields such as environmental, consumer and occupational-safety law have been suggested as possibilities for increasing legal employment. Others have suggested public administration, the poor and criminal work. These suggestions would seem to be predicated on a public belief that lawyers do not provide efficient legal service to all socio-economic classes and a public willingness to support improved and expanded legal services. The taxpayer mood of the early

1970s seems to indicate that a rapid expansion in this area is unlikely in the very near future.

A system of prepaid legal services, if and where implemented, would increase the demand for lawyers partially because many potential participants are presently unaware of their need for legal representation. Other trends, programs and legislation will most likely decrease the demand for legal services, such as no-fault divorce and no-fault automobile insurance legislation.

The geographic distribution of lawyers has also been criticized. This latter contention is based upon the proposition that there is a growing demand for lawyers in small cities and towns. As discussed earlier,... the trend has been for lawyers to congregate in the larger cities. If they are economic men, and the income figures seem to indicate that they are, then small-city demand is not effective. Unless there is a drastic change in the structure of the legal-services industry, there seems to be no prospect that lawyers will in large numbers opt for practice in small cities and towns....

Law is a risky profession. At the top of the pyramid, earnings are high, but the average lawyer—while usually earning more than a college graduate—does not earn a high income. Therefore, investment in a legal education is likely to appeal to the risk-taker.

The emerging graduate faces an uncertain future, unless he is in the top of his class at a well-known school. So-called "top" graduates comprise less than 10 percent of all law school graduates.... The differential between what the "top" graduates receive and what some lesser ones receive right after law school increases as the prestige of the school diminishes....

Summary and Conclusions

Entry into the legal profession requires 19 years of schooling. Since lawyers are not homogeneous in terms of training, practice situation and clientele, their earnings vary greatly, making entry into the profession a risky venture. The population of lawyers has been growing. Indeed, recently it has grown at a rate which far exceeds the demand for traditional legal services. While most lawyers are in solo practice, the reward of high incomes goes to those in partnerships and in corporate law departments. In response to these income patterns, there has been a shift away from individual practice to the higher-paying practice situations. Lawyers, also, seem to have responded to geographic differences in earnings. The profession is plagued by market imperfections, as lawyers' mobility is restricted and some clients are not aware of price, quality or even, perhaps, of the fact that they need legal service.

A lawyer's income is determined not only by location and experience and years of practice, but principally by the type of practice and clientele. The latter is heavily influenced by the type of law school from which he receives his legal training. The top graduates of the "national" schools, or most selective ones, obtain the associate openings in the prestigious law firms, directly upon graduation or after a one-or-two-year clerkship with a judge. This apprenticeship as an associate not only leads often to lucrative partnership positions, but provides these fortunate few who are already highly endowed, with further training which increases their productivity even more, and hence increases their lifetime earnings. Graduates of less prestigious schools are at an initial disadvantage. The exceptional person may be able to overcome this obstacle. The average or low-end student would seem to be doubly handicapped in this most competitive profession. First of all, his law school training is regarded as, and probably is, inferior. Secondly, he does not have the opportunity for further training which is provided for the associate. Neither his initial nor his lifetime earnings come close to those of his more fortunate brethren.

Therefore, it must be concluded that students who are enrolling in the "new" schools, "municipal" schools and "less selective" schools will probably not be able to secure employment to make it worthwhile for them to make the investment in a legal education. Since the legal-services industry is a segmented market, the emergence of large numbers of low-prestige graduates will not depress the earnings of graduates from better law schools. The demand for top legal talent does not consider the supply from the less prestigious institutions as its supply curve. In fact, associate incomes (i.e., income to top young legal talent) may rise if demand for legal services increases, for the top-rated schools have expanded their enrollments only moderately. Despite exhortation that rewarding careers should be open to all law graduates, there seems little prospect that there will be a sizeable increase in demand in the near future to meet the rising supply. One should not be the captive of a "lump of labor theory." The demand for lawyers is growing, but it hardly seems possible that it can expand at a rapid enough rate in the next few years to absorb the already incipient supply. To absorb the rising tide, there would have to be a re-structuring of the profession to meet the needs of those who are not now adequately served. In the near future, it seems unlikely that society will so change its priorities that lawyers will be adequately compensated for meeting these needs. Hence up to half of the graduates in the near future may have to seek employment in fields where traditionally legal training is not a prerequisite.

Notes and Questions

1. One consequence of increased competition among lawyers for business has been pressure within the profession to drop its long-standing prohibition against professional advertising. At the prodding of the U.S. Supreme Court, bar associations have been developing guidelines to permit lawyers to advertise. Typically these include: allowing lawyers to indicate their educations, specialties, public offices and teaching positions held, and memberships in professional organizations. They may also, with clients' permission, indicate other clients represented; tell what credit arrangements are acceptable, and indicate fees for initial consultations and other services. Lawyers will not be permitted to give false or deceptive statements, nor use "puffery."

2. What are the implications of having a large population of underemployed lawyers? Is it necessary for most persons to have a "family lawyer" in the same way they have family doctors? Lawyers are sometimes cynically referred to as "hired guns." Should everyone have one?

2 Legal Education

You are sitting, let us say, in a class in Contracts, or Personal Property, or Domestic Relations. John Smith in the third row is reciting on a case, and has got the facts confused, or he has misread the Restatement section in the footnote. A dozen hands are up, and a dozen eager faces reflect the desire to close in for the kill. The professor delays the moment of slaughter and deliberately passes over the volunteer matadors in order to call on Dick Jones in the tenth row. The professor knows from previous experience that he can count on Jones not only to set Smith right, but to introduce a new misconception that will transfer the error to a still deeper level of confusion. Jones performs according to expectation. More hands go up as more of the class come to share the illumination, taking it either from an inner flame or from the whispered coachings of neighbors. The whole discussion is lively and stimulating; everyone is put on his mettle and seeks to show his best capacities.

Lon L. Fuller, "On Teaching Law,"
Stanford Law Review (1950)

It is not only open verbal attack or the socratic method which is seen as hostile. Each of us interprets the emotions of his interlocutor by far more than the content of his language. Tones of voice, physical mannerisms, facial expression, cast of eye—all these are as important in the classroom as they are anywhere else in life. What is conveyed—for whatever reason—is extraordinarily often contempt, or disgust, or what one student described as "ice-cold indifference."

Duncan Kennedy, "How the Law
School Fails: A Polemic," *Yale Review*
of Law and Social Action (1970)

They were offered the choice between becoming kings or the couriers of kings. The way children would, they all wanted to be couriers. Therefore there are only couriers who hurry about the world, shouting to each other—since there are no kings—messages that have become meaningless. They would like to put an end to this miserable life of theirs but they dare not because of their oaths of service.

Franz Kafka, *Parables and Paradoxes*
(1961)

Law schools are the gate-keepers for the legal profession. For the financially unresourceful and the academically uncompetitive, they are the barriers. To those allowed to pass, they are the profession's initiation—a rite of passage that all lawyers share, a basis of community.

Law school is to transform lay-persons into novice lawyers, providing them with competency in the law, and instilling in them a nascent self-concept as a professional, a commitment to the values of the calling, and that esoteric mental style called "thinking like a lawyer."

Many issues have been recently raised about the quality, substance, and effects of legal education. Does law school adequately prepare people to assume the responsibilities of legal practice? Given that the practice of law is so diverse, why is there little diversity in the content of law school curricula? Does law school change people's personalities? Can it instill ethical values?

The readings here are directed to some of these questions. But the major theme is an exploration of the way in which law school education inculcates what Tocqueville identified as the lawyers' habits of mind.

The Trouble with Law School *Scott Turow*

The professor stands in the center of the room, and the students—one hundred of them or more—are seated in tiers that rise steeply above him. Suddenly, the professor will call out a name, chosen at random from the seating chart he has before him. "Mr. Jones," the professor will say, "state the case."

Slowly, Jones will describe the facts and issues of a dispute that has come before an appeals court somewhere in the English-speaking countries, usually in the United States. At moments, the professor will interrupt Jones, pressing the student to make his answers clearer, his reasoning more precise. Just how was the contract breached? What part of the agreement was most essential to the court in reaching its findings? Often the professor will add remarks of his own. Then he will choose another student, Ms. Green. She will be asked to state the next case, and, more important, to compare it with the case Jones described. In what ways are the facts and results of the two cases similar? In what ways are they distinct? What consistent principles seem to emerge in the comparison? And in their seats the other students will sit, intent, listening to these dialogues. Now and then, a few of the others will venture questions or comments of their own. But for the most part, they will answer only in their own minds the questions Jones and Green are asked. They will make occasional notes. They will feel acutely anxious every time the professor returns to the seating chart to select a new student to interrogate. They are learning the law.

For a hundred years it has been this way for American law students: the professorial inquisitions called "the Socratic method," the deduction of legal principles from a tireless comparison of case after case. There are variations from the pattern I describe, often significant ones; but since

the case and Socratic methods were first developed in the 1870s at Harvard Law School, under the guidance of Dean Christopher Columbus Langdell, the pedagogy of American law schools has remained remarkably uniform and fixed. Today, the methods of Dean Langdell predominate at virtually every law school in the country—no less so at Harvard, where they were initially practiced, and where I entered as a first-year law student in the fall of 1975.

Traditionally, the first year of legal education is the most dramatic of law school's three years. The curriculum of the first year has become as well established in the past century as the teaching methods. Nearly all of the 40,000 young Americans who begin their legal educations every fall are required, as I was, to take what are generally thought of as the basic subjects—contracts, torts, property, the criminal law, and civil procedure. And for all of them, the effects of that education are thought to be equally predictable and far-reaching. It is during the first year that law students learn to read a case, to frame a legal argument, to distinguish between seemingly indistinguishable ideas; then that you begin to absorb the mysterious language of the law, full of words like "estoppel" and "replevin." It is during the first year, according to a saying, that a law student learns "to think like a lawyer," to develop the habits of mind and world perspective that will stay with him or her throughout a legal career.

For me my first year of law school at Harvard was a time of extraordinary intellectual excitement. But it was also a period when I came to recognize and regret many of the shortcomings of the peculiar educational system that has been so long employed in preparing young Americans for the bar. Certainly doubts about legal education are not original with me. For about a decade now, law students and young lawyers have been raising questions about the way in which they were trained, and the complaints that my classmates and I made were more or less the same as

Reprinted by permission of G. P. Putnam's Sons from *One L* by Scott Turow. Copyright © 1977 by Scott Turow.

those that have been heard for years: that law classes are too large—they keep tuition low but leave students feeling anonymous and lonely; that the professors are too remote—brilliant men and women but often startlingly aloof; that Socratic inquisition, which comes without warning and forces students to perform before their peers, is anxiety-provoking and sometimes brutal in its results.

But the most serious and persistent criticism I heard was less specific, since it seemed to call into question the aims of legal education itself. By the middle of my first term of law school, I'd begun to hear from classmates (and feel myself) strong objections to the process of learning to think like a lawyer.

The first complaints began after about a month of school. Nicky Morris, the young professor who taught us civil procedure, had spoken in class about the education we were undergoing.

"Right now," he told us, "you have probably begun to recognize that going to law school involves learning a lot of legal rules, and you'll find pretty quickly that there's quite a premium placed on mastering the rules and knowing how to apply them. But in learning rules, don't feel like you've got to forsake a sense of moral scrutiny. The law in almost all its phases is a reflection of competing value systems. Don't feel because you're learning the rule, you've necessarily taken on the values that produced the rule in the first place."

The remark struck a number of my classmates, and as we left class for lunch, I talked about what Nicky had said with one of them, Gina Spitz. Gina came on as the last of the tough cookies. She'd just graduated from Barnard and she was full of the bristle of New York City. She was big, feisty, outspoken, and glitteringly bright. But Nicky's words had touched her in a way that left her sounding plaintive.

"They're making me different," she said, referring to our professors. "They're turning me into someone else, someone I don't want to be. I have the feeling all the time that I'm being indoctrinated."

As I listened to Gina that day, and judging from other remarks, I decided that she'd articulated feelings that seemed to have become common to many of the first-year students. On the one hand, the problem was as simple as the way Morris had put it. Some of us felt we were being forced to identify with rules and social notions with which we didn't really agree. In Contracts, for instance, it had already become clear that our professor, Rudolph Perini, was an ardent free-market exponent. Perini quickly succeeded in showing us that many of the traditional contract rules reflected free-market assumptions. When he threw the floor open for comment about whether those free-market rules were desirable or not, many students were reluctant to contest him. Perini was fearsome in debate and a renowned expert on contract law, and as a result many of us felt that we had no choice but to accept the logic of what Perini was saying, to take it as the law we would live and work with.

But there was a subtler difficulty in our education, one that went to the basis of legal thinking itself, and became especially apparent in class. We were learning more than a process of analysis or a set of rules. In our discussions with the professors, as they questioned us and picked at what we said, we were also being tacitly instructed in the strategies of legal argument, in putting what had been analyzed back together in a way that would make our contentions persuasive to a court. We all quickly saw that this kind of argument was supposed to be reasoned, consistent, progressive in its logic. Nothing was taken for granted; nothing was proven just because it was strongly felt. All of our teachers tried to impress upon us that you did not sway a judge with emotional declarations of faith. Nicky Morris often derided responses as "sentimental goo," and Perini on more than one occasion quickly dispatched those students who tried to argue by asserting supposedly irreducible principles.

Why, Perini asked one day, was the right to bargain and form contracts granted all adults, rather than a select group within the society?

Because that was fundamental, one student suggested, basic: all persons are created equal.

"Oh *are* they?" Perini asked. "Did you create them, Mr. Vivian? Have you taken a survey?"

"I believe it," Vivian answered.

"Well, hooray," said Perini, "that proves a great deal. How do you *justify* that, Mr. Vivian?"

The demand that we examine and justify our opinions was not always easily fulfilled. Many of the deepest beliefs often seemed inarticulable in their foundations, or sometimes contradictory to other strongly felt principles. I found that frequently. I thought, for example, that wealth should be widely distributed, but there were many instances presented in class that involved taking from the poor, where I felt that property rights should be regarded as absolute.

Yet with relative speed we all seemed to gain skill in reconciling and justifying our positions. In the fourth week of the term, Professor Bertram Mann, our criminal-law teacher, promoted a class debate on various schemes for regulating prostitution, and I noticed the differences in style of argument from similar sessions we'd had earlier in the year. Students now spoke about crime statistics and patterns of violence in areas where prostitution occurred. They pointed to evidence and avoided emotional appeals and arguments based on the depth and longevity of their feelings.

But to students like Gina, the process that had produced this kind of change was frightening.

"I don't care if Bertram Mann doesn't want to know how I *feel* about prostitution," she said at lunch that day. "I *feel* a lot of things about prostitution and they have everything to do with the way I *think* about prostitution. I don't want to become the kind of person who tries to pretend that my feelings have nothing to do with my opinions. It's not *bad* to feel things."

The deepest fear among us seemed to be the one Gina expressed—that, somehow, deep personal changes were being forced upon us by the process of legal education. More and more often as the year wore on, I would hear comments from classmates to the effect that we were being limited, harmed by the education, forced to substitute dry reason for emotion, to cultivate opinions that were "rational" but had no roots in the experience, the life we'd had before. We were being cut away from ourselves, we felt. And thus, more and more often I would scrutinize myself for the signs of those unwanted changes. On occasion I would find them.

At home, for instance, my wife, Annette, told me that I had started to "lawyer" her when we quarreled, badgering and cross-examining her much as the professors did students in class. And there seemed to me other habits to be wary of. It was a grimly literal, linear, step-by-step process of thought that we were learning. The kind of highly structured problem-solving method taught in each class, that business of sorting through the initial details of a case and then moving outward toward the broadest implications, was an immensely useful technical skill, but I feared it would calcify my approach to other subjects. And besides rigidity, there was a sort of mood to legal thinking that I found plainly unattractive.

"Legal thinking is nasty," I said to Gina at one point in our conversation, and I began to think later I'd hit on a substantial truth. Thinking like a lawyer involved being suspicious and distrustful. You re-evaluated statements, inferred from silences, looked for loopholes and ambiguities. You did everything but take a statement at face value.

So on one hand you believed nothing. And on the other, for the sake of logical consistency, and to preserve long-established rules, you would accept the most ridiculous fictions—that a corporation was a person, that an apartment tenant was renting land and not a dwelling.

In time I began to recognize that all of these smaller complaints about rigidity, emotional suffocation, the tortured logic of the law were part of a more fundamental phenomenon in the law itself. Law is at war with ambiguity, with uncertainty. In the courtroom, the adversary system—plaintiff against defendant—guarantees that someone will always win, someone lose. No matter if justice is evenly with each side, no matter if the issues are indefinite and obscure, the rule of law will be declared. The law and the arbitrary certainty of some of its results are no doubt indispensable for the secure operation of a society where there is ceaseless conflict requiring resolution.

But a lot of those attitudes toward certainty seem to rub off on the institutions of legal education, which show a similar seeking after sureness and definition, a desire to subdue the random element. The structure of classroom relations is an example, with all power and control vested in the professor. Yet it is hardly clear that the need that supports the customs of the courtroom is present in class. Not even the law can abolish the fundamental unclearness of many human situations, but in the law schools there is precious little effort to address the degree to which human choice is arbitrary. We are taught instead that there is always a reason, always a rationale, always an argument. And too much of that amounts to a tacit tutoring of students in strategies for avoiding, for ignoring, for somehow subverting the unquantifiable, the inexact, the emotionally charged, those things that still pass in my mind under the label "human." Eventually, I came to regard that kind of schooling not merely as objectionable, but even as inappropriate in light of the ultimate purposes of legal education—the fact that as future lawyers, my classmates and I were training to become the persons on whom this society rests the chief responsibility for making and doing justice.

Notes and Questions

1. Law school teaching uses a technique, unique to legal education, called the Socratic dialogue. This pedagogy, also known as the case method, generally involves an intensive interrogation by the teacher of individual students concerning the facts and principles presumed to be operative in an appellate opinion. The Socratic method is intended to accomplish two goals. The first is informational: instruction in the substantive rules of discrete bodies of law. The second is to develop in the student a cognitive restructuring for the style of analysis generally called "thinking like a lawyer." In that analysis, a student is trained to account for the factual minutiae as well as legal issues determined by the court to be at the core of the dispute which may allow an intelligent prediction of what another court would do with a similar set of facts. The technique is learner-centered: students are closely questioned

and their responses are often taken to direct the dialogue.

The Socratic method has been at the center of much of the criticism of legal education. Paul Savoy, in a frequently cited article, compared the pedagogy to game playing:

The Socratic method . . . consists largely of a set of "games," the most popular of which is "Corner". . . . The objective in each case is to drive the student into a corner by refuting any position he takes. In being presented with . . . a Socratic question, the student is cast on the horns of a dilemma: he is made to feel that there is some answer he must find, but in seeking it out, he begins to despair of finding it because everything he says is rejected as wrong. . . .

A variation of the game of "Corner" is "One-Up":

Student: "Do you think that custodial interrogation in the absence of counsel is a violation of the dignity of the individual?"

Teacher: "What do you mean by 'dignity'?" . . .

Then there is the familiar "chamber of horrors" gambit—the logical paradigm of which is the *reductio ad absurdum* argument —or what I prefer to call the game of "Now I've Got You, You Son-of-a-Bitch." By the time a law student reaches his second year, he knows the game and either stops playing it, plays along cynically, or initiates the counter-game of "Wooden Leg" ("What can you expect of a 'dumb' student like me"). . . . Another popular pastime of professors that often passes for Socratic dialogue is the game of "Guess What I'm Thinking"; the student counter-game is "Mindreading I, II or III," depending on the number of previous courses the student has had with the professor.*

Dr. Andrew Watson, a psychiatrist and law professor, sees the pedagogy of legal education as causing students to lose their willingness to care about other people.

It is my contention that law school education explicitly shapes the character development of law students in certain ways which are detrimental to efficient professional performance. The character adaptation is necessary in order

* Paul Savoy, "Toward a New Politics of Legal Education," *The Yale Law Journal* 79 (1970): 457–459.

to resolve and escape the tensions of the classroom. The principle [*sic*] characterological development change is to become "unemotional." In addition to being told that this is a desirable attribute to develop, it is also a reaction to classroom anxiety.... Marked stoicism and emotional unresponsiveness may be regarded as characterological defenses against underlying emotions. Intellectual means in the form of cynicism about the human aspects of the lawyer's role may also be used to accomplish this purpose. This cynicism is a kind of characterological defense which enables a person to avoid the necessity of caring about people with its intrinsic capacity to stir up anxiety.*

A defender of the Socratic method, Dr. Alan Stone, also a psychiatrist and law teacher, responded to legal education's critics as follows:

Despite its admitted potential for destructive interaction, Socratic dialogue also has enormous value in channeling group emotions into structural academic inquiry. As individuals vie for status during the period when a group evolves into a coherent entity the entire gamut of intense feelings and personal motivations, including a certain amount of free-floating hostility, is inevitably generated.... What the Socratic technique can do at its best is to channel the inevitable hostility into the academic inquiry. Most professors do not allow one student to become the constant target, nor do they accept the role of target themselves; rather, the ritual has evolved such that hopefully a student's ideas rather than the student are the impersonal target; at worst, a number of students in turn will be the focus.... Its functional value is, however, that group hostility is controlled, and the class knows that the teacher's authority—in this context his capacity to control group hostility and other emotional excesses—is unquestioned.†

Lastly, from another section of Scott Turow's book, a student's remark:

At moments during the year, it sometimes appeared to me that my female classmates were not themselves entirely comfortable with the open aggression that law and law school demanded. In class, they tended to be retiring.... Moreover, if I could believe Gina, many of the women were sometimes even more uncomfortable than the men when they were called on.

"I know how this sounds," she told me once, "but a lot of the women say the same thing. When I get called on, I really think about rape. It's sudden. You're exposed. You can't move. You can't say no. And there's this man who's in control, telling you exactly what to do. Maybe that's melodramatic," she said, "but for me, a lot of the stuff in class shows up all kinds of male/female power relations that I've sort of been training myself to resent." ‡

That the Socratic dialogue provokes anxiety, hostility, and aggression seems to be generally agreed upon. Savoy's analogy to game-playing and Watson's observation that students are encouraged to become unemotional suggests an important part of legal training is to develop in novice lawyers a sense of detachment from the emotion-laden fray. Stone and the student focused on the domination by the law teacher as authority figure, suggesting that another aspect of the training is to enforce a respect for authoritative power. What are the implications of such training for the role these new lawyers are ultimately to have? Should the non-professional population—both lawyers' clients and members of society generally—be concerned about the psychological aspects of legal education?

2. Turow's point that political values are often fused with the learning of legal dogma is a subtle one. Ralph Nader wrote of this process, "Students are conditioned to react to questions and issues which they have no role in forming or stimulating. Such teaching *forms* have been crucial in perpetuating the status quo in teaching *content*. For decades, the law school curriculum reflected with remarkable fidelity the commercial demands of law firm practice." §

* Andrew Watson, "The Quest for Professional Competence: Psychological Aspects of Legal Education," *University of Cincinnati Law Review* 37 (1968): 131.

† Alan Stone, "Legal Education on the Couch," *Harvard Law Review* 85 (1971): 412–413.

‡ Reprinted by permission of G. P. Putnam's Sons from *One L* by Scott Turow. Copyright © 1977 by Scott Turow. P. 245.

§ Ralph Nader, "Law Schools and Law Firms," *New Republic* (October 11, 1969), p. 21.

Another critic of legal education's content suggests that the reliance of the case method on appellate opinions, which are produced primarily by those legal interests who are sufficiently affluent to pursue costly appeals, biases the instruction:

> The emphasis placed on the study of appellate decisions omits consideration of the actual problems of trial work, such as the prejudices of judges and juries, the deals which are made in criminal courts, or the political focus affecting various classes of interested parties, such as tenants. This coincides with the insistence of many law schools that emphasis be placed on a supposedly value-free theoretical approach to law. In practice this means that law students draw only from theory heavily tinged with corporate values. They will thus be able to offer solutions for corporate problems, but not for the problems posed by injustices in the judicial system or other injustices caused by corporate interests." *

If this criticism is taken seriously, what kind of measures should be considered to control or balance political messages in legal training? What interests should society have in this matter?

* David N. Rockwell, "The Education of the Capitalist Lawyer: The Law School," in Robert Lefcourt, ed., *Law Against the People* (New York: Vintage Books, 1971), p. 97.

Law School: Caught in the Paradigmatic Squeeze   *John J. Bonsignore*

There was a man in our town
and he was wondrous wise:
he jumped into a BRAMBLE BUSH
and scratched out both his eyes—
and when he saw that he was blind,
with all his might and main
he jumped into another one
and scratched them in again.

With this nursery rhyme, Karl Llewellyn opened a book of first lectures to beginning Columbia law students, *The Bramble Bush*. Law students, like wise men, could expect to become blinded in the thicket of law and only upon bold reentry would they regain their vision. One wonders why the most apt metaphor for law is a bramble, why a wise man would jump into it to be blinded, why once blinded he would come back for more, and why more of what takes vision away will yield it again. . . .

Entering law students, unlike graduate students in other disciplines, who have already sampled their fields at the undergraduate level, come to law school with very little knowledge of what it will mean to study law and become lawyers. Admission is difficult (hence, law school *must* be

Reprinted from the *ALSA Forum* (December, 1977), Vol. 2, No. 3, pp. 65–74, published by the American Legal Studies Association. (Abridged. Original title, "Law as a Hard Science.")

good for you), law offers "more options" than does a Ph.D. in English, and parents and friends think that law is a good career. Beyond this, there floats what Llewellyn earlier termed "a pleasant haze."

Erving Goffman's classic work *Asylum* offers the best model on the remaking of visions in institutional settings. Although law students are voluntary entrants, they will find the psychic-social process of change a sharp intrusion into their lives and may wonder, after the first few days, what happened to the pleasant haze.

A key concept for Goffman is that all social institutions, such as the home, schools, work places, prisons, asylums, or monasteries have *"encompassing tendencies,"* that is, the ability to capture the time and interest of participants. Although most people carry on several activities in several institutions at different times and places with different participants and different authorities, there are some people who are encompassed by more *total institutions* which crowd out competing value sets and alternative identities that people in them would otherwise experience. The more encompassing or total an institution, the more influence it can exert over its participants.

Upon entry into an institution of whatever type, a person carries a *home world* or *presenting culture,* which Goffman impressionistically defines as "a record of experience that confirmed a tolerable conception of self and allowed a set of defense maneuvers, exercised at his own discretion, for coping with conflicts, discreditings and failures." The more the "home world" can be kept intact in an institution, the less influence that institution can have in altering values or identities of participants.

One additional preliminary idea is necessary before beginning to make application of Goffman to the law school setting. The idea of novices to an institution presupposes veterans or other regulars in the institution, who establish the institutional values and the permitted personal identities. Thus, home world or presenting culture meets *institutional* world and its culture. A clash of competing cultures may occur upon entry into an institution, even when the entry is voluntary; and the institution must develop *strategies* to eliminate the "home world" and replace it with the "institutional world." The more total an institution, the more effective it will be in prevailing in this contest of values and identities.

Some questions immediately arise as these abstractions are brought closer to the question of law schools and their impact. How total is the law school as an institution? How antithetical are its values and prescribed identities to the values and presenting identities of incoming participants? When there is conflict, what strategies are employed by regulars of the law school, particularly its faculty and veteran students, in overcoming "presenting cultures" and in replacing presenting cultures with the institutional culture? Some tentative answers to these questions can be put forth before going into the details of the "contest of wills" in law schools.

1. Law schools appear to be quite total, exerting strong encompassing tendencies that sharply curtail the regular rhythm among competing institutions of work, play, family, friendships, etc.

2. Even though entry is voluntary, there is a substantial conflict between the values and expected identities of entrants and the values and prescribed identities available in the institution.

3. Given that law schools are relatively total, the school has the edge in reshaping values and identities, but given the clash between "home world" and "institutional world," the law school must employ distinctive strategies to prevail.

4. At stake, behind this contest of wills is nothing other than the paradigm of law, from world view through technique. Learning to see the world as a lawyer and to use legal techniques to the exclusion of other organizing principles appears at most to be only a semivoluntary process....

Judging from the types of strategies used in law school teaching, it seems safe to assume that a law school has more than ordinary leverage over its student body. (Of course, it must be acknowledged that some do leave the school entirely and to this extent the institution is more open than a prison.) That entrants are in conflict with the institutional culture can also be assumed from the intensity with which strategies are employed in the early months of law school. (There is either overkill on willing subjects or necessary intensity of strategies on at least semi-unwilling subjects; the latter appears to be the better explanation.) These heroic assumptions made, this essay can focus on the strategies employed in eliminating the presenting culture and replacing it with the institutional culture.

The pleasant haze in the first days of law school is traceable to the fact the "home world" of most entrants has been good: having graduated from college, usually with at least a modicum of academic honor; having satisfactorily performed tests, particularly the LSAT which is supposedly predictive of law school success; having passed through the "careful screening" of the law school admission committee; and so on. In addition to these acceptable images possessed by all entrants, each entrant has additional sources of contentment and is assured of his or her capacity for self-determination, autonomy, freedom of action, and self-expression. It must be that the pleasant haze and its underlying causes are deemed undesirable in a good law school, because in the next few months there will be a vigorous institutional effort to cut the individual loose from all of these psycho-social anchoring points.

How can individuals who are relatively well satisfied with past experiences, identities, and values be made to want to get rid of them? According to Goffman, institutions (at least the more encompassing ones) provide a unique kind of "welcome" which entails the mortification of entrants through a series of abasements, degradations, humiliations, and profanations of self. If the institution is to prevail, the ways that entrants have defined their identity and role must never find outlet in behavioral opportunities within the institution.

Goffman focused in part on the physical side of "identity stripping" such as the admission practices of photographing, head shaving, removal of personal possessions and property, issuance of drab institutional clothing, forcing intimacy with batches of other people, and curtailing privacy in such institutions as mental hospitals, prisons, and the army. But he also considered psychological forms of mortification which are more pertinent in the law school setting. The classroom is the primary situs, the teacher the mortifier and the students the mortified. When the process is over, former selves will be largely abandoned and new selves will be born to think and act in ways not anticipated upon entry.

The pedagogy of a law school is said to be Socratic, but it has nothing to do with Socrates except that two people are talking to each other. The manifest aim in all early law school communication is to avoid common understandings through dialogue and to make the student into a fool whose past academic life and ways of thought are not only unhelpful in doing law, but are positively in the way. This is done primarily in two ways: (1) by a process called *looping,* in which the students' verbal responses and defenses are *themselves* made the objects of attack and rejected as improper and worthless, and (2) a disruption in the students' sense of economy of action. Looping makes for the ever-shifting ground in law school dialogue, the only constant being that whatever students say exceeds the wildest image of incomprehensibility. Every expression down to the face-saving aside thus becomes a fit subject matter for this process. And given the useful hangup of law students of seeking teacher praise, the student struggles desperately to determine what has gone wrong with the academic

success formula that worked in undergraduate settings. Students who observe the looping process on other students are happy not to have been the subject of ridicule before the entire class, but at the same time they identify with the victim and try to find out what earns rewards in this peculiar institution. When students *en masse* begin to feel inferior, weak, blameworthy, and guilty and are constantly looking over their shoulders to see if criticism or other sanctions are once again coming, the process of mortification (literally, the killing off of a self) has reached full effectiveness.

The second major strategy in bringing entrants into institutions involves a disruption of the students' sense of *economy of action,* that is, the way each individual balances needs and objectives in a personally efficient way in the ordering of events, scheduling of time, determining the relative importance of things, and so on. For the law student, personal economies, derived from prior academic experience, also become the subject of criticism. In preparing for class, the usual student technique of reading for point or mood rather than trifling detail becomes—it is learned from class—an improper technique. The very thing left out of preparation is said to be the thing needed, and *vitally* needed. Once again, the need for recognition of academic competence surfaces and students grow compulsive, scrapping their old economies of action, studying longer, reading more slowly, underlining everything, taking more notes or even copying whole sections of casebooks, or memorizing material, so as to be "thoroughly prepared" and not a target of academic ridicule. . . .

Of interest here is the transformation in attitudes that law students have about themselves and the worth of their past. In the foregoing ways, the pleasant haze is burned off, people become dissatisfied with their home worlds or presenting cultures and become amenable to the institution's culture and its privilege system. As Goffman states:

> Total institutions do not really look for total cultural victory. They create and sustain a particular kind of tension between the home world and the institutional world and use the per-

sistent tension as strategic leverage in the management of men.

The tension explains why students do not rebel *en masse* at institutional demands. First, as noted above, each student has a need for teacher praise in academic matters and each believes that the odd pedagogy of law school must somehow be necessary to becoming a lawyer. Secondly, the usual student competition for an edge over fellow students militates against solidarity and collective political action at the formative period when such action is desperately needed. Thirdly, students are in such a state of personal stress and chaos that they seek personal solutions and have literally no energy left for resistance. (It also may be that those who would be so inclined simply leave the law school.)

As the mortification process runs its course, the privilege system of the law school is slowly introduced and some students are restored to a state of partial grace. Law school questions and ways of answering them, though alien at first, become slowly intelligible. (Repetitive practice in legal technique begins to take hold.) Students starved for favorable recognition begin to build whole worlds around a favorable nod or facial expression, or in lasting a few seconds longer in "dialogue" before being put down. Beginners also get solace from the fact that most of the class will pass and ultimately some people do get out of law school. But the fewness of examinations and the postponing of those that are given until late in the first year prolongs and intensifies anxieties and facilitates the changing process. By the start of the second year, students have adjusted and anxiety yields to quiet boredom.

How does the stripping and conversion process of the first year of law school relate to the main question of paradigms and their practice in community? The shortest answer to this question is that much of the first year struggles may be traceable to the unwillingness of law students to accept the legal world view, the kinds of questions asked in law, and the way lawyers answer questions. If cases are presented in the raw—that is, factually—there may be a wide variety of organizational principles that can be invoked in their resolution. It is only after discipline that

students will "know" what questions arise from facts. (This is what the phrase "spotting the issues" so commonly heard in law school means.) For example, it is not a legal question to ask about the happiness of marriage. Rather, one must learn to ask about the presence or absence of statutory grounds for divorce. Similarly, one does not ask about the fairness of bargains after learning the rule that adequacy of consideration is not significant in contract law. Becoming case-hardened thus means the ability to read the legal world and to share understandings of it with other professionals. (If law students wonder why they have difficulty in talking with former college acquaintances, it is because of the deep transformation that has taken place in law school; the intensity of the law school has so displaced the home culture of students that they are literally different people when visiting old friends.)

In summary, seeing what a discipline says should be seen, and nothing else, can be understood as a highly painful and unnatural process of closing down perception, intuition, emotions, and other aspects of being that are not relevant to the calling. While it is sometimes said that law students have too much inclination toward certainty, the deeper need may be quite in the opposite direction; rather students intuitively feel the gross neglect of fundamental questions of justice, good policy, and fairness, in the theory and practice of law. But it is through the closing down of vision that the paradigm of the calling is developed and shared vision through community becomes the abiding reality. It is this process that lies behind the blindness-seeing metaphor of Llewellyn.

Notes and Questions

1. The process of taking on professional attitudes and identity, called professional socialization by sociologists and "the paradigmatic squeeze" by Bonsignore, can be traumatic. The following is a quote from a first-year law student reported in a recent study:

   In my two and a half months here I have felt myself deteriorate mentally, emotionally and spiritually. My high level of self-confidence and self-pride that I carried with me is gone. For the first time in any academic or intellectual phase of my life I feel completely in-adequate and find myself losing sleep. I am unable to communicate with former friends of mine from college who are not in law school. Law school has made me a miserable person and the worst thing about it is that I can sense it happening. I had quite a creative talent when I came here; I feel I have lost it. I had quite a flair with the subject matter of my undergraduate major. I find it inapplicable now. Is it necessary that I am doing this to myself? How much longer will I last? Does anybody in this law school care? *

The paradigmatic squeeze is largely a phenome-non of the first year in law school. The intensity of the experience diminishes as students adopt the accepted style of thinking, develop coping devices (academic ploys as suggested by Savoy, or psycho-logical defenses as Watson noted), and class rank becomes established through the first battery of examinations.

2. Wilbert Moore, a well-known sociologist of profes-sions, has developed a theory of professional train-ing called punishment-centered socialization, which casts law school education in a somewhat different light. He notes that suffering is a prominent com-ponent in the training of all developed professions. The training includes hazing, demands that are

* Ronald M. Pipkin, "Legal Education: The Consumers' Perspective," *American Bar Foundation Research Journal*, Vol. 1976, No. 4 (1976), p. 1191.

"unpleasant and even hazardous to...good stand-ing," and "challenging and painful experiences." These experiences are shared with other initiates "who thus have a sort of fellowship of suffering."

He concludes that occupational identity and com-mitment are proportional to the degree that initi-ates are compelled to suffer, have a realistic fear of failure, have acceptable role models available, and develop collective bonds based on hardships. (See Wilbert E. Moore, *The Professions: Roles and Rules* [New York: Russell Sage Foundation, 1970], pp. 76–79.)

In Moore's view, the greater the amount of suf-fering and mortification in professional prepara-tion, the more likely students are to take on the proffered professional identities and values. Even if this analysis correctly describes the collective ex-perience of students in law school, the reader should not be left with the impression that all students suffer the education, do not find excite-ment, or have traumatic anxieties. The degree of personal turmoil for any individual is likely tied to the resistance of that person's "home culture" and its distance from the institutionally accepted culture.

3. Do these readings make Tocqueville's observation on the lawyer's mind and habits more understand-able? Does not the profession have an obligation to the public to ensure that all lawyers are well-trained and meet exacting standards? Does good training require suffering? Should it be any other way?

3 The Lawyer in the Legal System

From the moment I left on the trip until I returned, every penny I spent, even for the newspaper, was charged to the client's account. Every quarter I handed a shoeshine man or dollar I put down for a drink was not my own money. And if anyone thinks this was great, I would like to point out one fact. Every motion I made, every word I uttered, every thought I had was also not my own. It belonged to somebody else.

Charles Reich, *The Sorcerer of Bolinas Reef* (1976)

Maintenance of the legal system as construed by lawyers is the principal function of the lawyer.... What degrades the profession degrades the legal sys-tem.... What is not good for lawyers is bad for law. In short, lawyers *are* the legal system.

Jethro K. Lieberman, *The Tyranny of Experts* (1970)

From the very beginning, our state and national con-stitutions and laws have laid great emphasis on pro-cedural and substantive safeguards designed to assure fair trials before impartial tribunals in which every defendant stands equal before the law. This noble ideal cannot be realized if the poor man charged with crime has to face his accusers without a lawyer to assist him.

Gideon v. *Wainwright,* 372 U.S. 335
(1963)

[The Pre–Civil War circuit] system required each judge to hold court successively in each county over a large district. He would try cases for a week or so in one county seat, then ride in a body with the attorneys of the court to the next county seat. Traveling together, rooming in the same inns, drinking together, the lawyers, attorney general, and judge all came to know each other intimately . . . they were one big family of high-spirited gentlemen. . . .

Daniel H. Calhoun, *Professional Lives
in America* (1965)

Conflict resolution within the legal system is through the adversary process. The theory of this method is that (1) adjudication can be most successful when the primary responsibility for articulating the dispute is left to those most closely involved in it, and (2) the integrity of the adjudicative offices—judges and juries—can best be maintained by being in the position of impartial arbiter.

The adversary process requires the presentation by the disputants of partisan evidence and arguments. Lawyers act as advocates for their clients in this process. In court, lawyers stand in the place of their clients. Their credentials, their skills, their special knowledge, their influence, and even their personality are for hire.

The Ethics of Advocacy   *Charles P. Curtis*

I

I want first of all to put advocacy in its proper setting. It is a special case of vicarious conduct. A lawyer devotes his life and career to acting for other people. So too does the priest, and in another way the banker. The banker handles other people's money. The priest handles other people's spiritual aspirations. A lawyer handles other people's troubles.

But there is a difference. The loyalty of a priest or clergyman runs, not to the particular parishioner whose joys or troubles he is busy with, but to his church; and the banker looks to his bank. It is the church or the bank, not he, but he on its behalf, who serves the communicant or the borrower. Their loyalties run in a different direction than a lawyer's.

So too when a lawyer works for the government. His loyalties hang on a superior peg, like the priest's or the clergyman's. For it is fiction to

say that he only has the government for his client. The government is too big. It absorbs him. He is part of it.

Likewise with the general counsel for a corporation. His identification with his client is all but complete. Taft in some lectures at the Albany Law School,[1] referring to work in the legal department of a corporation, said, "Such employment leads to a lawyer's becoming nothing more than an officer of the corporation as closely identified with it as if he was the president, the secretary or the treasurer."[2] Indeed, he usually is a director or a vice-president.

Not so the lawyer in private practice. His loyalty runs to his client. He has no other master. Not the court? you ask. Does not the court take the same position as the church or the bank? Is not the lawyer an officer of the court? Doesn't the court have first claim on his loyalty? No, in a paradoxical way. The lawyer's official duty, required of him indeed by the court, is to de-

---

Abridged from *Stanford Law Review,* December 1951, Vol. 4, pp. 3–23. Copyright 1951, by the Board of Trustees of the Leland Stanford Junior University. Reprinted by permission.

[1] The Hubbard Lectures in May 1914.

[2] Cheatham, *Cases and Materials on the Legal Profession* 60 (1938).

vote himself to the client. The court comes second by the court's, that is the law's, own command. . . .

. . . How far must a lawyer accompany his client and turn his back on the court? . . .

The person for whom you are acting very reasonably expects you to treat him better than you do other people, which is just another way of saying that you owe him a higher standard of conduct than you owe to others. This goes back a long way. It is the pre-platonic ethics which Socrates had disposed of at the very outset of the *Republic;* that is that justice consists of doing good to your friends and harm to your enemies. A lawyer, therefore, insensibly finds himself treating his client better than others; and therefore others worse than his client. A lawyer, or a trustee, or anyone acting for another, has lower standards of conduct toward outsiders than he has toward his clients or his beneficiaries or his patrons against the outsiders. He is required to treat outsiders as if they were barbarians and enemies. The more good faith and devotion the lawyer owes to his client, the less he owes to others when he is acting for his client. It is as if a man had only so much virtue, and the more he gives to one, the less he has available for anyone else. The upshot is that a man whose business it is to act for others finds himself, in his dealings on his client's behalf with outsiders, acting on a lower standard than he would if he were acting for himself, and lower, too, than any standard his client himself would be willing to act on, lower, in fact, than anyone on his own.

You devote yourself to the interests of another at the peril of yourself. Vicarious action tempts a man too far from himself. Men will do for others what they are not willing to do for themselves—nobler as well as ignoble things. What I want to do now is to illustrate this in the practice of law by a number of perplexing situations. They raise ethical problems, but none of them, I think, has a simple right or wrong answer, and I know of no canons of ethics or morals which lead to any answer. How could there be when the cause of the perplexity is the difference between acting for another and acting for yourself? . . .

II

A lawyer is called on the telephone by a former client who is unfortunately at the time a fugitive from justice. The police want him and he wants advice. The lawyer goes to where his client is, hears the whole story, and advises him to surrender. Finally he succeeds in persuading him that this is the best thing to do and they make an appointment to go to police headquarters. Meanwhile the client is to have two days to wind up his affairs and make his farewells. When the lawyer gets back to his office, a police inspector is waiting for him, and asks him whether his client is in town and where he is. Here are questions which the police have every right to ask of anybody, and even a little hesitation in this unfortunate lawyer's denials will reveal enough to betray his client. Of course he lies.

And why not? The relation between a lawyer and his client is one of the intimate relations. You would lie for your wife. You would lie for your child. There are others with whom you are intimate enough, close enough, to lie for them when you would not lie for yourself. At what point do you stop lying for them? I don't know and you are not sure.

To every one of us come occasions when we don't want to tell the truth, not all of it, certainly not all of it at once, when we want to be something less than candid, a little disingenuous. Indeed, to be candid with ourselves, there are times when we deliberately and more or less justifiably undertake to tell something else or something different. Complete candor to anyone but ourselves is a virtue that belongs to the saints, to the secure, and to the very courageous. Even when we do want to tell the truth, all of it, ultimately, we see no reason why we should not take our own time, tell it as skillfully and as gracefully as we can, and most of us doubt our own ability to do this as well by ourselves and for ourselves as another could do it for us. So we go to a lawyer. He will make a better fist of it than we can.

I don't see why we should not come out roundly and say that one of the functions of a lawyer is to lie for his client; and on rare occasions, as I think I have shown, I believe it is. Happily they are few and far between, only when his duty gets him into a corner or puts him on the spot. Day in, day out, a lawyer can be as truthful as anyone. But not ingenuous.

A lawyer is required to be disingenuous. He is required to make statements as well as arguments which he does not believe in. But the further his statements descend toward the particular, the more truthful he may be, indeed must be, because no one appreciates the significance of the particular better than a lawyer. In the higher brackets of generality, he has to be freed from his own beliefs and prejudices, for they are irrelevant, unless they are pressed into service for the client. But his insincerity does not extend to the particular, except, of course, particulars which do not belong to him, but are his client's secrets. Barring these, when he is talking for his client, a lawyer is absolved from veracity down to a certain point of particularity. And he must never lose the reputation of lacking veracity, because his freedom from the strict bonds of veracity and of the law are the two chief assets of the profession.

I have said that a lawyer may not lie to the court. But it may be a lawyer's duty not to speak. Let me give you a case from the autobiography of one of the most distinguished and most conscientious lawyers I or any other man has ever known, Samuel Williston. In his autobiography, *Life and Law,* he tells of one of his early cases. His client was sued in some financial matter. The details of the claim are not important. Williston, of course, at once got his client's letter file and went through it painstakingly, sorting, arranging, and collating it. The letters, we may well believe, told the whole story, as they usually do in such a case. Trial approached, but the plaintiff's lawyers did not either demand to see the correspondence, nor ask for their production. "They did not demand their production and we did not feel bound to disclose them." [3] At the close of the trial, "In the course of his remarks the Chief Justice stated as one reason for his decision a supposed fact which I knew to be unfounded. I had in front of me a letter that showed his error. Though I have no doubt of the propriety of my behavior in keeping silent, I was somewhat uncomfortable at the time."

[3] Williston, *Life and Law* 271 (1940).

This was a letter, a piece of evidence, a fact. Suppose it had been a rule of law. Suppose the Chief Justice had equally mistakenly given as a reason for his decision some statute or regulation which Williston knew had been repealed or amended, and it was not a letter but a copy of the new statute which he had in front of him. Williston would have interrupted the Chief Justice and drawn his attention to it. This is sometimes debated, but it is beyond dispute that this would have been Williston's duty, and there is no doubt at all that he would have performed it as scrupulously as he respected his duty to his client. . . .

III

"I must be cruel only to be kind," said Hamlet, on his way to his mother. And so likewise a lawyer has to tell himself strange things on his way to court. But they are strange only to those who do not distinguish between truth and justice. Justice is something larger and more intimate than truth. Truth is only one of the ingredients of justice. Its whole is the satisfaction of those concerned. It is to that end that each attorney must say the best, and only the best, of his own case.

This is not the method we have used in other endeavors, with not only more, but with conspicuous success. But the law has other things than success to think about. It must give the losing party, and his friends and his sympathizers, as much satisfaction as any loser can expect. At least the most has been said for him. The whole has been shaken out into the sun, and everyone concerned is given a feeling akin to the feeling of security which you get when you have told yourself the worst before you make a decision. The administration of justice is no more designed to elicit the truth than the scientific approach is designed to extract justice from the atom.

Advocacy requires a lawyer to start with something to be proved, and this is as true of facts as it is of propositions of law. When he goes to interview a witness as well as when he goes to the law library, he goes to get something. He will waste a lot of time if he goes with an open mind.

He must, of course, first formulate the issue in his mind, but he does this only to make it the easier to find what lies on his side of the issue. He fixes on the conclusion which will best serve his client's interests, and then he sets out to persuade others to agree.

The problem presented to a lawyer when he is asked to defend a man he knows is guilty or to take a case he knows is bad is perplexing only to the laymen. Brandeis said, "As a practical matter, I think the lawyer is not often harassed by this problem, partly because he is apt to believe at the time in most of the cases that he actually tries, and partly because he either abandons or settles a large number of those he does not believe in." [4]

It is profoundly true that the first person a lawyer persuades is himself. A practicing lawyer will soon detect in himself a perfectly astonishing amount of sincerity. By the time he has even sketched out his brief, however skeptically he started, he finds himself believing more and more in what it says, until he has to hark back to his original opinion in order to orient himself. And later, when he starts arguing the case before the court, his belief is total, and he is quite sincere about it. You cannot very well keep your tongue in your cheek while you are talking. He believes what he is saying in a way that will later astonish himself as much as now it does others.

Not that he cares how much we are astonished. What he does care is whether we are persuaded, and he is aware that an unsound argument can do much worse than fall flat. For it may carry the implication that he has no better one. He will not want to make it unless he really has no better.

IV

The classical solution to a lawyer taking a case he knows is bad is Dr. Johnson's. It is perfectly simple and quite specious. Boswell asked Johnson whether as a moralist Johnson did not think that the practice of the law, in some degree, hurt the nice feeling of honesty.

[4] Brandeis, *The Opportunity in the Law*, 39 *Am. L. Rev.* 561 (1905).

"What do you think," said Boswell, "of supporting a cause which you know to be bad?"

Johnson answered, "Sir, you do not know it to be good or bad till the Judge determines it. I have said that you are to state facts fairly; so that your thinking, or what you call knowing, a cause to be bad, must be from reasoning, must be from your supposing your arguments to be weak and inconclusive. But, Sir, that is not enough. An argument which does not convince yourself, may convince the Judge to whom you urge it: and if it does convince him, why, then, Sir, you are wrong, and he is right."

Dr. Johnson ignored the fact that it is the lawyer's job to know how good or how bad his case is. It is his peculiar function to find out. Dr. Johnson's answer is sound only in cases where the problem does not arise.

A lawyer knows very well whether his client is guilty. It is not the lawyer, but the law, that does not know whether his case is good or bad. The law does not know, because it is trying to find out, and so the law wants everyone defended and every debatable case tried. Therefore the law makes it easy for a lawyer to take a case, whether or not he thinks it bad and whether or not he thinks other people think it bad. It is particularly important that it be made as easy as possible for a lawyer to take a case that other people regard as bad.

We want to make it as easy as we can for a lawyer to take a bad case, and one of the ways the bar helps go about it is the canon of ethics which says, "It is improper for a lawyer to assert in argument his personal belief in his client's innocence or in the justice of his cause." It is called improper just so that the lawyer may feel that he does not have to. This, I think, must be its only purpose, for it is honored in no other way. . . .

No, there is nothing unethical in taking a bad case or defending the guilty or advocating what you don't believe in. It is ethically neutral. It's a free choice. There is a Daumier drawing of a lawyer arguing, a very demure young woman sitting near him, and a small boy beside her sucking a lollypop. The caption says, "He defends the widow and the orphan, unless he is attacking the orphan and the widow." And for every lawyer whose conscience may be pricked, there is another whose virtue is tickled. Every case has two sides, and for every lawyer on the wrong side, there's another on the right side.

I am not being cynical. We are not dealing with the morals which govern a man acting for himself, but with the ethics of advocacy. We are talking about the special moral code which governs a man who is acting for another. Lawyers in their practice—how they behave elsewhere does not concern us—put off more and more of our common morals the farther they go in a profession which treats right and wrong, vice and virtue, on such equal terms. Some lawyers find nothing to take its place. There are others who put on new and shining raiment. . . .

I have talked perhaps too lovingly about the practice of the law. I have spoken unsparingly, as I would to another lawyer. In a way the practice of the law is like free speech. It defends what we hate as well as what we most love. I don't know any other career that offers ampler opportunity for both the enjoyment of virtue and the exercise of vice, or, if you please, the exercise of virtue and the enjoyment of vice, except possibly the ancient rituals which were performed in some temples by vestal virgins, in others by sacred prostitutes.

V

Let us now go back and reconsider, and perhaps reconstruct, in the light of my examples and our discussion, this "entire devotion" which a lawyer owes to his client.

The fact is, the "entire devotion" is not entire. The full discharge of a lawyer's duty to his client requires him to withhold something. If a lawyer is entirely devoted to his client, his client receives something less than he has a right to expect. For, if a man devotes the whole of himself to another, he mutilates or diminishes himself, and the other receives the devotion of so much the less. This is no paradox, but a simple calculus of the spirit.

There is authority for such detachment. It is not Christian. Nor is the practice of law a char-

acteristically Christian pursuit. The practice of law is vicarious, not altruistic, and the lawyer must go back of Christianity to Stoicism for the vicarious detachment which will permit him to serve his client.

E. R. Bevan, in his *Stoics and Sceptics,*[5] summarized the Stoic faith as follows: "The Wise Man was not to concern himself with his brethren . . . he was only to serve them. Benevolence he was to have, as much of it as you can conceive; but there was one thing he must not have, and that was love. . . . He must do everything which it is possible for him to do, shrink from no extreme of physical pain, in order to help, to comfort, to guide his fellow men, but whether he succeeds or not must be a matter of pure indifference to him. If he has done his best to help you and failed, he will be perfectly satisfied with having done his best. The fact that you are no better off for his exertions will not matter to him at all. Pity, in the sense of a painful emotion caused by the sight of other men's suffering, is actually a vice. . . . In the service of his fellow men he must be prepared to sacrifice his life; but there is one thing he must never sacrifice: his own eternal calm." . . .

The Stoics gave us a counsel of perfection, but it is none the less valid. If a lawer is to be the best lawyer he is capable of being, and discharge his "entire duty" to his clients, here in the Stoic sage is his exemplar. Here in Stoicism is his philosophy. Let him be a Christian if he choose outside the practice of the law, but in his relations with his clients, let him be a Stoic, for the better Stoic, the better lawyer.

A lawyer should treat his cases like a vivid novel, and identify himself with his client as he does with the hero or the heroine in the plot. Then he will work with "the zest that most people feel under their concern when they assist at existing emergencies, not actually their own; or join in facing crises that are grave, but for somebody else. . . ."[6]

---

[5] As quoted in 6 Toynbee, *A Study of History,* 146–47 (1939).

[6] Cozzens, *Guard of Honor* 479 (1948).

How is a lawyer to secure this detachment? There are two ways of doing it, two devices, and all lawyers, almost all, are familiar with one or the other of them.

One way is to treat the whole thing as a game. I am not talking about the sporting theory of justice. I am talking about a lawyer's personal relations with his client and the necessity of detaching himself from his client. Never blame a lawyer for treating litigation as a game, however much you may blame the judge. The lawyer is detaching himself. A man who has devoted his life to taking on other people's troubles, would be swamped by them if he were to adopt them as his own. He must stay on the upland of his own personality, not only to protect himself, but to give his client the very thing that his client came for. . . .

The other way is a sense of craftsmanship. Perhaps it comes to the same thing, but I think not quite. There is a satisfaction in playing a game the best you can, as there is in doing anything else as well as you can, which is quite distinct from making a good score. . . .

A lawyer may have to treat the practice of law as if it were a game, but if he can rely on craftsmanship, it may become an art. . . .

. . . I wonder if there is anything more exalted than the intense pleasure of doing a job as well as you can irrespective of its usefulness or even of its purpose. At least it's a comfort.

I have compared the lawyer to the banker who handles other people's money and to the priest who handles other people's spiritual aspirations. Let me go further. Compare the lawyer with the poet whose speech goes to the heart of things. "Yet he is that one especially who speaks civilly to Nature as a second person and in some sense is the patron of the world. Though more than any he stands in the midst of Nature, yet more than any he can stand aloof from her." [7]

Notes and Questions

1. Curtis states that lawyers who work for government or corporations are absorbed by their clients.

[7] VII Writings of Henry David Thoreau, 289 (1906).

Does this mean that such lawyers should have no obligations to the public beyond those of their employers? Consider the following from the ethical code for lawyers in federal government employment:

Federal Ethical Consideration 8-2
The situation of the federal lawyer which may give rise to special considerations, not applicable to lawyers generally, includes certain limitations on complete freedom of action in matters relating to Canon 8. [Canon 8 of the American Bar Association Code of Professional Responsibility states, "A Lawyer Should Assist in Improving the Legal System."] For example, a lawyer in the Office of the Chief Counsel of the Internal Revenue Service may reasonably be expected to abide, without public criticism, with certain policies or rulings closely allied to his sphere of responsibility even if he disagrees with the position taken by the agency. But even if involved personally in the process of formulating policy or ruling there may be rare occasions when his conscience compels him publicly to attack a decision which is contrary to his professional, ethical or moral judgment. In that event, however, he should be prepared to resign before doing so, and he is not free to abuse professional confidence reposed in him in the process leading to the decision.*

2. The lawyers' code of professional ethics sets forth a number of ethical standards which are meant to assure clients of their lawyers' competent, confidential, and zealous counsel. Should society have any interest in the lawyer-client relationship so long as the lawyer is ethical?

3. In a recent case in Lake Pleasant, New York, two lawyers appointed to defend a man charged with murder were told by their client of two other murders, unknown to police, that he had committed. The lawyers, following the client's directions, discovered the bodies in an abandoned mine shaft and took pictures of them. They did not, however, inform the police until several months later, after their client confessed to those killings. In addition, the parents of one of the victims had approached one of the lawyers seeking information about his

* Federal Bar Association: *Federal Ethical Considerations* (adopted November 17, 1973).

missing daughter. The attorney denied having any information.

Monroe Freedman, a law school dean and prominent writer on legal ethics, wrote of this case:

The adversary system, within which the lawyer functions, contemplates that the lawyer frequently will learn from the client information that is highly incriminating and may even learn, as in the Lake Pleasant case, that the client has in fact committed serious crimes. In such a case, if the attorney were required to divulge that information, the obligation of confidentiality would be destroyed, and with it, the adversary system itself.*

Should there be any limits to a lawyer's advocacy?

4. Curtis claims lawyers need to be detached from their client's plight in order to play the "litigation game." How does law school training, as described in the preceding section, prepare lawyers to do this? Why can't lawyers be Christians?

* Monroe H. Freedman, *Lawyers' Ethics In An Adversary System* (Indianapolis, Ind.: Bobbs-Merrill, 1975), p. 5.

The courtroom is not merely a field upon which personal grievances are settled by rhetorical combat. It is not a closed scene in which only the parties to the dispute have an interest. Adjudication is a process of state governance. The court represents the government and, less directly, the society. Judgments of the court are backed by state power. Adjudication is imbued with the public interest.

The "Fight" Theory versus the "Truth" Theory   *Jerome Frank*

I

When we say that present-day trial methods are "rational," presumably we mean this: The men who compose our trial courts, judges and juries, in each law-suit conduct an intelligent inquiry into all the practically available evidence, in order to ascertain, as near as may be, the truth about the facts of that suit. That might be called the "investigatory" or "truth" method of trying cases. Such a method can yield no more than a guess, nevertheless an educated guess.

The success of such a method is conditioned by at least these two factors: (1) The judicial inquirers, trial judges or juries, may not obtain all the important evidence. (2) The judicial inquirers may not be competent to conduct such an inquiry. Let us, for the time being, assume that

the second condition is met—i.e., that we have competent inquirers—and ask whether we so conduct trials as to satisfy the first condition, i.e., the procuring of all the practically available important evidence.

The answer to that question casts doubt on whether our trial courts do use the "investigatory" or "truth" method. Our mode of trials is commonly known as "contentious" or "adversary." It is based on what I would call the "fight" theory, a theory which derives from the origin of trials as substitutes for private out-of-court brawls.

Many lawyers maintain that the "fight" theory and the "truth" theory coincide. They think that the best way for a court to discover the facts in a suit is to have each side strive as hard as it can, in a keenly partisan spirit, to bring to the court's attention the evidence favorable to that side. Macaulay said that we obtain the fairest decision "when two men argue, as unfairly as possible, on opposite sides," for then "it is certain that no important consideration will altogether escape notice."

Unquestionably that view contains a core of

Selections from "The 'Fight' Theory versus the 'Truth' Theory," and from "The Jury System" in Jerome Frank, *Courts on Trial: Myth and Reality in American Justice* (copyright 1949 by Jerome Frank; copyright renewed © 1976 by Princeton University Press; Princeton Paperback, 1973): pp. 80–102, 108–125. Reprinted by permission of Princeton University Press. Abridged.

good sense. The zealously partisan lawyers sometimes do bring into court evidence which, in a dispassionate inquiry, might be overlooked. Apart from the fact element of the case, the opposed lawyers also illuminate for the court niceties of the legal rules which the judge might otherwise not perceive. The "fight" theory, therefore, has invaluable qualities with which we cannot afford to dispense.

But frequently the partisanship of the opposing lawyers blocks the uncovering of vital evidence or leads to a presentation of vital testimony in a way that distorts it. I shall attempt to show you that we have allowed the fighting spirit to become dangerously excessive.

II

This is perhaps most obvious in the handling of witnesses. Suppose a trial were fundamentally a truth-inquiry. Then, recognizing the inherent fallibilities of witnesses, we would do all we could to remove the causes of their errors when testifying. Recognizing also the importance of witnesses' demeanor as clues to their reliability, we would do our best to make sure that they testify in circumstances most conducive to a revealing observation of that demeanor by the trial judge or jury. In our contentious trial practice, we do almost the exact opposite.

No businessman, before deciding to build a new plant, no general before launching an attack, would think of obtaining information on which to base his judgment by putting his informants through the bewildering experience of witnesses at a trial. "The novelty of the situation," wrote a judge, "the agitation and hurry which accompanies it, the cajolery or intimidation to which the witness may be subjected, the want of questions calculated to excite those recollections which might clear up every difficulty, and the confusion of cross-examination . . . may give rise to important errors and omissions." "In the court they stand as strangers," wrote another judge of witnesses, "surrounded with unfamiliar circumstances giving rise to an embarrassment known only to themselves."

In a book by Henry Taft (brother of Chief Justice Taft, and himself a distinguished lawyer) we are told: "Counsel and court find it necessary through examination and instruction to induce a witness to abandon for an hour or two his habitual method of thought and expression, and conform to the rigid ceremonialism of court procedure. It is not strange that frequently truthful witnesses are . . . misunderstood, that they nervously react in such a way as to create the impression that they are either evading or intentionally falsifying. It is interesting to account for some of the things that witnesses do under such circumstances. An honest witness testifies on direct examination. He answers questions promptly and candidly and makes a good impression. On cross-examination, his attitude changes. He suspects that traps are being laid for him. He hesitates; he ponders the answer to a simple question; he seems to 'spar' for time by asking that questions be repeated; perhaps he protests that counsel is not fair; he may even appeal to the court for protection. Altogether the contrast with his attitude on direct examination is obvious; and he creates the impression that he is evading or withholding." Yet on testimony thus elicited courts every day reach decisions affecting the lives and fortunes of citizens.

What is the role of the lawyers in bringing the evidence before the trial court? As you may learn by reading any one of a dozen or more handbooks on how to try a law-suit, an experienced lawyer uses all sorts of stratagems to minimize the effect on the judge or jury of testimony disadvantageous to his client, even when the lawyer has no doubt of the accuracy and honesty of that testimony. The lawyer considers it his duty to create a false impression, if he can, of any witness who gives such testimony. If such a witness happens to be timid, frightened by the unfamiliarity of court-room ways, the lawyer, in his cross-examination, plays on that weakness, in order to confuse the witness and make it appear that he is concealing significant facts. Longenecker, in his book *Hints On The Trial of a Law Suit* (a book endorsed by the great Wigmore), in writing of the "truthful, honest, over-cautious" witness, tells how "a skilful advocate by a rapid cross-examination may ruin the testimony of such a witness."

The author does not even hint any disapproval of that accomplishment. Longenecker's and other similar books recommend that a lawyer try to prod an irritable but honest "adverse" witness into displaying his undesirable characteristics in their most unpleasant form, in order to discredit him with the judge or jury. "You may," writes Harris, "sometimes destroy the effect of an adverse witness by making him appear more hostile than he really is. You may make him exaggerate or unsay something and say it again." Taft says that a clever cross-examiner, dealing with an honest but egotistic witness, will "deftly tempt the witness to indulge in his propensity for exaggeration, so as to make him 'hang himself.' And thus," adds Taft, "it may happen that not only is the value of his testimony lost, but the side which produces him suffers for seeking aid from such a source"—although, I would add, that may be the only source of evidence of a fact on which the decision will turn.

"An intimidating manner in putting questions," writes Wigmore, "may so coerce or disconcert the witness that his answers do not represent his actual knowledge on the subject. So also, questions which in form or subject cause embarrassment, shame or anger in the witness may unfairly lead him to such demeanor or utterances that the impression produced by his statements does not do justice to its real testimonial value." Anthony Trollope, in one of his novels, indignantly reacted to these methods. "One would naturally imagine," he said, "that an undisturbed thread of clear evidence would be best obtained from a man whose position was made easy and whose mind was not harassed; but this is not the fact; to turn a witness to good account, he must be badgered this way and that till he is nearly mad; he must be made a laughing-stock for the court; his very truths must be turned into falsehoods, so that he may be falsely shamed; he must be accused of all manner of villainy, threatened with all manner of punishment; he must be made to feel that he has no friend near him, that the world is all against him; he must be confounded till he forget his right hand from his left, till his mind be turned into chaos, and his heart into water; and then let him give his evidence. What

will fall from his lips when in this wretched collapse must be of special value, for the best talents of practiced forensic heroes are daily used to bring it about; and no member of the Humane Society interferes to protect the wretch. Some sorts of torture are as it were tacitly allowed even among humane people. Eels are skinned alive, and witnesses are sacrificed, and no one's blood curdles at the sight, no soft heart is sickened at the cruelty." This may be a somewhat overdrawn picture. Yet, referring to this manner of handling witnesses, Sir Frederic Eggleston recently said that it prevents lawyers from inducing persons who know important facts from disclosing them to lawyers for litigants. He notes, too, that "the terrors of cross-examination are such that a party can often force a settlement by letting it be known that a certain . . . counsel has been retained."

The lawyer not only seeks to discredit adverse witnesses but also to hide the defects of witnesses who testify favorably to his client. If, when interviewing such a witness before trial, the lawyer notes that the witness has mannerisms, demeanor-traits, which might discredit him, the lawyer teaches him how to cover up those traits when testifying: He educates the irritable witness to conceal his irritability, the cocksure witness to subdue his cocksureness. In that way, the trial court is denied the benefit of observing the witness's actual normal demeanor, and thus prevented from sizing up the witness accurately.

Lawyers freely boast of their success with these tactics. They boast also of such devices as these: If an "adverse," honest witness, on cross-examination, makes seemingly inconsistent statements, the cross-examiner tries to keep the witness from explaining away the apparent inconsistencies. "When," writes Tracy, counseling trial lawyers, in a much-praised book, "by your cross-examination, you have caught the witness in an inconsistency, the next question that will immediately come to your lips is, 'Now, let's hear you explain.' Don't ask it, for he may explain and, if he does, your point will have been lost. If you have conducted your cross-examination properly (which includes interestingly), the jury will have seen the inconsistency and it will have made the proper impression on their minds. If, on re-direct examination the witness does explain, the explanation will have come later in the case and at the request of the counsel who originally called the witness and the jury will be much more likely to look askance at the explanation than if it were made during your cross-examination." Tracy adds, "Be careful in your questions on cross-examination not to open a door that you have every reason to wish kept closed." That is, don't let in any reliable evidence, hurtful to your side, which would help the trial court to arrive at the truth.

"In cross-examination," writes Eggleston, "the main preoccupation of counsel is to avoid introducing evidence, or giving an opening to it, which will harm his case. The most painful thing for an experienced practitioner ... is to hear a junior counsel laboriously bring out in cross-examination of a witness all the truth which the counsel who called him could not bring out and which it was the junior's duty as an advocate to conceal." A lawyer, if possible, will not ask a witness to testify who, on cross-examination, might testify to true facts helpful to his opponent.

Nor, usually, will a lawyer concede the existence of any facts if they are inimical to his client and he thinks they cannot be proved by his adversary. If, to the lawyer's knowledge, a witness has testified inaccurately but favorably to the lawyer's client, the lawyer will attempt to hinder cross-examination that would expose the inaccuracy. He puts in testimony which surprises his adversary who, caught unawares, has not time to seek out, interview, and summon witnesses who would rebut the surprise testimony. "Of course," said a trial lawyer in a bar association lecture in 1946, "surprise elements should be hoarded. Your opponent should not be educated as to matters concerning which you believe he is still in the dark. Obviously, the traps should not be uncovered. Indeed, you may cast a few more leaves over them so that your adversary will step more boldly on the low ground believing it is solid."

These, and other like techniques, you will find unashamedly described in the many manuals on trial tactics written by and for eminently reputable trial lawyers. The purpose of these tactics— often effective—is to prevent the trial judge or jury from correctly evaluating the truthworthiness of witnesses and to shut out evidence the trial court ought to receive in order to approximate the truth.

In short, the lawyer aims at victory, at winning in the fight, not at aiding the court to discover the facts. He does not want the trial court to reach a sound educated guess, if it is likely to be contrary to his client's interests. Our present trial method is thus the equivalent of throwing pepper in the eyes of a surgeon when he is performing an operation. . . .

III

That brings me to a point which the fighting theory obscures. A court's decision is not a mere private affair. It culminates in a court order which is one of the most solemn of governmental acts. Not only is a court an agency of government, but remember that its order, if not voluntarily obeyed, will bring into action the police, the sheriff, even the army. What a court orders, then, is no light matter. The court represents the government, organized society, in action.

Such an order a court is not supposed to make unless there exist some facts which bring into operation a legal rule. Now any government officer, other than a judge, if authorized to do an act for the government only if certain facts exist, will be considered irresponsible if he so acts without a governmental investigation. For instance, if an official is empowered to pay money to a veteran suffering from some specified ailment, the official, if he does his duty, will not rely solely on the applicant's statement that he has such an ailment. The government officer insists on a governmental check-up of the evidence. Do courts so conduct themselves?

In criminal cases they seem to, after a fashion. In such cases, there is some recognition that so important a governmental act as a court decision against a defendant should not occur without someone, on behalf of the government itself, seeing to it that the decision is justified by the actual facts so far as they can be discovered with reasonable diligence. For, in theory at least, usually before a criminal action is begun, an official investigation has been conducted which reveals data sufficient to warrant bringing the defendant to trial. In some jurisdictions, indigent defendants charged with crime are represented by a publicly-paid official, a Public Defender—a highly important reform which should everywhere be adopted. And the responsibility of government for mistakes of fact in criminal cases, resulting in erroneous court judgments, is recognized in those jurisdictions in which the government compensates an innocent convicted person if it is subsequently shown that he was convicted through such a mistake.

In civil cases (non-criminal cases), on the whole a strikingly different attitude prevails. Although, no less than in a criminal suit, a court's order is a grave governmental act, yet, in civil cases, the government usually accepts no similar responsibilities, even in theory. Such a suit is still in the ancient tradition of "self help." The court usually relies almost entirely on such evidence as one or the other of the private parties to the suit is (a) able to, and (b) chooses to, offer. Lack of skill or diligence of the lawyer for one of those parties, or that party's want of enough funds to finance a pre-trial investigation necessary to obtain evidence, may have the result, as I explained, that crucial available evidence is not offered in court. No government official has the duty to discover, and bring to court, evidence, no matter how important, not offered by the parties.

In short, the theory is that, in most civil suits, the government, through its courts, should make orders which the government will enforce, although those court-orders may not be justified by the actual facts, and although, by reasonable diligence, the government, had it investigated, might have discovered evidence—at variance with the evidence presented—coming closer to the actual facts.

Yet the consequence of a court decision in a civil suit, based upon the court's mistaken view of the actual facts, may be as grave as a criminal judgment which convicts an innocent person. If, because of such an erroneous decision, a man loses his job or his savings and becomes utterly impoverished, he may be in almost as serious a plight as if he had been jailed. His poverty may make

him a public charge. It may lead to the delinquency of his children, who may thus become criminals and go to jail. Yet in no jurisdiction is a man compensated by the government for serious injury to him caused by a judgment against him in a non-criminal case, even if later it is shown that the judgment was founded upon perjured or mistaken testimony.

I suggest that there is something fundamentally wrong in our legal system in this respect. If a man's pocket is picked, the government brings a criminal suit, and accepts responsibility for its prosecution. If a man loses his life's savings through a breach of a contract, the government accepts no such responsibility. Shouldn't the government perhaps assume some of the burden of enforcing what we call "private rights"? . . .

IV

Suppose, that, in a crude "primitive" society, A claims that B took A's pig. If that is true, B violated a well-settled tribal rule. But B denies that he took the pig. A attacks B and kills him. Does A's killing of B prove that B was wrong about the facts? Does that killing constitute the enforcement of the tribal rule? Now suppose somewhat the same sort of dispute in the U.S.A. A sues B, claiming that, by fraud and deceit, B got A's pig. A legal rule says that if B did those acts, then A has a legal right to get back the pig or its money value. If A wins that suit, does the decision in his favor constitute the enforcement of that legal rule, even if A won through perjured testimony or because the trial court erroneously believed an honest but mistaken witness?

A lawyer friend of mine, to whom I put this question, replied, "Yes, in theory. In theory, the facts as found must be assumed to be true." His answer does not satisfy me. That we must accept the facts found by a trial court does not mean that a rule against fraud is really enforced when a court holds a man liable for a fraud he did not commit. My friend is saying, in effect, that, even were it true that the courts misfound the facts in 90% of all cases, still the courts would be enforcing the rules.

That conclusion does not bother the hardened

cynic. "In the long run," one may imagine him saying, "what is the difference whether courts make many mistakes in fact-finding, and, as a result, render erroneous decisions—as long as the public generally doesn't learn of those mistakes? Take, for instance, all this to-do about 'convicting the innocent.' One of the important purposes of punishing a man for a crime is to deter others from becoming criminals. Conviction and punishment of the innocent serve just as effectively as if they were guilty to deter others from crime—provided only the errors are not, too frequently, later discovered and publicized. It's tough on the innocent; but we can afford to sacrifice them for the public good. In the same way, if a non-criminal legal rule is of a desirable kind—for instance, a rule concerning the duty of a trustee to the beneficiaries of a trust—why bother whether, in particular law-suits, the courts, through failure to discover the actual facts, apply it to persons who haven't violated it? Public respect for that rule, and its infiltration into community habits, will come just as well from its misapplications as from its correct applications—if only the public doesn't learn of its misapplications. If you call it injustice to punish the innocent or mistakenly to enter money judgments against men who have done no legal wrongs, then I answer that effectively concealed instances of injustice are not only harmless but socially beneficial. They serve as useful examples. Don't get squeamish about such mistakes." I doubt whether any reader will agree with the cynic.

V

No one can doubt that the invention of courts, which preserve the peace by settling disputes, marked a great step forward in human progress.

But are we to be so satisfied with this forward step that we will rest content with it? Should not a modern civilized society ask more of its courts than that they stop peace-disrupting brawls? The basic aim of the courts in our society should, I think, be the just settlement of particular disputes, the just decision of specific law-suits.

The just settlement of disputes demands a legal system in which the courts can and do strive tirelessly to get as close as is humanly possible to the actual facts of specific court-room controversies. Court-house justice is, I repeat, done at retail, not at wholesale. The trial court's job of fact-finding in each particular case therefore looms up as one of the most important jobs in modern court-house government. With no lack of deep admiration and respect for our many able trial judges, I must say that that job is not as well done as it could and should be.

Questions

1. Curtis stated uncritically that "the administration of justice is no more designed to elicit the truth than the scientific approach is designed to extract justice from the atom." Would Judge Frank agree? How can there be justice without truth?

2. In criminal cases the state is a party to the legal dispute. Does this fact explain why the government may be more diligent in searching for truth than in civil cases between private parties? If the court were to conduct its own truth-seeking inquiries to settle private disputes, would it jeopardize the court's status of impartial arbiter? If so, how could it be avoided?

3. What is Frank's view of the interests of the state and society in private litigation? Does he suggest a role for lawyers different from that put forth by Curtis?

In addition to being an advocate, the lawyer is part of the administration of justice—an officer of the court. The court is a social system. It has structured relationships which are instrumental to its organizational functions and goals. One of its functions is to process people. As with most social systems, among a court's goal is efficiency.

The Practice of Law as Confidence Game   *Abraham S. Blumberg*

The overwhelming majority of convictions in criminal cases (usually over 90 per cent) are not the product of a combative, trial-by-jury process at all, but instead merely involve the sentencing of the individual after a negotiated, bargained-for plea of guilty has been entered. Although more recently the overzealous role of police and prosecutors in producing pretrial confessions and admissions has achieved a good deal of notoriety, scant attention has been paid to the organizational structure and personnel of the criminal court itself. Indeed, the extremely high conviction rate produced without the features of an adversary trial in our courts would tend to suggest that the "trial" becomes a perfunctory reiteration and validation of the pretrial interrogation and investigation.

The institutional setting of the court defines a role for the defense counsel in a criminal case radically different from the one traditionally depicted. Sociologists and others have focused their attention on the deprivations and social disabilities of such variables as race, ethnicity, and social class as being the source of an accused person's defeat in a criminal court. Largely overlooked is the variable of the court organization itself, which possesses a thrust, purpose, and direction of its own. It is grounded in pragmatic values, bureaucratic priorities, and administrative instruments. These exalt maximum production and the particularistic career designs of organizational incumbents, whose occupational and career commitments tend to generate a set of priorities. These priorities exert a higher claim than the stated ideological goals of "due process of law," and are often inconsistent with them.

Organizational goals and discipline impose a set of demands and conditions of practice on the respective professions in the criminal court, to which they respond by abandoning their ideological and professional commitments to the accused client in the service of these higher claims of the court organization. All court personnel, including the accused's own lawyer, tend to be coopted to become agent-mediators who help the accused redefine his situation and restructure his perceptions concomitant with a plea of guilty.

Of all the occupational roles in the court the only private individual who is officially recognized as having a special status and concomitant obligations is the lawyer. His legal status is that of "an officer of the court" and he is held to a standard of ethical performance and duty to his client as well as to the court. This obligation is thought to be far higher than that expected of ordinary individuals occupying the various occupational statuses in the court community. However, lawyers, whether privately retained or of the legal-aid, public defender variety, have close and continuing relations with the prosecuting office and the court itself through discreet relations with the judges via their law secretaries or "confidential" assistants. Indeed, lines of communication, influence and contact with those offices, as well as with the Office of the Clerk of the court, Probation Division, and with the press, are essential to present and prospective requirements of criminal law practice. Similarly, the subtle involvement of the press and other mass media in the court's organizational network is not readily discernible to the casual observer. Accused persons come and go in the court system schema, but the structure and its occupational incumbents remain to carry on their respective career, occupational and organizational enterprises. The individual stridencies, tensions, and conflicts a given accused person's case may present to all the participants are overcome, because the formal and informal relations of all the groups in the court setting require it. The probability of continued

Reprinted from *Law and Society Review* 1 (June 1967), pp. 18–31. By permission of the publisher, the Law and Society Association. (Abridged and footnotes deleted.)

future relations and interaction must be preserved at all costs.

This is particularly true of the "lawyer regulars" *i.e.,* those defense lawyers, who by virtue of their continuous appearances in behalf of defendants, tend to represent the bulk of a criminal court's non-indigent case workload, and those lawyers who are not "regulars," who appear almost casually in behalf of an occasional client. Some of the "lawyer regulars" are highly visible as one moves about the major urban centers of the nation, their offices line the back streets of the courthouses, at times sharing space with bondsmen. Their political "visibility" in terms of local club house ties, reaching into the judge's chambers and prosecutor's office, are also deemed essential to successful practitioners. Previous research has indicated that the "lawyer regulars" make no effort to conceal their dependence upon police, bondsmen, jail personnel. Nor do they conceal the necessity for maintaining intimate relations with all levels of personnel in the court setting as a means of obtaining, maintaining, and building their practice. These informal relations are the *sine qua non* not only of retaining a practice, but also in the negotiation of pleas and sentences.

The client, then, is a secondary figure in the court system as in certain other bureaucratic settings. He becomes a means to other ends of the organization's incumbents. He may present doubts, contingencies, and pressures which challenge existing informal arrangements or disrupt them; but these tend to be resolved in favor of the continuance of the organization and its relations as before. There is a greater community of interest among all the principal organizational structures and their incumbents than exists elsewhere in other settings. The accused's lawyer has far greater professional, economic, intellectual and other ties to the various elements of the court system than he does to his own client. In short, the court is a closed community.

This is more than just the case of the usual "secrets" of bureaucracy which are fanatically defended from an outside view. Even all elements of the press are zealously determined to report on that which will not offend the board of judges, the prosecutor, probation, legal-aid, or other officials, in return for privileges and courtesies granted in the past and to be granted in the future. Rather than any view of the matter in terms of some variation of a "conspiracy" hypothesis, the simple explanation is one of an ongoing system handling delicate tensions, managing the trauma produced by law enforcement and administration, and requiring almost pathological distrust of "outsiders" bordering on group paranoia.

The hostile attitude toward "outsiders" is in large measure engendered by a defensiveness itself produced by the inherent deficiencies of assembly line justice, so characteristic of our major criminal courts. Intolerably large caseloads of defendants which must be disposed of in an organizational context of limited resources and personnel, potentially subject the participants in the court community to harsh scrutiny from appellate courts, and other public and private sources of condemnation. As a consequence, an almost irreconcilable conflict is posed in terms of intense pressures to process large numbers of cases on the one hand, and the stringent ideological and legal requirements of "due process of law," on the other hand. A rather tenuous resolution of the dilemma has emerged in the shape of a large variety of bureaucratically ordained and controlled "work crimes," short cuts, deviations, and outright rule violations adopted as court practice in order to meet production norms. Fearfully anticipating criticism on ethical as well as legal grounds, all the significant participants in the court's social structure are bound into an organized system of complicity. This consists of a work arrangement in which the patterned, covert, informal breaches, and evasions of "due process" are institutionalized, but are, nevertheless, denied to exist.

These institutionalized evasions will be found to occur to some degree, in all criminal courts. Their nature, scope, and complexity are largely determined by the size of the court, and the character of the community in which it is located, *e.g.,* whether it is a large, urban institution, or a relatively small rural county court. In addition, idiosyncratic, local conditions may contribute to a unique flavor in the character and quality of the criminal law's administration in a particular community. However, in most instances a variety of stratagems are employed—some subtle, some crude, in effectively disposing of what are often too large caseloads. A wide variety of coercive devices are employed against an accused-client, couched in a depersonalized, instrumental, bureaucratic version of due process of law, and which are in reality a perfunctory obeisance to the ideology of due process. These include some very explicit pressures which are exerted in some measure by all court personnel, including judges, to plead guilty and avoid trial. In many instances the sanction of a potentially harsh sentence is utilized as the visible alternative to pleading guilty, in the case of recalcitrants. Probation and psychiatric reports are "tailored" to organizational needs, or are at least responsive to the court organization's requirements for the refurbishment of a defendant's social biography, consonant with his new status. A resourceful judge can, through his subtle domination of the proceedings, impose his will on the final outcome of a trial. Stenographers and clerks, in their function as record keepers, are on occasion pressed into service in support of a judicial need to "rewrite" the record of a courtroom event. Bail practices are usually employed for purposes other than simply assuring a defendant's presence on the date of a hearing in connection with his case. Too often, the discretionary power as to bail is part of the arsenal of weapons available to collapse the resistance of an accused person. The foregoing is a most cursory examination of some of the more prominent "short cuts" available to any court organization. There are numerous other procedural strategies constituting due process deviations, which tend to become the work style artifacts of a court's personnel. Thus, only court "regulars" who are "bound in" are really accepted; others are treated routinely and in almost a coldly correct manner.

The defense attorneys, therefore, whether of the legal-aid, public defender variety, or privately retained, although operating in terms of pressures specific to their respective role and organizational obligations, ultimately are concerned with strategies which tend to lead to a plea. It is the rational, impersonal elements involving economies of time, labor, expense and a superior commitment of the defense counsel to these rationalistic values of maximum production of court organization that prevail, in his relationship with a client. The lawyer "regulars" are frequently former staff members of the prosecutor's office and utilize the prestige, know-how and contacts of their former affiliation as part of their stock in trade. Close and continuing relations between the lawyer "regular" and his former colleagues in the prosecutor's office generally overshadow the relationship between the regular and his client. The continuing colleagueship of supposedly adversary counsel rests on real professional and organizational needs of a *quid pro quo,* which goes beyond the limits of an accommodation or *modus vivendi* one might ordinarily expect under the circumstances of an otherwise seemingly adversary relationship. Indeed, the adversary features which are manifest are for the most part muted and exist even in their attenuated form largely for external consumption. The principals, lawyer and assistant district attorney, rely upon one another's cooperation for their continued professional existence, and so the bargaining between them tends usually to be "reasonable" rather than fierce.

Fee Collection and Fixing

The real key to understanding the role of defense counsel in a criminal case is to be found in the area of the fixing of the fee to be charged and its collection. The problem of fixing and collecting the fee tends to influence to a significant degree the criminal court process itself, and not just the relationship of the lawyer and his client. In essence, a lawyer-client "confidence game" is played. A true confidence game is unlike the case of the emperor's new clothes wherein that monarch's nakedness was a result of inordinate gullibility and credulity. In a genuine confidence game, the perpetrator manipulates the basic dishonesty of his partner, the victim or mark, toward his own (the confidence operator's) ends. Thus, "the victim of a con scheme must have some larceny in his heart."

Legal service lends itself particularly well to confidence games. Usually, a plumber will be able to demonstrate empirically that he has performed a service by clearing up the stuffed drain, repairing the leaky faucet or pipe—and therefore merits his fee. He has rendered, when summoned, a visible, tangible boon for his client in return for the requested fee. A physician, who has not performed some visible surgery or otherwise engaged in some readily discernible procedure in connection with a patient, may be deemed by the patient to have "done nothing" for him. As a consequence, medical practitioners may simply prescribe or administer by injection a placebo to overcome a patient's potential reluctance or dissatisfaction in paying a requested fee, "for nothing."

In the practice of law there is a special problem in this regard, no matter what the level of the practitioner or his place in the hierarchy of prestige. Much legal work is intangible either because it is simply a few words of advice, some preventive action, a telephone call, negotiation of some kind, a form filled out and filed, a hurried conference with another attorney or an official of a government agency, a letter or opinion written, or a countless variety of seemingly innocuous, and even prosaic procedures and actions. These are the basic activities, apart from any possible court appearance, of almost all lawyers, at all levels of practice. Much of the activity is not in the nature of the exercise of the traditional, precise professional skills of the attorney such as library research and oral argument in connection with appellate briefs, court motions, trial work, drafting of opinions, memoranda, contracts, and other complex documents and agreements. Instead, much legal activity, whether it is at the lowest or highest "white shoe" law firm levels, is of the brokerage, agent, sales representative, lobbyist type of activity, in which the lawyer acts for someone else in pursuing the latter's interests and designs. The service is intangible.

The large scale law firm may not speak as openly of their "contacts," their "fixing" abilities, as does the lower level lawyer. They trade instead upon a facade of thick carpeting, walnut panelling, genteel low pressure, and superficialities of traditional legal professionalism. There are occasions when even the large firm is on the defensive in connection with the fees they charge because the services rendered or results obtained do not appear to merit the fee asked. Therefore, there is

a recurrent problem in the legal profession in fixing the amount of fee, and in justifying the basis for the requested fee.

Although the fee at times amounts to what the traffic and the conscience of the lawyer will bear, one further observation must be made with regard to the size of the fee and its collection. The defendant in a criminal case and the material gain he may have acquired during the course of his illicit activities are soon parted. Not infrequently the ill gotten fruits of the various modes of larceny are sequestered by a defense lawyer in payment of his fee. Inexorably, the amount of the fee is a function of the dollar value of the crime committed, and is frequently set with meticulous precision at a sum which bears an uncanny relationship to that of the net proceeds of the particular offense involved. On occasion, defendants have been known to commit additional offenses while at liberty on bail, in order to secure the requisite funds with which to meet their obligations for payment of legal fees. Defense lawyers condition even the most obtuse clients to recognize that there is a firm interconnection between fee payment and the zealous exercise of professional expertise, secret knowledge, and organizational "connections" in their behalf. Lawyers, therefore, seek to keep their clients in a proper state of tension, and to arouse in them the precise edge of anxiety which is calculated to encourage prompt fee payment. Consequently, the client attitude in the relationship between defense counsel and an accused is in many instances a precarious admixture of hostility, mistrust, dependence, and sycophancy. By keeping his client's anxieties aroused to the proper pitch, and establishing a seemingly causal relationship between a requested fee and the accused's ultimate extrication from his onerous difficulties, the lawyer will have established the necessary preliminary groundwork to assure a minimum of haggling over the fee and its eventual payment.

In varying degrees, as a consequence, all law practice involves a manipulation of the client and a stage management of the lawyer-client relationship so that at least an *appearance* of help and service will be forthcoming. This is accomplished in a variety of ways, often exercised in combination with each other. At the outset, the lawyer-professional employs with suitable variation a measure of sales-puff which may range from an air of unbounding selfconfidence, adequacy, and dominion over events, to that of complete arrogance. This will be supplemented by the affectation of a studied, faultless mode of personal attire. In the larger firms, the furnishings and office trappings will serve as the backdrop to help in impression management and client intimidation. In all firms, solo or large scale, an access to secret knowledge, and to the seats of power and influence is inferred, or presumed to a varying degree as the basic vendible commodity of the practitioners.

The lack of visible end product offers a special complication in the course of the professional life of the criminal court lawyer with respect to his fee and in his relations with his client. The plain fact is that an accused in a criminal case always "loses" even when he has been exonerated by an acquittal, discharge, or dismissal of his case. The hostility of an accused which follows as a consequence of his arrest, incarceration, possible loss of job, expense and other traumas connected with his case is directed, by means of displacement, toward his lawyer. It is in this sense that it may be said that a criminal lawyer never really "wins" a case. The really satisfied client is rare, since in the very nature of the situation even an accused's vindication leaves him with some degree of dissatisfaction and hostility. It is this state of affairs that makes for a lawyer-client relationship in the criminal court which tends to be a somewhat exaggerated version of the usual lawyer-client confidence game.

At the outset, because there are great risks of nonpayment of the fee, due to the impecuniousness of his clients, and the fact that a man who is sentenced to jail may be a singularly unappreciative client, the criminal lawyer collects his fee *in advance.* Often, because the lawer and the accused both have questionable designs of their own upon each other, the confidence game can be played. The criminal lawyer must serve three major functions, or stated another way, he must solve three problems. First, he must arrange for

his fee; second, he must prepare and then, if necessary, "cool out" his client in case of defeat (a highly likely contingency); third, he must satisfy the court organization that he has performed adequately in the process of negotiating the plea, so as to preclude the possibility of any sort of embarrassing incident which may serve to invite "outside" scrutiny.

In assuring the attainment of one of his primary objectives, his fee, the criminal lawyer will very often enter into negotiations with the accused's kin, including collateral relatives. In many instances, the accused himself is unable to pay any sort of fee or anything more than a token fee. It then becomes important to involve as many of the accused's kin as possible in the situation. This is especially so if the attorney hopes to collect a significant part of a proposed substantial fee. It is not uncommon for several relatives to contribute toward the fee. The larger the group, the greater the possibility that the lawyer will collect a sizable fee by getting contributions from each.

A fee for a felony case which ultimately results in a plea, rather than a trial, may ordinarily range anywhere from $500 to $1,500. Should the case go to trial, the fee will be proportionately larger, depending upon the length of the trial. But the larger the fee the lawyer wishes to exact, the more impressive his performance must be, in terms of his stage managed image as a personage of great influence and power in the court organization. Court personnel are keenly aware of the extent to which a lawyer's stock in trade involves the precarious stage management of an image which goes beyond the usual professional flamboyance, and for this reason alone the lawyer is "bound in" to the authority system of the court's organizational discipline. Therefore, to some extent, court personnel will aid the lawyer in the creation and maintenance of that impression. There is a tacit commitment to the lawyer by the court organization, apart from formal etiquette, to aid him in this. Such augmentation of the lawyer's stage managed image as this affords, is the partial basis for the *quid pro quo* which exists between the lawyer and the court organization. It tends to serve as the continuing basis for the higher loyalty of the lawyer to the organization; his relationship with his client, in contrast, is transient, ephemeral and often superficial.

Defense Lawyer as Double Agent

The lawyer has often been accused of stirring up unnecessary litigation, especially in the field of negligence. He is said to acquire a vested interest in a cause of action or claim which was initially his client's. The strong incentive of possible fee motivates the lawyer to promote litigation which would otherwise never have developed. However, the criminal lawyer develops a vested interest of an entirely different nature in his client's case: to limit its scope and duration rather than do battle. Only in this way can a case be "profitable." Thus, he enlists the aid of relatives not only to assure payment of his fee, but he will also rely on these persons to help him in his agent-mediator role of convincing the accused to plead guilty, and ultimately to help in "cooling out" the accused if necessary.

It is at this point that an accused-defendant may experience his first sense of "betrayal." While he had perhaps perceived the police and prosecutor to be adversaries, or possibly even the judge, the accused is wholly unprepared for his counsel's role performance as an agent-mediator. In the same vein, it is even less likely to occur to an accused that members of his own family or other kin may become agents, albeit at the behest and urging of other agents or mediators, acting on the principle that they are in reality helping an accused negotiate the best possible plea arrangement under the circumstances. Usually, it will be the lawyer who will activate next of kin in this role, his ostensible motive being to arrange for his fee. But soon latent and unstated motives will assert themselves, with entreaties by counsel to the accused's next of kin, to appeal to the accused to "help himself" by pleading. *Gemeinschaft* sentiments are to this extent exploited by a defense lawyer (or even at times by a district attorney) to achieve specific secular ends, that is, of concluding a particular matter with all possible dispatch.

The fee is often collected in stages, each installment usually payable prior to a necessary court appearance required during the course of an accused's career journey. At each stage, in his interviews and communications with the accused, or in addition, with members of his family, if they are helping with the fee payment, the lawyer employs an air of professional confidence and "inside-dopesterism" in order to assuage anxieties on all sides. He makes the necessary bland assurances, and in effect manipulates his client, who is usually willing to do and say the things, true or not, which will help his attorney extricate him. Since the dimensions of what he is essentially selling, organizational influence and expertise, are not technically and precisely measurable, the lawyer can make extravagant claims of influence and secret knowledge with impunity. Thus, lawyers frequently claim to have inside knowledge in connection with information in the hands of the D.A., police, probation officials or to have access to these functionaries. Factually, they often do, and need only to exaggerate the nature of their relationships with them to obtain the desired effective impression upon the client. But, as in the genuine confidence game, the victim who has participated is loathe to do anything which will upset the lesser plea which his lawyer has "conned" him into accepting.

In effect, in his role as double agent, the criminal lawyer performs an extremely vital and delicate mission for the court organization and the accused. Both principals are anxious to terminate the litigation with a minimum of expense and damage to each other. There is no other personage or role incumbent in the total court structure more strategically located, who by training and in terms of his own requirements, is more ideally suited to do so than the lawyer. In recognition of this, judges will cooperate with attorneys in many important ways. For example, they will adjourn the case of an accused in jail awaiting plea for sentence if the attorney requests such action. While explicitly this may be done for some innocuous and seemingly valid reason, the tacit purpose is that pressure is being applied by the attorney for the collection of his fee, which he knows will probably not be forthcoming if the case is concluded. Judges are aware of this tactic on the part of lawyers, who, by requesting an adjournment, keep an accused incarcerated awhile longer as a not too subtle method of dunning a client for payment. However, the judges will go along with this, on the ground that important ends are being served. Often, the only end served is to protect a lawyer's fee.

The judge will help an accused's lawyer in still another way. He will lend the official aura of his office and courtroom so that a lawyer can stage manage an impression of an "all out" performance for the accused in justification of his fee. The judge and other court personnel will serve as a backdrop for a scene charged with dramatic fire, in which the accused's lawyer makes a stirring appeal in his behalf. With a show of restrained passion, the lawyer will intone the virtues of the accused and recite the social deprivations which have reduced him to his present state. The speech varies somewhat, depending on whether the accused has been convicted after trial or has pleaded guilty. In the main, however, the incongruity, superficiality, and ritualistic character of the total performance is underscored by a visibly impassive, almost bored reaction on the part of the judge and other members of the court retinue.

Afterward, there is a hearty exchange of pleasantries between the lawyer and district attorney, wholly out of context in terms of the supposed adversary nature of the preceding events. The fiery passion in defense of his client is gone, and the lawyers for both sides resume their offstage relations, chatting amiably and perhaps including the judge in their restrained banter. No other aspect of their visible conduct so effectively serves to put even a casual observer on notice, that these individuals have claims upon each other. These seemingly innocuous actions are indicative of continuing organizational and informal relations, which, in their intricacy and depth, range far beyond any priorities or claims a particular defendant may have.

Criminal law practice is a unique form of private law practice since it really only appears to be private practice. Actually it is bureaucratic practice, because of the legal practitioner's enmeshment in the authority, discipline, and perspectives of the court organization. Private practice, supposedly, in a professional sense, involves the maintenance of an organized, disciplined body of knowledge and learning; the individual practitioners are imbued with a spirit of autonomy and service, the earning of a livelihood being incidental. In the sense that the lawyer in the criminal court serves as a double agent, serving higher organizational rather than professional ends, he may be deemed to be engaged in bureaucratic rather than private practice. To some extent the lawyer-client "confidence game," in addition to its other functions, serves to conceal this fact. . . .

Questions

1. Does Ladinsky's model of the career paths of lawyers help explain the phenomena Blumberg described? What would happen to advocacy and the criminal court system if large firm lawyers were to take on this work?

2. Curtis stated that clients benefit from the detachment of lawyers when lawyers treat litigation as a game. Is the "detachment game" similar to the confidence game?

3. The criminal justice system is frequently criticized for being cumbersome and slow. If Blumberg's observations are true, would more courts, judges, and lawyers necessarily speed up the process, as typically suggested?

4. Consider the following excerpt from a study of criminal defendants:

   They tended to see the individuals and institutions which apprehended and punished them —police officers, prosecutors, public defenders, judges—as essentially playing games not much different from the games they played themselves. They perceived the behavior of law enforcement officials as being essentially the same as the behavior of law violators—conning, manipulating, lying, using power and resources rather than applying principles of justice. . . .

For many of the men, the game-like nature of the system extended even to their relationship to their lawyer. In particular most of those who were represented by public defenders thought their major adversary in the bargaining process to be not the prosecutor or the judge, but rather their own attorney, for he was the man with whom they had to bargain. They saw him as the surrogate of the prosecutor—a member of "their little syndicate"—rather than as their own representative.*

A confidence game can work only if the victim is unaware of the consequences of the game? Who is getting conned in Blumberg's confidence game? Is it the client? Is it the larger society?

* Jonathan D. Casper, "Did You Have a Lawyer When You Went to Court? No, I Had a Public Defender," *Yale Review of Law and Social Action*, vol. 1 (Spring 1974), pp. 4–9.

"I Have Nothing To Do With Justice" *James Mills*

Martin Erdmann thinks he might be antisocial. When he was 6 he liked to sneak across his family's red-carpeted, spiral-staircased entrance hall to the potted palm, and spit in it. At Yankee Stadium, he rooted for the Red Sox. When he went to Dartmouth, he cheered for Yale. He didn't make a lot of friends. He says he doesn't need them. Today he's 57 years old, an unmarried millionaire lawyer, and he has defended more criminals than anyone else in the world. Because he is one of the five or 10 best defense lawyers in New York, he gets those criminals turned back into the streets months or years earlier than they had any right to hope for. His clients are not Mafia bosses or bank embezzlers or suburban executives who've shot their wives. He defends killers, burglars, rapists, robbers—the men people mean when they talk about crime in the streets. Martin Erdmann's clients *are* crime in the streets.

In 25 years, Martin Erdmann has defended more than 100,000 criminals. He has saved them tens of thousands of years in prison and in those years they have robbed, raped, burglarized and murdered tens upon tens of thousands of people. The idea of having had a very personal and direct hand in all that mayhem strikes him as boring and irrelevant. "I have nothing to do with justice," he says. "Justice is not even part of the

equation. If you say I have no moral reaction to what I do, you are right."

And *he* is right. As right as our adversary judicial system, as right as jury trials, as right as the presumption of innocence and the Fifth Amendment. If there is a fault in Erdmann's eagerness to free defendants, it is not with Erdmann himself, but with the system. Criminal law to the defense lawyer does not mean equity or fairness or proper punishment or vengeance. It means getting everything he can for his client. And in perhaps 98% of his cases, the clients *are* guilty. Justice is a luxury enjoyed by the district attorney. He alone is sworn "to see that justice is done." The defense lawyer does not bask in the grandeur of any such noble oath. He finds himself most often working for the guilty and for a judicial system based upon the sound but paradoxical principle that the guilty must be freed to protect the innocent.

And Erdmann does free them, as many as he possibly can. He works for the Legal Aid Society, a private organization with a city contract to represent the 179,000 indigent defendants who flood each year into New York City courtrooms. He heads the society's supreme court branch, has 55 lawyers working under him, makes $23,500 a year. Next to the millions left him by his father, a Wall Street bond broker, the money means nothing. Twenty-five years ago, until the accounting office told him he was messing up their books, he kept his paychecks stuffed in a desk drawer.

Excerpted from *On the Edge* by James Mills. Copyright © 1971, 1972, 1975 by James Mills. Reprinted by permission of Doubleday & Company, Inc.

In private practice he could have a six-figure income and, probably, the fame of Edward Bennett Williams, or F. Lee Bailey, or Percy Foreman. He is disgusted when people accuse him of dedication. "That's just plain nonsense. The one word that does *not* describe me is dedicated. I reserve that word for people who do something that requires sacrifice. I don't sacrifice anything. The only reason I'm any good is because I have an ego. I like to win."

Martin Erdmann does not look like a winner. He is slight, unimposing, with balding hair cut short every Monday on his way to work, custommade suits that come out baggy anyway and a slightly stooped, forward-leaning walk that makes him look in motion like Groucho Marx. His face is lean, bony, taut-skinned, with thin lips and bulging eyes. He lives in a one-bedroom co-op on Manhattan's East Side, has no television and rarely answers his phone ("I learned that from my father—he could sit in a room for hours with a ringing phone"). He plays chess by postcard, buys Christmas presents from catalogues and seldom goes out except to work and eat. Defendants who ask him for loans, get them. He finances black student scholarships and is listed as a patron of New York's City Center. His only self-indulgences are a 75-acre weekend Connecticut retreat and a one-month-a-year fishing trip, alone, to the Adirondacks. "I discovered a long time ago," he says, "that I am a very self-contained person."

Like most men who are alone without loneliness, Martin Erdmann is emotionally compact: self-centered, stubborn, at times perverse. He is also a failed idealist. "I had an English professor in college," he says, "who read an essay I wrote and told me, 'Martin, you are looking for better bread than is made of wheat.' I've never forgotten that."

Martin Erdmann gets up at 4:45, reads till 6:30, then subways three miles downtown to the Criminal Court Building. He moves through the dark, empty hallway to his office and unlocks the door. He is there at 7:30, two and a half hours before the courts open, and he is alone. In another 10 or 15 minutes Milton Adler will arrive, his boss, chief attorney in the criminal branch.

Then, one or two at a time, come the phone operator and clerks, the other lawyers, the defendants on bail, mothers of men in jail, sick-looking junkies with vomit-stained shirts, frightened people who sit quietly on the seven wooden chairs along the wall, angry people mumbling viciously, insane people dressed in costumes with feathers in their hair.

Before the rush begins, Martin Erdmann sits at his desk in a side office and goes over the folders of the day's cases. Anthony Howard, a 21-year-old Negro, is accused of using a stick and knife to rob a man of his wallet. Howard's mother visits him in jail, brings clean clothes and takes out his laundry. She doesn't know that the greatest danger to her son is not the robbery charge, but the man who sleeps above him in the eight-by-six-foot cell. Robert Phillips, Howard's cellmate, escaped from a state mental hospital seven years ago, was recaptured, released, then arrested for the murder of a 22-year-old girl and an infant boy. After three more years in a mental hospital, he has been declared legally sane and is now awaiting trial for the murders. Erdmann looks over the file. "Prisoners who've been in mental hospitals," he says, "tell me they keep them there until they admit the charges against them. Then they mark them sane and send them down for pleading." He decides to give the Anthony Howard case to Alice Schlesinger, a young lawyer who can still believe her clients are innocent. She's good at what Erdmann calls "hand-holding," giving a defendant and his family more time than the case might need.

Milton Adler walks in and says something about a meeting he went to yesterday with DAs and judges to discuss ways of getting more prisoners out on bail. Erdmann listens and says nothing. What's left of his idealism, the wreckage, he defends against the day's events by affecting an air of playful cynicism. He smiles and laughs and pricks the pretty little bubbles of naïveté that rise around him from other lawyers. Listening to Adler, his face flashes now with the playful-cynic smile. "If they do reduce bail," he says, "it'll be the last they see of the defendants."

Alice Schlesinger appears in the doorway, a small young woman, about 30, with long black hair. She wants to know what she can do to pressure the DA to start the trial of a bailed defendant charged with robbery. "Can't we put the screws to them a little? My client is very nervous and upset. He wants to get the trial over with."

"Well," says Erdmann, "of course you can always make a motion to dismiss for lack of prosecution. Say your client is suffering great emotional stress at having this dreadfully unjust accusation hanging over his head."

"Don't *smile* like that," she says. "He *is* innocent, this time."

Erdmann gets rid of the smile. "Well, you know," he says, "maybe the DA is having a little trouble locating the complainant, and your defendant's on bail anyway, so why urge them to go right out and track him down? Because if they find the complainant and go to trial and if from some extremely unfortunate occurrence your client should be convicted, then he's going to jail and he'll be a lot worse off than just nervous."

She agrees reluctantly and leaves. Erdmann sits silently at his desk, staring into the piles of papers. Then he says, "She has a lot to learn. She'll learn. With some tears, but she'll learn."

Erdmann gathers up the folders and takes the elevator to a courtroom on the 13th floor. He sits in one of the soft upholstered chairs in the jury box and takes another look at the 30 folders of the day's cases: a forgery, robberies (mostly muggings), burglaries, drug sales, assault with a gun, arson, sodomy, an attempted murder. He arranges them on the shelf in front of the jury box and then sits back to await the DAs and the judge. He is alone in the courtroom, a dimly lighted, solemn place—meant to be imposing, it is only oppressive. Brown walls, brown tables, brown church-pew seats soak up what little light the low-watt overhead bulbs surrender.

A DA comes in and Erdmann asks him about a kidnapping case that's approaching trial. "The DA on that one's on trial on another case, Marty. He won't be finished for a month at least."

"Wonderful," Erdmann laughs. "I hope he stays on trial until the complainant's 30. Then it won't look so bad. She was 8 when it happened and she's already 11." The DA shakes his head

and walks away. Two more DAs arrive and Erdmann talks to them, joking with them, making gentle fun of them, establishing his presence: twice their age, more experienced, more knowledgeable, more cunning. "There's no question that my reputation is much too high," he says. "It's been carefully cultivated. Myths are very important in this business."

The judge enters: Mitchell Schweitzer, tall, thin, gray-haired, on the bench 26 years, 16 of them working closely with Erdmann. He flashes a look around the room, greeting private lawyers, Erdmann and the two assistant DAs.

The clerk calls a name: "José Santiago!"

Erdmann fumbles through his folders and pulls one out. "He's mine," he says. An assistant DA looks at the rows of folders on his table and picks one up. Erdmann and the DA walk slowly toward the judge's bench, pulling out papers as they go. Erdmann has, among other things, a copy of the complaint and a hand-written interview that another Legal Aid lawyer had earlier with the defendant. The DA has a synopsis of the grand jury testimony and a copy of the defendant's record. With these documents, in the next three or four minutes, while the defendant himself sits unaware in a detention pen beneath the courtroom, the judge, DA and Erdmann will determine the likelihood of guilt and the amount of time the man will serve.

Trials are obsolete. In New York City only one arrest in thousands ends in trial. The government no longer has time and money to afford the luxury of presuming innocence, nor the belief that the truest way of determining guilt is by jury trial. Today, in effect, the government says to each defendant, "If you will abandon your unsupportable claim of innocence, we will compensate you with a light sentence." The defendant says, "How light?"—and the DA, defense lawyer and judge are drawn together at the bench. The conference there is called "plea bargaining," and it proceeds as the playing of a game, with moves and countermoves, protocol, rules and ritual. Power is in the hands of the prisoners. For as increasing crime has pushed our judicial system to the crumbling edge of chaos and collapse, the defendant himself has emerged as the only man with a helping hand. The government needs guilty pleas to move the cases out of court, and the defendants are selling their guilty pleas for the only currency the government can offer— time. But no matter what sentence is finally agreed upon, the real outcome of this bargaining contest is never truly in doubt. The guilty always win. The innocent always lose.

To play the game well, a lawyer must be ruthless. He is working within, but *against* a system that has been battered to its knees. He must not hesitate to kick it when it's down, and to take every advantage of its weakness. No one is better at the game than Martin Erdmann.

Judge Schweitzer glances through the grand jury extract handed him by the DA, a young bespectacled man named Jack Litman. Then the judge looks up over his glasses. "What are you looking for, Marty?"

Erdmann isn't sure yet. His client is accused of robbing a man on the street after stabbing him in the face, neck, chest, stomach and back. The victim was held from behind by an accomplice. "They have a big identification problem," Erdmann says. He is looking at a copy of a police report. "The DD-5 says the complaining witness refused to look at pictures in the hospital the next day because he said he wouldn't be able to identify the assailants from photographs."

"Your honor," Litman says, "they put 65 stitches in him."

"Just a minute," says the judge, and proceeds to read quickly to Erdmann from the grand jury extract: "They fled into an apartment house, the cop asked the super if he'd seen them, the super said they went into apartment 3-A, the cop went in, placed them under arrest and took them to the hospital where they were identified by the victim." He looks up. Erdmann has never heard the grand jury testimony before, and it hasn't exactly made his day. "So, you see, Marty, it's not such a bad case." He leans back. "I'll tell you what. A year with credit for time served." Santiago already has been in jail for 10 months. With time off for good behavior, that sentence will let him out today. Erdmann agrees. The DA nods and

starts stuffing papers back into the folder. "Bring him up," he says.

Santiago's accomplice is brought in with him. Both men are 21, short and defiant-looking. The accomplice, Jesus Rodriguez, has his own lawyer, who now joins Erdmann in agreeing to the sentence. The lawyers explain the offer to the defendants. They tell them that the offer can be made only if they are in fact guilty. Neither the judge nor the DA nor the lawyers themselves would permit an innocent man to plead guilty. Santiago and Rodriguez look bewildered. They say they are innocent, they did nothing. Much mumbling and consternation at the counsel table. Then Schweitzer says, "Would you like a second call?"

"Yes, your honor," says Erdmann. "A second call." The defendants are led out and downstairs to a detention pen. Erdmann looks at Santiago's interview sheet, a mimeographed form with blanks for name, age, address, education, employer, and then at the bottom, space for his version of what happened. Santiago's statement begins, "I am not guilty. I did nothing wrong." He has never been arrested before. He says he and Rodriguez were asleep in their apartment when the police charged in and grabbed them. At his arraignment some weeks ago, he pleaded not guilty.

"Talk to them," Judge Schweitzer suggests. Erdmann and his co-counsel walk over to the door of the pen. A court officer opens it and they step from the court's dark, quiet brownness into a bright, noisy, butt-littered hallway. The door slams shut behind them. From somewhere below come voices shouting, and the clang of cell doors closing. A guard yells, "On the gate!" and precedes them down a dark stairway to a barred steel door. An inside guard unlocks the door and they walk into a yellow, men's-room-tiled corridor with windows on the left and a large bench-lined cell on the right. Twenty men are in the cell, almost all of them dirty and bearded, some young and frightened sitting alone on the benches, others older, talking, standing, as at home here as on a Harlem street corner. Suddenly the voices stop and the prisoners, like animals expecting to be fed, turn their heads toward Erdmann and his co-counsel. Three other lawyers walk in, too, and in a moment the voices begin again—prisoners and lawyers arguing with each other, explaining, pleading, conning in the jailhouse jargon of pleas and sentences: "I can get you one and one running wild [two years consecutive].... I know a guy got an E and a flat [a Class E felony with a year].... So you want a bullet [a year]? You'll take a bullet?..."

Erdmann walks to the far end of the cell and Santiago meets him at the bars. Erdmann puts his toe on a cross strip between the bars and balances Santiago's folder and papers on his knee. He takes out a Lucky Strike, lights it and inhales. Santiago watches, and then a sudden rush of words starts violently from his mouth. Erdmann silences him. "First let me find out what I have to know," he says calmly, "and then you can talk as much as you want." Santiago is standing next to a chest-high, steel-plate partition. On the other side of it, a toilet flushes. A few steps away, Rodriguez is talking through the bars to his lawyer.

"If you didn't do anything wrong," Erdmann says to Santiago, "then there's no point even discussing this. You'll go to trial."

Santiago nods desperately. "I ain't done nothing! I was asleep! I *never* been in trouble before." This is the first time since his initial interview seven months ago that he has had a chance to tell his story to a lawyer, and he is frantic to get it all out. Erdmann cannot stop the torrent, and now he does not try. "I never been arrested." Santiago shouts, "never been to jail, never been in *no* trouble, no trouble, *nothing*. We just asleep in the apartment and the police break in and grab us out of bed and take us, we ain't done nothing. I *never* been in trouble, I never saw this man before, and he says we did it. I don't even know what we did, and I been here 10 months, I don't see no lawyer or nothing, I ain't had a shower in two months, we locked up 24 hours a day, I got no shave, no hot food, I ain't *never* been like this before, I can't stand it, I'm going to kill myself, I got to get out, I ain't—"

Now Erdmann interrupts, icily calm, speaking very slowly, foot on the cross strip, drawing on his cigarette. "Well, it's very simple. Either you're guilty or you're not. If you're guilty of anything you can take the plea and they'll give you a year, and under the circumstances that's a very good plea and you ought to take it. If you're *not* guilty, you have to go to trial."

"I'm not guilty." He says it fast, nodding, sure of that.

"Then you should go to trial. But the jury is going to hear that the cop followed you into the building, the super sent him to apartment 3-A, he arrested you there, and the man identified you in the hospital. If they find you guilty, you might get 15 years."

Santiago is unimpressed with all of that. "I'm innocent. I didn't do nothing. But I got to get out of here. I got to—"

"Well, if you *did* do anything and you are a little guilty, they'll give you time served and you'll walk."

That's more like it. "Today? I walk today?"

"If you are guilty of something and you take the plea."

"I'll take the plea. But I didn't do nothing."

"You can't take the plea unless you're guilty of something."

"I want the year. I'm innocent, but I'll take the year. I walk today if I take the year?"

The papers start to fall from Erdmann's knee and he grabs them and settles them back. "You walk if you take the plea, but no one's going to let you take the plea if you aren't guilty."

"But I didn't *do* nothing."

"Then you'll have to stay in and go to trial."

"When will that be?"

"In a couple of months. Maybe longer."

Santiago has a grip on the bars. "You mean if I'm guilty I get out today?"

"Yes." Someone is urinating on the other side of the partition.

"But if I'm innocent, I got to stay in?"

"That's right." The toilet flushes.

It's too much for Santiago. He lets go of the bars, takes a step back, shakes his head, turns around and comes quickly back to the bars. "But, *man*—"

Back upstairs at the bench, Erdmann says to Schweitzer, "He's got no record, your honor, and I've had no admission of guilt. You know I'm very careful with people who have no records—"

"And I am too, Marty, you know that."

"He says he hasn't had a shower in two months, he's in a 24-hour-a-day lockup, and he wants to get out, and I don't blame him."

"Marty, I'm not taking a guilty plea just because he wants a shower."

"Of course not."

"Do you want me to talk to them?"

"I think it might be a good idea, your honor."

Santiago and Rodriguez are brought up again and led into a small jury room adjoining the courtroom. Schweitzer reads the grand jury extract to the defendants, making sure they know the case against them.

Now Rodriguez says he'll take the plea. Schweitzer asks him to tell what happened the night of the robbery. Rodriguez says he and Santiago were on the street and they ran into the complainant and spoke with him and the complainant had a knife in his pocket and ended up getting cut, "but I didn't do nothing."

This departure from the original story, the admission that they had been with the victim and that there was indeed a knife, is enough for Erdmann. He looks at Schweitzer. "Now I'm convinced he's guilty." Schweitzer and Litman go back to court. Erdmann says to Santiago, "Do you want the plea?"

"Yes, man, I *told* you that, I got to get out—"

"Then the judge will ask you certain questions and you have to give the appropriate answers." He nods toward Rodriguez. "He held him and you stabbed him. Let's go."

They return to the courtroom and stand before the bench. Three times Schweitzer asks Santiago if he wants to change his plea, and three times Santiago refuses to answer. What if this is just a ruse to trick him into confessing? In exasperation Schweitzer gives up and moves on to Rodriguez. Rodriguez pleads guilty and is sentenced. Erdmann leans against the clerk's desk, his arms crossed over his chest, his eyes burning into Santiago. This ignorant, stupid, vicious kid has been offered a huge, heaping helping of the Erdmann talent, the experience, the knowledge, the *myth*—and has shoved it away. Erdmann's face is covered with disgust. Through his eyes, way beyond them, is fury—and unclouded, clear contempt.

The defendants are led from the courtroom. The clerk calls a case for a private lawyer, and Erdmann takes advantage of the break to get a cigarette. He goes into a small side room the court officers use for a lounge. The room has lockers, a desk, a refrigerator, toaster and hotplate—all of them old and beaten and scarred. Cops' jackets hang from the chair backs. Erdmann has forgotten Santiago. He stands by the window with his foot up on a radiator and looks across at the Tombs, home of many of his clients, a desperate place of rats and rapes, beatings, murders and, so far this year, six suicides. Eighty percent of the 1,800 men in the Tombs are clients of the Legal Aid Society. A few weeks ago, some of the prisoners, angry at the overcrowding, vermin and lack of official attention, decided to find out what could be accomplished by rioting. The riots were followed by avalanches of studies, committees, investigations and reports—some helpful, some hysterical.

Erdmann is looking at workmen on a Tombs setback clearing away shattered glass and broken furniture from beneath burned-out windows. "It will never be the same," he says. "Once they've found out they can riot and take hostages, it will never be the same. Today defendants are telling the judges what sentences they'll take. I had a guy the other day who told me he knew the system was congested and that they needed guilty pleas, and he was willing to help by pleading guilty for eight months. The guilty are getting great breaks, but the innocent are put under tremendous pressure to take a plea and get out. The innocent suffer and the community suffers.

"If the defendants *really* get together, they've got the system by the balls. If they all decide to plead not guilty, and keep on pleading not guilty, then what will happen? The offered pleas will get lower and lower—six months, three months. If that doesn't work, and they still plead not guilty, maybe the court will take 15 or 20 and try them and give them the maximum sentences. And if *that* doesn't work—I don't know. I don't know. They have the power, and when they find out, you're in trouble."

Two workmen standing on a plank are lowering themselves on ropes down the side of the Tombs. "Fixing the windows," Erdmann says. "Or escaping."

Forty minutes have been wasted with the stubborn Santiago, and now comes another problem. An Erdmann client named Richard Henderson says he was asleep in a Welfare Department flophouse when another man "pounced" on him with a stick. The other man says he was trying to wake Henderson when Henderson "jumped up like a jack rabbit" and stabbed him in the chest. Henderson is charged with attempted murder.

Erdmann talks to him in the pen hallway just outside the courtroom door. It has started to rain. A casement window, opaque, with chicken wire between the plates, has been cranked open and cold air and rain are blowing in and making things miserable for Henderson. He's a 21-year-old junkie—wire-thin, with deep, lost, wandering eyes, and a face sad and dead, as if all the muscles that could make it laugh or frown or show fear or anger had been cut. He stands there shivering in a dirty white shirt, no socks, no shoelaces, the backs of his shoes pushed in like slippers, hands stiff-armed down into the pockets of beltless khaki pants. Quietly, he tells Erdmann he wants to go to trial.

"Well you certainly have that right. But if you're guilty, I've spoken to the judge, and he'll give you a year with credit for time served. How long have you been in?" Erdmann turns the folder and looks at a date. "Six months. So with good behavior you'll have four left. It simply depends on whether you're guilty of anything or not."

Henderson nods. "Yes, that's why I want a jury trial."

"Why?"

"To find out if I'm innocent or not."

"Don't you know?" Erdmann takes another look in the folder. Henderson was psychiatrically examined at Bellevue Hospital and returned as legally sane.

"No. I don't know. But I have an opinion."

His eyes leave Erdmann and begin to examine the hallway. He has withdrawn from the conversation. Erdmann watches him a moment, then brings him back.

"What is your opinion?"

"That I am."

"Well, if you go to trial, it may be four months anyway before you *get* a trial, and then you'll be gambling zero against five or 10 years. And even if you're acquitted, you'll still have done the four months."

Henderson moves his feet and shivers. "I understand," he says meekly. "So I think I'd better do that."

"What?"

"Go to trial."

Erdmann just looks at him, not angry as he was with Santiago, but questioningly, trying to figure him out.

"I think I'd better have a trial," Henderson says.

Erdmann leaves him and walks back into court. "Ready for trial," he announces. "Don't even bother bringing him out." Litman makes a note on his file and they move on to another case.

Erdmann sits down in the jury box. The next few defendants have private lawyers, so he just waits there: watching, smiling, his bulging eyes gently ridiculing those around him who have failed to see as clearly as he into the depths of this charade, and to have found the joke there.

The judge is asking a defendant where he got the loaded gun. "He found it," Erdmann whispers before the man answers.

"I found it," the man says.

"Where?" asks the judge.

"Someone just gave it to him," Erdmann says.

"Someone walked by and handed it to me," says the defendant.

Erdmann smiles. "It's amazing," he says, "how often people rush by defendants and thrust things into their hands—guns, watches, wallets, things like that."

One of the two DAs is Richie Lowe, a black man—young, tall, slender, double-breasted, mod, Afro-haircut. Black defendants coming into court glance quickly around, and they see a white judge, white defense lawyers, white clerk, white stenographer, white guards, and then, over there, at that table over there, a *black*, the *only* black in the room, and he's—the enemy. Lowe, the black kid with a law degree from St. John's, sits next to millionaire Erdmann with the Wall Street father and Dartmouth and Yale Law.

But the irony is superficial—inside, Erdmann's character belies his background. He says he was "far to the left" of his parents, and he spent much of his youth trying to radicalize them. After law school he went to work in "a stuffy Wall Street law firm" where his first assignment was discovering whether or not a Florida gambling casino had acted legally in denying admittance to a female client's poodle. He quit, spent World War II in the Army and then joined the Legal Aid Society. "When I run into someone I can't place, I just say, 'Good to see you again, when did you get out?' That covers college, the Army and prison."

Guards bring in an old, toothless black man with wild white hair and an endless record of rapes, assaults, sodomy and armed robbery. He's accused of trying to rape a 4-year-old Puerto Rican girl. Some people driving in a car saw the man sitting on a wall with the girl struggling in his lap, and rescued her. Erdmann, Lowe and Judge Schweitzer talk it over. Schweitzer suggests a year. Lowe runs his eyes again over the grand jury extract. He usually goes along with Schweitzer, but this time he balks. "I can't see it, your honor. I just can't see it."

Erdmann speaks a few urging words, but Lowe won't budge. "No," he says, "I just can't see it, your honor. If these people hadn't come by in the car and seen the girl, this could have been— it could have been anything."

Schweitzer, himself under great Appellate Division pressure to dispose of cases, now pressures Lowe, politely, gently. He points out that the girl was not injured.

"I just can't, your honor," Lowe says. "I just can't. This is abhorrent, this—"

Schweitzer breaks in. "It's abhorrent to *me*, too, and it's being discussed *only* in the light of the calendar."

"Your honor, we've been giving away the courthouse for the sake of the calendar. I can't

do it. I won't do it." He stuffs his papers back in the folder. "Ready for trial, your honor."

He moves back to the prosecution table and announces for the record, "The people are ready for trial."

Erdmann has been saying nothing. As he passes Lowe's table on his way to the jury box, Lowe says, "Am I being unreasonable, Marty?"

Erdmann stops for a moment, very serious, and then shakes his head. "No, I don't think you are."

Lowe is upset. The next case has not yet been called. He moves around the table, fumbling folders. Then loudly he says, "Your honor, if he takes it *right now* I'll give him a year."

The judge fires Lowe a look. "You'll *recommend* a year. *I'll* give him a year."

Erdmann talks to the defendant at the counsel table. Lowe keeps shaking his head. He is suffering. He takes a step toward the bench. "Your honor," he says desperately, "he should get zip to three, at *least*."

"I *know* he should," Schweitzer says.

Erdmann now stands and for the record makes the customary speech. "Your honor, the defendant at this time wishes to withdraw his plea of not guilty, previously entered, and plead guilty to the second count of the indictment, attempted assault in the second degree, a Class E felony, that plea to cover the entire indictment."

Now it's Lowe's turn to make the speech of acceptance for the people, to accept the Class E felony, the least serious type of felony in the penal code. He stands. "Your honor, the people respectfully recommend acceptance of this plea, feeling that it will provide the court with adequate scope for punishment—" He stops. The next words should be, "in the interest of justice." He sits down and pretends to write something on a folder. Then softly, as if hoping he might not be heard, he speaks down into the table: "...in the interest of justice."

He walks over to a visitor. "What do you think about *that*?" he demands. "That took a little *piece* out of me. He got a *year* for trying to *rape* a *4-year-old* girl."

Schweitzer recesses for lunch, and Lowe and Erdmann ride down in the elevator. Lowe is still upset. "What do I tell that girl's mother when she calls me and wants to know what happened to the man who tried to rape her daughter?"

Erdmann smiles, the playful cynic. *Better bread than is made of wheat.* "Tell her, 'No speeka English, no speeka English, no speeka English.'"

Because Manhattan's Criminal Court Building is on the Lower East Side, in the midst of the ethnic no-man's-land where Little Italy collides with Chinatown, it is surrounded by some of the city's best Italian and Chinese restaurants. But every lunch-time Erdmann ignores these and walks two blocks north to Canal Street, a truck-choked crosstown conduit littered with derelicts overflowing from the Bowery, and eats in the sprawling, Formica-filled, tray-crashing chaos of the foulest cafeteria east of Newark. No number of threats, insults or arguments can persuade him into any other eating place. He has, every day, one scoop of cottage cheese, a slice of melon, and one slice of rye bread, buttered. (They give you two slices, want them or not, but he never succumbs.) Today he is at a table with a friend, not a lawyer, who asks how he feels when he goes to trial with a man he knows is guilty, and gets the man freed.

"Lovely! Perfectly beautiful! You're dancing on air and you say to yourself, 'How could that have happened? I must have done a wonderful job!' It's a euphoric feeling. Just to see the look of shock on the judge's face when the jury foreman says 'Not guilty' is worth something. It's the same sense of greed you get if a horse you bet on comes in at 15 to 1. You've beaten the odds, the knowledgeable opinion, the wise people." He laughs. "The exultation of winning dampens any moral feelings you have."

"But what," he is asked, "if you defended a man who had raped and murdered a 5-year-old girl, and he was acquitted and went free, and a year later was arrested for raping and murdering another 5-year-old girl. Would you defend him again with the same vigor?"

"I'm afraid so."

"Why afraid?"

"Because I think most people would disapprove of that."

"Do you care?"

"No."

"It doesn't concern you?"

"I'm not concerned with the crime committed or the consequences of his going free. If I were, I couldn't practice. I'm concerned with seeing that every client gets as good representation as he could if he had $200,000. I don't want him to get screwed just because there wasn't anyone around to see that he not get screwed. If you're a doctor and Hitler comes to you and says you're the one man in the world who can cure him, you do it."

"How much of that is ego?"

"Ninety-nine percent."

Erdmann eats his cottage cheese. An old derelict—bearded, toothless, with swollen lips—puts his tray down next to Erdmann and sits slurping soup and eyeing the untouched slice of rye.

In the courthouse lobby after lunch, Erdmann stops to buy a candy bar. Someone says he saw a story in the *Times* that 5,000 of that brand had been recalled after rodent hair was found in some of them. Erdmann smiles and buys two more.

A court officer sees Erdmann coming down the hall. "Hey, Marty," he yells, "he's on the bench, he's starting to call your cases."

"So what do you want me to do," Erdmann says, "break into a run?"

Guards bring in a 20-year-old girl charged with robbery with a knife. Erdmann is talking to her at the counsel table when Lowe strolls over and says, "Marty, an E and a flat?"

The girl looks at Lowe. "What's he saying, who's he?"

Lowe starts away. "Don't listen to me, I'm the enemy."

She wants to know why she has to go to jail. "Well, rightly or wrongly," Erdmann tells her, "people think they shouldn't be robbed. So when they get robbed, they give a little time." She asks if the year can run concurrent with another sentence pending against her. Erdmann asks Lowe and he agrees. She still hesitates, and finally refuses the offer.

"What's wrong?" Lowe says. "She wanted a year, I gave her a year. She wanted it concurrent, I made it concurrent. It's unreal. They tell us what they want and we're supposed to genuflect."

"José Sanchez!" the clerk calls. A drug-sale case.

"Your honor, he hasn't been seen yet," Erdmann says.

"Let me see the file," Schweitzer says to Lowe.

"Your honor," Erdmann says, "he hasn't even been interviewed. I haven't seen him."

"Well, just let's look at it, Marty," the judge says. He goes over Lowe's file. "It's one sale, Marty. He doesn't have any robberies. Burglaries, petty larceny. Mostly drugs, I'll tell you what, Marty, I'll give him an E and a flat." Lowe agrees.

Erdmann walks into the pen hallway, and they bring up a defendant. "They're offering an E and a flat," Erdmann says to him. "For a single sale, that's about the—"

The defendant looks mystified. He says nothing. The guard interrupts. "This isn't Sanchez, Marty. It's Fernandez."

Erdmann drops his arms in disgust, and without a word he turns and goes back into court and sits down in the jury box. A defendant has in effect been tried, convicted and sentenced before his lawyer even knew what he looked like.

After court, Alice Schlesinger comes into Erdmann's office to brief him on a client of hers, a woman, who will be in Schweitzer's court tomorrow. "She's absolutely not guilty," Alice says. When she leaves, Erdmann's smile turns wistful and nostalgic. "It must be wonderful," he says, "to have an *absolute* sense of who's guilty and who isn't. I wish I had it."

Adler walks into the office. "What can I tell them?" he asks Erdmann. "Jack says he's leaving because the job's making a cynic of him. He says he thought he was going to defend the downtrodden and he finds out they're hostile and they lie to him. So he's leaving. Alice comes to me and says, 'The system's wonderful for the guilty, but for the innocent it's awful. Some of them *must* be innocent.' What do you *say* to that?"

"You say nothing," Erdmann answers, "because it's true."

"No. You say that in a good system of government the vast majority get fair treatment, but there are bound to be a few who don't." He looks at Erdmann. "You think that's sentimental."

"I think you're a Pollyanna."

Adler turns to another man in the office. "He's called me sentimental, and he's called me a Pollyanna. And you know what? It's *true*."

Erdmann laughs. "What difference does *that* make?"

That night Erdmann goes home, has three Scotches on the rocks, meets a former judge for dinner, has a double Scotch, and thus fortified appears before the judge's evening seminar at the New York University Law School. Ten students are sitting in upholstered, stainless-steel swivel chairs in a red-carpeted conference room —all very new and rich and modern. Erdmann is supposed to tell them about jury selection and trial tactics, subjects on which he is a recognized master.

He unwraps a pack of cigarettes, lights up, and leans close over the table. Two of the students are girls. Most of the men are in jeans and long hair. Erdmann knows the look in their eyes. They think they will have innocent clients, they think they'll be serving their fellow man, the community, justice. They don't know that what they'll be serving is the system. He wants to give them some of the facts of life. "You are salesmen," he begins, "and you are selling a product that no one particularly wants to buy. You are selling a defendant who in all likelihood is guilty." They give him looks. "So you're going to disguise the product, wrap it in the folds of justice, and make it a symbol of justice. You have to convince the jurors that you're sincere, and that the product you are selling is not really this defendant, but justice. You must convince them that your defendant is not on trial. Justice is on trial."

The students are cautious. No one has taken any notes. "Your job is at the beginning and the end of the trial—the jury-picking and the summation. In between comes that ugly mess of evidence. In examining prospective jurors you have to sell your product before they get a look at him, before they hear the evidence. You want also to plant the seeds of your defense, and soften the blow of the prosecution's case. If you know that a cop is going to testify that the defendant stabbed the old lady 89 times, you can't hide from it. You might just as well bring it out yourself, tell them that they're going to hear a police officer testify that the defendant stabbed the old lady 89 times, and then when the testimony comes you will be spared the sudden indrawing of breath. And maybe you can even leave the impression that the cop is lying."

A girl mentions the Tombs riots and asks Erdmann what could be done to give the prisoners speedy trials. During the riots, inmates' demands for less crowding, better food, extermination of rats and vermin were supported even by the hostage guards. But their demands for speedy trials, though they found strong support in the press, were less sincere. Virtually every prisoner in the Tombs is guilty, either of the crime charged or of some lesser but connected crime. He knows that he will either plead guilty or be convicted in a trial, and that he will serve time. He knows, too, that delays will help his case. Witnesses disappear, cops' memories fade, complainants lose their desire for vengeance. As prosecutors see their cases decaying, they lower and lower the pleas. Meanwhile, time served in the Tombs before sentencing counts as part of the sentence. Erdmann wants to explain that to the students, but he knows he will not find many believers.

"Let me disabuse you," he says, "of the idea that the prisoners in the Tombs want speedy trials. Most of them are guilty of something, and the *last* thing they want is a trial. They know that if every case could be tried within 60 days, the pleas of one-to-three for armed robbery would be back up to 15-to-25."

"What about the defendants out on bail?" a student asks.

"People out on bail almost *never* have to go to trial. If you can get your client out on bail, he won't be tried for at least three years, if at all. The case will go from one DA's back drawer to another's until it either dissolves into dust or the DA agrees to a plea of time served."

A student asks about the defense lawyer's re-

sponsibility to be honest. That triggers Erdmann's smile. "My *only* responsibility," he says, "is to my client. And not to suborn perjury, and not to lie personally. My client may lie as much as he wants."

So mired have the courts become that there now arises the nightmare possibility of a prisoner sinking forever out of sight in the quicksand of judicial chaos. In the post-riot panic to relieve overcrowding in the Tombs, a special court was set up to facilitate the return to state prisons of inmates who had been brought to the Tombs to await hearings on various motions of appeal. One defendant entered the court in a rage. He was doing 20-to-life at Sing Sing for stabbing someone to death with an umbrella. A year ago he was brought to New York for an appeal hearing. He never got the hearing, and went 11 months without seeing a lawyer. Finally in court—unsure as to when, if ever, he would reappear—he shouted furiously at the judge. Guards moved in around him.

The judge got things sorted out, scheduled the hearing for the following week, and the prisoner was removed. After a year in limbo in the Tombs, he had finally been found. The judge waited until the door closed behind the prisoner, then looked at Erdmann, at the DA and back at Erdmann. He said, "Now there's a man who's got a *beef*."

Since the case of Richard Henderson, the junkie who didn't know if he was guilty, was marked ready for trial, he has been returned each day to the detention pen beneath Schweitzer's courtroom—on the almost nonexistent chance that his lawyer, and the DA assigned to the case, and a judge and courtroom might all become simultaneously available for trial. Each day he sits there in the pen while upstairs in court his case is called and passed, with no more certain consequence than that he will be back again the next day, so that it can be called and passed once more. After several days of this, Erdmann speaks to him again to see if he has changed his mind. He is the same—same clothes, same dead expression, same mad insistence on trial. Erdmann tries to encourage him to take the plea, "if you are guilty of anything."

Henderson still wants a trial.

"What will happen today?" he asks.

"Nothing. They'll set another date for trial, and that date will mean about as much as any date they set, which is nothing. You'll just have to wait in line."

Henderson picks at some mosquito-bite-size scars on his arm. "The other prisoners intimidate me," he says. "They keep asking me about my case, what I did, what I'm in for."

"What do you say?"

"I don't answer them. I don't want to talk about it."

Henderson is adamant. Erdmann leaves him and goes back to court.

Erdmann's disrespect for judges (Schweitzer is a rare exception) is so strong and all-inclusive that it amounts at times to class hatred. When one of his young lawyers was held in contempt and fined $200, Erdmann left Schweitzer's court and rushed to the rescue. He argued with the judge and conned him into withdrawing the penalty. Then, outside the courtroom in the corridor, Erdmann's composure cracked. "He's a bully," he said angrily. "I'll put Tucker [one of his senior lawyers] in there a couple of days and tell him, 'No pleas.' That'll fix *that* wagon." He makes a note, then crumples it up. "No. I'll take it myself —and it'll be on the record this time." Erdmann remembers that two days earlier the judge's car was stolen in front of the courthouse. "I should have told him not to let the theft of his Cadillac upset him so much."

"There are so few trial judges who just judge," Erdmann says, "who rule on questions of law, and leave guilt or innocence to the jury. And Appellate Division judges aren't any better. They're the whores who became madams."

Would he like to be a judge?

"I would like to—just to see if I could be the kind of judge I think a judge should be. But the only way you can get it is to be in politics or buy it—and I don't even know the going price."

Erdmann is still in the hallway fuming over the contempt citation when a lawyer rushes up and says a defendant who has been in the Tombs five months for homicide has been offered time served and probation—and won't take it. Erdmann hurries to the courtroom. The defendant and his girl friend had been playing "hit and run," a ghetto game in which contestants take turns hitting each other with lead pipes. He said he was drunk when he played it and didn't know how hard he was hitting the girl. They both passed out and when he awoke the next morning she was dead. He had no previous record, and the judge is considering the extraordinarily light sentence agreed upon by the lawyer and DA. Neither the judge nor the DA is in a mood for any further haggling from the defendant. Erdmann talks with the defendant and gets the plea quickly accepted. Five months for homicide. As he leaves the courtroom, a DA says, "Marty, you got away with murder."

Erdmann is gleeful. "I always get away with murder."

He goes down to his office. Alice Schlesinger walks by his desk and Erdmann remembers something he saw in the *Times* that morning about Anthony Howard, the man with an insane cellmate whose case he assigned to her three weeks ago.

"Hey, Alice," he calls to her, "congratulations on winning your first case."

She shrugs. A lawyer named James Vinci walks in and Erdmann says to him, "Don't forget to congratulate Alice. She just won her first case."

"Really?" says Vinci. "That's great."

"Yeah," Erdmann laughs. "Anthony Howard. His cellmate strangled him to death last night."

Every evening Martin Erdmann walks crosstown to a small French restaurant in the theater district. He sits always at the same table in a rear corner, with his back to whatever other customers there are, and he is happiest when there are none. The owner and his wife are always pleased to see him, and when he does not come they call his apartment to see if everything is all right.

Not long ago he reluctantly agreed to allow a reporter to join him for dinner. The reporter asked him if he could be positive after 25 years that he had ever defended an innocent man.

"No. That you never know. It is much easier

to know guilt than innocence. And anyway, it's much easier to defend a man if you know he's guilty. You don't have the responsibility of saving him from unjust punishment."

"What do you think about the courts today, the judicial system?"

"I think it's time people were told what's really going on. Everyone's so cowardly. Nobody wants to tell the public that the minimeasures proposed to clear up the mess *won't* do it. If you only had two roads going in and out of New York and someone said, 'What can we do about the traffic problem?' the answer would be, 'Nothing—until we get more roads.' You couldn't help it by tinkering around with the lights. Well, tinkering with the courts isn't going to help. We need more courts, more DAs, more Legal Aids, more judges —and it's going to cost a massive amount of money. I wonder how much money you could raise if you could guarantee safety from mugging and burglary and rape for $50 per person. Eight million people in New York? Could you get $20 million? And if you asked for $20 million to provide a workable system of criminal justice, how much would you get? People are more interested in their safety than in justice. They can pay for law and order, or they can be mugged."

"So what's the solution?"

"I've never really felt it was my problem. Everything up to now has benefited the defendant, and he's a member of the community, too. When you say, 'The people versus John Smith'—well, John Smith is part of the people, too. As a Legal Aid lawyer, I don't think it's my problem to make things run smoothly so my clients will get longer sentences. That's the court's problem."

He stops talking and thinks for a minute. Something is burning inside. "That's the wrong attitude, I suppose, but then the Appellate Division has never approached me and asked me what can be done to improve justice for the *accused*. They *never* ask *that* question. It's just how can we clear the calendars. It's how can we get these bastards in jail faster for longer. Not in those words—*certainly* not. They *never* in all these years asked, how can we have more justice for the defendants. That's why I'm not too concerned about the system." He has become angry and impassioned and

now draws back. He concentrates on a lamb chop.

"I'm loquacious when I'm tired," he says.

After several minutes, he begins again. "You know, I really don't think there *is* any solution to the problem, any more than there is to the traffic problem. You do what you can within the problem."

"Is the day coming when the traffic won't move at all?"

"Yes. If every defendant refused to plead and demanded a trial, within a year the system would collapse. There would be three-year delays in reaching trial, prison riots, defendants would be paroled into the streets."

"What's Martin Erdmann going to do when that happens?"

"That's an interesting question. It would be too late by then to do anything. It's going to be too late very soon."

Every Friday, Erdmann assigns himself to a courtroom with a half-day calendar and catches the 1:35 bus for Danbury, Conn. From there he drives to his estate in Roxbury and spends the weekend walking, gardening "and talking to myself." He has a three-story house with a junk-jammed attic, a cellar filled with jarred fruit he preserved years ago and never ate, and a library cluttered with unread books and magazines. A brook runs down from the acres of Scotch pine, past his garden and under a small bridge to the country below. He walks along the brook, and stops on the bridge to stare down at the trout. He never fishes here. "These are my friends," he says, "and you don't catch your friends."

Most of the weekend he spends trying to coax cooperation from the flowers and vegetables. "I worry most about the tomatoes because I like to eat them. The most difficult is what I don't grow anymore, roses. They demand constant care and that's why I don't have them." Tulips he likes. He spent a recent four-day weekend putting in 400 bulbs sent by a friend from Holland. "They're not difficult. You just dig 400 holes and put them in and they come up in the spring. The only problem is moles. The moles make runs to eat insects and then the mice use the mole runs to eat the tulip bulbs. Years ago I used to be out with spray guns. And then I figured, what the hell, this is nature, the mice don't know they're not supposed to eat tulip bulbs. So I gave up the spraying. I can't be hostile to something that's just doing what comes naturally."

The tulips are all in, it's 9 A.M., and Erdmann is back in his office going through the *Times*. He is stopped by an item about a former Legal Aid client, a 25-year-old homosexual named Raymond Lavon Moore. Charged with shooting a policeman in a bar, Moore had been in the Tombs 10 months, made 24 appearances in court, and steadfastly refused to plead guilty to anything more serious than a misdemeanor. He went into the Tombs weighing 205 pounds, and wasted slowly down to 155. He had never been in jail before. Five times Moore was removed to hospitals for mental observation, and each time he was returned to the Tombs. He twice tried unsuccessfully to kill himself. For fighting with a guard, Moore was sentenced to 20 days' solitary confinement in a small iron box whose only openings were a barred window and a four-inch-wide glass slit in the door. Last weekend, while Erdmann was on his hands and knees in T-shirt and dungarees digging the 400 tulip holes, Moore stripped the white ticking from his mattress, knotted it into a noose and hanged himself from the barred window.

Erdmann slowly folds the paper around the clipping and without expression hands it across his desk to another lawyer. He says nothing.

That noon, Erdmann is back talking through the bars of the detention pen beneath Schweitzer's courtroom. He's asking a drug pusher if there's someone who will make bail for him.

"I can't get in touch with no one from in here, man."

"Can I?"

"Yeah. My mama in Cincinnati." He is about to give Erdmann the phone number when Erdmann moves aside to allow a guard to open the door and insert more prisoners. One of the prisoners is Richard Henderson, the junkie who wants to go to trial. He walks in, foggy and listless, and his momentum carries him to the center of the cell. He stops there, staring straight ahead. He does not move or look around for three minutes. Then he takes two steps to the bench, sits down and puts his hands between his knees. He sits there, rubbing his palms together.

Five hours later, Judge Schweitzer is almost at the end of the day's calendar. The spectators have all left, and no one remains but court personnel. Everyone is tired. To speed things up, Schweitzer has told the guards to bring up everyone left in the pen and keep them in the hall by the door till their names are called. Five come up. Their cases already have been adjourned and what's happening now is more or less a body count to make sure no one is missed.

The last is Henderson. A guard walks him in, holding his arm, and someone says, "That's Henderson. He's been adjourned."

The guard, just four steps into the courtroom when he hears this news, quickly wheels Henderson around and heads him back out the door. Something in the wide, crack-the-whip arc of Henderson's swift passage through the court, something in his dead, unaware, zombie-eyed stare as he banks around the pivoting guard, strikes everyone who sees it as enormously funny. It's strange and it's pathetic, and no one can keep from laughing.

Questions

1. Erdmann says at one point, "We need more courts, more DAs, more Legal Aids, more judges..." and at another point, "It's just how can we clear the calendars. It's how can we get these bastards in jail faster for longer.... They *never* in all these years asked, how can we have more justice for the defendants." How will the provision of more courts, and the like, result in more justice if justice is *not* just a matter of "clearing the calendars"?

2. Do you feel that Erdmann is justified in obstructing the DA and judge even to the point of the system's collapse if he believes that the defendant is not getting justice?

3. Why are the judge and lawyers careful to get the defendant to state a guilty plea openly in court?

4. What are the underlying goals of the state in plea bargaining: rehabilitation, deterrence, retribution, or something else?

5. Is it proper for a judge or lawyer who has lost faith in the prison system to allow defendants to bargain out of going to prison? Should the conditions in prison influence the sentencing process?

4 The Lawyer and Social Reform

Society's overriding concern today is with providing freedom and equality of rights and opportunities, in a realistic and not merely formal sense, to all the people of this Nation: justice, equal and practical, to the poor, to the members of minority groups, to the criminally accused, to the displaced persons of the technological revolution, to alienated youth, to the urban masses, to the unrepresented consumers—to all, in short, who do not partake of the abundance of American life.

> Justice William Brennan, Jr., "The Responsibilities of the Legal Profession," in Arthur E. Sutherland, ed., *The Path of The Law from 1967* (1968)

The ambivalence of the public image of lawyers is readily understandable. It corresponds to the highly ambivalent nature of the lawyers' role in the governing process.... On the one hand, lawyers are experts at writing up the grand populist generalities of statutes and court decisions. On the other hand, they know what the hard practical questions are—how those generalities will be applied to specific cases.... It has even been argued that the virtual hypocrisy built into the lawyers' role serves a vital and useful social function; even if the populist notion that the people should be sovereign is an impossible dream, it may help keep people happy to go on promising that it can come true or by pretending that it has come true.

> Simon Lazarus, *The Genteel Populists* (1974)

Tocqueville noted the American propensity to transform all political questions into legal questions. The social movements of the last decade again illustrate his insight. The concept of civil rights, which is core to "liberation" movements—racial and ethnic, women, children, aged, gay, prisoners, institutionalized patients, handicapped, and so on—is a legal concept. Similarly, political claims that challenge the established order for the benefit of the population generally—for example, consumer rights and the ecology movement—are pressed largely by legal initiatives. Social reform, as it has developed in this country, requires legal activism and the engagement of lawyers. So, too, does resistance to these movements.

The readings in this section concern the role of lawyers in one attempt at social reform—the antipoverty program. However, they raise questions about the transformation of political claims into legal claims that are relevant more generally to issues of social reform.

Store Front Lawyers in San Francisco   *Jerome E. Carlin*

A United States district court on 22 April 1968 invalidated California's residency requirements

Published by permission of Transaction, Inc. from *Transaction*, Vol. 7, #6. Copyright © 1970 by Transaction, Inc. (Abridged.)

for persons seeking public assistance. Previously, applicants had to be residents of the state for at least one year before they could become eligible for benefits. According to the *San Francisco Chronicle* of 25 April:

The Reagan Administration will try to over-turn last week's landmark Federal Court decision.... Health and Welfare Director Spencer Williams said the decision would add another 24 million dollars to welfare costs, and add about 6,900 families and 12,000 other individuals to the welfare rolls.

On 28 December 1968 the *New York Times* printed the following story datelined San Francisco:

Poor Win Victory in a Housing Suit
Court Halts Coast Renewal until
Residents Back Plan

A Federal Court has halted the funding of a $100 million urban renewal project here with a decision that is expected to affect similar projects across the country and aid the poor in establishing legal rights for themselves. The court order prohibits the Department of Housing and Urban Development from supplying additional funds for the project until an acceptable plan has been approved for relocating uprooted families.... In taking the action to court, the Western Addition community group was [represented] by the San Francisco Neighborhood Legal Assistance Foundation....

On 12 August 1969 the following appeared on the front page of the *Chronicle*:

Bay Judge Orders Boost in Welfare

More money must be paid in rent allotments to people in the biggest welfare program in San Francisco and Alameda Counties, a Superior Court judge ruled here yesterday. Judge Alvin E. Weinberger further ordered the State Department of Social Welfare to take steps that will produce another increase in rent money across the State in a few months time.

He acted in a law suit brought by the San Francisco Neighborhood Legal Assistance Foundation on behalf of all persons receiving Aid to Families with Dependent Children (AFDC) in the two counties. Foundation lawyers charged that most AFDC clients are getting a monthly rent allotment less than the actual rent they are paying. Under State law, the Department's standards for rent must insure "safe, healthful housing." And the Department's own regulations require that its rent standards be based on "current actual costs for housing."

Judge Weinberger said the state and counties must live up to their own laws and regulations....

The total sum required statewide would be $19 million per year.... This would pay the actual rent. How much more would be required after the Department hearings, to pay for safe, healthful housing is a matter of dispute. But the total increase could reach $50 million.

These have been some of the more newsworthy activities of a new type of professional organization. The San Francisco Neighborhood Legal Assistance Foundation is a federally financed, community-controlled legal service agency which has been aggressively advocating the rights of the poor since it began operation in October 1966. It is one of about 300 agencies throughout the United States funded by the Office of Economic Opportunity (OEO) to deliver more effective legal services to the nation's poor.

Since the foundation has probably gone farther than almost any of the other legal service agencies in carrying out this mandate and has served as a model for many other programs in the United States, it may be instructive to examine what it set out to accomplish, the extent to which it was able to achieve its objectives, and the problems it encountered. One of the most important issues that emerges from such an inquiry is the apparent incompatibility of the two principal goals of the organization: control by the client community and institutional change.

Having participated in the creation of the foundation, and having served as its head for the first three years of its existence, I will be presenting an insider's view that may well be biased and self-serving. I trust that my training as a sociologist and lawyer will serve to curb any major excesses.

Money and Organization

The foundation is a private, nonprofit corporation with a governing board consisting of representatives of the local bar associations, law schools and the poverty community. The bylaws require that a majority of the board members be selected by the five poverty areas in San Francisco and that the board must also have a majority of attorneys. This is accomplished by having each poverty area select at least one lawyer representative. The board hires the coordinator, who is the chief executive officer of the foundation, and the directing attorney (chief counsel) for each of the five neighborhood law offices. The coordinator is responsible for carrying out the overall policies of the organization (which are determined by him and the board), for allocating resources among the various offices and departments and for hiring and supervising administrative and legal staff at the headquarters office (Main Office) of the foundation. Each chief counsel hires and fires his own staff of attorneys, secretaries, law students and aides.

In the fall of 1969 there were more than 120 paid staff persons working at the foundation including 50 full-time attorneys and about 30 part-time law students. In addition, about 25 law students and 10 social work students spent varying amounts of time at the foundation for credit under faculty supervision. Numerous private attorneys, on a volunteer basis, interview clients in the evening at a neighborhood office, make court appearances on default divorces or perform other services.

The staff attorneys are generally young—about a fourth came to the foundation right out of law school (mostly through the OEO-funded Reginald Heber Smith Fellowship and VISTA programs); only about a third had at least four years of practice experience before joining the foundation. Most attended top-ranking law schools; approximately a third graduated from an Ivy League law school (Harvard, Yale or Columbia). One out of four foundation attorneys is from a minority group; there are nine black lawyers.

The yearly budget of the foundation is over a million dollars, practically all of which comes from OEO in the form of an annual grant channeled through the local poverty agency, the Economic Opportunity Council of San Francisco (EOC). Although the foundation must deal both with OEO and EOC, it is essentially the former, and particularly the Legal Services Division within OEO, that has played the principal role in articulating and enforcing general guidelines for the foun-

dation (and other legal service agencies) and evaluating performance.

OEO seeks to shape and control programs and promote certain national objectives, not only through the funding process, but also by means of nationwide training programs, research and back-up centers and fellowship programs that place bright young law school graduates in funded agencies. Many foundation lawyers (particularly those working in the Main Office) maintain close ties with other poverty lawyers throughout the country by taking an active part in these OEO programs as well as in meetings of the National Legal Aid and Defender Association (which has become largely dominated by OEO lawyers) and other newly developed associations of poverty lawyers. In the national poverty law movement, OEO's Legal Services (in alliance with the American Bar Association, if not all or even most state and local bar associations) continues to play a leading role, giving solid support (with only few lapses) to program goals generally more advanced than most funded agencies are willing or able to realize.

Every month over a thousand new clients come into the five neighborhood offices of the foundation. A large majority of the clients are seeing a lawyer for the first time, most are on welfare, and half are in families with an annual income of less than $3,000 a year. About 15 percent of the clients are referred out—mainly to private attorneys or the public defender—because they fall above the foundation's income standard or they have a fee-producing or criminal case. The largest number of clients (about 30 percent) want help with a family problem, and half of these are seeking a divorce. The next biggest group are those having problems with administrative agencies: welfare, unemployment insurance, social security, immigration and naturalization (the bulk of the cases in the Chinatown Office) and the draft. Problems with landlords and merchants (and their collection agents) each constitute about 15 percent of the cases.

A major portion of the family cases, including all divorce matters, are referred to the Domestic Relations Unit, now located at the Main Office, for more expeditious handling. This innovation has been adopted by a great many other programs and has contributed significantly to reducing the overall time and resources that need be devoted to this largely routine service.

The Main Office also houses a legal staff handling a limited number of cases that are selected because they raise major poverty issues in public housing, welfare, urban renewal and more recently in the consumer area. The cases are referred to the staff from community organizations or neighborhood office lawyers. In time the Main Office attorneys have become specialists in the particular areas in which they work, in contrast with most attorneys in the neighborhood offices who, given the diversity of legal problems they have to deal with and the relatively little time they have to give any particular case, remain essentially general practitioners.

Community Control

The foundation was largely the creation of Charles Baumbach, a politically astute young lawyer who put together a coalition of white militant lawyers (primarily Jewish) and minority professionals (mainly black) who held positions in the local poverty power structure. The founders had a common cause in their insistence on neighborhood control of legal services.

For the lawyer-founders, community control was in part a means of negating control by the organized bar which they felt would be opposed to a more aggressive form of advocacy, one that would seek to use the law as an instrument of social change. The lawyers were also committed to altering the conventional power relation between the poor and the agencies that purport to serve them. Community control would create new opportunities for the poor to participate in determining agency policy and decisions, and this principle should also apply to legal service programs for the poor, or so it was felt.

For their part, the neighborhood poverty leaders had just fought and won a battle with the mayor for majority control of the EOC by representatives from the "target" areas, and they wanted control of the legal services component as well. Their reasons were complex: in part they were

simply extending the demand for self-determination; in part they had learned to resent the paternalism and insensitivity of traditional legal aid. But there was also a desire to expand a new power base by gaining control over jobs, services and other rewards for constituents.

Majority control of the Board of Directors by representatives of the poor was one expression of the neighborhood leaders' insistence on community control. Another was the very considerable autonomy given the neighborhood offices. The local leaders envisioned that each of the poverty areas would in effect have its own law firm. The chief counsel of the neighborhood office was to be selected by the board, rather than the coordinator, and it was assumed that the representatives on the board of a particular neighborhood would have primary say in choosing the attorney to head "their" office. Also, limiting the powers of the coordinator would, it was hoped, minimize racial and ethnic jealousies—given the ethnic mix of San Francisco's poverty areas—and provide a hedge against a bad director.

Community control was the unifying issue for the lawyers and neighborhood leaders who established the foundation. It was also the major issue in the foundation's sometimes bitter struggle with the legal establishment in San Francisco. After a year-long battle, the foundation won a stunning victory when it finally convinced OEO officials to fund it rather than the bar-supported Legal Aid Society of San Francisco. The foundation became the first OEO-funded legal service agency in the United States with majority control by representatives of the poverty community.

Institutional Change

Although the neighborhood leaders expressed no particular views regarding the content of the legal program, the lawyer-founders had some very strong ideas about it. These ideas were derived from an analysis of traditional legal aid and some conceptions about law and social change. The lawyers wanted to create an agency that would not only provide remedial assistance to individual clients (albeit in a more sympathetic and aggressive fashion than legal aid), but would also work toward altering conditions that keep the poor powerless and victims of injustice. This aim was based in part upon a recognition of the impossibility, with limited resources, of handling more than a small fraction of the problems urgently calling for legal assistance, and the necessity, therefore, of a more "wholesale" approach. It rested also on the understanding that, as Jan Howard, Sheldon Messinger and I wrote in 1966,

> the legal problems of the poor...characteristically arise from systematic abuses embedded in the operation of various public and private agencies, affecting large numbers of similarly situated individuals. Effective solution of the problems may require the lawyer to direct his attention away from a particular claim or grievance to the broader interests and policies at stake, and away from the individual client to a class of clients, in order to challenge more directly and with greater impact certain structural sources of injustice.

Very generally speaking, we came in time to conceive of our mission in this way: to find leverage points in the system to bring about a redistribution of power and income more favorable to the poor. Two general approaches were developed: strategic advocacy and economic development. Under the first, we sought to enter into the variety of forums where the law is made and administered, to facilitate the development of new rights in areas where the law was vague or clearly biased against the poor, or to enforce existing law favorable to the poor which had remained unimplemented (e.g., enforcement of health and safety provisions of the housing code, prohibitions against fraud and misrepresentation in sale of consumer goods).

To a remarkable extent, it appeared that "the system"—be it welfare, urban renewal, private slum housing or the garment industry in Chinatown—could not operate successfully without breaking the law: the cost of compliance is generally greater than the operators of the system are willing to pay, especially since those most likely to be hurt have been least likely to complain. Consequently, we hoped that vigorous law enforcement might serve not only to redistribute

income, but also to mount sufficient pressure to change the system.

The test for the efficacy of such activity was whether it would result in increasing the income or political bargaining power of a substantial number of poor persons. Litigation (with an emphasis on class suits) and administrative and legislative advocacy were the principal tools. In time, however, we learned that these measures, particularly court cases, by themselves were frequently ineffective unless combined with the mobilization of political support in the middle class as well as poverty communities.

By means of the second general approach we sought to promote entrepreneurial activity among ghetto residents. This came later and remained a subsidiary strategy.

A Force in the City

Whatever else the foundation may have achieved, it gained a reputation in the community of being a tough advocate for the poor, of being willing to take on any and all opponents—police department, Housing Authority, United States Army, welfare department, used-car dealers, Redevelopment Agency, City Hall, board of education. In a skit presented at the Bar Association of San Francisco Annual Ball (December 1968), the following, written by an attorney member, was sung to the tune of "Glowworm":

> We're from Neighborhood Legal Assistance
> We encourage draft resistance
> Nasty landlords are our nemesis
> We keep tenants on the premises
> We give deadbeats our protection
> To frustrate any debt collection
> The laws we use are not on your shelf
> 'Cause we make them up ourself.

We soon recognized the importance of publicity in building a reputation: it has been said that we won more cases at press conferences than in the courts. We published our own newsletter which reached several thousand persons, mostly private attorneys in San Francisco, with reports of our more important and more interesting cases. We also made it a point to get our cases into the press. Some idea of the coverage, and the developing image, may be seen in the following:

> In one of the most unusual cases handled by the Foundation in recent weeks, 20-year-old Ted Townsend, who had been held for three months in the Presidio stockade as a suspected deserter, was freed after his Neighborhood Legal Assistance attorney pointed out.... (*San Francisco Progress*, 24 August 1967)

> A poverty program lawyer has filed a complaint with the State Public Utilities Commission, seeking to end Pacific Telephone's $25 deposit requirement for certain new customers. (*Chronicle*, 16 December 1967)

> The Neighborhood Legal Assistance Foundation filed a suit that seeks to prevent San Francisco policemen from carrying guns while off duty. (*Chronicle*, November 9, 1968)

> The San Francisco Neighborhood Legal Assistance Foundation has fired another salvo at the State Department of Social Welfare. (*Examiner*, 27 June 1968)

> The unit [the Main Office legal staff] is illustrative both of the length to which the young attorneys in Legal Assistance will go to attempt to help their clients and of the crusading idealism of the men who operate it. (*Examiner*, 9 October 1968)

> The Neighborhood Legal Assistance Foundation is seeking a breakthrough in labor practices to make unions more responsive to the needs of their members, especially minority group members with language and cultural problems. (*Argonaut*, 26 October 1968)

> The San Francisco Neighborhood Legal Assistance Foundation has joined the legal fight against Rudolph Ford, the Daley City car dealer. (*Examiner*, 14 January 1969)

Dilemmas

As we have seen, the foundation was initially conceived as a collection of largely autonomous neighborhood law firms with a central administrative staff to "keep the machinery running" and to provide liaison among the neighborhood offices and between them and the board and various outside agencies. This highly decentralized system

was designed to insure maximum responsiveness to the particular needs of the various poverty communities.

I had become convinced from a brief study I had conducted for oeo in the summer of 1966 that a central research and planning staff was essential to implement the broader, strategic goals of the legal services program. Notwithstanding the greater dedication and competence of the attorneys in the oeo-funded agencies, I argued in my report that without structural changes that go beyond simply shifting the location of the office (into the neighborhood) there would be little difference in actual impact and operation between oeo legal programs and conventional legal aid. I suggested, therefore, a division of function between a central office and neighborhood offices. Lawyers in the central office would develop strategies for change and take the necessary steps to implement these strategies through test cases, class actions and the like. I contended that they should also maintain close relations with neighborhood organizations, "for the task of creative advocacy ought to reflect consultation with the slum community as well as feedback from the caseload of the neighborhood offices." The main task of the neighborhood office would be that "of serving a large volume clientele on something like a mass production basis," with some research and other assistance from the specialist attorneys.

Over the years, a strong central legal staff was built up in the Main Office of the foundation. The attorneys became specialists in housing and redevelopment, welfare and other areas, and they were responsible for the major cases of the foundation. The office was started with two attorneys. In the fall of 1969, there were approximately 15 attorneys (including most of the foundation's allotment of Reginald Heber Smith Fellows) and a total staff of about 25, not including the many law students working in the clinic program. The Main Office legal staff was now larger than any of the neighborhood offices. The Main Office attorneys were the "cosmopolitans" in the foundation: they were much more likely than the neighborhood attorneys to have contacts with other poverty lawyers across the United States—in oeo programs, the Legal Defense Fund—to attend regional and national conferences and training sessions and to keep up with the growing body of legal literature in their field.

From the very beginning, relations between the neighborhood offices and the Main Office were strained. In my report to OEO I had pointed out that one of the problems that might arise in setting up a separate structure for the strategic cases was

> the tension between service to a mass clientele and creative advocacy. At any point the decision to allocate limited resources to a central planning staff may seem arbitrary, even heartless. For the decision will necessitate turning away desperate people who are, after all, entitled to the service. But unless this is done, little will be accomplished for the large majority of slum dwellers, and many of those who are served will receive only temporary relief.

Neighborhood attorneys felt that they were carrying the burden of providing legal services to the poverty community with little or no help or relief from their Main Office colleagues. The latter were viewed as an expensive luxury—their case loads immorally small, the pace of their work annoyingly relaxed and the results highly dubious. Was the WACO case really worth all the time and effort that had gone into it, and what about the welfare cases that put a few more dollars in a recipient's pocket, if that? Is it fair to spend such a large share of the foundation's resources on these highly speculative cases when there are clear, tangible results obtained in eviction cases and divorce cases, where people really hurt? These questions bothered many neighborhood attorneys. Their growing resentment of Main Office attorneys was hardly diminished by the incidental benefits they seemed to enjoy—the many trips to conferences and meetings, the publicity in the newspapers and on TV.

Neighborhood Sovereignty

From the point of view of the Main Office attorneys, neighborhood lawyers were not only essentially engaged in a band-aid operation, but even on a remedial basis were frequently unable to give effective representation to their clients, given the unwillingness of the neighborhood offices either to limit caseloads or to accept more efficient, routinized procedures. Furthermore, several chief counsels were viewed as the prime perpetuators of a system in which the client community was often the loser.

Main Office attorneys were also unhappy about what appeared to be the political restrictions on some neighborhood offices. The principal example was the unwillingness of the Western Addition office to represent WACO in its fight with the Redevelopment Agency. This decision, it was felt, was motivated in part by a reluctance to oppose the black Establishment in the Western Addition (including the local EOC leaders) which supported redevelopment in exchange for more jobs for blacks in the agency and sponsorship of projects within the renewal area. Similarly, the Chinatown office was extremely reluctant to take an aggressive position against established interests in Chinatown. Thus it was fully two years before any action at all was taken against the sweatshops. It was no accident that these were the two offices in which the local Establishment had most to do with the selection of the chief counsel.

Tensions were heightened by racial and ethnic differences. The Main Office legal staff has been predominantly white (it is interesting that a black lawyer who joined the staff has had little sympathy for the goals and methods of the office) and largely Jewish. Criticism of the Main Office has undoubtedly been affected by the feeling that it was inappropriate for white lawyers to be deciding what is best for poor blacks.

Although the neighborhood lawyers continued to be critical of the increase in staff at the Main Office and its failure to operate primarily as a back-up resource for them, an uneasy truce emerged between the neighborhood offices and the Main Office. The chief counsels agreed to leave the Main Office alone if it would not interfere in internal operations of the neighborhood offices. The sovereignty of the neighborhood offices was not to be trifled with. This was not a very happy solution. Indeed, it became increasingly difficult to effect even a modest degree of coordination. At stake was raising the quality of service in the neighborhood offices—and at the very least, preventing a deterioration in quality. This meant being able to do something about recruitment of attorneys, training of new attorneys and increasing office efficiency. Development of a rational recruitment program to take advantage of the foundation's nationwide reputation to attract top legal talent, particularly minority lawyers, simply was not possible with each office refusing to yield on its absolute power to hire and fire staff. A staff training program never really existed—some chief counsels resented the interference, and one refused to permit his attorneys to attend training sessions. Development of standard legal forms and office procedures, sharing of information on cases, research memos and briefs to avoid duplication of effort and to insure the best thinking or approach to a case—all of these seemed unattainable despite repeated campaigns to bring them about. In response to a grant condition from OEO, the director of litigation (who is in effect the chief counsel for the Main Office legal staff) drew up a minimal plan to insure that information on more important or unusual cases would be made available to him and to the chief counsels in advance of filing, but leaving final control over the cases in the hands of the chief counsels. For a long period the chief counsels for one reason or another were unwilling to consider the plan on its merits.

We were caught in a bind. Our efforts to assist neighborhood offices in raising the quality of service to clients were generally opposed as undermining the autonomy of the neighborhood offices. As a result, the neighborhood job got tougher—with increasing resentment against the Main Office and a lowering of the quality of service to the clients in the neighborhoods. The offices continued operating essentially as independent law firms. Within the offices there was no real division of labor specialization. Attorneys handled as best they could whatever cases and matters came their way on their interview days. Case loads were large and becoming more burdensome as the backlog of unfinished cases slowly but surely built up. Work with neighborhood groups was confined mostly to incorporation of essentially paper organizations. Moreover, the staff became less experienced, given the tendency to

fill vacant slots with younger attorneys. And there was little effective supervision, since in most offices the chief counsel was playing primarily a political role in the community, having turned over the day-to-day administration of the office to his senior staff attorney or senior secretary. Consequently, in spite of the dedication and ability of most neighborhood attorneys, the quality of the work product in general declined.

The goal of community control had been institutionalized in the autonomous neighborhood offices, while the aim of institutional change was embodied in the Main Office legal staff. It was obvious that the growing antagonism between these two structures in large measure represented a conflict between the two goals. The lawyer-founders had been wrong in assuming that control by the client community was a necessary condition for, let alone compatibility with, a program of institutional change. We were unfortunately burdened with some romantic notions of the poor.

The Old Way Up

The neighborhood leaders, particularly those identified with the poverty program, were following an old pattern fashioned by other ethnic groups as they fought their way up the power ladder. These leaders were, by and large, not out to change or seriously challenge the system; they simply wanted to be cut in. They were willing to have an understanding with the older, white Establishment: in exchange for greater control of public programs aimed at helping the poor, and more control over jobs and other rewards for their constituents, they would keep the peace. The WACO suit was, of course, embarrassing: it was not until the Redevelopment Agency by its arrogance alienated its black allies in the Western Addition that the neighborhood leaders were able openly to support WACO's position.

It may well be the case that, with respect to their conception of legal services, the neighborhood leaders at this point are much closer to the conservative Republicans than to the militant white lawyers.

It is always possible, of course, that the neighborhood leaders may become radicalized—and the violent repression of the Panthers may be doing just that. And it is also possible that the young black lawyers coming out of the Reginald Heber Smith program may press for a more radical approach to legal services. Neither group, so far, however, seems to be prepared to move much beyond the issue of community control. The two principal demands of the black Reginald Heber Smith Fellows in a recent confrontation with OEO officials were higher salaries and control of the program.

By the spring of 1969 I was convinced that there would have to be some basic change in the structure of the foundation: although much of our work, particularly in housing and welfare, was beginning to pay off, the tensions within the foundation were becoming critical. The changes that would have to be brought about would necessarily mean limiting, if not doing away with, the autonomy of the neighborhood offices. In my view, this could only be accomplished by a black coordinator dedicated to institutional change, that is, by a militant black lawyer. I tried unsuccessfully for several months to find such a person. Finally, in October, having held the office for three years, and with a sense that we had accomplished in some ways a great deal more than I had ever expected, I resigned as coordinator of the foundation. It was now up to the board to find my successor, and hopefully a solution to our dilemma.

In December of 1969 my successor was chosen. The new coordinator is a black lawyer who had been a staff attorney in one of the neighborhood offices, and more recently held a top administrative post in the EOC. He is an able attorney, with a strong sense of professionalism and a flair for administrative efficiency. Although not unsympathetic to the aims and approach of the Main Office legal staff, he clearly represents the interests and perspective of the neighborhood offices. The tensions within the foundation should be significantly reduced, the divisions healed. I assume that the commitment to institutional change will gradually become weaker and that the Main Office legal staff will be reduced in size and given a different direction—to serve primarily as back-up resource for the neighborhood offices.

In retrospect, this probably represents the only solution that was realistically open to the foundation. Reorganization in the image of the Main Office legal staff would have brought the foundation into more direct and intolerable confrontations with the Establishment and would have seriously jeopardized neighborhood support. Perhaps at this point the main objective should be the survival of the foundation as a major institution serving the ghetto under ghetto control.

If the militant white lawyers move on, this should not be interpreted simply as a reaction to a shift in leadership and possible direction of the foundation. Some have become disillusioned with the capacity of the legal system to respond; others may be following new fashions. In one way or another, however, the old coalition will very likely be dissolved. Looking back, I suppose we have each used the other—the black professionals and neighborhood leaders have gained an organization, and we had the chance to put our theories into practice. Still, it's sad the partnership couldn't last.

Notes and Questions

1. Since this article was written, the Legal Services Program suffered many political and fiscal attacks under the hostile Nixon administration and almost expired with its parent organization, OEO. Much of the animosity was leveled at the kind of law reform effort Carlin described. Vice President Spiro Agnew exemplified this critique when he wrote:

> Through the imaginative use of ever-expanding constitutional concepts, the legal services program has seized upon the idea of the law and the lawsuit as an offensive weapon to redress an alleged imbalance created by the political processes. While we must do everything we can to protect every American's constitutional rights, we must ask ourselves this: Isn't it possible that we have gone too far when the Federal Government constructs a program which encourages individual lawyers to test at public expense their own individual theories of how society should be structured and how the resources, rights and

benefits of that society should be distributed among the population? *

Think back over the readings in the last section. To whom is the lawyer responsible? How could Agnew's charge be answered?

2. How far does Carlin's notion of advocacy carry? Would it be likely to encompass the following:

Not too long ago, at the request of a priest in Brownsville, Brooklyn, I found myself addressing over 100 Puerto Rican factory workers out on a wildcat strike. They were protesting an almost unbelievable "sweetheart" contract between their employer and bargaining representative that, among other omissions, did not take cognizance of an increase in the state minimum wage. Most of the strikers, incidentally, were eligible for welfare supplements but had been too proud to apply.

Technically, being an "officer of the court," as lawyers describe themselves, I suppose I should have told the group their strike was illegal, and fled the scene with all professional aplomb. Instead, I remained to say that while the workers risked being discharged from employment, as a practical, nonlegal matter their collective strength might force the employer to capitulate to their just demands.

Unethical? Perhaps; but I had in mind those management attorneys from highly re-

spectable firms in New York, Chicago, Atlanta and New Orleans who have amassed fortunes by unlawfully teaching employers how to break labor unions without getting caught. My ethical sense had also been dulled by the sight of too many upright attorneys parading well-coached, lying witnesses to the stand at Labor Board hearings.†

3. Is there an analogy to be drawn between the stratification of the private bar (Ladinsky) and the stratification of the Foundation?

4. The legal services program is now housed in a federal nonprofit corporation called the Legal Services Corporation. When the legislation establishing the Corporation passed Congress in 1974, it included provisions prohibiting legal services funds to be used for support of political activity, demonstrations, picketing and strikes, and legal services attorneys are prevented from helping persons seeking assistance with abortions, school desegregation, the draft or military desertion. When the Corporation came up for refunding in 1977 an additional restriction was added: that prohibiting legal activism on behalf of homosexual rights.

The Corporation funding goal is to provide two lawyers for every 10,000 of the 24 million poor persons in the country by 1979. The balance of the population currently has a ratio of 14 lawyers for every 10,000 people and the ratio is declining with each law school graduation.

* Spiro T. Agnew, "What's Wrong with the Legal Services Program," *American Bar Association Journal*, vol. 58 (September 1972), p. 930.

† James J. Graham, "The Ghetto Lawyer," *Commonweal* (November 1967), p. 199.

The issue of individual representation versus class representation is further explored in the following reading. The comparison to the preceding article is made all the more interesting by the fact that the author, Harry Brill, was also employed by the San Francisco Neighborhood Legal Assistance Foundation.

The Uses and Abuses of Legal Assistance   *Harry Brill*

Those of us who subscribe to the ideal of equal treatment under law for all citizens must agree that public money is well spent when it effectively

From *The Public Interest*, No. 31 (Spring 1973), pp. 38–55. Copyright © 1973 by National Affairs, Inc. Reprinted by permission.

reduces the disadvantages that the poor suffer under our present legal arrangements. Judged by this standard, the legal assistance program sponsored by the Office of Economic Opportunity (OEO)—whose uncertain fate will soon be determined in Washington—has been a success. By providing free legal services, its 265 agencies with their more than 900 neighborhood offices have improved the ability of poor people to defend their interests. Whether as defendants or as plaintiffs, the poor can now have highly dedicated and skilled lawyers to represent them.

In their role as tenants, many poor people can for the first time confront their landlords with dignity. As consumers, they are in a position to challenge unreasonable overcharges and other unscrupulous business practices; in fact, their chances of winning consumer cases have multiplied tenfold. Moreover, welfare departments and housing authorities—to cite just two kinds of public agencies that the poor encounter—can no longer anticipate that their practices will be passively accepted. Almost unheard of a decade ago, it is now quite common for a poor person to exclaim, "I will see my lawyer."

OEO lawyers are handling more than a million individual cases each year and winning the overwhelming majority of them. Their actual achievements, though, are even greater than the record shows, for pouring legal services into low-income communities does not merely win individual cases, it also has a deterrent effect. Faced with the possibility of legal action, people have begun to think second thoughts about mistreating the poor. Of course, the availability of legal services alone by no means eliminates the legal disadvantages of being poor. Other institutional sources of inequality persist—not least, certain characteristics of the laws themselves. Nevertheless, there does exist considerable law on the books to protect the poor, and by providing them with legal services, OEO has appreciably reduced a major source of inequality.

Not only is the program successful; it has also attracted wide support. And its supporters are by no means all liberal reformers or the poor themselves. Conservatives who believe the poor should have access to legal and peaceful means to cope with their individual problems consider it a worthwhile public investment. And the American Bar Association has also given the program a hearty endorsement—though, to be sure, the Association speaks partly from self-interest, since it realizes that under an adversary system the provision of legal assistance to those who are unable to pay also creates business for lawyers who serve paying clients. But however diverse the motives of the various endorsers, it remains a noteworthy fact that the program is approved by most of its attentive publics.

The Question of Class Actions

The legal assistance program, then, might seem to be that rare and heartwarming case of a public program that does good, does good well, and does good without arousing fierce opposition. Yet since its uncertain beginning the program has in fact been embroiled in controversy. The controversy has not centered on the "traditional" individual case services which aid clients on a one-to-one basis, which are intended to resolve the legal problems only of the clients who are actually represented, and which make up the bulk of the program's work. Instead, almost all the debate has focused on the program's support of class action suits, which challenge general practices and policies of both private and public institutions. The few clients directly represented in these class action cases are said to be only a "legal sample" of larger numbers of people who are similarly situated. The few, then, may win major reforms on behalf of many others as well as themselves. OEO's class action cases have been instrumental —or so it is said—in righting a long series of wrongs: in overturning welfare residency requirements, restoring Medicaid cuts, and forcing business establishments to change consumer practices.

On the face of it, the controversy about the class action aspect of the OEO program hardly seems surprising. Conservatives, so the logic goes, and those with vested interests in our current political arrangements might well support a program providing legal aid only in individual cases of no broad impact; but that support would surely evaporate if OEO ever attempted changes posing a fundamental threat to the Establishment. And conservatives have indeed complained loudly about OEO's sponsorship of class action suits. Even those who have supported or learned to live with the idea of federally subsidized legal services find the use of public funds for large-scale attacks against any arm of the government itself a bitter pill to swallow. Moreover, some public officials whose agencies are threatened by class action have been outspoken in their opposition to such suits. This discomfort on the part of the Establishment has alone been sufficient to win class action a high repute among liberals, and to make its list of accomplishments seem especially significant. In addition, even apart from the howls of conservatives, many legal-minded reformers view class action as a quick and powerful tool for peaceful change in the system. So the class action controversy would seem a fairly straightforward debate between those who are willing to change the system for the benefit of the poor and those who are not.

But neither the moral outrage of the Establishment nor the vigorous defense of class action by liberals should in itself be taken as evidence of the success of this part of the program or of its benefits to the poor. The Establishment, for good reason, has by no means always criticized class actions so vehemently in private as it does in public. And liberals have ignored the various direct and indirect costs to the poor that class action suits have entailed. The activities of the San Francisco Neighborhood Legal Assistance Foundation—OEO's second largest legal service agency—are a case in point. Since the beginning of the poverty program, the Foundation has been a favorite child of the city's liberal constituency. To raise a serious criticism of any of the Foundation's activities has been taboo for anyone who does not wish to be labeled an arch-conservative. In this atmosphere—the atmosphere of many other cities as well—it has been virtually impossible for reform-minded citizens to consider the dark side of class action suits.

While serving as the Foundation's research director, I learned first-hand how great the disparity can be between an organization's reputation and its actual accomplishments. What the Foundation has done poorly, unsuccessfully, or not at all must be tallied alongside its real accomplishments. And such an accounting unfortunately reveals that the effects of the San Francisco Foundation's class action suits have been minimal or even harmful. It may be instructive to explore how this is so and why the organization has pursued these actions nonetheless.

The Neighborhoods vs. the Main Office

The Foundation, like other man-made entities, operates on limited resources. An organizational commitment to pursue certain approaches must necessarily entail some sacrifice of other approaches. Since the Foundation is serving clients whose low income makes it virtually impossible for them to obtain legal services elsewhere, it is appropriate to weigh the costs to the poor of the services that are sacrificed.

The Foundation is composed of five neighborhood offices and a main office. The main office in San Francisco might have adopted any one of several notions of its proper role. It might, for instance, have served as a source of *ad hoc* and supplementary staff for the neighborhood offices. But instead, the main office chose to become a branch specializing in organizational advocacy. Its lawyers would devote their expertise to helping community organizations solve their problems and become stronger politically. Whether these organizations needed to be incorporated, advised on the legal implications of their actions, assisted in negotiations, provided with legal representation on behalf of their individual members, or rendered any other service that the Foundation could appropriately perform, the lawyers would be ready and willing. As time went on, and for reasons we will explore later, the range of functions that the main office lawyers actually performed for their organizations narrowed sharply. "Organizational advocacy" became a euphemism for class actions.

The neighborhood lawyers were not unaware of the implications these main office decisions had for the allocation of legal service benefits: indeed, this issue was a major source of conflict within the Foundation. The neighborhood offices, handling conventional individual cases, are deluged with clients. Anxious to give sufficient attention to each client while maximizing the number of cases they could process, these local branches consistently urged the main office to provide them with staff assistance—assistance which, because of main office preoccupation with class actions, was not forthcoming.

The local branches' obvious lack of interest in

class actions convinced main office staff that their colleagues were legally provincial and that a few might even be committed to the status quo. Conversely, the neighborhood lawyers were irritated by this main office concentration on class action. Not only did the main office lawyers refuse to relieve the pressures on the local branches; they also attempted to persuade the neighborhood offices to assist *them* in generating class action suits. To their outrage, the branch offices were advised to cut or limit their caseloads and to develop antennae that might alert them to opportunities presented by their own clients for innovative class action cases.

The neighborhood lawyers considered their main office colleagues opportunists and publicity hunters. They were troubled that the pace of the main office was leisurely while their own was often frantic. Nor could they understand why the main office devoted so much time and energy to public relations. Most irksome of all was the great discrepancy between the number of cases they handled and the number handled by the main office. While a community-based office would process a few hundred in a given month, the main office might still be in the midst of preparing a single class action suit.

The main office repeatedly argued that even though in the short run resources were being shifted away from direct benefits to the poor, and even though fewer cases were handled than might have been otherwise, the class action suits justified themselves in the long run through the widespread benefits they conferred. But in fact this argument is by no means a conclusive justification. As the neighborhood lawyers realized, at least several hundred cases were being traded off for each class action suit. The investment in time and resources for a class action suit, particularly for research, is considerable. A single case may wholly occupy a few lawyers for an entire year. And just as important, the Foundation, like other legal assistance agencies, won extremely few of its class action suits but well over 75 per cent of its individual cases. Thus in terms of the likelihood of winning a legal victory, a single class action suit is equivalent to at least several thousand individual cases. These numbers alone leave a heavy burden of proof on the proponents of class action.

Moreover, it is not so clear that the objectives of class action suits are necessarily of greater value than, say, taking a landlord to court to rectify a dangerous safety hazard. And even the strongest argument in favor of class action—the wider nature of its benefits—is seriously open to question. Even in a conventional individual case, the client himself is not the only beneficiary. Word travels fast, and the legal activity of the neighborhood offices has already had a considerable deterrent effect. Still greater penetration of neighborhood legal services into the community through more individual cases would further sensitize the poor to their legal rights and also serve to warn others that the poor have legal protection. For these reasons the high costs of class action to the individual poor cannot be justified by any abstract argument; they must instead be justified by a showing of the actual social and economic gains that these large cases produce.

Hollow Victories

Unfortunately, a very large proportion of class action legal victories do not in fact lead to actual social and economic gains. Unlike individual cases, in which favorable legal decisions are readily translated into real gains, class action involves more difficult hurdles—often insurmountable ones. The Foundation won several paper victories in which court orders were ignored because of an inability to comply. For example, the Foundation obtained a favorable decision against the Welfare Department's low rent allotment to recipients. The court ruled that it must be increased to a more realistic figure. The Department, however, was unable to comply without receiving assurances of additional funds from the state legislature. Though the Foundation made legal headway, no concrete gains were achieved for the people on welfare.

There were even instances when favorable decisions *were* enforced but still yielded little or no net gains for the poor. Take, for example, the Foundation's very important and celebrated participation in the defeat of the one-year residency requirement for welfare. This "victory," along with other developments in California, triggered austerity measures by the legislative and executive branches. Eligibility requirements were more vigorously enforced and tightened to exclude many poor people who had formerly been eligible; the new restrictions were so severe that, despite an increase in unemployment, the total number collecting welfare in California actually dropped. So the victory for the recently arrived poor in California simply came at the expense of those poor who had lived there longer.

The main office lawyers responsible for these welfare cases had followed a plan of action that backfired. They had argued that inundating the courts with class action suits was the best route to achieving welfare reforms. The idea was to force a crisis situation that would prompt the legislature and governor to liberalize welfare and provide more funds; the actual consequence was the opposite. Curiously, the lawyers had never considered this possibility.

A One-track Commitment

Their preoccupation with class action has also led the lawyers to divert resources from other, probably superior ways of attacking the problems at hand. In general, the main office lawyers proceeded as if class action were always the best vehicle and sometimes the only one for improving the social and economic conditions of the poor. In a highly publicized case, one which was eventually lost, the Foundation brought a class action suit against the San Francisco Housing Authority to compel it to physically upgrade one of its projects. The liberal public applauded this action because it had been unhappy about the inadequate physical conditions of these projects. But its enthusiasm would have soured had it understood that the suit could not have changed these conditions one iota.

The operation of public housing is financed mainly out of collected rents. (Though some federal subsidies are available for project rehabilitation, they are woefully inadequate for the purpose.) Because the costs of operating the projects have been rising more rapidly than rents, the Housing Authority has been thrown into a finan-

cial crisis. Like many other public housing agencies, it has been in the red. Its debt has been growing largely because the soaring costs of material and labor for maintenance and repair have been rising without comparable increases in rent. It was not likely that the Housing Authority could free substantial additional funds for rehabilitation by streamlining its operation; the agency is considered among the more efficient ones in San Francisco. Nor was the agency wasting money as a result of corrupt practices. Not even the lawyers believed that the Housing Authority was guilty of such excesses. What then could a court order to the Housing Authority accomplish? To rule that it spend even more, and thus further increase its debt, would be like ordering its executive director to jump out of a window and fly.

The response of the lawyers to such criticism of their activities is that to do nothing changes nothing. But to point out that the Housing Authority alone is financially incapable of the massive rehabilitation and maintenance needed is not to argue for inaction. Rather it poses the issue of where energies might be more appropriately directed and whose energies should be primarily involved. Since San Francisco's public housing, like that of most other cities, is a federal program, Congress could appropriate funds for it. In fact, the lobbying activities of tenant organizations and their allies have been somewhat successful in this regard. The judicial route, on the other hand, is an ineffective one because the courts have no legal power to compel Congress to spend millions of dollars against its will. Instead of filing a class action suit, the main office lawyers could have assisted community groups to prepare a bill and advised them on lobbying strategies. This plan would have been consistent with the commitment they expressed to organizational advocacy; but it was not a plan that they chose.

The general question of whether to pursue the legislative or the judicial route to reforms is of course a subject of legitimate debate. The point here is simply that the Foundation tended to channel organizational clients toward the courts even when—as in the public housing case—there was nothing to gain, and, by diverting resources, a great deal to lose. There were other occasions when the judicial route was more appropriate but still less expedient than other actions would have been. Issues were translated into class action suits even when there were strong indications that a bill introduced into the state legislature and supported by a minimal amount of lobbying would have accomplished the same end more directly and swiftly. The lawyers on several occasions convinced community organizations to drop their lobbying plans in favor of court action. Yet it is almost axiomatic that legislative action offers a more enduring basis for reforms, since they are written into the law and marked with a clear stamp of public acceptance, rather than left to court interpretation.

The lawyers pursued this strategy even where it jeopardized the specific goals and the autonomy of the community organizations they presumed to serve. One community organization that was attempting to halt a major redevelopment project finally had to threaten the Foundation to get it to withhold legal action in the matter. Against the advice of one of the main office lawyers, the Western Addition Community Organization (WACO) was trying to pressure the Board of Supervisors to stop the project. WACO feared that a legal suit filed at this time would thwart its attempts to win a political victory. It argued that if the courts refused to hear the case, the Supervisors would be under less pressure to support WACO's demands.

The lawyers nevertheless insisted that the suit be filed immediately. Many difficult months had been consumed in preparing it, and they wanted to bring it to court as soon as possible. They were not moved by WACO's argument that a political strategy at the moment made better sense. Tempers were high. The lawyers seriously contemplated filing the case without WACO's permission; they would argue that WACO had already assented to the suit. WACO prevailed—but only by threatening to drop the services of the Foundation. Subsequent events justified WACO's strategy. The Board of Supervisors voted to stop the project. Though this decision was later vetoed by a lame duck mayor, the battle greatly strengthened WACO as an organization. Consequently, it was eventually able to force a considerable number of concessions from the redevelopment agency.

This episode was typical of Foundation behavior. The one-track commitment to class action, even when it might harm organizational clients, was characteristic of the main office lawyers. In a way, then, the Foundation itself became a barrier to social change.

Main Office Motives: The Problem of Audience

Why did the main office pursue this strategy, a course of action that was certainly not forced upon it by any obvious external constraints? It was not that they were indifferent to the fate of the poor; indeed, one reason for their persistence was that they were genuinely committed to reforming the Establishment and believed that class action was an all-purpose tool to achieve their goals. In fact, class action was eulogized and idealized by them with as much enthusiasm as direct action evokes among militants. The lawyers believed that, whatever its short-run limitations, the long-range consequence of continually battering the courts and the system would be to force changes favorable to the poor. This perspective made them much less prone to consider the various problems each particular suit presented, and made their faith in class action largely immune to defeat or criticism.

This ideological commitment to class action suits led the lawyers to go beyond their role as organizational advocates providing technical assistance in support of policies set by their clients. Community organizations did not normally propose class action. The services that they did demand more often than not seemed either self-defeating or inconsequential to the lawyers, who thought that change was too crucial to leave to the inexperienced. Rather than acceding to their clients' wishes, they believed that they had a responsibility to educate them. In practice, this meant taking the lead and persuading community organizers of the merits of class action. The lawyers themselves had faith in the tool; changing their clients' minds, therefore, was justified.

But an ideological belief in the merits of class action does not explain everything the lawyers did. It is hard to imagine the simple belief in one legal tool causing them to be so indiscriminating in their choice of cases, so willing to rescind their immediate commitment to the organizations and the individual poor that class actions are supposed to serve. So it is not surprising that a further explanation for the lawyers' behavior lies in the way it enabled them to meet the various expectations of four different audiences—their client organizations, the Establishment, their professional colleagues, and the liberal middle-class public.

Lawyers and Clients

These lawyers and their clients, first of all, were each other's captives. The lawyers were obligated to serve all clients that they could who were classified as poor. And since the Foundation had committed itself to serving organizational clients, the main office lawyers had to assist all poor peoples' organizations that sought legal aid. Moreover, the lawyers' special interest in class action made community organizations even more important to them. Though individuals directly represented in class action cases need not have organizational links, community organizations serve as a natural vehicle for developing these suits. They provide ideas and leads, they are able to produce the individual clients and assure their availability, and they can be actively enlisted in collecting data for cases. Moreover, to bypass community organizations on issues that directly concern them involves very serious risks.

Conversely, because they were generally unable to afford fees, organizational clients often had no choice but to deal with the Foundation. So although clients enjoyed the advantage of receiving free legal assistance, and the lawyers were able to earn a reasonably good income doing work they regarded as both socially important and professionally productive, neither enjoyed free market relations and each side paid heavily for this. There were no easy ways of disposing of one another if they wanted to—and they often did want to.

A great many organizations that approached the Foundation were militant, and the relations that developed between their organizers and the lawyers ranged from the tense to the explosive. The militants had very definite ideas on how

lawyers should behave. When illegal activities were planned, they admonished the lawyers about their responsibility to keep them out of jail. If the organizers were seeking more time, perhaps to organize their forces for battle, they wanted the lawyers to deter the Establishment from acting before they were ready. If they wanted the lawyers to assist in harassing public agencies for various political reasons, the lawyers were expected to conform. And no matter what the organizers demanded, they insisted that the lawyers respond right away. This was not at all a minor matter to the lawyers, as various militant organizations would sometimes contact their office several times per day.

The organizers expected conformity in style as well. If they walked out of public meetings, they would be furious if the lawyers did not tag behind. If the organizers wished to impress their members in court, they demanded that the lawyers behave dramatically. Similarly, if they chose to ignore their enemies, they insisted that the lawyers do likewise; organizers were frequently angry with the lawyers for being on friendly terms with those who represented their opponents. To the organizers the city was a battlefield, and the lawyers were almost always expected to prove in one way or another that they were on the right side.

The lawyers, who without exception were more moderate politically, had very different aims in mind—aims that brought them into serious conflict with their clients. The lawyers were anxious to help militant organizations which they believed had legitimate grievances by reducing tensions between them and their opponents. Their strategy was to provide militant organizers with access to the system by way of the courts. By translating social and economic issues into legal ones, they would make possible the peaceful settlement of potentially volatile disputes. All sides would gain: Both disruptive activities and the stern countermeasures often resorted to by the Establishment could be avoided. The lawyers frequently boasted to public officials and others about how they intervened to prevent disruptive and illegal activities such as sit-ins and even riots. To the militants, the lawyers proudly recounted how they were able to convince various Establishment representatives to listen, negotiate, and be more conciliatory. This, incidentally, was characteristic of how the lawyers behaved. They always attempted to show each side how successfully they were able to deal with the other.

Advocates or Mediators?

The lawyers, then, defined their role primarily as that of mediators. Rather than representing only their organizational clients, they took a middle-ground position by acknowledging the legitimacy of some of their opponents' concerns and demands. Instead of seeking compromises only when they represented the best their clients could expect, they often sought compromises in order to be fair to both sides. At negotiating sessions they articulated the demands not only of their clients, but also of the adversary parties, and in the interest of reaching an agreement they were quick to call to their clients' attention what they felt were reasonable proposals from the opposition. Organizers frequently interpreted this behavior as a betrayal. It seemed to them that without prior permission the lawyers were diluting their demands, and that as a result they would eventually have to settle for much less than a firmer strategy would have won.

The mediating stance of the lawyers also came into conflict with the expectations of the organizers when the lawyers would offer their own separate formulas for settling disputes. To break a stalemate they often met among themselves to develop a program that they believed might be acceptable to both parties. Instead of first consulting with their clients, they occasionally met initially with the opposition to present their ideas. The lawyers naively believed that if they extracted an agreement from the Establishment first, they would be in a better position to persuade their clients. Also, they wished to communicate a message to public officials, many of whom wondered whether the lawyers would permit themselves to be controlled by the militants. Aware of these suspicions, the lawyers wanted to show that they had ideas of their own, and that these ideas represented efforts to settle rather than polarize disputes.

The organizers objected so strongly to the way the lawyers proceeded that they often rejected proposals they might otherwise have found acceptable. The organizers always resented the lawyers for initiating proposals, and they were usually horrified whenever they learned that the lawyers had first met with the opposition, without the organization's prior knowledge and approval. The good intentions behind the lawyers' attempt to absorb the militants into the legitimate political arena would backfire, and the organizers would have their worst fears about liberals confirmed. Many of them accused the lawyers of belonging to the enemy camp, and it became almost routine for the lawyers to have to defend their integrity as well as their actions.

The lawyers adopted a variety of strategies to cope with the differing expectations of these two audiences, but they did not have much success. They regularly spoke very differently to different people. They attempted to reestablish their credibility with their clients by expressing in strong language, both publicly and privately, their outrage over Establishment abuses. At the same time, they attempted to maintain their links with the Establishment by privately reassuring public officials of their conciliatory intentions. Also privately, they would on occasion make derogatory comments about their clients and decry their extremism. They believed that to be effective mediators they had to indicate to each side their sympathies for its position.

When their militant clients wanted to initiate legal actions that were highly charged politically, the lawyers sometimes refused to go along. They felt that suing the mayor for dereliction of duty, subpoenaing official documents to show evidence of corruption, and other extremely sensitive legal activities would impede rather than promote social change by increasing tension and possibly inviting retaliation. But not believing that community organizers would respond favorably to these considerations, the lawyers tried to convince them by means of their technical legal expertise. In other words, they gave their clients professional rationales for decisions that were really made on political grounds.

None of this stopped the organizers from accusing them of being tools of the Establishment— a label the lawyers appreciated no more than they enjoyed being viewed by the Establishment as lackeys of the militants. The absence of a true market relationship had created this dilemma. It permitted an unusual diversity of view and action between lawyer and client, by encouraging the organizers to make extravagant demands upon their lawyers, by giving the lawyers considerable independence in dealing with their clients, and by preventing either party from withdrawing from the relationship. If the lawyers were to build a workable relationship with their organizational clients while bound by these constraints, they had to find their way out of what seemed like an impossible dilemma: how to be militant and moderate simultaneously.

The Class Action Strategy

Class action was the perfect strategy. It eventually won over many of the militants because it seemed to challenge basic practices and policies of Establishment institutions. They began to see parallels between what the lawyers were attempting to accomplish in court and their own activities in the street. The lawyers did what they could to reinforce this impression. Class action provided the lawyers with a politically militant language that justified their bypassing other legal alternatives, yet could still persuade the organizers that they were serious about their anti-Establishment convictions. Though the lawyers almost always initiated the idea of class action, the organizers tended to believe that in so doing the lawyers were responding favorably to their pressure for radical action. This made class action even more palatable to them.

What is more surprising is that—despite the public outcries of some officials—the local Establishment was not antagonized by the lawyers' class action strategy. Of course, public officials preferred not being attacked at all; but if being on the firing line seemed inevitable, they viewed class action as the least undesirable way to be attacked. In fact, there were numerous officials who, though publicly criticizing the Foundation, privately praised it. They thought that class action suits provided militants with a legitimate outlet

for their dissatisfactions and frustrations. Many San Francisco institutions had been the object of direct action assaults, and to the extent that the Foundation was believed to be diverting the volatile energies of the militants into legitimate legal battles, it was regarded highly for playing a constructive role.

Many of those in power found class action relatively benign compared to the traditional case approach for two reasons. First, while the strategy favored by many militant organizers was to batter their various enemies with one case after another, class action was generally a one-shot affair. Even when the outcome was appealed, there was a considerable time lapse before the next trial. Public agencies did not have to be forever devoting their resources to litigation, nor were they as vulnerable to the bad publicity that a continuous barrage of individual cases could have precipitated. Furthermore, class action suits were less likely than a rapid-fire succession of individual cases to agitate a whole community and thus build up the strength of militant organizations.

A second advantage of class action to the local Establishment was the Foundation's tendency to use it in ways that either avoided or minimized political pressures on the city. Community organizers tended to believe that a broad cross-section of the city's officials, agencies, and private interests held responsibility for almost any abuse the poor suffered. As they saw it, the failure to enforce housing codes, for example, reflected not only landlord negligence but also malpractice in the Department of Public Health, Fire Department, District Attorney's office, and the office of the Mayor as well. They thought that if the lawyers would legally pester these agencies with the individual complaints of community residents, the political motion these activities would stir could then be used to change conditions. The lawyers, who for good reason believed this approach would be a fruitless one from a legal point of view, generally attributed responsibility for abuses more narrowly. Thus the class action cases cited far fewer culprits than organizers originally identified. As a rule, then, the local Establishment was relieved by the decision of the lawyers to pursue a class action strategy.

The Other Audiences

Two other audiences—their professional colleagues throughout the country, and the liberal middle-class public—exerted a considerable influence on the actions of the main office lawyers. Side by side with their idealism, the lawyers possessed a great desire to develop their reputations. Class action was a powerful tool that could win them the respect and admiration of these audiences. To other lawyers they were able to display their legal acumen by skillfully preparing and presenting innovative and potentially precedent-shattering cases to the higher courts. And to the liberals, the highly dramatic anti-Establishment aspect of class action had great appeal. It offered the potential of bringing about major reforms without engaging in political excesses.

But these audiences are not reliable judges of the real merits and benefits of class action. The middle-class public, who were neither directly affected by the outcome of the Foundation's class action suits nor knowledgeable about legal issues, were readily impressed by the visible and superficial. The mere fact that the Foundation filed a class action suit on behalf of the poor, along with the strong tone and content of its public statements, was sufficient to win their enthusiasm and unqualified support. Lawyers across the country, on the other hand, understood the various legal issues involved in the class action suits. But, perhaps for reasons related to their training, the actual social and economic implications of these cases were often not clear to them.

Yet these were audiences the lawyers chose to act for, and this choice had serious consequences. For the main office lawyers, image making had a top priority, and it consumed a disproportionate amount of their energies. During the aftermath of press conferences, meetings, and other public encounters, the lawyers talked among themselves not about the issues they had addressed but almost solely about the impressions they had created. Whether they believed each other to be persuasive, sufficiently dramatic, or clever—these were more often the topics of discussion than the substantive issues they were being persuasive, dramatic, or clever about. In fact, their vanity was

so routinized that the lawyers were unaware of anything unusual about their behavior.

This concern with image was also manifested in their highly competitive spirit, which in turn produced its share of envy, anger, and anxiety. On several occasions the competition grew so fierce that it provoked a great deal of verbal abuse. In one instance, a lawyer physically attacked a colleague who accused him of deliberately omitting his name from a press release. It is not that warm relations were absent among the lawyers; but along with their collegiality there was considerable tension. Mutual distrust was rampant. They readily suspected each other of seeking personal advantage—for example, by not sharing credit fairly.

Even the attention received by other OEO legal service programs provoked their jealousy. Publicly they praised the accomplishments of OEO's largest legal assistance agency, Cal-Rural, but among themselves they were indignant about Cal-Rural's better reputation, which in their view reflected only its superior public relations efforts. Amazingly, they claimed that Cal-Rural was too obsessed with public image. They seemed to be unaware of how image-oriented their own behavior was.

Idealism and Deception

The lawyers' absorption in image-building might have been merely amusing and of no great consequence, except that it frequently conflicted with the best interests of their clients. Clients needed services that were custom-made. Image building promoted class action on an assembly-line basis. The specific needs of clients and the question of whether or not they really could gain from class action were incidental to the lawyers. They were concerned only with filing as many dramatic class action cases as possible. Among other things, this meant that they were constantly seeking out interesting issues and organizations that might help generate them. So they had little time or patience for community organizations that sought other, less dramatic kinds of legal service.

As might be expected, community organizations that were already mature and independent often refused to deal with the Foundation. The Mission Coalition, a powerful Alinsky-influenced grass roots organization in the Latin community, carefully defined the terms under which it would be willing to accept the Foundation's offer of legal assistance. Knowing the Foundation's reputation, it insisted that the Foundation provide whatever technical aid it needed without ever intruding on policy matters. Predictably, the Foundation lost its interest in working with the Coalition.

But a great many organizations that were neither strong nor sophisticated tended to become enveloped by the Foundation's activities. Whether they were battling against the lawyers, or assisting them in numerous ways (such as gathering material for class action suits), or doing almost nothing pending the disposition of a case, these community organizations were caught up in a process that was stunting their development and eroding their autonomy.

Corollary to this process, and perhaps as important, was the miseducation foisted on community organizers and their followers. Rather than assisting their clients to overcome their ignorance about the law, the lawyers were continually reinforcing it. No matter how irrelevant their clients' needs were to their choice of a legal strategy, the lawyers always tried to show how their actions or inactions were in the clients' best interest. So the lawyers developed an expertise in presenting distorted and falsified explanations to account for their behavior.

Miseducating the organizers about their legal options was fundamental to the selling of the class action strategy. Organizers were generally interested in improving conditions primarily for their own neighborhoods. The primary concern of the lawyers, however, was not the poor in a specific community but the poor who shared a common legal problem no matter where they resided. To sell the organizers on class action, the lawyers, for reasons they regarded as idealistic, misled them into believing that these suits were aimed primarily toward improving conditions in their own community, and that the suits offered the best possible means for doing so.

The lawyers believed that they had a mission—to devote themselves to bettering the conditions of the poor not only locally but across the state and nation. So if in service to their idealistic aims they breached professional standards of conduct, they experienced no remorse. Though they often felt unappreciated, the lawyers also felt proud of their efforts. They seemed unaware that in the process of doing what they did—falsifying, distorting, and withholding information—these idealists were becoming cynical operators who paid little attention to the means they employed. So the class action strategy the lawyers pursued victimized not only the poor and the organizations that served them; ultimately, the strategy also made casualties of the lawyers themselves.

It is important for those who debate the fate of legal assistance to separate in their minds class action from more conventional legal services. It would be tragic for those who are outraged at government-funded class action to assess and determine the future of the program as a whole on the basis of one of its weakest components. On the other hand, the poor and their representatives, who often tend to regard any attack on existing social programs as an attack on themselves, should realize that, just because something describes itself as a service to the poor, it doesn't follow that, in actuality, it is.

Notes and Questions

1. Some critics of the law reform orientation adopted by zealous legal services programs have argued that such work threatens the stability of all legal order. Is this view supported by Brill's analysis?

2. The lawyer as mediator was discussed in several of the earlier readings. To Tocqueville, through mediation, lawyers prevented the "tyranny of the majority." Pipkin argued that early legal aid societies used mediation to cool out clients who might be attracted to radical ideologies. Mediation was an integral part of what Blumberg called "the confidence game." Does Brill's description of the mediator's role assumed by main office attorneys suggest that law reform lawyers use mediation differently?

3. Compare Brill's analysis of class actions to the following:

    Through the individual incident or transaction, law makes individuals the basic unit of any case. Class actions exist in civil law, but numerous and growing restrictions frustrate attempts to reach basic issues. The persons who are normally engaged in legal controversy are separated out from the mass of people by the legal process and made to look special; and each case is made to appear different from others ... social struggles and political movements are splintered into their individual components and prevented from making any stronger or more collective statements than might be made by any of the individuals involved. Yet often, the only way a judge or jury might understand motivations behind a particular act is through its collective statement.*

4. Others have argued that a focus on individual cases with high caseloads rather than class actions with low caseloads does not necessarily preclude

law reform efforts by legal service programs. For example:

[O]ne of the basic forces for social change in the law is a high caseload. If the volume is very heavy, there is of course a distinct drawback in that it forces the lawyer to give less thorough attention to the details of each individual case, but a large caseload has great advantages if it can be harnessed and used to effect change.

The fact is that, if the Welfare Department buys out an individual case, we are precluded from getting a principle of law changed, but if we give them one thousand cases to buy out, that law has been effectively changed whether or not the law as written is changed. ... The value of a heavy caseload is that it allows you to populate the legal process. It allows you to apply unremitting pressure on the agency you are dealing with.†

* Kenneth Cloke, "The Economic Basis of Law and State," in Robert Lefcourt, ed., *Law Against the People* (New York: Random House, 1971), p. 69.

† Harold J. Rothwax, "The Law as an Instrument of Social Change," in Harold H. Weissman, ed., *Justice and the Law in the Mobilization for Youth Experience* (New York: Association Press, 1969), p. 140.

After a decade of turmoil, the government-sponsored effort to bring legal services to the poor was finally established. The law reform thrust, which characterized the early years, was blunted but the neighborhood model of client service ultimately prevailed.

All the issues raised by previous articles in this chapter should be reflected upon while reading the following essay on problems in the mature legal services program.

The Legal Aid Puzzle: Turning Solutions into Problems *Gary Bellow*

Before OEO committed $19 million to legal services for the poor in 1965, legal assistance to the needy in the United States was charity, provided by an often grudging bar. The bar did not relinquish this conception easily. The early years of the OEO program were marked by controversy over federal attempts to "socialize" the legal profession. Speeches at bar associations condemned the entry of hippies into the profession, Spiro Agnew charged that the program was

dominated by "ideological vigilantes," and several governors vetoed grants to legal services projects in their states. The dominant issue for the "legal services movement" was survival.

In the seventies, that concern has receded into the background. Under the auspices of the Legal Services Corporation Act (passed in 1974), over 3,000 full-time lawyers now handle a million or more cases a year in neighborhood-based offices and in centers that concentrate on particular groups (the aged, children), particular geographic areas (states, regions), or specific subject matters (welfare, housing). Although the present program, with a $100 million yearly authorization, still meets less than 15 percent of the official (and understated) need, it does reflect an explicit congressional commitment to provide the poor with "equal access to the nation's system of justice."

Today's lack of controversy, however, may be as much a cause for concern as for satisfaction. A cursory review of the cases handled by legal services offices around the country reveals a problem that those involved in the movement have not paid much attention to—the degree to which the legal aid bar itself has come to acquiesce in and even support the very inequalities that brought a federally financed legal aid program into being.

Like the welfare system, the public housing system, and the other government-funded social services that preceded it, the legal aid system may be evolving routines and justifications that can become as much a source of new problems as solutions to old ones.

What follows is a case that illustrates some of the characteristics of these practices. The service pictured is typical of what we have found in our review of files in legal aid offices around the country. The counsel's entries tell how the case was handled. The observations offer some insight into what might have been.

At the time Mrs. L came into the legal services office, she had been divorced a year and was living with her five-year-old daughter in an apartment in a low-income area of a midwestern city. Five other families lived in the building, and all apartments were subject to the city rent control law and the state sanitary code.

The previous winter the oil burner had broken down and the tenants had been without heat for weeks at a time. The building was also in serious disrepair (exposed wiring, peeling paint, sagging ceilings), and a number of tenants, including Mrs. L, had refused to pay rent for two months. Later she fell an additional month behind.

Two months before Mrs. L came to the office, Realty Trust, the owner, had hired a new management company to maintain the building. The company had made substantial repairs and had indicated to all tenants that it planned to pursue the back rent and to seek an increase from the rent control board to cover the cost of rehabilitation. It followed this up by serving eviction notices on a number of tenants who were in arrears. Sometime shortly before she came to the office, Mrs. L received a summons and complaint informing her of eviction proceedings against her.

Counsel's File Entries

September 10. Spoke with Mrs. L who brought in eviction papers that had been served on her. Said that she had been in the building for two years and wanted to stay but didn't have enough money to pay the three months' back rent. I told her I would call the landlord to see what I could work out. The building is apparently in very bad shape.

Observations

☐ Although faced with a possible eviction, Mrs. L had a good many legal claims and defenses available to her under the law of the state in which she lived. These included (a) a claim for damages or for back rent because of the condition of the premises (the conditions were bad enough to violate local housing and sanitary codes); (b) a defense to the eviction on the same grounds; (c) a defense to the eviction on the grounds that the landlord was proceeding against Mrs. L because of her prior withholding of rent. Although the lawyer never learned of it, only certain tenants in arrears, considered by the new management company to be potential "troublemakers," had received eviction notices.

In addition, Mrs. L was entitled to certain procedural safeguards in any action against her. It was later learned that she had never been correctly served with the court papers. This possibility was not explored by the lawyer in the course of the interview, nor did the lawyer subsequently investigate the past or present conditions in the building, or the possibility that the eviction had been improperly motivated. The lawyer always assumed that Mrs. L didn't pay three months' rent simply because she couldn't afford it and that the eviction was a consequence of her failure to pay.

Interestingly, two other tenants in the building were clients of other attorneys in the office, although none of them were aware of this. None of these issues were ever discussed with any of the clients.

September 12. Called counsel for Realty Trust and was referred to the building manager. The manager said that anything wrong with the building had now been corrected and was not his responsibility. Mrs. L was a problem tenant whom he suspected of being on drugs; he wanted her out as soon as possible and would agree to no negotiated resolution.

☐ The call should have been preceded by some planning about what demands to make and what counterdemands might be acceptable. It also should have been based on a good deal of knowledge about the case, the applicable law, and Mrs. L. The conversation with the building manager might have been very different if the lawyer had been able to answer the assertions about his client and had argued forcefully that, given the conditions in the building, Mrs. L did not owe the landlord any rent and could not be evicted. (This, in fact, would have been a fair interpretation of the law.)

The manager might also have responded very differently had the lawyer discussed with him the likely effect of the prior violations in the building on the company's efforts to obtain a rent increase from the rent control board or the potential claims for damages that the other tenants in the building had against the owner.

By not taking a strong position in the first contact with the manager, counsel for Mrs. L may well have given the impression that the manager's views of Mrs. L were justified and that her lawyer did not intend to pursue the case aggressively.

As the lawyer indicated in an interview after the case was completed, he never did enough legal or factual research to be confident of his position and was unsure whether the fact that the new company had not been involved in the past deterioration of the premises significantly affected his position. Under the prevailing law, it did not.

September 17. Called the clerk of the court and learned that the answer was due tomorrow. Filled out a regular form answer defending on the grounds that conditions in the building violate the state sanitary code. Trial date is late next week.

☐ By failing to have checked more carefully when and how Mrs. L received the papers (by a call to the marshal who served them or by pressing the clerk about the due date) the lawyer ran the risk of missing an important deadline date. In fact, the clerk was in error; the answer was due on the 17th, although the landlord's lawyer apparently didn't try to take advantage of its being filed late. More significantly, the lawyer did not (a) check with the rent control board to be sure the rental level was proper; (b) ask for an inspection of the premises by the appropriate government agency; (c) seek formal disclosure by Realty Trust or the management company of what repairs were made on the building, or of any communications, documents, and the like relevant to the eviction of Mrs. L; (d) discuss any of these possibilities with his client. The answer was also not carefully drafted, omitted a number of available defenses (including a possible action for damages), and could only signal to the opposing counsel that Mrs. L's case was being handled as a routine matter.

September 20. Wrote to client to tell her to be in court on September 24.

☐ Mrs. L might have needed a babysitter or help in getting to court, as well as some idea of what would happen there. None of these possibilities was considered by the lawyer, nor did he counsel Mrs. L about her forthcoming testimony. Other potential witnesses were not sought. There is no way the case could have been properly presented to a court on the basis of the preparation that had been done up to this point in the process.

September 22. Mrs. L called to tell me she couldn't make the hearing on the morning of the 24th because she had to take her daughter to the doctor. I told her I'd ask for a continuance of the case but that if it wasn't granted, she'd have to come in that afternoon.

☐ The lawyer did not ask why Mrs. L's daughter needed medical attention. It turned out that the child had a number of medical and school problems with potential legal remedies that were never explored. In reviewing the case after its completion it was also found that Mrs. L had made payment on a consumer purchase that she could have legally avoided and was receiving $50 less welfare than she was entitled to while the eviction case was being handled. The lawyer was never aware of these problems.

In addition, he was careless in asking for a continuance without notifying the other side in advance and getting an affidavit or other documentation from Mrs. L that established the legitimacy of her inability to attend. As a result, the judge refused to set a new date and required a trial that afternoon.

September 24. Called Mrs. L from court to tell her that the case was set for 2 p.m. this afternoon, but that the landlord's lawyer had agreed to give up two months' back rent if she'd pay last month's rent, stay current, and leave within 90 days. I told her that since several hundred dollars was being forgiven, it was a pretty good deal and about the best I could do. She authorized me to accept it.

☐ Why Mrs. L accepted the settlement is not known because of the minimal exploration of her desires and options. Similarly, without investigating the apartment's condition, past and present, it is impossible to know whether the settlement was warranted. Given the possible defenses and actions against the landlord, however, and the admission by the building manager that a good deal of repair had been undertaken, what Mrs. L agreed to was probably far too generous.

I don't want to suggest that legal aid offices treat all clients or problems in this way. There are many variations among programs, among lawyers and offices, and even in the way the same lawyer handles different cases. There are also many well-served clients and well-handled cases. Nevertheless, enough research has been done in enough offices to suggest that Mrs. L's case reflects a number of recurring practices in legal aid work. These include the following:

1. The lawyers handle problems in routine, standardized ways. Cases not referred to other agencies are typically "slotted" into predictable patterns—getting the client time to move out in an eviction case, working out a payment schedule in a debt case, applying to the appropriate agency in a benefit case. Only rarely do the lawyers get involved in any research, investigation, or courtroom work. Indeed, many of the lawyers never leave the office, resolving their cases over the phone. Only if an "interesting" issue is raised, or if the client is especially attractive or demanding, will the attorney spend an unusual amount of time, effort, or planning on a particular case.

2. The lawyers dominate interactions with clients. In most discussions with clients, the lawyer does almost all of the talking, gives little

opportunity for the client to express his or her feelings or concerns, and consistently controls the length, topic, and character of the conversation. Facts are obtained by a series of pointed, standard questions rather than by any process that resembles a dialogue. The lawyer then restates the client's problems in legal terms and suggests the best available solutions based on his or her view of the situation and its possibilities. As may have happened in Mrs. L's case, this often results in a client's being unable or unwilling to provide needed information or clarity about his or her own desires and goals.

3. Service is limited to the problems actually presented by the clients. There is no concept of a legal checkup in legal services practice. Thus, unless Mrs. L knows that she has specific consumer or welfare rights, or that a lawyer could be of help in dealing with her daughter's medical and school difficulties, and unless she is willing to ask for such help, she will receive no legal advice or representation on these matters. Legal services lawyers do not generally inquire about any "other" problems.

4. The lawyers treat clients and problems individually. No efforts are made to encourage clients with related problems to meet and talk with each other, or to explore the possibilities of concerted challenges to an institution's practices. Nor do the lawyers systematically review cases to identify recurring problems, to deepen their knowledge of the bureaucracies with which they deal, or to expose publicly what they have uncovered. Despite the volume of cases, there are legal services lawyers who have been handling landlord-tenant or welfare cases for several years who cannot describe the nature of the housing market in their area or the supervisory structure of the local welfare department.

5. Many cases end in highly questionable settlements. Clients agree to move out, despite available defenses, or to accept a percentage of back benefits admittedly owed by the welfare department, or to give up a sound damage action against a credit company in exchange for reducing past debts. Whether such results are good or bad depend on a number of factors—how much the client could have obtained by further negotiation, what would have occurred at trial, whether or not the client was willing to undergo the delays and tensions of not settling out of court. But reviews by experienced lawyers of typical settlements in legal services programs suggest that outcomes for clients in legal aid cases may be considerably lower than they ought to be, and that many cases should have been far more aggressively pursued.

In a number of cases, the agreement to settle was preceded by clear overstatements by the lawyer of the risk of not settling, the benefits of the proposed agreement, and the difficulties the lawyer encountered in obtaining it. To use Erving Goffman's phrase, the clients were, intentionally or unintentionally, "cooled out" to guarantee that what they got was perceived to be as much as or more than they had been led to expect. In some cases the clients received a so-called short trial, in which a perfunctory hearing and a few questions to one witness were used to permit the judge to impose a settlement that had been agreed to in advance by both lawyers.

Sources of the Problem

The picture that Mrs. L's case presents is puzzling. Legal aid lawyers are, by and large, concerned and capable individuals. They come from a cross section of the nation's law schools and from the upper stratum of successful students. They have often given up better-paying jobs and better working conditions to do this sort of work. They enter poverty-type programs well aware of the dangers of bureaucratization, unresponsiveness, and routine in social services. Why then do these same patterns prevail in legal services? And why are legal services attorneys so unaware of these patterns even in their own handling of cases?

The blame for the way service is provided, if blame is assigned at all, is usually put on the high caseloads. Legal services attorneys regularly handle 150 to 200 ongoing cases, and many handle far more than that. Even so, general estimates are that in most communities 80 to 90 percent of the need is not being met.

The argument is that the mass processing of cases is a necessary, if unfortunate, response to this demand. Legal aid lawyers are paid, after all, to serve the community. They feel they must therefore take on as many cases as possible. If this precludes the careful, aggressive handling of fewer cases, it at least offers a little help to those who would otherwise get none.

As one examines the actual work of the offices, however, this argument, no matter how sincerely felt, seems less compelling. The price for the kind of routine, cautious, detached practice that is developing in the legal aid system is just too high. Professional growth among staff is stifled, turnover is a continuing problem, creativity is dampened. Legal aid work becomes less and less attractive to young lawyers in need of guidance and encouragement.

More important, in case after case legal entitlements are compromised or ignored, and clients are misled into believing they are receiving service that conforms to the norms of the profession. They are not told they are being given minimal assistance in the interest of offering some service to the greatest number.

In addition, a decision to provide the poor with lawyers too overburdened to handle individual cases properly is a policy question that needs to be openly discussed, not only among the legal aid bar but also with the people they serve. There is no requirement by the Legal Services Corporation or anyone else that a legal aid lawyer must take every client who seeks help. In fact, the legal profession's ethics insist that a lawyer not take more cases than he or she can reasonably handle.

Finally, even in offices with relatively low caseloads, the same routine service appears. Cases are seen and handled as "simple," although a review reveals missed complexities and opportunities. In one office, cases were handled in ways similar to Mrs. L's by lawyers who had less than ten other clients. This suggests that the reasons for such practices do not lie in heavy caseloads. More likely, they are rooted in how the legal system works for the poor, how lawyers are trained, and how "professional" attitudes shape the ways lawyers justify their actions.

THE LOWER COURT SYSTEM. The legal aid lawyer practices in courts where there are persistent demands to settle every case. Opposing lawyers and agency officials, who are pressed by high caseloads, want quick, certain resolution of disputes. For a legal aid lawyer willing to go along with prevailing settlement patterns, there are many potential benefits: a break now and then for a client with a weak claim, consideration for the lawyer's busy schedule, or help in looking good when public performance slips a little. On the other hand, there can be severe sanctions against the client of the legal services lawyer who won't cooperate. Most poor clients are vulnerable to harassment by a hostile social worker, or by the attorney for an angry landlord who can almost always serve the client with a late-rent eviction notice.

Judges often use similar pressures. The courts want the crowded calendar to move, whatever the circumstances of particular cases. A surprising number of judges in the last ten years have punished legal aid clients because their lawyers took too much of the court's time on "frivolous" matters. Some even initiated actions against particular legal aid programs when they thought the staff departed too dramatically from regular ways of doing things in the local system.

The potential impact of these sanctions on clients creates considerable pressure to go along with the bureaucratic rules of the game. A negotiated settlement satisfies all interests with virtually no possibility of criticism. (Who, after all, is to say that a better result could have been obtained?) Law practice is an uncertain business, and predictability depends on good working relationships with the other professionals engaged in it.

LEGAL EDUCATION. Recent graduates from law schools—the bulk of the legal aid bar—are ill-equipped to provide aggressive representation in such a system. Advocating client interests within a highly bureaucratized setting is always a source of strain and uncertainty, even more so when the client is poor. Unfortunately, very little in a lawyer's education or on-the-job training produces the skills, confidence, or perspective necessary to protect clients from such tensions.

Generally, American law schools prepare students only to do the entry-level jobs in large firms, such as legal research and memorandum writing. A new lawyer certified by the bar to practice law in most instances has never handled a case, interviewed a client, examined a witness, or negotiated a settlement. Baldly stated, he or she is licensed but not competent to be a lawyer. The firm must teach the neophyte to perform lawyer tasks and introduce the new attorney to increased responsibility for clients and their problems.

For the lawyer who goes from law school to the large or middle-sized firm, this division of educational responsibility between practice and law school functions reasonably well as long as its costs can be passed on to clients. If the student goes directly into solo practice, joins a small partnership, or enters legal aid work, however, he or she must learn on the job, and on the clients. Only rarely are standards made explicit; only rarely is the work reviewed or criticized by an experienced attorney. Young lawyers are expected to "know" good and bad work when they see it and to adapt to "the way we do things here."

Inexperienced legal aid lawyers are particularly vulnerable to these pressures. Their clients are not apt to be sufficiently knowledgeable and demanding to hold them accountable to high standards of practice. They have had virtually no law school instruction in the large body of law and skills that would enable them to be self-critical. The turnover rate among experienced attorneys in legal aid work is so high that there is no one to provide the on-the-job training or supervision they need.

Under these conditions, the massive caseloads serve an ambiguous function. On the one hand, trying to meet the demands of so many cases prevents the inexperienced lawyers from ever adequately developing their skills and knowledge. (The high turnover rate among legal services attorneys is undoubtedly related to the persistent feeling of being confronted daily with too much need for too long.) On the other hand, very high caseloads also serve as an "out" for untrained lawyers well aware of their own limitations. The heavy workload provides a legitimate reason why they cannot thoroughly prepare and investigate particular cases or link them to local organizing efforts or exert political pressure.

"PROFESSIONAL" ATTITUDES Prevailing ideas about professionalism in legal work further reinforce and rationalize these patterns. For example, most lawyers consider emotional detachment an important aspect of giving careful legal advice. This posture toward clients, however, also encourages legal aid lawyers to maintain a good deal of distance from the day-to-day poverty and exploitation of their clients. It is a short step from such detachment to impersonal, routine service.

Similar consequences result from other professional values. The virtue of "sticking to the legal," intended to protect client choice, justifies the lawyer's not asking questions beyond the client's specific complaint. The idea of legal "expertise," potentially a source of self-regulation within the profession, provides a rationale for lawyers to make a large number of essentially nontechnical decisions about the character and quality of legal aid service. Even professional neutrality, thought essential to keeping personal biases out of lawyer-client relationships, provides a rationale for narrowly defining what the lawyer inquires into or undertakes in a particular case.

The widely held belief among lawyers that individual client service is fundamentally apolitical performs similar rationalizing functions. According to this view, the day-to-day complaints clients bring to the neighborhood legal services offices—against creditors, landlords, welfare workers—are not considered fuel for political action or reform. If reform is to be sought by lawyers at all, the model is the constitutional challenge in court to an existing law or practice, the "test case." Since these cases usually require lengthy research and preparation, lawyers doing service work in neighborhood offices are not expected to undertake them. Programs are organized so that neighborhood offices handle large numbers of cases, and reform work, if any, is left to specialized centers or to individuals in the "central office." Indeed, advancement and status in legal aid work often mean moving on to work on specialized litigation and other "reform" efforts, leaving routine case work to the younger lawyers.

Unfortunately, this idea that the legal problems of the poor can and should be divided into large (political) test case claims and routine (apolitical) grievances places a further stigma on day-to-day legal aid work, minimizing the importance of efforts on behalf of individual clients. It blurs the possibilities for linking "test case" litigation to more community-based political efforts, and it justifies the limited approach to individual client grievances.

Possibilities for Change

It is rarely easy to alter patterns as institutionally reinforced as those in most legal aid offices. And blaming the attorneys who are at least struggling with realities that most lawyers ignore is not only unfair, it is likely to add to the very pressures that now promote withdrawal and noninvolvement in legal aid work. What is needed are ways of developing pressures and incentives to counter those that now encourage routine practices.

First, the lawyers themselves might initiate systematic critical scrutiny of the character and quality of their own practices. Since they are often not fully aware of the extent to which their work has become routine, impersonal, and controlling, such self-scrutiny should be done in ways that minimize resentment and defensiveness. This might require that offices experiment with systematically evaluating case files; conduct postmortems on closed cases; regularly circulate case files for review within offices; pair lawyers in handling cases; regularly test office staff on skills and information; survey clients to assess their reactions to the service; or call on outside consultants to review the office's practices.

It might also require that the more experienced lawyers begin to handle day-to-day service cases and that the offices spell out policies that ought to govern representation in these situations. For example, it might be important to require visits to a client's home whenever housing conditions are an issue, regular reviews of welfare eligibility before closing a case, and written justifications for any critical decision or long period of inactivity in a case. This would signal to the younger staff that clients in "ordinary" cases are important and would begin to establish criteria for the sort of legal help clients in these cases ought to be receiving.

Second, clients might be involved in evaluating the service they receive. This would require communicating to clients what can be asked, expected, and obtained from and by lawyers in different kinds of cases. Programs might make written materials available in waiting rooms, enlarge opportunities for paralegals and other office personnel to evaluate the quality of service, include a significant number of clients on the program's board of directors, and institute effective procedures for reviewing, investigating, and deciding any client grievances against lawyers and the office. The offices might also initiate regular legal checkups and any other procedures that inform clients of their rights. Local papers and meetings could be used to report regularly on the activities and policies of the office.

Many of these suggestions have been tried with varying degrees of success in different programs and communities. Whatever their limits, a real commitment by the staff to explain, disclose, and listen to criticism, not only from each other but from clients as well, is basic to altering the relationships that now dominate legal aid practice.

Third, career lines, incentive structures, and educational opportunities within the office might, and indeed must, be significantly altered. Without some possibility for personal and professional growth, there seems little chance that the lawyers in legal aid work will alter deeply embedded routines. Law school graduates do need a good deal of instruction in lawyering skills. But they also need examples of good practice, personal success, a positive way of looking at themselves and their potential. Otherwise, their hard work, defeats, and loss of status in the profession will inevitably result in short-term commitments to legal aid work. (Even when legal services lawyers have stayed with programs for five or six years, they are somehow always about to leave.)

This would require at least the following: salary structures that encourage longer tenure and less turnover; staffing patterns that do not force a lawyer to give up representing individual clients in order to advance professionally; three-to-five-year commitments from young lawyers entering the program; systematic and regular internal staff training, including incremental introduction of responsibilities in the first year of practice; rotation of jobs and locations; and sabbaticals for senior staff. If clients are to be adequately served, it will be necessary to attend to the needs of their lawyers as well.

Finally, a much more explicitly political attitude toward day-to-day work might be adopted by individual programs and offices. By political I don't mean to evoke a simplified version of marches, protests, and demonstrations—a "poor people's politics." Nor do I mean that the big "reform" test cases are inconsistent with day-to-day services. What I have in mind is an approach that includes the following features:

1.   A sufficiently limited number of day-to-day cases so the lawyers can coordinate and compare the way they handle cases;

2.   Selection of "target" institutions whose illegal practices affect a significant number of the program's clients. (The gap between rule and practice in most private and public institutions that deal with the poor is so large that there is usually no difficulty in identifying such a practice. Examples might be the living conditions maintained in public housing, the treatment of welfare recipients, the discipline and education of low-income students.)

3.   Representation of large numbers of clients who have been victims of these practices, through referrals, in-depth interviews, and solicitation (the latter is now permitted under the Code of Professional Responsibility).

4.   Service to clients that maximizes individual claims and increases the office's knowledge of the personnel, practice, and vulnerabilities of the target institutions.

5.   Coordination and communication within the office to crystallize strategies and goals directed to the target institutions.

6.   Direct contact by the office with the target institutions to seek change in the policies and practices documented in handling the cases.

7.   Coalitions with other community groups seeking similar changes.

The net effect of such efforts is to confront particular institutions with an increasing number of individual grievances, coordinated by a group of experienced advocates whose commitment and continuous attention is ordinarily available only

to the regular players in the system—those with money, resources, and incentives to use law and lawyers consistently as a source of power and control.

I believe that such a focused-case strategy can do a good deal to change the illegal and exploitative practices that affect poor people. The type of illegalities that it confronts are often the product of cost calculations that are radically altered when a substantial number of complainants with a real stake in the outcome do not have to pay the usual attorney's fees and other costs to pursue their grievances to completion. I also believe that only focused political efforts of this kind will sustain the self-consciousness, discipline, and cooperation necessary to counteract tendencies toward routine, constricted service in legal aid practice. Finding meaning in work requires a considerably richer and more morally rooted set of self-conceptions than are offered by an abstract notion of "access" to the legal system for the poor.

Are such changes likely to occur within legal services offices? It's very hard to say. Social services have been stubbornly resistant to the attempts to alter established ways of doing things even when the changes are initiated by clients and staff. Nevertheless, such efforts are especially important in a program that has the possibility of becoming an instrument of the very class biases its founders hoped to counter.

Lawyers inevitably shape much of what clients see as possible and desirable. The relationship between lawyer and client can be a source of security and autonomy. But, it can also generate dependence and subordination. It can focus or diffuse, enlarge or narrow the pattern of grievances that clients experience. At stake in every interaction between a lawyer and a client, particularly a poor client, is the question of how the lawyer's considerable interpersonal power will be used.

Without question, there is a real need for more legal services for the poor in this country. In a law-dominated society such as ours, it would be hard to imagine a process of change on behalf of the poor without improving their access to, or at least protection from, the legal system. But the

Legal Services Corporation's current plans for a massive expansion of minimal, routinized legal assistance, with selective efforts at "law reform," is also a potentially powerful system of social control, capable of defining and legitimating particular grievances and resolutions and ignoring others.

Legal aid lawyers unwilling or unable to respond to client concerns in ways that link them to a larger vision of social justice can easily become purveyors of resignation and acquiescence in existing social arrangements. Clients can literally be taught that their situations are natural, inevitable, or their own fault, and that they themselves are ultimately dependent on professional advice and guidance. To echo a now familiar observation about the welfare state, a social service that is not part of the solution can soon become part of the problem. The legal aid experience may be one more example of the truth in that homily.

Notes and Questions

1. Consider the following discussion on the ideological content of a television program on legal aid:

   In one scene a city-dressed lawyer talked in an impeccable accent to an old man. He told him to leave the papers and forms concerning his problems with him and on his return they would be prepared, ready for signature. What is the ideological meaning of this scene? First, there is a picture of an old man who is seen as alone, poor and friendless. The only thing that he has which he can call his own is his problem. The lawyer takes away the last thing that the old man has which enables him to think that people still react in some way to him, his problem.... The meaning is plain—he is being confirmed as a failure. The only thing that he can do is sign his name.... People are being dehumanized, although more "nicely." Their problems are being removed. Their experience of how things are solved is being negated. They are told that the only way of solving their problems is to leave them to the expert....*

2. If lawyer dominance of clients and individualistic responses to cases are the result of law school training, is it unrealistic for Bellow to suggest that legal aid lawyers can counter this phenomenon?

3. Bellow seems to vacillate between two visions of the situation: One in which the poor are here to stay and the problem is to build a form of legal practice to represent them; and the second, in which the poor are but the temporary victims of an unjust economic system and the problem is to use legality as a tool in their struggle for social justice on a grand scale. Aggressive lawyers are a part of both visions. But in one they are only trying to provide what is already available to "the regular players in the system." In the other, they are trying to cut through the class structure and prevent legal aid from becoming "an instrument of the class biases its founders hoped to counter." At its deepest, this vacillation represents an ambivalence about law itself. Bellow concludes that the poor need "access to, or at least protection from, the legal system." Which is it? Can it really be both simultaneously? And if Bellow doesn't know, how can any recent law school graduate know? If the confusion is this deep, is it likely that any changes in legal aid practice, including increased aggression and craft, will produce positive movement?

* Zenon Bankowski and Geoff Mungham, *Images of Law* (London: Routledge & Kegan Paul, 1976), p. 27.

Suggested Additional Readings

History of the Legal Profession

Auerbach, Jerome. *Unequal Justice*. New York: Oxford University Press, 1976.

Bloomfield, Maxwell. *American Lawyers in a Changing Society, 1776–1876*. Cambridge: Harvard University Press, 1976.

Friedman, Lawrence. *A History of American Law*. New York: Simon and Schuster, 1973.

Hurst, James Willard. *The Growth of American Law*. Boston: Little, Brown, 1950.

Pound, Roscoe. *The Lawyer from Antiquity to Modern Times*. St. Paul: West, 1953.

Smith, Reginald Heber. *Justice and the Poor*. Montclair, N.J.: Patterson Smith, 1972. Reprint of the 1924 edition.

Warren, Charles. *A History of the American Bar*. Boston: Little, Brown, 1911.

Legal Education

Shaffer, Thomas and Redmount, Robert. *Lawyers, Law Students and People*. Indianapolis: Sheppard's, 1977.

Turow, Scott. *One L*. New York: G. P. Putnam's Sons, 1977.

Practice of Law

Carlin, Jerome E. *Lawyers on Their Own*. New Brunswick, N.J.: Rutgers University Press, 1962.

Goulden, Joseph. *The Super-Lawyers*. New York: Weybright & Talley, 1971.

Handler, Joel. *The Lawyer and his Community*. Madison: University of Wisconsin Press, 1967.

Lieberman, Jethro K. *The Tyranny of the Experts*. New York: Walker, 1970.

Mayer, Martin. *The Lawyers*. New York: Dell Publishing, 1968.

Rosenthal, Douglas. *Lawyer and Client: Who's In Charge?* New Brunswick, N.J.: Transaction Books, 1974.

Smigel, Erwin O. *The Wall Street Lawyer*. New York: The Free Press, 1964.

Wood, Arthur Lewis. *Criminal Lawyer*. New Haven: College & University Press, 1967.

Activist Lawyers

Bankowski, Zenon and Mungham, Geoff. *Images of Law*. London: Routledge & Kegan Paul, 1976.

Black, Jonathan, ed. *Radical Lawyers*. New York: Avon Books, 1971.

Ginger, Ann Fagan. *The Relevant Lawyers*. New York: Simon and Schuster, 1972.

Graham, James J. *The Enemies of the Poor*. New York: Random House, 1970.

Lefcourt, Robert. *Law Against the People*. New York: Vintage Books, 1971.

Marks, F. Raymond. *The Lawyer, the Public, and Professional Responsibility*. Chicago: American Bar Foundation, 1972.

Stumpf, Harry P. *Community Politics and Legal Services*. Beverly Hills: Sage Publications, 1975.

Drawing by Steven Guarnaccia. © 1977 by The New York Times Company.
Reprinted by permission.

But jury trial, at best, is the apotheosis of the amateur. Why should anyone think that twelve persons brought in from the street, selected in various ways for their lack of general ability, should have any special capacity for deciding controversies between persons?

Erwin Griswold, Dean, Harvard Law School, *Report of the Dean* (1963)

All the sovereigns who have chosen to govern by their own authority, and to direct society instead of obeying its directions, have destroyed or enfeebled the institution of the jury.

Alexis de Tocqueville, *Democracy in America* (1835)

chapter four

The Jury

Somewhere between Dean Griswold's claim that the jury is no more than a vestigial organ of the body politic and Alexis de Tocqueville's claim that the jury is the centerpiece of true democracy lies the American jury. This chapter will raise most of the issues that have to be considered by anyone who wants to discern what the function of the jury is in American society today.

Imbedded in this question are still further questions: Should we continue to maintain a jury system? As it is presently operated and understood, does this system serve the interests of the people as a whole or the interests of only a few? How should we understand the real purposes and effects of the many reforms of the jury system being suggested? How useful a forum for the exploration and expression of personal and community ethics is the jury system as presently constructed? Is it possible that the jury system is already defunct? If we have lost this means of injecting popular will into law, what other means of de-professionalizing law do we have? How do other societies deal with the problem of making the law public?

The chapter is divided into five sections, each dealing with a basic jury issue but all tied together by the underlying questions of the chapter. Section 1 places the jury in the context of culture and history. Here we treat the jury and its parallel institutions in other cultures as we would a piece of broken pottery discovered at the site of an archaeological dig. What can be learned about the society that uses this form of legal process? What functional parallels can be drawn between the ordeal, the jury, and the use of "truth serum"? The reader is invited to use conflict as "a candle to illumine the nature of society," as Llewellyn suggested, and also to examine the operation and premises of legal institutions to shed light on the character of the cultures that produced them.

Section 2 concerns the political importance of the jury in our own society. Which part of Tocqueville's seemingly contradictory description of the jury is accurate today? How much should the public be aware of the jury's unchallengeable power to nullify the law? Does our own individual consciousness as jurors determine the function of the jury system? How do other societies, the Chinese in particular, deal with the appearance and reality of public participation in defining and resolving conflict?

Section 3 invites the reader to look beneath the surface of the traditional "judicial" role of juries. What really happens to an ordinary citizen when he or she enters a jury room to begin deliberations? Is it the best or the worst in us

that comes out as we struggle with the obligation to judge our fellow citizens? Is it possible that although the jury is written into the Constitution, it is being slowly and quietly eliminated through court decisions, plea bargaining, the use of expert testimony, and changes in our political economy?

Section 4 briefly explores the composition of juries and the way they are presently selected. Are formal legal protections adequate to assure a trial by a jury of one's peers? Are sophisticated and expensive psychological techniques turning peer selection into pawn selection? What ethical considerations are imposed upon social scientists participating in the selection of jurors? How do we maintain a functioning system of judgment of peers in a society increasingly separated into classes based on race, wealth, age, and sex?

Section 5 presents the problem of civil disobedience and the jury's reaction to it. Two brief descriptions of the rationale behind civil disobedience and the function of a jury confronted with the ambiguities of deviance are provided. To encourage an intense consideration of this problem, a slightly fictionalized description of one man's challenge to nuclear power plants is provided; readers are invited to form juries to deliberate his fate and your own.

The reader might be aware that the jury is not used very much and wonder why it should receive more than passing attention. After all, most civil cases result in out-of-court settlements or trials by judge. Most criminal cases result not in jury trials but in plea bargaining. Most of the world's societies survive with no jury trials at all. Yet to the extent that we attribute importance to the right of trial by jury, these very facts about its disuse may constitute cause for alarm or at least reason for study. And if we find jury trial insignificant, we may want to know whether that sentiment signifies that we are on the threshold of enlightenment or the brink of oppression.

Finally, one should acknowledge that for

many people the jury, like a flag or a clenched fist, sets off a welter of reactions which indicate that it has high symbolic importance.

Its history has been written about, its function speculated about, its adequacy argued about, and its mythology trumpeted about. Is it an inadequate and burdensome appendage which is falling into disuse, and which we cling to only out of loyalty to a dead ideology? Or is it an institution of the highest importance to law and democracy which has been thwarted and then maligned by the technological society?

For a crude beginning one may say that the petit, or trial, jury is charged with the job of determining facts and applying law in a particular case; and that the grand jury is required to decide whether criminal indictments shall issue when requested by the government. Each jury's peculiarity is in the fact that it presents a formal structure for injecting the ordinary citizen into the legal process. Like the vote, which is almost equally subject to argument about its symbolic and practical importance, the jury is at least an opportunity for the masses to participate in a generally professionalized legal process and thereby grant it the seal of democratic sanctity.

Rather than sweeping the entire issue away with *au courant* generalizations, however, one wants to know in what kind of complex matrix of legal functions, social symbols, practical reforms, political philosophy, and human psychology the jury can be located. After the basic lines of the matrix have been evoked, each person individually can calculate the location of the jury.

The matrix begins with a handful of fiery stones.

1 The Jury in a Cultural Context

The Ordeal as a Vehicle for Divine Intervention in Medieval Europe *William J. Tewksbury*

The ordeal is a primitive form of trial used to determine the guilt or innocence of the accused, the result being regarded as a divine or preter-human judgment. The fundamental idea upon which the ordeal rests is that it is a device for regulating, under conditions of comparative fairness, the primitive law of force. The concept that victory would inure to the right—that divine intervention would prevail on behalf of the innocent—was a belief that was subsequently engrafted upon the concept of the ordeal. The earliest occurrences, which can be referred to as pseudo-ordeals, seem to turn on the idea of brute strength. Such was the wager of battle and other "*bilateral* ordeals" to which both sides had to submit. Only later do we see man, alleging his innocence and facing his Creator, on trial by himself.

To understand the ordeal and the use for which it was designed, one must recognize the tremendous impact that religion has on the daily lives of the people who rely on it. The usual conception of divine intervention to vindicate innocence and to punish guilt is illustrated through an occurrence which happened in 1626 in France. A master had two servants, one stupid, and the other cunning. The latter stole from the master and so framed the stupid servant that he could not jus-

From William J. Tewksbury, "The Ordeal as a Vehicle for Divine Intervention" in Paul Bohanon, ed., *Law and Warfare* (Garden City, N.Y.: Natural History Press, 1967), pp. 267–270. Reprinted by permission.

tify himself. The doltish servant, allegedly guilty, was tied to a flagstaff and guarded by the accuser. In the night, the flagstaff broke, the upper part falling upon and killing the guilty cunning servant, leaving the innocent servant unhurt. Beliefs such as this lead to irregular judicial proceedings. One might refer to them as ordeals of chance. The innocence of a man often turned on pure luck.

I.   Ordeals by Fire and Heat

The ordeal of boiling water is important in medieval Europe and elsewhere because it combines the elements of fire and water. Water represents the deluge which was the judgment inflicted upon the wicked of old. Fire represented the fiery doom of the future—the day of judgment. This ordeal compelled the accused with his naked hand to find a small pebble within a caldron of boiling water. After the hand had been plunged into the seething caldron, it was carefully enveloped in a cloth, sealed with the signet of a judge, and three days later was unwrapped. It was at this subsequent unwrapping that the accused's guilt or innocence was announced, determined by the condition of the hand.

A related ordeal was that of the red-hot iron. Two forms of this ordeal were found in medieval Europe. The first, which can best be categorized as one of chance, is the ordeal of the red-hot ploughshares. Ploughshares are heated until they glow and are then placed at certain intervals. The accused walks blindfolded and barefooted through the prescribed course. If he escapes injury, he is acquitted. The second form of the ordeal is more widely discussed. The accused is compelled to carry a piece of hot iron for a given distance. The weight of the iron varies with the magnitude of the crime alleged. If the accused can carry the piece of iron without sustaining any burn, he is regarded as innocent.

II.   Ordeals by Water and Means Other than a Direct Appeal to God

The basis of the ordeal of cold water was that water, being a pure element, will not receive into her bosom anyone stained with the crime of a false oath. Water was recognized as capable of ascertaining those things which had been injected with untruths. The result seems, today, somewhat anomalous: the guilty floated and the innocent sank.

The success of this ordeal was less than perfect. Throughout the sources on this mode of ordeal were examples of malfunctions. Witches would sink like rocks, while leading members of the community, offering themselves to the rigors of the ordeal to test their validity, would float, often not sinking at all, even with the efforts of the officiating executioner.

Some ordeals were designed for people with some type of infirmity, such as blindness, lameness, or old age. Such people had to endure less trying ordeals to determine their guilt or innocence. A person burdened by such an incapacity is placed in one scale of the balance with an equivalent weight to counterbalance him in the other scale. The accused then went before the administering official, who then addressed a customary adjuration to the ordeal of the balance. The accused ascended the balance again, and if he was lighter than before, he was acquitted. This association of lightness with innocence would seem to be contrary to the European belief that lightness is associated with the Devil, as the Devil was regarded as nothing but a spirit of air.

III.   Ordeal by Direct Appeal to God

The ordeal of the cross is characterized by placing two parties, the accused and the accuser, in front of a cross with their arms uplifted. Divine service was performed, and victory was adjudged to the one who was able to maintain his arms in the upraised position for the longest period of time. If this procedure led to a stalemate, the accused was given a piece of bread or cheese over which prayers had been said. If the accused could swallow the consecrated morsel, he was acquitted. We must remember that at the time these ordeals were the vogue, the people had great faith in Christ. The criminal, conscious of his guilt, standing before God and pledging his salvation, was expected to "break" under the weight of his own conscience. The truth of the matter lies in the fact that bread or cheese is difficult to swallow when the saliva secretion in one's mouth is not functioning properly. The exorcisms which were said beforehand were subject only to the imagination of the presiding priest. The more ingenious and devising he was, the more constricted became the throat of the most hardened criminal (as well as God-fearing innocents), and, therefore, the more difficult became the function of swallowing.

It was only a slight modification of the above which resulted in the Eucharist as an ordeal. "He that eateth and drinketh unworthily eateth and drinketh damnation to himself" (I Corinthians XI). When the consecrated wafer was offered under appropriate adjuration, the guilty would not receive it; or if it were taken, immediate convulsions and speedy death would ensue.

The basis for all ordeals is that men are asking for divine help to relieve themselves of the responsibility of decision. The ordeal has as its greatest characteristic the element of certainty. Such dependence on ordeals could be had whenever man waived his own judgment and undertook to test the inscrutable ways of his Creator—i.e., the laws of Nature are to be set aside whenever man chooses to tempt his God with the promise of right and the threat of injustice to be committed in His name. This passing the buck to God was particularly prevalent when there was no evidence as to the crime or where the crime was very difficult to prove judicially. The ordeal offered a ready and satisfactory solution to the doubts of a timid judge. Man believed that God would reverse the laws of Nature to accomplish a specified object.

The ordeal was thoroughly and completely a judicial process. It seems to have been used mostly to supplement deficient evidence and amounts to nothing more than an appeal to God.

Note on the History of the Jury Trial

Trial by jury and trial by ordeal could hardly seem less alike; yet like the opposite faces of a coin, they share the same center. The almost mythic reverence in which we hold the jury today is probably neither more nor less than the public reverence toward the ordeal in its day. Each produces, for a different society, that degree of certainty of truth and acceptability of decision necessary for the settling of disputes and the imposition of authority.

The differences between jury and ordeal are not in their function, but in the underlying cultural values of the societies which these seemingly antithetical institutions served. Medieval England looked to the judgment of God and the power of the Church. Twentieth-century America looks to rationalism, the objective consciousness, and the state. Since trial by jury is the successor to trial by ordeal, we may learn something by examining briefly a historical point of contact between them—thirteenth-century England.

The earliest juries in England were not concerned with determining guilt or innocence or civil liability, but rather with making accusations on behalf of the Crown and thereby extending its authority. At a time when the monarchy was still struggling to bring the private resolution of conflict under its own control through the extension of "law," Henry II made the jury of presentment a nationwide phenomenon in which twelve local knights or "free lawful men" of each village were charged with producing accusations of murder, theft, or arson. Having been thus accused, the defendant had to proceed to "the judgment of the water." (Assize of Clarendon, 1166.)

Whether accusations were made by a jury of presentment on behalf of the king or by private individuals for themselves, the decision as to whether the accused was guilty or innocent still had to be made. The three most common forms of making such decisions in the early thirteenth century were the ordeal, the wager of law, and the battle. The ordeal, described by Tewksbury (see page 287), was administered officially by the church, which was paid well enough for presiding over the delivery of the "truth." The ordeal was often part of a mass in which the power and judgment of God were invoked by the presiding priest. The wager of law was a kind of character test in which the accused had to find twelve people who were willing to swear an oath that the accused's oath of innocence was "clean." The oath, like the physical ordeals, was surrounded by strong religious sanctions and it was not easy to produce twelve oath takers. The trial by battle was available in private accusations called "appeals of felony" or in civil matters, but not in cases to which the Crown was party. The battle was fought to the death between the accused and his accuser or between champions in civil matters.

By the first part of the thirteenth century, something a little more like jury trial as we know it began to appear in murder cases in England. Those who felt that they had been accused of murder "out of spite and hate" could purchase from the king a "writ" entitling them to a trial by twelve "recognitors" on the issue of whether the accusation was malicious. If they found it was, no ordeal was required. If the accusation was not found malicious, trial by ordeal was prescribed. This preliminary determination, not of guilt but of the good faith of the accusation, began to bring considerable revenue to the royal coffers as it was claimed more and more as a matter of course by accused murderers seeking to avoid the ordeal.

As the procedure was developing, the Church dealt a heavy blow to the ordeal and gave the jury more room to develop. In 1215, the Fourth Lateran Council forbade the clergy to perform any religious ceremonies in connection with the ordeal. The reason for this decision is unclear, but without this religious seal of approval the mainstay of the system of determining guilt began to lose its legitimacy, and substantial confusion among the king's justices was created as to how such decisions were to be reached. In the confusion and experimentation which ensued, the jury trial began to emerge as one way of deciding issues of fact. But it was not a jury trial we would recognize today.

The central issue in using what were then called jury trials seems to have been the reluctance of the populace to accept them as a legitimate determination of guilt. Despite the increased use of juries to determine whether accusations of murder were malicious, the general attitude of most people still seemed to have been to feel confident in the ordeal as the judgment of God and to doubt the jury trial as the judgment of men. In fact it was not until 1275 that the king felt it was reasonable to impose the jury trial even on notorious felons. Up to that point people had to voluntarily accept a jury trial (throw themselves on the country); and some endured death by torture (being sandwiched between two boards which were then slowly loaded with stones) rather than accept trial by jury when conviction meant forfeiture of land and chattel. What was at issue during the formative period of trial by jury was whether this institution could confer legitimacy upon decisions or whether it was too inscrutable, heretical, and unfamiliar to be trusted with such an important task.

While this transformation of the mind was beginning, the jury was at best a makeshift procedure from our point of view. It had not yet been rationalized or even settled in its procedure. In fact, it was very much like the inquisition which preceded it in the making of accusations (jury of presentment) or in determining the existence of taxable property (the Domesday Book of 1086). Instead of hearing evidence and making an allegedly impartial decision based on the evidence, it relied solely on its own knowledge of local affairs. As the king's justices traveled on circuit they convened a jury in each village and these men were then charged with the duty of determining the guilt or innocence of the accused on the basis of whatever they knew personally or were able to find out on their own. In fact, there were often members of the accusing jury on the trial jury, and the trial was probably one of general reputation in the village. It was not until the 1500s that witnesses were even *allowed* to present information to the jury, and it was almost 1700 before the accused gained the right to compel the attendance of witnesses he thought would help his case.

Whatever its shortcomings from the viewpoint of modern American legal process, the jury did serve the purpose even then of relieving the king's justices of the responsibility of deciding issues of guilt and innocence or civil liability. In so doing it shifted the focus, though perhaps not the reality, of authority

from king to subjects, from rule of man to rule of men and ultimately rule of law. And it began to shift the justification for decisions resolving disputes from God to rational man, an equally inscrutable entity. By the 1700s the transformation began to be layered over with the philosophy of individualism, rationalism, and what we now call due process of law. By 1954 this rationalistic jury had become so little understood, yet so sacred, that a scholarly attempt to probe its workings was met with an investigation by the Internal Security subcommittee of the Senate Judiciary Committee and by legislation forbidding the recording of jury deliberations.

Perhaps there is something about the function of the jury in the legal process that requires this protectiveness and even mystery, lest we lose our legitimized decision-making process at the hands of objective consciousness just as Henry II lost the ordeal in the thirteenth century at the hands of progressive religion. In any case, its symbolic role can be no less important than its practical utility.

When the jury system was moved to America in the colonial days it began a historical development which is quite different from its birth in medieval England, as the following documents show.

U.S. Constitution

Article III

SECTION 2. (3) The trial of all Crimes, except in Cases of Impeachment, shall be by Jury; and such Trial shall be held in the State where the said Crimes shall have been committed; but when not committed within any State, the Trial shall be at such Place or Places as the Congress may by Law have directed.

Amendment VI (1791)

In all criminal prosecutions, the accused shall enjoy the right to a speedy and public trial, by an impartial jury of the State and district wherein the crime shall have been committed, which district shall have been previously ascertained by law, and to be informed of the nature and cause of the accusation; to be confronted with the witnesses against him; to have compulsory process for obtaining witnesses in his favor, and to have the Assistance of Counsel for his defence.

Amendment VII (1791)

In Suits at common law, where the value in controversy shall exceed twenty dollars, the right of trial by jury shall be preserved, and no fact tried by jury, shall be otherwise re-examined in any Court of the United States, than according to the rules of the common law.

Duncan v. Louisiana   *391 U.S. 145 (1968)*

MR. JUSTICE WHITE delivered the opinion of the Court.

Appellant, Gary Duncan, was convicted of simple battery in the Twenty-fifth Judicial District Court of Louisiana. Under Louisiana law simple battery is a misdemeanor, punishable by a maximum of two years' imprisonment and a $300 fine. Appellant sought trial by jury, but because the Louisiana Constitution grants jury trials only in cases in which capital punishment or imprisonment at hard labor may be imposed, the trial judge denied the request. Appellant was convicted and sentenced to serve 60 days in the parish prison and pay a fine of $150. Appellant sought review in the Supreme Court of Louisiana, asserting that the denial of jury trial violated rights guaranteed to him by the United States Constitution. The Supreme Court, finding "[n]o error of law in the ruling complained of," denied appellant a writ of certiorari.

[A]ppellant sought review in this Court, alleging that the Sixth and Fourteenth Amendments to the United States Constitution secure the right to jury trial in state criminal prosecutions where a sentence as long as two years may be imposed. . . .

Appellant was 19 years of age when tried. While driving on Highway 23 in Plaquemines Parish on October 18, 1966, he saw two younger cousins engaged in a conversation by the side of the road with four white boys. Knowing his cousins, Negroes who had recently transferred to a formerly all-white high school, had reported the occurrence of racial incidents at the school, Duncan stopped the car, got out, and approached the six boys. At trial the white boys and a white onlooker testified, as did appellant and his cousins.

The testimony was in dispute on many points, but the witnesses agreed that appellant and the white boys spoke to each other, that appellant encouraged his cousins to break off the encounter and enter his car, and that appellant was about to enter the car himself for the purpose of driving away with his cousins. The whites testified that just before getting in the car appellant slapped Herman Landry, one of the white boys, on the elbow. The Negroes testified that appellant had not slapped Landry, but had merely touched him. The trial judge concluded that the State had proved beyond a reasonable doubt that Duncan had committed simple battery, and found him guilty.

The test for determining whether a right extended by the Fifth and Sixth Amendments with respect to federal criminal proceedings is also protected against state action by the Fourteenth Amendment has been phrased in a variety of ways in the opinions of this Court. The question has been asked whether a right is among those " 'fundamental principles of liberty and justice which lie at the base of all our civil and political institutions.' " . . . whether it is "basic to our system of jurisprudence," and whether it is "a fundamental right, essential to a fair trial." The claim before us is that the right to trial by jury guaranteed by the Sixth Amendment meets these tests. The position of Louisiana, on the other hand, is that the Constitution imposes upon the States no duty to give a jury trial in any criminal case, regardless of the seriousness of the crime or the size of the punishment which may be imposed. Because we believe that trial by jury in criminal cases is fundamental to the American scheme of justice, we hold that the Fourteenth Amendment guarantees a right of jury trial in all criminal cases which—were they to be tried in a federal court—would come within the Sixth Amendment's guarantee. Since we consider the appeal before us to be such a case, we hold that the Constitution was violated when appellant's demand for jury trial was refused.

The history of trial by jury in criminal cases has been frequently told.[1] It is sufficient for present purposes to say that by the time our Constitution was written, jury trial in criminal cases had been in existence in England for several centuries and carried impressive credentials traced by many to Magna Carta.[2] Its preservation and proper operation as a protection against arbitrary rule were among the major objectives of the revolutionary settlement which was expressed in the Declaration and Bill of Rights of 1689. . . .

Jury trial came to America with English colonists, and received strong support from them. Royal interference with the jury trial was deeply resented. Among the resolutions adopted by the First Congress of the American Colonies (the Stamp Act Congress) on October 19, 1765—resolutions deemed by their authors to state "the most essential rights and liberties of the colonists" —was the declaration:

> That trial by jury is the inherent and invaluable right of every British subject in these colonies.

The First Continental Congress, in the resolve of October 14, 1774, objected to trials before judges dependent upon the Crown alone for their salaries and to trials in England for alleged crimes committed in the colonies; the Congress therefore declared:

> That the respective colonies are entitled to the common law of England, and more especially

[1] E.g., W. Forsyth, History of Trial by Jury (1852); J. Thayer, A Preliminary Treatise on Evidence at the Common Law (1898); W. Holdsworth, History of English Law.

[2] E.g., 4 W. Blackstone, Commentaries on the Laws of England 349 (Cooley ed. 1899). Historians no longer accept this pedigree. See, e.g., 1 F. Pollock & F. Maitland, The History of English Law Before the Time of Edward I, at 173, n. 3 (2d ed. 1909).

to the great and inestimable privilege of being tried by their peers of the vicinage, according to the course of that law.

The Declaration of Independence stated solemn objections to the King's making "judges dependent on his will alone, for the tenure of their offices, and the amount and payment of their salaries," to his "depriving us in many cases, of the benefits of Trial by Jury," and to his "transporting us beyond Seas to be tried for pretended offenses." The Constitution itself, in Art. III, §2, commanded:

> The Trial of all Crimes, except in Cases of Impeachment, shall be by Jury; and such Trial shall be held in the State where the said Crimes shall have been committed.

Objections to the Constitution because of the absence of a bill of rights were met by the immediate submission and adoption of the Bill of Rights. Included was the Sixth Amendment which, among other things, provided:

> In all criminal prosecutions, the accused shall enjoy the right to a speedy and public trial, by an impartial jury of the State and district wherein the crime shall have been committed.

The constitutions adopted by the original States guaranteed jury trial. Also, the constitution of every State entering the Union thereafter in one form or another protected the right to jury trial in criminal cases.

Even such skeletal history is impressive support for considering the right to jury trial in criminal cases to be fundamental to our system of justice, an importance frequently recognized in the opinions of this Court. . . .

The guarantees of jury trial in the Federal and State Constitutions reflect a profound judgment about the way in which law should be enforced and justice administered. A right to jury trial is granted to criminal defendants in order to prevent oppression by the Government.

Those who wrote our constitutions knew from history and experience that it was necessary to protect against unfounded criminal charges brought to eliminate enemies and against judges too responsive to the voice of higher authority. The framers of the constitutions strove to create an independent judiciary but insisted upon further protection against arbitrary action. Providing an accused with the right to be tried by a jury of his peers gave him an inestimable safeguard against the corrupt or overzealous prosecutor and against the compliant, biased, or eccentric judge. If the defendant preferred the common-sense judgment of a jury to the more tutored but perhaps less sympathetic reaction of the single judge, he was to have it. Beyond this, the jury trial provisions in the Federal and State Constitutions reflect a fundamental decision about the exercise of official power—a reluctance to entrust plenary powers over the life and liberty of the citizen to one judge or to a group of judges. Fear of unchecked power, so typical of our State and Federal Governments in other respects, found expression in the criminal law in this insistence upon community participation in the determination of guilt or innocence. The deep commitment of the Nation to the right of jury trial in serious criminal cases as a defense against arbitrary law enforcement qualifies for protection under the Due Process Clause of the Fourteenth Amendment, and must therefore be respected by the States.

Of course jury trial has "its weaknesses and the potential for misuse." We are aware of the long debate, especially in this century, among those who write about the administration of justice, as to the wisdom of permitting untrained laymen to determine the facts in civil and criminal proceedings....[3] At the heart of the dispute have been express or implicit assertions that juries are incapable of adequately understanding evidence or determining issues of fact, and that they are unpredictable, quixotic, and little better than a roll of dice. Yet, the most recent and exhaustive study of the jury in criminal cases concluded that juries do understand the evidence and come to sound conclusions in most of the cases presented

to them and that when juries differ with the result at which the judge would have arrived, it is usually because they are serving some of the very purposes for which they were created and for which they are now employed.

...In determining whether the length of the authorized prison term or the seriousness of other punishment is enough in itself to require a jury trial, we...refer to objective criteria, chiefly the existing laws and practices in the nation. In the federal system, petty offenses are defined as those punishable by no more than six months in prison and a $500 fine. In 49 of the 50 States crimes subject to trial without a jury, which occasionally include simple battery, are punishable by no more than one year in jail. Moreover, in the late 18th century in America crimes triable without a jury were for the most part punishable by no more than a six-month prison term, although there appear to have been exceptions to this rule. We need not, however, settle in this case the exact location of the line between petty offenses and serious crimes. It is sufficient for our purposes to hold that a crime punishable by two years in prison is, based on past and contemporary standards in this country, a serious crime and not a petty offense. Consequently, appellant was entitled to a jury trial and it was error to deny it.

The judgment below is reversed and the case is remanded for proceedings not inconsistent with this opinion.

Reversed and remanded.

Notes and Questions

1. Why, if the jury is so central in importance, does the court allow any trials without a jury?

2. What is the effect of using existing practices in the nation as a standard for ruling on Louisiana's laws?

3. Does the Court seem aware of the early history of the jury in England? Is that history relevant to the problem before the Court?

4. At this point refer to *People* v. *Collins,* which appears on page 12. In that case the prosecution introduced statistical evidence concerning the likelihood that the crime in question was committed by persons answering the defendant's physical descrip-

[3] A thorough summary of the arguments that have been made for and against jury trial and an extensive bibliography of the relevant literature is available at Hearings on Recording of Jury Deliberations before the Subcommittee to Investigate the Administration of the Internal Security Act of the Senate Committee on the Judiciary, 84th Cong., 1st Sess., 63–81 (1955). A more selective bibliography appears at H. Kalven, Jr. & H. Zeisel, The American Jury 4, n. 2 (1966).

tion. The appeals court found several problems of statistical reliability in the prosecution's evidence, but what is more important for purposes of understanding the function of the jury, the court said:

> ... the likelihood of human error or falsification obviously cannot be quantified: that likelihood must therefore be excluded from any effort to assign a number to the probability of guilt or innocence. Confronted with an equation which purports to yield a numerical index of probable guilt, *few juries could resist the temptation to accord disproportionate weight to the index;* only an exceptional juror ... would keep in mind the fact that the probability computed by the prosecution can represent, at best, the likelihood that a random couple would share the characteristics testified to by the People's witnesses—not necessarily the characteristics of the actually guilty couple. [Emphasis added.]

Later in the opinion, the court comments, "Undoubtedly the jurors were unduly impressed by the mystique of the mathematical demonstration but were unable to assess its relevancy or value." In considering the importance of the trial by jury of the *Collins* case, consider the following questions.

5. Trial by jury is said to involve the use of rational techniques by ordinary citizens in determining facts. Can their judgments be anything more than probabilistic? If certainty is unattainable, why might the court be opposed to the use of even reliable statistical evidence of guilt? What do you think the judge's opinion is of juror intelligence?

6. The mysticism involved in ordeals conducted under religious auspices concerned revelation of the divine will. What is the mysticism evoked by statistics? What is the court protecting by excluding such mysticism from the trial? Where does the jury's function lie between the divine revelation and technological proof?

The Trial of the Future *Bernard Botein and Murray A. Gordon*

For a long time science has been deflating our notions about the infallibility of the trial process. More recently, the technicians have gone even further. There have been developed startling, effective techniques for "eavesdropping on man's unconscious," as it has been termed. If these techniques fulfill the expectations of many sober-minded men of science, the laboratory will be equipped to reveal truth much more efficiently and inexorably than the courtroom. We may reach the point where our present methods of resolving legal disputes may seem as archaic and barbaric as trial by ordeal seems to us today; and courtroom procedures as we know them may have to be scrapped.

Because we stand at the threshold of such a possibility, it should be profitable to review briefly the progress of science in the ascertainment of

From *The Trial of the Future* by Bernard Botein and Murray A. Gordon. Copyright © 1963 by Bernard Botein and Murray A. Gordon. Reprinted by permission of Simon & Schuster, a Division of Gulf & Western Corporation.

truth and to consider its implications for the administration of law in this country. If science can reproduce truth more reliably and effectively than our present system, we shall not be able long to defer our rendezvous with progress. The judicial test for admitting the fruits of scientific research is whether they have won general acceptance in the appropriate discipline. Because of this stringent test various newer truth-revealing techniques have not yet won admittance to the courthouse, but they are storming its steps.

In little more than half a century we have traveled, in our still-frightening interventions into the privacy of the mind, from Freud to brainwashing to subliminal projection—all encompassed within the notion that the operations and motivations of our mental processes are knowable, controllable, and even exploitable. In his *Brave New World Revisited,* Aldous Huxley is understandably appalled at the extent to which his fantasies of more than twenty-five years ago have been realized in modern manipulation of minds and emotions; George Orwell would be only a little less troubled at the prospect that in this aspect "1984" may be reached before that date. It is certain that by means of psychoanalytical, narcoanalytical and electronic techniques and devices, motivational research and chemistry, we shall attain greater insight into and control over the billions of units comprising the human brain. This rapidly advancing frontier that is being staked out amidst the mysteries of the mind augurs revolutionary changes in the trial process.

Fact-finding for trial purposes today depends in large measure upon articulate, communicable testimony reflecting the recollection of witnesses. As indicated, limitations of conscious memory, even aside from the distorting factors of self-interest and partisanship, made this process painfully fallible; and its deficiencies often cannot be cured by cross-examination, that revered rectifier of purposeful fabrication or unwitting error. And many times, even when recollection is accurate, tense and frightened witnesses fail to communicate accurately to judge or jury.

Recent experience with drugs such as scopolamine and the barbiturates (sodium pentothal and sodium amytal), techniques such as hypnosis and devices such as the lie detector should be, accordingly, of profound significance in our current trial procedures. These devices suggest the eventual emergence of scientifically accepted procedures for inducing the full and truthful recollection and the relaxed narration of events. The present unperfected nature of these fact-finding interventions, the circumstance that they are not uniformly operative and that some persons are able to lie or withhold information, form no basis for blinking the problems promised by their ultimate development.

Narcoanalysis, a term loosely blanketing procedures for interrogating subjects while they are in a state of partial unconsciousness induced by drugs, is the most dramatic of the techniques mentioned. The drugs employed in narcoanalysis serve as central nervous system depressants and thereby lessen inhibitions and other blocks to disclosures. The relationship between self-revelation and depressants of the central nervous system is not a novel discovery. . . .

Modern man put the revelatory by-products of cerebral depressants to systematic and organized use. In the late nineteenth century the latch was lifted by the application of hypnosis to the study of individual personality and of personality disorder. It was reported in 1893 that the Dutch had, by law, authorized the use of hypnotism in police investigation. This sequence is typical. The main aspiration of the scientist is to apply the revelations and relaxations of narcoanalysis to diagnosis and therapy; but its truth-divulging properties may also make it a significant instrument in the administration of justice. No doubt many scientists look at this tributary use as suspiciously as others view the use of nuclear energy for war purposes.

In the United States the importation of drug-induced disclosures into criminology was initiated by Dr. Robert E. House, an enterprising medical practitioner from Ferris, Texas. He had observed the amazingly candid and uninhibited remarks of women giving birth under the influence of scopolamine as an anesthetic—then known as the "twilight sleep" drug. Reasoning logically enough that a similar technique could be used in criminal investigation, he administered scopolamine in 1922 to establish the innocence of two convicted criminals and subsequently published his findings in a regional medical journal. Later Dr. House employed scopolamine in the interrogation of at least eighty-four criminals or suspects and then proceeded to expand his claimed discovery to the point of erroneously but euphemistically entitling the drug a "truth serum."

Understandably, various investigatory agencies have availed themselves of this technique for dragging the pool of man's unconscious. As far back as 1924 the district attorney of Birmingham, Alabama, used scopolamine to obtain confessions to twenty-five ax-murders from five suspects. For several decades the Scientific Crime Detection Laboratory of Northwestern University experimented with the same drug. So-called truth serum techniques have been used frequently by investigators of the Kansas City Police Department, by the University of Minnesota and by Dr. W. F. Lorenz at the University of Wisconsin. In June 1946, the press widely publicized the case of William Heirens, a seventeen-year-old murder suspect who feigned amnesia. He was interrogated while under the influence of sodium pentothal and confessed to three murders and more than five hundred burglaries.

The present skeptical judicial attitude toward the admissibility of drug-induced revelations is, no doubt, based largely upon the judiciary's uncertainty as to the reliability of the information thus obtained. In a 1960 decision excluding a drug-induced statement, a Kentucky judge colorfully held that he was "not disposed to lead a safari into that jungle without first being satisfied that the new devices...have attained full scientific acceptance." Many interviewees are not satisfactory subjects, even under ideal circumstances. Even good subjects are extremely suggestible while under the influence of drugs, and others, for neurotic or unconscious reasons, use the occasion to confess to crimes and other wrongdoings never perpetrated by them. On the other hand, some are able to withhold information and some to lie while under the influence of the drugs. Workers in the field report a heavy incidence of fantasy in the material produced, and it seems agreed that at this time, even for use outside the courts, the examinations must be conducted and the results interpreted only by experts in this field.

The slow and limited judicial acceptance of drug-induced revelations must be viewed in the light of similar judicial skepticism which existed and was ultimately dispelled by scientific progress leading eventually to court acceptance of fingerprint evidence, blood tests, and handwriting, X-ray and psychiatric testimony. Thus, although there has been a fairly consistent body of law rejecting findings from lie detector tests, the results of such a test were recently admitted in a New York case where the trial judge believed experience had established a sufficient foundation to validate the use of the machine. In the celebrated Alger Hiss trial, a psychiatrist employed by the defense observed the government's chief witness, Whittaker Chambers, on the witness stand. He was then permitted to give his opinion concerning Chambers' credibility, testifying that he was a psychopathic personality "with a tendency towards making false accusations."

It has been aptly said by a federal court in the leading case of *Frye* v. *United States* that "just when a scientific principle or discovery crosses the line between the experimental and demonstrable stages is difficult to define. Somewhere in this twilight zone the evidential force of the principle must be recognized...." The likely timetable of judicial acceptance of drug-induced disclosures will, no doubt, reflect the observation of our outstanding authority on the law of evidence, the late Professor Wigmore: "If there is ever devised a psychological test for the evaluation of witnesses, the law will run to meet it.... Whenever the psychologist is ready for the courts, the courts are ready for him."

In short, recent and probable future advances in the technique of inducing revelations by narcoanalysis and the general judicial receptivity to scientifically validated evidence remove this subject from the realm of science-fiction fantasy and dictate a sober consideration of the consequences to the judicial process....

As the novel methods of proof we have discussed assume greater scientific validity, serious questions must also arise as to whether findings of fact, of intention or of motive can be left, as now, to the nonscientific community of judges or juries, or whether that function will be for those whose special skills and training more particularly qualify them to appraise the materials resulting from such methods. Indeed, there would no doubt be agitation for the elimination of judge, jury and courtroom, as we know them, in favor of the more clinical precincts of the technician. Certainly, there would be a significant change in the roles presently played by courtroom principals; and this, too, can find parallels in the past. Max Radin has written that in Rome in the fourth and fifth centuries B.C., the initiative for truth-finding reposed in the judge. With the advent of the adversary, self-help form of litigation as we know it, which is usually waged through the opposing parties' lawyers, the judge's function evolved to what it is today, that of an umpire. It is not at all unlikely that the onus of monitoring the fact-finding processes will shift from the lawyer to the scientist.

More subtle than the scuttling of the traditional trial process, but probably more critical in its societal implications, would be the effect of truth-revealing techniques on rights of the individual which have long been cherished and associated with protection of his person and dignity. We shall be unable to avoid re-examining the present practice of imposing upon the claimant in a civil action the burden of proving his version by a fair preponderance of the evidence, or requiring the prosecution in a criminal case to prove the defendant guilty beyond a reasonable doubt. The trial process is usually weighted on the side of the defending party. The law places a heavy burden on the complaining party who would enlist its resources to obtain relief. This is particularly true in criminal cases, where society seeks to balance the uneven resources of government and the accused individual so as to protect him from tyrants and powerful masters who possess the means to employ the courts as instruments of oppression.

But what need will remain to such weighting and protective rules, it will be argued, if the management of litigation by the parties themselves becomes minimal? Constitutional and common law safeguards, such as the provisions against self-incrimination, the presumption of innocence, the right to due process, are all commonly believed to be for the protection of the innocent. Again, what need in law or logic for invoking these protections when science can reliably establish such innocence without them? The language of the late United States Supreme Court Justice Jackson in *Stein* v. *New York* will be quoted for the proposition that constitutional doctrines are "not mere technical loopholes for the escape of the guilty."

A public trial, by jury in most instances, is another such highly regarded right. What need will there be for such a trial, it will no doubt be argued, when the determinative fact-finding will be transferred from the courtroom to the laboratory? Yet one must wonder how readily the bar and public will accept the resolution of legal controversies by technicians in the arcane seclusion of the laboratory instead of by judge or jury in the open courtroom.

It will be contended that since the end to be attained by the provisions of constitutional and common law is protection of the innocent, and since science will accomplish this so much more effectively than all of the legal doctrines laid end to end, *ergo,* this is one end that justifies the means. In such a view the presumption of innocence would be dissolved because it would become unnecessary. Likewise, a major justification for asserting the right against self-incrimination—that the innocent might become entangled in the toils of the law through his own lips—falls away. The innocent person would no longer have to hack his way through the jungle of uncertainties and technicalities which made all these legal safeguards necessary. He would be able to establish his innocence more easily and directly through science. Indeed, if the reliability of narcoanalysis is demonstrated, but it is not received as evidence, an innocent man ready to submit to the testing may be deemed to be deprived unfairly of the right to clear himself.

We can, of course, assume that none would be directly compelled to submit to narcoanalysis, and that such a procedure would be allowed only with the consent of the subject. Not that it would make much practical difference, if a person's consent is required, whether he agrees or refuses to submit to narcoanalysis. Refusal to submit to narcoanalysis would be interpreted, practically if not legally, by the trier of the facts as an admission of guilt—much as jurors construe a defendant's failure to take the stand in a criminal case in a light adverse to him, despite the strongest judicial instructions to the contrary.

As one moves toward extending the reach of narcoanalysis in the courts through logic rather than experience, he may encounter critical conflicts in values. Logicians will hold, for the reasons just advanced, that a person actually charged with crime should not complain, since his innocence as well as his guilt can be established through scientific means. But the question will arise whether a witness not under indictment should be compelled to undergo narcoanalysis if by doing so he may implicate himself in the commission of a crime of which he has hitherto been unsuspected. Logically, there should be no difference; the guilty will pay, the innocent be cleared. It is not unlikely, however, that there would be some gagging on such a premise.

This is because the public intuitively looks to those administering justice not only to elicit truth and enforce law, but to satisfy other social and community values. Such protective rules as the privilege against self-incrimination, the presumption of innocence, and the exclusion from evidence of confidential communications between husband and wife, doctor and patient, lawyer and client, all have evolved to maintain the high value the community has set on the grandeur of the individual. Each of these principles subordinates full disclosure of the facts to some other higher social value.

Still closer to our discussion is the inadmissibility of an involuntary confession, even if true. Just recently the United States Supreme Court held the admission into evidence of the confession of one suffering from insanity as violative of the due process clause of the Fourteenth Amendment, not only because the confession was unreliable, but also because it was improperly obtained from one while weak of will and mind. It is, therefore, frequently the case that where investigatory or trial procedures for the disclosure of facts impinge upon deeply held values sustaining the integrity and the dignity of the individual, those values prevail at the expense of the facts. Ultimately, then, the great issue will be what Professor Helen Silving, in a perceptive article, delineated as that of truth versus dignity, as to which she concluded that "in the administration of justice truth is but a means, whereas dignity is an end."

Each of the techniques associated with narcoanalysis involves dredging facts from the unconscious that the person interrogated might be unwilling consciously to reveal. To that extent, each of these techniques entails an invasion of his privacy, as well as his freedom of will. Each abrades the dignity of man; and such indignities can become contagious, if not epidemic. Our tra-

ditional and adversary system of litigation, though it may not prove to be the most exact medium for ascertaining truth, embodies the democratic emphasis upon respect for human dignity at every step of the way. If we do not act to anticipate, it remains for us to await—and not without anxiety—the balance finally to be struck between the service of dignity and of truth in the trial process as truth comes more surely within reach as a result of scientific validation of fact-finding through unconscious disclosures. The issue posed is, in the end, no less than an uneasy search for the character of our society of the future. For the balance finally struck between dignity and truth in our courts will be cast in the image of a society which has opted either for efficiency or for freedom.

Questions

1. Tewksbury's analysis of the ordeal as a medieval legal institution has shown us something about the epistemology and beliefs of medieval society. The society and its legal process are both based upon a belief in divine intervention. What does trial by jury imply about the epistemology and basic beliefs of the society that spawned it? Is it significant that trial by jury reached its pinnacle in Anglo-American history at the time of the Enlightenment?

2. Considering that both ordeals and jury trials provided necessary legitimacy to decisions that had to be made for society to function, why do courts today seem, as in the *Collins* case, to resist the legitimizing power of statistics, technology, and "hard" science? Does this reflect at all upon the values or training of lawyers and judges?

3. Consider the Botein and Gordon reading as a portent of things to come in trials and other legal processes aimed at certifying "truth." What kind of society will we have when these new methods are accepted by law and the public? Try to identify the sources of your own resistance to and approval of these new methods. Is it possible that this new age has already been ushered in?

2   The Jury as a Political Institution

Judge: Has the jury reached a verdict?
Jury foreman: We have, your honor. We the jury have agreed that even if the defendant actually did commit the crimes, it is WE who are the guilty ones. The U.S. social system is at fault, and we must all share the blame.
Judge: The jury is sentenced to five years.
    —Overheard outside
    a legal studies class

As the previous materials imply, the function of the jury extends beyond determining the facts and applying the law in a particular case. In fact, one of the difficulties inherent in considering the adequacy of technological methods of finding the "truth" is that the jury is really asked to do much more. Polygraphs, truth serums, and other methods of probing the unconscious of witnesses or defendants imply that there is no necessary political content to jury decisions. The existence of such methods, moreover, might deflect us from considering how the very existence of jury trials is a political phenomenon.

In the following article, Tocqueville, writing in 1830, gives a view of the complexities of the American jury system as a political institution. His view may be ambiguous, because he suggests that the jury is both an agent for extending the power and legitimacy of formal law, and a basic item of popular political sovereignty in a democracy. Inevitably a discussion of the political function of juries involves questions of the jury's power and the juror's attitude toward his or her involvement in the jury. Scheflin's article discusses the issue of jury nullification beginning with the unquestioned and unquestionable right of the jury to reach its verdict in a criminal case as a matter of conscience even when that conscience is at odds with the law. How this right of nullification ought to be treated by the trial judge is the subject of heated controversy in "Follow-up."

To examine further the problems of exercising political sovereignty through legal process in a cross cultural context, a transcript of a Chinese divorce trial is presented. The trial itself is merely a part of an immense system of conflict resolution the Chinese employ. It should be examined to determine whether it provides a different mechanism for popular participation in law and to explore the merits and shortcomings of such a system in comparison to jury trials.

Trial by Jury in the United States   *Alexis de Tocqueville*

Trial by jury, which is one of the forms of the sovereignty of the people, ought to be compared

From *Democracy in America*, Volumes I & II, by Alexis de Tocqueville, translated by Henry Reeve, revised by Francis Bowen, and edited by Phillips Bradley. Copyright 1945 and renewed 1973 by Alfred A. Knopf, Inc. Reprinted by permission of the publisher. Pp. 291–297. (Some footnotes omitted.)

with the other laws which establish that sovereignty—Composition of the jury in the United States—Effect of trial by jury upon the national character—It educates the people—How it tends to establish the influence of the magistrates and to extend the legal spirit among the people.

Since my subject has led me to speak of the administration of justice in the United States, I will not pass over it without referring to the institution of the jury. Trial by jury may be considered in two separate points of view: as a judicial, and as a political institution. If it was my purpose to inquire how far trial by jury, especially in civil cases, ensures a good administration of justice, I admit that its utility might be contested. As the jury was first established when society was in its infancy and when courts of justice merely decided simple questions of fact, it is not an easy task to adapt it to the wants of a highly civilized community when the mutual relations of men are multiplied to a surprising extent and have assumed an enlightened and intellectual character.

My present purpose is to consider the jury as a political institution; any other course would divert me from my subject. Of trial by jury considered as a judicial institution I shall here say but little. When the English adopted trial by jury, they were a semi-barbarous people; they have since become one of the most enlightened nations of the earth, and their attachment to this institution seems to have increased with their increasing cultivation. They have emigrated and colonized every part of the habitable globe; some have formed colonies, others independent states; the mother country has maintained its monarchical constitution; many of its offspring have founded powerful republics; but everywhere they have boasted of the privilege of trial by jury. They have established it, or hastened to re-establish it, in all their settlements. A judicial institution which thus obtains the suffrages of a great people for so long a series of ages, which is zealously reproduced at every stage of civilization, in all the climates of the earth, and under every form of human government, cannot be contrary to the spirit of justice.[1]

[1] If it were our object to establish the utility of the jury as a judicial institution, many arguments might be brought forward, and among others the following:

In proportion as you introduce the jury into the business of the courts, you are enabled to diminish the number of judges, which is a great advantage. When judges are very numerous, death is perpetually thinning the ranks of the judicial functionaries and leaving places vacant for new-comers. The ambition of the magistrates is therefore continually excited, and they are naturally made dependent upon the majority or the person who nominates to vacant

But to leave this part of the subject. It would be a very narrow view to look upon the jury as a mere judicial institution; for however great its influence may be upon the decisions of the courts, it is still greater on the destinies of society at large. The jury is, above all, a political institution, and it must be regarded in this light in order to be duly appreciated.

By the jury I mean a certain number of citizens chosen by lot and invested with a temporary right of judging. Trial by jury, as applied to the repression of crime, appears to me an eminently republican element in the government, for the following reasons.

The institution of the jury may be aristocratic or democratic, according to the class from which the jurors are taken; but it always preserves its republican character, in that it places the real direction of society in the hands of the governed, or of a portion of the governed, and not in that of the government. Force is never more than a transient element of success, and after force comes the notion of right. A government able to reach its enemies only upon a field of battle would soon be destroyed. The true sanction of political laws is to be found in penal legislation; and if that sanction is wanting, the law will sooner or later lose its cogency. He who punishes the criminal is therefore the real master of society. Now, the institution of the jury raises the people itself, or at least a class of citizens, to the bench of judges. The institution of the jury consequently invests the people, or that class of citizens, with the direction of society.

In England the jury is selected from the aristo-

offices; the officers of the courts then advance as do the officers of an army. This state of things is entirely contrary to the sound administration of justice and to the intentions of the legislator. The office of a judge is made inalienable in order that he may remain independent; but of what advantage is it that his independence should be protected if he be tempted to sacrifice it of his own accord? When judges are very numerous, many of them must necessarily be incapable; for a great magistrate is a man of no common powers: I do not know if a half-enlightened tribunal is not the worst of all combinations for attaining those ends which underlie the establishment of courts of justice. For my own part, I had rather submit the decision of a case to ignorant jurors directed by a skillful judge than to judges a majority of whom are imperfectly acquainted with jurisprudence and with the laws.

cratic portion of the nation; the aristocracy makes the laws, applies the laws, and punishes infractions of the laws; everything is established upon a consistent footing, and England may with truth be said to constitute an aristocratic republic. In the United States the same system is applied to the whole people. Every American citizen is both an eligible and a legally qualified voter. The jury system as it is understood in America appears to me to be as direct and as extreme a consequence of the sovereignty of the people as universal suffrage. They are two instruments of equal power, which contribute to the supremacy of the majority. All the sovereigns who have chosen to govern by their own authority, and to direct society instead of obeying its directions, have destroyed or enfeebled the institution of the jury. The Tudor monarchs sent to prison jurors who refused to convict, and Napoleon caused them to be selected by his agents.

However clear most of these truths may seem to be, they do not command universal assent; and in France, at least, trial by jury is still but imperfectly understood. If the question arises as to the proper qualification of jurors, it is confined to a discussion of the intelligence and knowledge of the citizens who may be returned, as if the jury was merely a judicial institution. This appears to me the least important part of the subject. The jury is pre-eminently a political institution; it should be regarded as one form of the sovereignty of the people: when that sovereignty is repudiated, it must be rejected, or it must be adapted to the laws by which that sovereignty is established. The jury is that portion of the nation to which the execution of the laws is entrusted, as the legislature is that part of the nation which makes the laws; and in order that society may be governed in a fixed and uniform manner, the list of citizens qualified to serve on juries must increase and diminish with the list of electors. This I hold to be the point of view most worthy of the attention of the legislator; all that remains is merely accessory.

I am so entirely convinced that the jury is pre-eminently a political institution that I still consider it in this light when it is applied in civil causes. Laws are always unstable unless they are founded upon the customs of a nation: customs are the only durable and resisting power in a people. When the jury is reserved for criminal offenses, the people witness only its occasional action in particular cases; they become accustomed to do without it in the ordinary course of life, and it is considered as an instrument, but not as the only instrument, of obtaining justice.

When, on the contrary, the jury acts also on civil causes, its application is constantly visible; it affects all the interests of the community; everyone co-operates in its work: it thus penetrates into all the usages of life, it fashions the human mind to its peculiar forms, and is gradually associated with the idea of justice itself.

The institution of the jury, if confined to criminal causes, is always in danger; but when once it is introduced into civil proceedings, it defies the aggressions of time and man. If it had been as easy to remove the jury from the customs as from the laws of England, it would have perished under the Tudors; and the civil jury did in reality at that period save the liberties of England. In whatever manner the jury be applied, it cannot fail to exercise a powerful influence upon the national character; but this influence is prodigiously increased when it is introduced into civil causes. The jury, and more especially the civil jury, serves to communicate the spirit of the judges to the minds of all the citizens; and this spirit, with the habits which attend it, is the soundest preparation for free institutions. It imbues all classes with a respect for the thing judged and with the notion of right. If these two elements be removed, the love of independence becomes a mere destructive passion. It teaches men to practice equity; every man learns to judge his neighbor as he would himself be judged. And this is especially true of the jury in civil causes; for while the number of persons who have reason to apprehend a criminal prosecution is small, everyone is liable to have a lawsuit. The jury teaches every man not to recoil before the responsibility of his own actions and impresses him with that manly confidence without which no political virtue can exist. It invests each citizen with a kind of magistracy; it makes them all feel the duties which they are bound to discharge toward society and the part which they take in its government. By obliging men to turn their attention to other affairs than their own, it rubs off that private selfishness which is the rust of society.

The jury contributes powerfully to form the judgment and to increase the natural intelligence of a people; and this, in my opinion, is its greatest advantage. It may be regarded as a gratuitous public school, ever open, in which every juror learns his rights, enters into daily communication with the most learned and enlightened members of the upper classes, and becomes practically acquainted with the laws, which are brought within the reach of his capacity by the efforts of the bar, the advice of the judge, and even the passions of the parties. I think that the practical intelligence and political good sense of the Americans are mainly attributable to the long use that they have made of the jury in civil causes.

I do not know whether the jury is useful to those who have lawsuits, but I am certain it is highly beneficial to those who judge them; and I look upon it as one of the most efficacious means for the education of the people which society can employ.

What I have said applies to all nations, but the remark I am about to make is peculiar to the Americans and to democratic communities. I have already observed that in democracies the members of the legal profession and the judicial magistrates constitute the only aristocratic body which can moderate the movements of the people. This aristocracy is invested with no physical power; it exercises its conservative influence upon the minds of men; and the most abundant source of its authority is the institution of the civil jury. In criminal causes, when society is contending against a single man, the jury is apt to look upon the judge as the passive instrument of social power and to mistrust his advice. Moreover, criminal causes turn entirely upon simple facts, which common sense can readily appreciate; upon this ground the judge and the jury are equal. Such is not the case, however, in civil causes; then the judge appears as a disinterested arbiter between the conflicting passions of the parties. The jurors look up to him with confidence and listen to him with respect, for in this instance, his intellect en-

tirely governs theirs. It is the judge who sums up the various arguments which have wearied their memory, and who guides them through the devious course of the proceedings; he points their attention to the exact question of fact that they are called upon to decide and tells them how to answer the question of law. His influence over them is almost unlimited.

If I am called upon to explain why I am but little moved by the arguments derived from the ignorance of jurors in civil causes, I reply that in these proceedings, whenever the question to be solved is not a mere question of fact, the jury has only the semblance of a judicial body. The jury only sanctions the decision of the judge; they sanction this decision by the authority of society which they represent, and he by that of reason and of law.

In England and in America the judges exercise an influence upon criminal trials that the French judges have never possessed. The reason for this difference may easily be discovered; the English and American magistrates have established their authority in civil causes and only transfer it afterwards to tribunals of another kind, where it was not first acquired. In some cases, and they are frequently the most important ones, the American judges have the right of deciding causes alone. On these occasions they are accidentally placed in the position that the French judges habitually occupy, but their moral power is much greater; they are still surrounded by the recollection of the jury, and their judgment has almost as much authority as the voice of the community represented by that institution. Their influence extends far beyond the limits of the courts; in the recreations of private life, as well as in the turmoil of public business, in public, and in the legislative assemblies, the American judge is constantly surrounded by men who are accustomed to regard his intelligence as superior to their own; and after having exercised his power in the decision of causes, he continues to influence the habits of thought, and even the characters, of those who acted with him in his official capacity.

The jury, then, which seems to restrict the rights of the judiciary, does in reality consolidate its power; and in no country are the judges so powerful as where the people share their privileges. It is especially by means of the jury in civil causes that the American magistrates imbue even the lower classes of society with the spirit of their profession. Thus the jury, which is the most energetic means of making the people rule, is also the most efficacious means of teaching it how to rule well.

Jury Nullification — The Right to Say No
A. Scheflin
45 S. Cal. L. Rev. 168 (1972)

According to the doctrine of jury nullification, the jurors have the inherent right to set aside the instructions of the judge and to reach a verdict of acquittal based upon their own consciences, and the defendant has the right to have the jury so instructed. There was a time when "conscience" played a legally recognized and significant role in jury deliberations....

In the British colonies, the role of the jury in criminal trials is exemplified by the *Zenger* case. A New York jury in 1735, at the urging of Andrew Hamilton, generally considered to be the foremost lawyer in the Colonies, gave John Peter Zenger his freedom by saying "no" to governmental repression of dissent. Zenger was the only printer in New York who would print material not authorized by the British mayor. He published the *New York Weekly Journal,* a newspaper designed to expose some of the corruption among government officials. All of the articles in the papers were unsigned; the only name on the paper was that of its printer, Zenger. Although a grand jury convened by the government refused to indict Zenger, he was arrested and charged by information with seditious libel. Although Zenger did not write any of the articles and it was not clear that he even agreed with their content, had the jury followed the instructions of the court they would have had to find him guilty.

Against this obstacle, Hamilton insisted that the jurors:

> ...have the right beyond all dispute to determine both the law and the facts, and where they do not doubt of the law, they ought to do so.

He urged the jury "to see with their own eyes, to

hear with their own ears, and to make use of their consciences and understanding in judging of the lives, liberties or estate of their fellow subjects." The closing words of his summation to the jury are as vital today as they were when they were uttered over 200 years ago:

> [t]he question before the Court and you gentlemen of the jury, is not of small or private concern, it is not the cause of a poor printer, nor of New York alone, which you are now trying: No! It may in its consequence, affect every freeman that lives under a British government on the main of America. It is the best cause, it is the cause of liberty; and I make no doubt but your upright conduct this day will not only entitle you to the love and esteem of your fellow citizens; but every man who prefers freedom to a life of slavery will bless and honor you as men who have baffled the attempt of tyranny; and, by an impartial and uncorrupt verdict, have laid a noble foundation for securing to ourselves, our posterity, and our neighbors that to which nature and the laws of our country have given us a right—the liberty—both of exposing and opposing arbitrary power (in these parts of the world) at least, by speaking and writing truth.

[In behavior similar to the *Zenger* case] colonial juries regularly refused to enforce the navigation acts designed by the British Parliament to channel all colonial trade through the mother country. Ships impounded by the British for violating the acts were released by colonial juries, often in open disregard of law and fact. In response to this process of jury nullification, the British established courts of vice-admiralty to handle maritime cases, including those arising from violations of the navigation acts. The leading characteristic of these courts was the absence of

---

Reprinted by permission. (Footnotes omitted.)

the jury; this resulted in great bitterness among the colonists and was one of the major grievances which ultimately culminated in the American Revolution.

In the period immediately before the Revolution, jury nullification in the broad sense had become an integral part of the American judicial system. The principle that juries could evaluate and decide questions of both fact and law was accepted by leading jurists of the period.

John Adams, writing in his Diary for February 12, 1771, noted that the jury power to nullify the judge's instructions derives from the general verdict itself, but if a judge's instructions run counter to fundamental constitutional principles

> is a juror obliged to give his verdict generally, according to his direction or even to the fact specially, and submit the law to the court? Every man, of any feeling or conscience, will answer, no. It is not only his right, but his duty, in that case to find the verdict according to his own best understanding, judgment, and conscience, though in direct opposition to the direction of the court.

Adams based this reasoning in part on the democratic principle that "the common people . . . should have as complete a control, as decisive a negative, in every judgment of a court of judicature" as they have in other decisions of government. At the time of the adoption of the Constitution, this view of jury nullification prevailed. Without jury nullification, as the Founding Fathers well knew, government by judge (or through the judge by the rulers in power) became a distinct possibility and had in fact been a reality. In the *Zenger* case, two lawyers were held in contempt and ordered disbarred by the judge when they argued that he should not sit because he held his office during the King's "will and pleasure." The Court of Star Chamber was not too distant in memory for the colonists to have forgotten the many perversions perpetrated there in the name of justice and law. It was likely, therefore, that the once unchecked, unresponsive power of the judge would have been limited by the Founding Fathers through some method of public control. One method chosen was the jury

function most closely guarded by the colonists: the power to say no to oppressive authority. . . .

Proper understanding of the concept of jury nullification requires it to be viewed as an exercise of discretion in the administration of law and justice. Jury discretion in this context may be a useful check on prosecutorial indiscretion. No system of law can withstand the full application of its principles untempered by considerations of justice, fairness and mercy. Every technical violation of law cannot be punished by a court structure that attempts to be just. As prosecutorial discretion weeds out many of these marginal cases, jury discretion hopefully weeds out the rest.

"Jury lawlessness" according to Dean Roscoe Pound, "is the great corrective" in the administration of law. Thus, the jury stands between the will of the state and the will of the people as the last bastion in law to avoid the barricades in the streets. To a large extent, the jury gives to the judicial system a legitimacy it would otherwise not possess. Judge control of jury verdicts would destroy that legitimacy.

A juror who is forced by the judge's instructions to convict a defendant whose conduct he applauds, or at least feels is justifiable, will lose respect for the legal system which forces him to reach such a result against the dictates of his conscience. The concept of trial by a jury of one's peers is emasculated by denying to the juror his right to act on the basis of his personal morality. For if the jury is the "conscience of the community," how can it be denied the right to function accordingly? A juror compelled to decide against his own judgment will rebel at the system which made him a traitor to himself. No system can be worthy of respect if it is based upon the necessity of forcing the compromise of a man's principles. . . .

Jessica Mitford interviewed three jurors in the *United States* v. *Spock* case after the trial's completion. She detected that they had misgivings about the unfairness of the laws which they were asked to apply. Though they all seemed to sympathize with the defendants, they were concerned, in principle, about violations of law going unpunished. Each one indicated that the conviction was necessary in light of the instructions from the judge: "I knew they were guilty when we were charged by the judge. I did not know *prior* to that time—I was in full agreement with the defendants until we were charged by the judge. That was the kiss of death!" It is reasonable to conclude that if the jury had been instructed of their power to nullify, the convictions might not have been returned. However, these jurors felt bound by the judge's instructions, even though they had previously decided the issue of guilt in favor of the defendant. If they had been told that an element of the crime was that the jury in good conscience must feel that the law was fair and was fairly applied, then they could have dispensed justice in accordance with their conscientious beliefs. Even if this jury felt guiltless because they had done what was required of them, they should not have felt comfortable about a system which may have misused them for political purposes.

If jury discretion leads to a lawless society, as some critics of nullification have argued, what does no discretion lead to? Several years ago the New York police went on "strike" on the Long Island Expressway and ticketed every motorist failing to observe any traffic regulation presently on the books. Though the police did not ticket non-violators, there was still a great outcry against their conduct. While much of the wrath was vented on the devious tactic used to get the raises, much of it was also against the lack of discretion in the enforcement of the laws. Without such discretion, the legal system becomes a mockery. But unlimited discretion in the hands of persons in power can become despotic. Accountability of such discretion to the people is the fundamental principle of democracy. It is also the underlying rationale for jury nullification.

One of the most significant principles of democracy calls for the involvement or participation of the "man in the street" in the formation of public policy. Within the framework of the judicial process, the jury has evolved as an institutional reflection of such a commitment. The "man in the street" becomes the "man in the jury box," and as such sits as the representative of the community in question. As the embodiment of the

"conscience of the community" he functionally legitimizes and effectuates the authoritativeness of decisions made by and through the judicial process.

The chief distinguishing characteristic of any democratic system is effective popular control over policymakers. With reference to the judicial process this can mean only one thing: If the "man in the jury box" is to fulfill his role as the representative of the "conscience of the community," participating effectively in the making of public policy, then he must possess the power and the right to check the "misapplication" of any particular value distribution. Beyond this, he must be informed that he has such a power and the constitutional right to exercise it.

Thus, jury service is a two-way street. Community values are injected into the legal system making the application of the law responsive to the needs of the people, and participation on the jury gives the people a feeling of greater involvement in their government which further legitimizes that government. This dual aspect of the concept of the jury, flowing from its role as a political institution in a constitutional democracy, serves to keep both the government and the people in touch with each other. But should there be a divergence of sufficient magnitude, as the Founding Fathers were aware there often is, the jury can serve as a corrective with a final veto power over judicial rigidity, servility or tyranny.

In the words of Thomas Jefferson, "Were I called upon to decide, whether the people had best be omitted in the legislative or in the judiciary department, I would say it is better to leave them out of the legislative. The execution of the laws is more important than the making of them." The power of the people as a community conscience check on governmental despotism is manifested in their ability to sit on juries and limit the thrust of governmental abuse of discretion.

The jury provides an institutional mechanism for working out matters of conscience within the legal system. Jury nullification allows the community to say of a particular law that it is too oppressive or of a particular prosecution that it is too punitive or of a particular defendant that his conduct is too justified for the criminal sanction to be imposed. As William Kuntsler put it,

> Unless the jury can exercise its community conscience role, our judicial system will have become so inflexible that the effect may well be a progressive radicalization of protest into channels that will threaten the very continuance of the system itself. To put it another way, the jury is . . . the safety valve that must exist if this society is to be able to accommodate itself to its own internal stresses and strains.

. . . The high-water mark of contemporary jury nullification may very well be the trial of the "Oakland Seven." In any politically-charged case where there is a jury acquittal, it is not always clear whether the verdict was a product of the inability of the prosecutor to prove his case beyond a reasonable doubt or rather was a demonstration that the case was so well proven that the real motive for prosecution became all too clear: stifling political dissent. Or the verdict could quite easily be a combination of deficient proof and juror outrage over governmental repression. Because of this ambiguity, and because questions of intent are vague enough to give jurors room to nullify subconsciously by honestly believing that criminal intent is not consistent with good faith resistance to seemingly unjust laws or applications of laws, any description of an acquittal as an instance of jury nullification may not be entirely accurate. Revelations by jurors after the rendition of the verdict, although somewhat self-serving at that time, furnish some help.

The trial of the Oakland Seven grew out of indictments brought against leaders of Stop the Draft Week which occurred outside the Oakland Armed Forces Induction Center in October, 1967. Demonstrations designed to show opposition to the war and the draft were planned and staged along with attempts to physically interfere with the normal course of business of the Induction Center.

In January, seven persons were indicted for conspiracy (a felony) to commit three misdemeanors: trespass, creating a public nuisance and resisting arrest. Although hundreds of persons were involved, only these seven were indicted on conspiracy charges. The District Attorney of Alameda County, J. Frank Coakley, told the Oakland Tribune:

> Technically, a hundred or even a thousand of the demonstrators could have been indicted for their action, but we simply don't have enough courts so we have to take the most militant leaders.

The acquittal verdict in the case might not be surprising considering the weakness in the case presented by the prosecutor and the very liberal instructions given which allowed the jury to consider the defendants' belief in the illegality of the war as an item to be weighed in determining whether they had a criminal intent, and declared that much of the evidence presented concerned conduct protected by the first amendment. Nevertheless, post-trial interviews with the jurors conducted by Elinor Langer suggest that the underlying political motivations behind the trial were fully recognized:

> The Oakland Seven jury wanted to find the defendants innocent. "I tried to examine the prosecution's argument," commented one juror, the keeper of records in an industrial firm, "but I thought it meant, in other words, that people should be puppets, go along. If that were true, our democratic procedures wouldn't be worth much. I'm not a puppet, I'm a free thinker. I wonder what the prosecution would have made of the Boston Tea Party, a 'costly and disruptive demonstration.' Our early leaders were all radicals, they had to be." This juror, a man in his thirties, attended the post acquittal party. The colonel: "I was very caught up in the details of the case, but I also understood in a brief flash, if they could do that to these boys they could do it to anyone: they can stop all dissent." A woman, the bookkeeper, was stirred even beyond most of her fellow jurors into the experience that leftists call "radicalization": "Now I understand how dangerous being a fence-sitter can be. I was one of those people, I'm not too proud of it, who sat on my can all the time. People who do that are playing into the hands of the power structure. I can see why young people hate us. But I can

never be neutral anymore." She is reading Eldridge Cleaver—"to see why the defendants stood up for the Panthers"—and studying a book on the Vietnam War. The black member of the jury, a Post Office employee, found himself more stirred than he expected by the witnesses' stories of police brutality. The night of the acquittal, as he was leaving the courthouse, he raised his arm to the defendants in the black power salute: the first, it seemed, he had ever given in his life.

The success of the Oakland Seven in raising the political consciousness of the jurors is a direct result of their conduct of their defense. As one of the defendants explains:

> We had a simple defense strategy. We attempted to focus attention on the war in Vietnam, police brutality and the First Amendment. We tried to force the jury to vote not on our guilt or innocence, but rather for or against the war, for or against the police, and for or against free speech. . . .
>
> Each witness tried to get across our three major political points. The first question to every witness was, why did you attend the demonstration? This allowed the witness to give a short speech against the war. In some cases the witnesses gave long speeches against the war—[Judge] Phillips allowed that because the witness supposedly was only reporting what he earlier had said to a defendant. Then the typical witness said that he was not under orders from any of the defendants and that the demonstration was organized just like any other demonstration. Finally the witness reported incidents of police brutality.

Critics may protest this use of the judicial forum for the advocacy of political views and speak of the inadequacy of the courts to handle political questions. But it must be remembered that for purposes of the jury nullification argument, the jurors are as free to reject the defendant's policies as they are to reject the defendant's version of the facts; and though the court may not be the ideal place to resolve political issues, the only issue for decision is not political in the criminal trial—it is the legal issue of guilt or innocence. The jury is not asked to decide which political side they are on, it is asked to decide the legal status of an alleged violation of the criminal laws. If the jury is persuaded by the defendants' politics (and is this any different from being persuaded by his oratorical ability, for example, or by his cool demeanor?) then perhaps the prosecutor ought to learn a valuable lesson about the exercise of his discretion for the public good. Elinor Langer's conclusion about the trial of the Oakland Seven bears repeating:

> Perhaps the main consequence of the Oakland Seven trial is that twelve jurors were moved from apathy to affirmation. Presented with honest evidence about the motives and intentions of the left, they defied the repressive logic of their political authorities and said, "You cannot do it. Americans are still free men." Twelve jurors were, as the left says, "organized," and if that seems a small number, a high price, and a slow pace, it still may be a portent of more to come.

Questions

1. Who motivates a jury to nullify the law? Is it urged on them by an articulate defense lawyer pleading the cause of liberty, or do jurors decide themselves that nullification is appropriate?

2. Why is jury nullification such a rare occurrence in modern trials? Is it the nature of the cases being tried or the crimes committed? The influence of the judge? The consciousness of the jurors?

3. How important an option is nullification if it is rarely used?

Jury Instructions

California

Ladies and Gentlemen of the Jury.*

It becomes my duty as judge to instruct you concerning the law applicable to this case, and it is your duty as jurors to follow the law as I shall state it to you.

The function of the jury is to try the issues of fact that are presented by the allegations in the information filed in this court and the defendant's plea of "not guilty." This duty you should perform uninfluenced by pity for the defendant or by passion or prejudice against him. . . .

You are to be governed solely by the evidence introduced in this trial and the law as stated to you by me. The law forbids you to be governed by mere sentiment, conjecture, sympathy, passion, public opinion, or public feeling. Both the Peo-

ple and the defendant have a right to demand and they do demand and expect, that you will conscientiously and dispassionately consider and weigh the evidence and apply the law of the case, and that you will reach a just verdict, regardless of what the consequences may be. . . .

Maryland

Members of the jury†: this is a criminal case and under the Constitution and the laws of the state of Maryland in a criminal case the jury are the judges of the law as well as of the facts in the case. So that whatever I tell you about the law, while it is intended to be helpful to you in reaching a just and proper verdict in the case, it is not binding upon you as members of the jury and you may accept the law as you apprehend it to be in the case.

---

* Excerpt from California jury instructions in criminal cases.

† Excerpt from Maryland jury instructions in criminal cases.

Follow-up/The Jury

At a recent Center Club meeting in New York, Visiting Fellow Jon M. Van Dyke's article, "The Jury as a Political Institution" (The Center Magazine, March, 1970), was attacked and defended by a panel of lawyers and jurists. Mr. Van Dyke opened the discussion with a summary statement of his position.

Jon M. Van Dyke

Visiting Fellow, and Assistant Professor (on leave) at the Catholic University of America School of Law

---

Reprinted with permission from the July/August, 1970, issue of *The Center Magazine,* a publication of the Center for the Study of Democratic Institutions, Santa Barbara, California.

I view the present age as reminiscent of the second half of the eighteenth century. I agree with Justice William O. Douglas, who says that those in power today are similar in many respects to King George III. They oppose change, no matter what the merits of a change may be, and they repress the activities of those seeking new alternatives. . . .

I advocate a return to the original rule. We should tell the jurors that they have the power to acquit, even if the accused's activities have violated the law as it is articulated by the trial judge. . . .

When a juror is obliged to convict a person whose conduct he agrees with, that can only lead to disrespect for the law and for the whole judicial process. . . .

Jurors are selected anonymously from the community and they melt anonymously back into the community when their job is done. They need not fear reprisal if they come to a decision contrary to the policies and actions of the current administration, and hence they can offer the community's judgment on the administration's laws.

The model instruction I propose would have the judge tell the jurors that, although they are a public body and are thus bound to give respectful attention to the law, they have nonetheless the final authority to decide whether or not to apply a given law to the acts of the defendant on trial before them. This instruction would not lead to a society in which men could pick and choose with impunity the laws they will obey or disobey. Most jurors, because they are among those who elected the legislators who passed the laws, will apply the law, as written, to the facts of the case. In some trials, however, the jurors will conclude that the legislators could not have intended the law to apply to their set of facts or that it is time to review the wisdom of the law. They will then acquit a person who has broken a law. This safeguard is one that should be recognized and strengthened.

Abe Fortas

Former Associate Justice,
United States Supreme Court

This is a fascinating proposal. In microcosm it is a reflection of the agony of our time. In effect, it is an attack upon law itself. In effect, it is an assertion of the right of the individual to determine for himself what the standard of his conduct shall be. What is being proposed is not merely that jurors should be given the power to determine what is the law, but that they should be instructed that they may acquit a defendant even though they believe that he did something the law forbids. This goes to the heart of our society because it says that this shall not be a society in which there are general rules of law and conduct which apply to everybody and to which everybody is held accountable.

Democracy is a fragile institution. A democratic society functions only because there is a structure of rules of conduct applicable to everybody. But people are people, not computers, and in order to live together they must have two things: a structure or a set of rules on the one hand, and on the other a certain amount of give within those rules because of the complexity of the human personality.

It is true that to some extent the jury system supplies this "give," or flexibility. Jurors are not computers; sometimes they do come in with a verdict of innocent when a computer would say that the facts add up to guilt and that the defendant should be punished. We recognize and tolerate this as a worthwhile anomaly in the rule of law. But if this occasional departure from the general application of the law were to be institutionalized—if it were to become the rule rather than the tolerated departure from the rule, we would have a kind of anarchy: that is, a system in which the ultimate test of socially permissible conduct is, to a significant degree, the random reaction of a group of twelve people selected at random. Acceptance of this as the principle governing individual conduct which collides with the rules adopted by governmental processes would, of course, amount to rejection of law as the controlling principle of society.

Without insistence on rules of law and rules of conduct applicable across the board, I think that community living would be impossible.

I wonder whether Mr. Van Dyke thinks that a judge, too, should have the freedom and power to disregard a law. For example, I am very much opposed to capital punishment; it offends me deeply. But should I, as an appellate judge, say that I will disregard the law, and, for this reason, vote to set aside an otherwise proper judgment? If a judge is at liberty to do that, then I think the whole structure is imperiled. Similarly if capital punishment has been abolished, should a judge, offended by a particularly horrible crime, be able nevertheless to impose it? If a jury can disregard the law, why shouldn't a judge also be able to disregard it?

Mr. Van Dyke says that the jury should have the power to lessen but not increase the punishment for a defendant. Why? Is amelioration of punishment the only value that society should safeguard? If a vindictive white man rapes, mutilates and kills a half-dozen blacks, and if the law doesn't permit capital punishment, a jury composed of sensitive, socially aware people might feel that the ultimate penalty should be imposed. By parity of reasoning, why not? Because Mr. Van Dyke and I are opposed to capital punishment? I don't think you can have an organized society functioning on a free-wheeling basis. You have to have a structure, a rule, a framework, some standards. I am in favor of juries, in part for the reasons that Mr. Van Dyke gives in his article. I believe that they are a necessary counter to case-hardened judges and arbitrary prosecutors. While we all recognize that juries sometimes do not act according to strict logic, I do not believe that juries should be instructed and invited to act not on the basis of the law but on the basis of their own judgment at the time. There is a profound difference between these two things. . . .

Simon H. Rifkind

Attorney, and former federal judge

Any democratic society must indulge a very high tolerance for dissent, or eccentricity if you like, for non-conformism, for iconoclasm. These are the leavening forces that generate peaceful change in society and promote the kind of revolutions of which we have had many since 1776. We are living through a drastic revolution today, but so far it is the product of our tolerance for dissent. If you repress that dissent, you build up the kind of pressures that may result in a different kind of revolution, from which we have fortunately been spared. But in acknowledging this, we must not make the mistake of confusing the yeast with the dough. The criminal law is a system for regulating the dough, the generality of the population, not the exceptional situation. The exceptional situation (of the kind already described around this table) has, in most cases, somehow or other received appropriate treatment. In the ordinary case tried in any of the criminal courts of our country the defendant is not a Socrates on trial for his ideas. That is the exceptional situation. The routine grist of the criminal courts is arson,

burglary, robbery, rape, use of the mails to defraud, tax evasion, counterfeiting, forgery. The "political trial" happens once in a long, long time, unless you want to identify as a political trial every trial in which the attorney for the defendant makes that claim. The Scopes trial may have been a true political trial, but in my experience, there have been few political trials since then.

In Mr. Van Dyke's article there are three strands of ideas and three kinds of instructions jurors might receive according to those ideas. Let us assume that we are in a jury room somewhere in the South, deliberating after a trial of three members of the Ku Klux Klan charged with depriving a black man of his civil rights. Say, he was about to enter a voting booth and they shouldered him out. The first kind of instruction, as reflected in the article, causes a juror to say to his fellow jurors: "We have been charged to find out for ourselves what the law is. Now, do you gentlemen really think it is unlawful to shoulder a black man out of a polling booth? I haven't heard of any such law." Maybe the jurors decide that they also have never heard of that law, maybe they decide that they have. But at least under the doctrine of the Maryland instruction, as recited by Mr. Van Dyke, the jurors must decide what they thought the law was and, having so decided, be guided by that law.

A second kind of instruction reflected in the article would move a juror to say to his fellows: "Now, you will observe that we have been told to be guided by our conscience. Gentlemen, look me in the eye. Tell me the truth. Would your conscience tolerate the punishment of three members of the Ku Klux Klan for shouldering a Negro out of a polling booth?" (That was defense attorney Weinglass's proposal when he requested Judge Julius Hoffman to ask the jurors in the Chicago conspiracy trial to be guided by their conscience. That, to me, was a request for a direct verdict of guilty.)

There is a third kind of instruction, which is Mr. Van Dyke's own proposal. He would have the juror say: "Now, fellow jurors, you have heard the judge give us the charge as to what our function is. We are here to do as we please. If we think the law is unjust, we do not have to pay any attention to it. Each of us is here to do his own thing, or, in the words of the Book of Judges, 'Each man would do that which was right in his own eyes.' Now, does any one of you here think it is wrong to shoulder a Negro out of a polling booth?"

These are the three proposed instructions to a jury reflected in that article. I think all three are wicked.

The article is based on some erroneous factual premises. It is not true that juries are rubber stamps for the judge. Anyone who has actually struggled with juries, tried to move their minds one way or the other, either in favor of the prosecution or the defense, knows that they are not rubber stamps. During the Prohibition era, you could not get jury convictions even though the facts were clear that the law against serving alcoholic beverages had been violated. We finally had to resort to padlocking the saloons in proceedings that dispensed with juries. Another example is of the husband who comes home and finds his wife with another man and shoots the intruder. There is no question that he has killed the other man and he tells the jury he did it because he wanted to save his home. Juries have been known to acquit in those circumstances. Juries have been known to acquit in cases of statutory rape when the defendant looks like an eighteen-year-old college boy and the victim appears to be a professional purveyor of her favors. But the best example of the independence of juries was given by Mr. Lefcourt: the hung jury in the Buffalo trial. And in the Chicago conspiracy trial, the jury found a verdict of its own.

So, why do we need to abandon a system that is capable of such variety, flexibility, and pliability, and adopt one that is laden with defects?

There is a second flaw in the Van Dyke proposal. It springs from a misconception of the jury's duty as it is currently defined in the customary charge. The judge says to the jury: "If you find A, B, C, and D to be the facts, you *must* acquit the defendant. If you find E, F, and G to be the facts, you *may* convict the defendant." I have never yet heard a judge say to

a jury: "If you find E, F, and G to be the facts, you *must* convict the defendant." Those words, "may convict," are always underscored by counsel for the defense, who keeps reminding the jury that the jurors, and only the jurors, may convict a defendant. Every jury I have ever had anything to do with was instructed by counsel for the defense that it was within its unlimited power to set the defendant free. And I have seen district attorneys chew their lips while this was going on because they wondered whether the defense counsel's passionate appeal to the mercy and power of the jury would be effective.

A third defect in the Van Dyke proposal springs from a misconception of the nature of criminal law. One gets the impression from the article that a defendant is accused of a crime, he is presented to the jury, the jury sits there and wonders whether the judge will tell them that the defendant's behavior is wrong or right. Now, you don't have to tell a jury that setting fire to a building is wrong, that forgery is wrong, that rape is wrong, that tax evasion is wrong. They know it. The only purpose served by the judge's charge to the jury on the law is to protect the interest of the *defendant*. If it were up to the district attorney, he would waive the judge's charge every time because the district attorney has described the defendant as having committed some atrocious act. But the judge, in his charge, tells the jury that they must be convinced of a great many other things that hadn't occurred to them before they can convict the defendant.

Take the case of arson, for example. The statute's definition of arson reads this way: "A person is guilty of arson in the first degree when he intentionally damages a building by starting a fire or causing an explosion." You can see that right away there will be an argument as to whether the act was intentional. There will be an argument as to whether there was damage. Another part of the definition of arson is that there has to be another person in the building at the time of the fire, and the defendant has to know that such a person is in the building, or have reason to believe that another person or persons would be in a building, such as a theater. In such a case the judge does not have to tell the jury that it is wrong to set fire to a building. He does tell them: "Don't convict this defendant unless he has done this intentionally, unless he has damaged the building, unless there was a person in the building, unless he knew there was a person in the building." The judge's charge is always for the benefit of the defendant. To let a jury write its own law is to deprive the defendant of the defenses now given him by the law already in existence.

A fourth defect in the Van Dyke proposal is that juries may decide to ignore technical defenses, such as entrapment or the statute of limitations, in their overriding desire to convict.

In short, the Van Dyke proposal would expose hundreds of defendants to convictions which they would not otherwise suffer....

Questions

1. If the law provides that the jury can in fact disregard the judge's instructions and deliver a verdict of their own choosing without fear of any sanctions, why is there so much resistance to telling the jury its power? What effect on jury deliberations might result from telling the jurors about nullification?

2. Can you think of ways of explaining to jurors what their role in the legal process is other than the two instructions appearing on page 309.

3. Tocqueville writes that "in no country are the judges so powerful as where the people share their privileges." Does jury nullification strengthen or weaken Tocqueville's argument? What, other than jury instructions, is the source of the judge's power in the trial?

4. Under what conditions do you think a jury would consider nullification? Is it a matter of spontane-

ous outrage in a plainly political case? If an attorney were to address the issue of nullification in a summation to the jury, what sorts of things would you expect to be stressed? What kind of jurors would you want to select if you knew your case depended largely upon their willingness to nullify the law in the case?

5. See Zerman's description of the deliberations in the Mathes trial on page 326. Are there any points at which the jurors might have been tempted to ignore the law in favor of their own sentiments or those they attributed to the community as a whole?

6. Suppose that jury nullification became routinized through judge's instructions about the propriety of nullification and lawyer's argument on summation about whether the law should be nullified in the case being tried. Would such regular use of nullification serve as a mask for the effects of the formal legal system in general? Is it possible that the glorification of jury nullification might weaken the power of ordinary people dissatisfied with legal process by leading them to believe they can have an effect that in reality is insignificant?

7. Does jury nullification, even if it became routine, really provide significant power to jurors? What about routine cases in which the political nature of the crime or dispute is not readily apparent? Can jury nullification change the allocation of power in the legal system or in society or is it a superficial solution to a major denial of public participation in law?

8. Suppose a jury nullifies a law by acquitting a defendant in a plainly political case in which the defendant has the sympathy and support of the community. How does this "victory" have an effect on law and politics? What is the role of the media in effectuating the jury's actions? Is there such a thing as a social precedent even when no legal precedent results from the jury's actions?

This transcript of a 1972 divorce trial in Peking was recorded by Doris Brin Walker, a California lawyer and former president of the National Lawyers Guild. The trial itself is part of a long continuum of informal and formal mechanisms for conflict definition and resolution in the People's Republic of China. It is important to sketch some elements of this legal system to be able to evaluate how similar or different this trial is from an American jury trial.

The Chinese have traditionally looked down upon formal legal process and law in favor of educational means of defining and controlling patterns of behavior. The trial included here comes only after the failure of many of these informal, mediating, or educational processes. All of these other methods are said to express the "mass line" in legal work by which an ideological commitment to mass participation in law is expressed. In addition to an extensive use of mass media, one of the most distinctive elements of this system of participation is the "study group."

Most people in China belong to at least two small groups, sometimes called study groups. These groups of ten to twenty persons are centered at one's workplace and one's residence. Victor Li has estimated that study groups, with their discussions of everything from Marx, Lenin, and Mao Tse-tung to art, personal problems, and technical matters, take up ten hours each week of each year. These study groups do not tolerate passivity or refusal to participate. They are meant to provide early detection of conflict, deviance, or other problems; and their role is partly to provide help in resolving such problems. It would appear from several observers' reports that a substantial number of conflicts are resolved through these study groups and their helping, mediating, and controlling techniques. The practicality of such small group study and action sessions for smooth running of work and collective living seems to be matched by their reported emotional intensity. These sessions of criticism, self-criticism, attempts to be honest with oneself and concerned with the thoughts of others have been described by Ruth Sidel, in *The Families of Fengsheng,* as "characterized by a level of intimacy rarely shared in urban America outside of, perhaps, therapy groups."

China has over a million lay mediators involved in small dispute settlement, but only a few thousand lawyers for a population of 800,-000,000. The process described below occurs only after the failure of earlier, less formal, and more localized attempts to resolve the marriage dispute. To examine further the spectrum of legal processes in China, the following general materials may prove useful: Victor Li, *Law Without Lawyers* (Stanford, Calif.: Stanford Alumni Association, 1977); Ruth Sidel, *The Families of Fengsheng: Urban Life in China* (Baltimore, Md.: Penguin, 1974); Jerome Cohen, "The Criminal Process in the People's Republic of China," 79 *Harvard Law Review* 469 (1966); and Michael E. Tigar, "Socialist Law and Legal Institutions," in Chapter Six of this book, pages 517–524.

People's Court in China: Trial of a Divorce Case *Doris Brin Walker*

CHIEF JUDGE: Our procedure is for the parties to the case and the masses to participate and make proposals, using criticism and self-criticism. Tell us your age and nationality.

WIFE: 33 years old; Han; middle peasant family from Hopei Province; middle school education.

CHIEF JUDGE: Salary?

WIFE: 41 yen per month.

HUSBAND: 39; Han; Peking middle peasant; junior middle school.

CHIEF JUDGE: Salary?

HUSBAND: 70 yen per month.

CHIEF JUDGE: What are your reasons for seeking a divorce?

WIFE: We got acquainted through introduction by friends. Married in 1961: daughter born 1962. Had usual feelings of newly-married couple. Then I got maternal disease of irregular menses and had to stay home from work for two months. I still suffer from this illness. This led to conflicts in our sex life. At first we forgave each other, but as time passed, this was no longer possible. I myself was at fault and was often unhappy, although my husband was often quite understanding. He said that I should not become pregnant again because of this disease. Thereafter our sex life was not good. So I said this was not good for family life, and my grandmother proposed that I get a divorce and I thought this was reasonable. She told my husband that he could not sacrifice his spiritual life because I was sick. She told him that he was still in good condition and must consider future generations. For myself, I was still reluctant to get divorced, but thought I could take care of our child. Often I was very sorry, but often too sick to get up. Sometimes my husband could not suppress his sexual

From Doris Brin Walker, "People's Court in China: Trial of a Divorce Case" from The Guild Practitioner, Vol. 30, No. 2 and 3 (September 1973), pp. 45–53. © 1974 National Lawyers Guild. Reprinted by permission.

desires. Our Constitution says if marriage is not feasible, the couple can be separated for the sake of work and daily life.

HUSBAND: Our problem is of long standing. She says her disease is the main problem, and she is really sick, but I do not think it is as serious as she says. The main thing is her mental feeling; the spiritual burden on her is very heavy. I think the problem can be solved, but now, since she says we should be separated, I cannot but agree.

CHIEF JUDGE: How long did you know each other before marriage?

HUSBAND: About two years. We fell in love in May, 1959. I worked in this office; she lived in the dormitory of the office building and worked on the construction team there. Later we met through an official introduction.

CHIEF JUDGE: Tell us how you felt about each other before marriage and right afterward?

WIFE: Those were the best times, but just so-so; not very bad or good. At times I thought he was quite good in some respects. Before the birth of our child, sex relations were good.

REPRESENTATIVE OF HUSBAND'S WORK UNIT: Feelings appear quite good before then.

CHIEF JUDGE: Describe conflicts and basic relations.

HUSBAND: Generally good. Busy with work. I had heavy tasks, had to travel; she handled family affairs. Until she suggested in 1968 that I suppress my sex desires. Then there was trouble. Before 1968 no big conflicts. Let her tell about conflicts.

ASSISTANT JUDGE: Has your husband stated all the main reasons?

WIFE: Yes.

CHIEF JUDGE: [reviewing husband's story] Did the misunderstandings change in character? Did they become deeper? Help us analyze the case. Your comrades know about you, but your expressions will help us to handle the contradictions according to Chairman Mao's teaching and laws. For example, when did the contradictions become very sharp?

WIFE: Sharpened after 1968. My disease was worse and I felt very bored. Quarrels could not be avoided, also misunderstandings. I was sick and he could not understand me very well.

CHIEF JUDGE: First, your sickness; second, married life no good; third, misunderstandings. Also the wife felt the husband did not show enough consideration. Right?

HUSBAND: In addition, we now have no affection; the sentiment has been broken. This has affected our work, confused our minds. After many years, I agreed to separation.

CHIEF JUDGE: How old is your child now?

HUSBAND: Ten.

CHIEF JUDGE: Have you ever talked to her about separating?

WIFE: No.

HUSBAND: No, but she knows that we quarrel.

CHIEF JUDGE: We must consider whether the situation is serious enough to warrant separation. Describe the worst quarrel.

WIFE: You say.

HUSBAND: She was to handle family affairs, but she spent her own salary and then often came to my office to find me. Often she went to the responsible leadership for help. She could not work well, due to her illness. We never cursed each other or fought. We went to comrades and finally to court for help.

CHIEF JUDGE: Your husband says you did not pay attention to family affairs; made a disturbance in his work unit, and aroused bad feelings toward him.

WIFE: Basically true.

CHIEF JUDGE: Apart from buying something for your child, you spent your own salary and made trouble. Yes?

WIFE: Yes.

CHIEF JUDGE: You did not show consideration for your wife, though she had done enough as a revolutionary partner? According to article 8 of the Marriage Law, spouses are to love, help and raise children together. When there are shortcomings, they are to be solved through criticism and self-criticism.

HUSBAND: Generally I was all right about carrying out my obligations. After she proposed separation, my feelings were hurt; then sometimes I showed insufficient consideration.

CHIEF JUDGE: What about plans for your child?

WIFE: Since kindergarten at age 4, she has been living with my husband's mother in the countryside because we are working here. I pay half her expenses for clothing and so forth.

CHIEF JUDGE: Why not tell [the] child?

WIFE: Too young; it might affect her mentally and make her unhappy. I will tell her when she is older.

CHIEF JUDGE: [to Representatives of Work Units] You know details better than we do. Leading comrades, please give us your description of the situation and your ideas.

REPRESENTATIVE OF WIFE'S WORK UNIT: We first learned of the troubles in 1969 when the wife brought bedding to sleep in our station. We asked her why. She was too shy to tell the details because I am a man, so I asked a woman comrade to talk with her and get details. We gave help, education for unity. Then she returned home, but there were frequent disputes and we tried to work with them. The situation was better, then worse, etc. As to her demand for separation, we think more work should be done before this is accepted, but her demand was urgent, so we signed approval.

REPRESENTATIVE OF WIFE'S WORK UNIT: I talked with the wife in 1969 when she came with bedding and child. I expressed my concern for the child and her view of her parents. I said there should be more self-criticism by husband and wife to see strong points of each. I pointed out her workplace was too far from the child's school and that she would arouse her husband's suspicions if she stayed at the workplace; that is not a correct way to handle conflicts.

REPRESENTATIVE OF WORK UNIT: [also from wife's unit voiced similar views]

WIFE: The grandmother is reluctant to have the child leave her.

COMRADE: How can you as parents leave your own child if the grandmother cannot?

ASSISTANT JUDGE: [after reviewing everyone's list of the problems] If the husband shows more consideration during menses, maybe this will help solve the problems. Contradictions about sex life are not big contradictions. Perhaps a family meeting with the grandparents would help. There are no fundamental contradictions.

REPRESENTATIVE OF HUSBAND'S WORK UNIT: I have a good understanding of the husband, but don't know the wife well. My opinion now is that they have a good sentimental basis for marriage from their early years. The main contradiction is in sex life. Revolutionary comrades should keep each other, though they cannot agree on all matters. Both are responsible for situation. Why did the husband finally agree to divorce? Very painful for him. His wife came here to see the leadership and sometimes she exaggerated her husband's misdeeds. This affected her husband's colleagues and embarrassed him. That's why he agreed to separation. The wife should try harder to cure her illness and he should show more understanding. Divorce is bad for the mind of a child. How can you as parents live apart from your own child? This must influence her feelings. Try to solve contradictions through criticism and self-criticism.

HUSBAND'S FRIEND: The contradiction can be solved. She can try more for a cure and he should try to understand. [While she reviews problems, husband's left leg and foot continuously jerk up and down.] And what happens to the child if you remarry? [Leader of husband's unit repeats previous speakers.]

CHIEF JUDGE: Both parties have suffered spiritually. Under article 17 of the Marriage Law, if both sides agree to a divorce, the court will approve. You should consider this again very seriously. Are you really at a stage where you should be separated? According to Chairman Mao, there are no fundamental contradictions within the working class. I see none between you. The basis for your marriage is good. Self-criticism can find defects and make it possible to continue the marriage. As to the wife's disease, medical facilities in our country can cure many now, and they are getting better. Do you think after hearing your comrades you can make more self-criticism and reconcile? [to wife] You want

a divorce, but haven't told your child. This shows a contradiction in you, that you are still uncertain. [As Chief Judge continues, husband holds his forehead.]

WIFE: You are earnest and frank. I am touched and grateful. But there is an acute struggle in my mind. If we reconcile and contradictions arise again, how will we resolve them? [Husband shows pained expression.] I must insist on my demand. This will save trouble for the leadership.

CHIEF JUDGE: Your mind is entangled with contradictions. Self-criticism will solve problems if you reconcile. Do you think all the fault is with your husband? If you reconcile and new problems arise, you can put forward certain demands on your husband. Have you really shown enough effort?

COMRADE: You may repent later if you separate now. Better reconcile—better for work and politically.

CHIEF JUDGE: What do you say? I have misgivings about a separation. You ought to be reconciled, but I see you did not criticize yourself enough or make enough demands on your husband. In the future, make more demands on yourself and show more responsibility in the family. And I say to grandparents and husband: have a family meeting. Discuss the practical problems: the wife told exaggerated stories about the husband at his work unit. He lost face and it was not good for his work. And she is afraid of future complications.

ASSISTANT JUDGE: Don't be afraid of contradictions. You will get help if they arise in the future. New unity can be reached and comrades will help.

HUSBAND'S FRIEND: Don't be afraid of future or about his attitude in future. He is a cadre with responsibilities.

CHIEF JUDGE: My final opinion is that this contradiction cannot be solved by divorce.

Others speak, mainly to wife.

CHIEF JUDGE: Tell us your final decision. [to husband] If you agree, we must grant separation. [more comments to wife]

WOMAN COMRADE: [to wife] Have faith in comrades as to future help.

WOMAN ASSISTANT JUDGE: The wife

wants her husband to express his feelings.

CHIEF JUDGE: [irritated] He already has. Have faith in comrades.

ASSISTANT JUDGE: Your husband cannot be blamed for everything. In some respects your husband is quite good. He should improve.

COMRADE: Do not fear your husband will make some reprisal against you. We know his political consciousness and integrity.

COMRADE: Your husband treated you quite well despite your hot temper. Your minds are now open to each other; life will be happier.

CHIEF JUDGE: Let's hear first from the wife.

WIFE: You have been patient and given good advice. I would like to be reconciled. I will make more strict demands for help and will take more family responsibility. I withdraw my request for separation.

HUSBAND: For years I did not agree to divorce until I felt I must. Since she now agrees not to separate, I agree. All details and future plans cannot be solved here, but the basis for the future is certain now.

CHIEF JUDGE: Look to your comrades and, if necessary, to court for help. Rest for a while. Wait in another room while we study the situation.

Recess.

In absence of parties and witnesses, judges confer.

CHIEF JUDGE: There is a very acute struggle in her mind.

[Discussion among judges. Agree to reconciliation: welcome it; must work on the next stage in the relationship, including the grandmother.]

Parties return.

CHIEF JUDGE: We agree to your present view, that there is insufficient reason to separate and you now agree to reconcile. We have heard the wife's misgivings, and you must arrange for future meetings between yourselves, with your families, and within your work units. [to wife] Will you sign the minutes of the court?

Wife signs.

Husband signs.

CHIEF JUDGE: If you would like to read the minutes, you can come to court to read them and see if there are any mistakes.

Hearing concluded.

3 The Judicial Role of Juries-Finding "the Truth"

Discussion of the political role of juries and jurors leaves unexamined problems of how adequate the jury system is for its more narrowly defined judicial tasks. In the *Duncan* case (see page 292), Justice White notes that the jury system is fundamental to "principles of liberty and justice which lie at the base of all our civil and political institutions." Yet he gives only passing mention to the years of debate which have taken place about the ability of juries to understand evidence and determine issues of fact. Referring to the Kalven and Zeisel study, *The American Jury,* Justice White assures us that juries "come to sound conclu- sions in most of the cases presented to them." But what do other writers, jurors, and judges believe about the quality of discussion in the jury room?

The first two articles in this section present opposing views of the quality and reliability of jury deliberations. One is written by an experienced and realistic judge; the other is the work of a layman who served as a juror in a murder trial and kept a meticulous journal of evidence and deliberation. Because jury proceedings cannot be recorded we have only these indirect reports to guide us in determining whether we would like to leave the fate of our liberty or property in the hands of our peers. If the same question is viewed on a system-wide rather than personal level, we are exploring the basis of democracy, our view of human nature, and the adequacy of juries to represent our collective notions of fairness and justice.

The view we reach about the adequacy of juries for determining "truth" and "settling" disputes will inevitably influence the degree to which we support or oppose reforms of the jury system. As the following readings indicate, several changes in the jury system are and have been taking place. Some of these, such as legislative proposals designed to reduce the size of juries or eliminate the requirement of a unanimous verdict, come before the public for conscious decision making. Such proposals are often justified by claims for saving tax money by increasing the efficiency of jury deliberations. Other changes in the jury system arise from changes in the allocation of economic power and seem to take place without any public discussion of their merits for the jury system. Professor Horwitz gives us a glimpse of one such subterranean method of reducing jury power in the early days of the republic.

Still other changes in the jury system seem to be inevitable—the reflection of changes in society over which no one seems to have any control. The use of expert testimony, which seems necessary in view of the increasingly technical nature of knowledge, conflict, and social organization, may serve to convert the jury to a rubber stamp for technocracy or reduce the juror to confusion and helplessness.

Overall one is aware also that the jury seems to have less and less use as it is replaced by negotiated settlements, private arbitration or mediation, and trials before a judge only. In 1960 only 3,035 of 6,988 federal civil trials were by jury; in 1974 the ratio was 3,569 out of 10,972. Some estimates claim that more than 95 percent of all criminal charges lead to plea bargaining and hardly any to trial by jury. In view of the disuse of juries and the reforms that reduce their power or importance, the candid observer might wonder whether the jury system exists at all outside the realm of political ideology. If such is the case, the same observer might also wonder what has become of the political sovereignty discussed in the previous section.

A.   In the Jury Room

The Jury System   *Jerome Frank*

Blackstone called the jury "the glory of the English law." Jefferson, who detested Blackstone as

From "The Jury System," in Jerome Frank, *Courts on Trial: Myth and Reality in American Justice,* copyright renewed © 1976 by Princeton University Press; (copyright 1949 by Jerome Frank; Princeton Paperback, 1973): pp. 108–125. Reprinted by permission of Princeton University Press. (Abridged.)

a Tory, agreed with him at least on that one subject. Judge Knox, chief federal district judge in the Southern District of New York, said a few years ago, "In my opinion, the jury system is one of the really great achievements of English and American jurisprudence."

As you'll see, I dissent from those views. When I hear the jury praised as the "palladium of our liberties," I keep thinking that, while a palladium (a word derived from the ancient use of the image of Pallas Athena) means something on which the safety of a nation or an institution depends, it also is the name of a chemical element which, in the spongy state "has the remarkable quality of absorbing, up to nearly 1,000 times its own volume in hydrogen gas...."

I have said that, supposedly, the task of our courts is this: To make reasoned applications of legal rules to the carefully ascertained facts of particular law-suits. You will recall my crude schematization of the alleged nature of the process—$R \times F = D$—i.e., the Rules times the Facts equals the Decision. Where, in that scheme, does the jury fit in?

In most jury trials, the jury renders what is called a "general verdict." Suppose that Williams sues Allen claiming (1) that Allen falsely told him there was oil on some land Williams bought from Allen, but (2) that in fact there was no oil there, so that Williams was defrauded. The jury listens to the witnesses. Then the judge tells the jurors, "If you find Allen lied, and Williams relied on that lie, a legal rule requires that you hold for the plaintiff Williams, and you must compute the damages according to another rule," which the judge explains. "But if you find that Allen did not lie, then the legal rule requires you to hold for the defendant Allen." The jury deliberates in the jury-room and reports either, "We find for the plaintiff in the sum of $5,000," or "We find for the defendant." In other words, the jury does not report what facts it found. Such an undetailed, unexplained, jury report is called a "general verdict."

There are three theories of the jury's function:

1. The naive theory is that the jury merely finds the facts; that it must not, and does not, concern itself with the legal rules, but faithfully accepts the rules as stated to them by the trial judge.

2. A more sophisticated theory has it that the jury not only finds the facts but, in its deliberation in the jury-room, uses legal reasoning to apply to those facts the legal rules it learned from the judge. A much respected judge said in 1944 that a jury's verdict should be regarded as "the reasoned and logical result of the concrete application of the law (i.e., the rules) to the facts."

On the basis of this sophisticated theory, the jury system has been criticized. It is said that juries often do not find the facts in accordance with the evidence, but distort—or "judge"—the facts, and find them in such a manner that (by applying the legal rules laid down by the judge to the facts thus deliberately misfound) the jury is able to produce the results which it desires, in favor of one party or the other. "The facts," we are told, "are found in order to reach the result."

This theory ascribes to jurors a serpentine wisdom. It assumes that they thoroughly understand what the judge tells them about the rules, and that they circumvent the rules by falsely contriving—with consummate skill and cunning —the exact findings of the fact which, correlated with those rules, will logically compel the result they desire.

3. We come now to a third theory which may be called the "realistic" theory. It is based on what anyone can discover by questioning the average person who has served as a juror— namely that often the jury are neither able to, nor do they attempt to, apply the instructions of the court. The jury are more brutally direct. They determine that they want Jones to collect $5,000 from the railroad company, or that they don't want pretty Nellie Brown to go to jail for killing her husband; and they bring in their general verdict accordingly. Often, to all practical intents and purposes, the judge's statement of the legal rules might just as well never have been expressed. "Nor can we," writes Clementson, "cut away the mantle of mystery in which the general verdict is enveloped, to see how the principal facts were determined, and whether the law was applied under the judge's instructions.... It is a matter of common knowledge that the general verdict may be the result of anything but the calm deliberation, exchange of impressions and opinions, resolution of doubts, and final intelligent concurrence which, theoretically, produced it. It comes into court unexplained and impenetrable."

The "realistic" theory, then, is that, in many cases, the jury, often without heeding the legal rules, determine, not the "facts," but the respective legal rights and duties of the parties to the suit. For the judgment of the court usually follows the general verdict of the jury, so that the verdict results in a decision which determines those rights and duties. . . .

Practically, then, we do have the very conditions which we were warned would exist if juries had the right to ignore the judge's instructions as to the correct rules: Cases are often decided "according to what the jury supposes the law is or ought to be"; the "law" is "as fluctuating and uncertain as the diverse opinions in regard to it"; often juries are "not only judges but legislators as well"; jurors do become "superior to the national legislature," and its laws are "subject to their control" so that "a law of Congress" is "in operation in one state and not in another."

This truth the general verdict conceals. "Whether," says Sunderland, "the jurors deliberately threw the law into the discard, and rendered a verdict out of their own heads, or whether they applied the law correctly as instructed by the court, or whether they tried to apply it properly but failed for lack of understanding—these are questions respecting which the verdict discloses nothing. . . . The general verdict serves as the great procedural opiate, . . . draws the curtain upon human errors, and soothes us with the assurance that we have attained the unattainable."

Now what does bring about verdicts? Longenecker, in a book written by a practical trial lawyer for practical trial lawyers, says: "In talking to a man who had recently served for two weeks on juries, he stated that in one case after they had retired to consider the verdict, the foreman made a speech to them somewhat like this: 'Now boys, you know there was lying on both sides. Which one did the most lying? The plaintiff is a poor man and the defendant is rich and can afford to pay the plaintiff something. Of course the dog did not hurt the plaintiff much, but I think we ought to give him something, don't you?' There were several 'sures'; we thought the plaintiff might have to split with his lawyers, so we gave him a big verdict." A case is reported in which the jurors explained their verdict thus: "We couldn't make head or tail of the case, or follow all the messing around the lawyers did.

None of us believed the witnesses on either side, anyway, so we made up our minds to disregard the evidence on both sides and decide the case on its merits." "Competent observers," says Judge Roseman, "who have interviewed the jurors in scores of jury trials, declare that in many cases . . . principal issues received no consideration from the jury." Bear that in mind, when considering these remarks by Ram: "And to what a fearful extent may a verdict affect a person! It may pronounce a man sane or insane; it may establish character, or take it away; it may give liberty to the captive, or turn liberty into slavery; it may continue life to a prisoner, or consign him to death."

Again and again, it has been disclosed that juries have arrived at their verdicts by one of the following methods: (1) Each juror in a civil case writes down the amount he wants to award; the total is added and the average taken as the verdict. (2) The jurors by agreement decide for one side or the other according to the flip of a coin. (3) A related method, reported in a case where a man was convicted of manslaughter and sentenced to life imprisonment, is as follows: The "jury at first stood six for assault and battery, and, as a compromise, the six agreed to vote for manslaughter, and the vote then stood six for manslaughter, and six for murder in the second degree; it was then agreed to prepare 24 ballots— 12 for manslaughter and 12 for murder in the second degree—place all of them in a hat, and each juror draw one ballot therefrom, and render a verdict either for manslaughter or murder in the second degree, as the majority should appear; the first drawing was a tie, but the second one resulted in eight ballots for murder in the second degree and four for manslaughter, and thereupon, according to the agreement, a verdict was rendered for murder in the second degree.

How do the courts react to such a disclosure? When it is made known before the jury is discharged, a court will usually reject the verdict. But, frequently, the revelation occurs after the jury's discharge. In most states, and in the federal system, the courts then refuse to disturb the verdict. They say that any other result would mean that jurors would be subjected to pressures, after a case is over, to induce them to falsify what had occurred in the jury-room, so that all verdicts would be imperiled.

One may doubt whether there is much danger of such falsifications. I surmise that the underlying reason for that judicial attitude is this: The judges feel that, were they obliged to learn the methods used by jurors, the actual workings of the jury-system would be shown up, devastatingly. From my point of view, such a consequence would be desirable: The public would soon discover this skeleton in the judicial closet....

Are jurors to blame when they decide cases in the ways I've described? I think not. In the first place, often they cannot understand what the judge tells them about the legal rules. To comprehend the meaning of many a legal rule requires special training. It is inconceivable that a body of twelve ordinary men, casually gathered together for a few days, could, merely from listening to the instructions of the judge, gain the knowledge necessary to grasp the true import of the judge's words. For these words have often acquired their meaning as the result of hundreds of years of professional disputation in the courts. The jurors usually are as unlikely to get the meaning of those words as if they were spoken in Chinese, Sanskrit, or Choctaw. "Can anything be more fatuous," queries Sunderland, "than the expectation that the law which the judge so carefully, learnedly and laboriously expounds to the laymen in the jury box becomes operative in their minds in true form?" Judge Rossman pointedly asks whether it "is right to demand that a juror swear that he will obey the instructions (which the lawyers frequently say they are not sure of until they have been transcribed) and return a general verdict in obedience thereto." Judge Bok says that "juries have the disadvantage... of being treated like children while the testimony is going on, but then being doused with a kettleful of law, during the charge, that would make a third-year law student blanch."

Under our system, however, the courts are obligated to make the unrealistic assumption that the often incomprehensible words, uttered in the physical presence of the jurors, have some real effect on their thought processes. As a logical deduction from that unfounded assumption, the trial judge is required to state the applicable rule to the jury with such nicety that some lawyers do not thoroughly comprehend it. If the judge omits any of these niceties, the upper court will reverse a judgment based on the jury's verdict. For, theoretically, the jury actually worked in accordance with the $R \times F = D$ formula, applying the R they received from the judge, so that, if he gave them the wrong R, then, in theory, the D —their verdict—must logically be wrong. Lawyers thus set traps for trial judges. Decisions, in cases which have taken weeks to try, are reversed on appeal because a phrase, or a sentence, meaningless to the jury, has been included in or omitted from the charge.[1]

When a decision is reversed on such a ground, there results, at best, a new trial at which the trial judge will intone a more meticulously worded R to another uncomprehending jury. This leads to an enormous waste of time and money. And note that the prospect of a prolonged expensive new trial often induces a litigant who won in the first trial, and who has only modest means, to accept an unfair settlement.

Many of the precise legal rules on which, according to the conventional theory, men in their daily affairs have a right to and supposedly do rely are found solely in upper-court opinions admonishing trial judges to use, in charges to juries, words and phrases stating those rules. But if jurors do not understand those words and phrases, and consequently do not apply those rules, then reliance on the rules is unreliable: Men who act in reliance on that purported right to rely are

---

[1] Dean Green says that some upper courts, when they dislike jury verdicts, are astute to discover errors in the instructions, as a means of requiring new trials. It is a curious fact that many upper courts, which refuse to reverse decisions for "procedural" errors those courts call "harmless," nevertheless will be prompt to reverse for an error in a trial judge's charge about the "substantive" legal rules —although the first kind of error (e.g., an improper, highly inflammatory, remark to the jury by the winning lawyer) may be the very sort of thing which is within the comprehension of the jurors and may have influenced their verdict, while the second kind frequently are beyond the jurors' understanding and could not have affected the verdict.

deceived. I cannot, therefore, agree with Dickinson when he says that, although no precedents emerge from the verdicts of successive juries "so long as the application of a rule is left to the jury under no other guidance than the statement of the rule as such by the court," yet "the moment of elaboration of a rule is definitely isolated and registered as that at which a court for the first time instructs a jury that a rule does or does not apply to a particular state of facts, and this instruction is tested and approved on appeal," and that "this is an important and powerful aid in minting new law into stable and recognizable form, and offers one of the cogent arguments for the preservation of the jury system."

Suppose, however, that the jurors always did understand the R's. Nevertheless, often they would face amazing obstacles to ascertaining the F's. For the evidence is not presented all at once or in an orderly fashion. The very mode of its presentation is confusing. The jurors are supposed to keep their minds in suspense until all of the evidence is in.

Can a jury perform such a task? Has it the means and capacity? Are the conditions of a jury trial such as to make for the required calm deliberation by the jurors? Wigmore, who defends the jury system, himself tells us that the court-room is "a place of surging emotions, distracting episodes, and sensational surprises. The parties are keyed up to the contest; and the topics are often calculated to stir up the sympathy, or prejudice, or ridicule of the tribunal." Dean Green remarks: "The longer the trial lasts, the larger the scanning crowds, the more intensely counsel draw the lines of conflict, the more solemn the judge, the harder it becomes for the jury to restrain their reason from somersault."

We may, therefore, seriously question the statement of Professors Michael and Adler that, unlike the witnesses, the jury "observes the things and events exhibited to its senses under conditions designed to make the observation reliable and accurate. In the case of what (the jury) observes directly the factor of memory is negligible." As shown by Wigmore, Green, and Burrill, the first of those comments surely does not square with observable courtroom realities. As to the second—

that the factor of the jurors' memory is negligible —consider the following: Theoretically, as we saw, the jury, in its process of fact-finding, applies to the evidence the legal rules it learns from the judge. If the jury actually did conduct itself according to this theory, it would be unable to comprehend the evidence intelligently until it received those instructions about the rules. But those instructions are given, not before the jury hears the evidence, but only after all the witnesses have left the stand. Then, for the first time are the jurors asked to consider the testimony in the light of the rules. In other words, if jurors are to do their duty, they must now recollect and assemble the separate fragments of the evidence (including the demeanor of the several witnesses) and fit them into the rules. If the trial has lasted for many days or weeks, the required feat of memory is prodigious. As Burrill says: "The theory of judicial investigation requires that the juror keep his mind wholly free from impressions until all facts are before him in evidence, and that he should then frame his conclusion. The difficulty attending this mode of dealing with the elements of evidence (especially in important cases requiring protracted investigation) is that the facts thus surveyed in a mass, and at one view, are apt to confuse, distract, and oppress the mind by their very number and variety.... They are, moreover, necessarily mixed up with remembrance of the mere machinery of their introduction, and the contests (often close and obstinate) attending their proof; in the course of which attempts are sometimes made to suppress or distort the truth, in the very act of presentation."

In a discussion I recently had with Professor Michael, he maintained that, since jurymen, in their daily out-of-court living, conduct most of their affairs on the basis of conclusions reached after listening to other men, they are adequately equipped as fact-finders in the court-room. One answer to this argument is that often the issues in trials are of a complicated kind with which most jurymen are unfamiliar. But let us ignore that answer. A more telling criticism of Michael's assertion is this: The surroundings of inquiry during a jury trial differ extraordinarily from those in which the juryman conducts his ordinary affairs. At a trial, the jurors hear the evidence in a public place, under conditions of a kind to which they are unaccustomed: No juror is able to withdraw to his own room, or office, for private individual reflection. And, at the close of the trial, the jurors are pressed for time in reaching their joint decision. Even twelve experienced judges, deliberating together, would probably not function well under the conditions we impose on the twelve inexperienced laymen....

... Typically, in his book for practicing trial lawyers, Longenecker writes: "No more important matter presents itself in the trial of a case than that of selecting a jury ... Do not take a chance (in this matter) because you have no right to gamble with your client's interests."

Do the lawyers strive to pick impartial jurors? Do they want jurymen whose training will best enable them to understand the facts of the case? Of course not. If you think they usually do, watch the trial lawyers at work in a court-room. Or read the books written for trial lawyers by seasoned trial lawyers.

Here are a few excerpts from such a book, Goldstein's *Trial Techniques,* a book commended for its accuracy by Professor Morgan of Harvard. Always demand a jury, says Goldstein, if you represent a plaintiff who is a "woman, child, an old man or an old woman, or an ignorant, illiterate or foreign-born person unable to read or write or speak English who would naturally excite the jury's sympathies," especially if the defendant is a large corporation, a prominent or wealthy person, an insurance company, railroad or bank. Then, he advises, seek the type of juror who "will most naturally respond to an emotional appeal." Make every effort, this author counsels, to exclude from the jury anyone "who is particularly experienced in the field of endeavor which is the basis of the law suit." As such a person is likely, says Goldstein, to have too much influence with the other jurors, it is always better to submit the issues "to a jury who have no knowledge of the particular subject."

In that book much is made of the fact that "the jury tries the lawyers rather than the clients," that, "without realizing it, the jurors allow their opinions of the evidence to be swayed in favor of the side represented by the lawyer they like."

That notion is repeated in some of the pamphlets, written by eminent trial lawyers, published in 1946 under the auspices of the American Bar Association. They advise the lawyer to "ingratiate himself" with the jury. One of these pamphlets says that the jurors' reaction to the trial lawyer "may be more important than the reaction to the client, for the client is on the stand only during a relatively brief period, while the lawyer is before the jury all the time." Harris, in his well-known book on "advocacy," says, "It may be that judgment is more easily deceived when the passions are aroused but if so, you (the lawyers) are not responsible. Human nature was, I presume, intended to be what it is, and when it gets into the jury-box, it is the duty of the advocate to make the best use of it he fairly can in the interest of his client." The Supreme Court of Tennessee has solemnly decided that "tears have always been considered legitimate arguments before a jury," that such use of tears is "one of the natural rights of counsel which no court or constitution could take away," and that "indeed if counsel has them at command, it may be seriously questioned whether it is not his professional duty to shed them whenever proper occasion arises...."

This is no laughing matter. For prejudice has been called the thirteenth juror, and it has been said that "Mr. Prejudice and Miss Sympathy are the names of the witnesses whose testimony is never recorded, but must nevertheless be reckoned with in trials by jury." The foregoing tends to justify Balzac's definition of a jury as "twelve men chosen to decide who has the better lawyer."

In any law-suit, success or defeat for one of the parties may turn on his lawyer's abilities. But, in the light of the fact that juries "try the lawyers," it is peculiarly true, in many a jury trial, that a man's life, livelihood or property often depends on his lawyer's skill or lack of it in ingratiating himself with the jury rather than on the evidence. Not that lawyers, trying to protect their clients, should be censured for exploiting jurors' weaknesses—as long as we retain the general-verdict jury system.

Since, as every handbook on trial practice discloses, and as visits to a few jury trials will teach anyone, the lawyers are allowed—more, are expected—to appeal to the crudest emotions and prejudices of the jurors, and jurors are known often to respond to such appeals, I confess that it disturbs me not a little that we require trial judges to perform the futile ritual of saying to each jury something like this: "The law will not permit jurors to be governed by mere sentiment, sympathy, passion or prejudice, and you will reach a verdict that will be just to both sides, regardless of what the consequences may be." We tell jurors to do—have them take an oath to do—what we do not at all expect them to do.

... The search for the facts in a courtroom must necessarily be limited by lack of time; also, for important reasons of public policy, some ways of obtaining evidence are precluded—by the rule against self-incrimination, for instance, or by the rule against any unreasonable search and seizure.

But there are other rules of exclusion which, no matter what their origin, have been perpetuated primarily because of the admitted incompetence of jurors. Notable is the rule excluding hearsay evidence. Hearsay may be roughly (and somewhat inaccurately) described as the report in court by a witness of a statement made by another person, out of court, who is not subject to cross-examination at the trial, when the report of that statement is offered as evidence to prove the truth of a fact asserted in that statement. It is, so to speak, second-hand evidence. No doubt hearsay should often be accepted with caution. But 90% of the evidence on which men act out of court, most of the data on which business and industry daily rely, consists of the equivalent of hearsay. Yet, because of distrust of juries—a belief that jurors lack the competence to make allowance for the second-hand character of hearsay —such evidence, although accepted by administrative agencies, juvenile courts and legislative committees, is (subject, to be sure, to numerous exceptions) barred in jury trials. As a consequence, frequently the jury cannot learn of matters which would lead an intelligent person to a more correct knowledge of the facts.

So, too, of many other exclusionary rules. They limit, absurdly, the courtroom quest for the truth. The result, often, is a gravely false picture of the actual facts. Thus trial by jury seriously interferes with correct—and, therefore, just—decisions. Even if the juries could understand what the trial judges tell them of the R's, the juries would often be unable to apply these rules to anything like the real F's, because of the exclusion of relevant evidence.

But, even apart from that difficulty, since jurors frequently cannot understand the R's, the general-verdict jury trial renders absurd the conventional description of the decisional process— the $R \times F = D$. To my mind a better instrument than the usual jury trial could scarcely be imagined for achieving uncertainty, capriciousness, lack of uniformity, disregard of the R's, and unpredictability of decisions.

My attitude towards the jury is not unique. James Bradley Thayer, a great legal scholar and a profound student of jury trials, said in 1898 that in civil cases, "I would restrict (jury trial) narrowly, for it appears to me...to be a potent cause of demoralization to the bar." Learned Hand remarked in 1921, "I am by no means enamored of jury trials, at least in civil cases...." Mr. Justice Cardozo, in a Supreme Court opinion, wrote, "Few would be so narrow or provincial as to maintain that a fair and enlightened system of justice would be impossible without" jury trials. The noted historian, Carl Becker, one of the ablest students of American history and institutions, said in 1945: "Trial by jury, as a method of determining facts, is antiquated...and inherently absurd—so much so that no lawyer, judge, scholar, prescription-clerk, cook, or mechanic in a garage would ever think for a moment of employing that method for determining the facts in any situation that concerned him." Two very able and experienced trial judges, Judge Galston and Judge Shietag, have each recently indicated a belief that the use of the jury in civil suits should be severely restricted. Judge Shietag said: "The civil jury would seem to be unnecessary except in a few types of injury to the person, such as libel and slander, false arrest, and malicious prosecution."

Osborn, a keen observer of many jury trials, wrote in 1937: "When a group of twelve men, on seats a little higher than the spectators, but not quite so high as the judge, are casually observed it may appear from their attitude that they are thinking only about the case going on before them. The truth is that for much of the time there are twelve wandering minds in that silent group, bodily present but mentally far away. Some of them are thinking of sadly neglected business affairs, others of happy or unhappy family matters, and, after the second or third day and especially after the second or third week, there is the garden, the house-painting, the new automobile, the prospective vacation, the girl who is soon to be married and the hundred and one other things that come to the mind of one who is only partly interested in the tedious proceeding going on before him. There is probably more woolgathering in jury boxes than in any other place on earth. ...Someone has said that the invention of this jury system is one of the 'splendid achievements of civilization,' but its splendor is now and then somewhat dimmed when some juryman frankly tells just what occurred in some jury-room. If for a term of court or two a complete transcript of all the comments, criticisms, and reasons of jurors in jury-rooms could be made and furnished to ...the newspapers, it would no doubt furnish some suggestions looking toward improvement. If this exposure did not bring about the total abolition of the jury system, it would perhaps tend to bring about improvement in some of the methods of selecting jurors, or perhaps a selection of the kind of cases to be submitted to juries. ...It is plainly said by those whose opinions command the utmost respect that the administration of the law in this land is on a lower plane than other phases of government and is unworthy of the civilization it poorly serves."

In 1975 Melvyn Zerman was chosen to serve on a jury which was to participate in the trial of Ricky Mathes for the murder of a potato chip deliveryman in New York. Mr. Zerman had never been on a jury before. He was an employee of Harper & Row Publishers, but he was not a professional writer. In the ensuing weeks he kept a careful journal of evidence, his own reactions and observations of the other participants, and finally, of the jury deliberations. The result was a book published in 1977, *Call the Final Witness*.

The following excerpts fall into two parts. First we hear the most crucial part of the jury's deliberations as recalled by Mr. Zerman. As one reads this section the testimony in the trial begins to emerge and we see that the state's case rests heavily upon the testimony of three teenagers alleged to have arrived on the scene almost immediately after the gun was fired.

In the second part, "Reflections on Being a Juror," we get the benefit of Mr. Zerman's replies to questions about his judgment of the quality of his experience and those of his fellow jurors. Taken together, the two parts provide a rare glimpse into the workings of juries.

Call the Final Witness *Melvyn Zerman*

The first significant words prompted not only re-

Abridged from pp. 127–139, 157–163 in *Call the Final Witness* by Melvyn Bernard Zerman. Copyright © 1977 by Melvyn Bernard Zerman. By permission of Harper & Row Publishers, Inc.

lief but surprise, and the surprise stemmed not only from their content but from their source. They were spoken by, of all people, Juror 8—the former first alternate, the occasional snoozer, and the imitator, yesterday, of the young punk's walk. What he said—tersely, flatly, and with that somewhat choked quality fat men's voices sometimes have—was: "The state ain't got no case." Then there was silence in the room.

It was broken by Juror 1, our forewoman, and she proved the biggest surprise of all. She, who over eight days had smiled a lot and said very little, took command immediately and she was nothing short of remarkable. As we began deliberating, with the exhibits gathered up and put aside, she exchanged seats with Juror 5 and moved to the end of the table opposite me. From then on, where she sat became the head of the table.

She opened the discussion by asking Juror 8 if he wanted to elaborate on his statement. When he was unwilling or unable to do so, she turned to the rest of us: Would anyone volunteer his or her reconstruction of the case? Getting no immediate response, she proceeded to do it herself, and she stated my views almost exactly: she discounted all the police testimony as failing to implicate Ricky in any way; she reviewed the descriptions given by the adult eyewitnesses, particularly Clare Anderson, and reminded us that they did not resemble Ricky at all; therefore, she said, the state's case had to rest solely on the testimony of the three kids—and she for one could not believe it. She suggested that they were motivated by the promise of a reward—or perhaps for some other reason—but no matter what, to her their stories were transparent, and she went on to enumerate an inescapable series of flaws. She went further than I had in my mind by speculating that after the kids had spoken to the police, they realized they had embarked on a very dangerous course and now they were afraid. Perhaps they even regretted what they had done. Fear or regret or both would explain why they were reluctant witnesses. In any case, their testimony was so incredible that she would have to find Ricky not guilty.

She suggested then that we go around the table and each of us talk in turn. Juror 2 found it difficult to believe that in "their ethnic group" these kids would turn on one of their own and concoct such a story simply for the reward. He told us a rambling anecdote about a black man who had once worked with him and who had

stood by another black in circumstances where no white man would have supported another white. I answered that it would be a miracle for us to *know* what may have motivated the kids—the range of human experience was just too broad and the possible explanations were endless. I mentioned a theory that had come to me a day or two before. What if Jennifer's boyfriend, whose name was mentioned during the trial, had been involved in the crime? What if the description of the suspect given on the Channel 2 News and the sketch shown had resembled this man? What if he had taken off for Texas and the kids, to keep the police off his trail, had decided to implicate Ricky? (They had come forward no more than five days after that CBS News program.) There, certainly, was a motive for the kids. But no sooner had I offered this theory—and I could see some jurors nodding their heads in interest and others all set to attack it—than I disavowed it. It was pure conjecture, I said, unsupported by a crumb of evidence, but it was an example of the myriad of possible truths in this case.

The "not guilty" faction was strongly on the offensive at this point. Encouraged by the fact that we had already swayed two of the "undecideds," we hammered at two key arguments: Ricky's dissimilarity to the sketch of the suspect drawn from Clare Anderson's description and the unmistakable discrepancies between Clarissa's original police interview, her later interview (taped) with an assistant D.A., and her aborted testimony on the stand.

Juror 5, probably the oldest person in the room, was convinced to the end that Ricky was guilty, but in objective terms he never really explained why. He kept alluding to "bad vibes" and to the "feeling in his gut"—he rarely went beyond the viscera to the brain. Thus, for as long as he was a holdout, he was mostly content to allow Juror 6 to do battle for them both. Juror 6. Came to the U.S. from Czechoslovakia twenty-five years ago, a CPA with one of New York's largest accounting firms, a command of English —though he, like Juror 4, speaks with an accent —probably greater than that of anyone else in the jury room. Loquacious. Stentorian. Ready with an anecdote on any subject. A self-proclaimed expert on gourmet cooking, the stock market, and —so unfortunately for the rest of us—guns and human nature.

On human nature, or more precisely black human nature, he knew more than the rest of us because he sees blacks socially. His first memorable statement once deliberations began: "I am sorry there are no blacks on this jury." Because blacks know how other blacks think. Said Juror 1, then, and repeatedly over the next nine hours, "Phillip, we shouldn't, we mustn't, talk about color." Juror 6 smiled condescendingly. At one point I mentioned one of Jennifer's most astonishing statements that she and Clarissa and Jimmy had *never* discussed among themselves seeing Ricky commit the crime, not even after their mother gathered them into her car and drove them to the precinct house to talk to the police. "What wheels turning in her head could make her think that we would believe something like that?" I asked, rhetorically. Juror 6 announced, "Black wheels."

He had quickly conceded that the kids' testimony was full of contradictions. But that didn't trouble him. He had a theory: the four of them were in it together. They had all attempted to rob—and succeeded in murdering—the potato chip man. But a month later something happened —perhaps the offer of a reward, perhaps something else—to cause Jennifer, Clarissa, and Jimmy to decide to make Ricky their scapegoat. In effect, then, all the blacks were guilty, but since only one was on trial, he could convict only one.

There were three "facts" he considered irrefutable: they all said they saw Ricky leaning half in, half out of the truck, they all heard the shots, they all saw the gun. With glee he reminded us that they described the gun differently: Jimmy said it was a .38, Jennifer said it was "little and brownish," Clarissa said it was "medium and brown." But these inconsistencies *proved* they were telling the truth because the kids weren't *experts* and they couldn't tell one gun from another.

At one point, after a long, aimless pause in the deliberations, Juror 6 said with a sly smile, "You all keep asking me to explain to you why I think

Ricky is guilty. Well, now I ask you: How can you prove to me that he is innocent?" Without a breath of hesitation—almost as if she had been waiting for this question—Juror 1 met the challenge: "Phillip, we don't have to prove he is innocent. He is *presumed* innocent. That's our system here. The prosecution has to prove him guilty." Juror 6's smile faded but did not disappear. Was he embarrassed by his unthinking lapse? He conceded nothing. The smile became a look of condescension, as if to say, "And that, my dear, is what is wrong with your system."

Juror 1: "What about their insistence in their early testimony that it all happened at five-thirty?" Juror 6: "They didn't have watches." Juror 1: "But Detective McKinley testified that when he interviewed Clarissa she at first insisted that she saw Ricky at *five-thirty,* even after he reminded her that the murder was committed at five." (Now how did she remember that? She's brilliant.) Juror 6: "I don't remember that." Juror 5: "I don't either."

[Jurors are escorted to dinner.]

The jury room was no more inviting on our return than it had been when we left, but we were not in it very long before we were recalled to the courtroom, to rehear the testimony we had requested. As we crossed to the jury box and I passed Ricky sitting at the defense table, I noticed that, for the first time, he appeared to be crying. At least he was holding a white handkerchief to his eyes and there it remained for as long as the jury sat in the courtroom. The court reporter read Clarissa's taped testimony as he had recorded it. Loudly, distinctly, his voice a monotone, he recited: "There were lots of cops around but I couldn't find one."

After reading the taped testimony in its entirety, the court reporter found that isolated passage from Kellam's cross-examination of Detective McKinley. There could be no doubt now. McKinley had flatly admitted that when Clarissa was first questioned she stuck to five-thirty as the time she saw Ricky running away, even after she was told that the potato chip man had been murdered much closer to five o'clock. Back in the jury room, I knew it was merely a matter of time before Juror 5 abandoned his ally. The immediate response was from Juror 6. With the kids' stories crumbling around him, he moved to a clearer spot: the testimony, and, more important, the demeanor of Ricky on the stand. The kid was arrogant, he was hostile, he was evasive. Couldn't we all tell he was guilty?

Juror 5 could tell. Of course Ricky was guilty. He had that feeling in his gut. But he had to admit now there *was* a doubt. The state's case was weak. Yes, Ricky was guilty, guilty as hell—but he was changing his vote. Sadly but with a kind of flourish. He wanted the respect that age commands. He got a few smiles at least. For now it was eleven to one. We had been deliberating for over eight hours.

Instead of bringing relief, the capitulation of Juror 5 recharged the atmosphere. The pressure on Juror 6 should have been insupportable. But without any evident rancor toward the sudden renegade, he made it immediately clear that *he* was not planning to change *his* vote, now or in the future. Anger burst around him. He was being totally unreasonable. How could he still insist on "guilty" when the state's case had been exposed to him, over and over again, as a fraud? What more could any of us say? He repeated, with that exasperated but not yet spent patience that teachers show to mischievous children, "I don't care about the kids' stories. Sure, they may be lying. But not about the important thing. Ricky is on trial, not the kids."

There seemed to be no more avenues of attack open to us. We had tried to wear him down by confronting him with all the flaws in the kids' testimony, but he had made it inescapably clear that this strategy was futile. I sat silently for a moment, trying to come up with a new argument, yet certain that it would prove as useless as all the others.

I thought to myself: He believes all four were conspirators in the crime. Can we build on that? Of course! Trying to keep my voice down and free of hostility, I asked Juror 6 how he could be sure, if they were all in it together, that it was Ricky rather than one of the other three who had pulled the trigger. Someone else answered, "It couldn't have been one of the girls." Had I believed the shared-guilt theory, I would not have

conceded even that, but for the moment it didn't matter. "Just Jimmy, then. How do you know Jimmy didn't do it?" "Because," replied Juror 6, "the description of the killer given by the four adults sounded much more like Ricky." "But you've already said we should discount their statements. They were in shock or too frightened to be reliable witnesses. You can't have it both ways—dismissing what they said when it favors Ricky and accepting it when it doesn't!" Silence again and then a barely audible remark from Juror 6: "Let me sleep on it."

For me this was the first hopeful note of the evening, but to my surprise, I was virtually alone in my reaction. The others seemed more irate at the implied suggestion that we be sequestered overnight than they were by the possibility of our never reaching a verdict. Indeed, the sense of outrage now was almost palpable. "That's so unfair. That's so selfish!" shouted Juror 3, sitting to my right—she who had, for the past week, talked about little except her home and family. She whispered to me that the time had come for us to report to the judge that we were at an impasse. "Let it be a hung jury and let's go home," she said. I answered that it was very likely that the judge would insist that we continue to deliberate. "But how can he do that?" she whined. Around us indignation was boiling. The surrender of Juror 5 had proved to be like the dropping of a single shoe. Everyone had waited for the second to fall and now frustration was more intense than it had ever been, for it appeared that the shoe would not fall tonight.

Somehow, by offering the faint suggestion that he might *eventually* change his mind, Juror 6 seemed more stubborn, quixotic, and self-indulgent than he had when he was proclaiming that he would never vote for acquittal. Shouts of abuse and personal hostility were coming from jurors who for hours had said almost nothing. At some point, much earlier, Juror 7 had observed that Juror 6 and I were the most diametrically opposed. I questioned that at the time (and still do) because it seemed to me that the forewoman was at least as firm in her verdict of not guilty as I was. Now, however, there was no doubt that both Juror 6 and I were together in misjudging the mood of the others. His offer to "sleep on it," intended no doubt to reduce the pressure on him and welcomed by me as cause for optimism, had only served to isolate him further from the group. The barrage of arguments and supplications—the same arguments and the same supplications that had been voiced for hours—was now impelled by a renewed rush of anger.

Which only served to stiffen his resistance. Did he immediately regret his vague concession? Perhaps. For when the forewoman, with her own blend of exasperation and studied calm, asked if there was any real possibility that he would ever change his mind, he replied, almost smugly, that it was very remote. And then he added, in a thundering voice, "Only I have to live with my conscience!" The massive egotism here—as if everyone else's conscience were some muddy mess and his were granite—produced another uproar. It was interrupted by a knock on the door and the arrival of the judge's assistant.

He immediately made it clear that Agresta would not accept a "no verdict" decision tonight. If we couldn't come to unanimous agreement soon, we would have to be put up at a hotel to resume deliberations in the morning. What had been the effect, he wanted to know, of the reading of the testimony after dinner? Juror 1 explained that it had changed one vote as we now stood eleven to one. "Well, keep trying," he said as he walked to the door. We had been deliberating for almost nine hours.

Alone again, our mood seemed to change from anger to resignation and disgust. To many, I'm sure, every road seemed blocked and every weapon spent. But the forewoman was determined to try again, and I tried to help her. Between us we reviewed once more all the reasons for our own doubts: the adult descriptions that in no significant way resembled Ricky, Clarissa's remark about the police, the conflicts in time and place, the wild improbabilities, the general sense of untruth that had settled crushingly on the testimony of the three kids. I added a new note, in desperation and regret, for I wanted to persuade Juror 6 by rational arguments and not by group pressure: We were eleven fairly intelligent, fairly perceptive people. Didn't the

fact that we all agreed on not guilty—that we all thought there were grounds for a reasonable doubt—didn't that mean anything to him? I could not hear his reply, for other voices were drowning out mine even before I finished my question. And most powerful among those voices was that of Juror 5. "There is a reasonable doubt!" he cried. The next-to-last holdout had joined the pack and at that moment the pack was immeasurably strengthened.

Was what followed the most sustained barrage of the evening? Had some sort of climax been reached? Yes, the voices were rising again, but were they actually louder and sharper than ever before? Perhaps Juror 6 only thought they were: How much pressure can one man take? Suddenly, he broke.

"All right," he said, almost softly. "I've come to respect all of you too much. I can't do this to you and I won't continue any longer. I change my vote."

Juror 1 started to cry. I felt limp and choked. "Christ almighty, we did it. We did it," I said to myself. But within seconds Juror 6 had leaped to his feet, his eyes blazing, and like a titan of vengeance, tottering and about to collapse, he screamed at us all: *"And how many of you believe with me that we are turning an animal loose on the streets again?"* It seems almost comical now to remember that two or three hands shot up immediately—such a puny gesture in response to such Jehovic wrath. Said Juror 2, "If you add the word 'possibly' . . ." But Juror 6 was not adding anything. He was stumbling away from the table and toward the bathroom, his eyes flooded with tears.

Juror 1 rang the bell and Jack opened the door at once. He smiled when he heard that we had reached a verdict. As he went to report this to the court, we got to our feet. We were exhausted, in every way. Conversation was desultory. In the back of my mind there was a sense of triumph but not of elation, and I felt no comfort at all. Jack returned and had us line up in the hall. We left the jury room at ten forty-five. We had been in there for almost ten hours.

Cleaning men were sweeping the corridors as we waited to file into the courtroom for the last time. While in the past when we crossed to the jury box, I tended to avoid looking at Ricky, his lawyers, and the assistant D.A., now I gazed at them all, and saw nothing.

We stood at our places in the box and enacted the familiar last rite of all the stage, movie, and TV trials I've ever seen. Judge Agresta: "Ladies and gentlemen of the jury, have you reached a verdict?"

Juror 1: "We have, Your Honor."

Clerk of the court: "The defendant will rise and face the jury." (Ricky did, but the defense table was set at an angle to the jury box, and standing in front of his chair he may have faced Jurors 1 and 7, but he didn't face me.) "What is your verdict?"

Juror 1: "We find the defendant not guilty ... on both counts."

[Reflections on Being a Juror]

Q: What happened in the jury room was obviously the high point of the trial for you. How do you see those events now?

A: For me now the deliberations seem to have been a three-act play in which I was a main character; in my own view—though perhaps in no one else's—the hero. In any case, I was certainly subordinate to the heroine, Juror 1. But for sheer theatrical power—the richness of the part— we were both over-shadowed by the antagonist, Juror 6. Juror 5, another colorful, meaty role, was also a major character, and the rest of the jurors ranged from featured to barely supporting.

The play began slowly, with much exposition as the jurors examined and discussed the documentary evidence and then, rather haltingly, almost reluctantly, expressed their views. A few people were tentative, guarded, quite deliberately vague; clearly they hoped to make a stand with the majority, but they did not yet know where that stand would be. The two jurors who favored a "guilty" verdict spoke up late, but with such vehemence that bitter conflict was immediately assured. So ended Act I.

Act II saw the "undecideds" gradually, but not too slowly, join the "not guilty" faction. With the formation of a strong majority, the conflict heightened and complications of plot developed: Juror 5's misinterpretation of the evidence, the return to the courtroom to hear the Clarissa tape, the dinner outing, the second return to the courtroom. The characters grew edgier, emotions gained in intensity and in blunt expression. Finally, a climax was reached, and Act II ended, when Juror 5 surrendered to the majority.

The third act was the briefest and the most dramatic. Throughout the focus remained piercingly on Juror 6. From all sides the pressure on him mounted at an irregular but inexorable pace. The pressure was compounded of anger, frustration, and, for some, even despair—and it was all exerted on that one obdurate but vulnerable character. Until at last he exploded, submitted, collapsed, and resolution achieved, the play was over.

Q: As a vehicle to achieve justice, rather than theater, what do you think of the jury?

A: We were, above all else, a responsible, almost extravagantly serious group. If I may refer to "the play" just once more, it had hardly any comic relief. Right from the start all of us were united in one belief at least—that we had been chosen to perform a formidable, indeed fearful, task, and to it we had to apply whatever wisdom we possess.

We were to decide not merely where and how a seventeen-year-old boy would spend the next five to ten or twenty years, but also whether or not he was to be marked for life as a murderer. The decision each one of us made was determined by much more than what we heard and observed in the courtroom. The influences on that decision included all the values and experiences and hopes and suspicions and ideas and ideologies that we carried into the jury room as unseen baggage. This is of course how juries are intended to work. What Mendelow cited as our "sophistication" he would have been better advised to call our humanity, and it was not only inevitable, it was *proper* that this humanity, with all its strengths and failings, be brought to bear on the matter at hand.

Strengths and failings our jury had in abundance. We were not a highly educated group; I'm sure that fewer than half of us had attended college. But almost all of us had basically sound judgment—common sense, if you will. A good many of us had compassion and even more had patience. A few of us were articulate, a few analytical and highly logical in our thinking. A very few of us were forceful and commanding, perhaps not ordinarily but when the challenge to exhibit those qualities finally arose.

We also had our share of ignorance, selfishness, and extreme egotism. But there is no question that our major failing was prejudice. It infected us *all* to varying degrees, but where it was strongest it became the flint from which the spark of disagreement flew.

Ironically, I think now that where the jury is most to be commended was in the painfully conscious effort nearly all of us made to look beyond our prejudices. When, early in the deliberations, Juror 6 said that he was sorry there were no blacks on the jury, to lend us some insight into how "they" think, he was giving voice to a factual observation that probably disturbed everyone: we were a lily-white group sitting in judgment on a young black man. Ricky says he never worried about this and the outcome of the trial proves that he was right not to be concerned. But I doubt that he fully appreciates *why* he was "safe" with us. One of the prime reasons was a peculiar type of backlash, which was evident in the general reaction to Juror 6's early statement: the multivoiced protests that it did not matter that there were no blacks among us, that we were all capable of viewing and judging the evidence fairly. In other words, we were out to prove that our prejudices could be overcome. And although at times they leaked or burst from our words, prove it we did.

Q: All of you?

A: Ten of us anyway. Obviously the rigid resistance of the two holdouts was occasioned by deep-seated feelings—fear, perhaps hatred—toward blacks. As they eventually admitted, their certainty of Ricky's guilt rested not on any evidence or testimony as such, but on Ricky himself. They had "gut feelings" and they sensed "bad vibes." Juror 6 propounded the theory that the defendant and his three accusers were all "in it"

together—that is, all the blacks involved were guilty. When, time after time, the holdouts' feeble arguments were countered by a rational look at the facts available to us, the two men retreated into the kind of subjectivity—"I just looked at him and could tell he was guilty"—that reason is powerless to attack.

So, no, not all of us rose above our prejudices. Of the two who did not, at least one finally allowed himself to see that blackness was not the only operative factor in the case. The other, Juror 6, remained convinced to the end that Ricky was guilty. Presumably he thinks so even today. When he eventually collapsed, he claimed he was reacting to group pressure, the weight of which he could no longer sustain. It is regrettable, in a way, that we were able to reach our verdict only by resorting to emotional force, regrettable that, apparently, we could not persuade our last holdout to understand the justness of our decision, regrettable that we could not help him recognize the existence of that greater-than-reasonable doubt. But of course, group pressure is also built into the system. And if it must be used, so be it.

Q: You mention the system. On the basis of your service on this jury, what are your thoughts about the jury system in criminal cases?

A: Because in the Mathes trial the state's case was weak and the defense was skillful, it is, I believe, dangerous for me to generalize from this one experience. The challenge we faced was not severe, in spite of our ten hours of deliberation and conflict. If I venture some opinions, it is with a warning that they may not apply to trials in which defense and prosecution are more evenly matched or in which an elusive truth must be found before a verdict can be reached.

Criticism of the jury system usually centers on the folks in the jury box. Said Jerry Paul, attorney for Joan Little, "A jury box is twelve people deciding who has the 'best lawyer.'" Wrote Morton Hunt in *The Mugging,* "[A jury is] a collection of persons of no special training or knowledge, no notable intellectuality, no particular awareness of the problems at issue, no strong ideology, no previous trial experience, and no clear ideas about the causes or control of crime. The principal qualification of the ideal juror is that he be an ignoramus about all the subjects to be discussed in the case at hand, and thoroughly underqualified to make expert judgments about the evidence he will be hearing."

I daresay those are not inaccurate descriptions of juries. Certainly the twelve of us did not comprise any kind of elite. While a few of us read newspapers or even books at almost every opportunity and one of us was a whiz at needlepoint and someone else was a great opera buff and a third person claimed to be an expert on *everything,* we would be more appropriately characterized as "salt of the earth" types than as eggheads hatched in sociology, law, or political science. And we did have a pronounced tendency to make judgments on and comparisons of the defense and prosecuting attorneys. But in having said all this, we have neglected the salient point: The hallmark of the jury system is the ordinariness of the people in the jury box.

As we were constantly reminded during the *voir dire* and the judge's charge to the jury, it was our function to decide on the *facts* of the case, or, to use a grander term, the truth. (As a practical matter, for us this reduced to judging the credibility of the state's star witnesses; that was essentially all we had to do.) We were not to be concerned with the refinements of the law—for example, whether Darrell Mathes should have been indicted on a charge of first- rather than second-degree murder—or the severity of the sentence the defendant faced if he was found guilty. And if the jury's role is restricted to assessing the evidence that has been presented to it—to determining what parts of that evidence are valid and what parts are suspect—then, usually, the need for expertise vanishes and the common sense that I believe distinguished our jury becomes all that matters.

True, the common sense of a jury is not guaranteed. In selecting jury members, prosecution and/or defense may err. Indeed, it is established practice for either side, intent above all else on winning its case, to seek among potential jurors not necessarily those who seem most intelligent, but those who are most likely to hold advantageous prejudices. The adversary nature of the selection process should serve to lessen the possibility of empaneling a jury that is predisposed toward one side or the other. In any case, another factor is at work here: the unpredictability of the human animal.

Who would have guessed that an unemployed middle-aged blue-collar worker, living in a crime-ridden city and enraged by the smart-ass young punks and welfare chiselers who are invading his neighborhood, would decline an opportunity to put a swaggering, hostile black adolescent behind bars for a few years? A juror of ours who meets that description did—and without a moment of hesitation or reluctance. Who would have suspected that a man who, less than twenty-five years ago, fled to freedom from a Communist-controlled Eastern European country would have fully embraced the bigotry inherent in the equation black equals guilt? That describes one of our worthies too. Who would have imagined that a pleasant, demure, pretty young speech therapist would assume control of a group of eleven people, all older than she—some considerably so—and guide them to her goal with such wit, subtlety, charm, and power that at times she seemed a veritable Joan of Arc? Our forewoman takes those honors.

So jurors may surprise you. Of course, no one, in or out of a jury room, is capable of complete reversal of his or her nature. In the deepest sense, the words and actions of all twelve of us were totally compatible with the ideas and personalities we brought to the trial. But it was not in the deepest sense—on the contrary, it was only in the most superficial sense—that the attorneys could even hope to know us.

Beyond unpredictability is the capacity to rise to a challenge. Serving on the jury was exactly that to each of us; we all recognized that more was being demanded of us—in the way of wisdom, if nothing else—than had often—perhaps ever—been demanded of us before. Some of us were almost embarrassed to be in the position we were. Some of us, when the deliberations grew fierce, were afraid. As we had been warned repeatedly during the *voir dire,* this was not Perry Mason stuff. Anyone who might have waited for the real murderer of Edward Fendt to be suddenly and dramatically exposed would have waited in vain. But we were too serious, too dedicated, even to entertain such thoughts. There was never a time during the deliberations when we lost sight of the reality that confronted us. And for me there was never a time when I doubted that all of us—the holdouts included—were trying to deal with that reality as responsibly as our intelligence and our human understanding allowed.

To paraphrase Bernard Shaw's Eliza Doolittle, the difference between an ordinary man and a juror is not how he behaves, but how he's regarded. This, it seems to me, is the key to the success of the jury system in criminal trials. If a person, whatever his background, knows that much is expected of him—no less than helping to determine the course of someone else's life—in all probability that person will strive with all his capability to be wise and just and compassionate, to stretch himself beyond his foibles and his prejudices. One thing you can be sure of: he will not forget that the stakes are high.

Questions

1. Judge Frank is concerned about the process of jury deliberations and whether the verdicts arrived at by this process are, among other things, accurate. Is accuracy the same as justice? Compare Frank's attitude with that of the court in *Duncan* v. *Louisiana* when it stated that one purpose of the jury was to be sure that "If the defendant preferred the common-sense judgment of a jury to the more tutored but perhaps less sympathetic reaction of the single judge, he was to have it."

2. Zerman's article gives an image of what a jury deliberation would be like and what skills and attitudes the jurors bring to the jury room. Does Frank's argument undermine the image created by Zerman?

3. Frank in using the imaginary formula $R \times F = D$ says that he could hardly imagine a better instrument than the jury for "achieving uncertainty, capriciousness, lack of uniformity, disregard of the R's, and unpredictability of decisions." What reply to this might Zerman make? How do the two men differ in their images of the decision-making process appropriate to law? Which image would make the jury trial more acceptable as an institution if that image were held by the general public?

B. Elimination of the Jury

The following excerpt from *The Transformation of American Law* gives a brief sketch of how the professional bar, the judges, and certain commercial interests united in the early 1800s to erode the power of juries. Each of these parties seems to have had its own independent reason for forming a coalition with the others; none described its purpose as the erosion of a jury system recently written into the Bill of Rights to secure the ratification of the Constitution. That the real effect and ideological basis of these changes remained obscure from public view at the time suggests that other proposed changes in legal structure and jury function ought to be more closely scrutinized by the public to determine whose interests such reforms actually will serve. Although it is brief, this section from Professor Horwitz's book provides a revealing look at the manipulation of legal institutions and rules by those seeking to consolidate their power. Moreover, it suggests that legal institutions conceived or described as a bulwark against oppression may be eroded without the consent or even the knowledge of those they are meant to protect.

Excerpt from *The Transformation of American Law*   *Morton Horwitz*

It should have come as no surprise that in most cases "merchants were not fond of juries." For one of the leading measures of the growing alliance between bench and bar on the one hand and commercial interests on the other is the swiftness with which the power of the jury is curtailed after 1790.

Three parallel procedural devices were used to restrict the scope of juries. First, during the last years of the eighteenth century American lawyers vastly expanded the "special case" or "case reserved," a device designed to submit points of law to the judges while avoiding the effective intervention of a jury.

A second crucial procedural change—the award of a new trial for verdicts "contrary to the weight of the evidence"—triumphed with spectacular rapidity in some American courts at the turn of the century. The award of new trials for any reason had been regarded with profound suspicion by the revolutionary generation. "The practice of granting new trials," a Virginia judge noted in 1786, "was not a favourite with the courts of England" until the elevation to the bench of Lord Mansfield, "whose habit of controlling juries does not accord with the free institutions of this country, and ought not to be adopted for slight causes." Yet, not only had the new trial become a standard weapon in the judicial arsenal by the first decade of the nineteenth century; it was also expanded to allow reversal of jury verdicts contrary to the weight of the evidence, despite the protest that "not one instance . . . is to be met with" where courts had previously reevaluated a

From Morton Horwitz, *The Transformation of American Law* (Cambridge, Mass.: Harvard University Press, 1977), pp. 84–85, 141–143, 154–155. Copyright © 1977 by the President and Fellows of Harvard College. (Abridged.)

jury's assessment of conflicting testimony. In both New York and South Carolina this abrupt change of policy was first adopted in order to overturn jury verdicts against marine insurers. In Pennsylvania too the earliest grant of a new trial on the weight of evidence occurs in a commercial case.

These two important restrictions on the power of juries were part of a third more fundamental procedural change that began to be asserted at the turn of the century. The view that even in civil cases "the jury [are] the proper judges not only of the fact but of the law that [is] necessarily involved" was widely held even by conservative jurists at the end of the eighteenth century. "The jury may in all cases, where law and fact are blended together, take upon themselves the knowledge of the law . . . ," William Wyche wrote in his 1794 treatise on New York practice.

During the first decade of the nineteenth century, however, the Bar rapidly promoted the view that there existed a sharp distinction between law and fact and a correspondingly clear separation of function between judge and jury. For example, until 1807 the practice of Connecticut judges was simply to submit both law and facts to the jury, without expressing any opinion or giving them any direction on how to find their verdict. In that year, the Supreme Court of Errors enacted a rule requiring the presiding trial judge, in charging the jury, to give his opinion on every point of law involved. This institutional change ripened quickly into an elaborate procedural system for control of juries.

By 1810, it was clear that the instructions of the court, originally advisory, had become mandatory and therefore juries no longer possessed the power to determine the law. Courts and litigants quickly perceived the transformation that had occurred and soon began to articulate a new principle—that "point[s] of law ... should ... be ... decided by the Court," while points of fact ought to be decided by the jury.

These procedural changes made possible a vast ideological transformation in the attitude of American jurists toward commercial law. The subjugation of juries was necessary not only to control particular verdicts but also to develop a uniform and predictable body of judge-made commercial rules.

Thus, it appears that several major changes in the attitude of judges and merchants toward commercial arbitration had begun to emerge at the beginning of the nineteenth century. First, an increasingly organized and self-conscious legal profession had become determined to oppose the antilegalism among merchants which, during the colonial period, had taken the form of resort to extralegal settlement of disputes. Second, the mercantile classes, which had found the colonial legal rules hostile to their interest began, at the end of the eighteenth century, to find that common law judges themselves were prepared to overturn anticommercial legal conceptions. Third, the development of a split in the commercial interest, first manifested in the field of marine insurance, converted a largely self-regulating merchant group into one that was made dependent on formal legal machinery. Thus, one might loosely describe the process as one of accommodation by which merchants were induced to submit to formal legal regulation in return for a major transformation of substantive legal rules governing commercial disputes. The judges' unwillingness any longer to recognize competing lawmakers is a product of an increasingly instrumental vision of law. Law is no longer merely an agency for resolving disputes; it is an active, dynamic means of social control and change. Under such conditions, there must be one undisputed and authoritative source of rules for regulating commercial life. Both the hostility of judges to arbitration and the willingness of merchants to forgo extrajudicial settlement spring from a common source: the increasingly active and solicitous attitude of courts to commercial interests. . . .

Standing beside the numerous changes in legal conceptions was an important institutional innovation that began to appear after 1830—an increasing tendency of state legislatures to eliminate the role of the jury in assessing damages for the taking of land. It was long a commonplace that juries increased the size of damage judgments. Although there were other early instances in which legislatures eliminated the jury's role in assessing damages, it was only in connection with the building of railroads that this movement gained real force. Between 1830 and 1837 such statutes in New Jersey, New York, Ohio, and North Carolina were upheld over the objection that they violated constitutional provisions guaranteeing trial by jury. The result was that railroad companies were often allowed to take land while providing little or no compensation.

Question

1. Professor Horwitz's analysis of the whittling away of jury functions in early American law suggests that the merchants' economic interests combined with the judiciary's desire for exclusive control over dispute resolution to reduce popular influence on law. Almost two hundred years later a further whittling away of the role of the jury seems to be taking place, again with the sanction of the judiciary. Can you suggest an analysis of what interests are at work at present in reducing jury influence? What difference do you perceive between the stated ideology of these changes (for example, efficiency) and the real interests being served by these changes?

Note on the Use of Expert Testimony in Jury Trials

One of the seemingly inevitable results of technological progress has been the use of expert testimony in court trials. This testimony may be occasioned by the development of sophisticated techniques of identification—such as fingerprinting, blood tests, ballistics, or voice prints. In such case the jury may be confronted with competing expert opinions about the meaning of physical data or it may be invited to accept such expertise without understanding its basis or being able to question its validity.

On other occasions expert testimony may be required because of the complex technical basis of a dispute. A medical malpractice suit may involve comparing the defendant's medical techniques with accepted or normal medical practice. A suit against an auto mechanic may involve expertise in standards for tuning fuel-injected cars. A suit against the manufacturer of medicines or vitamins may involve endless issues of testing and marketing pharmacological products. In such trials it is commonplace for all participants to wonder about the ability and effectiveness of jurors in evaluating expertise as compared to feeling sympathy or anger about the parties or their attorneys.

Perhaps the most arcane area of expert testimony concerns psychiatric evaluations of defendants charged with crimes or subject to civil commitment for mental illness and dangerousness. Consider the following testimony by a psychiatrist explaining "passive-aggressive" personality to a jury in the case of *Washington* v. *U.S.,* as

a type of personality that an individual has, that is, everybody has some type of personality. We all have a type of personality. I

mean no one has no personality. We have some type. Well, you may say schizoid personality, or compulsive personality, but speaking of the one that you ask, such [as] the passive aggressive personality, these are broken down into two different categories.

One is passive and one is aggressive. Usually in these people the aggressive type acts out in an aggressive manner, to either major or minor stressful situations, they maneuver under close confinement or under strict rules and regulations except maneuvering into a psychosis.

It is generally considered that the passive type or the aggressive type frequently or sometimes an aggressive personality will also behave in a passive manner.

This is where we get the term "passive-aggressive." This is more a classification of the type of personality that the individual has....

...Everybody has a type of personality. I mean, you have to be categorized somewhere.

Although the use of expert witnesses is expensive, with some experts receiving $250. to $1,000. a day for their testimony, it is increasing. Organizations have arisen to advise attorneys about which experts they need and to arrange for the provision of such expertise. Some professionals make their livings almost completely by testifying in trials; they have become professional witnesses. In many cases the use of expert testimony can perhaps not be avoided; but in others it may be that areas of "expertise" are almost literally fabricated to weaken the ability of lay jurors to influence or even understand the issues before them. In a footnote to the *Washington* case referred to above, Judge Bazelon observes such an effect from the use of psychiatric nomenclature in criminal trials:

> An alternative to *Durham-McDonald* would be to make the ultimate test whether or not it is just to blame the defendant for his act. If the question were simply whether it is "just" to "blame" the defendant, then mental illness, productivity, ability to control oneself, etc., might be factors which the jury could consider in reaching its conclusion on the justness of punishment. Since the words "just" and "blame" do not lend themselves to refined definition, the charge to the jury under this test probably would not be detailed. But the words that have been used in other charges, such as "defect of reason," "disease of the mind," "nature and quality of the act," "behavior controls," "mental disease or defect," "capacity . . . to appreciate the criminality of his conduct," and "capacity to conform his conduct to the requirements of law," are also vague—the chief difference being that these words give a fake impression of scientific exactness, an impression which may lead the jury to ignore its own moral judgment and defer to the moral judgment of scientific "experts."

Would this suggestion make the evaluation of expert testimony easier for the jury in criminal cases? Does this suggestion in any way contradict the nature of "law" or the function of the jury in our legal system?

In a later footnote the *Washington* court compares the use of legally significant labels in criminal and civil cases:

> The phrase "mental disease or defect" has been criticized for not giving enough guidance to the jury. In this regard the phrase is similar to other conclusory labels in the law. For example, "negligence" is a vague label given content primarily by the conclusions for which it stands. A person is "negligent" if he is at "fault" (blameworthy?), or if he has not exercised "due care," or if he has not met some standard of reasonable conduct. We are comfortable with a concept like negligence because we understand that it is a conclusion based on other considerations. Similarly, we can accept the term "mental disease or defect" if we understand what it represents.

In referring to the "other considerations" that underlie legal labels, the court says labels can be accepted because we understand what they represent. Is this equally true of the labels "negligent" and "mental disease or defect"? If these labels can not be equally well understood, does this fact suggest that the labels used in insanity determinations should be changed so the jurors can make judgments more easily, that specially qualified jurors should be used, that expert testimony should be more tightly controlled, or that there should be no jury trials in such cases?

These are some of the issues involved in the growing use of expert testimony in jury trials. Beneath the surface lies the problem of using legal labels and other tools of mystification in law with the result that the entire process may become more and more alien to the layperson while arguments against public participation in law—arguments for the abolition of the jury—seem thereby to gain in strength.

In spite of the dwindling percentage of cases that actually result in jury trials, many critics are disturbed by the amount of time taken by impanelling the jury and by the jury deliberation itself. Crowded court dockets have lent a greater urgency to these criticisms and prompted some states to reduce the size of juries in order to reduce the time they take in being chosen and in deliberating. This action raises a number of thorny questions about the dynamics of jury deliberation, the representative character of juries, and the constitutional role of juries in the American legal system, as the following materials on jury reform and abolition illustrate.

Williams v. Florida   *399 U.S. 78 (1970)*

Mr. Justice White delivered the opinion of the Court.

Prior to his trial for robbery in the State of Florida, petitioner ... filed a pretrial motion to impanel a 12-man jury instead of the six-man jury provided by Florida law in all but capital cases. That motion was denied. Petitioner was convicted as charged and was sentenced to life imprisonment.... The question in this case then is whether the constitutional guarantee of a trial by "jury" necessarily requires trial by exactly 12 persons, rather than some lesser number—in this case six. We hold that the 12-man panel is not a necessary ingredient of "trial by jury," and that respondent's refusal to impanel more than the six members provided for by Florida law did not violate petitioner's Sixth Amendment rights as applied to the States through the Fourteenth....

The purpose of the jury trial, as we noted in *Duncan,* is to prevent oppression by the Government.... Given this purpose, the essential feature of a jury obviously lies in the interposition between the accused and his accuser of the commonsense judgment of a group of laymen, and in the community participation and shared responsibility that results from that group's determination of guilt or innocence. The performance of this role is not a function of the particular number of the body that makes up the jury. To be sure, the number should probably be large enough to promote group deliberation, free from outside attempts at intimidation, and to provide a fair possibility for obtaining a representative cross-section of the community. But we find little reason to think that these goals are in any meaningful sense less likely to be achieved when the jury numbers six, than when it numbers 12—particularly if the requirement of unanimity is retained. And, certainly the reliability of the jury as a fact-finder hardly seems likely to be a function of its size.

...Neither currently available evidence nor theory suggest that the 12-man jury is necessarily more advantageous to the defendant than a jury composed of fewer members.

Similarly, while in theory the number of viewpoints represented on a randomly selected jury ought to increase as the size of the jury increases, in practice the difference between the 12-man and the six-man jury in terms of the cross-section of the community represented seems likely to be negligible.

(Some footnotes and cases omitted.)

Johnson v. Louisiana   *92 S.Ct. 1620 (1972)*

Mr. Justice White delivered the opinion of the Court.

Under both the Louisiana Constitution and Code of Criminal Procedure, criminal cases in which the punishment is necessarily at hard labor are tried to a jury of 12, and the vote of nine jurors is sufficient to return either a guilty or not guilty verdict. The principal question in this case is whether these provisions allowing less than unanimous verdicts in certain cases are valid under the Due Process and Equal Protection Clauses of the Fourteenth Amendment.

I

Appellant Johnson was arrested at his home on January 20, 1968.... Johnson pleaded not guilty, was tried on May 14, 1968, by a 12-man jury and was convicted by a nine-to-three verdict....

II

Apellant argues that in order to give substance to the reasonable doubt standard which the State, by virtue of the Due Process Clause of the Fourteenth Amendment, must satisfy in criminal cases, that clause must be construed to require a unanimous jury verdict in all criminal cases.... Concededly, the jurors were told to convict only if convinced of guilt beyond a reasonable doubt. Nor is there any claim that, if the verdict in this case had been unanimous, the evidence would have been insufficient to support it. Appellant focuses instead on the fact that less than all jurors voted to convict and argues that, because three voted to acquit, the reasonable doubt standard has not been satisfied and his conviction is therefore infirm.

We note at the outset that this Court has never held jury unanimity to be a requisite of due process of law.... We can find no basis for holding that the nine jurors who voted for his conviction failed to follow their instructions concerning the need for proof beyond such a doubt or that the vote of any one of the nine failed to reflect an honest belief that guilt had been so proved....

We have no grounds for believing that majority jurors, aware of their responsibility and power over the liberty of the defendant, would simply refuse to listen to arguments presented to them in favor of acquittal, terminate discussion and render a verdict. On the contrary it is far more likely that a juror presenting reasoned argument in favor of acquittal would either have his arguments answered or would carry enough other jurors with him to prevent conviction. A majority will cease discussion and outvote a minority only after reasoned discussion has ceased to have per-

suasive effect or to serve any other purpose—when a minority, that is, continues to insist upon acquittal without having persuasive reasons in support of its position....

We conclude, therefore, that, as to the nine jurors who voted to convict, the State satisfied its burden of proving guilt beyond any reasonable doubt....

That rational men disagree is not in itself equivalent to a failure of proof by the State, nor does it indicate infidelity to the reasonable doubt standard....

In order to "facilitate, expedite, and reduce expense in the administration of justice," *State* v. *Lewis,* 129 La. 800, 804, 56 So. 893, 894 (1911), Louisiana has permitted less serious crimes to be tried by five jurors with unanimous verdicts, more serious crimes have required the assent of nine of 12 jurors, and for the most serious crimes a unanimous verdict of 12 jurors is stipulated. In appellant's case, nine jurors rather than five or 12 were required for a verdict. We discern nothing invidious in this classification....

[He] is simply challenging the judgment of the Louisiana Legislature. That body obviously intended to vary the difficulty of proving guilt with the gravity of the offense and the severity of the punishment. We remain unconvinced by anything appellant has presented that this legislative judgment was defective in any constitutional sense.

The judgment of the Supreme Court of Louisiana is therefore

Affirmed.

Mr. Justice Stewart, with whom Mr. Justice Brennan and Mr. Justice Marshall join, dissenting.

The guarantee against systematic discrimination in the selection of criminal court juries is a fundamental of the Fourteenth Amendment....

The clear purpose of these decisions has been to ensure universal participation of the citizenry in the administration of criminal justice. Yet today's judgment approves the elimination of the one rule that can ensure that such participation will be meaningful—the rule requiring the assent of all jurors before a verdict of conviction or acquittal can be returned. Under today's judgment, nine jurors can simply ignore the views of their fellow panel members of a different race or class. ...For only a unanimous jury so selected can serve to minimize the potential bigotry of those who might convict on inadequate evidence, or acquit when evidence of guilt was clear....

The requirement that the verdict of the jury be unanimous, surely as important as these other constitutional requisites, preserves the jury's function in linking law with contemporary society. It provides the simple and effective method endorsed by centuries of experience and history to combat the injuries to the fair administration of justice that can be inflicted by community passion and prejudice.

I dissent.

Apodaca et al. v. Oregon   *92 S.Ct. 1628 (1972)*

[In *Apodaca* the court upheld Oregon's jury statute allowing a conviction in a felony case by a jury voting 10–2. The court refuted the claim that minority groups would be excluded from influencing verdicts when unanimity was not required.]

We also cannot accept petitioners' second assumption—that minority groups, even when they are represented on a jury, will not adequately represent the viewpoint of those groups simply because they may be outvoted in the final result. They will be present during all deliberations, and their views will be heard. We cannot assume that the majority of the jury will refuse to weigh the evidence and reach a decision upon rational grounds, just as it must now do in order to obtain unanimous verdicts, or that a majority will deprive a man of his liberty on the basis of prejudice when a minority is presenting a reasonable argument in favor of acquittal. We simply find no proof for the notion that a majority will disregard its instructions and cast its votes for guilt or innocence based on prejudice rather than the evidence.

We accordingly affirm the judgment of the Court of Appeals of Oregon.

It is so ordered.

[Mr. Justice Douglas, in a dissent, found faults in the majority's view of jury deliberations.] ...

The dimunition of verdict reliability flows from the fact that nonunanimous juries need not debate and deliberate as fully as must unanimous juries.

As soon as the requisite majority is attained, further consideration is not required either by Oregon or by Louisiana even though the dissident jurors might, if given the chance, be able to convince the majority. Such persuasion does in fact occasionally occur in States where the unanimous requirement applies: "In roughly one case in ten, the minority eventually succeeds in reversing an initial majority, and these may be cases of special importance." [1] ...

It is said that there is no evidence that majority jurors will refuse to listen to dissenters whose votes are unneeded for conviction. Yet human experience teaches that polite and academic conversation is no substitute for the earnest and robust argument necessary to reach unanimity. As mentioned earlier, in Apodaca's case, whatever courtesy dialogue transpired could not have lasted more than 41 minutes. I fail to understand why the Court should lift from the States the burden of justifying so radical a departure from an accepted and applauded tradition and instead demand that these defendants document with empirical evidence what has always been thought to be too obvious for further study.

Questions

1. Does the court in the *Johnson* case equate having a "reasonable doubt" about guilt with "having persuasive reasons" in support of innocence?

[1] Kalven and Zeisel, The American Jury 490 (1966). See also The American Jury: Notes For an English Controversy, 48 Chi. Bar Rec. 195 (1967).

2. Does the *Johnson* court reconcile its admission that the Louisiana legislature "obviously intended to vary the difficulty of proving guilt with the gravity of the offense" with its conclusion that the state's jury law does not "indicate infidelity to the reasonable doubt standard"?

3. In his dissent in *Apodaca,* Mr. Justice Douglas wrote:

> The late Learned Hand said that "as a litigant I should dread a lawsuit beyond almost anything else short of sickness and death." At

the criminal level that dread multiplies. Any person faced with the awesome power of government is in great jeopardy, even though innocent. Facts are always elusive and often two-faced. What may appear to one to imply guilt may carry no such overtones to another. Every criminal prosecution crosses treacherous ground, for guilt is common to all men.

What significance does this statement have to the question of whether less than unanimous verdicts are constitutionally acceptable?

The Waning of the American Jury   *Hans Zeisel*

People See and Evaluate Things Differently

The jury system is predicated on the insight that people see and evaluate things differently. It is one function of the jury to bring these divergent perceptions and evaluations to the trial process. If all people weighed trial evidence in the same manner, a jury of one would be as good as a jury of twelve because there would never be any disagreement among them. In fact, we know the opposite to be true, if not from observation of our community then from the performance of our juries. Two thirds of all juries find their vote split at the first ballot in a criminal case.

There is, therefore, good reason to believe that the jury, to some extent, brings into the courtroom the differences in perception that exist in the community.

It should not be difficult to see that however well or poorly twelve people may represent a widely stratified community, a six-member jury must do less well. In fact, we can measure the degree of this poorer representation with some precision. Suppose we state the question this way: assume that there is a significant minority in the community, amounting to, say, 10 per cent of the population. The minority need not be a demographic one; it may represent any minority view-

point, although the obvious concern is for representation of demographically defined minorities. Assume then that our juries are drawn at random from the eligible population. How often will a representative of that minority be on a twelve-member and how often on a six-member jury, both drawn from the same population? The answer is that, on the average, seventy-two of every one hundred twelve-member juries, but only forty-seven of every one hundred six-member juries will have at least one minority representative.

One may argue, and I would, that we should not confront each other as majority and minority. But at this juncture of history, it is apparently not the accepted view to disregard such differences. And to force on the jury a view that is not accepted in other spheres would seem to be a rash move.

A somewhat different model will help us to appraise the effect of the six-member jury in civil cases. We know from experience and from many careful studies that the values different people place on the harm done in a personal injury case are likely to diverge considerably.

The final award of a jury is very much related to these initial individual evaluations; in the end it is some kind of average. The size of the jury, therefore, matters a great deal in the determination of these awards. It can be shown that reducing the jury from twelve to six increases what one might call the "gamble" the litigants take by about 40 per cent. The term is not found in the

From Hans Zeisel, "The Waning of the American Jury" in the *American Bar Association Journal,* Vol. 58, April 1972, pp. 367–370. Copyright 1972 American Bar Association. Reprinted by permission. (Abridged.)

law, but it describes a very real phenomenon—the fact that not all juries will decide a given case alike, while the litigants can have only one of these many possible jury trials. The extent of the "gamble" is easily established by asking any lawyer about to try a personal injury case two questions. What do you think will be the most likely verdict in this case? If you had to try this same case before ten different juries, what do you think their verdicts would look like? The second question will, as a rule, produce a very wide range, often from zero-verdicts (for the defendant) to considerable awards for the plaintiff. Well-established statistical analysis shows that this dispersion of verdicts for six-member juries will be about 40 per cent greater than for the twelve-member juries, hardly an "insignificant difference," as the Court called it. This is best understood by seeing the jury as a "sample" from the pool of all eligible jurors. As Gallup poll watchers, we know by now that the smaller the sample the greater the "sampling error," that is, the dispersion about the mean.

Number of Hung Juries May Be Reduced

In addition to being less representative and increasing the "gamble," smaller juries are also likely to reduce the number of hung juries. The hung jury is an expression of respect for a strongly held dissenting view; it is one of the many noble features of our jury system. And since, on the average, not more than 5 per cent of all trials end that way, it is a tolerable burden. Efficiency experts might welcome a still smaller percentage, but those concerned with the justice of our system should be wary.

The Court in *Williams* suggested that one juror against five is not worse off than two against ten, since it is the proportion that matters, not the absolute size. In support, the Court cited *The American Jury*—but in error. There on page 463 my coauthor and I said the exact opposite—that it is not the proportions that matter but the numbers: "[For a juror] to maintain his original position [of dissent] . . . it is necessary for him to have at least one ally."

There was a quick way of testing whether the

Court or we are correct. I obtained a special count from the Miami circuit court of the proportion of hung juries among its felony trials before six-member juries. As expected, the proportion was 2.5 per cent, exactly one half of the 5 per cent of hung juries obtained in regular twelve-member jury trials.

But after *Williams* and the diminution of the federal jury, an even more serious potential blow is now before the Court: the issue as to whether unanimity is essential in verdicts of criminal juries. The Court has noted probable jurisdiction (400 U.S. 900) in *Johnson* v. *Louisiana,* 230 So. 2d 825 (1970), and granted certiorari (400 U.S. 901) in *Apodaca* v. *Oregon,* 462 P. 2d 691 (1969), which involve the two states that allow majority verdicts in felony jury trials.

Offhand, the unanimity requirement appears to be just another way of reducing the size of the jury; allowing ten out of twelve jurors to find a verdict would seem to be tantamount to a ten-member jury. But it is much worse. Once one sees the problem with precision, the answer is quite clear. In a twelve-member jury, in which ten are allowed to find a verdict, one or two minority dissenters can simply be disregarded. It requires a minority of at least three before the majority is forced to take note of them. In a ten-man jury that must find unanimity, even a single minority dissenter must be taken into account.

One must ask—for example, with respect to a 10 per cent minority in the population—what is the probability that there will be at least three on a twelve-member jury and at least one on a ten-member jury? The answer is that the probability of at least one minority member on a jury of ten is 65 per cent, and the probability of at least three minority members on a jury of twelve is 11 per cent.

The majority rule, aside from reducing the number of hung juries, should result in more convictions. To obtain a conviction under the unanimity rule, the prosecutor must convince the last doubting juror of the defendant's guilt. We know individual jurors differ with respect to what they consider "proof beyond reasonable doubt." Some require more proof than others, and the two jurors who require most cease to count under a rule that allows ten jurors to find a verdict. During the American Bar Association meeting in London in the summer of 1971, *The New York Times* reported: "For several years British courts have been permitting jury actions on votes of ten to two, and statistics show that there have been more convictions, fewer acquittals and fewer hung juries than before."

In one remote corner of our law, we already have the powerful combination of both these features: juries of fewer than twelve members that can decide with majority vote. Under military law, a court-martial jury need consist of not more than five members, two thirds of whom can find a verdict. Lieutenant Calley and Colonel Henderson were tried before this kind of jury.

In our general jurisdiction, we are yet one step removed from this possibility, but it should give us pause. A six-member jury in which five jurors can find a verdict may still be a jury in name, but in fact it would be an institution very different from the twelve-member unanimous jury.

The Chief Justice, in his other capacity as presiding officer of the Judicial Conference, was quick to apply *Williams*. By now at least nineteen of the federal district courts have reduced the size of their civil juries from twelve to six in civil cases, and the Northern District of Illinois is experimenting with six-member juries in criminal cases, albeit with consent of both sides.

One wonders what is behind this new zeal for cutting into the jury. The ostensible argument is reducing costs and delay. But the money saved by having six-member civil juries in the federal court amounts to about 2.5 per cent of the federal judicial budget and to a little more than a thousandth part of 1 per cent of the total federal budget. As to the time likely to be saved, the best estimate is three tenths of 1 per cent of the judge's working time. There is obviously more to this concerted drive at this point of time.

Unconsciously, perhaps, the motives are likely to be similar to those that went into the rewriting of the military code of procedure; not only more efficiency, but also less tolerance toward a dissenting minority. At present only about 10 per cent of the defendants prosecuted for a felony are acquitted; 90 per cent either plead guilty or are found guilty after trial. Is this too small a percentage? Will the country be safer if it is 91 per cent or 92? One wonders.

By reducing the chances of effective dissent from what the judge would do, we are attacking the jury itself. If we continue to reduce the power of the jury as it stood at common law, we may soon confront the question as to why a jury at all, or why so much of it. Not that this is an improper question. Most countries never had juries, and many of those that had them do not have them any longer. To be sure, also their mode of selecting judges differs radically from ours.

My purpose is not to advocate or oppose any particular solution. It is merely to make clear that the changes imposed on our jury system are more serious than we are led to believe. They are effected, moreover, by the unobtrusive means of rule of court, instead of by the overt acts of the Congress or the state legislatures, which on second thought might consider these changes or their prevention to be their prerogative.

4 Jury Selection

The jury, either in response to a judge's specific instructions or because its verdict cannot be challenged except in rare circumstances, can inject current community standards into specific legal proceedings. But trial by current community standards may inject a political flavor into a trial.

This political nature of the jury's function is most acute in criminal trials, for as Tocqueville observed, "he who punishes the criminal is the real master of society." Political trials in the United States have included everything from attacks on labor organizers like Eugene Debs to the trials of the Chicago Seven, Daniel Ellsberg, Sacco and Vanzetti, and the Haymarket "rioters." All of these shared the characteristic of involving government prosecution of issues which were so inflammatory that juries might be swayed more by political beliefs and emotions than by facts related to defined crimes. Sacco-Vanzetti was an armed robbery prosecution, but the popular hostility to these two "anarchists" made the conviction really a statement of current political hysteria in the 1920s. In the famous trial of Peter Zenger in 1763, on the other hand, it was the jury which turned back the English Crown's attempt to silence a dissenting newspaper publisher. They refused to convict Zenger because the political motives of the prosecution were clear and unacceptable. The attempt to jail Angela Davis also failed.

In most of these trials the government insists that the proceedings and issues are conventional, but public reactions and trial tran-
scripts indicate that very broad political issues are at stake. Political trials have also been defined as ones in which there is a conflict between basic values of two subcultures in the society. Here the jury's role is even more critical, for a supposedly neutral law has become the vehicle for allowing a majority to impose its views upon the basic values or lifestyles of a minority. In a case involving a GI-run coffee house in South Carolina two GI's who were accused of creating a nuisance received six-year sentences. The case was a battle in a war of two life-styles.

The attempt to use jury trials for political purposes may, therefore, wind up with either the protection or the suppression of minority viewpoints or lifestyles. It is upon the composition of the jury, in part, which the results turn.

When lawyers or their clients participate in picking a jury for a particular case, what are they looking for? What tools does the legal system make available or permit in securing fair juries?

Science: Threatening the Jury *Amitai Etzioni*

Man has taken a new bite from the apple of knowledge, and it is doubtful whether we will be better for it. This time it is not religion or the family that are being disturbed by the new knowledge but that venerable institution of being judged by a jury of one's peers. The jury's impartiality is threatened because defense attorneys have discovered that by using social science techniques, they can manipulate the composition of juries to significantly increase the likelihood that their clients will be acquitted.

From *The Washington Post,* May 26, 1974, p. C-3. © The Washington Post. Reprinted by permission. The writer is a professor of sociology at Columbia University and director of the Center for Policy Research.

The problem is not that one may disagree with a particular jury verdict that has resulted in such cases; enough different defendants have been freed with the help of social science jury-stacking to disturb observers on all sides. The trouble is that the technique raises serious doubts about the very integrity of the jury system, that it increases the advantage of rich and prominent defendants over poor and obscure ones and, most ominously, that it may prompt the state to start hiring social scientists of its own. It would seem only a matter of time before prosecutors, with all the resources at their disposal, get fed up with losing cases partly because the defense has scientifically loaded panels with sympathetic jurors.

Prosecutors have already had to swallow a number of such defeats. A team headed by sociologist Jay Schulman and psychologist Richard Christie, for example, took an active role in selecting juries which discharged radical defendants in the Harrisburg Seven case, the Camden 28 trial over a draft-office raid, and the Gainesville Eight case involving Vietnam Veterans Against the War; Schulman is now working in Buffalo, N.Y., for the Attica defendants. A team of black psychologists, moreover, helped choose the jury that acquitted Angela Davis, and nothing of late has done more to publicize scientific intervention in jury selection than the Mitchell-Stans trial in New York.

In that case, helping to choose the jury was Marty Herbst, a "communication" specialist versed in social science techniques. He advised the defense to seek a jury of working-class persons of Catholic background, neither poor nor rich ("average income of $8,000 to $10,000"), and readers of New York's *Daily News*. To be avoided were the college educated, Jews, and readers of the *New York Post* and *The New York Times*. These sociological characteristics are widely associated with conservative politics, respect for authority and suspicion of the media.

In the original jury, the defense succeeded in getting 11 out of 12 jurors who matched the specifications. By a fluke, the 12th juror became ill and was replaced by another who, though college educated, was a conservative banker, thus completing the set.

Interviewing Acquaintances

The more elaborate ways in which social science can help select acquittal-prone juries are illustrated by the Schulman-Christie team's work in the trial of Indian militants at Wounded Knee.

As described in a May, 1973 report, the team first assembled a sociological profile of the community through interviews with 576 persons chosen at random from voter registration lists. The interviews allowed the research team to cross-tabulate such characteristics as occupation and education with attitudes favorable toward the defense—especially toward Indians—and to select

out the best "predictor variables." Such analysis was needed because people of the same social background hold different attitudes in different parts of the country; hence a generalized sociological model would not suffice. (In Harrisburg, where the Berrigan trial was held, for example, women proved more friendly toward the defense than men, but the reverse was true in Gainesville.)

Next, observers were placed in the courtroom to "psych out" prospective jurors, using anything from the extent to which they talked with other prospective jurors to their mode of dress. (In the Angela Davis case, handwriting experts analyzed the signatures of prospective jurors.)

Information gained in this way was compared to what the computer predicted about the same "type" of person, based on the interview data which had been fed into it. This double reading was further checked, especially when the two sources of information did not concur, by field investigators who interviewed acquaintances of the prospective jurors.

How Many Challenges?

Such information becomes more potent in the hands of defense lawyers the more challenges there are and the more unevenly the challenges are distributed. The number is important because the more persons one can challenge, the more one can select a jury to one's liking. The unevenness is important to prevent the other side from applying the same procedures and nullifying one's work.

The number of challenges varies with the seriousness of the offense and from state to state. A common pattern is that if the prospective penalty is death, each side receives 30 challenges, plus 3 for each of four alternate jurors. If 10 years' imprisonment is at stake, the respective numbers are 20 and 2, and so on down the scale. The original intention was to allow the fairest selections in the weightiest cases. But with the introduction of social science into jury picking, the unwitting result is that the more serious the trial, the more jury-stacking is allowed.

Similarly, uneven challenges are introduced, at

the judge's discretion, to make up for other imbalances. While a judge can severely limit the challenges on both sides to avoid a long jury selection process, this significantly increases the chances of having any convictions that might result overturned by a higher court on the ground of a biased jury—and reversals are considered a blot on a judge's record. In the Mitchell-Stans case, the judge allowed the defense 20 peremptory challenges, the prosecution 8, to make up for adverse publicity preceding the trial. This obviously helped the defense lawyers secure the kind of jury they favored.

Social scientists, of course, did not invent the idea of using challenges to help get a favorable jury. But until recently lawyers commonly could not use much more than rules of thumb, hunches, or experience to guide their challenges. As Justice John M. Murtagh put it: "One human being cannot read the mind of another." The lawyers on both sides, moreover, were more or less equal in their ability to exercise this kind of homespun social psychology.

The new methods are quite a bit more accurate, though fortunately they are far from foolproof. People do not always act out their predispositions. Social science data is statistical, not absolute. At best survey techniques, even when supplemented with psychological analysis, can produce only "probabilistic" profiles, not guaranteed results. At the Berrigan trial, two of the defense attorneys' careful selections—one a woman with four conscientious objector sons—held out for a guilty verdict on the conspiracy charge, causing a hung jury.

Nevertheless, the recent spate of acquittals demonstrates that the impact can be considerable and that, on the average, the method will work well. Hence we are surely in for more frequent use of the technique.

It Takes Money

It might be said that soon both sides to all trials will be equipped with the same capability and that so long as the granting of an uneven number of challenges is curbed, giving both sides similar selection power, the edge of the social science helpers will be dulled. But the extent to which this takes place will be limited by the costliness of the technique.

Radical defendants have benefited from the free labor of scores of volunteers and the time donations of high-powered consultants, though even they needed expensive computers. As Howard Moore Jr., Angela Davis' chief counsel put it: "We can send men to the moon, but not everyone can afford to go. Every unpopular person who becomes a defendant will not have the resources we used in the Davis case." The Mitchell and Stans bills for their social science helpers may run to a five-digit figure.

Clearly, the average defendant cannot avail himself of such aid. Therefore, the net effect of the new technique, as is so often the case with new technology, will be to give a leg up to the wealthy or those who command a dedicated following. This is hardly what the founders of the American judicial system had in mind.

No Good Remedies

Unfortunately, one cannot unbite the apple of knowledge. Even sadder is that we see here, as we have seen so often before, that attempting to contain the side-effects of the application of science is costly, at best partially effective, and far from uncontroversial itself. To put it more succinctly, there seem to be no half-good, let alone good, remedies.

Probably the best place to start is with prospective jurors. If fewer persons were excused from jury duty, the universe from which jurors are drawn would be more representative of the community and, to a degree, less easy to manipulate. Next, serious consideration could be given to reducing challenges, especially peremptory ones. This approach, though, constitutes not only a wide departure from tradition, but limits the possibility of uncovering prejudicial attitudes in would-be jurors.

More powerful but even more problematic is to extend the ban on tampering with the jury to all out-of-court investigations of prospective jurors.

It could be defined as a serious violation of law to collect data about prospective jurors, to investigate their handwriting, to interview their neighbors and the like, and any discovery of such data-gathering could be grounds for a mistrial. This would not eliminate the lawyers' courtroom use of sociology and psychology or the usefulness of community profiles based on studies of citizens at large. But it could curb the more sophisticated application of those techniques which require homing in on the characteristics of particular jurors.

Another potent but controversial answer is for the judge alone to be allowed to question and remove prospective jurors. In this way the judge could seek both an open-minded jury and one which represents a cross-section of the community, not sociologically loaded dice. To the extent that judges themselves are free of social bias, this would probably work quite well. However, since jury selection has some effect on the outcome of each case, such a relatively active role by the judge flies in the face of the prevalent Anglo-Saxon tradition, according to which the judge is a neutral referee between the sides, not a third party. The challenge, though, could be-

come the task of a specialist attached to the courts.

The most radical remedy would be to follow Britain's lead and restrict the conditions under which citizens are entitled to a jury trial. (In Britain only 2 to 3 per cent of the cases still go to a jury.) Moreover, the jury is considered by many to be a major cause of rising court costs and delays in cases coming to trial. Nor is there any compelling evidence that trial by jury is fairer than trial by judges. These are hardly the days, though, in which reforms entailing less participation by the people and greater concentration of power in the hands of elected or appointed officials are likely to be either very popular or wise.

But until one remedy or another is applied, the state will almost surely have to do its own research, if only to even the odds. District attorneys or U.S. attorneys cannot be expected to stand by doing nothing while defendants in the most serious cases buy themselves a significant edge in trial after trial. The champions of the technique will have to realize that the days when it could be reserved for their favorite defendants will soon be over.

Note on the Ethics of Selecting the Juries' Ethics

As Professor Etzioni has indicated, the use of sophisticated psychological and sociological techniques to help lawyers pick jurors favorable to their clients is becoming increasingly widespread. Some observers seem to believe that these techniques amount to "jury rigging" and observe that they have been used most often by defense attorneys and especially in conspiracy trials. Other observers note that the cost of using such social science expertise is so high that eventually the technique will become available only to those who already have the power and resources which gain them favoritism with the legal system.

The process of jury selection when aided by these techniques is fascinating, though it may not be more than an elaboration of rough talents already used by highly experienced trial lawyers during any *voir dire* examination. (See, for example, "Psychology and the Angela Davis Jury" in *Human Behavior,* January 1973.) In one case, the Wounded Knee trial of Russell Means and Dennis Banks of the American Indian Movement, psychologist June Tapp participated in screening prospective jurors on the issue of authoritarianism. She and her colleagues rated prospective jurors on how deferential they were to the judge, whether they exhibited body language indicating a high probability of deference to authority in general, and how they responded to the judge's questions about law in general and the nature of officialdom. These responses were taken as indicators of whether the jurors would be sympathetic to the government as the authority figure (prosecution) in the case.

Inevitably the use of these techniques raises not only serious questions about the structure of jury trials and legal decision making in general (as the Etzioni piece indicates), but also deep ethical questions for social scientists about the use of their knowledge and skills in contests in which they have no direct participation or stake. The problem may be even more acute than that of the ethics of advocacy because the social scientist is shrouded in an expertise which seems to insulate him or her from accusations of partisanship, and because the social scientist's role in the jury process is not formally a part of the system. Some social scientists seem to feel that regardless of their personal beliefs they can work to ensure that the jury is not politically or ideologically loaded against a defendant and that this is a sufficient standard of fairness to close the issue. Others see this as a serious dilemma fostered by the separation of knowledge and technique on the one hand from responsibility and accountability on the other.

In 1975 psychologist June Tapp was interviewed about her participation in the Wounded Knee trial. She was asked whether, if the government offered to hire "psycholegal technicians" to help in jury selection, she would be willing to recommend one of her own students for the job. Her answer was as follows:

> The decision to work in the public or private sector is a personal one. But the issue is not being pro or con government. Rather it is whether the hunches or fireside inductions that guide legal decision making should reflect systematic psychological findings. . . .

In terms of the politics or ethics of the situation, I suppose how one feels about it depends in part about how one feels about the government and about the law generally. After all, the federal government is not a monolith, a leviathan. Also we operate in an adversary system of law. In criminal cases the government acts on behalf of the people to prosecute the accused for wrongdoing. If the adversary system is to work properly, then it's very important that both sides of the trial have equal access to information and technique.

An individual can choose, of course, whether or not to work for the government in a particular role. But if psychologists can work in governmental settings to effect policy, promote welfare, and in general try to enhance the quality of U.S. life, then it seems to me they belong *everywhere* their knowledge and skills can be used and explored.

I think of laws, and legal reforms, as forms of social experiments, and I think that behavioral scientists should be in places where they help to insure the highest possible quality of those experiments.*

Questions

1. Do you think defendants think of their trials as legal "experiments"?

2. How would you have responded to the question June Tapp was asked? Do you think an expert in this area should feel any responsibility for the use of his or her knowledge? Upon what kind of considerations would you base your own decision about whether to participate in jury selection if you had these skills? Should the legal system set any standards for the use of such techniques? Should these standards affect qualifications of technicians? The economics of accessibility for defendants or prosecutors or plaintiffs to these technicians? Would you recommend that such techniques be barred from the court process?

* "The Notion of Conspiracy is Not Tasty to Americans: Interview of June Tapp by Gordon Bermant," *Psychology Today* (May 1975), 60.

Note on Constitutional Protection of Fair Jury Selection

The kind of expertise that aided the selection of the jury in the Mitchell-Stans and Wounded Knee trials is obviously not available to every criminal defendant or participant in civil litigation. As with the use of expert testimony, this raises the issue of whether trial by jury is really meaningful to and for the average citizen who can neither command expert resources nor understand their use. For those who must be content with institutional protections of fair trial such as the jury selection statutes of states, the *voir dire* questioning of prospective jurors by judge or counsel, and the protections of the Constitution, what are the prospects of getting a fair jury? More important, perhaps, what *is* a fair jury? What constitutes a jury of peers?

The phrase "jury of peers" goes back to the Magna Carta in 1215, though the significance of this pedigree is in doubt. In 1215, after all, there was little even remotely resembling trial by jury as we know it today. In fact the "jury of peers" represented an attempt by English barons to secure their privileges against the king's encroachment, not a notion of equality among the populace. Nevertheless, the concept of being tried by a jury of one's peers has become engrained in American law. The question is, what does it mean?

Does it stand for the proposition that defendants should be judged by members of their own social or economic subgroup? If so, what subgroups or communities are to be recognized as defining a person's peerage in a pluralistic society? Or does it mean that since all people are equal in a democratic republic, a jury must be a cross-section of the whole society? If this is so, the problem of defining communities is still with us, for now the issue is whether a recognizable group has been excluded. Finally, perhaps we are all each other's peers by virtue of our humanity. If so, does "jury of peers" mean anything practical at all as a principle of preventing discrimination in jury selection?

The formal legal system has approached issues of jury selection according to several criteria.

Race

Since 1880 the Supreme Court has ruled that a state cannot constitutionally exclude persons from juries solely on the basis of their race or skin color (*Strauder* v. *West Virginia,* 100 U.S. 303, 1880). The court looked for systematic exclusion from jury rolls rather than actual absence of any race from any particular jury. More recently, it has narrowed its scope of review even further by refusing to recognize as a violation of equal protection a pattern of absence of blacks from juries when such a pattern was produced by peremptory challenges. The standard of racial discrimination has thus become one of *opportunity* to serve rather than actual presence on a jury, and the proof necessary to show systematic exclusion from opportunity has been made more difficult (*Swain* v. *Alabama,* 380 U.S. 202 1965). (See also the Federal Jury Selection Act, 28 USC 1861 et. seq., 1968.)

Some courts have recognized that the actual presence of blacks on juries is more significant than the opportunity for blacks to serve. (See, for example, *Brooks* v. *Beto,* 366 F2d 1 [5th

Cir.].) Some commentators have also suggested that a strong case can be made that a majority or even all jurors should be black in cases involving black defendants (see "The Case for Black Juries," 79 *Yale Law Journal* 531). The argument is based primarily upon the absence of legitimacy a jury—and therefore the law in general—suffers when members of the black community do not see themselves reflected in actual jury composition. The ability of persons with similar life experiences to understand and credit the case of a defendant from the same community is also cited.

Age

In *United States* v. *Guzman,* 337 F. Supp. 140 (S.D.N.Y. 1972), a United States district court interpreting the Federal Jury Selection Act refused to reverse the conviction of a young man for refusing induction into the armed forces. The court rejected his claim that the jury that convicted him was unconstitutionally based on systematic exclusion of 18- to 21-year-olds and "young persons" between 24 and 30. In discussing its refusal to find any constitutional flaw in the New York jury selection method which resulted in underrepresentation of young people on the jury, the court said:

> The crux of the inquiry is whether, in the source used in the selection of juries, there has been systematic or intentional exclusion of any cognizable group or class of qualified citizens. Thus, selection systems which exclude identifiable racial groups or social or economic classes are vulnerable to attack. However, perfectly proportional representation is not required, since no source list will be an exact statistical mirror of the community.
>
> If it is ascertained, however, that any cognizable group is *substantially* under-represented in the source of names, systematic or intentional exclusion can be inferred.

> The test is to compare the degree of representation of a particular group to that group's percentage of the population....

> The major problem raised by defendant's challenge is determining whether his asserted age groups are "cognizable groups." While certain racial and economic groups have been held to be "cognizable groups" for purposes of jury challenges, the cases have dealt gingerly with the methodology used to determine whether other groups are "cognizable." Nevertheless, various critical factors can be gleaned from the opinions.

> A group to be "cognizable" for present purposes must have a definite composition. That is, there must be some factor which defines and limits the group. A cognizable group is not one whose membership shifts from day to day or whose members can be arbitrarily selected. Secondly, the group must have cohesion. There must be a common thread which runs through the group, a basic similarity in attitudes or ideas or experience which is present in members of the group and which cannot be adequately represented if the group is excluded from the jury selection process. Finally, there must be a possibility that exclusion of the group will result in partiality or bias on the part of juries hearing cases in which group members are involved. That is, the group must have a community of interest which cannot be adequately protected by the rest of the populace.

Sex

In *Alexander* v. *Louisiana,* 92 Sp. Ct. 1221 (1972), the Supreme Court quashed an indictment against a black defendant because the procedure for picking grand jurors systematically excluded members of the black community. The court refused to consider the defendant's alternative claim which was based on the systematic exclusion of women from the Grand Jury. In a concurring opinion, Mr. Justice Douglas took issue with the majority's refusal to consider the issue of sex discrimination and wrote, in part:

> The requirement that a jury reflect a cross-section of the community occurs throughout our jurisprudence: "The American tradition of trial by jury, considered in connection with either criminal or civil proceedings, necessarily contemplates an impartial jury drawn from a cross-section of the community.
>
> This is precisely the constitutional infirmity of the Louisiana statute. For a jury list from which women have been systematically excluded is not representative of the community.
>
> It is said, however, that an all male panel drawn from the various groups within a community will be as truly representative as if women were included. The thought is that the factors which tend to influence the action of women are the same as those which influence the action of men—personality, background, economic status—and not sex.
>
> Yet it is not enough to say that women when sitting as jurors neither act nor tend to act as a class. Men likewise do not act as a class. But, if the shoe were on the other foot, who would claim that a jury was truly representative of the community if all men were intentionally and systematically excluded from the panel? The truth is that the two sexes are not fungible; a community made up exclusively of one is different from a community composed of both; the subtle interplay of influence between one and the other is among the imponderables. To insulate the courtroom from either may not in a given case make an iota of difference. Yet a flavor, a distinct quality is lost if either sex is excluded. *The exclusion of one may indeed make the jury less representative of the community than would be true if an economic or racial group were excluded."*
>
> The absolute exemption provided by Louisiana, and no other State, betrays a view of a woman's role which cannot withstand scrutiny under modern standards. We once upheld the constitutionality of a state law denying to women the right to practice law, solely on grounds of sex. The rationale underlying Art. 402 of the Louisiana Code is the same as that which was articulated by Justice Bradley in *Bradwell:*
>
> "Man is, or should be, woman's protector and defender. The natural and proper timidity and delicacy which belongs to the female sex evidently unfits it for many of the occupations of civil life. The constitution of the family organization, which is founded in the divine ordinance, as well as in the nature of things, indicates the domestic sphere as that which properly belongs to the domain and functions of womanhood. The harmony, not to say identity, of interests and views which belong, or should belong, to the family institution is repugnant to the idea of a woman adopting a distinct and independent career from that of her husband.... The paramount destiny and mission of woman are to fulfill the noble and benign offices of wife and mother. This is the law of the Creator. And the rules of civil society must be adapted to the general constitution of things, and cannot be based upon exceptional cases."
>
> Classifications based on sex are no longer insulated from judicial scrutiny by a legislative judgment that "woman's place is in the home," or that woman is by her "nature" ill-suited for a particular task. But such a judgment is precisely that which underpins the absolute exemption from jury service at issue.

Attitude and Belief

In *Witherspoon* v. *Illinois*, 391 U.S. 510 (1968), the Supreme Court ruled that a jury convened for recommending a sentence in a capital case was unconstitutional because that jury was chosen by excluding persons who expressed conscientious or religious scruples against the death penalty. The court did not rule that a jury considering guilt or innocence (as opposed to sentence) would be unconstitutional if persons with scruples against the death penalty had been excluded. In its opinion, the court stated:

> If the State had excluded only those prospective jurors who stated in advance of trial that they would not even consider returning a verdict of death, it could argue that the resulting jury was simply "neutral" with respect to penalty. But when it swept from the jury all who expressed conscientious or religious scruples against capital punishment and all who opposed it in principle, the State crossed the line of neutrality. In its quest for a jury capable of imposing the death penalty, the State produced a jury uncommonly willing to condemn a man to die.

Mr. Justice Douglas, in a concurring opinion, wished to take the issue further both as to what is a truly neutral or representative jury, and as to whether persons with scruples against the death penalty could be excluded from juries determining guilt or innocence (as opposed to determining sentence only). He stated:

> My difficulty with the opinion of the Court is a narrow but important one. The Court permits a State to eliminate from juries some of those who have conscientious scruples against the death penalty; but it allows those to serve who have no scruples against it as well as those who, having such scruples, nevertheless are deemed able to determine after a finding of guilt whether the death penalty or a lesser penalty should be imposed. I fail to see or understand the constitutional dimensions of those distinctions. . . .

A fair cross-section of the community may produce a jury almost certain to impose the death penalty if guilt were found; or it may produce a jury almost certain not to impose it. The conscience of the community is subject to many variables, one of which is the attitude toward the death sentence. If a particular community were overwhelmingly opposed to capital punishment, it would not be able to exercise a discretion to impose or not impose the death sentence. A jury representing the conscience of that community would do one of several things depending on the type of state law governing it: it would avoid the death penalty by recommending mercy or it would avoid it by finding guilt of a lesser offense.

In such instance, why should not an accused have the benefit of that controlling principle of mercy in the community? Why should his fate be entrusted exclusively to a jury that was either enthusiastic about capital punishment or so undecided that it could exercise a discretion to impose it or not, depending on how it felt about the particular case?

I see no constitutional basis for excluding those who are so opposed to capital punishment that they would never inflict it on a defendant. Exclusion of them means the selection of jurors who are either protagonists of the death penalty or neutral concerning it. That results in a systematic exclusion of qualified groups, and the deprivation to the accused of a cross-section of the community for decision on both his guilt and his punishment.

Although the Court reverses as to penalty, it declines to reverse the verdict of guilt rendered by the same jury. It does so on the ground that petitioner has not demonstrated on this record that the jury which convicted him was "less than neutral with respect to *guilt*," because of the exclusion of all those opposed in some degree to capital punishment. The Court fails to find on this record "an unrepresentative jury on the issue of guilt." But we do not require a showing of specific prejudice when a defendant has been deprived of his right to a jury representing a cross-section of the community. We can as easily assume that the absence of those opposed to capital punishment would rob the jury of certain peculiar qualities of human nature as would the exclusion of women from juries. I would not require a specific showing of a likelihood of prejudice, for I feel that we must proceed on the assumption that in many, if not most, cases of class exclusion on the basis of beliefs or attitudes some prejudice does result and many times will not be subject to precise measurement. Indeed, that prejudice "is so subtle, so intangible, that it escapes the ordinary methods of proof." In my view, that is the essense of the requirement that a jury be drawn from a cross-section of the community.

Questions

1. Which is the better place to insist on a representative cross-section of the community, the rolls of names from which jurors are picked or the actual jurors on a particular jury panel? Why?
2. Should age be recognized as a factor in making up representative jury rolls or juries? Should the type of offense or the age of the defendant make any difference on this issue? What type of evidence might be offered to show that "young people" is a cognizable group under the test set forth in the *Guzman* case?
3. Instead of a representative cross-section of the community, should a jury of peers be defined as one made up of people sharing the cultural or economic background of the defendant?

---

5 A Problem in Jury Deliberation

It may be that a case of civil disobedience presents the most revealing avenue for exploring the vitality and importance of the jury system and for uncovering citizens' attitudes toward participation in the jury process. Civil disobedience defies easy rule-oriented decision because it attempts to touch the conscience of the community with a justification for rule-breaking. Civil disobedience, especially the kind presented in the *Lovejoy* case below, also raises the question of the ordering of principles in a moral or ethical system. When, for example, if ever, can property be destroyed to preserve life? Such dilemmas require all jurors to consider not only the nature of the rule of law but the depths of conscience to which they feel they must go to fulfill the juror's role as they understand it. Jury nullification is obviously an option. But the juror will probably have to think hard about differences between his or her own views and the views of the community as the juror perceives them. Emotions in this process are typically quite deep, although they are often balanced by the inclination of some to seek refuge from personal and community ethical dilemmas in ready-made formulations of rules and authorities of formal law. Perhaps after deliberating a case of civil disobedience such as that presented here, we may be able to see the ways in which individuals can contribute to the demise of the jury system through the consciousness of law and jury role which they bring to the task of serving on a jury.

In this section the readers are asked to form juries and deliberate a case based almost entirely upon an actual event. The incident is not a traditional civil disobedience case in which a rule is willfully violated out of conviction that it is unjust. But Sam Lovejoy's actions do compel his peers to come squarely to terms with a vital public issue while simultaneously considering the relative importance of maintaining the "rule of law" as it applies to a particular case. Experiments can be done in deliberating this case both by discussing the proper jury selection standards to be applied and by varying the size or unanimity requirement to test what, if any, effect such changes have upon the experiences of the jurors and the quality of group interaction in the jury room.

In deliberating this case two important principles should be kept in mind in addition to the general understanding of legal process gained from other materials in this book. First, civil disobedience is a deliberate and carefully thought-out tactic based on a clear understanding of law and morality. It has a long and largely honorable history represented in the United States most eloquently and courageously by Martin Luther King, Jr. To make clear the basic assumptions and attitudes that generally accompany acts of civil disobedience, Dr. King's "Letter from Birmingham Jail" is included here before the description of the *Lovejoy* case.

Second, it is important to bear in mind the function of judgment by the community in any jury case whether involving civil disobedience or not. One explanation for this function is contained in the theories of Emile Durkheim, as represented by Kai Erikson in *Wayward Puritans*. Although jury trials are not specifically discussed in Erikson's work, his description of the role played by community judgment of deviants clearly has major implications for the functioning of juries. Take, for example, the following brief excerpt from Erikson:

> The deviant individual violates rules of conduct which the rest of the community holds in high respect; and when these people come together to express their outrage over the offense and to bear witness against the offender, they develop a tighter bond of solidarity than existed earlier. The excitement generated by the crime, in other words, quickens the tempo of interaction in the group and creates a climate in which the private sentiments of many separate persons are fused together into a common sense of morality.

The process by which a community defines an act as deviant provides, then, a focus for group feeling and an opportunity for the group to discover or reaffirm its values. This process of discovery and reaffirmation is the means by which a community maintains its boundaries—the means for defining a culture or society as different from others and possessing its own unique view of human society. It is doubtful whether group cohesion can be maintained without some such boundary-maintaining process, though there is no reason to assume that the process must lead to exclusion rather than to inclusion of the deviant. Deviance may actually be viewed as a claim upon the group leading to a change of group values to accommodate the would-be deviant. Law, and especially the jury process, may be viewed as one of our society's major forms of group-process boundary definition—a participatory, group-oriented manipulation of consciousness. That such a process is often transformed into a vehicle for nonparticipatory social control does not eliminate its more democratic possibilities or design.

In deliberating the *Lovejoy* case, readers might bear in mind the following statement by Erikson:

> [S]ingle encounters between the deviant and his community are only fragments of an ongoing social process. Like an article of common law, boundaries remain a meaningful point of reference only so long as they are repeatedly tested by persons on the fringes of the group and repeatedly de-

fended by persons chosen to represent the group's inner morality.

The primary fictionalization in the *Lovejoy* case as reported here is in the judge's charge and the suggestion that the case went to the jury. In point of fact, a flaw in the indictment was discovered after the evidence had been presented and the case was dismissed. An accurate indictment was never filed and no new trial was held. The fact that the case never went to a jury was a bitter disappointment to Lovejoy. We have attempted to remedy that by the inclusion of these materials for your deliberation.

Excerpt from "Letter from Birmingham Jail"   *Martin Luther King, Jr.*

You express a great deal of anxiety over our willingness to break laws. This is certainly a legitimate concern. Since we so diligently urge people to obey the Supreme Court's decision of 1954 outlawing segregation in the public schools, at first glance it may seem rather paradoxical for us consciously to break laws. One may well ask: "How can you advocate breaking some laws and obeying others?" The answer lies in the fact that there are two types of laws: just and unjust. I would be the first to advocate obeying just laws. One has not only a legal but a moral responsibility to obey just laws. Conversely, one has a moral responsibility to disobey unjust laws. I would agree with St. Augustine that "an unjust law is no law at all."

Now, what is the difference between the two? How does one determine whether a law is just or unjust? A just law is a man-made code that squares with the moral law or the law of God. An unjust law is a code that is out of harmony with the moral law. To put it in the terms of St. Thomas Aquinas: An unjust law is a human law that is not rooted in eternal law and natural law. Any law that uplifts human personality is just. Any law that degrades human personality is unjust. All segregation statutes are unjust because segregation distorts the soul and damages the

personality. It gives the segregator a false sense of superiority and the segregated a false sense of inferiority. Segregation, to use the terminology of the Jewish philosopher Martin Buber, substitutes an "I-it" relationship for an "I-thou" relationship and ends up relegating persons to the status of things. Hence segregation is not only politically, economically and sociologically unsound, it is morally wrong and sinful. Paul Tillich has said that sin is separation. Is not segregation an existential expression of man's tragic separation, his awful estrangement, his terrible sinfulness? Thus it is that I can urge men to obey the 1954 decision of the Supreme Court, for it is morally right; and I can urge them to disobey segregation ordinances, for they are morally wrong.

Let us consider a more concrete example of just and unjust laws. An unjust law is a code that a numerical or power majority group compels a minority group to obey but does not make binding on itself. This is difference made legal. By the same token, a just law is a code that a majority compels a minority to follow and that it is willing to follow itself. This is sameness made legal.

Let me give another explanation. A law is unjust if it is inflicted on a minority that, as a result of being denied the right to vote, had no part in enacting or devising the law. Who can say that the legislature of Alabama which set up that state's segregation laws was democratically elected? Throughout Alabama all sorts of devious methods are used to prevent Negroes from becoming registered voters, and there are some counties in which, even though Negroes constitute a majority of the population, not a single Negro is registered. Can any law enacted under such circumstances be considered democratically structured?

Sometimes a law is just on its face and unjust in its application. For instance, I have been arrested on a charge of parading without a permit. Now, there is nothing wrong in having an ordinance which requires a permit for a parade. But such an ordinance becomes unjust when it is used to maintain segregation and to deny citizens the First-Amendment privilege of peaceful assembly and protest.

I hope you are able to see the distinction I am trying to point out. In no sense do I advocate evading or defying the law, as would the rabid segregationist. That would lead to anarchy. One who breaks an unjust law must do so openly, lovingly, and with a willingness to accept the penalty. I submit that an individual who breaks a law that conscience tells him is unjust, and who willingly accepts the penalty of imprisonment in order to arouse the conscience of the community over its injustice, is in reality expressing the highest respect for law.

Of course, there is nothing new about this kind of civil disobedience. It was evidenced sublimely in the refusal of Shadrach, Meshach and Abednego to obey the laws of Nebuchadnezzar, on the ground that a higher moral law was at stake. It was practiced superbly by the early Christians, who were willing to face hungry lions and the excruciating pain of chopping blocks rather than submit to certain unjust laws of the Roman Empire. To a degree, academic freedom is a reality today because Socrates practiced civil disobedience. In our own nation, the Boston Tea Party represented a massive act of civil disobedience.

We should never forget that everything Adolf Hitler did in Germany was "legal" and everything the Hungarian freedom fighters did in Hungary was "illegal." It was "illegal" to aid and comfort a Jew in Hitler's Germany. Even so, I am sure that, had I lived in Germany at the time, I would have aided and comforted my Jewish brothers. If today I lived in a Communist country where certain principles dear to the Christian faith are suppressed, I would openly advocate disobeying that country's antireligious laws.

I must make two honest confessions to you, my Christian and Jewish brothers. First, I must confess that over the past few years I have been gravely disappointed with the white moderate. I have almost reached the regrettable conclusion that the Negro's great stumbling block in his stride toward freedom is not the White Citizen's Counciler or the Ku Klux Klanner, but the white moderate, who is more devoted to "order" than to justice; who prefers a negative peace which is the absence of justice; who constantly says: "I agree with you in the goal you seek, but I cannot agree with your methods of direct action"; who paternalistically believes he can set the timetable for another man's freedom; who lives by a mythical concept of time and who constantly advises the Negro to wait for a "more convenient season." Shallow understanding from people of good will is more frustrating than absolute misunderstanding from people of ill will. Lukewarm acceptance is much more bewildering than outright rejection.

I had hoped that the white moderate would understand that law and order exist for the purpose of establishing justice and that when they fail in this purpose they become the dangerously structured dams that block the flow of social progress. I had hoped that the white moderate would understand that the present tension in the South is a necessary phase of the transition from an obnoxious negative peace, in which the Negro passively accepted his unjust plight, to a substantive and positive peace, in which all men will respect the dignity and worth of human personality. Actually, we who engage in nonviolent direct action are not the creators of tension. We merely bring to the surface the hidden tension that is already alive. We bring it out in the open, where it can be seen and dealt with. Like a boil that can never be cured so long as it is covered up but must be opened with all its ugliness to the natural medicines of air and light, injustice must be exposed, with all the tension its exposure creates, to the light of human conscience and the air of national opinion before it can be cured.

In your statement you assert that our actions, even though peaceful, must be condemned because they precipitate violence. But is this a logical assertion? Isn't this like condemning a robbed man because his possession of money precipitated the evil act of robbery? Isn't this like condemning Socrates because his unswerving commitment to truth and his philosophical inquiries precipitated the act by the misguided populace in which they made him drink hemlock? Isn't this like condemning Jesus because his unique God-consciousness and never-ceasing devotion to God's will precipitated the evil act of crucifixion? We must come to see that, as the federal courts have consistently affirmed, it is wrong to urge an individual to cease his efforts to gain his basic constitutional rights because the quest may precipitate violence. Society must protect the robbed and punish the robber.

I had also hoped that the white moderate would reject the myth concerning time in relation to the struggle for freedom. I have just received a letter from a white brother in Texas. He writes: "All Christians know that the colored people will receive equal rights eventually, but it is possible that you are in too great a religious hurry. It has taken Christianity almost two thousand years to accomplish what it has. The teachings of Christ take time to come to earth." Such an attitude stems from a tragic misconception of time, from the strangely irrational notion that there is something in the very flow of time that will inevitably cure all ills. Actually, time itself is neutral; it can be used either destructively or constructively. More and more I feel that the people of ill will have used time much more effectively than have the people of good will. We will have to repent in this generation not merely for the hateful words and actions of the bad people but for the appalling silence of the good people. Human progress never rolls in on wheels of inevitability; it comes through the tireless efforts of men willing to be co-workers with God, and without this hard work, time itself becomes an ally of the forces of social stagnation. We must use time creatively, in the knowledge that the time is always ripe to do right. Now is the time to make real the promise of democracy and transform our pending national elegy into a creative psalm of brotherhood. Now is the time to lift our national policy from the quicksand of racial injustice to the solid rock of human dignity.

The Trial of Sam Lovejoy   *Stephen Davis*

Montague, Massachusetts, lies in the green Connecticut River valley, 90 miles west of Boston. It is a beautiful township of gently rolling farmlands and majestic eastern foothills of the Berkshires. Economically Montague is spoken of as a depressed area; the small farms and light industry are slowly dying out, replaced by tract housing and high taxes and unemployment rates. Its two major villages, Montague City and Turner's Falls, look like they've been preserved intact from the Great Depression.

Stephen Davis is a veteran journalist, whose most recent book is *Reggae Bloodlines* (New York: Doubleday, 1977). This article was first published, in longer form, in The *Boston Globe,* December 1, 1974.

Early in 1973 Northeast Utilities (NU), the power combine that provides electricity to much of rural New England, made an offer to Montague its citizens didn't think they could refuse. The utility had plans for twin giant nuclear reactors to service the valley with electricity. NU proposed that the plant be built on the Montague Plains, several hundred acres of gravel, scrub oak and pine in the heart of town. The projected cost of the project was $1.52 billion, a figure almost 30 times the assessed value of the town itself. The reactors would go into operation in 1981 with a power capability of 2,300 megawatts; the Montague nuclear station would be the biggest ever built.

Local opinion toward the nuke was largely favorable. Businessmen and town boosters were delirious over the prospects of thousands of jobs, millions of dollars in new business over the years and the mammoth boost to local tax rolls the nuke would bring. An overwhelming majority of the town's 8,500 residents seemed to be in favor of the project.

But the atom has been a controversial little demon since it was first split in 1943, and opposition to the Montague nuke sprung up quickly. A group of university-oriented liberals asked that the project be built underground for safety reasons. The utility turned down the request, stating that it would cost too much and that there were no "major" safety hazards to be concerned about. The local [Franklin County] daily, the *Greenfield Recorder,* quoted NU vice-president Charles Bragg: "Even if there were significant local opposition, it wouldn't affect us."

Faced with the general attitude that the nuke was a foregone conclusion and the lack of any other direct opposition, a loose aggregation of farmers and communards formed Nuclear Objectors for a Pure Environment (NOPE). The people behind this perfectly Yankee rural acronym spent months researching the ecology of the area, the histories of existing nuclear plants and the track record of the federal Atomic Energy Commission (AEC) in monitoring and regulating them.

What the NOPEs discovered turned their stomachs with that cold tangible twist of apocalyptic fear, and they announced their unqualified opposition to the Montague project. NOPE set forth four central issues of health and safety where the Montague nuke could be hazardous.

—All existing nuclear plants exude what the AEC chooses to call "low level" radioactivity into the air. The AEC sets standards for this waste level but tends not to enforce them. Many plants exceed these levels without penalty. In his book *Low Level Radiation,* Dr. Ernest Sternglass of the University of Pittsburgh links this "low level" radioactivity with human birth defects and cancer as it gradually seeps into the local food chain.

—Controlled atomic fission is the source of generating nuclear power. If that reaction gets out of control, a reactor "melt-down" would release thousands of times more radiation than the bomb dropped on Hiroshima. The nuclear power industry and the AEC say this "melt-down" risk is minimal. But the last line of defense against any accident is the Emergency Core Cooling System, which is supposed to flood water on a "runaway" reactor. This system had been tested only six times on model reactors: the system failed all six tests.

—Reactors build solid, highly radioactive wastes with half-lives of thousands of years. Breeder reactors breed plutonium, which can be turned into bombs. The AEC admits it has yet to discover a safe disposal method for this waste. According to AEC statistics a solid waste storage facility at Hanford, Washington, had already leaked radiation 17 times in the last 20 years.

—The proposed Montague nuke would dump millions of gallons of hot, possibly contaminated water into the Connecticut River through the gravel aquifer of the Plains. Also the nuke's twin giant 550-foot cooling towers might emit enough steam to seriously affect the region's weather.

In addition to nuclear dangers, NOPE reasoned that the plant would double the town's population, reducing farmland and forest and ruining the quality of rural life. Although NOPE was a distinct minority in their own town, they were supported by many of their neighbors. The town meetings of adjacent Shutesbury, Leverett and Wendell voted overwhelmingly against the reactors.

In June 1973 the Montague selectmen issued Northeast Utilities a zoning variance to erect a 500-foot high meteorological tower on the Plains prior to construction of the nuke. The tower is required by AEC regulations to monitor meteorological conditions at a proposed site. This is where Sam Lovejoy comes in.

To an engineer the nuke tower might have been a thing of beauty; a high white aluminum-alloy rapier sporting sophisticated eco-data instruments and an Orion's Belt of relentless mercury vapor strobes visible in southern Vermont, 35 miles away.

Sam Lovejoy first saw the tower while driving home one night to his communal family's farm on Montague's Chestnut Hill. He remembers a painful thrill the first time the tower blinked at him through the dusk across the Plains.

"As soon as I saw the thing I instinctively knew it had to come down," Lovejoy said later. "It was such a heavy symbol of their arrogance, a kick in the nuts to all of us who spent our time and money battling the nuke. Now this was months before anything happened but I knew it had to go. I mean, what could be more obvious? Only at the time it wasn't so obvious that it would be *me* that would do it."

Lovejoy was 28 years old and no stranger to radical ideas. A Massachusetts native, Sam's father was a career army officer who passed away when Sam was five. Sam went to Wilbraham Academy and Amherst College, where he turned his frat brothers on to grass and convinced them to declassify their secret society into a public dorm. Sam worked on the *Amherst Student,* then edited by Marshall Bloom, the young activist who led the 1966 anti-Vietnam graduation walkout on Robert McNamara and later founded Liberation News Service. When Bloom moved the "Radical UPI" from New York to a crumbling Montague farm in 1968 Sam joined him soon after, becoming an invaluable member because he was the only communard who actually knew anything about farming.

Later Sam went to Cuba with one of the first Venceremos cane-cutting brigades made up of young Americans. He loved Cuba and the hard work but was turned off by the doctrinaire, humorless rhetoric of the SDSers who were his companions.

By the winter of 1974, months had gone by since the tower had been monitoring the valley wind currents, the NOPE campaign was stagnating due to the apathy of the townspeople and Sam Lovejoy was getting restless. The more research he did into nukes the more nervous he got.

So in the freezing and black small hours of February 22, 1974, on George Washington's birthday, a grim commando dressed in dark clothes carrying carefully muffled tools and a signed statement in his back pocket trudged through the snow-crunchy woods toward the tower. Once he reached the 8-foot chain link fence around the base of the tower, Sam looked around cautiously. Nothing happening for miles except the slight wind and the mechanical clicking of the instruments.

Sam paused a minute, listening, enjoying his own adrenaline and thinking . . . *a shame to waste this fine piece of engineering* . . . and then he went to work. With a wire cutter he sliced through the fence. The turnbuckles maintaining the tower's steel support cables required only a couple of straining turns with a heavy wrench. Once free, the cable snapped back from Sam like a monstrous, vicious whip, the tower shuddered and KKRAAAAANG AANG ANG ANG . . . went down.

Sam looked up. Through the darkness he could see that the lower 100 feet of the tower had survived and was still erect. Deciding to let sleeping towers lie, Sam collected himself, hid his tools in the brush and walked back to nearby Route 63. At three in the morning he flagged down a passing police cruiser and asked for a ride to the station. At the station house Sam lit a Kool and told the sergeant the tower was down. The sergeant had a cruiser go out and confirm that the tower was no more. Then Sam reached into his pocket and handed the sergeant this statement:

George Washington's Birthday

In the long-established tradition of challenging the constitutionality of particular events, I readily admit full responsibility for sabotaging that outrageous symbol of the future nuclear power plant, the N.U. meteorological tower on the Montague Plains. The Declaration of Independence rightfully legislates action ". . . whenever any form of government becomes destructive of these ends . . . of safety and happiness." The Massachusetts Bill of Rights further states, ". . . The people alone have an incontestable unalienable and indefeasible right to institute government; and to reform, alter or totally change the same, when their protection, safety, prosperity and happiness require it." With the obvious danger of a nuclear power plant, with the biological finality of atomic radiation (and other equally ominous problems), a clear duty was mine to secure for my community the welfare and safety that the government has not only refused to provide, but has conspired to destroy.

I held no malice toward the tower in itself; it was a beautiful engineering feat. Indeed I always dreamed of riding to the top to see the entire valley I am wont to love. Symbolically, however, it represented the most horrendous development this community could imagine. The very spectre of it oppressed us all.

Charles Bragg, a vice-president of N.U., said that local opposition, "wouldn't affect us. We would have to go ahead with it even if there was a protest movement mounted by the citizens of the area." When even the most learned physicists in the country continue to disagree, Prof. Inglis at UMass., for example, the citizens of the town were supposed to make a definitive judgment in a very few months on an issue that would radically alter their lives forever (or perhaps not occur at all!)! Social blackmail! Such perverse logic is a usurpation of normal human rights and cannot be tolerated.

Mr. Charles Bragg also compared the development of nuclear power plants to the western expansion of the railroads. The only possible extension of his logic is to remember the liquidation of the American Indian, and thus realize the ominous repercussions for our own fragile little community.

Characteristic of the times, though, the corporate giants not only extort us by preying on the weakness of the local citizenry, but also they degrade us with bribes. The pleasures of money magnanimously offered in the same vein as the carrot (and the stick). Here where the risks—the costs—are so devastating, the system has thrown the entire issue into the economic and political arenas. Economically for our little community, the proposed power plant budget is greater than Connecticut's entire state budget. Politically speaking, there is no democratic solution to a scientific problem. In a situation where unanimity is imperative, the opposite is true. There can be no trade-off here between money and public welfare.

The Massachusetts Bill of Rights declares, "No man, nor corporation, or association of men have any other title to obtain advantages, or particular and exclusive privileges, distinct from those of the community." And yet, are we not now only beginning to grasp how grossly the great corporations view their profit?

It was announced only recently (after much research, and then and only then admitted officially) that the relatively old Rowe nuclear reactor had not been the impeccably safe place it has been so eagerly billed by the avaricious power companies; indeed the plant had no emergency core cooling system at all until 1972! The ECCS is a rather simple water cooling idea much like a car—except it is supposed to control temperatures comparable to our sun! The AEC itself admits that all ECCS tests have been unsuccessful. The industry says that the AEC did not require one until now! What! say I.

I have been living here in Montague going on five years now, and in the valley for another five. As a farmer concerned about the organic and the natural, I find irradiated fruit, vegetables and meat to be inorganic; and I can find no natural balance with a nuclear plant in this or any community.

There seems to be no way for our children to be born or raised safely in our community in the very near future. No children? No edible food? What will there be?

While my purpose is not to provoke fear, I believe we must act; positive action is the only option left open to us. Communities have the same rights as individuals. We must seize back control of our own community.

The nuclear energy industry and its support elements in government are practicing actively a form of despotism. They have selected the less populated rural countryside to answer the energy needs of the cities. While not denying the urban need for electrical energy (perhaps addiction is more appropriate), why cannot reactors be built near those they are intended to serve? Is it not more efficient? Or are we witnessing a corrupt balance between population and risk?

In a society only beginning to explore the philosophical implications of abortion, euthanasia and genetic manipulation, do we citizens allow the disunited and unconfident scientists to plop down heaps of high and low level radioactivity in our midst? We truly have not delved into all the repercussions of our actions, yet we seek to proliferate the construction of obviously lethal experiments in ever increasing numbers of backyards? I fear the monsters of infanticide and forced sterilization will raise their heads before this society regains its senses! Jesus begged upon the cross, "Father, forgive them; for they know not what they do."

The energy crisis, so-called, is an obvious signal for the need for immediate and nationwide introspection and re-evaluation. We must give up those false and selfish notions of individual freedom where they impinge on the freedoms necessary for a wholesome and balanced community life. We must bring to an end the greed of the corporate state. We must see that profit, as the modus operandi of our society, is defunct. The American people surely had the power to control their own lives, and I believe they still do; but today it is a question of whether they really want control. "The times, they are achanging," but it is the task of all men to understand and control these changes.

We must remove the dangerous and sensitive issue of nuclear plant development from the economic and political arenas, and put the issue to a more prudent and judicious test. One of man's highest achievements is the principle and right of trial by jury. In any trial, indeed only one juror need voice skepticism to create a hung jury and a mistrial. The issue that faces us is more horrible even than murder, for here we speak not of one but an exponential number of grotesque deaths and mutilations. Herbert S. Denenberg, insurance commissioner of Pennsylvania, states, "It may be that no one but God could write the insurance policy we need on nuclear reactors!"

It is my firm conviction that if a jury of 12 impartial scientists was empanelled, and following normal legal procedure they were given all pertinent data and arguments: then this jury would never give a unanimous vote for deployment of nuclear reactors amongst the civilian population. Rather, I believe they would call for the complete shutdown of all commercially operated nuclear plants.

Through positive action and a sense of moral outrage, I seek to test my convictions.

Love and affection to all my fellow citizens.

Scratching his head, the sleepy, unbelieving officer read what came to be called "The Washington's Birthday Statement." The sergeant stared at the statement and then booked Sam Lovejoy. In the morning Sam was arraigned in nearby Greenfield and proudly pleaded "absolutely not guilty" to a charge of willful and malicious destruction of personal property, carrying a maximum penalty of five years in prison. Sam convinced the judge that he had turned himself in because he

wanted to stand trial, and he was released without bail in his own recognizance.

The trial of Samuel H. Lovejoy began in mid-September at the Franklin County Courthouse in Greenfield, Judge Kent Smith presiding. Sam had decided to defend himself against the charge. "I wanted to show the jury the whole Sam Lovejoy," he said later, "to make this a case of humanity against property."

At the beginning of the trial the jury stared intently at Sam's striking New England features, the ungainly sports jacket just a shade too large for the man's slender frame, the rough work boots, his long hair pulled severely back and tied in a bun.

Judge Smith, as progressive and intelligent a judge as Sam could hope for in this eco-political case, was almost overly solicitous in protecting Lovejoy's rights.

"At first the judge's initial reaction to me acting as my own counsel was uptightness," Sam recalled. "At both pre-trial hearings he strongly cautioned me against the idea. And once the trial began he kept tripping me up, testing me, getting on my back with procedural trivia about my legal motions and my lack of experience." But Sam had been reading the law voraciously in the seven months since he toppled the tower. And he had two lawyers, Tom Lesser and Harvey Silverglate, behind him in the courtroom constantly passing him notes and suggestions.

Assistant District Attorney John Murphy's case for the prosecution was contained in the testimony of one major witness. Sergeant John Cade, the arresting officer, was called to the stand and asked to read the Washington's Birthday Statement and to establish the fact that Lovejoy had voluntarily turned himself in and accepted full responsibility for destruction of the tower.

Lovejoy's strategy was to prove he hadn't acted with malicious intent. As his first witness he called Dr. John Gofman. The short, grey-bearded man was sworn in and presented his credentials to the court: Director of the Lawrence-Livermore Radiation Laboratory at Stanford, co-founder with Glenn Seaborg of the AEC; discoverer of Uranium 233, inventor of the various processes of separating plutonium for producing nuclear power.

Several years ago Gofman and Arthur Tamplin wrote an extraordinary AEC study of the potential hazards of nuclear power plants; the controversial report was promptly suppressed by the AEC, which had commissioned it. The two scientists subsequently published their findings as a book, *Poisoned Power.*

Gofman would be a friendly witness. Thirty years before he had helped to pry open Pandora's Box. Now, like many of his original colleagues, he wanted to shut it again for the good of humanity.

The D.A. objected before Gofman could begin to testify, stating that Gofman was in California when the tower was toppled and could present no evidence pertinent to this case.

This got Lovejoy mad. "Your honor, this witness is the key to my case. *Poisoned Power* showed me that the citizen has no recourse from the AEC or any authority in trying to keep nuclear power from coming into a community. He showed me the holocaust that the nuke could bring us. It was John Gofman who led me to the tower that night."

"Now Mr. Lovejoy," the judge asked, "did you talk to Dr. Gofman before you did anything?"

"Did I *talk* to him?" Sam exclaimed, exasperated. "I talked to George Washington and the signers of the Constitution before I did it. I talked to Thoreau when I wrote my statement. Why, your honor, don't *you* talk to Oliver Wendell Holmes when you read his books?"

The judge appeared slightly taken aback at this tirade, yet sustained the prosecution's objection. The same ruling applied to Lovejoy's other expert witness, Professor Howard Zinn of Boston University, who sought to testify on the history of civil disobedience.

After Zinn's testimony the trial was recessed for the weekend. The jury was admonished not to watch television or read the papers while they were home.

When court reconvened on Monday Sam called a succession of local character witnesses, and then put himself on the stand to testify in his own behalf. For a day and a half Sam described his farming background and the deleterious effects of pesticides, talked of his research

into the nukes and his reasons for destroying the tower, saying in the end that his act was for the children and their children's children. "They depend on us not to desecrate the land in the name of gross profit," he said. "I knew I had to do at least this for the children." With the testimony at a close, the judge then instructed the jury as follows:

Ladies and gentlemen of the jury:

The defendant is charged by the Commonwealth of Massachusetts with the crime of malicious destruction of property. Whoever destroys or injures the personal property of another in any manner and by any means, if such destruction or injury is willful and malicious, is guilty of malicious destruction of property.

The burden of proving guilt beyond a reasonable doubt is always upon the prosecution. A reasonable doubt exists if after careful and impartial consideration of all the evidence in the case a juror is not convinced to a moral certainty that the defendant is guilty of the charge.

In order to find the defendant guilty of the charge you must find that the prosecution has proven each and every element of the charge beyond a reasonable doubt. The crime of malicious destruction of property is comprised of four elements: you must find that (1) the tower was the property of Northeastern Utilities and not of the defendant, and (2) that the defendant did actually destroy or injure the tower, and (3) that the defendant acted without the permission of the rightful owner of the tower, and (4) that the injury or destruction was willfully and maliciously committed.

Malice is defined as follows: if there was an intention on the part of the defendant to inflict injury upon property which was (1) not justified on any lawful ground or (2) was not palliated by the existence of any substantial mitigating circumstances, then that intention was malicious within the meaning of the law. Malice does not imply or require proof of ill will by the defendant. Malice is a state of mind which prompts the conscious violation of law to the prejudice or injury of another.

You may take into account all the evidence actually presented to you in this trial. If you do not find that this evidence convinces you beyond a reasonable doubt of each and every element of the crime of malicious destruction of property as defined by me then you must find the defendant not guilty.

[As jurors, determine Lovejoy's guilt or innocence.——Ed.]

Questions

1. Jury as a political institution:

   As a juror, what was your analysis of the political context and meaning of Lovejoy's act? Did you consider this an apt case for nullification? Would a better purpose be served by Lovejoy's conviction or by his acquittal in view of his strategy? In view of Dr. King's statements about civil disobedience?

   How much of your difference with other jurors is accounted for by differences in your views about nuclear power? About the proper role of jurors? About the importance of maintaining the rule against destruction of property?

2. Judicial role of juries:

   How seriously did your fellow jurors take your views? Did you feel any pressure to go against your own best judgment? Did you want to explore possible difficulties with the case even after you reached apparent agreement about how it should end? Did any people on the jury seem to refuse to face the issues? If so, how did they manifest this resistance?

   What skills of persuasion or communication did you feel called upon to use in the deliberations? Did any leadership structure or pattern of influence develop in your jury? What and how? How might your consciousness of your role have been influenced by the number of jurors or the vote required?

   Did you feel in need of more evidence? If so, what kind and from whom? Do you think that Judge Frank or Melvyn Zerman has the more accurate view of jury deliberation as you experienced it? Was the verdict reached just? Would you want

to explain your vote to someone who asked outside the jury room?

What would have been lost if, as actually was the case, the Lovejoy trial never reached the jury? From Lovejoy's point of view? From the community's point of view? From the legal process's point of view?

3. Jury selection:

   Who would have been the ideal jurors for this trial? What kind of selection process would yield such jurors? How did your jury change in its deliberations or verdict by who actually served on your jury? What information did you request or learn about other jurors during the deliberation and what influence did this have on your thinking? Did any people seem to deserve more respect or carry more weight than others in the jury deliberation?

   Who are Sam Lovejoy's peers in this case? Can this question be answered by reference to his age? Lifestyle? Socioeconomic background? Race? Religion? What were the attitudes of the other jurors about the utility company? Were any peers of the corporation represented in the jury? Should there have been?

   Suppose you were working with a psychologist to help pick a jury for a trial like this? Knowing what you now do about how the discussion progressed, what kind of jurors would you have wanted to eliminate? Is your opinion on this matter at all based upon the jurors' attitudes toward law in general? Authority? Rules? Expertise? Left to the constitutional standards for fair jury selection, how likely would Sam Lovejoy be to get a fair trial?

4. History and future:

   Is there anything about your experience in this deliberation that would make you feel more strongly or articulate your views more rationally if it were suggested that jury trials be eliminated? Replaced by ordeals? By truth serums? By a process such as that used by the Chinese? Are jury trials important?

Suggested Additional Readings

The American Jury System: Final Report. Annual Chief Justice Earl Warren Conference on Advocacy in the United States. New York: Roscoe Pound Trial Lawyers Association, 1977.

Bloomstein, Morris J. *Verdict: The Jury System.* New York: Dodd, Mead, 1972.

"Federal Grand Jury Investigation of Political Dissidents," *Harvard Civil Rights–Civil Liberties Law Review* 7 (1972): 432.

Federal Jury Selection Act, 28 USC 1861 *et seq.*

Forsyth, Walter, *History of Trial by Jury.* New York: Burt Franklin, 1971.

Kalven, Harry, Jr., and Zeisel, Hans. *The American Jury.* Boston: Little, Brown, 1966.

Palmer, Ronald. "Post-Trial Interview of Jurors in the Federal Courts—A Lawyer's Dilemma." 6 *Houston Law Review* 290 (1968).

Simon, Rita James. *The Jury System in America: A Critical Overview.* Vol. 4, Sage Criminal Justice System Annuals. New York: Sage, 1975.

Subcommittee to Investigate Administration of Internal Security Act of Senate Judiciary Committee. Hearings on Recording of Jury Deliberations. 84th Cong., 1st session, 1955.

Stock Boston

If I were having a philosophical talk with a man I was going to have hanged (or electrocuted) I should say, "I don't doubt that your act was inevitable for you but to make it more avoidable by others we propose to sacrifice you to the common good. You may regard yourself as a soldier dying for your country if you like. But the law must keep its promises."

Oliver Wendell Holmes, *Holmes-Laski Letters, 1916–1935* (1953)

chapter five

Prisons

The way in which a society defines and responds to deviant behavior is one of the most significant and illuminating aspects of that society. What kind of behavior is labeled as deviant reveals important insights into the nature of that society. The criminal law and the criminal process reflect directly on the organization of society. Indeed, at least one writer has suggested that the criminal process is the mechanism by which a society defines itself:

A human community can be said to maintain boundaries...in the sense that its members tend to confine themselves to a particular radius of activity and to regard any conduct which drifts outside of that radius as somehow inappropriate or immoral.... Human behavior can vary over an enormous range but each community draws a symbolic set of parentheses around a certain segment of that range and limits its own activities within that narrow zone. These parentheses, so to speak, are the communities boundaries.... Deviant persons often supply an important service to society by patrolling the outer edges of group space and by providing a contrast which gives the rest of the community some sense of their own territorial identity.*

This suggests that a society actively uses the criminal law to define and limit itself. As Tocqueville once said, "He who punishes the criminal is, therefore, the real master of society." Following this view, the relationship of the criminal law to deviant behavior suggests a vision of society that is engaged in a struggle for control on two levels: the general struggle for social, political, and economic power and the struggle to gain control over the criminal law and the criminal process itself.

Such a view is perhaps most clearly reflected

* Kai T. Erikson, *Wayward Puritans; A Study in the Sociology of Deviance* (New York: John Wiley & Sons, 1966), pp. 10 and 196.

in the operation of a society's prisons and in the treatment meted out to its prisoners. Notions of punishment, retribution, rehabilitation, deterrence, freedom, and guilt are shaped by a societal definition of deviancy, as reflected in the criminal law. Because the legal response to deviant conduct is premised on a struggle for social control, what are considered to be acceptable forms of imprisonment will vary and change according to the state of this ongoing struggle. Therefore, an examination of prisons and forms of imprisonment raises important questions about law as well as about justice, deviancy, human nature, and society. An evaluation of prison also suggests important insights about the political, economic, and social relations existing in that society. Ultimately, an examination of prisons indicates in a fundamental way what the quality of life is in that society.

This chapter explores these notions about the relation of criminal law, prisons, and deviancy. It might be helpful to think about the following questions as you read the articles: What would society be like without any prisons? What should happen to an individual who is imprisoned? What kind of experience should it be? Who should decide what kind of "treatment" an individual will face in prison? Who should decide who should go to prison? If the economic system were different, would the prisons operate differently?

1 Punishment

Reflections on the Guillotine   *Albert Camus*

Shortly before the war of 1914, an assassin whose crime was particularly repulsive (he had slaughtered a family of farmers with their children) was condemned to death in Algiers. He was a farm-worker who had killed in a sort of bloodthirsty frenzy but had aggravated his case by robbing his victims. The affair created a great stir. It was generally thought that beheading was too mild a punishment for such a monster. This was the opinion, I have been told, of my father, who was especially aroused by the murder of the children. One of the few things I know about him, in any case, is that he wanted to witness the execution, for the first time in his life. He got up in the dark to go to the place of execution at the other end of town amid a great crowd of people. What he saw that morning he never told anyone. My mother relates merely that he came rushing home, his face distorted, refused to talk, lay down for a moment on the bed, and suddenly began to vomit. He had just discovered the reality hidden under the noble phrases with which it was masked. Instead of thinking of the slaughtered children, he could think of nothing but that quivering body that had just been dropped on to a board to have its head cut off.

Presumably that ritual act is horrible indeed if it manages to overcome the indignation of a simple, straightforward man and if a punishment he considered richly deserved had no other effect in the end than to nauseate him. When the extreme penalty simply causes vomiting on the part of the respectable citizen it is supposed to protect, how can anyone maintain that it is likely, as it should be, to bring more peace and order into the community? Rather, it is obviously no less repulsive than the crime, and this new murder, far from making amends for the harm done to the social body, adds a new blot to the first one. Indeed, no one dares speak directly of the ceremony. Officials and journalists who have to talk about it, as if they were aware of both its provocative and its shameful aspects, have made up a sort of ritual language, reduced to stereotyped phrases. Hence we read at breakfast time in a corner of the newspaper that the condemned 'has paid his debt to society' or that he has 'atoned' or that 'at five a.m. justice was done.' The officials call the condemned man 'the interested party' or 'the patient' or refer to him by a number. People write of capital punishment as if they were whispering. In our well-policed society, we recognize that an illness is serious from the fact that we dare not speak of it directly. For a long time, in middle-class families people said no more than that the elder daughter had a 'suspicious cough' or that the father had a 'growth' because tuberculosis and cancer were looked upon as somewhat shameful maladies. This is probably even truer of capital punishment since everyone strives to refer to it only through euphemisms. It is to the body politic what cancer is to the individual body, with this difference: no one has ever spoken of the necessity of cancer. There is no hesitation, on the other hand, about presenting capital punishment as a regrettable necessity, a necessity that justifies killing because it is necessary, and let us not talk about it because it is regrettable.

But it is my intention to talk about it crudely.

Condensed by permission of Alfred A. Knopf, Inc. from *Resistance, Rebellion and Death*, by Albert Camus, translated by Justin O'Brien. Copyright © 1960 by Alfred A. Knopf, Inc.; autorisé par les Editions Calmann-Lévy.

Not because I like scandal, nor, I believe, because of an unhealthy streak in my nature. As a writer, I have always loathed avoiding the issue; as a man, I believe that the repulsive aspects of our condition, if they are inevitable, must merely be faced in silence. But when silence or tricks of language contribute to maintaining an abuse that must be reformed or a suffering that can be relieved, then there is no other solution but to speak out and show the obscenity hidden under the verbal cloak. France shares with England and Spain the honour of being one of the last countries this side of the iron curtain to keep capital punishment in its arsenal of repression. The survival of such a primitive rite has been made possible among us only by the thoughtlessness or ignorance of the public, which reacts only with the ceremonial phrases that have been drilled into it. When the imagination sleeps, words are emptied of their meaning: a deaf population absent-mindedly registers the condemnation of a man. But if people are shown the machine, made to touch the wood and steel and to hear the sound of a head falling, then public imagination, suddenly awakened, will repudiate both the vocabulary and the penalty.

When the Nazis in Poland indulged in public executions of hostages, to keep those hostages from shouting words of revolt and liberty they muzzled them with a plaster-coated gag. It would be shocking to compare the fate of those innocent victims with that of condemned criminals. But, apart from the fact that criminals are not the only ones to be guillotined in our country, the method is the same. We smother under padded words a penalty of which it would be impossible to assert the legitimacy before having examined it in reality. Instead of saying that the death penalty is first of all necessary and then adding that it is better not to talk about it, it is essential to say what it really is and then say whether, being what it is, it is to be considered necessary.

So far as I am concerned, I consider it not only useless but definitely harmful, and I must record my opinion here before getting to the subject itself. It would not be fair to imply that I reached this conclusion as a result of the weeks of investigation and research I have just devoted to the question. But it would be just as unfair to attribute my conviction to mere mawkishness. I am far from indulging in the flabby pity characteristic of humanitarians, in which values and responsibilities fuse, crimes are balanced against one another, and innocence finally loses its rights. Unlike many of my well-known contemporaries, I do not think that man is by nature a social animal. To tell the truth, I think just the reverse. But I believe, and this is quite different, that he cannot live henceforth outside society, whose laws are necessary to his physical survival. Hence the responsibilities must be established by society itself according to a reasonable and workable scale. But the law's final justification is in the good it does or fails to do to the society of a given place and time. For years I have been unable to see anything in capital punishment but a penalty the imagination could not endure and a lazy disorder that my reason condemned. Yet I was ready to think that my imagination was influencing my judgment. But, to tell the truth, I found nothing during my recent research that did not strengthen my conviction or that modified my arguments. On the contrary, to the arguments I already had others were added. Today I share absolutely Koestler's conviction: the death penalty besmirches our society and its upholders cannot reasonably defend it. Without re-stating his decisive attack, without piling up facts and figures that would only duplicate others (and Jean Bloch-Michel's make them useless), I shall merely state reasons to be added to Koestler's; like his, they argue for an immediate abolition of the death penalty.

We all know that the great argument of those who defend capital punishment is the exemplary value of the punishment. Heads are cut off not only to punish but to intimidate, by a frightening example, any who might be tempted to imitate the guilty. Society is not taking revenge; it merely wants to forestall. It waves the head in the air so that potential murderers will see their fate and recoil from it.

This argument would be impressive if we were not obliged to note:

1. That society itself does not believe in the exemplary value it talks about;

2. That there is no proof that the death penalty ever made a single murderer recoil, when he had made up his mind, whereas clearly it had no effect but one of fascination on thousands of criminals;

3. That, in other regards, it constitutes a repulsive example, the consequences of which cannot be foreseen.

To begin with, society does not believe what it says. If it really did so, it would exhibit the heads. Society would give executions the benefit of the publicity it generally uses for national bond issues or new brands of drinks. But we know that executions in our country, instead of taking place publicly, are now perpetrated in prison courtyards before a limited number of specialists.

Today there is no spectacle, merely a penalty known to all by hearsay, and, from time to time, the news of an execution dressed up in soothing phrases. How could a future criminal keep in mind, at the moment of his crime, a sanction that everyone strives to make more and more abstract? And if it is really desired that he constantly keep that sanction in mind, so that it will first balance and later reverse a frenzied decision, should there not be an effort to engrave that sanction and its dreadful reality in the sensitivity of all by every visual and verbal means?

Instead of vaguely evoking a debt that someone this very morning paid society, would it not be a more effective example to remind each taxpayer in detail of what he may expect? Instead of saying, 'If you kill, you will atone for it on the scaffold,' would it not be better to tell him, for purposes of example: 'If you kill, you will be thrown into prison for months or years, torn between an impossible despair and a constantly renewed terror, until one morning we shall slip into your cell after having removed our shoes the better to take you by surprise while you are sound asleep after the night's anguish. We shall fall on you, tie your hands behind your back, cut your shirt collar and your hair with scissors if need be. Perfectionists that we are, we shall bind your arms with a strap so that you are forced to stoop and your neck will be more accessible. Then we shall carry you, an assistant supporting you on each side by the arm and with your feet dragging behind through the corridors. Then, under a night sky, one of the executioners will finally seize you by the seat of your trousers and throw you horizontally on a board while another will steady your head in the lunette and a third will let fall from a height of seven feet a hundred-and-twenty-pound blade that will slice off your head like a razor.'

For the example to be even better, for the terror to impress each of us sufficiently to outweigh at the right moment an irresistible desire for murder, it would be essential to go still further. Instead of boasting, with the pretentious thoughtlessness characteristic of us, of having invented this rapid and humane method of killing condemned men, we should publish thousands of copies, to be read in schools and universities, of the eye-witness accounts and medical reports describing the state of the body after the execution. Particularly suitable for this purpose is the recent report to the Academy of Medicine made by Doctors Picdelièvre and Fournier. Those courageous doctors, invited in the interest of science to examine the bodies of the guillotined after the execution, considered it their duty to sum up their dreadful observations: 'If we may be permitted to give our opinion, such sights are frightfully painful. The blood flows from the blood vessels at the speed of the severed carotids, then it coagulates. The muscles contract and their fibrillation is stupefying; the intestines ripple and the heart moves irregularly, incompletely, fascinatingly. The mouth puckers at certain moments in a terrible pout. It is true that in that severed head the eyes are motionless with dilated pupils; fortunately they look at nothing and, if they are devoid of the cloudiness and opalescence of the corpse, they have no motion; their transparency belongs to life but their fixity belongs to death. All this can last minutes, even hours, in sound specimens: death is not immediate.... Thus every vital element survives decapitation. The doctor is left with this impression of a horrible experience, of a murderous vivisection, followed by a premature burial.'

I doubt whether many readers can read that terrifying report without blanching. Consequently its exemplary power and its capacity to intimidate can be counted on. There is no reason not to add to it eye-witness accounts that confirm the doctors' observations. Charlotte Corday's severed head blushed, it is said, under the executioner's slap. This will not shock anyone who listens to more recent observers. An executioner's assistant (hence hardly suspect of indulging in romanticizing and sentimentality) describes in these terms what he was forced to see: 'It was a madman undergoing a real attack of *delirium tremens* that we dropped under the blade. The head dies at once. But the body literally jumps about in the basket, straining on the cords. Twenty minutes later, at the cemetery, it is still quivering.' The present chaplain of the Santé prison, Father Devoyod (who does not seem opposed to capital punishment), gives in his book, *Les Délinquants,* an account that goes rather far and renews the story of Languille whose decapitated head answered the call of his name: 'The morning of the execution, the condemned man was in a very bad mood and refused the consolations of religion. Knowing his heart of hearts and the affection he had for his wife who was very devout, we said to him: "Come now, out of love for your wife, commune with yourself a moment before dying," and the condemned man accepted. He communed at length before the crucifix, then he seemed to pay no further attention to our presence. When he was executed, we were a short distance from him. His head fell into the trough in front of the guillotine and the body was immediately put into the basket; but, by some mistake, the basket was closed before the head was put in. The assistant who was carrying the head had to wait a moment until the basket was opened again; now, during that brief space of time, we could see the condemned man's eyes fixed on me with a look of supplication, as if to ask forgiveness. Instinctively we made the sign of the cross to bless the head, and then the lids blinked, the expression of the eyes softened, and finally the look, that had remained full of expression, became vague....'

The reader may or may not, according to his faith, accept the explanation provided by the priest. At least, those eyes that 'had remained full of expression' need no interpretation.

I could adduce other first-hand accounts that would be just as hallucinating. But I for one could not go on. After all, I do not claim that capital punishment is exemplary and the penalty seems to me just what it is, a crude surgery practised under conditions that leave nothing edifying about it. Society, on the other hand, and the State, which is not so impressionable, can very well put up with such details and, since they extol an example, ought to try to get everyone to put up with them so that no one will be unaware of them and the population, terrorized once and for all, will become Franciscan one and all. Whom do they hope to intimidate, otherwise, by that example forever hidden, by the threat of a punishment described as easy and swift and easier to bear, after all, than cancer, by a penalty submerged in the flowers of rhetoric? Certainly not those who are considered respectable (some of them are) because they are sleeping at that hour, and the great example has not been announced to them, and they will be eating their toast and marmalade at the time of the premature burial, and they will be informed of the work of justice, if perchance they read the newspapers, by an insipid news-item that will melt like sugar in their memory. And yet, those peaceful creatures are the ones that provide the largest percentage of homicides. Many such respectable people are potential criminals. According to a magistrate, the vast majority of murderers he had known did not know when shaving in the morning that they were going to kill later in the day. As an example and for the sake of security, it would be wiser, instead of hiding the execution, to hold up the severed head in front of all who are shaving in the morning.

Nothing of the sort happens. The State disguises executions and keeps silent about these statements and eye-witness accounts. Hence it does not believe in the exemplary value of the penalty, except by tradition and because it has never bothered to think about the matter. The criminal is killed because this has been done for centuries and, besides, he is killed in a way that was established at the end of the eighteenth century.

Questions

1. What would Camus say about life imprisonment? If society were forced to know the "gory" details of life in prison, would most people feel differently about sending people to jail?

2. What does Camus mean when he says that he is not a flabby humanitarian and that he believes innocence finally loses its rights? How can he condemn the death penalty and not condemn other modes of punishment?

3. In 1972, the Supreme Court held in the case of *Furman* v. *Georgia,* 408 U.S. 238, that the imposition and carrying out of the death penalty in these cases constitutes cruel and unusual punishment in violation of the Eighth and Fourteenth Amendments.

    In comparison to all other punishments today, then, the deliberate extinguishment of human life by the State is uniquely degrading to human dignity. I would not hesitate to hold, on that ground alone, that death is today "cruel and unusual punishment," were it not that death is a punishment of long standing usage and acceptance in this country. I, therefore, turn to the second principle, that the State may not arbitrarily inflict an unusually severe punishment (p. 291).

Recently, however, the Supreme Court modified its position; and in the case of *Gregg* v. *Georgia,* 428 U.S. 153 (1976), the court stated that "The death penalty is not a form of punishment that may never be imposed, regardless of the circumstances of the offense, regardless of the character of the offender, and regardless of the procedure that followed in reaching the decision to impose it." (p. 187) Justice White stated:

> Imposition of the death penalty is surely an awesome responsibility for any system of justice and those who participate in it. Mistakes will be made and discriminations will occur which will be difficult to explain. However, one of society's most basic tasks is that of protecting the lives of its citizens, and one of the most basic ways in which it achieves the task is through criminal laws against murder (p. 226).

Why has the court changed its view? Does that change suggest any changes in society at large? What has happened in the social, economic, and political spheres of the country that may have affected the thinking of the judges?

Does this reacceptance of the death penalty suggest that fundamental notions toward deviancy and punishment have changed?

4. If the judges were forced to witness every execution of each individual they sentenced to death, do you think that would change their feelings about the death penalty?

5. Is capital punishment justified in any circumstances? What situations might call for the death penalty?

2 Institutionalization and Reform

People who come out of prison can build up the country
Misfortune is a test of people's fidelity
Those who protest at injustice are people of true merit
When the prison doors are opened, the real dragon will fly out.

Ho Chi Minh's Prison Writings

The spirit of the Lord is upon me because He has anointed me; He has sent me to announce good news to the poor, to proclaim release for prisoners and recovery of sight for the blind; to let the broken victims go free, to proclaim the year of the Lord's favor.

Jesus, in *Luke,* 16-30

There should be no jails. They do not accomplish what they pretend to accomplish. If you would wipe them out, there would be no more criminals than now. They terrorize nobody. They are a blot upon civilization, and a jail is an evidence of the lack of charity of the people on the outside who make the jails and fill them with the victims of their own greed.

> Clarence Darrow, *An Address to the Prisoners of Cook County Jail, Chicago* (1902)

To understand how different modes of punishment, treatment, and rehabilitation emerged as dominant forms of imprisonment at different periods of time, it is necessary to examine the convergence of social and political movements behind these historical events. This convergence, as the following article suggests, determines what ideology of imprisonment becomes dominant at a particular point in time. Furthermore, the prevailing ideology of imprisonment can be evaluated only in light of the more general social consciousness and modes of thinking present among the people of the society.

Behavior Modification in Total Institutions   *David Rothman*

The concept of rehabilitation and the practice of incarceration are relatively modern developments, which first emerged in this country during the Jacksonian period, the 1820s, '30s, and '40s. In the eighteenth century, the criminal justice system had been one with more circumscribed purposes: to deter and incapacitate the offender and to punish the sinner. The highly insular and static colonial communities sentenced the petty offender to the stocks, to shame him into conformity; or whipped or fined him, to make crime painful and costly; or banished him, to force some other town to deal with his behavior. For the particularly heinous offender, the murderer or the recidivist who simply would not leave the community in peace, towns had regular recourse to the gallows. Mental illness, to the limited degree that it evoked official attention, was defined not as a treatable disease, but as a special problem in relief or public order. The impoverished insane who posed no threat to others were boarded with a local family at the taxpayers' expense; violent cases were confined to the basement of a jail or some other building. All these were essentially stop-gap measures. They were intended to protect the citizenry and to minimize inconvenience, not to cure the deviant.

Beginning in the post–Revolutionary War period, American attitudes and programs changed dramatically. For the first time the goal of intervention became behavior modification, that is, reform of the criminal and the mentally ill. A heady patriotic enthusiasm encouraged citizens of the new republic to believe that no task, however grandiose, was beyond their ability to accomplish. This nation, unlike corrupt monarchial European

ones, could abolish crime and insanity, thereby demonstrating the superiority of its political and social arrangements. Moreover, the Enlightenment view of man as a plastic creature, shaped by his environment, replaced traditional Calvinist notions of innate depravity. Thus would-be reformers had all the more reason to believe that if only the right influences could be brought to bear, the deviant would be cured.

But these right influences, Americans in the Jacksonian period believed, were not to be found within the community. Their open and mobile society, where men could move westward to new lands or into the growing number of eastern cities, into new occupations or up and down the social ladder, was too chaotic and too corrupting to reclaim the deviant. Rather, for the purposes of reform they had to create a specially designed environment, a quasi-utopian setting. In these microcosms of the perfect society, the criminal and the insane would acquire what they lacked, the vital habits of obedience, discipline, and good order. These ambitions eventually led to the establishment of the state penitentiary and the insane asylum, and coincidentally, the almshouse, orphan asylum, and reformatory. The "total" character of these institutions, their ability to completely structure the environment and to order the daily routine of the deviant, was to be the very guarantor of their success.

Under the influence of this ideology, the institutions took their shape. They were, first and foremost, places of order and discipline. Bell-ringing punctuality and set periods for working, eating, and sleeping characterized the schedules of both prisons and mental hospitals. The corruptions at loose in the community were not allowed to intrude into the institutions. All such establishments were located at a distance from population centers. All of them had massive walls, as much to keep people out as inmates in. All of

From David Rothman, "Behavior Modification in Total Institutions," *Hastings Center Report*, Vol. 5, No. 1 (February 1975), pp. 17–24. © Institute of Society, Ethics and the Life Sciences, 360 Broadway, Hastings-on-Hudson, N.Y. 10706. Reprinted by permission.

them kept correspondence between insiders and outsiders to a minimum. In a similar spirit, the courts handed down lengthy sentences to offenders; the criminal needed long exposure to the regenerative influences of his new environment. So too, legislatures established a minimum of procedural requirements for committing the insane. Why allow them to languish on a courtroom bench if they could be receiving effective treatment?

The prospect of reform shone so brightly that these institutions proliferated and became the pride of the republic. One cannot find any challenge during these decades to the wisdom of a policy of incarceration. The promise to cure made state intervention not merely acceptable but altogether noble.

Legitimation Despite Failure

It is not difficult to sympathize with this initial enthusiasm for incarceration. Indeed, under the management of the first generation of medical superintendents and wardens, prisons and hospitals were places of good order. Every observer insisted that reform was actually taking place. And when one Ohio medical superintendent announced one hundred percent cures in his institution, his statement generated applause, not skepticism. But then beginning in the 1850s, more clearly in the 1870s, still more clearly in the 1890s, it became obvious that the institutions were not fulfilling the promises of their founders. Incarceration was not reforming the offender or curing the insane—rates of crime and insanity were not diminished by it. Worse yet, as numerous state and private investigators discovered, the institutions were typically overcrowded, filthy, corrupt, and brutal. Now one learned about wardens who exploited for their own profit the labor of convicts and of the prevalence of horrible punishments behind the walls. One reads these revelations today with a certain tension: after absorbing one hundred detailed pages of gruesome discipline, of inmates hanging by their thumbs for hours on end or stretched out on racks of medieval design, one wonders how state legislators will conclude their report. Will they pronounce

incarceration an experiment gone bad and search for alternatives? Will they ring the bell on this venture and call for a new departure?

Invariably they did not. One state committee after another, one benevolent society after another, one professional organization after another recounted the abuses and denounced the barbarisms. Then they urged the construction of bigger and better institutions. More cells, more wards, more humane administrators, more skilled guards and attendants—these were their recommendations. The faults lay, they argued, not in the policy of incarceration but in its implementation. The concept was marvelous, it was practice that had to be improved. How did they arrive at this judgment, justify it, and explain it? Why did these men so doggedly defend the institutions? How was the legitimacy of incarceration preserved once the grim reality became so apparent?

For some observers and commentators, the goal of reform was so noble that a program linked with such a goal, however tenuously, could not be abandoned. The rhetoric of rehabilitation was enough to justify the continued investment in incarceration. If they incessantly reminded the managers to strive to this end, perhaps then the institutions would measure up. For others, the convenience of incarceration, its very functional qualities, legitimated the institutions' existence. After all, by the late nineteenth century, immigrants had begun to flood not only our shores, but our prison cells and hospital wards as well. These aliens were dangerous enough in their ghettos; when they flouted the law or went insane, incarceration seemed an appropriate solution. No matter how miserable institutional conditions were, they were decent enough for the Irish—and then, later, decent enough for the blacks.

Still other reformers believed it right and just to defend the idea of incarceration because of their own very special reading of history. Their view of the past trapped them into defending existing realities instead of inviting them to devise alternatives. As they saw it, in half-truth fashion, incarceration in the 1820s and 1830s had replaced a fundamentally cruel and barbaric system, one in which all criminals went to the gallows and all the insane were chained in jails.

Hence, these reformers feared that if incarceration were eliminated as a public policy, the nation would automatically and immediately revert to those loathsome practices. It was the dungeon and the gallows or it was the institutions. Faced with such a choice, reformers believed it the better part of wisdom to work for the reform, not the abolition, of institutions. Finally, they suffered a failure of nerve and imagination; frightened of the future, they accommodated themselves to the present.

The legitimacy of incarceration in this period was further rationalized by the skillful way in which prison and asylum managers juggled incapacitation and rehabilitation. When challenged for not fulfilling the goals of reform, they justified procedures on the grounds of incapacitation. The institutions confined dangerous people, protecting society from the havoc they would cause. But when questioned on the propriety of confining those who were not especially dangerous, they shifted to rehabilitation. The institutions treated the deviant and released him when cured. It was a masterful tactic which kept critics off-balance and prevented them from attacking the system itself. The weakness of a defense that joined together two such divergent goals, that claimed that institutions could simultaneously incapacitate and rehabilitate, went unnoticed.

Those in the best position to mount an attack upon incarceration—state officials and medical professionals—played a more supportive than antagonistic role. By the 1890s, most states had established boards of charities and correction to investigate institutional conditions; invariably, the members of these boards were unwilling to question the legitimacy of the system. When particular abuses came to light, they preferred to sit down with the directors and managers and talk things over man to man, gentleman to gentleman. In training, outlook, and class, the state board members and the asylum directors were alike; with good will assumed on both sides, particular difficulties could surely be overcome. There seemed to be no cause for launching a fundamental attack on the way a peer conducted his business, especially when the other option was to ally oneself with the dangerous immigrant classes.

A devastating critique of the failures of the mental hospitals might have come from the growing number of neurologists in the late nineteenth century. To be sure, neurologists did attack the medical superintendents for ignoring research, for not running better pathology laboratories, for not examining more carefully the somatic basis for mental disorders, but they had no quarrel with the idea of incarceration itself. Their advice on how to administer an institution differed little from the practices of the medical superintendents. All that the neurologists wanted was more laboratory space in the asylums, not a basic change in the daily routine.

Finally, the legitimacy of incarceration received additional support from the existence of "model" institutions. If 999 institutions failed to live up to standards but *one* did, then the 999 failures reflected faulty administration, not a flaw in the system itself. The problem rested with a poorly trained staff or inadequate resources, not with the policy of incarceration. There was a Sodom and Gomorrah quality to this rationale—if ten good men could save a city from God's wrath, then one good institution could salvage the entire network of institutions. In this period, New York's Elmira Reformatory served as the model. Its graded system of classification and its work and early release procedures seemed to high-minded observers to set the standards which other institutions should meet. Whatever message the 999 failures had to transmit about the inherent limitations of the system was drowned out in the chorus of admiration for the one good prison. (A mode of thought from which we are no more immune than our predecessors.)

The result was to confirm the idea of building bigger and better institutions, not to raise doubts on the wisdom of a policy of confinement.

Questions

1. Rothman indicates that the same class interests were served by rigid, hierarchical state institutions for "deviants" on the one hand and by open, chaotic economic arrangements in American society in general on the other hand. What class was this? Who were its members? Does this class exist today?

2. How is it possible for a legal ideology of strict discipline to co-exist with an economic ideology of free-for-all competition in the same society? Does this co-existence indicate a basic split in social consciousness?

3. Rothman says that the criticisms of institutions did not go to their conceptual roots, but only to their practices. Can you think of situations today in which legal, political, or economic concepts are regarded as sacred, even though the practices based on these concepts are subjected to heavy criticism?

4. For further material on class conflict, communities, and ideology, see Chapter Six.

The following interview is with a twentieth-century reformer. Tom Murton attempted to institute his ideas about prison reform in an Arkansas penitentiary. The changes he supports suggest at least one view regarding the relationship of prisons as institutions to prisoners as individuals.

Playboy Interview: Tom Murton

On a bleak, rainy morning in late January of 1968, a small group of convicts trudged through the dark, alluvial mud behind a levee that keeps floodwaters from the Arkansas River out of a mule pasture at Cummins Prison Farm. When they reached a spot marked by a 58-year-old black prisoner, Reuben Johnson, they dug into the earth and, within an hour or so, struck the first of three coffins uncovered that day. The superintendent of Cummins, Tom Murton, told the press that the remains were those of inmates who had been secretly and brutally murdered under previous prison administrations; he also said there was evidence that as many as 200 other men were buried on the prison grounds. The governor of Arkansas, Winthrop Rockefeller, promised a full investigation. Instead, Murton was fired and the burial site was officially described as a paupers' graveyard. There was no more digging in the mule pasture.

The summary dismissal—he was given three days to get his wife and four children and their belongings out of the quarters he occupied on the prison grounds—came as no surprise to Murton; it had happened before. A year earlier, he had lost his job at Southern Illinois University. "I was one of three instructors in a program to train prison middle-management types, and the school wanted me to talk about the ideal number of cells and bars and that sort of thing. Instead, I tried to get my students talking about whether we needed cells or bars—or even prisons—and if we do, what their role in society should be. That was obviously unacceptable, because I was asked to leave."

... When Rockefeller was elected the first Republican governor of the state since Reconstruction—some claimed the prison scandal played a large part in the Democrats' defeat—he talked to Murton, who was serving as a consultant to the Arkansas prison system under a Federal grant, and was impressed enough with his blunt assessment of the situation at notorious Tucker Prison Farm, and with his self-confidence ("I'd like to go to Tucker and demonstrate to the people of Arkansas that you can run a prison without torture and brutality"), to hire him as superintendent of the institution. Once Murton had reformed Tucker, he was to take over its larger parent institution, Cummins, and responsibility for all correctional programs in the state.

PLAYBOY: What was the situation when you took over the Tucker Prison Farm?

MURTON: It couldn't have been much worse. There had been no prison superintendent at Tucker for weeks. One had lasted 90 days and my predecessor had been there only a month before he was found in his office cradling a Thompson submachine gun and defying the inmates to "cross the line." When I arrived on the prison grounds, "order" was being maintained by the presence of 13 unarmed state troopers. It was ludicrous: They were there to control more than 300 inmates, many of whom were armed to the teeth.

PLAYBOY: Where did they get the guns?

MURTON: From the state. Since no funds were appropriated for prison administration, farming operations were supposed to turn a profit for the state. One of the economies instituted at Arkansas' two prison farms, Tucker and Cummins, located about 50 miles from each other, was a system whereby trusties—inmates who have proved they can be trusted—serve as armed guards over work details of the other two classes of prisoners: the "rank" men, who harvest the crops and perform most of the drudgery around the prison, and the "doh-pops," so called because they used to have to pop doors open for wardens and trusties. "Doh-pops" work with livestock herds, farm machinery and in the garage and slaughterhouse. As part of the prison underground, the inmates also ran a number of illegal activities such as gambling, dope and liquor sales, and homosexual prostitution. The prison staff granted these privileges to trusties who cooperated with them in keeping order and enforcing discipline through the use of torture and brutality.

PLAYBOY: What sort of torture and brutality?

MURTON: In 1966, then-Governor Orval Faubus authorized an investigation of the prisons based on a number of letters and complaints about excessive brutality. It uncovered a variety of shocking practices employed by the wardens, their staffs and inmate trusties. Among these was the use of the strap, which was authorized by state law, making Arkansas the last state in the Union legally utilizing corporal punishment. The mandate was carried out with a vengeance. For offenses as trivial as failure to pick an established quota of cotton, men were forced to lie naked while a warden struck them as many as 60 times with a five-foot-long, wooden-handled leather strap. Every time the leather cut into his flesh, the prisoner had to shout the number of blows and "Oh, Captain!" Some men's buttocks were ripped and scarred beyond recognition; others passed out from the pain.

But this wasn't the most brutal device. That distinction belonged to the "Tucker Telephone," a satanic instrument employed by Jim Bruton, who was superintendent of Tucker until Faubus fired him in the wake of a report by the state criminal-investigations divisions. When a man received this form of punishment, he was taken to the hospital infirmary, stripped, then strapped to the operating table; electrodes were attached to his big toe and penis and wired to an old-fashioned rural telephone. When the handle was cranked, six volts of electricity discharged into his body. The process was repeated until the man was thought sufficiently disciplined, revealed some desired information or passed out from a sustained jolt of electricity, which inmates referred to as getting a "long-distance call." Typical prison humor. Some men were rendered permanently sterile; others went insane.

Not all torture, of course, was this exotic. Some men were beaten with pipes, clubs or rifle butts.

PLAYBOY: What were you able to do at Tucker to ease the tension and take control?

MURTON: Well, I realized that I couldn't take over by force, since I was the only nonconvict in the place with a gun—a little .38 I smuggled in past the guard at the gate. In that insane situation, I had to have the inmates' approval before I could begin to take charge and run the place. So, as my first official act, I abolished all forms of corporal punishment to show them I intended to make life better for them. Then I replaced with a civilian the inmate who kept the prison records and ran all the communications—radios and telephones—to let them know that *I* was going to administer the institution.

Then I called a meeting with the trusties, who were afraid of losing their power and privileges under my administration. I knew that if they wanted to stop me, they could, since I depended on them for all the services in the prison. I told them so and assured them that there wouldn't be any immediate shake-up. I promised not to demote any of them to "doh-pop" or rank jobs, where their lives would be in danger because of the resentments that had built up against them. I told them that if they cooperated with me, we could work together and make the prison a better place, that I intended to eventually stop their illegal activities, but that they would have plenty of notice.

Then I called a meeting of the other prisoners and told them that there would be no more brutal treatment; that the trusties would still be guards, since I didn't have the funds to change that; so they couldn't expect to just take off or they would be shot. But I told them I was going to improve conditions. After the meetings, I had to make good on my promises to both groups to win their confidence.

PLAYBOY: Were you able to do that?

MURTON: Slowly. But some things called for immediate action. Prisoners live from day to day; their lives are simple. To improve their lot, you tackle the simple grievances—like food. When I got to Tucker, the prisoners were all being fed in segregated groups to avoid mess-hall riots and fights between the trusties and rank men. The quality of food a man ate was determined by the power he had in the institution. If he was a trusty or had money, the inmates in the kitchen saw to it that he had meat three times a day, milk, vegetables and as much as he wanted to eat. Most "short hairs," as new inmates are called, got a spoonful of rice a day, plus some soybeans, corn bread and water. They ate meat once a *year,* usually pigs'-knuckles soup. The food was rancid and often contaminated with weevils. If they wanted any better fare, they had to bribe someone to get it. Some men were 40 to 60 pounds underweight. All this despite the fact that the kitchen, which had been built in 1966, was completely modern; the prison was farming several thousand acres and had large livestock herds and a slaughterhouse; the means to feed the convicts well were all right there.

I brought in an old friend, Bea Crawford, a large, dynamic woman who had worked with me when I ran the Alaskan correctional institutions, to take over the kitchen. She put the inmate kitchen crew to work cleaning the place up, started planning meals, accounting for supplies and feeding all prisoners three meals a day at the same time. Within a couple of weeks, we were serving meat at every meal and all the inmates had enough to eat. This accomplished two things: It showed the prisoners that I would deliver on my promise to improve conditions and it eliminated two major sources of tension—bad food and blackmarketing of provisions. In any prison, there are a few simple measures that can be taken immediately that will win the prisoners' confidence and improve conditions. These are the things I went after right away in Arkansas.

PLAYBOY: What did you do next?

MURTON: I went after the rackets. Any kind of prison racket is a source of trouble. Violence erupts because of debts not paid off to loan sharks, and theft of contraband, whiskey or narcotics. If you can eliminate the illegal activities, you can cut down on violence and assaults. The usual approach is tight security, close inspection of all mail and packages coming in, close supervision of visiting—in some places, they even shake down visitors—all the obvious police techniques. But these techniques, like all the other traditional tools of prison administration, are negative and unproductive.

When I went in there, we stopped the procedure of shaking down the visitors for contraband whiskey or weapons or drugs and the shaking down of inmates by other inmates. I opened up the prison to unsupervised visits by family, friends—everybody—and there's no evidence that anything was ever smuggled in after that, since the prisoners didn't want to risk losing these new privileges by trying to bring contraband inside.

PLAYBOY: Homosexuality is a major cause of prison violence. How did you handle this problem?

MURTON: I used some other nontraditional approaches. The homosexual situation was particularly bad in Arkansas, because there were only a few cells. If you can provide single-cell confinement, a man can, at least, be protected at night. But most of the inmates at Tucker were in three barracks of 100 to 150 men each. A complicating factor was that there was no minimum age for commitment, so I had 14-year-old boys in the same barracks with older men, since there were no special facilities for either. The first thing I did was put a staff guard in charge of the yard, the central hallway that controls the dormitory area, but this didn't really accomplish much, because the one man we could afford couldn't cover three barracks. We had serious situations develop, where kids were raped, and one even had his eye knocked out of his head. We were able to put into isolation some men who were likely to make homosexual attacks, but we had to double them up, since we only had seven cells and they had to be used to confine other prisoners for such things as attempting escape. Under these crowded conditions, one man was raped in his cell. So things were getting pretty bad.

Realizing that the professional staff couldn't handle it, I turned to the major source of change in the prison—the inmate power structure. I took a man by the name of "Chain-saw Jack," who was serving life for cutting a man's head off with a saw for making homosexual advances to him. He obviously had a useful hang-up, so I put him in charge of a barracks that I had been having a lot of trouble with. He called the boys together and he said, "OK, you know what I'm doing time for. I'm going to run this place, and if I catch two of you in the same sack, I'm gonna go up front and check out the chain saw." He was joking, of course, but being an older man and being in for murder, he had a certain status and they knew he wasn't going to tolerate any homosexuality. As long as he was in charge of the barracks, the rapes dropped to zero and the other, consensual activities were so infrequent, you couldn't count them. This is the way we changed the prison—using inmates with leadership ability to bring it about.

PLAYBOY: How did you convince these men that it was in their interest to cooperate with you?

MURTON: Every inmate wants two things in prison: to survive and to get out. His ability to get out is dependent upon pleasing the warden, since the institution makes recommendations to the parole boards. If the institution doesn't recommend it, the man will never get out until his sentence expires. So it's not difficult to make people do things the way you want them done. But not all of them. Chain-saw Jack was one of those few people in prison who can be killed but not controlled, like Cool Hand Luke in the Paul Newman movie. Those are the kind you want on your side. Once these very powerful men see that there's a better way to live, they'll follow you and become leaders of the new movement. And other people will emerge who never demonstrated leadership ability before under the corrupt system.

PLAYBOY: A number of your colleagues would contend that this is the worst possible means of reforming prisons—that it's letting the lunatics run the asylum. The man who replaced you in Arkansas, Robert Sarver, says that what is needed to reform prisons and reduce recidivism is more funds for professional supervision and training of inmates to prepare them for the kind of responsibilities you gave them outright.

MURTON: My colleagues and the other public figures in America who address themselves to prison reform are, as far as I'm concerned, generally sincere and well motivated, but lack an understanding of the true situation. When they speak of work-release programs—whereby a prisoner holds down a day job in the community—and vocational training, academic training, conjugal visits, group therapy, psychological counseling, halfway houses, all of these experiments that have been tried over the past 50 years, they're missing the point. There's no empirical evidence to demonstrate that any of these things has the slightest relationship to reducing recidivism. And that should be one of the first aims of any prison reform. The major justification for most of these programs, aside from employing people, is that they keep the inmates busy and, when they're busy, they don't cause trouble. It's an internal device for control of the institution.

PLAYBOY: But don't all these things have a place in penology? Can't the prisoners be at least partially rehabilitated by educational and vocational training?

MURTON: It's not too difficult to get the inmates interested in such things, but what have they got to do with recidivism? What have they got to do with anything? Educational and vocational training may assuage the guilt that liberals feel about the treatment convicts receive, but that's about all. A warden I know talked to a guy who said he'd learned two things in prison: welding, so that when he got out he would be more competent as a safe-cracker, and Dale Carnegie lessons, so he could better con the probation officer and the court when he was arrested again. That's an honest statement by an ex-inmate and it's typical. If you don't change the basic problem with the man, all you're doing is turning out a more skilled and better-educated criminal. As long as you maintain the autocratic system, whatever other Mickey Mouse stuff you do is irrelevant, because you can't let a man be raped at night and expect rehabilitation through group counseling and remedial reading during the day. All these things may be valid, or they may not, but they're probably secondary and superfluous if the true function of the prison is to prepare a man for the free world, which it should be.

We have a democracy here on the outside—compared with other political systems, at least—yet the professionals choose an autocratic, dictatorial system to train a man to function in society. It's analogous to training a man in the Gestapo to be president of the P.T.A. The man most likely to obtain parole is the man who adapts to the autocratic system of the prison, the one who "adjusts" and becomes a robot, the one who isn't bothered by somebody telling him when to get up, when to eat and everything else; he's the one most likely to regain his freedom. He's also the most likely to fail outside, because in free-world society, decisions aren't made for him anymore. He has to decide for himself where he's going to live, where he's going to work, what he's going to do, what time he gets up, what time he goes to bed. I'm suggesting that a better preparation for those responsibilities would be a democratic prison system—one based, at least partially, on inmate self-government.

PLAYBOY: Did you succeed in achieving true self-government at Tucker?

MURTON: Definitely. We even held elections in which some of the men voted for the first time in their lives. We set up an inmate council composed of six members; each of the three barracks sent two representatives. I explained voting procedures to the men and some of the inmates whose trust I had cultivated supervised the balloting. It's significant that no prison "wheels" were elected. When the council was established, we split it into two committees—one in charge of work assignments, the other discipline. The committee on discipline would hear the case of a man who had been charged with violating any rules, allow him to speak and present evidence in his defense, then decide on his guilt or innocence and pass sentence. Since I had outlawed corporal punishment, discipline consisted of extra work loads, denial of privileges or, in extreme cases, a period in solitary—the hole. The committee was remarkably fair and, in many cases, sterner than I would have been. I had veto power, but I never felt obliged to use it.

The committee on prisoner work assignments looked over the records of each new inmate and decided on his function in the prison labor force, based on his outside experience and other factors. It also had the responsibility of determining the appropriate level of custody for each man and deciding which inmates carried guns. These inmates knew more about the minds of convicts than I did and were able to arrive at reasonable conclusions about a man's potential threat to the well-being of the institution and the probability that he would attempt to escape. Again I had veto power but never used it, and none of the men assigned to minimum custody by the inmates ever attempted to escape. Those who weren't able to demonstrate responsibility were given a high-custody grade or restricted until they were able to show they could achieve responsibility. The prisoners know instinctively who these men are. There's no scientific method. You can't tear the walls down and you can't grant everyone the same freedoms in the institution. But I suspect that most prisoners can rise to a higher level of responsibility than they're usually allowed.

PLAYBOY: How much *are* they usually allowed?

MURTON: Practically none. The traditional

approach is to put a man into the system at the maximum-custody level, where he's placed under a microscope and examined and evaluated by people who may or may not be any smarter than he is, and who may or may not decide to reduce his custody level—regardless of his trustworthiness. This happens even to a draft dodger or a pot smoker. Why send him to maximum custody? The custody level should be determined by whether he's going to run or not and whether his running constitutes a real threat to the community. If a man is in for nonsupport, forget it. If he runs off, he's not going to nonsupport another woman. No hazard to the community. Maybe it would be well to send first offenders and people convicted of nonviolent crimes to the sort of minimum-custody detention camps where the total impact of imprisonment would not be imposed upon them. There *are* people, of course, who, for a variety of reasons that may be either congenital or environmental, are a physical hazard to the free-world community. They will always be a problem and should be in a maximum-custody unit. Every legal effort should be made to detain them. But the impulse of most wardens is to provide the highest level of custody for everyone, despite the fact that only about 15 percent of the inmates require the severity of custody we impose; and most condemned men aren't even allowed out of their cells.

PLAYBOY: Did you have condemned men at Tucker?

MURTON: Nine—eight of whom were black. When I arrived, they were confined to their cells, which were filthy. One man hadn't been out of his cell for *eight years*. They weren't allowed to have books, newspapers or magazines. They weren't allowed to communicate with other inmates. They were fed by guards who poked them with sticks and then threw food between the bars, like afternoon feeding at the zoo. One of the first things I did was provide materials for the men to clean and paint their cells. I sent reading material in to them. Then, gradually, I let them move around the cell block. Finally, I allowed them to go outdoors. It was an almost maudlin sight: Men were weeping and kissing the ground.

They began to do work around the prison grounds and eat in the mess hall with the other inmates. That was the first instance of this kind of integrated dining in the history of the Arkansas prison system. The death-row men formed a baseball team and built a playing field where they played the other inmates. They became completely integrated into the prison society without any problems. In fact, they were vital to one of the greatest morale boosters we came up with while I was at Tucker.

PLAYBOY: What was that?

MURTON: The chaplain, Jon Kimbrell, who had been around Tucker before my time, but was only allowed to give ten-minute Bible readings to the inmates, who were forced to march to his chapel to hear them, dedicated himself to reform when I arrived and began going around talking to the inmates on a personal basis. He came up with the idea of a prison band. He had heard one of the inmates playing and singing some of his own tunes on an old rebuilt guitar and thought it might be a good idea to encourage an inmate group that could give concerts at the prison. I agreed and spent $2000 from the inmate welfare fund on equipment. Five inmates, including two from death row, formed a group and began playing for the other prisoners. They even traveled off the grounds and played for the patients at the state mental hospital on one occasion. It's hard for people outside to understand how much something like this means. These men had known nothing but sheer drudgery, brutality and hostility for years. At the first concert, trusties and rank men, black and white prisoners, staff and inmates all sat together and enjoyed the music. In Arkansas, that's a revolution. Later, the band played for dances. At the first one, prisoners were allowed to invite their wives or girlfriends—not both—and staff men attended with their families.

PLAYBOY: And there was no trouble?

MURTON: None whatsoever. The traditional prison warden would never have scheduled such an event for fear that somebody would get raped. I demonstrated my trust in the inmates and they responded in kind. Before the evening was over, prisoners were dancing with staff wives and there was even some interracial dancing, which gave my hate mail a real boost.

PLAYBOY: Even without the racial factor, isn't your kind of program especially vulnerable to charges of "coddling criminals"?

MURTON: The issue of coddling is a smoke screen. I've never found an inmate who preferred prison to freedom, whatever privileges he enjoys inside. There is, by definition, no real way of coddling a man in prison. You're not giving him a break by having him there even if you treat him decently. There are some exceptions: old men who have been in prison most of their lives. Their families are all gone, they have no skills, they have no trade, they're weak—and that's their home. There's another group, which is like military men who do 30 years and really thrive on it and aren't comfortable out in the free world. I think there are even a few people who would commit a crime in order to go back to prison, but such an infinitesimally small number that it's not worthy of debate.

When you strip a man of his masculinity, his heterosexual experience and his freedom of choice, he simply isn't going to prosper. Because as bad as it may be on the street, he can still decide which side of the street he wants to walk on. Of course, you can do what they did with Joe Valachi: Give him a penthouse, like the Bureau of Prisons did—a special suite; he probably lived better there than he did outside. That, I would say, was definitely coddling. But I'm not out to make the prisoner's life posh and comfortable. I'm talking about the common humanity of reminding the inmate that he's a human being. That's where reform starts—as a communication to the inmate that he has dignity as a man. . . .

The amount of authority exercised by the staff is the amount granted by the inmates. They let the staff pretend they're in charge and allow them to control routine procedures in the prison. But the administrators maintain the fiction that they're in charge, doing the job, working with their limited resources to correct the abuses. Finally, you get a situation where the corrections people are doing literally anything to keep the prison from erupting, and lying to the public about what's going on, keeping up a good front with educational programs and the like, and trying to keep alive the lie that a prison can follow—like a number of institutions—the medical model whereby the treator is able to help the treatee whether the latter wants help or not. The assumption is that the treators have inherent wisdom that can be communicated by coercion to the treatee. It can't be done. I can't rehabilitate anyone, but I can create an environment wherein change may come about. I can provide a man with positive experiences. In Arkansas, I ate with the prisoners, talked with them in language they could understand, and wore Levis and work shirts.

PLAYBOY: Didn't they feel you were patronizing them?

MURTON: Hell, I'm just a hick from Oklahoma; that sort of thing is what I like to wear. But aside from that, I was running a farm and I was out and around all the time, so I wore clothes that were practical for the job. But the real reason was so that I wouldn't set myself apart. There are certain barriers to communication: One is having your degrees hanging on the wall; another is wearing a suit when your clientele in prison is wearing cruddy uniforms. What you're really doing when you wear a suit is identifying with the establishment. When I'm with the square Johns in the free world, I dress like they do; I wear their uniform so that I can communicate with them; when I'm working with inmates, I dress like they do. In Arkansas, one group of inmates wore Levis, another group wore white and the trusties wore khakis. Some of the trusties told me they outranked me because they wore khakis and I wore Levis.

For the same reason, staff, trusties and rank men all ate in the mess hall. And when the prison board came to visit, I made them take a tray and go through the line with me. You can imagine what that does to the inmates. These are the ways you tell a convict you don't consider yourself any better than he is by status or birth or any special knowledge. That's how you establish rapport, and you can't fake it. It has to be for real. I don't think I'm any better; I may have had some advantages, some experiences that are different, but if you cut me, I bleed just like any inmate. Prison reform starts with the rapport.

My critics would say there's danger in my methods, but they've got 180 years of prison experience to show what doesn't work. They don't have any experience to show what *does*. I'm arguing that I've *demonstrated* what works. I'm not talking from a purely theoretical stance. I've been there; I've carried the keys. I'm not a patsy or a Pollyanna. There are people I would never let out of a cell. I used the hole and I used humane punitive measures. A certain segment of the inmate population is dangerous; you grant them as much freedom as you can without threatening the rest of the people in the prison community. But even the men on death row, who have the least to lose by resisting reform—you can only kill them once—will cooperate if you're straight with them.

PLAYBOY: How do you feel about capital punishment?

MURTON: There's only one valid reason in favor of it and that's retribution. It's one of the few things in the criminal-justice system that we have statistics on. We know there's no such thing as a deterrent effect. Georgia, for example, had more executions since 1930 than any other state; it also has one of the highest homicide rates. There is no empirical evidence—in fact, the empirical evidence demonstrates to the contrary—that execution serves a valid function in a criminal-justice system, unless you accept the validity of retribution. Of course, it does reduce recidivism; you can't argue with that. The man you execute never commits another crime.

PLAYBOY: What effect do executions have on the other prisoners?

MURTON: Brutalizing. Inmates come up to you and ask how you can murder an inmate when murder is against the laws of the state. You can't tell them that it's legal; try to explain legal murder. That poor slob may have done something in a moment of passion; he may have had some emotional problem that precipitated the act. But you're doing it as a cool, calculated act. You're going to squash him like a bug. In many ways, that's less forgivable than the original act.

PLAYBOY: Were there any executions in Arkansas while you were there?

MURTON: No, because all the cases were on appeal. I would have resigned before allowing an execution. I wouldn't have participated in any way. In fact, we converted the death house into an infirmary and closed off "Old Satan," the electric chair. I could never have killed one of the death-row inmates. They were some of the best men I had. I was never quite so moved as when I received a Christmas card from the men on death row, shortly before I left Tucker to take over Cummins. The message was simple: "There is no possible way for us to put what you truly mean to us on this card. If it wasn't for you, there might not have been [a Christmas]. So from our hearts we say, may the God of your father, Jesus Christ, be with you and your family forever."

PLAYBOY: Why did you leave Tucker?

MURTON: It was part of the plan. Once I had control of Tucker, I was to take over Cummins and eventually administer both institutions. The last five months at Tucker were incredibly calm —one attempted escape and no assaults; at the same time, Cummins was getting worse. Everything I found when I went into Tucker prevailed on an even larger scale at Cummins, since they had an inmate population four times the size of Tucker's. The trusties at Cummins knew that at Tucker I had eliminated the corruption that was their source of power, so they were opposed to me even before I got there. The staff opposed me because I represented a threat to them, too. So they kept the prisoners in a high state of agitation for several weeks before my take-over. O. E. Bishop, who had been running the institution, confined all prisoners to their barracks for three weeks before my arrival. One man had been stabbed to death in a fight over a poker game. There had been sit-down strikes. The situation was so volatile that plans had been made to make a detachment of state troopers, National Guardsmen and airborne troops available in case the institution had to be taken over by force.

PLAYBOY: How much force was actually required?

MURTON: I had one man with me when I took over—Chain-saw Jack.

PLAYBOY: Was there any violence?

MURTON: No. We went in quietly. Two of the blacks from death row at Tucker came to Cummins a few days after I took over and talked to the black inmates there and convinced them that working with me would be to their advantage. Chain-saw Jack accomplished the same thing with the white inmates and I worked out a temporary truce with the staff by appointing one of the guards there temporary superintendent to act in my place during the first weeks, when I would be moving between Tucker and Cummins and couldn't be on the scene at all times.

PLAYBOY: Your successor has accused you of allowing this man to use corporal punishment. Is that true?

MURTON: Yes, it is. But I needed the support of the staff while I gradually brought my own people in and changed the trusty assignments. I drafted a memo appointing Clay Smith acting superintendent and instructed him to use any lawful means he thought necessary to maintain order at the prison. I couldn't hold him responsible for the institution without giving him full authority. The strap hadn't been outlawed in Arkansas at that time, so its use fell within his mandate; and he used it once. I had to prove to the staff that I wasn't a fanatic out to undermine them. They could have ruined me by stirring up the inmates. My tactic worked; there was no explosion and, within a few days, Smith resigned. I was able to fire most of the old guards who had relied on the strap and replace them with people who believed in my methods. I never personally authorized corporal punishment as long as I was in Arkansas.

PLAYBOY: Were you able to institute the kind of reforms at Cummins that had worked at Tucker?

MURTON: To a certain extent. Within the 67 days I was there, we cleaned up the mess hall, broke up the rackets and generally brought a sense of order and purpose to the place. At the same time, I turned my attention to the Women's Reformatory at Cummins.

PLAYBOY: What was the situation there?

MURTON: Women have been little discussed in relation to prisons. Hardly a single story or article or book has been written by a female ex-offender. Their problems are almost never brought to the attention of the public. They are truly the neglected prisoners of America. The women in the Arkansas reformatory were lodged in an antiquated facility that looked like a converted chicken house. There were cracks in the walls, the facilities were poor and it was totally segregated. The Negro women were only allowed to eat the scraps of food from the table after the white women left. The matrons stole most of the food that was brought to the reformatory and they had clothing made for their own families by the inmates. The Negro inmates clipped the grass with their fingernails; they wouldn't even give them clippers. Not that they thought clippers were dangerous. It was just one more mindless humiliation. Those women didn't even have any fingernails; just gnarled stubs.

Worse than that, they were beaten; they had the hide laid on them. They were put without clothing into the hole—a concrete-block structure with no heat and no water, no bedding—and they would have to defecate in a number-ten can. One of my predecessors as superintendent had a buzzer installed beside his bed and he'd just punch it and some gal would have to come trotting over from the reformatory to perform sex acts on him. If it matters, this guy was married. The women were transported to the prison in the back of a van with male convicts—no separation, no supervision. Consequently, they were all raped before they got to the prison. This is the prison as it was.

PLAYBOY: What changes did you make?

MURTON: I kept the women from being raped. And we got the place cleaned up, the women dressed and fed, and we put a stop to the brutality. But the thing that really broke it as far as the inmates were concerned was when an inmate by the name of Ann Shappy had her baby at the state hospital. She would probably be characterized by many people in that area as poor white trash—not too literate, low socioeconomic group and so forth. She'd had eight children before, by a variety of men, and the father of this particular baby was, at that time, in the Oklahoma State Penitentiary. I got a call from the head matron at the women's prison and she told me Mrs. Shappy was very despondent and the prison doctor thought she was going to commit suicide because she'd never been allowed to see her newborn baby, even though she'd given birth to it at the state hospital three weeks before. I called the state hospital and asked why. "Because she's a convict." I couldn't believe my ears. So I went over there and asked her, "Do you want your baby with you?" She said she'd like to *see* it, at least. So we got the baby and brought it to the prison.

PLAYBOY: How did you authorize the baby's release from the state hospital?

MURTON: I let them believe that we'd found a foster home and were placing it with the foster parents. The next day, the welfare department was going to take the baby and put it out for adoption and Mrs. Shappy would never have been able to see it. I had no notion of raising that kid in the prison, but at that time his mother needed her baby and he needed his mother. Unless the mother's beating her baby, it's better for a child to be with the natural mother for the first two years—even in prison—than with anyone else. So I went up and grabbed it and we got a case of formula milk and went on back to the prison. By the time we got there, one of the trusties had given up her bed; they'd strung a curtain across the corner and we had a nursery going there. After a few days, the male inmates down at the carpenter shop built little toys and a high chair. The women's attitude changed, the whole joint changed; we had no problem at all.

By this simple act of humanity, I was able to gain the confidence and respect of the inmates at the Women's Reformatory. I did the same thing at the men's prison by firing a staff man who was stealing. Many of the inmates literally went to the wall with me; they risked their lives by taking on the old system and risking the vengeance of the trusties and guards who ran it. That's how we changed the prison—recognizing these people and giving them a chance.

PLAYBOY: What finally happened to the baby?

MURTON: The "new, progressive" prison board expelled the baby while I was away. The reason wasn't because the people in the commu-

nity complained, although a few did. The staff tolerated it and the inmates loved it. The reason was because the people in the power structure thought it was unethical to have a baby in prison, because prisons are bad for people. They ought to know; they *make* them that way. All of this came from those in the system who were afraid of the ways I rocked their little boat. It was just a general resistance to innovation that might eventually threaten their fiefdoms. But it wasn't until I began to expose the system in its most naked brutality that they fought back hard. Hard enough to get me fired.

PLAYBOY: Are you referring to the murdered inmates whose bodies you uncovered?

MURTON: Right. When I arrived at Cummins, the records were in such bad shape that we didn't even know how many men we had in the prison. Some men had two files; brothers were listed in a single set of records; men were still carried who had escaped or been released years before. It was a total mess. Gradually, we got things straightened out, but we discovered a curious thing in the process. Over 200 prisoners were listed as escapees and had never been found—an unusually high number. The prison doctor also found that a number of inmates had been listed as victims of heart disease on death certificates—six within a four-day period.

Then he talked to a 58-year-old black inmate, Reuben Johnson, who said he had buried three prisoners, one of whom was listed as an escapee. He claimed he had seen the man murdered in 1947—on Christmas Eve—by a warden who told him to bury the dead man. Johnson said he built a coffin, put the body in it and buried it out near the levee that kept the floodwaters from the Arkansas River out of the prison fields. He said he had buried two other convicts, one of whom had been beheaded by a warden, the other bludgeoned to death by trusties, in the same location. He said he could point right to the spot.

A reporter from *The New York Times* called me shortly after I received this information and asked if I had heard anything about murdered inmates buried on prison grounds. I told him we intended to start digging. After his story appeared, we were besieged by newsmen. On January 29, 1968, we took a crew to the spot indicated by Johnson and with reporters and television newsmen watching, began digging. In a few hours, we uncovered three coffins. Preliminary study of the bones indicated that one man's head had been cut off, another's legs, and one's skull had been pounded to the size of a grapefruit. Since the press was there, all of this was front page and on the evening news. We had a large scandal on our hands in Arkansas, since most of the people who had run the prisons when the murders were committed were still around.

PLAYBOY: What was the official reaction?

MURTON: Governor Rockefeller called a press conference and promised a full investigation that would "let the chips fall where they may." In less than a week, he was begging off this promise, saying he thought the Criminal Investigation Department of the state police should have handled the digging, that I should have cleared it first with him—although I had authorization from his office—and that I was probably not the right man to run the Arkansas prison system. He was being pressured by members of the legislature, some of whom had worked in the prison system or had relatives and friends who had. A grand jury investigation was held in Lincoln County, where Cummins is located; it consisted for the most part of people who had connections with the prison. The judge in Lincoln County, Henry W. Smith, was the same man whose nephew I had made temporary warden at Cummins. Judge Smith so structured the grand jury that they were even considering indicting me for "grave robbing." They were far more interested in finding out why the men were dug up than who they were and why they were buried. A number of people in the state suggested that I had stumbled across a paupers' graveyard, and the deputy state medical investigator said he doubted that any of the men whose skeletons we had found had died violently. Nobody seemed very concerned about explaining why a head had been cut off and another crushed before these "paupers" were buried. And although there were several depressions in the earth in the field nearby where we found

the skeletons, there was no additional digging to see if these were more graves.

PLAYBOY: Has anything been done since to determine the cause of death of those three men, or to find out if others are buried in the same area?

MURTON: Nothing, even though there is no statute of limitations on murder in Arkansas or in any other state. My successor, Robert Sarver, even admits that more men may have been secretly murdered and buried in that pasture at Cummins, but he doesn't make any effort to do anything about it. He says it's not his responsibility, that the local prosecutor should conduct the investigation not the prison administration. All this is technically correct, but four years have passed since we first discovered the bodies. I think that indicates just how concerned the law-enforcement people are about the murder of inmates in Arkansas prisons. Sarver makes high-sounding statements about how he's concerned with the living and with trying to make prison conditions better for them. Well, I wonder how the living feel about working over the bodies of inmates who were murdered in the night and secretly buried by men who will never have to answer for their crimes. No prisoner in Arkansas can believe that justice is anything but a travesty as long as the resources of the state can be mobilized to punish him for his crime while the barbarism of state officials goes unpunished even when the evidence is clear.

Since I left, the inmate council has been abolished; the open-press policy has been eliminated; death-row inmates are once again restricted to their cells for most of the day. Conditions at the women's reformatory have reverted to those of the old, brutal days. Women are thrown naked into isolation units that have no plumbing, water or heat. They are fed miserably and sometimes beaten. Things became so bad that women began to attempt escape—something that had never happened before. In 1968, the then-superintendent at Cummins, Victor Urban, had inmates chained to a fence for several days as punishment. The men had to sleep on the ground and defecate publicly. Shortly after this, 100 inmates sat in the prison yard to protest work loads, inadequate food and other conditions. Although they constituted no threat to prison security, did not riot and made no attempt to escape, they were shotgunned. Twenty-four men were wounded. One lost an eye.

The inmate power structure is once again operating a number of rackets, so violence among prisoners has increased. There have been at least 18 stabbings and seven deaths since I was fired. Most of the staff I hired left with me or were fired shortly after my dismissal. The inmates who had worked with me and taken great risks to bring about reform weren't so lucky. They had to stay and face the vengeance of guards and inmates who regained their old positions of power. Chain-saw Jack was blinded in one eye when an inmate attacked him with a log chain. His assailant was never punished. The action that finally demonstrated the total bankruptcy of Arkansas prison reform was a court ruling. Judge J. Henley Smith, a Federal District Judge, ruled in February of 1970 that confinement in the Arkansas penitentiary was per se unconstitutional because it violated an inmate's right to protection against cruel and unusual punishment. He gave the prison officials several months to present a plan for reform to him.

PLAYBOY: Have they done so?

MURTON: Yes, and he's rejected three plans to date. He's insisting that the state prison system be brought up to minimal constitutional standards and he's threatened to close the prison if they don't do it. I mean totally close it. They'll have to board their prisoners with some other state or some other system, unless he receives a plan that's acceptable to him.

PLAYBOY: In fact, aren't prison administrators more often hindered than helped by the judicial system? Chief Justice Warren Burger recently addressed the American Bar Association on this issue, contending that bail procedures and long court delays are keeping men in prison who shouldn't be there and, in effect, perpetuating the cycle of criminality.

MURTON: I view prison as only part of the whole system. You have to consider not only the system of criminal justice but the entire societal matrix.

PLAYBOY: What sort of restrictions are put on a man on probation or on parole under the present system?

MURTON: Generally, without permission, he can't get a driver's license, he can't get married, he can't buy a car, he can't change jobs, he can't go into a saloon and drink whiskey. Parole is really an extension of the prison; it's custody without walls. If parole is supposed to be easing the man back into full responsibility for himself, how can you have Big Brother checking him in at night? It's the same way with state-operated halfway houses. A halfway house is supposedly a transition from the prison to the street. If a guy's on parole and is messing up and needs a little closer supervision, you move him back into the halfway house so he gets a little tighter structure, where you can watch him a little closer and maybe you won't have to send him back to prison. Excellent idea, excellent theory. But it doesn't always work that way. A man has to sign in and sign out. He can't have female guests in his room. He has to submit to bed checks. This sort of treatment at the hands of the state after a man has been physically released from prison does nothing but remind him of his degradation.

The best halfway houses are those operated by ex-inmates, because they know how to talk to a man. They know that confinement and supervision of a man who has committed a crime is only part of the solution. He also needs some basic understanding and respect. There's an uninformed notion that once you convict a man and send him to prison, that solves the problem. But about 95 percent of these guys come back—if they don't die in prison. What we *should* be doing is turning these men out of prison with the proper training—not just in manufacturing license plates, because about the only place you can practice that trade is inside a prison—then help them get jobs and offer the help of the state in solving their problems. But above all, we must start treating these people as humans. Every man who goes to prison isn't a moral reprobate. Until we stop behaving as though prisoners are fallen people whom we can pity and supervise and straighten out by imposing some formal "book" solution, we're going to re-enforce their antisocial attitudes.

So parole, halfway houses, work release and all the rest of the ways we have of working a former prisoner back into society are good only as far as they're administered by people who don't assume a posture of superiority to the man they're trying to help. This change in attitude is what I want to see. All the money for all the high-priced help in the world is useless if we insist on treating those who have performed criminal acts with condescension and authoritarianism.

PLAYBOY: Can anything be done *before* a man gets to prison to reduce the chance of his repeating criminal acts?

MURTON: Any number of things. Prison should be the last resort. We should be trying to keep lawbreakers *out* of prison. Consider the first offenders who do go to prison and fall into the cycle of criminality. The poor man's kid goes to the reformatory and the rich man's kid goes to the military academy. Or we can talk about suburbia, where you'll find essentially the same incidence of criminal conduct as in the ghetto. It's just handled informally. The adolescent vandal winds up on probation rather than in juvenile hall. I'm not suggesting that the rich should have imposed upon them the system that the poor have. I'm suggesting that the rich could *share* with the poor their method of escaping the criminal-justice system, because in many cases these informal systems seem to work and the kid does not recidivate. Those who could benefit by probation should be taken out of the prison system. One could talk about the whole court process; one could talk about the system of criminal justice for the poor; or about the bail system, which in most cases is based more on a man's ability to pay than the danger he represents to society or the likelihood that he won't appear in court.

PLAYBOY: Is there any validity to the charge that our system of justice is biased against racial minority groups as well as against the poor?

MURTON: It's weighted against the *powerless* in our society, and that includes not only the poor and the indigent but the black, the Indian and the Spanish American. But this is probably more a function of the fact that they can't retain adequate counsel than of racial bias. But it's a cold fact that no white man in Arkansas has ever been convicted and sentenced to the chair for raping a black woman. Yet Negroes are condemned for the opposite crime all the time. So there's no denying that there's a differential enforcement of the law. Until such basic injustice is corrected, it's a little fanciful to think that more sociological expertise among prison, probation and parole authorities is going to infuse a sense of responsibility to society in the people who are convicted of crimes. They're simply going to believe they've been shafted because they're unwhite and unrich. And they'll behave accordingly.

When prisoners look around and see only people like themselves inside the walls, they take it as evidence that they're being singled out by society as scapegoats. Inmates aren't dumb and they aren't entirely cut off from the outside world. They know that organized crime flourishes, that corporation officials are violating the law and getting away with it, that public officials are making and taking payoffs and being re-elected in spite of it. Until recently, you had no college-educated people to speak of in the inmate population. Now, with people like Joan Baez' husband, David Harris, and many other "political prisoners" coming into the institutions, there is going to be a change in inmates' political attitudes. It's too early to tell exactly what direction it will take. But wardens are already talking about it, and not with any gleeful anticipation, because people like Harris see the treatment of prisoners as part of a general political malaise, something that can be changed through political action. Prisoners never had any sense of this before; they fought back in very unsophisticated ways, individually or in mobs. Once they learn the language and tactics of confrontation, we may see unrest in prisons that will make some of the college disturbances look very tame.

PLAYBOY: You've said that prison is a microcosm of society and should be studied as such. Doesn't this contradict what you just said about most prisoners being from disadvantaged socio-economic backgrounds?

MURTON: Not really. I don't think prisons represent an exact one-to-one model of the society that establishes them. But they are a perfect model of the development of power systems. There is no masking in prison. Nobody worries about the social amenities and that sort of thing. So prisons should be studied by people who are interested in the motivating factors involved in human behavior, in understanding how power systems evolve and how people are manipulated. We can evaluate how far society has progressed on the evolutionary scale by examining how it treats its deviates, what form punishment takes for those who commit antisocial acts.

There have always been prisoners, slaves, people awaiting trial, execution or some other form of punishment. In the late 18th Century, the Quakers thought a man who was locked up alone in a cell would have time to dwell on his sins and become penitent. Hence the term penitentiary. But they soon learned that people in solitary confinement tend to go insane. So they started letting prisoners have some human contact—but not talk. They worked side by side and all the rest, but they weren't allowed to talk. Then, toward the last third of the 19th Century, there were a number of changes. The prison began to be seen as a place to reform a man through education and work projects. Parole and probation came along. Juveniles were taken out of the prison system. But there were still problems. One was overcrowding; another was outside opposition, in this century, to prison industries. Labor unions were able to outlaw the interstate sale of prison-made goods, arguing that it was unfair for free workers to have to compete with inmate labor.

So drudgery became the name of the game and, today, we have prisoners making license plates and breaking big ones into little ones—all this despite the innovations that have come along, all the things the professionals talk about. The official posture of the American Correctional Association is that prisons were created to implement the philosophy of retribution, and then moved into an era of reform of the individual and of the institution, and that the next few years will be devoted to "reintegration," as they call it—trying to get the offender from the prison back into society in such a manner that he won't commit criminal acts again. That's the *official* posture. But I really don't see that much difference; there's a difference in terminology, but the reality is still essentially the same as it was in the 18th Century: punitive.

PLAYBOY: Can you suggest a more humane form of imprisonment?

MURTON: A society will always have its outcasts. Even in prison, which is a sub-society consisting entirely of outcasts, you *still* find outcasts—those who are sent to solitary. Maybe we should find a new way of marking people as deviant. We had other means before the modern prison came along: branding, exile, the stocks and all sorts of other degradation ceremonies. It might be possible to come up with some sort of new ritual by which a man is ostracized for antisocial behavior. I don't know exactly what it would be, but until we come up with something better, the prison should at least be in a continuous state of reform.

Certain inmate groups and radical reformers have taken up the cry, "Tear down the walls." They believe that the present system is a monster and that we should quit feeding it. But they're like some of the radicals in the larger society who want to abolish the system: They don't have anything to replace it with. The people who want to abolish the prison system don't have an alternative method of taking dangerous people off the streets. I want to see the walls torn down, too; but until they are and something better replaces them, I want to help the inmates who are still behind them.

PLAYBOY: Don't you lose any chance of doing this by alienating your employers and getting fired? Couldn't you accomplish more, as Sarver contends, by bending a little and cooperating with elected officials instead of attacking them?

MURTON: I do polarize people, no question about it. I was fired in Alaska when I testified before the legislature about prison conditions there. I had helped establish the system when Alaska became a state and was in the process of building a model prison camp. But I couldn't get any support from the governor and his people. When I was invited to testify, I embarrassed the governor and he fired me. But I would do it again. Rockefeller didn't want the abuses in the Arkansas prisons spread all over the national media, so he got rid of me. But I didn't create the problems.

When I tried to improve them and he and his staff resisted, that made news. It was news, too, when I discovered evidence of mass murder. I wouldn't do anything differently in Arkansas, if I had it to do over. There is no easy road to true and lasting prison reform. Attention has to be called to the reality of prison conditions, and this is certain to make some people look bad—especially those who have created the situation. So whenever a true reformer comes in, he's going to be opposed by legislators and other government officials who have a stake in the old order. Eventually, he'll push too hard and they'll get rid of him. It's a cycle that's been going on for a long time. I'm not the first—or the last—person who's tried to reform a prison and been dismissed just as real change was being made.

PLAYBOY: Couldn't you settle for a rate of change that wouldn't create so much political hostility?

MURTON: Not without losing the trust of the inmates. You can't fake it with them.

PLAYBOY: But as you said, the inmates are worse off now than they were when you had the job. Which is worse: incurring their distrust or being responsible—by leaving the job—for returning them to inhuman living conditions?

MURTON: Inmate trust is an absolute thing. You can have their welfare in mind and still not have them believe in you or cooperate with you. If they see you make small compromises with their rights and well-being, they'll suspect that you may be willing to sell out when more critical issues are at stake. So they won't work with you. And until you have the inmates on your side, there's going to be no real reform. The prison can't run without the inmates, since they run the joint in so many ways. But if you have them on your side, anything is possible. First, however, you have to go to bat for them. Show a little trust in them and they'll respond. That's what I did in Arkansas— and it drove people crazy. You can't just move into a prison and take over and say, "Let bygones be bygones." There are going to be prisoners there who have been beaten or tortured and guards who have done it. There are going to be powerful inmates who run rackets. There are likely to be state officials involved in some sort of corruption. The brutal guards have to be exposed and held accountable or the inmates aren't going to trust you and believe that you have any real concern for their rights. The prison rackets have to be broken up or the inmates are going to be assaulted. The corruption has to be eliminated or you won't be able to look a prisoner in the eye and tell him that you're justified in keeping him in because he broke the law and criminal acts should be punished. But when you do these things, you make enemies and they fight back. You cause a fuss and people get embarrassed. They'd rather have things quiet, so they get rid of you and bring in someone who promises tranquillity.

Now, I don't have any political ambitions and I don't resist legitimate political authority. If they tell me to paint a barn red instead of green, hell, I'll paint it red. But I cannot accept the mere façade of reform and neither can the inmates; when real issues come up, questions about true prison reform, I have to take a stand for what I believe is right—first, because I'm a man and I value my own integrity; second, because if I don't, the next warden with a riot on his hands is going to be Tom Murton.

PLAYBOY: Do you think you'll ever be allowed to work inside a prison again?

MURTON: Yes. This may be the decade of prison reform. Human rights will be provided by the prison administrators, imposed by the courts or seized by the inmates. But as Martin Luther King, Jr., once observed, freedom is never willingly granted by the oppressor; it must be taken by the oppressed. So we will probably see more riots like those at three New York State institutions and people like myself will finally be hired because the others have failed again. I don't want to see this happen, but when it does, I'll go back —because my real place isn't in the ivory tower; it's in the gun tower.

Questions

1. Murton refers to powerful people "who can be killed but not controlled." He also describes how he relied on "inmates with leadership ability" to

change conditions in prison. He says that new people arise as leaders when the system changes. How is this vision of leadership different from that of professional training for leadership? Which vision makes more sense to you?

2. Murton says that the "autocratic, dictatorial system" of prison administration is incompatible with a free and democratic society. If this is true, what are the reasons that such a system exists in American society? Whose interests are served by this system?

3. Murton suggests that the idea of reform begins with a communication to the inmates that they have dignity as humans. Can imprisonment ever be a dignified experience? How can a prison administrator gain the trust of the inmates?

4. Is it possible to develop an individual's self-respect in a prison environment when there has not been a supportive climate before imprisonment, and when there will be no such atmosphere after release?

5. If prison reflects the larger power struggle in society and prison houses the powerless, can reform of any kind fundamentally alter this larger power conflict? Do Murton's reforms affect this power struggle?

6. Murton suggests that there will probably always be a need for maximum security prisons. Who should be confined in these jails? What is a maximum security institution?

7. Why was Murton fired? Does his firing validate his conception of prison as a reflection of a larger power struggle?

8. Why has there been so little attention paid to women in prison? Do you think that the prison experience is different for women than for men? Statistically, there are fewer "programs" such as vocational training, work release, and counseling in women's prisons than in male prisons. Why? Does this suggest another aspect of the larger struggle for power?

Rules and Regulations for Inmates at Cook County Jail, Chicago, Illinois

1. Address all correctional officers as "OFFICER."
2. DO NOT use slang in addressing an officer.
3. NEVER argue with an officer.
4. Obey all orders given to you by an officer or civilian personnel immediately. If you feel you have a legitimate complaint, you may put in a request to the person's superior only after you have done what you were ordered.
5. You cannot give anything to other inmates without permission.
6. Report all threats, acts of violence or pressures to an officer immediately.
7. Clothing, like everything else is county property. Take care of it. Destruction of ANY County property may get you more time.
8. You will not have cash in your possession at any time.
9. You cannot transfer money to another inmate at any time.
10. No gambling of any kind is permitted.
11. No food, tobacco, stamps, stamped envelopes, or medication can be brought in or sent to you.
12. Turn in all out going letters to officer in housing unit. Letters being written to Attorney, Judges, Court of legal nature may be given to the officer sealed by you.
13. Only books which have been approved are permitted.
14. When moving from one place to another, you will go straight to destination always with an officer or a runner.
15. When in a line, always move quietly, in an orderly manner.
16. Your family or friends may bring clothing 3 days before your out date.

Reprinted from Kathy Burkhardt, *Women in Prison* (New York: Popular Library, 1973), pp. 103–107.

BEHAVIOR:
1. Do not shout or yell at any time.

2. Do not change cells or bunks in dormitories.
3. Do not visit in other cells, dormitories, or housing units.
4. DO NOT FIGHT. No reason or excuse will be accepted.
5. Unnatural sex acts will not be tolerated. Anyone involved in such acts is subject to charges and prosecution.

CLEANLINESS:
1. You must keep yourself personally clean at all times.
2. You must keep your living area clean at all times.
3. You may obtain a razor to shave from an officer. When you have shaved you must return the razor to the officer.

CLOTHING:
1. You can have only 1 set of regular issue clothing at any time. No other clothing is permitted.
2. Do not wash clothing in housing unit. All clothing is washed in the Institution Laundry. Unless permitted by Superintendent Directive.

SMOKING:
1. No smoking in bed or in sleeping area.
2. No smoking in any dining area.
3. No smoking in the hospital. Except by directive.

MEDICATIONS:
1. You are not allowed to have any kind of medication without written permission.
2. All medication must be taken in the presence of a doctor, a nurse, or an officer.

CONTRABAND:
1. You must turn in any contraband you find to an officer. No excuse will be accepted for having any contraband in your possession.

REMEMBER:
ANYTHING NOT ISSUED BY THE INSTITUTION OR SOLD IN COMMISSARY IS CONSIDERED CONTRABAND!

In addition to the above, your housing unit may have some additional rules. If so, you will be told about them or they will be posted. Obey them. Violation of rules will subject you to a conduct report and the possible loss of privileges and/or Good Time.

OBEY THE RULES! STAY OUT OF TROUBLE! DO YOUR TIME! LET US HELP YOU HELP YOURSELF!

Time Schedules
Maximum—4:40 A.M.—Rising Time
5:00 A.M.—Breakfast
10:00 A.M.—Lunch
3:30 P.M.—Dinner
8:45 P.M.—Everyone in own bed area
9:00 P.M.—Lights out

Notes and Questions

1. What other institutions or organizations generate rules of this nature?
2. What purpose do regulations of this nature fulfill? What conceptions of imprisonment and organization underlie these rules?
3. Whose interests and what functions are served by starting the day at 4:40 A.M. and to end it at 9:00 P.M.?
4. How can our society sustain vigorous possibilities of protest for social justice while demanding that individuals obey orders and follow rules?

   Consider the case of Martin Luther King, Jr., who in 1963 had to decide whether to stage a nonviolent demonstration in Birmingham in violation of a state court injunction prohibiting the march. King declared, "We cannot in all good conscience obey such an injunction which is an unjust, undemocratic, and unconstitutional misuse of the legal process.... I am prepared to go to jail and stay as long as possible." (*The Civil Liberties Review*, December 1976/January 1977.) The Supreme Court upheld the injunction, and King went to jail. Thus, in the end King was forced to break the law in order to pursue his vision of justice.
5. What is the significance of the fact that, in some instances, it is necessary to break the law in a search for justice? Is that a contradiction? Under what circumstances might you refuse to follow orders or obey the rules?

Rules and Regulations for the Direction of the Officers and Employees of the Massachusetts Correctional Institution Framingham

"Deportment and conduct between employee and inmate"

12. Your relations with the inmates may be of necessity dual in character. You may be both counselor and disciplinarian at one and the same time. This will enjoin your utmost tact and diplomacy. You should aim to be friendly not familiar, sympathetic not maudlin, firm not harsh, constant, not obstinate, vigilant not unduly suspicious, strict not unjust. Let the inmate feel the impact of your leadership. Do not discuss the discipline or management of this or other penal institutions, or the affairs of your fellow employees while in the presence or hearing of an inmate, nor inform her as to the nature of comments, entries, or reports regarding her made by another employee. Do not show or otherwise allow these rules to be made available to an inmate. Do not

Rules and Regulations for the Direction of the Officers and Employees of the Massachusetts Correctional Institution, Framingham. Reprinted from hearings before Subcommittee No. 3 of the Committee on the Judiciary, House of Representatives, 92d Congress/first session on Corrections, Part V, Prisons, Prison Reform and Prisoners Rights, Massachusetts, December 18, 1971, serial no. 15 (Washington: United States Government Printing Office, 1972).

intercede personally for an inmate relative to release or outside employment, nor endorse a petition for granting parole, pardon or commutation without the permission of the Superintendent. You must not associate, accompany or consort with an inmate on parole or others permitted to be at liberty without specific written approval of the Superintendent and the Parole Board. Do not grant any inmate special privileges but treat all inmates impartially. Let your relations with inmates, or with their relatives or friends, at all times be such that you would have them known to any superior officer.

Questions

1. What relationship should a prison guard have to the inmates? Is it possible for a guard to function both as a counselor and as a disciplinarian simultaneously?

2. Who are prison guards? What kind of training do they receive? What kind of education is required? Are guards armed? Should they be?

3. If you were hired as a prison guard and it was your intention to be supportive toward the inmates, do you think you would be able to achieve your goal? What obstacles might arise?

The institutional reality of prison is so overwhelming and all encompassing that it becomes, as Erving Goffman suggests, a "total institution." * As such, individual attempts at modification and reform are overcome by the force of the institution. This view suggests that humanistic approaches to change within prison walls are doomed and cannot succeed in transforming fundamentally dehumanizing conditions. The following article suggests some reasons underlying the limits of institutional reform.

* Erving Goffman, *Asylums* (Garden City, N.Y.: Anchor Books, Doubleday, 1961).

Testimony of Dr. Philip Zimbardo

U.S. House of Representatives Committee on the Judiciary

I was recently released from "solitary confinement" after being held therein for 37 months [months!]. A silent system was imposed upon me and to even "whisper" to the man in the next cell resulted in being beaten by guards, sprayed with chemical mace, black-jacked, stomped, and thrown into a "strip-cell" naked to sleep on a concrete floor without bedding, covering, wash basin, or even a toilet. The floor served as toilet and bed, and even there the "silent system" was enforced. To let a "moan" escape your lips because of the pain and discomfort...resulted in another beating. I spent not days, but months there during my 37 months in solitary...I have filed every writ possible against the administrative acts of brutality. The State Courts have all denied the petitions. Because of my refusal to let the "things die down" and "forget" all that happened during my 37 months in solitary..., I am the most hated prisoner in —— Penitentiary, and called a "hard-core incorrigible."

Professor Zimbardo, maybe I am an incorrigible, but if true, it's because I would rather die than to accept being treated less than a human being. I have never complained of my prison sentence as being unjustified except through legal means of appeals. I have never put a knife on a guard's throat and demanded my release. I know that thieves must be punished and I don't justify stealing, even though I am a thief myself. But now I don't think I will be a thief when I am released. No, I'm not rehabilitated. It's just that I no longer think of becoming wealthy by stealing. I now only think of "killing." Killing those who have beaten me and treated me as if I were a dog. I hope and pray for the sake of my own soul and future life of freedom, that I am able to overcome the bitterness and hatred which eats daily at my soul, but I know to overcome it will not be easy.

"Testimony of Dr. Philip Zimbardo," U.S. House of Representatives, Committee on the Judiciary, October 25, 1971.

This eloquent plea for prison reform, for humane treatment of human beings, for the basic dignity that is the right of every American, came to me this week in a letter from a prisoner, who cannot be identified because he is still part of a state correctional institution. He sent it to me because he read of an experiment I conducted recently at Stanford University. In an attempt to understand just what it means psychologically to be a prisoner or a prison guard, we created our own prison. We carefully screened over 70 volunteers who answered an ad in the Palo Alto city newspaper and ended up with about two dozen young men who were selected to be part of this study. They were mature, emotionally stable, normal, intelligent college students from middle-class homes throughout the United States and Canada. They appeared to represent the "cream of the crop" of this generation. None had any criminal record and all were relatively homogeneous on many dimensions initially.

Half were arbitrarily designated as "prisoners" by a flip of a coin, the others as "guards." These were the roles they were to play in our simulated prison. The guards were made aware of the potential seriousness and danger of the situation, and their own vulnerability. They made up their own formal rules for maintaining law, order, and respect, and were generally free to improvise new ones during their 8-hour, 3-man shifts. The prisoners were unexpectedly picked up at their homes by a City policeman in a squad car, searched, handcuffed, fingerprinted, booked at the Station House, and taken blindfolded to our jail. There they were stripped, deloused, put into a uniform, given a number, and put into a cell with two other prisoners where they expected to live for the next two weeks. The pay was good ($15 a day) and their motivation was to make money.

We observed and recorded on videotape the events that occurred in the prison, and we interviewed and tested the prisoners and guards at various points throughout the study.

At the end of only six days we had to close down our mock prison because what we saw was frightening. It was no longer apparent to us or most of the subjects where they ended and their roles began. The majority had indeed become "prisoners" or "guards," no longer able to clearly differentiate between role-playing and self. There were dramatic changes in virtually every aspect of their behavior, thinking and feeling. In less than a week, the experience of imprisonment undid (temporarily) a lifetime of learning; human values were suspended, self-concepts were challenged, and the ugliest, most base, pathological side of human nature surfaced. We were horrified because we saw some boys ("guards") treat other boys as if they were despicable animals, taking pleasure in cruelty, while other boys ("prisoners") became servile, dehumanized robots who thought only of escape, of their own individual survival, and of their mounting hatred of the guards.

We had to release three "prisoners" in the first four days because they had such acute situational traumatic reactions as hysterical crying, confusion in thinking, and severe depression. Others begged to be "paroled," and all but three were willing to forfeit all the money they had earned if they could be "paroled." By then, the fifth day, they had been so programmed to think of themselves as "prisoners," that when their request for "parole" was denied, they returned docilely to their cells. Now, had they been thinking as college students acting in an oppressive experiment, they would have quit once they no longer wanted the $15 a day we used as our only incentive. However, the reality was not "quitting an experiment," but "being paroled by the parole board from the Stanford County Jail." By the last days, the earlier solidarity among the prisoners (systematically broken by the guards) dissolved into "each man for himself." Finally, when one of their fellows was put in solitary confinement (a small closet) for refusing to eat, the prisoners were given a choice by one of the guards: give up their blankets and the "incorrigible prisoner" would be let out, or keep their blankets and he would be kept in all night. They voted to keep their blankets and to abandon their brother, a suffering prisoner.

About a third of the guards became tyrannical in their arbitrary use of power, in enjoying their control over other people. They were corrupted by the power of their roles and became quite inventive in their techniques of breaking the spirit of the prisoners and making them feel they were worthless. Some of the guards merely did their jobs as "tough but fair" correctional officers. Several were "good guards" from the prisoners' point of view, since they did them small favors and were friendly. However, no "good guard" or any other one ever interfered with a command by any of the "bad guards"; they never intervened on the side of the prisoners, they never told the others to ease off because it was only an experiment, and they never even came to me as Prison Superintendent or Experimenter in charge to complain. In part, they were "good" because the others were "bad"; they needed the others to help establish their own egos in a positive light. In a sense, they perpetuated the prison more than the other guards because their own needs to be liked prevented them from disobeying or violating the implicit guard's code. At the same time, the act of befriending the prisoners created a social reality which made the prisoners less likely to rebel.

By the end of the week, the experiment had become a reality, as if it were a Pirandello play directed by Kafka that just keeps going after the audience has left. The Consultant for our prison, Carlo Prescott, an ex-con with 16 years imprisonment in California's jails, would get so depressed and furious each time he visited our prison, because of its psychological similarity to his experiences, that he would have to leave. A Catholic priest, who was a former prison Chaplain in Washington, D.C., talked to our "prisoners" after four days and said they were just like the "first-timers" he had seen.

But in the end, I called off the experiment not because of the horror I saw out there in the prison yard, but because of the horror of realizing that *I* could have easily traded places with the most brutal guard, or become the weakest prisoner full of hate at being so powerless that I could not eat, sleep or go to the toilet without permission of the authorities. *I* could have become Calley at My Lai, George Jackson at San Quentin, one of the men at Attica, or the prisoner quoted at the beginning of this report. I believe *you* could too.

With regard to prisons, we can state that the mere act of assigning labels to people, such as "prisoners" and "guards," and putting them into a situation where those labels acquire validity and meaning, is sufficient to elicit pathological behavior. This pathology is not predictable from any available diagnostic indicators we have in the social sciences, and is extreme enough to modify in very significant ways fundamental attitudes and behavior. The prison situation, as presently arranged, is guaranteed to generate severe enough pathological reactions in both guards and prisoners as to debase their humanity, lower their feelings of self-worth, and make it difficult for them to be part of a society outside of their prison.

Prison is any situation in which one person's freedom and liberty are denied by virtue of the arbitrary power exercised by another person or group. Thus our prisons of concrete and steel are only metaphors for the social prisons we create and maintain through enforced poverty, racism, sexism, and other forms of social injustice. They are also the physical symbol of the psychological prisons we create for others, by making even our loved ones feel inadequate or self-conscious, and worst of all, the imprisonment we impose on our own minds and actions through neurotic fears.

The need for "prison reform" then is a cry not only to change the operating procedures of our penal institutions, but a more basic plea to change the conditions in our society which make us all prisoners, all less happy, less productive, less free to grow, and less concerned about our brothers than about our own survival.

Our national leaders for years have been pointing to the enemies of freedom, to the fascist or communist threat to the American way of life. In so doing, they have overlooked the threat of social anarchy that is building within our own country without any outside agitation. As soon as a person comes to the realization that he is being "imprisoned" by his society or individuals in it, then, in the best American tradition, he demands liberty and rebels, accepting death as an alternative. The third alternative, however, is to allow oneself to become a "good prisoner," docile, cooperative, uncomplaining, conforming in thought and complying in deed.

Our prison authorities now point to the "militant agitators" who are still vaguely part of some communist plot, as the irresponsible, "incorrigible" trouble-makers. They imply that there would be no trouble, riots, hostages, or deaths if it weren't for this small band of "bad prisoners." In other words, if they could break these men, then everything would return to "normal" again in the life of our nation's prisons.

The riots in prison are coming from within— from within every man and woman who refuses to let *The System* turn them into an object, a number, a thing, or a no-thing. It is not communist-inspired, but inspired by the spirit of American freedom. No man wants to be enslaved. To be powerless, to be subject to the arbitrary exercise of power, to not be recognized as a human being is to be a slave.

To be a "militant prisoner" is to become aware that the physical jails are but more blatant extensions of the forms of social and psychological oppression experienced daily in the nation's ghettos. They are trying to awaken the conscience of the nation to the ways in which the American ideals are being perverted in the name of "justice," but actually under the banner of apathy, fear, and hatred. If we do not listen to the pleas of the prisoners at Attica to be treated like human beings, then we all have become brutalized by our priorities for property rights over human rights. The consequence will not only be more prison riots, but a loss of all those ideals on which this country was founded.

Questions

1. What do you think of the ethics of conducting an experiment of this nature? What contribution to

society does this type of research make? Should such psychological experiments using human subjects be undertaken?

2. In light of the information yielded by this experiment, what are the possibilities for prison reform? If Tom Murton had been familiar with this experiment, do you think he would have changed his approach to improving prison conditions?

3. Are there any other institutions that would be similar to prisons in their power to overcome individual consciousness? What are other examples of "total institutions"?

4. Does it matter if prison is humane? Why should imprisonment be a humane experience? Are humaneness and dignity realizable goals of incarceration? How can they be?

3 Treatment

The rationale of imprisonment is constantly evolving. At a certain point in the history of penology, imprisonment was no longer based on notions of punishment. Instead, treatment became the dominant justification for incarceration. As some of the following articles suggest, however, the conditions that were no longer justifiable in terms of retribution or punishment were legitimized instead in the name of treatment.

Why treatment became the prevailing ideology of prison work is an important question to analyze. It can best be understood in light of a larger historical framework. The rise of the treatment rationale can be attributed in part to an increase in the status of the medical profession. Also, psychology as a mode of understanding human thought and action was quickly becoming a generally acceptable way of understanding the world and was replacing previous patterns of understanding. Psychological analysis and therapeutic technique, for example, replaced religion as a way of comprehending and explaining the world and human behavior. Thus, the notion of treatment was connected to an emerging faith in "rational" discourse and "reasoned" action. Treatment promised to cure deviancy through so-called

rational interaction between deviant and doctor. Whereas past prison work had concentrated on helping inmates to find God and salvation, this new mode urged the inmates to become healthy. Both goals, however, shared certain fundamental notions relating to obedience and authority. Both approaches demanded that the inmate follow orders, conform to a highly structured environment, and demonstrate respect for the authority of the institution and its agents. In both models, evalution of the inmate's "progress" was, and is, assessed in terms of the ideology and standards created by the authorities in charge of the prison.

The treatment model of imprisonment leaves the definition of health to psychiatrists. A psychiatric definition reflects a narrow professional notion of mental health. Social, political, and economic factors, for example, are not usually evaluated in the determination of mental health. Mental health has been, and continues to be, evaluated exclusively by doctors. And, an individual's liberty was, and continues to be, contingent on this evaluation. Thus the notion of treatment as the primary means of rehabilitation has greatly enhanced the power of the medical profession in prison work. As this status continues to increase, the benefits and the detriments of medical intervention in prisons must be assessed.

Recently, however, there has been a resurgence of the punishment rationale. This trend is reflected in various proposals ranging from "straight time," mandatory sentencing, to no parole. As you read the following articles, consider whether this resurgence indicates that the medical model is losing favor among penologists, politicians, and society at large. Why might this resurgence be happening now?

Behavior Modification in Total Institutions   *David Rothman*

About 1900, a third stage emerged in the complex relationship between the ideal of behavior modification and the history of total institutions, a stage that has persisted almost to the present. The most distinguishing characteristic of this period was the crucial influence of psychiatric thought in both mental health and criminal justice. These years witnessed the general triumph of the "medical model."

These new doctrines evoked an optimism reminiscent of the Jacksonian era. Psychiatrists and their social worker allies promised to reduce substantially, if not to eliminate altogether, the problem of deviancy. They would uncover the psychodynamics of the deviant personality and explore the psychological processes that made persons mentally ill or criminal. Then, in therapeutic encounters, the doctor would review and explain these dynamics to the patient, assisting him to adjust successfully to his environment. The encounter itself, not an institutional routine, would be the instrument of rehabilitation. Accordingly, the new theories looked to the community and away from incarceration as the treatment center of first resort.

But at the same time, the psychological doctrines encouraged a massive expansion of the mental health and criminal justice systems, and in doing so extended the power and reach of doctors, wardens, superintendents, and judges. Even

From David Rothman, "Behavior Modification in Total Institutions," Hastings Center Report, Vol. 5, No. 7 (February 1975), pp. 17–24. © Institute of Society, Ethics and the Life Sciences, 360 Broadway, Hastings-on-Hudson, N.Y. 10706. Reprinted by permission.

more troubling than this expansion was the creation of a new category of deviancy. Implicit in the pledge to cure some of the deviants was the definition of another class of persons who were beyond assistance, persons who, because of their inherited physical deficiencies or the gross character of their malady, were unable to respond to a therapeutic encounter. For them, extended confinement, perhaps even life-long confinement, was the only alternative. Thus, as psychiatrists encouraged opening the door of the asylum part way for some, they simultaneously helped to close it more firmly behind others. The promise to rehabilitate did move society away from a total reliance upon incarceration, but by the same definition, it legitimated its prolonged use.

The prospect of a cure through a therapeutic encounter helped to create the first alternatives to confinement. Probation was one by-product. Some criminals did not need to enter a prison; rather, the probation officer-social worker would be able to rehabilitate the deviant within the community. Parole was another. Convicted offenders could be released from prison to the supervision of a parole officer-social worker; in weekly meetings they would explore and eliminate the psychological roots of disturbed behavior. Concomitantly, the first outpatient mental health clinics sprang up. Instead of committing the mentally ill to an asylum, psychiatrists would treat them within the community. Psychopathic hospitals, dedicated to short term and intensive programs, were created during these years. A brief period of confinement would be followed by a longer period of treatment after the patient returned home.

Yet rationales and practices that initially promised to be less intrusive and less onerous nevertheless served to encourage an extension of state authority. The impact of the new ideology was to expand intervention, not to restrict it.

The medical model stimulated and legitimated a vast increase in discretionary decision-making. "Treat the criminal, not the crime," became the slogan; the system was to concern itself not with the "act" of the offender but with his "state of mind." Hence, the interventions that were appropriate for one type of offender were not necessarily appropriate for another—and officials had to have the leeway to decide among them. Under the impact of this doctrine, the indeterminate sentence flourished, expanding the prerogatives of judges and parole boards. Instead of legislatures continuing to set fixed terms for an offender (three or four years for a burglar), they now established widely divergent minimum and maximum terms (two years to eight), and left it to the judge to make his choice. The judge exercised his discretion: in one case, he could settle on a sentence of two to four years; in another identical one, he could choose a term of three to eight. Then, in turn, he passed on to a parole board the discretion to select the moment for final release. It could discharge the inmate at the minimum term set, or midway through his sentence, or at the expiration of the maximum. Thus, in the name of treating the criminal not the crime, the justice system became unpredictable and ultimately arbitrary. And whatever inequities occurred were interpreted as a necessary and proper by-product of individualized treatment.

An enlarged definition of the type of information considered necessary for decision-making also took hold during this period. If the system was to treat the criminal, to decide who should go on probation and who should make parole, then officials had to know the most intimate details of the offender's life. To this end, psychiatrists and social workers compiled pre-sentence reports and parole dossiers, including data on the offender's family life, his relationship to his parents, how he got on with his wife and friends, the level of his occupational and educational training, his work history, his social attitudes, his feelings, and his IQ score. His fate now hinged not on what he had done, but upon his motivation, his attitudes, and his psychological state. There was nothing private left to the individual; the system had a right and a need to know everything. This probing without limits was not seen as an intrusion into privacy or violation of personal rights. Since the goal was rehabilitation, the means were legitimate. Just as the doctor was entitled to compile a social history in order to diagnose and cure the sick, so the psychiatrist was entitled to compile a social history in order to diagnose and cure the deviant.

Moreover, it was the psychiatrists' definition of time that ruled in criminal justice and mental health: not the particular and exact measurement of time—seconds as well as minutes and hours—which now marked both work and play in industrializing America; not even "medical time." For surgeons, after all, think of intervention in terms of minutes. The good surgeon is the quick surgeon, one who will boast of being in and out in twenty minutes. But psychiatrists work to a different clock. Psychiatrists will matter-of-factly admit that it took a year and half to overcome a patient's resistance to therapy. A four-year therapeutic encounter is considered average; weeks of bad sessions must be expected, even years of bad sessions must be tolerated. After all, psychiatrists accept a theoretical construction that is very fluid about time. The patient is ill precisely because he is still reacting to events buried deep in his past; that trauma at age three is still with him at age forty—it is as if time had not passed. Thus, they are often reluctant to predict how long therapy will take, indeed to say how long therapy should take. And this concept of time, imported into determinations of sentence length and commitment terms, helped to expand the period for which intervention was permissible. If indeterminate sentences proved to be longer than fixed ones, if commitments in state hospitals were for five or ten years, the rehabilitative process demanded it. Once again, psychiatric doctrines worked to break down, not to build up, clear and defined limits.

The rehabilitative ethic also expanded the reach of the criminal justice and mental health systems, bringing new sectors of the population under supervision and treatment. Programs designed in the first instance as alternatives to incarceration quickly developed into supplements to incarceration. It appears, for example, that probation did not reduce the number of offenders confined to state prisons. Rather, it gave judges the opportunity to place under supervision a class of persons who otherwise would have received suspended sentences or release under their own recognizance. So too, the first outpatient mental health clinics seem not to have reduced hospital populations. Instead, they serviced members of the community who heretofore had not received treatment. It may well be that these persons profited from the intervention, that probation and community clinics provided useful supporting services. But the point remains that these innovations probably did more to enlarge the network of clients than to provide practical alternatives to total institutions.

In a curious way, the new programs actually enhanced the legitimacy of state prisons and mental hospitals. The process worked in two ways. First, the existence of new programs encouraged the public to believe that those behind the walls undoubtedly belonged there. If the offender was tractable, he would be free on probation; if he had learned his lessons, he would be released on parole. If the mentally ill were manageable, they would be in outpatient clinics, or, at worse, in psychopathic hospitals. Therefore, anyone still found inside a prison or state mental hospital was simply too dangerous or too bizarre to stay in the community. Second, the institutions could now present themselves as testing grounds for social adjustment. Once the prisoner behaved well inside, he could be trusted to behave well outside; once the patient functioned adequately within the hospital, he would function adequately outside it. Both perspectives gave powerful support to a policy of incarceration. The institutions had accepted the challenge that the community refused. They held the hard-core deviant until he was cured.

It was not a long step from this conclusion to a compelling justification for life-long commitment. And this step was taken in the first decades of the twentieth century. Between 1900 and 1920, institutions for the permanent confinement of the mentally retarded proliferated. In 1890, there were fourteen institutions for the retarded in this country; by 1910 there were twenty-six, and by 1923, forty. In the 1920s and 1930s, numerous states passed their first habitual offender laws, providing life sentences for third-time felons. Simultaneously, they created the first institutions to confine indefinitely the defective delinquent, that class of persons with low IQs and high recidivism, and sexual psychopaths, that catch-all term for the dangerous and the disturbed.

In part, these developments reflected the new popularity of eugenic theories. Americans were panicked at the prospect of defectives multiplying themselves and passing on their incapacities until their numbers eventually overran the community. The Jukeses and Kallikaks were nightmare families whose threat to the social order had to be eliminated at all cost. And in part, these developments reflected an acute concern about crime waves. Crime seemed to be increasing so rapidly that life in the nation's cities would soon become intolerable unless some drastic measures were adopted. But probably more basic to an understanding of these changes was the fear that the new release procedures would allow the hard-core deviant, the retarded, the professional criminal, and the sexual psychopath to return easily and quickly to the community. Just when probation, parole, and out-patient clinics were being established, the state also created institutions for long-term commitment, in effect providing for preventive detention.

Psychiatric theories and the psychiatrists themselves played a crucial role in making this procedure appear legitimate, indeed constitutionally acceptable. Practically every institution for the retarded and for the defective delinquent was headed by a psychiatrist. The simple logic of the situation made this an odd choice. By definition, the retarded and the defective delinquent were beyond psychiatric assistance. Typically, the institutions that held them were farms on which they carried out menial agricultural chores. A skilled administrator, a competent businessman or a farmer, would have been a more sensible choice than a psychiatrist to superintend such places. Why then this choice of a psychiatrist?

To a degree, the decision may reflect our society's predilection for giving over the care of the "dying" to a doctor. The medical profession does assume responsibility for those suffering from chronic illness; hence, by extension, they should have responsibility for the chronic deviant. Furthermore, the rationale for preventive detention rested on the deviant's state of mind, not on any particular acts he might have committed. Therefore, it seemed appropriate to let the expert in states of mind head up the institutions. Morever, the vast discretion allowed by the law in selecting persons for this type of incarceration might have been challenged as arbitrary and capricious unless it was exercised by someone with impeccable and impressive credentials. Finally, the choice of a psychiatrist helped to dress preventive detention in the garb of rehabilitation. If the retarded or defective delinquent could possibly be reformed, then the psychiatrist would do it; and if he could not treat them, then confinement was an appropriate policy. In other words, the link between incarceration and rehabilitation was unbreakable. When forced to justify extended commitments, officials could raise the prospect of cure. When confronted with the fact that the institutions were not treatment centers, that the staff of professionals was pitifully small, and that rehabilitation programs were practically non-existent, then they could vividly describe just how dangerous their inmate population was. As we shall soon see, this equivocation is no less prevalent today—and frequently the public role of the psychiatrist is not altogether different either.

Questions

1. Is there any acceptable role for psychiatric intervention among prisoners? Is it possible for a psychiatrist to offer help or assistance to an inmate without creating another bind for the individual who is in jail? Once the psychiatrist enters the picture, doesn't the inmate have another authority structure toward whom he/she owes respect and who holds power over that individual?

2. Who would make a better head of a correctional institution—a psychiatrist or a professional prison administrator? What kind of person should run a jail? What skills are useful to this job?

3. Rothman describes how new theories of deviance along the medical model were used to extend state intervention into people's lives rather than to limit the activity of the state. Can you think of other examples in which health or safety are used to justify an expansion of state power in people's lives?

A Model, Clockwork-Orange Prison *Phil Stanford*

JESSUP, Md.: The Patuxent Institution for Defective Delinquents is widely considered a "model rehabilitative prison" and a showplace of enlightened penology. At Patuxent (named for a nearby river), inmates are called patients, which means that they are here not to be punished but to be cured. Patuxent's director, Dr. Harold M. Boslow, a properly benign gentleman with a soft pink face, swept-back white hair and glasses that

Phil Stanford, "A Model, Clockwork-Orange Prison," *The New York Times Magazine,* September 17, 1972. © 1972 by The New York Times Company. Reprinted by permission.

slide down his nose, is a psychiatrist. Two of the three associate directors are behavioral scientists, and for a prison population of about 400, there are more than 40 psychiatrists, psychologists and social workers on the staff. To use a phrase I heard there frequently in interviews, Patuxent is more a "therapeutic community" than a prison.

In one of Patuxent's many brochures, Dr. Boslow describes the institution this way: "Dealing with nonpsychotic patients, it combines the functions of a mental hospital and a penal institution." To a visitor, the second function is immediately apparent. Patuxent is surrounded by a 30-foot chain-link fence fronted with a sheet of slick plastic "climb-proofing" and with barbed wire along the top. The guards in the towers carry high-powered rifles, and all the windows on the two main buildings in the compound come equipped with steel bars.

Under Maryland's Defective Delinquency Law, convicted lawbreakers who appear by their records to have a compulsive criminal nature can be referred to Patuxent for a psychiatric evaluation. The trial judge, the prosecuting attorney, or even the defense lawyer may request the diagnosis after sentencing. (The men referred, it might be emphasized, are all legally sane, or as Dr. Boslow puts it, "nonpsychotic." If they were judged insane, they would go to the state hospital.) Once a person has been diagnosed as a "defective delinquent," he may be formally committed to Patuxent by a civil court—or, if not, returned to the penitentiary to complete his sentence. If he is committed to Patuxent, which happens 85 per cent of the time, he will receive treatment for his condition. When he is well, he can leave.

From the first, Patuxent has had the enthusiastic support of America's liberal psychiatric establishment, which has long seen crime as a social and emotional problem. One member of the panel of psychiatrists that recommended Patuxent to the Maryland Legislature was Dr. Robert Lindner, author of "The Fifty-Minute Hour" and "Rebel Without a Cause." Another member, well-known in the profession as an expert on the burgeoning field of forensic psychology, was Dr. Mannfred Guttmacher. Guttmacher, who was chief medical officer of the Maryland courts when Patuxent was established in 1955, is considered something of a patron saint by the administrators.

Dr. Karl Menninger, perhaps the country's most honored psychiatrist, thinks Patuxent is a "great idea." He says, "It's the only one of its kind." In fact, as Menninger later qualified himself, prison systems in other states, particularly California, have attempted treatment programs like Patuxent's, "but none of them have done anything in nearly as much detail." (The U.S. Bureau of Prisons is now building a Behavioral Research Center at Butner, N.C., where it will develop behavior-modification programs for Fed-

eral prisons, but that won't be in operation until 1974.) "Patuxent is a progressive step forward," says Dr. Menninger.

Dr. Thomas Szasz, professor of psychiatry at New York's Upstate Medical Center, sees it somewhat differently. Szasz, an author who is critical of nearly everything about institutional psychiatry today, says Patuxent is a "concentration camp." "Patuxent," he told me, "is worse than the way they use mental institutions in Russia, except that when they haul someone off over there everyone here gets upset. It reminds me of the Biblical proverb of the mote in the eye." In Patuxent Szasz sees merely a further extension of psychiatry's already abused power to "define and rule."

When I asked Menninger if he had any response to Szasz's charges, he sounded grumpy over the phone and refused to say anything at all. Szasz, for his part, says people like Patuxent's director, Dr. Boslow—and therefore, presumably, Menninger himself—ought to be hanged. Some days it is particularly difficult to find a nice, reasonable discussion.

On the third Thursday of every month, the Patuxent Institution Board of Review meets in a basement room of the administration building. It is a very ordinary, utilitarian room, and in the middle of it there is a long conference table. The seven members of the board sit around three sides of the table. The patient, when he is summoned, sits at the other end. Over a year, every one of the 400 or so patients at Patuxent will get a hearing, and depending on his progress toward responsible citizenship, as indicated by his disciplinary record, achievements in a vocational program and in psychotherapy, the board may vote to release him or bind him over for another year.

The members of the board besides Dr. Boslow are: Dr. Arthur Kandel, Dr. Giovanni Croce and Forrest Calhoun, Patuxent's three associate directors; Dr. Olive Quinn of the Goucher College sociology department; Leonard Briscoe, a lawyer from Baltimore; and Edward Tomlinson, a young law professor from the University of Maryland. The representation of various professions on the board is determined by Maryland law.

Board of Review meetings are closed to the public, even to lawyers of the patients. I was allowed to attend one session (July 20–21) only on the condition that I would not embarrass any of the patients by printing their names. Except in the case of one patient who expressly asked me to use his name, I have observed this ground rule.

Patient I

The man before the board is a large Negro with heavy scar tissue above his eyes and what appears to be a knife mark on his right cheek. The mimeographed sheet that each of the seven board members holds says he is 35 years old. Under "Antisocial/Criminal Activity" is the entry "Armed Robbery." There is another notation that reads "Murder (2nd), charge dropped." The patient takes his place at the end of the table.

"You know why you're here," says Dr. Boslow, who is sitting at the other end of the table. "What would you like to tell us?"

"At this time I would like to ask for work release. I feel at this time that I understand myself where I didn't understand myself before. Before I felt I wasn't really loved or understood. I even took a man's life."

"Did you really do it?" someone asks.

"Yes," says the patient. He says the charge was dropped for lack of evidence.

"Tell us about it."

The patient explains that he killed the man in a barroom brawl because of his mother's teachings. "She always told me to defend my younger brother," he says. "But now I see that I was wrong. I feel I was very immature in my thinking."

"What do you mean by that?" Dr. Croce asks.

"I mean I would never find fault in myself. I always found fault in the other person."

The board asks about his fighting.

"I know my place isn't out in the street fighting," he says. "I know now that fighting doesn't solve anything. It doesn't bring any understanding."

"How are you going to handle your alcohol problem?"

"I realize now that I used alcohol as a crutch. I don't need it any more."

After about 10 minutes the board runs out of questions.

"Is there anything else you want to say?" Dr. Boslow asks. This is a standard courtesy of the interviews.

"Yes," says the patient earnestly, "I do. I'd like to say that all these things I've done, I can see now that my ways and concepts were all wrong. I can see now that they caused a great deal of pain and sorrow to other people. I'm truly sorry for that." He develops this theme with a few additional variations before moving on: "I used to think it was a weakness to show weakness."

BOSLOW (showing some excitement): Wait a minute. What do you mean?

PATIENT: To cry, to be sorry.

BOSLOW: You mean to show love.

PATIENT: Yes.

BOSLOW (after a pause): Thank you.

The patient departs and the board votes on his request for work release. The count is 5 to 2 against. The majority, although pleased with the patient's evident progress, feels on the basis of the interview and the report before the board that more therapy is required in this particular case.

Dr. Boslow explains that Patuxent "is designed to identify dangerous offenders, retain and treat them." Of the 425 patients currently at Patuxent, 305 have been committed and the other 120 are waiting to be diagnosed. A recent breakdown of patients' crimes shows murder (4), second-degree murder (18), assault with intent to murder (43), robbery (35), robbery with a deadly weapon (87). There are a number of convictions for sex offenses, including rape (45), attempted rape (14), statutory rape (2), perverted practices (29), indecent exposure (4), and attempted perversion (1). The list also includes breaking and entering (9), housebreaking (14), rogue and vagabond (2), petty larceny (3), car theft (10), forgery (2) and writing bad checks (2).

Dr. Arthur Kandel, who was my guide for most of my visits, anticipates the question.... Kandel explains that 78 per cent of the patients are in for crimes involving violence. The others were examined and found to be "potentially violent." A patient's criminal record is of course important to the psychiatrist making a diagnosis, but it is only one consideration. "Our focus here is on behavior," says Kandel, "and we are not that concerned with the concept of guilt or innocence." What all patients committed to Patuxent have in common is that all of them have been diagnosed as "defective delinquents."

Under Maryland's unique statute, a defective delinquent is "an individual who, by the demonstration of persistent, aggravated, antisocial or criminal behavior, evidences a propensity toward criminal activity, and who is found to have either such intellectual or emotional unbalance, or both, as to clearly demonstrate an actual danger to society so as to require such confinement and treatment, when appropriate, as to make it reasonably safe for society to terminate the confinement and treatment."

As the Patuxent staff interprets the law, this means a very particular type of criminal. The brochures stress that certain lawbreakers, such as a professional gunman, wouldn't qualify. Dr. Kandel explained why. "The professional gunman," he said, "ordinarily has chosen this as a way of earning a living, and in most other respects you won't tell him apart from any other human being. He may very well have a wife and kids that he's devoted to. He'll probably pay his taxes reasonably well. He'll probably live in a decent neighborhood, in a decent home. You know, it's just that he picks this peculiar way of earning a living. Now a professional gunman, for example, doesn't act on impulse or he wouldn't be a professional. Whereas our people, by and large, one of their characteristics is they're very impulsive. The professional gunman can delay frustration, he can tolerate delay, he can plan. And if he plans a hit at this time and this place and it doesn't pan out, so he retracts and makes new plans and goes ahead again."

A defective delinquent, to use psychiatric language, is someone afflicted with a behavioral problem called an antisocial disorder. Until recently the official term was sociopath, and before that it was psychopath, but both terms have been dropped from the official nomenclature of the American Psychiatric Association. Perhaps the best description of a defective delinquent comes from Dr.

Guttmacher, who played such an important role in getting Patuxent started. In a 1965 court case (when it was still fashionable to refer to a defective delinquent as a sociopath), Guttmacher was asked to describe the symptoms, which he did at some length:

"My own feeling is that probably the most basic thing is their inability to make any strong identifications with other people, and by that I mean they don't become a real member of the group. They are not team players; they don't have strong loyalties toward their country, toward their family, toward anyone. Their affectionate relationships are very shallow. They become involved in numerous affairs with women, frequently with multiple marriages. . . .

"Then there is this underlying hostility which manifests itself in many ways. As I said before, there is, in a sense, a war with society, and they get great satisfaction in seeing what they can get away with in their acting out against society. They are an extremely restless group of people. . . . They normally have not the success in school which their intelligence would indicate they might have. . . . They very frequently become dropouts. They frequently have conflict with teachers because part of their pattern is to be in conflict with authority figures. . . . They can't take criticism with any degree of equanimity, so that their work records are almost universally very fugitive. They rarely stick to anything for any great length of time. They are basically hedonistic, and they must satisfy their needs as rapidly as they possibly can and at the expense of others."

Interestingly enough, elsewhere in his testimony Guttmacher referred to a defective delinquent as "a rebel without a cause." Robert Lindner, who was another of the founding fathers of Patuxent, must have been very surprised when the character James Dean played in the movie version of his book became the antihero of a generation. Lindner wanted to cure him.

Patient II

An 18-year-old black takes his seat and folds his hands quietly before him on the table. The record says he was convicted of rape.

"At this time I would like to ask the board for leave," he says.

"All right," says Dr. Boslow. "Tell us why you think you are ready for leave."

"When I first came to this institution I was a very confused and mixed-up 15-year-old boy. I had a low opinion of myself," he says.

He says he hated his father and mother. He tells how, when he was a small boy, his father would come home and beat him, then lock him in his room. He had come to have a low opinion of his mother because she hadn't done anything to stop it.

BOSLOW: Do you like yourself now?

PATIENT: Yes. I've come to accept myself. I accept my mother for what she is.

BOSLOW: How about your father?

PATIENT: He's dead.

BOSLOW: But that doesn't help. You know that you still carry your father with you in your mind. Until you come to accept your father too, you won't be able to solve anything.

PATIENT: Oh yes, I accept my father too.

The board votes unanimously to grant the leave.

"Frankly," says Dr. Boslow, "I think the most important thing in the development of the character is the early family relationship. That's the one thing that stands out in our case histories. Well over 95 per cent of our patients have easily detected pathological home situations. You know, overprotective, domineering mother, brutal, alcoholic father, sadistic father, bad relationships between the parents. That sort of thing.

"That's the type of therapy that we've attempted to incorporate in the institution—a stable, structured environment with therapists who have some concept of themselves as human beings and who are able to impart this to our patients. Our people come to us, they're all school dropouts—I think we've had only one or maybe two college guys here. They've never really learned to live in society, and essentially they have no skills. We've got to treat them in all these areas."

Dr. Giovanni Croce is the associate director in charge of treatment programs.... "What is very important to me," he says, "is the relationship you develop with these people. Therefore, at the beginning when they go out, they're going to be dependent on you. You make yourself available. I make myself available at any time. Most of my best friends now are people who were here and were released, black and white. They still call, they still let me know when a child is born or how they're doing. This is the relationship of which they were deprived. Whether I take the role of the father, the mother or the big brother doesn't matter. They know there is a somebody who will be there ready to listen."

Would he say, then, that the institution was acting in the role of a parent?

"I think to a certain extent we are acting in the role of a superego, which means we act as the parent, yes."

"What we do," Dr. Boslow told me, "is socialize them."

At Patuxent a patient enters what the professional staff calls a "therapeutic milieu." That means it is a total environment, every part of which—including group psychotherapy, vocational therapy and a programed system of incentives—is intended to work toward the patient's rehabilitation and prepare him to return to society.

Patients are expected to attend weekly group-therapy sessions, where (to quote from another of Patuxent's brochures) "they are made aware of their distorted perceptions, feelings and attitudes, and the part these distortions play in developing their antisocial behavior pattern."

The core of the program is the "graded-tier" system, which "provides rewards for socially acceptable behavior." There are four levels to the system, and a new patient must start on the lowest and work his way up. "As he moves upward in the tier system, a patient gains more privileges, but also more obligations and responsibilities.... The rewards reinforce the positive aspects of his behavior." Fourth-level patients, for example, can stay up as late as they want, third-level patients must be in bed by 11:30 and second-level patients by 11. Only fourth-level men get to have Sunday afternoon picnics on the prison lawn with members of their families or other approved guests. Fourth-level day rooms have pool tables, but third-level day rooms have only Ping-Pong tables. Most important, to be eligible for parole a patient must have reached the third or fourth level. "It works," Dr. Croce told me, "because that's the way life itself is set up."

Dr. Kandel, helpful and talkative as usual, says the institution has also tried a number of drug programs with Johns Hopkins, the University of Maryland and the National Institute of Mental Health. "We have ongoing research with all of these agencies in terms of drugs that are coming out that may be effective as behavioral controls in terms of impulsivity," he said. "They use all the usual psychotropic drugs." Johns Hopkins, he said, was currently doing a great deal of research with Dilantin, on the theory that in some of the patients "the electrical transmissions of the brain are messed up." He says, "It's no sweat getting volunteers because all of these programs pay volunteers." Kandel recalls that once Patuxent started an aversive therapy program using electroshock. "But we caught so much flak we had to drop it before we could even get going."

"Our experience," says Dr. Boslow, who has been Patuxent's director since it began, "has confirmed the fact that all human beings are essentially alike, that all people can be treated and helped, provided they want to be. I don't believe in punishment. I don't think in those terms. I think that people who commit crimes should be treated until they are capable of going out into society again."

That, in outline, is Patuxent's treatment program. The only thing that remains is perhaps to underscore what Dr. Boslow has already stated— that once a patient is committed to Patuxent, he must stay until he is cured. One of Patuxent's unique features as a prison—another one borrowed from practice at mental institutions—is the indeterminate sentence. To get out, a patient must meet the approval of the institution's Board of Review, which is responsible only to itself. Failing that, he can try a recommitment hearing, to which he is entitled every three years.

Patient III

"This is an interesting case," whispers Dr. Boslow in an aside as the next patient enters the room. He is an extremely tall and muscular young white man. The record says he is 21. It quickly develops that he is an XYY chromosome mutant[1] and under study by Johns Hopkins. The first thing he does when he sits down is to object about the Johns Hopkins students who have been showing up at the Patuxent gate, "tossing [my] name around." He has a plaintive, boyish voice. Dr. Kandel assures him that he is quite right in being annoyed and that the practice will be halted immediately.

The patient requests a leave to visit his family at Christmas time. "If I may have a few minutes I'd like to speak of what I have planned for the future," he says.

"Of course," says Dr. Boslow.

For the future he wants to see his family for Christmas, earn money for an apartment, get a learner's permit and marry a 20-year-old girl who began writing to him after he came to Patuxent.

When XYY came to Patuxent three years ago he had been both violent and suicidal.

"Do you ever think of cutting yourself now?" Dr. Boslow asks him.

"No," he says, "I have not only myself to live for anymore. I have someone I love."

Dr. Boslow thanks him and he leaves.

While the board is voting, Edward Tomlinson, the young law professor, asks about the research program that Johns Hopkins is conducting with the patient. Someone explains that XYY is getting dosages of a female hormone, presumably to counteract his "supermasculinity."

TOMLINSON: Does he understand the effects of the drug?

BOSLOW: Yes, we explained the whole thing to him. We don't want any misunderstandings.

TOMLINSON: Well, what are the effects?

KANDEL: We don't know. That's what they're trying to find out.

---

[1] Humans normally carry a pair of sex-determining chromosomes, XX in the female and XY in the male (with Y being the male chromosome). While the evidence is so far unconvincing, some studies suggest that males born with an extra Y chromosome may be more inclined to aggressive behavior than XY males.

The board votes unanimously to grant the patient's request for Christmas leave.

According to figures released by the institution, 38 per cent of all patients are now serving beyond their original sentences. Of those who were sentenced to terms of five years or less, 75 per cent are, as they might see it, overdue. Dr. Boslow acknowledges that Patuxent has been under fire lately, particularly for its indeterminate sentence. "What they don't understand," he says, "is that it is necessary for therapeutic reasons." In one of his pamphlets, Dr. Boslow writes that "there is a long history of disbelief in the efficacy of psychotherapy with persons having strong antisocial tendencies." At first, many defective delinquents won't even admit that they're sick. The indeterminate sentence is simply "a mechanism for making them realize that they need help," he explains. "That's why the indeterminate sentence is so important. It's a means of attracting their attention to the fact that they need to make some changes to get out."

Dr. Kandel develops the point. "No one likes to admit he's not normal," he says. "Everybody who's in here, their primary drive is toward getting back in society. This is part of their problem—the inability to delay gratification. From a treatment point of view, the indeterminate sentence is very helpful."

The patients, who have staged four publicized disturbances this year, including a 60-man sit-in in August, may have another viewpoint. But they are not the only non-psychiatrists who have failed to appreciate Patuxent's therapeutic approach to criminal behavior. Lawyers are a source of constant complaints. Patients' lawyers are not allowed to be present during psychiatric examinations, although they argue that the information gathered there, including facts about crimes for which the patient was never charged, is used against the patient at his commitment trial. Lawyers are also excluded from the Board of Review because they would "interfere with the therapeutic program."

One of the most irritating of these lawyers to the staff (Dr. Kandel calls him "a kooky young lawyer trying to make a name for himself") is Julian Tepper, head of the National Law Office of the Legal Aid and Defender Service in Washington, D.C. On behalf of 13 patients, Tepper in 1971 brought suit in Maryland court (*McCray et al.* v. *Patuxent*) on a lengthy list of complaints.

During the trial several patients complained of being locked up for long periods of time in totally dark cells. Besides the regular four tiers of cells that are part of Patuxent's "graded-tier system," there are two separate rows where patients who misbehave are frequently sent. Some of these cells are smaller and can be closed with a heavy steel door. Critics of Patuxent often refer to them as "punishment" or "solitary confinement."

When Dr. Kandel was called to the witness stand, he explained this misunderstanding to the court. There are some people who respond favorably to positive reinforcement, as for example, the graded-tier system, he said. "There are also people who don't respond and need [to devote] a certain period of time to what is known as negative reinforcers." Patuxent's negative-reinforcement program included "deprivation schedules" and perhaps a certain amount of "sensory deprivation," which is probably what the patients referred to when they said there wasn't any light in their cells.

To judge from comments by the Patuxent administrators, the McCray case was an even more traumatic episode than the U.S. Supreme Court decision (*McNeil* v. *Patuxent*) this summer.

In *McCray,* Patuxent was ordered to establish a written disciplinary code, to limit the time patients could be put in "negative-reinforcement" cells and to allow access to the press. In June the Supreme Court told Patuxent to release noncommitted patients whose terms had expired. These "noncooperatives," as they are called, had refused to let a psychiatrist interview them for their precommitment diagnosis. Patuxent has released about 10 of these patients since the decision. There are at present about 60 to 70 "noncooperatives" at Patuxent. The ruling, of course, does not affect the more than 305 patients already committed.

Patient IV

The next patient to enter the board room is a 26-year-old fellow with long wavy hair, drooping mustache and quizzical, diffident eyes. His name, one judges from the mimeographed fact sheet, is Jewish. This is notable only because almost all the patients at Patuxent are either from the black Baltimore slums or the dirt-poor Anglo-Saxon hinterlands. The record shows that the patient is in for assault. When he was 17, in jail awaiting trial for burglary, he hit a guard over the head with a rock in a sock. He received a two-year sentence. That was in 1964.

The patient is before the board because he has violated the terms of his "school-out-live-in" program. He had been studying music at one of the local colleges. One night when he returned to Patuxent he was caught with a marijuana cigarrette in his jacket pocket.

The board members ask him why. The best answer he can come up with is that some people he knew were smoking and he joined them because he was "feeling empty at the time." He explains himself in spiritless abstractions, attempting to assess his sickness, but obviously not quite sure what it is.

"I know what's right here," he says, tapping his temple with his forefinger. "But when it's between me and society, I'm, ah, undeft. I guess that's right. I can't think of another word."

"That's a good word," says Dr. Kandel approvingly.

"I guess I just have to keep trying to understand," the patient says. He gets up to go.

After he leaves, Dr. Kandel says that he is very fond of the patient. Dr. Boslow agrees that he is "a very engaging fellow." Dr. Olive Quinn, the sociology professor from Goucher, apparently doesn't. "He's not my style," she says. Dr. Quinn, a squarely built, middle-aged woman, smiles a lot when she talks.

There is some discussion about whether it is legal for the board to revoke parole programs, such as "school-out-live-in," without observing due process. This had come up in an earlier case as well, with the law professor Tomlinson making the objection.

TOMLINSON: I wish we could get a ruling from the Attorney General on this. I don't think it's legal to revoke work release without a full hearing.

QUINN: No, I don't think so. I think all we need is new terminology. We're working here in a therapeutic situation.

The board decides to revoke the patient's school privileges, but to reconsider him in a few months.

This summer Patuxent received a couple days of publicity in the Baltimore and Washington papers when the courts ordered the release of a 29-year-old patient, Grover Miller, who had already served more than eight years for breaking a window. The exact charge was "malicious destruction of property." Miller's disciplinary record, which the institution let me see, showed page after page of entries saying, "refused medication" and "refused meals," but nothing that indicated violent or even unruly behavior.

To get the complete story I talked to Miller's therapist, a bearded young man with an M.S. in psychology from Wisconsin, Lee Runkle. (Patuxent is proud of the fact that all its psychologists have at least their master's. Runkle, it turns out, is even working on his doctorate.) Runkle told me he had found that Miller was an "extremely unstable individual." He often had "insupportable fantasies" of what he would do on the outside. Runkle couldn't give me any examples without violating his professional ethics as a therapist. "But I'll tell you one thing that won't appear on the records," Runkle confided, "Grover Miller had a habit of throwing beer bottles at people when he got drunk."

When I approached Dr. Kandel, he took a look at the record and said that Miller was "probably one of those marginal cases." Running an institution such as Patuxent is no simple matter, he acknowledged. Administering the indeterminate sentence was perhaps the most difficult problem of all. "They say to you, 'How do you know I'm going to foul up if you don't give me the chance to get out there and foul up?' It's not an easy thing to handle," said Kandel.

Well, what do you say to a man who was sent up for two years and after four years is still inside?

"I tell him that based on my best professional judgment, this is my opinion," said Kandel. "You've got to consider the probabilities. You have to think that if you release a patient and he fouls up, he's the one who's going to pay for it, not you."

The responsibility weighs heavily on Kandel and the rest of the staff. In nearly 18 years of operation, out of a total of 985 patients committed to Patuxent, only 115 have been released as cured. Another 332 have left through recommitment hearings—those whose sentences have expired go free; the others serve out their terms in the penitentiary.

Patient V

When Roosevelt Murray came to Patuxent in 1958, a skinny 17-year-old kid from the black part of Baltimore, it became apparent to the professional staff that he was a defective delinquent. Tests showed a decided potential for violence. A psychiatrist who interviewed him diagnosed the problem as a "Sociopathic Disorder—Antisocial (with affinity for auto theft)," and on Oct. 11, 1961, Murray was committed to Patuxent, just as his four-year sentence for unauthorized use of a motor vehicle was about to expire. He has never really gotten used to the idea.

Murray, 31, a starchy 5-foot-8 or so, sits glaring across the conference table, at everyone in general, but particularly at Dr. Boslow. He is in handcuffs and a guard waits by the door. Clearly no one is taking any chances. Not long ago Murray slugged his social worker. He is also charged with stabbing another social worker, whom, as Dr. Boslow explained later, "he didn't even know."

"You know why you're here," says Dr. Boslow. "Tell us what you want to tell us."

"I want to tell you that you have no right to be holding me," begins Murray at somewhere near a shout. "I want to say, for all the damn good it will do me, that I want to get out of here, man. That's what I want to tell you."

The board listens to approximately two minutes of this tirade before it decides to ask Murray about his behavior. "Mr. Murray," asks the sociologist Olive Quinn in a conciliatory voice, "why don't you behave some way so we feel we can let you out?"

In truth, as the file shows, Murray has always been a problem at Patuxent. In 1962 he made his first appearance before the Board of Review. The record says he appeared hostile and spoke belligerently to the board. "I don't like the idea of my time being up and me still being here," he had said. In 1963 Dr. Boslow interviewed Murray at length for a psychiatric evaluation. Toward the end of the session, Murray apparently lost control of his emotions. "Murray launched into a hostile attack on the United States and said he wanted to go to Russia," Dr. Boslow wrote in his report. "At this point he seemed very angry, paranoid and disturbed." In 1965 at his recommitment hearing, Murray lashed out again. After the judge finished reading a list of Murray's disciplinary infractions at Patuxent, Murray was said to have turned over the table he was sitting at and shouted, "This is the unfairest court I've ever seen." The newspaper account says he threatened Dr. Boslow.

Murray's ample disciplinary record, which begins with entries for smoking, throwing a bag out the window and fighting with another inmate, shows a similar progression toward violence. The board asks about the recent incidents which are mentioned on the mimeographed sheet. Someone asks Murray why he stabbed a social worker. "Because I wanted to get out of this place any way possible," he shouts.

QUINN (sweetly): And did you think the proper way to get out of here was to kill a social worker?

MURRAY (loudly, pleadingly): You're killing me, aren't you? You people don't realize what you did to me in my 14 years here. You know that Roosevelt Murray never stabbed anyone before he came here.

I don't like what you're doing to me here. If you had any decency you'd let me go free. Why don't you send me to the pen? Does it make any sense to hold me here when you can see it isn't doing me any good?

BOSLOW (after a pause): Is there anything else?

MURRAY: Yes. I'd like to know why you postponed my hearing three times. I think it was a deliberate attempt to harass me and provoke me into actions you could use to keep me here. I'd like to know why.

(No answer.)

MURRAY: Don't you have the decency to do things right?

BOSLOW: Don't you have the decency to do things right?

Murray is led out shouting: "You're not a man, you're an animal. Let me out. If you just take these handcuffs off me, I'll show you man to man."

After the meeting I ask Dr. Kandel about Murray. "Well, you saw for yourself," he says. "He's a very violent man."

Isn't it possible, I suggest, that Murray is really angry at the institution for keeping him beyond his sentence, just as he said?

"It's a matter of projection," Kandel says. "Many of these people like to blame anything instead of what really bothers them. That's part of their problem."

I ask why Murray was put in Patuxent in the first place, since Patuxent is for dangerous and violent criminals.

"It's true," Kandel says, "that Murray came here for something relatively minor, like stealing a car or something. But when he came here we examined him and judged him to be potentially violent. Events have proved us right."

The question that remains, then, is how do you know when a patient is cured, or, to use Dr. Boslow's word, "socialized"? When is he ready to move out into society?

"It's a matter of experience and judgment," says Dr. Boslow. "There's no problem in saying who *will* commit a crime when he's released. If you just say yes all the time you'll be right 70 or 80 per cent of the time. The art is in saying who won't."

Dr. Boslow says Patuxent is "the most successful penal institution in the country, in fact in the Western world." For proof he cites a study showing that Patuxent's recidivism rate over the years has been 37 per cent, compared with a national average of almost 80. (When the study was presented at a meeting of the American Psychiatric Association, it was immediately attacked for "methodological deficiencies," but Boslow discounts the criticism.)

"You become convinced," says Dr. Boslow, "when a patient begins relating to you as a human being, when he no longer has to be defensive and hostile, when he develops a sense of self-regard. One of the greatest things is the increase in self-esteem and the capacity to relate to other people as a warm, meaningful human being. It's the guy who can come to you and ask you to help him. He's admitting he's a human being and that he has problems."

"What do you think holds society together?" Boslow asks, suddenly intense. Before I can say I don't know he answers himself. "Love," he says. "It's love."

I'm not sure, I tell him.

"Yes," says Dr. Boslow, "it is. Love in its broadest sense, which includes the need for the regard and esteem of one's fellow men. Without this mutual need our society would fall apart. For example, what do you think causes a man to walk into a machine-gun nest?"

I don't know. I really don't.

"It's love," Dr. Boslow says, wondering perhaps what it is that makes me so slow to see this very basic equation of our civilization.

Questions

1. When would a psychiatric staff feel convinced that the patient/inmate was cured and, therefore, ready to be paroled?

2. How should parole work? What qualifications should members of a parole board have? Is it possible to create a fair parole system if it is based on the discretion of the parole board, regardless of what kind of people constitute the board?

3. Would a fairer system result if the granting of parole had no element of discretion in the process

but instead was based on a system of mandatory sentences? If indeterminate sentences were abolished, is it unlikely that institutions like Patuxent would exist? Is there any legitimate purpose served by such institutions?

4. What role does the legal system play in the area of imprisonment? Can an individual inmate find relief through the legal system? What kind of relief does the law offer? What are the limits to that relief?

McNeil v. Director, Patuxent Institution   *92 S. Ct. 2083 (1972)*

MR. JUSTICE MARSHALL delivered the opinion of the Court.

Edward McNeil was convicted of two assaults in 1966, and sentenced to five years' imprisonment. Instead of committing him to prison, the sentencing court referred him to the Patuxent Institution for examination, to determine whether he should be committed to that institution for an indeterminate term under Maryland's Defective Delinquency Law. Md. Code Ann., Art 31B. No such determination has yet been made, his sentence has expired, and his confinement continues. The State contends that he has refused to cooperate with the examining psychiatrists, that they have been unable to make any valid assessment of his condition, and that consequently he may be confined indefinitely until he cooperates and the institution has succeeded in making its evaluation. He claims that when his sentence expired, the State lost its power to hold him, and that his continued detention violates his rights under the Fourteenth Amendment. We agree.

I

The Maryland Defective Delinquency Law provides that a person convicted of any felony, or certain misdemeanors, may be committed to the Patuxent Institution for an indeterminate period, if it is judicially determined that he is a "defective delinquent." A defective delinquent is defined as:

an individual who, by the demonstration of persistent aggravated antisocial or criminal behavior, evidences a propensity toward criminal activity, and who is found to have either such

intellectual deficiency or emotional unbalance, or both, as to clearly demonstrate an actual danger to society so as to require such confinement and treatment, when appropriate, as may make it reasonably safe for society to terminate the confinement and treatment. [Md. Code Ann., Art. 31B, § 5.]

Defective delinquency proceedings are ordinarily instituted immediately after conviction and sentencing; they may also be instituted after the defendant has served part of his prison term. In either event, the process begins with a court order committing the prisoner to Patuxent for a psychiatric examination. The institution is required to submit its report to the court within a fixed period of time. If the report recommends commitment, then a hearing must be promptly held, with a jury trial if requested by the prisoner, to determine whether he should be committed as a defective delinquent. If he is so committed, then the commitment operates to suspend the prison sentence previously imposed.

In *Murel* v. *Baltimore City Criminal Court,* 407 U.S. ——, 92 S.Ct. 2091, 31 L.Ed.2d ——, several prisoners who had been committed as defective delinquents sought to challenge various aspects of the criteria and procedures that resulted in their commitment....

But Edward McNeil presents a much more stark and simple claim. He has never been committed as a defective delinquent, and thus he has no cause to challenge the criteria and procedures that control a defective delinquency hearing. His confinement rests wholly on the order committing him for examination, in preparation for such a commitment hearing. That order was made, not on the basis of an adversary hearing, but on the basis of an *ex parte* judicial determination that there was "reasonable cause to believe that the defendant may be a defective delinquent." Petitioner does not challenge in this Court the power of the sentencing court to issue such an order in the first instance, but he contends that the State's power to hold him on the basis of that order has expired. He filed a petition for state post-conviction relief on this ground.

The trial court denied relief, holding that "a person referred to Patuxent under Section 6, Article 31B for the purpose of determining whether or not he is a defective delinquent may be detained in Patuxent until the procedures for such determination have been completed regardless of whether or not the criminal sentence has expired." The Court of Appeals of Maryland denied leave to appeal.

We granted certiorari, 404 U.S. 999, 92 S.Ct. 568, 30 L.Ed.2d 552 (1971).

II

The State of Maryland asserts the power to confine petitioner indefinitely, without ever obtaining a judicial determination that such confinement is warranted. It advances several distinct arguments in support of that claim.

A. First, the State contends that petitioner has been committed merely for observation, and that a commitment for observation need not be surrounded by the procedural safeguards (such as an adversary hearing) that are appropriate for a final determination of defective delinquency. Were the commitment for observation limited in duration to a brief period, the argument might have some force. But petitioner has been committed "for observation" for six years, and on the State's theory of his confinement there is no reason to believe it likely that he will ever be released. A confinement which is in fact indeterminate cannot rest on procedures designed to authorize a brief period of observation.

We recently rejected a similar argument in *Jackson* v. *Indiana,* when the State sought to confine indefinitely a defendant who was mentally incompetent to stand trial on his criminal charges. The State sought to characterize the commitment as temporary, and on that basis to justify reduced

substantive and procedural safeguards. We held that because the commitment was permanent in its practical effect, it required safeguards commensurate with a long-term commitment. 406 U.S. ——, ——, 92 S.Ct. 1845, ——, 31 L.Ed.2d —— (1972). The other half of the *Jackson* argument is equally relevant here. If the commitment is properly regarded as a short-term confinement with a limited purpose, as the State suggests, then lesser safeguards may be appropriate, but by the same token, the duration of the confinement must be strictly limited. "[D]ue process requires that the nature and duration of commitment bear some reasonable relation to the purpose for which the individual is committed." 406 U.S., at ——, 92 S.Ct. at 1858. Just as that principle limits the permissible length of a commitment on account of incompetence to stand trial, so it also limits the permissible length of a commitment "for observation." We need not set a precise time limit here; it is noteworthy, however, that the Maryland statute itself limits the observation period to a maximum of six months. While the state courts have apparently construed the statute to permit extensions of time,...nevertheless the initial legislative judgment provides a useful benchmark. In this case, it is sufficient to note that the petitioner has been confined for six years, and there is no basis for anticipating that he will ever be easier to examine than he is today. In these circumstances, it is a denial of due process to continue to hold him on the basis of an *ex parte* order committing him for observation.

B. A second argument advanced by the State relies on the claim that petitioner himself prevented the State from holding a hearing on his condition. The State contends that, by refusing to talk to the psychiatrists, petitioner has prevented them from evaluating him, and made it impossible for the State to go forward with evidence at a hearing. Thus, it is argued, his continued confinement is analogous to civil contempt; he can terminate the confinement and bring about a hearing at any time by talking to the examining psychiatrists, and the State has the power to induce his cooperation by confining him.

Petitioner claims that he has a right under the Fifth Amendment to withhold cooperation, a claim we need not consider here. But putting that claim to one side, there is nevertheless a fatal flaw in the State's argument. For if confinement is to rest on a theory of civil contempt, then due process requires a hearing to determine whether petitioner has in fact behaved in a manner that amounts to contempt. At such a hearing it could be ascertained whether petitioner's conduct is willful, or whether it is a manifestation of mental illness, for which he cannot fairly be held responsible.

Civil contempt is coercive in nature, and consequently there is no justification for confining on a civil contempt theory a person who lacks the present ability to comply.

Moreover, a hearing would provide the appropriate forum for resolution of petitioner's Fifth Amendment claim. Finally, if the petitioner's confinement were explicitly premised on a finding of contempt, then it would be appropriate to consider what limitations the Due Process Clause places on the contempt power. The precise contours of that power need not be traced here. It is enough to note that petitioner has been confined, potentially for life, although he has never been determined to be in contempt by a procedure that comports with due process. The contempt analogy cannot justify the State's failure to provide a hearing of any kind.

C. Finally, the State suggests that petitioner is probably a defective delinquent, because most noncooperators are. Hence, it is argued, his confinement rests not only on the purposes of observation, and of penalizing contempt, but also on the underlying purposes of the Defective Delinquency Law. But that argument proves too much. For if the Patuxent staff was prepared to conclude, on the basis of petitioner's silence and their observations of him over the years, that petitioner is a defective delinquent, then it is not true that he has prevented them from evaluating him. On that theory, they have long been ready to make their report to the Court, and the hearing on defective delinquency could have gone forward.

III

Petitioner is presently confined in Patuxent without any lawful authority to support that confinement. His sentence having expired, he is no longer within the class of persons eligible for commitment to the Institution as a defective delinquent. Accordingly, he is entitled to be released. The judgment below is reversed, and the mandate shall issue forthwith.

Reversed.

MR. JUSTICE DOUGLAS, concurring....

McNeil was tried and convicted in a Maryland court for assault on a public officer and for assault with intent to rape. He took the stand and denied he had committed the offenses. He had had no prior criminal record. The sentencing judge asked for a psychiatric evaluation of the accused, though neither side at the trial had raised or suggested any psychiatric issues. A medical officer examined him and recommended that he be considered for evaluation and treatment at Patuxent Institution, a state psychiatric agency....

The examination normally entails psychiatric interviews and evaluation, psychological tests, sociological and social work studies, and review of past history and records, including police, juvenile, penal and hospital records. Personal interviews include a series of questions to elicit and to determine the past criminal record, antisocial and criminal behavior of the individual.

If the report shows that he should not be classified as a defective delinquent, he is retained in custody under his original sentence with full credit given for the time confined at Patuxent.

If the report says that he should be classified as a defective delinquent, a hearing is held at which the defendant is entitled to counsel and a trial by jury....

McNeil, though being at Patuxent beyond the term of five years for which he was sentenced, has never had such a hearing, for he has never been declared a "defective delinquent."[1] He has not been so declared and on the other hand has

---

[1] Detention beyond the expiration of court-imposed sentences occurs in Communist China where "public security organs [have] the authority to impose as well as administer punishment" and "the discretionary power to extend the duration of imprisonment beyond the original sentences." Shao-chuan Leng, *Justice in Communist China* 34 (1967).

not been cleared, because he has refused on at least 15 separate occasions to submit to the psychiatric tests and questions. Nor has he received in the interim any rehabilitative treatment or training. The State indeed intends to keep him there indefinitely, as long as he refuses to submit to psychiatric or psychological examinations.[2]

McNeil's refusal to submit to that questioning is not quixotic; it is based on his Fifth Amendment right to be silent. McNeil remains confined without any hearing whatsoever that he has a propensity toward criminal activity and without any hope of having a hearing unless he surrenders his right against self-incrimination....

McNeil was repeatedly interrogated not only about the crime for which he was convicted but for many other alleged antisocial incidents going back to his sophomore year in high school. One staff member after interviewing McNeil reported: "He adamantly and vehemently denies, despite the police reports, that he was involved in the offense"; "Further questioning revealed that he had stolen some shoes but he insisted that he did not know that they were stolen..."; "...but in the tenth grade he was caught taking some milk and cookies from the cafeteria"; "He consistently denies his guilt in all these offenses"; "He insisted that he was not present at the purse snatching"; "He was adamant in insisting on this version of the offense despite the police report which was in the brief and which I had available and discussed with him"; "He continued his denial into a consideration of a juvenile offense..."; "He denies the use of all drugs and narcotics"; "...I explained to him that it might be of some help to him if we could understand why he did such a thing but this was to no avail...."

First, the staff refuses to diagnose him, no matter how much information they may have, unless he talks. The result is that he never receives a hearing and remains at Patuxent indefinitely.

Second, if there is no report on him, he remains on the receiving tier indefinitely and receives no treatment....

Whatever the Patuxent procedures may be called—whether civil or criminal—the result under the Self-Incrimination Clause of the Fifth Amendment is the same. As we said in In re Gault, 387 U.S. 1, 49–50, 87 S.Ct. 1428, 1455–1456, 18 L.Ed.2d 527 there is harm and self-incrimination whenever there is "a deprivation of liberty"; and there is such a deprivation whatever the name of the institution, if a person is held against his will.

Questions

1. If you were a lawyer and an individual who was incarcerated in an institution like Patuxent approached you and asked you to use your skills to get him/her out, what would be your advice about the quality of legal relief available? Would you be able to inform the client of any limitations to the relief that the legal system provides?

2. What kind of legal resources are available to inmates? How can an inmate make contact with a lawyer or legal worker?

3. Until the mid-1960s, many federal and state courts refused to consider complaints by prisoners relating to prison regulations or practices. This policy was attributed to the so-called hands-off doctrine which was based on the following rationales: (1) prison officers are professionals, and judges do not have the background adequately to review these complaints, and (2) prisoners had no rights and, therefore, the courts had no jurisdiction. A prisoner was thought to be a "slave of the state." See *Ruffin* v. *Commonwealth*, 62 Va. 790, 796 (1871). The modern version of this conception was the notion of the "civil death" of inmates which stripped them of virtually all legal rights.

[2] In the District Court proceedings in *Murel* v. *Baltimore City Criminal Court, supra,* at —— of 405 U.S., at 2091 of 92 S.Ct., Dr. Boslow, the Director of Patuxent, testified:

"[The Court] ... Take the case of a person who is referred for diagnosis and he fails, let us say, 100 per cent, to cooperate; he won't talk to anybody, he won't undergo any tests, he won't participate, though I don't think he gets group therapy.

"[Dr. Boslow] No, sir.

"[The Court] But he will do absolutely nothing and will take no advantage of whatever opportunity if any there may be.

"He, therefore, assuming that the law is valid, and assuming that the administration in that respect is supportable, could he remain there indefinitely unclassified? Is that correct?

"[Dr. Boslow] Under the present state of things, yes."

Nevertheless, in the past decade, the hands-off doctrine has been eroding. An inmate can now file suit. Do you think that access to courts has changed the nature of incarceration? What effect has access to the courts had?

4. Do you think that if every judge was required to spend some time in a jail or a prison that the general legal response to prisoner's cases would be different?

4 Behavior Control

Many cling to the old-fashioned belief that each of us builds up his personality logically and by free will. This is as patently incorrect as the belief that the world is flat. No one owns his own personality. Your ego, or individuality, was forced on you by your genetic constitution and by the society into which you were born. You had no say about what kind of personality you acquired, and there's no reason to believe you should have the right to refuse to acquire a new personality if your old one is antisocial. I don't believe the Constitution of the United States gives you the *right* to commit a crime if you want to; therefore, the Constitution does not guarantee you the right to maintain inviolable the personality it forced on you in the first place—if and when the personality manifests strongly antisocial behavior.

James McConnell, *Criminals Can be Brainwashed Now*

Behavior modification therapies present new and complex issues for law and for society. The field of behavior modification is relatively new, yet it grows out of the treatment-oriented programs discussed in the previous section. In fact, the definition of behavior modification is problematical and it can be understood in varying ways. Behavior therapy can be viewed as a specialized field of treatment relying on specialized techniques. The actual techniques involved in behavior modification programs cover a wide range of examples. Some techniques utilize physical punishment, shock treatments, and drug therapy, as well as other forms of aversive stimuli. At the softer end of the spectrum, it has been suggested that any

learned response to any stimuli is an example of behavior control. The Department of Health, Education, and Welfare defines behavior modification in the following manner: "The systematic application of psychological and social principles to bring about desired changes in, or to prevent development of, certain problematic behaviors and response." *

There are, however, some common elements of all behavior modification programs; each employs methods that involve the direct and systematic manipulation by one individual of the personality of the other through the use of consciously applied psychological, medical, and other technological methods. The aim of behavior modification programs is to restructure personality so that the controlled individual will no longer act in the fashion previously determined unacceptable by the controller.

The transformation from psychotherapeutic emphasis of treatment to a technology of behavior control can be attributed to many factors. B. F. Skinner initially conceptualized psychotherapy in behavior terms in the 1950s. He explained:

> The field of psychotherapy is rich in explanatory fictions. Behavior itself has not been accepted as subject matter in its

---

* "Individual Rights and the Federal Role in Behavior Modification," Committee on Judiciary, U.S. Senate, November 1, 1974, p. 1.

own right, but only as an indication of *something wrong somewhere else.* The task of therapy is said to be to remedy an inner illness of which the behavioral manifestations are merely "symptoms"... the condition to be corrected is called "neurotic," and the thing to be attacked by psychotherapy is then identified as a "neurosis." The term no longer carries its original implication of a derangement of the nervous system, but it is nevertheless an unfortunate example of an explanatory fiction. It has encouraged the therapist to avoid specifying the behavior to be corrected or showing why it is disadvantageous or dangerous. By suggesting a single cause for multiple disorders it has implied a uniformity which is not to be found in the data. Above all, it has encouraged the belief that psychotherapy consists of removing inner causes of mental illness, as the surgeon removes an inflamed appendix or cancerous growth or as indigestible food is purged from the body... it is not an inner cause of behavior but the behavior itself which—in the medical analogy of catharsis—must be "got out of the system."*

* B. F. Skinner, *Behavior Therapy: An Overview,* from *Behavior Theory: Application and Outcome* by K. Daniel O'Leary and G. Terence Wilson (Englewood, N.J.: Prentice Hall, 1975), pp. 4–5.

Skinner's impatience with psychotherapy was shared by many people, and his work in the area of behavior control drew support from many people in different fields of work.

The attraction for theories of behavior modification in the area of prison work has other causes as well. A new and available technological capacity to control behavior changed the vision of what was and is possible. There has also been a marked increase in government funding in this area. In part, this governmental interest in controlling violence and reducing crime through behavior-modifying techniques is attributable to the widespread spirit of protest of the late 1960s and early 1970s. The "law and order" notion of that time is presently manifested in these programs of behavior control.

The techniques of behavior modification are perhaps most visible in prison environments, but they also permeate other institutions, such as in schools and hospitals as well.

As you read the next section, keep the following questions in mind: Are these programs objectionable? Why or why not? Has technology of behavior taken on an autonomous identity and momentum? Does the ideology of behavior control support an expansion or a restriction of state intervention in people's lives?

Beyond Freedom and Dignity   *B. F. Skinner*

Almost all our major problems involve human behavior, and they cannot be solved by physical and biological technology alone. What is needed is a technology of behavior, but we have been slow to

From *Beyond Freedom and Dignity,* by B. F. Skinner. Copyright © 1971 by B. F. Skinner. Reprinted by permission of Alfred A. Knopf, Inc. Pp. 22–23.

develop the science from which such a technology might be drawn. One difficulty is that almost all of what is called behavioral science continues to trace behavior to states of mind, feelings, traits of character, human nature, and so on. Physics and biology once followed similar practices and advanced only when they discarded them. The behavioral sciences have been slow to change partly because the explanatory entities often seem to be directly observed and partly because other kinds of explanations have been hard to find. The environment is obviously important, but its role has remained obscure. It does not push or pull, it *selects,* and this function is difficult to discover and analyze. The role of natural selection in evolution was formulated only a little more than a hundred years ago, and the selective role of the environment in shaping and maintaining the behavior of the individual is only beginning to be recognized and studied. As the interaction between organism and environment has come to be understood, however, effects once assigned to states of mind, feelings, and traits are beginning to be traced to accessible conditions, and a technology of behavior may therefore become available. It will not solve our problems, however, until it replaces traditional prescientific views, and these are strongly entrenched. Freedom and dignity illustrate the difficulty. They are the possessions of the autonomous man of traditional theory, and they are essential to practices in which a person is held responsible for his conduct and given credit for his achievements. A scientific analysis shifts both the responsibility and the achievement to the environment....

Man's struggle for freedom is not due to a will to be free, but to certain behavioral processes characteristic of the human organism, the chief effect of which is the avoidance of or escape from so-called "aversive" features of the environment. Physical and biological technologies have been mainly concerned with natural aversive stimuli; the struggle for freedom is concerned with stimuli intentionally arranged by other people. The literature of freedom has identified the other people and has proposed ways of escaping from them or weakening or destroying their power. It has been successful in reducing the aversive stimuli used in intentional control, but it has made the mistake of defining freedom in terms of states of mind or feelings, and it has therefore not been able to deal effectively with techniques of control which do not breed escape or revolt but nevertheless have aversive consequences. It has been

forced to brand all control as wrong and to misrepresent many of the advantages to be gained from a social environment. It is unprepared for the next step, which is not to free men from control but to analyze and change the kinds of control to which they are exposed.

Questions

1. The idea of controlling people's behavior by controlling their environment has taken other forms as well as those suggested by B. F. Skinner. It has been suggested, for example, that:

   > We should try to establish, at the earliest possible moment of the baby's life, a program of psychogenesis, meaning the use of available physiological, psychological and psychiatric knowledge for the formation of the child's personality.... The postulates of psychogenesis are: 1) the mind does not exist at the moment of birth; 2) the mind cannot appear in the absence of sensory inputs; 3) individual identity and personal behavior are not properties of the brain which will unfold automatically through neuronal maturation, but are acquired functions which must be learned...; 4) man is not born free but is subservient to genes and education; 5) personal freedom is not inherited, nor is it a gift of nature, but one of the highest attainments of civilization which acquires awareness and intellectual and emotional training in order to process and choose intelligently among environmental alternatives.*

   What are the implications of this statement in terms of what would be appropriate and acceptable forms of treatment in prison?

2. What are the implications for other social institutions if the understanding of the relationship of freedom to human behavior is understood in the foregoing manner?

3. Can behavior modification be understood simply as a new technological response to imprisonment? Is behavior modification inherently a theory of autocratic social structure?

* José M. R. Delgado, *Physical Control of the Mind: Toward a Psychocivilized Society* (New York: Harper Colophon Books, Harper & Row, 1971), pp. 241–242.

Behavior Modification in Total Institutions   *David Rothman*

A New Critique

Since the mid-1960s, a new and persuasive critique of total institutions has emerged. Rationales that once buttressed the practice of incarceration now seem flimsy. As faith in the ability of total institutions to rehabilitate the deviant has declined, so has support for incarceration. For the first time, reformers are not focusing their attack on the inadequacies of one particular institution or the failing of one group of administrators but on the very idea of confinement. Unlike their predecessors, who invariably responded to scandals by calling for bigger and better prisons and asylums, and greater state intervention, critics today are blaming the system, not its wardens or superintendents. Since the arrangements that are ostensibly susceptible to improvement within incarceration are well nigh endless, from the administrative hierarchy to the quality of the staff to the nature of the daily programs, the ability to transcend this particular angle of vision and achieve a more generalized analysis is genuinely impressive.

Part of the credit for this breakthrough belongs to such theorists as Erving Goffman. His study *Asylums* argues compellingly that the inherent characteristics of total institutions make impossible the achievement of rehabilitative goals. A series of sociological studies have also been important in demonstrating the failure of existing penal programs. These findings have influenced a wide and diverse group of observers. The contemporary dissatisfaction with incarceration does not follow political lines. It includes conservative as well as liberal members of government commissions, left-wing writers and former wardens, psychiatric superintendents and federal judges.

And yet for all the novelty and popularity of this perspective, for all the unanimity in calling for a moratorium on the construction of new institutions and for a reduction in the number of inmates and patients, there is little cause to believe that our long and grim history of incarceration is nearing its end, that state intervention will decline. The anti-institutional program is vulnerable in several important respects.

First, it is a faint trumpet that now calls us to reform. The attack upon incarceration is generally a negative one, a dissatisfaction with current arrangements, without any promise that alternatives will promote massive cure. Unlike the first promoters of asylums, the new breed of reformers does not claim to be able to rid the streets of crime or the community of mental illness. Their aims are more modest: to reduce the harm done by intervention, to lower the costs of care, to make treatment less cruel and inhumane. Their goals are sensible and decent, but not dramatic or glamorous.

Further, the first attempts to bring the incarcerated back into the community have not been without drawbacks of their own. Although the experiment is only a few years old, there is mounting evidence of a backlash. To date reformers have been more concerned with emptying the institutions than in thinking through the modes of community care and treatment. Activist lawyers won the major legal battles which helped reduce institutional populations—it was not, however, within their skill or province to design alternatives. In addition, many observers are so shocked at the inadequacy of institutional conditions that they feel compelled to press for immediate reduction in the numbers of the incarcerated, and to leave for later the problem of alternatives. (In the words of one crusading psychiatrist, when you have Buchenwald, you don't

From David Rothman "Behavior Modification in Total Institutions," Hastings Center Report, Vol. 5, No. 1 (February 1975), pp. 17–24. © Institute of Society, Ethics and the Life Sciences, 360 Broadway, Hastings-on-Hudson, N.Y. 10706. Reprinted by permission.

worry first about alternatives to Buchenwald.) But the effect of these approaches, particularly in the field of mental health, has been to force ex-patients into settings almost as bad as, and in some cases perhaps worse than, the institutions they have left. And tolerance for the deviant, no matter how harmless he may be, is very limited; communities simply will not, in their own terms, gamble with safety. Hence, before non-incarcerative programs are able to learn from their own mistakes, they may be put out of business.

A still more significant development, whose thrust is much more pro-institutional and conducive to maximizing state intervention, is the burgeoning faith in the power of behavior modification techniques to rehabilitate the deviant. Not everyone, it seems, is so pessimistic about the prospects for cure. Indeed, at a time when so many others are abandoning the goal of rehabilitation as an unrealistic and ultimately a mischievous one upon which to base public policy, those who claim to have answers, those who present themselves as problem-solvers, receive a very attentive and enthusiastic audience.

The optimism comes from several quarters, and the term behavior modification does not fit easily over all of them. Some psychiatrists insist that the environment of a total institution or the compulsory character of treatment within it need not weaken efforts at rehabilitation. They insist that group therapy sessions with inmates, whether conducted by more orthodox psychiatrists or encounter group leaders, can work well; they argue that if psychiatrists hold the key to release from confinement, if the inmate must reckon with the fact that either he cooperates with his doctor or remains inside, then progress is all the more likely. (Many of the staff at Patuxent, Maryland's institution for defective delinquents, subscribe to this position.) Still other psychiatrists find this to be an appropriate time for wide-open experimentation with all kinds of therapeutic techniques, proven or unproven, traditional or novel. Perhaps effective treatment will emerge from the work of drama therapists, or Synanon-type models, or human resources development-type models, or in heart-to-heart discussions between cons and ex-cons. (The plans for the new federal treatment center at Butner, North Carolina, illustrate this approach.) And finally, there are the behavior modifiers in the strict sense of the term, the most aggressive and optimistic of the lot, those persuaded that operant conditioning holds the key to effective cure. Convinced that they can curb the eating habits of the overweight and eliminate the cigarette habit of the chain smoker, they stand ready to apply their skills to the deviant.

To date, most of their efforts have been applied to the hard-core deviant, the institutional dregs, the toughest cases. In Connecticut's prison at Somers, behavior modifiers have used their techniques on pedophiles, the child molesters who so shock the community conscience that they typically remain incarcerated for decades. In *Clockwork Orange* fashion, the behavior modifiers attach electrodes to the inmate's skin, flash on the screen pictures of nubile and naked boys and girls, and then simultaneously apply electric shock. They have also intervened with the most troublesome inmates in the federal prison system. At the Springfield, Missouri treatment center, the behavior modifiers took inmates with long records as troublemakers in other federal prisons, those who had spent months in solitary and disciplinary cells, and placed them in the START program. Through a careful meting out of rewards and punishments, they promised to turn them into obedient inmates and, ostensibly, obedient citizens.

Because they have worked with the hard-core, the behavior modifiers can argue, more or less in good conscience, that however unpleasant their techniques, the inmates otherwise confront an even worse fate. You may not like shock conditioning, but remember that the alternative is to keep pedophiles locked up forever; the START program may be rough, but surely it is no worse than months in solitary. They further argue that nothing else works with this segment of the deviant population. Just as doctors will use experimental drugs on terminally ill patients, so too, behavior modifiers should be allowed to use their techniques on the chronic deviant. We have nothing to lose, they tell us, and much to gain through their efforts.

Medical Center for Federal Prisoners START Program

Introduction

The START Program at the Medical Center for Federal Prisoners is designed to assist you in changing your current way of living within the Federal prison system. To be eligible for the program you must have spent considerable time in segregation for one reason or another. This is a miserable existence and the Federal Government is the first to recognize this situation. We, in the Federal Government, have not sent you to prison but we have been given the responsibility of your custody by the Federal courts. We have also been given the responsibility to establish a program in which you can still live by your principles and beliefs, but learn to express them in a manner more acceptable to society than you have in the past.

The enclosed information will serve to introduce you to the START Program. It will attempt to explain the benefits you can expect to gain, and the personal cooperation and effort required of you to earn a favorable recommendation for transfer back to a regular institution. First of all you must understand that you have been designated for placement on this unit by the Bureau of Prisons due to adjustment problems at previous institutions. Likewise Bureau approval must be obtained before you can be transferred to another institution.

The START Program is designed to employ rigid controls and at the same time provide you the opportunity for participation in work, recreation, and areas of self-improvement. All of your needs will be provided within the unit including meals, work, play, sick call, education, visits, etc. The unit is self contained which simply means

From "Individual Rights and the Federal Role in Behavior Modification," U.S. Senate, Committee on the Judiciary, November 1974.

you will not be permitted to visit other areas of the Medical Center.

Immediate change in one's behavior is an unrealistic objective. For this reason the START Program consists of three levels of privileges, responsibilities, and opportunities. Every new inmate starts at Level I and progresses to Level III. Promotions from one level to another are earned or awarded on the basis of your conduct, cooperation, acceptance of responsibility for your own behavior, and achievement towards Treatment Team established goals.

You are initially assigned to Level I until the Treatment Team recommends promotion to Level II. Level I has a minimum of privileges and responsibilities with requirements for promotion to Level II also being minimal. In Level II your privileges and responsibilities are increased and you will be required to participate in more activities such as work and self-improvement.

Satisfactory performance in Level II must be maintained for at least six months before you can be promoted to Level III. Here again, your privileges and responsibilities will be increased and more will be expected of you. There is no minimum or maximum time limit for this level. The Treatment Team will evaluate your accomplishments with you and will make recommendation for transfer to another institution when deemed appropriate. Although you can earn more benefits and privileges in the START Program than you could have in a locked segregation unit, you can never benefit as well or receive as much in this unit as in a regular institution population.

Some of the benefits available in the START Program are as follows:

1. You will have the opportunity for educational achievement.

2. You will have an opportunity to earn Industrial Good Time and pay.

3. You can work toward restoration of forfeited Statutory Good Time.

4. You will have the opportunity to seek personal counseling and understanding.

The operational philosophy of the START Program simply says that you are a man and you will be treated as a man. However, if you behave as a child, you will be treated as a child.

The following specific paragraphs will help to explain many of your questions. If there is an area you still do not understand after reading the entire brochure, the Treatment Team will assist you.

Admission

Upon admission you will be placed on Level I for orientation and admission procedures. During this period you will be given time to understand the program and learn what is expected of you. With a minimal amount of cooperation and satisfactory conduct, you can be promoted to Level II. Also during this initial period, the Treatment Team will establish program goals and will explain what will be required of you to attain these goals.

Meals

In Level I, depending upon your conduct, you will be released from your cell to serve yourself from the food cart and then return to your cell to eat. The Officer will collect and account for your eating utensils when you have had sufficient time to finish your meal.

In Level II, you will be released from your cell to serve yourself from the food cart. In most cases you will be required to eat with the group at the unit's dining area. However, at the Treatment Team's option other arrangements for eating may be designated.

In Level III, you will be released from your cell to serve yourself from the food cart and eat with the group at the unit's dining area. You are not required to eat; but if you do, you must eat at the tables in the dining area.

Bathing, Clothing Exchange, and Shaving

Level I will bathe twice weekly and an exchange of clothing will be provided at shower time. You will be issued a razor to shave during your shower period which must be returned after use. Extra clothing will not be permitted in your cell.

Level II will bathe three times weekly and clothing exchange will be provided at shower time. You will be issued a razor daily for use in shaving as it is policy to be clean shaven at all times. You must return the razor to the Officer immediately after use. You will be permitted to keep one extra suit of clothing in your cell.

Level III will be permitted to bathe daily during your off duty hours, and exchange clothing when available. Three suits are standard issue and special arrangements will not be made to provide extra clothing. You will be issued a razor to keep in your cell and will be required to be clean shaven at all times.

Yard and Recreation

In Level I you will be provided a one hour period in the yard for exercise and fresh air twice weekly, weather permitting. Recreation within the unit will be available during inclement weather.

Level II will be allowed a one hour yard period three times weekly, weather permitting. Recreation within the unit will be available during inclement weather.

Level III will be permitted daily yard privileges during evenings, weekends, and on holidays within the unit, or on the yard when daylight and weather will permit. Recreation in the 10 Building yard or the unit's yard is at the discretion of the Treatment Team.

Personal Property

While in Level I you will not have access to your personal property beyond that provided for in the Bureau Policy Statement. With satisfactory cooperation on your part, you will be in

Level I only a minimum amount of time, so do not request special consideration.

In Levels II and III the Treatment Team will approve for you to have some of your personal property. You most likely will not be allowed to have all of your property, as you will not be allowed to accumulate items to the extent the Officers cannot routinely and efficiently check your cell.

Mail and Correspondence

Men at all levels will have regular correspondence privileges in accordance with the Medical Center Policy Statement governing "Inmate Correspondence Procedures." You will be allowed to subscribe to a limited number of publications at the upper levels.

Commissary

Depending upon your level, you will be permitted to spend a limited amount of money for approved commissary items. You will submit an order list to the Unit Officer who will check it for approved items and forward it to the sales unit. The commissary supervisor will deliver the filled order to you in the unit. Level I will not have commissary spending privilege.

Visiting

Visiting will be in the designated unit's visiting area. All visits will be in accordance with the Medical Center Policy Statement governing "Inmate Visiting Privileges." However, the number of visits and length will be dependent upon the number of Officers available, space, and current condition you are in at the time. Because of these limitations, you are requested to contact all potential visitors and request that they write to the Warden designating the date and time of a visit so arrangements can be made.

Attorney visits will be granted as the need arises and will not be charged against your regular visiting.

Sick Call

A member of the medical staff will visit the unit daily. You should make your medical problems known to him and he will make the proper disposition. If you are seriously ill, you will be transferred to a locked ward in the medical hospital area and returned to the START unit when you have made satisfactory recovery.

Religion

If you need assistance in the area of religion, you may request help by submitting a request to one of the staff chaplains who visit the unit several times weekly.

Education

You will have the opportunity to further yourself and your education through use of individual study courses. The Education Department Staff will evaluate your educational needs and make recommendations to the Treatment Team. The Team will then present educational goals which you are urged to complete.

Work Assignments

Your work assignments will consist of orderly work within the unit, or an industrial assignment making "sweep brushes," or both. The Treatment Team will discuss and designate your work classification.

When assigned to industry, you will earn extra good time and pay at a standard rate proportionate to the hours you work.

Case Manager

A Case Manager is assigned and will be available on request. He is a member of the Treatment Team and will periodically come to the unit for notarization of correspondence and legal material. If you have a problem outside the unit or Medical Center, he will assist you in its resolution.

Correctional Counselor

Correctional Counselor will be available daily to discuss any area of concern you may have. He is a member of the Treatment Team and can be called upon to speak for you if you are not present. He is trained in various counseling methods and can be helpful when you need someone to talk with on a personal and private level.

You will gain as much from the START Program as you put into it. If segregation is the way you choose to do your time, you have a right to this choice. However, each staff member is here to help you change those aspects of your life which resulted in your continual placement in a segregation unit. Everyone finds himself in situations in which he would prefer not to be in, but this is life. He is a MAN who can make the best of a situation and profit from the experience. This is true not only for inside a prison but also in the community. If you feel you can make it in the community, you must first demonstrate that you can adjust in a general population. The man who says that he can make it in the community but can not make it in the general population is only fooling himself and copping out from life. You are now given the opportunity to start over again. Are you man enough to accept this challenge?

Goals and Objectives

The primary goal of Project START is the care, control, and correction of the long term, disruptive adult offender. The major objective is to help these individuals gain better control over their behavior so that they can be returned to regular institutions where they can then participate in programs designed to help them make a successful community adjustment. START, then, can be viewed as a type of *"pre-rehabilitation;"* a necessary first step for that small subset of inmates who consistently undermine training programs that the majority of offenders find useful in contributing to post-release success.

Pertinent sub-goals of Project START are those which will enable the individual to participate in programs in regular institutions. There are three such sub-goals:

1. Maintain an appropriate level of personal hygiene.
2. Develop an ability to engage positively in inter-personal relationships.
3. Learn productive work habits.

The Participants

The type of individual eligible for selection in the START program represented less than 1% of the total Federal Prison System's population. Nevertheless, he does much to disrupt normal operation of any institution. He consumes a disproportionate share of staff time by destructive behavior and does not respond to disciplinary or other external controls. Most counseling efforts fail. He is assaultive and maliciously schemes to demonstrate his physical prowess, usually by pressuring the weaker, more passive inmates. Feelings of genuine guilt are non-existent as he readily rationalizes his own maladaptive behavior, displacing responsibility for his actions onto others. Usually, he is verbally facile and quite clever in being able to mask his deceitful intent. Thus, he is manipulative, egotistical in the extreme and verbally and physically assaultive. He threatens the successful rehabilitation of other offenders, continually indoctrinating those less sophisticated than he with the idea that "crime does pay."

The START participants are heterogeneous relative to age, type of offense, race, area of residency, etc. The major common element is that they all have repeatedly demonstrated their inability to live in regular penal facilities.

Treatment Approach

The START program was developed to help an individual change those aspects of his behavior which are maladaptive. The task presented to the START staff was to find a means which would result in the decreased occurrence of these destructive behaviors. To accomplish this goal, certain basic principles of behavior modification

Federal Center for Federal Prisoners

START PROGRAM

INDUSTRY PERFORMANCE EVALUATION

Name _____ Date _____

WORK SKILLS	Very Good	Good	Fair	Poor	Indeterminate
A. Ability to:					
1. learn quickly					
2. follow directions					
3. retain instructions					
4. work without close supervision					
5. sustain work effort					
6. stay at work assignment					
7. exhibit versatility					
8. handle complex tasks					
9. assume responsibility					
10. organize work efficiently					
11. recognize errors					
12. seeks assistance if runs into difficulty					
13. work under pressure					
14. return to work promptly after break					
15. become involved with work					
16. derive satisfaction from being productive					
17. do a job he doesn't like					
18. work without complaining					
19. conform to rules and regulations					
B. Level of:					
1. finger dexterity					
2. eye, hand coordination					
3. physical strength					
C. Attendance has been:					

INTERPERSONAL RELATIONSHIPS:

A. Relationships to Supervisors	Slight	Moderate	Excessive
1. need for encouragement			
2. need for emotional support			
3. need for strict limit setting			

	Above Average	Average	Poor
4. ability to handle criticism			
5. ability to learn from correction			

B. Relationships to Co-workers	Very Good	Good	Fair	Poor	Indeterminate
1. ability to get along with others					
2. ability to tolerate annoying co-workers					
3. Inmate is generally liked by others					

4. Inmate functions as: Leader _____ Active Participant _____

Passive Individual_____ Social Isolate _____

Comments _____

_____

Evaluator _____ Date _____

were adapted. The underlying theme of the START program is to reward constructive behavior. If appropriate behavior is rewarded, the likelihood of it happening again is increased; conversely, if unacceptable behavior is not rewarded (i.e., not attended to) the likelihood of it re-occurring is reduced.

Table 2—"Good Day" Criteria

1. Willingness to participate; e.g.
   a. Accepted work assignment.
   b. Vacated room when opportunity available.
   c. Served self from food cart.
   d. Agreed to medical exam and laboratory test upon admission and/or request.
2. Neat and clean room appearance.
3. Neat and clean personal appearance.
4. Shower and shave according to guidelines on designated days.
5. Engaged in exercise or recreation activities; e.g.
   a. Vacated room.
   b. Went to yard or day room.
6. Accepted a "no" or other reasonable response when making requests. Made requests in a non-abusive manner.
7. Communicated with others in a reasonable tone of voice without belittling, agitating, or using abusive language.
8. Accepted or performed assignments, duties, or tasks without needing persuasion.
9. Followed directions and instructions in a willing manner without bickering.
10. Followed rules, regulations, and policies of unit.
11. Used care in handling federal property.
12. Settled differences without fighting, wrestling, striking, or other overt, physically aggressive acts towards another person.

Non-earning of a "Good Day" necessitates a note in resident's file.

Questions

1. What are the premises about human behavior around which the daily workings of this program are built? Why might a program of this type be successful in controlling behavior?

2. Is the control of behavior a legitimate goal of incarceration? What other goals underly notions of imprisonment?

3. If the control of antisocial behavior is the desirable goal to be attained, what other methods might be employed to achieve that end?

4. Does the description of the START Program remind you of any institutions that have been part of your experience?

5. What is the significance that eating is a controlled item of behavior in Project START but correspondence is not? If court decisions order that food, clothing, or mail be given to prisoners as a matter of their rights, does this interfere with the behavior modification process? Which is more basic, a prisoner's rights as articulated by the courts or the behavior modification process?

Techniques of behavior modification in our society reflect some of our basic social and cultural values. Our increasing faith and reliance on technology, for example, supports the development of behavior-modifying equipment. Behavior modification theory rests on some fundamental conceptions of humanity which are at the basis of many social institutions.

Techniques of controlling behavior exist in other cultural contexts as well. Some of these techniques resemble methods employed in this country and others are very different. Behavior-control techniques examined in different social and cultural contexts suggest some primary aspects of the organization of each society and the values on which that society is based. The following articles suggest some things about the meaning of behavior control and imprisonment in Chinese society.

Introduction to *Prisoners of Liberation*   *Victor Li*

"Thought reform"—*ssu-hsiang kai-tsao*—is a most unfortunate term. It conjures up images of 1984, brainwashing, and various Oriental niceties and as a result diverts us from a serious consideration of the important issues underlying the thought reform process. Stripped of emotionalism and of Cold War and other ideological rhetoric, the fundamental question is: what must be done to get people to act in a particular manner—that is, to have people avoid certain "undesirable" actions and undertake certain other "desirable" ones? Implicit in this question is a series of others. In what manner and on what bases are norms of behavior determined for a society or a group? How are these norms communicated to the public? What means are used to get a group and its members to adhere to the norms? What happens when a person fails to adhere? And finally, what are the human and material costs in carrying out this course of action? Phrased in this manner, the thought reform process is of obvious interest to us, not only because it adds to our understanding of China, but no less importantly because it also concerns problems arising in our own society. Perhaps this entire area would be more understandable if we called it socialization rather than thought reform.

The Chinese subsume under the rubric of thought reform a very wide range of activities. On one end of the spectrum is the intense long-term process, such as the four-year prison experience with several "study sessions" each day described by the Ricketts. Next is a possibly more intense but much shorter-term variation. This

often occurs, for example, during "rectification" and other kinds of campaigns when for a limited period of time specific persons are attacked or particular lines of action vigorously promoted. Toward the other end of the spectrum is the "regular" group study sessions that all persons engage in for ten or more hours a week. They study not only political matters, but also try to upgrade their cultural levels and professional skills. In addition, these groups carry out a variety of activities involving management of minor local affairs. Finally, we might also include a kind of self-cultivation whereby an individual studies on his own—again, the matters studied vary greatly —to improve himself.

This spectrum of activities can be described in a different manner. In some cases, a person has committed a serious anti-social act and his treatment is the primary order of business. Depending on the intensity of the effort and the amount of time spent, thought reform, if carried out properly, could produce a kind of spiritual catharsis and lead to basic changes in attitude and behavior. Even where this does not occur, the person has learned how it must conform his behavior to terminate his present "treatment" and to prevent future conflicts. In other cases, the principal object is not to "cure" a deviant, but rather to prevent deviation from occurring in the first place. This usually takes place during ordinary group or individual study, when people consider what is permissible and impermissible conduct for particular situations, on what bases these distinctions are made, and what are the consequences of non-compliance. This effort is relatively low-keyed and is continuous. Finally, it is important to note that thought reform is not merely a weapon with which to attack deviants nor a prophylaxis to guard against deviation—although the defining and criticizing of anti-social conduct necessarily entails a thorough discussion of what is proper conduct. There are many cases where thought reform also is used in a much more positive and constructive sense to increase political consciousness, to explain social policies, to teach specific techniques, or even to raise the cultural level of the public. Again, much of this takes place through ordinary group or individual study.

More importantly, the thought reform process rests on a fundamental premise that a person's "thoughts" are in fact "reformable." This is not as simple a statement as it might appear. Such a premise is intimately linked with one's philosophical view of the basic nature of man. Without getting too esoteric, the Chinese Communists appear to believe that man is educatable, and perhaps even that man's nature is basically good. (Fortunately, both the Confucian tradition and Marxist doctrine agree here.) Consequently, when a person behaves improperly, it is possible to show him the error of his ways and teach him proper behavior. In addition, this process of "reform" is not extremely difficult. A man is not evil by nature and can be educated; going further, if man is by nature good, then when good and evil are presented to him, he will "naturally" choose the former. Approaching the same question from a positive direction, where a group is in disagreement over a particular issue, careful and rational discussion by that group will result, even without outside guidance, in correct decisions almost all the time. This is the basis of the mass line.

A second major aspect of thought reform in China is that there is a great deal of it. Again, this is not as simple as it sounds. The Chinese devote a staggering amount of human and material resources to this effort. By now, each adult has engaged in perhaps ten thousand hours of regular study sessions. In addition, production sometimes is curtailed so that rectification or other campaigns can be implemented.

By way of contrast, our society devotes almost no resources to the prison system or to the problems of rehabilitation or post-release reintegration. Similarly, formal programs of socialization and education end after childhood, rather than continue throughout one's adult life.

It is not entirely clear to me why the Chinese place such great emphasis on thought reform work. Perhaps it is just a "given": the possession of Truth carries with it the evangelical zeal to convert all non-believers. A variation of this idea might be the traditional Chinese view that the "superior man" had a social duty to teach his less enlightened brethren. Another reason might be that the Chinese view a "just" society as one where each person is able to fulfill his potential. Hence, one's "good" nature should be promoted and one's "evil" tendencies eradicated; similarly, if a person deviates from correct conduct, the rest of society has a duty to help salvage him. On a less abstract level, the Chinese may favor the thought reform process because it is an effective and cheap mechanism for communicating orders from the center to the local levels, adapting central directives to local conditions, and ensuring that these orders are carried out.

The "central core" of the thought reform process also involves a common set of specific techniques. Initially, there often is some attempt to disorient a person. This might be done by outright attacks on one's positions or by posing for discussion ("some comrades say . . .") questions to which there are not clear answers. The ensuing uncertainty, confusion, and even despair renders a person ready to have his thoughts reoriented along "correct" lines.

The disorientation-reorientation effort makes careful and extensive use of positive incentives. Negative incentives and sanctions are present, of course, and are used when a person is especially recalcitrant. In general, however, coercion is downplayed. The goal of thought reform is to change one's way of thinking; and while one may be forced to act in a particular way, one cannot be forced to adopt a particular set of beliefs.

Thus, there usually is not total condemnation of a person. Each man is in part his own creation and in part a product of social conditions. When a person acts improperly, society must bear part of the blame. This approach has several good effects. First, since the fault is not totally one's own, a person is able to retain some measure of self-esteem—something very important to have if he is to be reintegrated into society. At the same time, society has a responsibility to change those conditions that contributed to the problem. It cannot, for example, abandon a criminal after his reform and release and merely return him to the same milieu from which he had originally come. It also must help to provide educational training, job training, suitable employment, and the like. Finally, a person is provided with a method for carrying out and for rationalizing his reform. He can admit that he had acted improperly in the past and analyze what aspects of his behavior were "caused" by social conditions and what aspects were his own doing. The former will be changed by society; the latter he must change himself. He will do so, of course, since having now seen the "truth," he "naturally" will choose to act properly. The above considerations were especially important in the years just after Liberation, when many ills could be blamed on the bad conditions in the old society and when the new regime could promise and carry out large and conspicuous changes.

Positive incentives are used more directly in other ways. In the case of a criminal, for example, there is constant stress that total reintegration is in fact possible. Since a person is not basically evil and is educatable, it is possible for him to see the error of his ways and to reform completely. Thereafter, no stigma need attach, and he is just like any other person. Going much further, the former criminal is offered a chance to help build the New China and to be a part of an exciting and rewarding effort. The attractiveness of this offer cannot be underestimated, since it gives a person purpose and hope.

Part of the positive incentives come in the form of praise for a person's every improvement and advance. In addition, deeds supplement words and thereby give the words greater weight and reality. Thus, the Ricketts described the teaching of illiterates to read and the promotion to cell leader and the return to dignity of a former cringing, whimpering pickpocket.

The situation is similar in the non-criminal area. The formula of unity-criticism-unity en-

sures that one does not get condemned for disagreeing, so long as the second unity is reached after the debate. People whose thinking and actions are "progressive" receive much praise. And there also is a stress on being a part of the building of a better and greater New China. In addition, activities such as discussions, debates, and study of central policies involve a considerable amount of local decision making and autonomy. This heightens one's sense of participation and importance and produces considerable positive incentive to participate to an even larger extent.

Another important characteristic of the thought reform process is the use of "small groups." Everyone belongs to one or more such groups where he lives, works, or has other principal associations. These groups consist of twenty or so people. They meet frequently and handle a wide range of functions, including being the focal points where much information and policy from above are disseminated to the public. Thus, on any particular issue, the group members will study relevant materials and discuss the pros and cons. In the process, broad central directives are translated into local terms; this includes the clarification of ambiguities and the opportunity to introduce local initiatives and variations. The final result is that each person knows quite clearly "the rules of the game" for that issue. Presumably, he also has internalized the norms of behavior described by the central policy and refined by the concrete local discussion. The group's role does not end here. Thereafter, members continue to comment upon each other's conduct and to "help" whoever may be straying from the correct path. These really are quite desirable features since they enable people to take part in the formulation of the rules governing their own behavior and also let people "police" themselves.

Interaction within a group generally is lively. Non-participation in the work of the group is not a possibility, since that in itself is a sign of backwardness and recalcitrance. Beyond that, there appears to be a kind of "group dynamic" that impels people to take part, perhaps much like the dynamics of encounter groups and T-groups in this country.

Questions

1. [C]an first-year law school be analogized to intense long-term thought reform? Again, there is a belief that "reform" can be accomplished and a willingness to devote large amounts of resources to it. In addition, considerable disorientation—whether or not intentionally caused by the faculty/group leaders—sets in at the beginning of this process, followed by varying degrees of confusion and despair. At the proper moment, hope is held out ("if you will only learn to think in a lawyer-like manner, everything will clear up"). There is no condemnation of the inner man ("it is not your fault that your liberal arts undergraduate background did not teach you to think clearly"). Positive incentives are used ("you can be a lawyer and do wonderful things"), although negative incentives also are present (embarrassment in front of one's class mates). And most of all, there is that overpowering group dynamics and peer pressure.*

   What would be the goal of an educational policy like the one described here?

   * Excerpted from *Prisoners of Liberation* by Allyn & Adele Rickett. Introduction by Victor Li. Introduction copyright © 1973 by Doubleday & Company, Inc. Reprinted by permission of the publisher.

2. What is the difference between thought reform and behavior modification? Li suggests that thought-reform techniques permeate the entire fabric of Chinese life and that it is accepted throughout the society. Why has there been an antipathetic response among many people in our society toward suggested behavior-modifying techniques in a cross-section of institutional environments?

3. If every individual in this country were required to participate in daily study groups with other people, would that change any of our commonly accepted social values? Would mandatory group study make behavior modification programs in differing institutions more acceptable?

4. If prisoners were forced to participate in group study sessions with a mandatory reading list, what would be your response?

5. Is there any difference between the Chinese concept that people are educable and can arrive at correct decisions by group discussion and the Jacksonian American concept that people are changeable and can be made to behave correctly by proper control?

6. Chinese prison theory holds that society has a responsibility to change those conditions that contribute to a person's criminal acts. Is there any counterpart to this in American theory?

In Chinese Prisons *John K. Fairbank*

Jean Pasqualini was born in China in 1926 of a French army father and a Chinese mother. He grew up with Chinese playmates, looking Chinese, speaking like a native. He learned French and English at French Catholic mission schools, and held the passport of a French citizen resident in China. In 1945 he worked for the Fifth U.S. Marines as a civilian specialist with the Military Police, and later for the U.S. Army Criminal Investigation Division until November, 1948. In 1953 he got a job in a Western embassy in Peking

Reprinted with permission from *The New York Review of Books.* Copyright © 1973 Nyrev, Inc. [Footnotes omitted.]

and was finally arrested during the anti-rightist campaign in December.

Under his Chinese name, Bao Ruo-wang, he then spent seven years of a twelve-year sentence for criminal activities in the Chinese communist labor camps, one of many millions undergoing Reform Through Labor (Lao Gai or Lao-tung kai-tsao), to be distinguished from the other multitudes undergoing Re-education Through Labor (Lao Jiao or Lao-tung chiao-yang). After de Gaulle's recognition of the People's Republic in 1964 led to Bao's release, he came to Paris for the first time, where he is today a respected teacher of Chinese language.

After his arrest Pasqualini, or Bao, to use his Chinese name, spent his first fifteen months in an interrogation center. Under the warders' close supervision, his dozen cellmates constantly exhorted one another to behave properly and with gratitude to the government for their chance to expiate their crimes and achieve reform. The government policy was "leniency to those who confess, severity to those who resist, expiation of crimes through gaining merits, reward to those who have gained merits." The key principle throughout was complete submission to authority.

Early on Bao was led into a torture chamber full of grisly equipment, only to be told after his first shock that it was a museum preserved from the Kuomintang era. Throughout his experience physical coercion of prisoners was strictly forbidden. Prison life was thoroughly organized to occupy nearly every waking moment. Prisoners moved at a trot with their heads bowed, looking neither to the right nor left. They followed punctilious daily routines, including periods for meditation when they sat cross-legged on their beds "exactly like a flock of Buddhist monks." Five days a week were occupied with confessions and interrogations, which each man worked out laboriously for himself with his interrogators. Bao wound up with a 700-page statement. Sunday was free for political study and Tuesday for clean-up, including passing around "a little box for toenail parings" collected monthly and sold for use in traditional Chinese medicine. The proceeds paid for a movie every four months. During fifteen months in this detention center Bao "ate rice only once and meat never. Six months after my arrest my stomach was entirely caved-in and I began to have the characteristic bruised joints that came from simple body contact with the communal bed." Vitamin deficiency led to his hair falling out and skin rubbing off.

"Facing the government we must study together and watch each other" was the slogan posted on the walls. Occasionally the study sessions would be punctuated by a struggle meeting, "a peculiarly Chinese invention combining intimidation, humiliation and sheer exhaustion . . . an intellectual gang-beating of one man by many, sometimes even thousands, in which the victim

has no defense, not even truth." A struggle can go on indefinitely until contrition has been achieved. The only way out is to develop a revolutionary ardor and the only means for that is by full confession. When it was decreed that all prisoners should take a two-hour nap in the summer afternoon, "anyone with his eyes open would receive a written reprimand. Enough reprimands and he would be ripe for struggling. We were very well-behaved. Model children."

When his interrogation was finally complete, Bao was shown the dossier of accusations against him. He found that all kinds of friends and colleagues had submitted their hand-written denunciation forms about him. It was now his turn to denounce others. "We want you to reform, but how can we consider you to be truly on the good road unless you tell us about your associates? Denunciation of others is a very good method of penance."

Another of the devices for inhibiting prisoners' solidarity was the system by which cellmates were obliged to settle the ration due to each cell-member, based on his own proposal and everyone else's assessment and vote. No one could help a friend eat well, any more than he could avoid struggling against him with hateful denunciations.

Finally, Bao came to trial: "You are not obliged to say anything. You will answer only when you are told to. We have chosen someone for your defense." The defense lawyer made a simple point, "The accused has admitted committing these crimes of his own free will. Therefore no defense is necessary."

Prisoners in the 1958–1959 period were caught up in the campaigns of the time. Urged to write down his feelings about his own sentence and crimes, Bao made the mistake of responding sincerely and stated that the government's alleged concern for him seemed to be a sham. All it really wanted from the prisoners was cheap slave labor. Soon this was used, at the end of the ideological reform campaign, to make him an example and he was put in chains in solitary in a cell about four feet long and four and a half feet high, room enough to sit but not to stand or lie down, with a permanently lit electric bulb overhead. At mealtime his handcuffs which had been behind him were changed to be in front, which was better than having to lap up the food ration like a dog. With his hands bound, however, he could hardly fight off the lice which soon flourished on his body.

After five days he asked to speak with someone from the Ministry of Public Security, to whom he said that the government had told him lies when the warder had assured him that honesty would be rewarded and his worst thoughts should be put on paper. "Having obeyed because of my profound confidence in the government and the Party, I was now being rewarded with solitary. Where was my sin?" This got him out, since "the Maoist order is inordinately proud of its own special sort of integrity."

In September, 1959, he was transferred to Peking Prison Number One, the model jail where he found it "almost shocking to be treated like a human being." The food was now good and plentiful and the warden sympathetic and humane. "Maybe it was the classical Pavlovian approach . . . his decency after two years of pain and humiliation was absolutely inspirational." Here Bao put together his first full-scale ideological review. In this the principles of criticism and self-criticism are the same as for citizens outside. Confession should be spontaneous, the moment one commits any error. Others should be quick to assist anyone who makes a mistake so that he can recognize it better. Only if this fails is the individual pushed into struggle or solitary. In this statement Bao typically declared that his sentence seemed most lenient and just, confessed that he disregarded the regulations that prisoners should always move in groups of two or more because several times he had gone to the latrine alone, and other times in study sessions he had not sat in the regulation manner or again he had talked during working hours.

With their low rations the prisoners he had seen thus far had never shown any sexual problems. But one day the camp barber was found to have seduced a feeble-minded young prisoner. Within hours the barber was brought in front of the assembly, denounced, condemned, and shot, his brains spraying over the front rows of the audience. "I have read of men being raped in Western prisons. In China the guilty party would be shot on the spot."

The fall of 1960 found Bao still struggling to get enough to eat as the winter cold came on. Work was reduced to six hours a day. Conditions became truly desperate as the food supply dwindled. The camp experimented with ersatz to mix in the food in the form of paper pulp. At first this made the steamed bread bigger and more filling, but soon the whole farm suffered "probably one of the most serious cases of mass constipation in medical history because the paper pulp powder had absorbed the moisture from the digestive tract. . . . I had to stick my finger up my anus and dig it out in dry lumps like sawdust." Another effort was to use marsh water plankton but this proved unassimilable. Still the warden was able to give them a New Year meal with rice, meat, and vegetables.

By 1961 Bao had achieved a high ideological level: he believed what the wardens told him, respected most of the guards, and was convinced that if the government didn't exactly love him it was at least doing everything within its power to keep him healthy in the bad times. In this season of semistarvation the wardens put rumors to rest by taking all the prisoners through their own kitchen to show that they too were living on sweet potato flour mixed with corn cob ersatz. "Chinese communists are often painful fanatics but they are straight and honest."

One cold night instead of going 200 yards to the latrine, Bao pissed against a wall. "I had barely finished when I received a very sharp and very swift kick in the ass. It was a warden. 'Don't you realize the sanitation rules?' he demanded. He was quite right but it was the ass of an ideological veteran he had kicked. 'I admit I am wrong Warden, but I had the impression that government members were not supposed to lay hands on prisoners. I thought physical violence was forbidden.' . . ." The warden admitted his mistake, said he would bring it up at his own next self-criticism session, and sent Bao back to his cell to write a confession. Bao thereupon confessed that his pissing on the wall had demonstrated "a disregard for the teachings of the government and a resistance to reform . . . displaying my anger in an underhanded manner . . . like spitting in the face of the government when I thought no one was looking. I can only ask that the government punish me as severely as possible." The result was no punishment.

By 1963 Bao was so ideologically active and correct that he was trusted to be a cell leader. "With the zeal of a true convert I began searching for new ways to serve the government and help my fellow men."

Questions

1. How does the concept of a cell leader differ from some of the ideas espoused by Tom Murton in encouraging certain inmates to accept more responsibility and assume positions of leadership among the inmates?

2. Would behavior-modifying techniques be more legitimate if the guards were required to undergo similar courses of treatment as the inmates?

A technology of behavior relies upon devices and instruments that make a certain course of treatment possible. Behind every program exists a manufacturing community that produces and markets the implements used in the various programs. The technology of behavior control is interdependent with the industry of behavior modification.

Catalogue No. F–72, Farrall Instruments Company, Grand Island, Nebr.

PRESENTING: THE FARRALL INSTRUMENTS COLLECTION OF THE WORLD'S MOST ADVANCED BEHAVIOR MODIFICATION EQUIPMENT FOR TREATMENT OF COMPULSIONS, ADDICTIONS, PHOBIAS AND LEARNING DIFFICULTIES

We at Farrall Instruments do not agree with those who feel that conditioning has all the answers and that behavior modification alone can permanently change any type of behavior. Rather, we look upon behavior modification conditioning as a superb tool to be used in conjunction with other types of more traditional therapy. The literature which reports follow-ups after a period of time contains comprehensive programs of supportive therapy used in behavior modification.

It is our feeling that unless these traditional supportive techniques are also used extinction of the conditioning will take place and the patient

From "Individual Rights and the Federal Role in Behavior Modification," U.S. Senate, Committee on the Judiciary, November 1974.

may return to the old problem. One of the major advantages of the behavior modification technique is that it usually provides an immediate reduction of the unwanted behavior. This gives the patient confidence that he is being helped and thus increases his motivation.

Since many of the conditioning and desensitization techniques are repetitive they lend themselves to automatic instruments. By using our automated apparatus the professional can eliminate the need for his direct supervision of the patient during most of the conditioning period.

Aversive Conditioning

Some in the mental health field feel aversive conditioning is cruel and look upon it as a punishment. We agree that aversive techniques which use a more aversive level than that required to stop or prevent an undesirable act are cruel. An example of this is the use of a cattle prod which has such a high voltage that it produces skin destruction. In the cattle prod no voltage control is present; thus this device is not really a controlled aversive unit for behavior conditioning but rather is a punishment apparatus. Severe punishment works against the conditioning principles and produces hostility.

Those who feel it is morally wrong to give electric shocks must forget the emotional content of the question and address themselves to the issue of the alternatives. Is it more humane for a self-destructive child to receive a few controlled shocks or to go through life in a straight jacket? Is it better to lock a sex deviant away as a criminal or treat him with aversive therapy so that he can become a productive member of society? It is true in both examples cited above that some cases would respond to prolonged conventional therapy: but in most institutions this is not possible because of the shortage of professional personnel. Probably the most valuable contribution aversion therapy can make is the reduction of treatment time.

For Improving Antisocial Behavior, Aggressive Behavior, Psychosomatic Problems, Self-Destructive Behavior

The Aversive Stimulator, AR–7, gives therapists aversive control over situations without the encumbrance of wires. The wireless feature of the aversive stimulator allows the client to move freely yet still be under the therapist's control. Because there is no visible link between the stimulator and the therapist, the client associates the aversive shock with the undesired behavior rather than with the therapist.

New Wireless Stimulator

A new feature of the AR–7–T is the presentation of a tone with the aversive stimulus. Repeated pairings of the tone with the aversive stimulus will come to make the tone secondarily aversive to the client. After conditioning the therapist can present either the tone or the aversive stimulus and tone on a random schedule. This procedure will allow for maintenance of the desired behavior with a minimum presentation of the aversive stimulus.

With this system of equipment, the therapist is able to much more effectively control clients' behavior. Paraprofessionals can be trained to utilize the auxiliary equipment cutting both the therapist's time and the length of conditioning.

The Model AR–5 is an improved version of our Model AR–2 which has been in production for over five years. An automatic gain control has been added to the receiver. This greatly increases the reliability by decreasing overload problems at close range. The new model also has an increased shock output.

The shocker has a range of around 75 feet indoors and 300 feet outdoors. The long outdoor range makes the unit useful on the playground and in similar situations. The control unit is a small hand-held device. The receiver-shocker is a small unit housed in a leather case and is usually attached to the patient by a belt around the waist. Both units are sufficiently small to permit unobtrusive use in a variety of field or group situations. Thus, behavior modified in the laboratory or office situation may be subject to generalization and discrimination training more closely approximating the situations to which the behavior must be transferred.

The Wireless Shocker

The Wireless Shocker gives clinicians and researchers aversive control over situations without the encumbrance of wires. Unhampered by control wires, the patient can now move with unrestrained freedom and yet be under control. Another great advantage of this physical isolation of the patient from the therapist is the diminished link between the therapist and the aversive shock. The patient thinks less of the therapist, as a punisher, and associates the shock with the undesired act he is doing.

Self-Destructive Behavior

The effectiveness of this apparatus has been well established in the behavior modification field. It is an effective tool in breaking up the behavior pattern of the autistic child. Head banging, hair pulling and many other self-destructive behaviors have been stopped. Many problems associated with mentally retarded people can be eliminated using operant conditioning with this apparatus.

Aggressive Behavior

Aggressive behavior has been controlled using the Wireless Shocker. The portable nature of the equipment makes behavior shaping possible in schools, play-ground and downtown store settings. The ease with which this equipment fits into the real life situation makes the Wireless Shocker ideal for treating aggressives.

Psychosomatic Problems

Conditioning programs have been used successfully to stop psychosomatic vomiting. In this case shock is applied the instant the patient gives signs of an impending attack. In some cases this has been used to maintain the patient's life until other types of therapy could become effective.

Unique Features

Adjustable shock; immune to interference, non-blocking at close range, robust metal case, long battery life.

Aversive Shock

Shock is adjustable from 0 to 800 volts. The shock is a narrow 1 to 2 millisecond width at a 10 to 20 Hz. rate. Maximum current is 5 milliamperes. This aversive stimulus can be applied to an arm or leg. An accessory belt (E–AR–3) which has electrodes in the belt can be supplied on special order. This belt, when used with care, can shock the patient's waist and eliminate the need of electrode wires. Use of the belt reduces the effective range of the apparatus.

The transmitter uses one of five special medical frequencies in the 27 MHz band. A tuning fork oscillator codes the radio carrier when the shock button is pressed. When a matching tuning fork in the receiver responds to the transmitter fork, a pulse-type shock generator is turned on. The tuning forks are extremely selective and prevent false shocks from radio or noise interference.

AR–5 Specifications

Model AR–5 Receiver-Shocker and Transmitter for remote wireless shocking of humans. Consisting of the following: 1 ea. crystal controlled transmitter operating in 27 MHz. band, with audio tuning fork encoder, solid state. 1 ea. crystal controlled superhetrodyne receiver for transmitter, tuning fork decoder with adjustable shock generator, solid state. 1 ea. leather case for receiver, 1 set of batteries for each unit, with electrodes. Transmitter (1¾″ x 2¾″ x 5¾″) with 15″ antenna, weight 18 oz. Receiver-Shocker (1¾″ x 2¾″ x 5¾″) weight 20 oz.

Two Patient Model

The Model AR–6 is a Wireless Shocker that is identical to the AR–5 except it contains two encoders so that two different shock receivers can be controlled. With this unit and two receiver-shockers, it is possible to work with two patients in the same area at the same time. NOTE: Both patients can not be shocked at the same instant.

AR–6 Specifications

Model AR–6 Receiver-Shocker and Transmitter for remote wireless shocking of humans. Consisting of the following: 1 ea. crystal controlled transmitter operating in 27 MHz. band, with dual audio tuning fork encoders, solid state, 2 ea. crystal controlled superhetrodyne receivers for transmitter, tuning fork decoder with adjustable shock generator, solid state. 1 ea. leather case for receiver, 1 set of batteries for each unit, with electrodes. Transmitter (1¾″ x 2¾″ x 5¾″) with 15″ antenna, weight 19 oz. Receiver-Shocker (1¾″ x 2¾″ x 5″) weight 20 oz.

The literature contains many examples of successful conditioning "cures" which relapsed after leaving the office. The Personal Shocker provides a direct link between the clinician's office and the patient's normal life. Light and portable, it can be easily concealed and unobtrusively operated by the patient so that he can administer shock to himself whenever he encounters, in real life, stimuli associated with his disorder. Thus, the office treatment may be continued throughout the day.

This series of Personal Shockers is designed around a unique four-transistor pulse circuit. Use of a pulse circuit gives extremely low battery drain and, thus, long battery life which is essential for reliable patient use. Shock potential is adjustable from zero to 800 volts. The pulse is 1 to 2 milliseconds in duration with a 10 to 20 Hz rate. This extremely short duration contributes greatly to patient safety. The patient's lack of knowledge regarding safety techniques dictates the necessity of using a battery operated device with a wave form least likely to produce cardiac problems if misused.

Patient Self Reinforcement

The "Take-Me-Along" is effective in reinforcing the patient's conditioning when he is away from the protective confines of the office or institution. It has been used to reinforce conditioning for patients on therapy programs for alcohol, drugs, sexual preference and sexual deviations. Many patients are quite willing to assist in their therapy program and they welcome the "security" of having such a device with them.

Doctor's Bag

The light weight small size of the Personal Shocker makes it ideal for the doctor to carry with him. It will fit into a coat pocket and, thus, is conveniently ready whenever or wherever the doctor or the therapist may need it. The shock level is adjustable from zero to the maximum voltage. The compact size and noninstrument appearance of this shocker make it less frightening to the patient. Despite this appearance the apparatus has a very aversive shock. The AP–10 and the AP–11 can be used in this service.

Conditioning on the Ward

The "Take-Me-Along" Personal Shockers are ideal for carrying in the pocket or medical bag. Since they are so compact, they are ideal for personnel to carry on the wards. The small size makes the shocker appear less threatening to the patient. The Model AP–11 with concentric ring electrodes is most convenient for this purpose.

Postural Control

Postural and tic control can be achieved by behavior modification techniques. The patient is well aware of his problem but usually is not at the time of the occurrence. "Take-Me-Along" can thus be used in two ways; first, to alert the patient and second as an operant conditioning apparatus.

A switch or series of switches is attached to the patient's body in a manner which will detect the tic, slouch or undesired posture. Depending on your choice of apparatus, closing of the switch circuit will give the patient an average electric shock or present an aversive audio tone. The patient will respond to either of these aversive signals by correcting the posture. Thus, the patient is automatically conditioned using escape and avoidance techniques. The Model PA–12 "Take-Me-Along" is used where aversive shock is to be used. The Model AP–14 or AP–15 is used when an aversive tone is desired. The AP–14 delivers the tone to a loudspeaker and provides considerable aversion due to embarrassment in social group settings. The AP–15 delivers the tone to a small earpiece.

Farrall Instruments does not sell to patients. We do not send catalogs to patients and wish that doctors would not give our catalogs to them. We sell only to doctors and want payments made directly by the doctor's check or money order.

From time to time, we have problems with patients calling us to talk about their problems or instrument. We refuse to discuss problems with patients. The doctor must show the patient how to use the equipment and adjust shock level. Therefore, we do not ship a Personal Shocker to the patient. We will make exception to this when a patient already has a unit and he needs a replacement or fast repair.

Ordering Specifications

AP–10 "Take-Me-Along" Personal Shocker with 4' electrode cable. Shock adjustable 0 to 800 volts, 4 transistor circuit, powered by 3 (E91) batteries, in sturdy plastic covered metal case (2¾" x 1¼" x 3¾"), weight approximately 8 oz., with electrodes and instructions.

AP–12 "Take-Me-Along" Personal Shocker with 4' electrode cable and jack for remote control switch. Note: No switch is included and no switch is on the unit. Shock adjustable 0 to 800 volts, 4 transistor circuit, powered by 3 (E91) batteries, in sturdy plastic covered metal case (2¾" x 1¼" x 3¾"), weight approximately 8 oz., with electrodes and instructions.

AP–15 "Take-Me-Along." A hearing aid type ear phone receives a tone when the switch is closed. Intensity is adjustable. Solid state. Powered by 3 (E91) batteries, in sturdy plastic covered metal case (2¾" x 1¼" x 3¾"), weight approximately 8 oz., with instructions.

This fully automated system uses standard 35MM slides for stimulus and neutral cues. The patient can be conditioned or desensitized without the attendance of a professional. In many cases the patient can give himself the therapy; thus, saving the time of the professional staff for less routine aspects of therapy.

The new family of automatic visual stimulus devices described here is the result of four years of evolutionary developments. Since we introduced the world's first commercial Visually Keyed Shocker we have been continually improving on the instrument and its software. This research makes it possible to now provide a combination instrument useful for both Aversive Conditioning and Systematic Desensitization.

Systematic Desensitization

Systematic desensitization is a highly successful method of relieving anxiety associated with phobias; such as, fear of sexual activity, death, flying, elevators, crossing bridges, going to the doctor and the like. There has been considerable work done in this field but mostly with simple equipment requiring constant attention of the therapists or with highly sophisticated costly automated apparatus. This equipment makes available, for the first time, an automated apparatus with a price practical for private practice and non-research patient treatment centers.

Aversive Conditioning

Aversive conditioning has proven an effective aid in the treatment of child molesters, transvestites, exhibitionists, alcoholics, shop lifters and other people with similar problems. Stimulus slides are shown to the patient intermixed with neutral slides. Shock is delivered with stimulus scenes but not with neutral scenes. In reinforcing heterosexual preference in latent male homosexuals, male slides give a shock while the stimulus relief slides of females do not give shock. The patient is given a "Slide Change" handbutton which enables him to escape or avoid a shock by rejecting a shock cue scene.

Questions

1. Who decides what kind of implements will be developed? Who would work for a company like Farrall Instruments? Which comes first, the ideology of behavior control or the technological equipment?

2. Do any of these instruments have to be tested before they are marketed? How would they be tested? Is there any limit to the types of instruments that can be developed? Should there be any controls on the development of technology of this type?

3. Could courts or any part of the legal system regulate the extent to which behavior modification programs could exist?

Knecht v. Gillman   *488 F.2d 1136 (8th Cir. 1973)*

Ross, Circuit Judge

This is an action by Gary Knecht and Ronald Stevenson, both in the custody of the State of Iowa, against officials of that state, under 42 U.S.C. § 1983. Their complaint alleged that they had been subjected to injections of the drug apomorphine at the Iowa Security Medical Facility (ISMF) without their consent and that the use of said drug by the defendants constituted cruel and unusual punishment in violation of the eighth amendment. The trial court dismissed their complaint for injunctive relief. We reverse with directions to enjoin the defendants from further use of the drug except pursuant to specific guidelines hereinafter set forth.

The summary of the evidence contained in the report of the magistrate showed that apomorphine had been administered at ISMF for some time prior to the hearing as "aversive stimuli" in the treatment of inmates with behavior problems. The drug was administered by intra-muscular injection by a nurse after an inmate had violated the behavior protocol established for him by the staff. Dr. Loeffelholz testified that the drug could be injected for such pieces of behavior as not getting up, for giving cigarettes against orders, for talking, for swearing, or for lying. Other inmates or members of the staff would report on these violations of the protocol and the injection would be given by the nurse without the nurse or any doctor having personally observed the violation and without specific authorization of the doctor.

When it was determined to administer the drug, the inmate was taken to a room near the nurses' station which contained only a water closet and there given the injection. He was then exercised and within about fifteen minutes he began vomiting. The vomiting lasted from fifteen minutes to an hour. There is also a temporary cardiovascular effect which involves some change in blood pressure and "in the heart." This aver-sion type "therapy" is based on "Pavlovian conditioning."[1]

The record is not clear as to whether or not the drug was always used with the initial consent of the inmate. It has apparently been administered in a few instances in the past without obtaining written consent of the inmate and once the consent is given, withdrawal thereof was not permitted. Apparently, at the time of trial apomorphine was not being used unless the inmate signed an initial consent, but there is no indication that the authorities now permit an inmate to withdraw his consent once it is given. Neither is there any indication in the record that the procedure has been changed to require the prior approval of a physician each time the drug is administered. Likewise there is no indication that there has been any change in the procedure which permits the administration of the drug upon reports of fellow inmates despite a recommendation by the magistrate that this practice should be avoided.

The testimony relating to the medical acceptability of this treatment is not conclusive. Dr. Steven Fox of the University of Iowa testified that behavior modification by aversive stimuli is "highly questionable technique" and that only a 20% to 50% success is claimed. He stated that it is not being used elsewhere to his knowledge and that its use is really punishment worse than a controlled beating since the one administering the drug can't control it after it is administered.

---

[1] Pavlovian conditioning is based on the theory that when environmental stimuli or the kinetic stimuli produced by the incipient movements of the punished act are made contiguous with punishment, they take on some of the aversive properties of the punishment itself. The next time the organism begins the act, particularly in the same environment, it produces stimuli which through classical conditioning have become aversive. It is these aversive stimuli which then prevent the act from occurring. Singer, *Psychological Studies of Punishment,* 58 Calif. L. Rev. 405, 423 (1970).

On the other hand, Dr. Loeffelholz of the ISMF staff testified that there had been a 50% to 60% effect in modifying behavior by the use of apomorphine at ISMF. There is no evidence that the drug is used at any other inmate medical facility in any other state.

The Iowa Security Medical Facility is established by Section 223.1, Code of Iowa, 1973. It is an institution for persons displaying evidence of mental illness or psychological disorders and requiring diagnostic services and treatment in a security setting. The patients admitted to the facility may originate from the following sources:

1. Residents of any institution under the jurisdiction of the department of social services.

2. Commitments by the courts as mentally incompetent to stand trial under Chapter 783 of the Iowa Code.

3. Referrals by the court for psychological diagnosis and recommendations as part of the pretrial or presentence procedure or determination of mental competency to stand trial.

4. Mentally ill prisoners from county and city jails for diagnosis, evaluation, or treatment.

Section 223.4. Code of Iowa, 1973.

Those transferred from institutions where they were committed pursuant to civil statutes or those who were committed by order of the court prior to conviction, suffer a compromise of their procedural rights in the process of the transfer to ISMF. The constitutional justification of this compromise of procedure is that the purpose of commitment is treatment, not punishment. *Cf. McKeiver* v. *Pennsylvania*, 403 U.S. 528, 552 (WHITE, J., concurring) (1971); *Sas* v. *Maryland*, 334 F.2d 506, 509 (4th Cir. 1964). Beyond this justification for treatment is the clear command of the statutes that the purpose of confinement at ISMF is not penal in nature, but rather one of examination, diagnosis and treatment. Naturally, examination and diagnosis, by their very definition, do not encompass the administration of drugs. Thus, when that course of conduct is taken with respect to any particular patient, he is the recipient of treatment.

The use of apomorphine, then, can be justified, only if it can be said to be treatment. Based upon

the testimony adduced at the hearing and the findings made by the magistrate and adopted by the trial court, it is not possible to say that the use of apomorphine is a recognized and acceptable medical practice in institutions such as ISMF. Neither can we say, however, that its use on inmates who knowingly and intelligently consent to the treatment, should be prohibited on a medical or a legal basis. The authorities who testified at the evidentiary hearing indicate that some form of consent is now obtained prior to this treatment. The only question then is whether, under the eighth amendment, its use should be prohibited absent such consent; and if so what procedure must be followed to prevent abuses in the treatment procedures and to make certain the consent is knowingly and intelligently made.

At the outset we note that the mere characterization of an act as "treatment" does not insulate it from eighth amendment scrutiny. In *Trop* v. *Dulles*, 356 U.S. 86, 95 (1958), the Supreme Court stated that the legislative classification of a statute is not conclusive in determining whether there had been a violation of the eighth amendment. Instead, the Court examined the statute by an "inquiry directed to substance," reasoning that "even a clear legislative classification of a statute as 'nonpenal' would not alter the fundamental nature of a plainly penal statute." *Trop* v. *Dulles*, supra, 356 U.S. at 95.

Other courts have examined nonpenal statutes in the manner suggested by the Supreme Court in *Trop*. The contention that a state's incarceration of runaway juveniles could not violate the eighth amendment because the statute did not authorize any punishment of juveniles was struck down in *Vann* v. *Scott*, 467 F.2d 1235, 1240 (7th Cir. 1972):

"Whatever the State does with the child is done in the name of rehabilitation. Since—the argument runs—by definition the treatment is not 'punishment,' it obviously cannot be 'cruel and unusual punishment.' But neither the label which a State places on its own conduct, or even the legitimacy of its motivation, can avoid the applicability of the Federal Constitution. We have no doubt that well intentioned attempts to rehabilitate a child could, in extreme circumstances, constitute cruel and unusual punishment proscribed by the Eighth Amendment."

The absence of criminal incarceration did not prohibit a federal court from entertaining an eighth amendment claim to test the conditions of confinement in a boys' training school:

"The fact that juveniles are *in theory* not punished, but merely confined for rehabilitative purposes, does not preclude operation of the Eighth Amendment.

"The reality of confinement in Annex B is that it is punishment."

Inmates of the Boys' Training School v. *Affleck,* 346 F.Supp. 1354, 1366 (D.R.I. 1972).

Such findings of cruel and unusual punishment have been sustained with respect to the death penalty, penal incarceration for status, civil commitment for status without treatment, striprooms and solitary confinements, tranquilizing drugs, and corporal punishment for prisoners. However, any such determination rests on the facts of a particular case.

Here we have a situation in which an inmate may be subjected to a morphine base drug which induces vomiting for an extended period of time. Whether it is called "aversive stimuli" or punishment, the act of forcing someone to vomit for a fifteen minute period for committing some minor breach of the rules can only be regarded as cruel and unusual unless the treatment is being administered to a patient who knowingly and intelligently has consented to it. To hold otherwise would be to ignore what each of us has learned from sad experience—that vomiting (especially in the presence of others) is a painful and debilitating experience. The use of this unproven drug for this purpose on an involuntary basis, is, in our opinion, cruel and unusual punishment prohibited by the eighth amendment.

We turn then to the question of how best to prevent abuse in the treatment procedures of consenting participants and how to make certain that the consent is knowingly and intelligently given, 42 U.S.C. § 1983 does not specify the scope of judicial relief available in an action successfully sustained under its terms. Yet this fact does not

limit the courts in framing appropriate relief. Its counterpart, 42 U.S.C. § 1982, is likewise framed only in declaratory terms, but the Supreme Court has held that a federal court is not thereby precluded from fashioning an effective equitable remedy. *Jones* v. *Alfred H. Mayer Co.,* 392 U.S. 409, 414 n.13 (1968). The substantive scope of relief available is a matter of the equitable powers of the federal courts. Accordingly, courts have exercised broad remedial power in civil rights actions. *See United States* v. *Ironworkers Local 86,* 443 F.2d 544, 553 (9th Cir.), *cert. denied,* 404 U.S. 984 (1971); *Parham* v. *Southwestern Bell Telephone Co.,* 433 F.2d 421, 428 (8th Cir. 1970) and cases cited therein.

Yet although it is generally true that:

"[w]here all relevant circumstances have properly been evaluated the action of the trial court, whether granting or denying an injunction, ordinarily will be sustained."

Hodgson v. *American Can Co.,* 440 F.2d 916, 920 (8th Cir. 1971), it is not unknown for a federal appellate court to change the scope of an equitable order on appeal. *United States* v. *St. Louis-San Francisco Ry.,* 464 F.2d 301 (8th Cir. 1972), *cert. denied,* 409 U.S. 1107 (1973) [employment discrimination under Title VII]; *Carter* v. *Gallagher,* 452 F.2d 315, 324 (8th Cir. 1971), modified en banc, 452 F.2d 327 (8th Cir.), *cert. denied,* 406 U.S. 950 (1972) [employment discrimination under 42 U.S.C. §§ 1981 and 1983]; *Action* v. *Gannon,* 450 F.2d 1227, 1237–1238 (8th Cir. 1971) civil rights action under 42 U.S.C. §§ 1981, 1982, 1983, 1985].

In this case the trial court should enjoin the use of apomorphine in the treatment of inmates at ISMF except when the following conditions are complied with:

1. A written consent must be obtained from the inmate specifying the nature of the treatment, a written description of the purpose, risks and effects of treatment, and advising the inmate of his right to terminate the consent at any time. This consent must include a certification by a physician that the patient has read and understands all of the terms of the consent and that the inmate is mentally competent to understand fully

all of the provisions thereof and give his consent thereto.

2. The consent may be revoked at any time after it is given and if an inmate orally expresses an intention to revoke it to any member of the staff, a revocation form shall be provided for this signature at once.

3. Each apomorphine injection shall be individually authorized by a doctor and be administered by a doctor, or by a nurse. It shall be authorized in each instance only upon information based on the personal observation of a member of the professional staff. Information from inmates or inmate aides of the observation of behavior in violation of an inmate's protocol shall not be sufficient to warrant such authorization.

The judgment of the district court is reversed with directions to grant the injunction under the terms hereinbefore set forth.

STEPHENSON, CIRCUIT JUDGE.
I concur with the result.
A true copy.
Attest:
Clerk, U.S. Court of Appeals, Eighth Circuit.

Questions

1. The court does not ask the question whether injections of this sort should be permitted at all. Is it inappropriate for the court to make judgments about what is socially permissible in this area? Or should the court confine itself to questions of legal doctrine?

2. The court concerns itself exclusively with efforts to prevent abuse of this treatment. Shouldn't it concern itself instead with the prevention of the treatment generally?

3. Why would anyone ever consent to receiving an injection of apomorphine?

Kaimowitz v. Department of Mental Health for State of Michigan
In the Circuit Court for the County of Wayne, State of Michigan, Civil Action No. 73–19434–AW

GABE KAIMOWITZ, REPRESENTING HIMSELF AND CERTAIN INDIVIDUAL MEMBERS OF THE MEDICAL COMMITTEE FOR HUMAN RIGHTS ON BEHALF OF JOHN DOE AND AT LEAST 23 OTHERS SIMILARLY SITUATED WHO ARE HELD OR COMMITTED INVOLUNTARILY IN PUBLIC INSTITUTIONS IN MICHIGAN, PETITIONERS-PLAINTIFFS, AND JOHN DOE, INTERVENOR-PLAINTIFF

v.

DEPARTMENT OF MENTAL HEALTH FOR THE STATE OF MICHIGAN, DR. E. G. YUDASHKIN, DIRECTOR, STATE DEPARTMENT OF MENTAL HEALTH; DR. J. S. GOTTLIEB, DIRECTOR LAFAYETTE CLINIC; DR. ERNEST RODIN, ASSOCIATE OF DR. GOTTLIEB AT THE CLINIC, IN THEIR OFFICIAL CAPACITIES, AS WELL AS THEIR AGENTS, ASSIGNEES, EMPLOYEES, AND SUCCESSORS IN OFFICE, RESPONDENTS-DEFENDANTS, AMERICAN ORTHOPSYCHIATRIC ASSOCIATION, AMICUS CURIAE

Opinion

This case came to this Court originally on a complaint for a Writ of Habeas Corpus brought by Plaintiff Kaimowitz on behalf of John Doe and the Medical Committee for Human Rights, alleging that John Doe was being illegally detained in the Lafayette Clinic for the purpose of experimental psychosurgery.[1]

John Doe had been committed by the Kalamazoo County Circuit Court on January 11, 1955, to the Ionia State Hospital as a Criminal Sexual Psychopath, without a trial of criminal charges, under the terms of the then existing Criminal

---

[1] The name John Doe has been used throughout the proceedings to protect the true identity of the subject involved. After the institution of this action and during proceedings his true identity was revealed. His true name is Louis Smith. For the purpose of the Opinion, however, he will be referred to throughout as John Doe.

Sexual Psychopathic law.[2] He had been charged with the murder and subsequent rape of a student nurse at the Kalamazoo State Hospital while he was confined there as a mental patient.

In 1972, Drs. Ernest Rodin and Jacques Gottlieb of the Lafayette Clinic, a facility of the Michigan Department of Mental Health, had filed a proposal "For the Study of Treatment of Uncontrollable Aggression." [3]

This was funded by the Legislature of the State of Michigan for the fiscal year 1972. After more than 17 years at the Ionia State Hospital, John Doe was transferred to the Lafayette Clinic in November of 1972 as a suitable research subject for the Clinic's study of uncontrollable aggression.

Under the terms of the study, 24 criminal sexual psychopaths in the State's mental health system were to be subjects of experiment. The experiment was to compare the effects of surgery on the amygdaloid portion of the limbic system of the brain with the effect of the drug cyproterone acetate on the male hormone flow. The comparison was intended to show which, if either, could be used in controlling aggression of males in an institutional setting, and to afford lasting permanent relief from such aggression to the patient.

Substantial difficulties were encountered in locating a suitable patient population for the surgical procedures and a matched controlled group for the treatment by the anti-androgen drug. As a matter of fact, it was concluded that John Doe was the only known appropriate candidate available within the state mental health system for the surgical experiment.

John Doe signed an "informed consent" form to become an experimental subject prior to his transfer from the Ionia State Hospital. He had

obtained signatures from his parents giving consent for the experimental and innovative surgical procedures to be performed on his brain, and two separate three-man review committees were established by Dr. Rodin to review the scientific worthiness of the study and the validity of the consent obtained from Doe.

The two issues framed for decision in this declaratory judgment action are as follows:

1. After failure of established therapies, may an adult or a legally appointed guardian, if the adult is involuntarily detained, at a facility within the jurisdiction of the State Department of Mental Health give legally adequate consent to an innovative or experimental surgical procedure on the brain, if there is demonstrable physical abnormality of the brain, and the procedure is designed to ameliorate behavior, which is either personally tormenting to the patient, or so profoundly disruptive that the patient cannot safely live, or live with others?

2. If the answer to the above is yes, then is it legal in this State to undertake an innovative or experimental surgical procedure on the brain of an adult who is involuntarily detained at a facility within the jurisdiction of the State Department of Mental Health, if there is demonstrable physical abnormality of the brain, and the procedure is designed to ameliorate behavior, which is either personally tormenting to the patient, or so profoundly disruptive that the patient cannot safely live, or live with others?

Throughout this Opinion, the Court will use the term psychosurgery to describe the proposed innovative or experimental surgical procedure defined in the questions for consideration by the Court.

The testimony showed that any physical intervention in the brain must always be approached with extreme caution. Brain surgery is always irreversible in the sense that any intrusion into the brain destroys the brain cells and such cells do not regenerate. Dr. Ommaya testified that in the absence of well defined pathological signs, such as blood clots pressing on the brain due to trauma, or tumor in the brain, brain surgery is viewed as a treatment of last resort.

The record in this case demonstrates that

---

[2] C.L. 780.501 et seq. The statute under which he was committed was repealed by Public Act 143 of the Public Acts of 1968, effective August 1, 1968. He was detained thereafter under C.L. 330.35(b), which provided for further detention and release of criminal sexual psychopaths under the repealed statute. The Supreme Court also adopted an Administrative Order of October 20, 1969 (382 Mich. xxix) relating to criminal sexual psychopaths. A full discussion of these statutes is found in the Court's earlier Opinion relating to the legality of detention of John Doe, filed in this court on March 23, 1973.

[3] See Appendix to Opinion, Item 1.

animal experimentation and non-intrusive human experimentation have not been exhausted in determining and studying brain function. Any experimentation on the human brain, especially when it involves an intrusive, irreversible procedure in a none life-threatening situation, should be undertaken with extreme caution, and then only when answers cannot be obtained from animal experimentation and from non-intrusive human experimentation.

Psychosurgery should never be undertaken upon involuntarily committed populations, when there is a high-risk low-benefit ratio as demonstrated in this case. This is because of the impossibility of obtaining truly informed consent from such populations. The reasons such informed consent cannot be obtained are set forth in detail subsequently in this Opinion.

Generally, individuals are allowed free choice about whether to undergo experimental medical procedures. But the State has the power to modify this free choice concerning experimental medical procedures when it cannot be freely given, or when the result would be contrary to public policy. For example, it is obvious that a person may not consent to acts that will constitute murder, manslaughter, or mayhem upon himself. In short, there are times when the State for good reason should withhold a person's ability to consent to certain medical procedures.

It is elementary tort law that consent is the mechanism by which the patient grants the physician the power to act, and which protects the patient against unauthorized invasions of his person. This requirement protects one of society's most fundamental values, the inviolability of the individual. An operation performed upon a patient without his informed consent is the tort of battery, and a doctor and a hospital have no right to impose compulsory medical treatment against the patient's will. These elementary statements of tort law need no citation.

Jay Katz, in his outstanding book "Experimentation with Human Beings" (Russell Sage Foundation, N.Y. [1972]), points out on page 523 that the concept of informed consent has been accepted as a cardinal principle for judging the propriety of research with human beings.

He points out that in the experimental setting, informed consent serves multiple purposes. He states (pages 523 and 524):

> Most clearly, requiring informed consent serves society's desire to respect each individual's autonomy, and his right to make choices concerning his own life.
>
> Second, providing a subject with information about an experiment will encourage him to be an active partner and the process may also increase the rationality of the experimentation process.
>
> Third, securing informed consent protects the experimentation process by encouraging the investigator to question the value of the proposed project and the adequacy of the measures he has taken to protect subjects, by reducing civil and criminal liability for nonnegligent injury to the subjects and by diminishing adverse public reaction to an experiment.
>
> Finally, informed consent may serve the function of increasing society's awareness about human research....

It is obvious that there must be close scrutiny of the adequacy of the consent when an experiment, as in this case, is dangerous, intrusive, irreversible, and of uncertain benefit to the patient and society.

Counsel for Drs. Rodin and Gottlieb argues that anyone who has ever been treated by a doctor for any relatively serious illness is likely to acknowledge that a competent doctor can get almost any patient to consent to almost anything. Counsel claims this is true because patients do not want to make decisions about complex medical matters and because there is the general problem of avoiding decision making in stress situations, characteristic of all human beings.

He further argues that a patient is always under duress when hospitalized and that in a hospital or institutional setting there is no such thing as a volunteer. Dr. Ingelfinger in Volume 287, page 466, of the *New England Journal of Medicine* (August 31, 1972) states:

"The process of obtaining 'informed consent' with all its regulations and conditions, is no more than an elaborate ritual, a device that when the subject is uneducated and uncomprehending, confers no more than the semblance of propriety on human experimentation. The subject's only real protection, the public as well as the medical profession must recognize, depends on the conscience and compassion of the investigator and his peers."

Everything defendants' counsel argues militates against the obtaining of informed consent from involuntarily detained mental patients. If, as he argues, truly informed consent cannot be given for regular surgical procedures by non-institutionalized persons, then certainly an adequate informed consent cannot be given by the involuntarily detained mental patient.

We do not agree that a truly informed consent cannot be given for a regular surgical procedure by a patient, institutionalized or not. The law has long recognized that such valid consent can be given. But we do hold that informed consent cannot be given by an involuntarily detained mental patient for experimental psychosurgery for the reasons set forth below.

The Michigan Supreme Court has considered in a tort case the problems of experimentation with humans. In *Hortner* v. *Koch,* 272 Mich. 273, 261 N.W. 762 (1935), the issue turned on whether the doctor had taken proper diagnostic steps before prescribing an experimental treatment for cancer. Discussing medical experimentation, the Court said at page 282:

"We recognize the fact that if the general practice of medicine and surgery is to progress, there must be a certain amount of experimentation carried on; but such experiments must be done with the knowledge and consent of the patient or those responsible for him, *and must not vary too radically from the accepted method of procedure.* (Emphasis added.)

This means that the physician cannot experiment without restraint or restriction. He must consider first of all the welfare of his patient. This concept is universally accepted by the medical profession, the legal profession, and responsible persons who have thought and written on the matter.

Furthermore, he must weigh the risk of the patient against the benefit to be obtained by trying something new. The risk-benefit ratio is an important ratio in considering any experimental

surgery upon a human being. The risk must always be relatively low, in the non-life threatening situation to justify human experimentation.

Informed consent is a requirement of variable demands. Being certain that a patient has consented adequately to an operation, for example, is much more important when doctors are going to undertake an experimental, dangerous, and intrusive procedure than, for example, when they are going to remove an appendix. When a procedure is experimental, dangerous, and intrusive, special safeguards are necessary. The risk-benefit ratio must be carefully considered, and the question of consent thoroughly explored.

To be legally adequate, a subject's informed consent must be competent, knowing and voluntary.

We must first look to the competency of the involuntarily detained mental patient to consent. Competency requires the ability of the subject to understand rationally the nature of the procedure, its risks, and other relevant information. The standard governing required disclosure by a doctor is what a reasonable patient needs to know in order to make an intelligent decision. See Waltz and Scheunerman, "Informed Consent Therapy," 64 Northwestern Law Review 628 (1969).

Although an involuntarily detained mental patient may have a sufficient I.Q. to intellectually comprehend his circumstances (in Dr. Rodin's experiment, a person was required to have at least an I.Q. of 80), *the very nature of his incarceration diminishes the capacity to consent to psychosurgery.* He is particularly vulnerable as a result of his mental condition, the deprivation stemming from involuntary confinement, and the effects of the phenomenon of "institutionalization."

The very moving testimony of John Doe in the instant case establishes this beyond any doubt. The fact of institutional confinement has special force in undermining the capacity of the mental patient to make a competent decision on this issue, even though he be intellectually competent to do so. In the routine of institutional life, most decisions are made for patients. For example, John Doe testified how extraordinary it was for him to be approached by Dr. Yudashkin about the possible submission to psychosurgery, and how unusual it was to be consulted by a physician about his preference.

Institutionalization tends to strip the individual of the support which permits him to maintain his sense of self-worth and the value of his own physical and mental integrity. An involuntarily confined mental patient clearly has diminished capacity for making a decision about irreversible experimental psychosurgery.

Equally great problems are found when the involuntarily detained mental patient is incompetent, and consent is sought from a guardian or parent. Although guardian or parental consent may be legally adequate when arising out of traditional circumstances, it is legally ineffective in the psychosurgery situation. The guardian or parent cannot do that which the patient, absent a guardian, would be legally unable to do.

The second element of an informed consent is knowledge of the risk involved and the procedures to be undertaken. It was obvious from the record made in this case that the facts surrounding experimental brain surgery are profoundly uncertain, and the lack of knowledge on the subject makes a knowledgeable consent to psychosurgery literally impossible.

We turn now to the third element of an informed consent, that of voluntariness. It is obvious that the most important thing to a large number of involuntarily detained mental patients incarcerated for an unknown length of time, is freedom.

The law has always been meticulous in scrutinizing inequality in bargaining power and the possibility of undue influence in commercial fields and in the law of wills. It also has been most careful in excluding from criminal cases confessions where there was no clear showing of their completely voluntary nature after full understanding of the consequences. No lesser standard can apply to involuntarily detained mental patients.

The keynote to any intrusion upon the body of a person must be full, adequate and informed consent. The integrity of the individual must be protected from invasion into his body and personality not voluntarily agreed to. Consent is not an idle or symbolic act; it is a fundamental requirement for the protection of the individual's integrity.

We therefore conclude that involuntarily detained mental patients cannot give informed and adequate consent to experimental psychosurgical procedures on the brain.

The three basic elements of informed consent—competency, knowledge, and voluntariness—cannot be ascertained with a degree of reliability warranting resort to use of such an invasive procedure.

Questions

1. In 1973, two forty-five-year-old men—Joseph A. Kenner and Paul R. de la Haye—both pleaded guilty to sex offenses involving minors. Having had prior histories of such behavior, both were committed to California's Atascedera State Mental Hospital. After two years of treatment, however, hospital officials reported that the two convicted child molesters had failed to respond to psychotherapy and had remained dangerous to society with little or no prospect of improvement. The men were released and returned to County Jail to await sentencing.

   On grounds of the hospital's negative prognosis, the judge indicated in court that he would sentence the men to indeterminate terms with a good likelihood that they would pass the remainder of their days within the confines of prison walls. Given so bleak a life prospect, the two men signed requests for castration, along with waivers releasing their lawyers, the court-approved surgeon, and the judge from any liability. The surgery, known as bilateral orchidectomy, was to constitute part of a rehabilitation program which might contribute to a possible grant of probation.*

   Is it possible for men to consent freely to this procedure? Is it a legitimate option for inmates? What other kinds of alternatives should be available to men in this category?

   * *Hastings Institute Report*, Vol. 5, No. 5, October 1975, p. 17.

2. Is the alternative of castration a legitimate alternative to life imprisonment?

3. How should our society respond to sex offenders?

Should they be treated differently from other individuals who are imprisoned for committing crimes? What kind of punishment would be in order? What kind of treatment would be appropriate?

5 Experimentation

There can be little doubt that experimentation on human beings is necessary, if medical knowledge is to expand. Sometime during the development of any new drug, a human being must test on his own body a researcher's belief that a new compound can cure a given disease.

Nearly 80 percent of biomedical experimentation on humans takes place in prisons, using inmate volunteers as guinea pigs.

Carol Benfell, *Abusing the Bodies and Minds of Prisoners* (1977)

The notion of experimentation on human beings is profoundly problematical. What interests are furthered by human experimentation? The question can be understood only in light of the increasing emphasis on technology and technological growth. Each new technological "breakthrough" must be tested to assess its reliability and to understand the possibilities for use. Drugs, for example, are the basis for many forms of medical treatment and for many forms of psychiatric care. Before drugs can be marketed for general use, they must be tested. What kind of testing would be acceptable? If our society relies on technologies, isn't human experimentation a necessity? What are the ethical problems of experimentation?

The problem is particularly complex when experimentation of prisoners is considered. Are inmates free to refuse tests? What does free choice mean to someone who is imprisoned? Why would an inmate consent to being a subject? Should any protection be offered? Keep these questions in mind as you read the following selection.

Statement of Otis Clay

To the Members of the Subcommittee on Courts, Civil Liberties and the Administration of Justice: I am very pleased at the opportunity to testify before you with respect to HR 3603 and submit this statement in connection with my testimony:

On or about April 19, 1967 I was sentenced to

From "Prison Inmates in Medical Research," U.S. House of Representatives, Committee on the Judiciary, September–October 1975, p. 16.

10 years for a drug-related offense and was thereafter incarcerated at the Federal prison in Atlanta, Georgia.

At Atlanta I was housed in a small cell with 6 or 7 other inmates, ate food of low quality and was permitted little entertainment to break up the boredom of prison.

I first learned of the possibility of transfer to the Addiction Research Center at Lexington, Kentucky from a notice posted on a bulletin board at the Atlanta prison. That notice indicated that former drug addicts would be paid $3.00 per experimental session and one day "good time" for participating in medical experiments at the Addiction Research Center. I also learned from fellow inmates of the better living conditions available at the Center, such as a private room, and of the chance to receive narcotics there. I then filled out an interview form and was later informed of my selection to be transferred to the Center at a group meeting held at Atlanta. At that meeting I was told nothing about the experiments I would be subjected to, or the drugs I would be injected with.

I was transferred to the Addiction Research Center in or about July 1968, was examined by various doctors, and was pronounced in good health.

I then attended a group meeting at which Drs. Martin and Jasinski were present. They informed us that each of us would have a private room, the opportunity to have a radio, television or record player, and that we would be asked to participate in various medical experiments, and take various drugs, for which we would earn $3.00 and one day "good time" for each day of participation. I asked whether the drugs would cause us any harm, and I was assured by the doctors that they would not.

Neither at this meeting, nor at any time thereafter, was I ever told the names of the drugs that I was requested to take nor the purposes of these experiments. In addition, I had no control over the duration of each experiment and understood that if I refused to participate regularly in them I would be sent back to Atlanta.

Following this meeting I was assigned to work as a porter at the Center's laboratory and was given a series of written tests inquiring about my former drug addiction.

Morphine Experiment

After one to two months of answering these tests I, along with some 15 other inmates, was requested to participate in a morphine addiction program. During this program morphine and other related drugs were injected in my arm about three to four times a day for about 6 to 8 months. Before each injection, I was examined by a medical aide who examined my eyes and noted my blood pressure, weight and temperature. Additionally, before each injection I was required to fill out a questionnaire which sought information about the effects of the drugs I was then being given.

At various times during the course of this experiment I was asked by the doctors if I would buy the same drug I was being injected with if I were on the street, or whether that drug had the same effect on me as heroin.

After 6 to 8 months I was then brought down from my addiction to these drugs and suffered withdrawal including nausea, insomnia, chills and anxiety.

Second Drug Experiment

A few months after my withdrawal I was then asked to take another drug once a week. The night before each injection, I went to the part of the Center where the experiments were conducted and was examined by medical aides. The next day I was injected with a drug whose name I still do not know and my eyes were examined every hour thereafter. The drug made me nervous and miserable all day. The day following the injection I returned to my living quarters and continued normal prison routine until the following week when the next injection was given.

Electrical Shock Experiment

Sometime thereafter I was requested to subject myself to an electrical shock experiment. During this experiment I was twice strapped to a chair in a cubicle where electrodes and various wires were attached to my arms. A medical aide then stood behind me out of my view and at various times caused electrical shocks to pass through my fingers and arms. At first the shocks were preceded by the sounding of a buzzer in my cubicle. At other times, the buzzer would sound and I would be frightened but not shocked. After two such sessions I was withdrawn from this experiment.

Various Other Drug Experiments

Additionally, I was asked to participate in a series of other drug experiments. In these experiments I was again given various drugs once a week which drugs also caused me to feel miserable and sick.

Naltrexone Experiment

Finally, on or about May 27, 1970 Drs. Martin and Jasinski requested that I participate in the experimentation of a drug which they stated had never been given to humans. These doctors provided me with a written statement which indicated that the drug had caused animals to suffer nervousness and convulsions. After reading the statement, I asked the doctors if the drug would cause me any permanent harm. The doctors assured me that I would not be harmed because I would be given smaller doses than the animals had received. Relying on these assurances I signed the statement. The next day I was injected with what I now know to be the drug naltrexone. The injection caused me to feel worse than I had ever felt following any prior injections. I felt about fifty years older. Following examination, I returned to my living quarters and went back to normal prison routine.

On or about June 3, I was injected a second time with naltrexone, and again felt terrible. I continued to feel bad during the week of June 3rd and finally early in the morning on June 8th, I awoke with a severe chest pain. I struggled to the end of the corridor where I was led up to an examination room. A medical aide then phoned Dr. Martin who apparently instructed the aide to give me the electrocardiograph test. Drs. Martin, Jasinski and Mansky then arrived, examined the results of this test and ordered that I be taken to the hospital. On the way to the hospital I was told by one of the doctors that I had suffered a heart attack.

The following day I was taken to the intensive care unit at the hospital and hooked up to a machine that monitored my heart beat. The doctor in charge of the hospital visited me three times a day. Drs. Martin, Mansky and Jasinski came by to see me daily. About one week after the heart attack I asked Dr. Martin if the drug I had just been injected with on May 28th and June 3rd could have caused the heart attack. Dr. Martin replied that it could have. I remained at the hospital for a few weeks.

I was not involved in any more medical experiments at the Addiction Research Center and I was then transferred in September of 1970 to the Federal House of Detention in New York City.

Thereafter in May of 1971 I filed a *pro se* complaint against Drs. Martin, Mansky and Jasinski, as well as the Surgeon General, Attorney General and the director of the Bureau of Prisons seeking damages for the pain, suffering and permanent disability caused by the heart attack. This action by amended complaint now includes the United States and is proceeding to trial at the direction of the United States Court of Appeals for the Second Circuit, who, in an opinion dated January 20, 1975 reversed the district courts dismissal of the complaint.

In summary, based on my long and unfortunate experience as a subject of medical experimentation while an inmate at the Addiction Research Center, I urge such experimentation be banned by the passage of H.R. 3603.

Notes and Questions

1. Federal agencies have developed an enormous number of regulations governing the introduction of new drugs to the general public. Is it possible for a drug company to conform to these regulations which require assurances of the safety of the new product without testing them on real people first? Does the legal system, through its regulatory agencies, essentially require human experimentation? What are the implications here for the relationship of state control to personal freedom?

2. Who would be appropriate subjects for tests of this

nature? Should people be allowed to volunteer for these kinds of tests?

3. Experiments on human beings of new drugs and other technological products not only directly affect the subjects of the experiment; the companies who manufacture these products receive subsidies for conducting experiments. A major concern of the companies is their profit. The argument put forward by these companies has been that subsidies by the government for these experiments have been essential to the companies' profit.

Pharmaceuticals Development Experimentation

In order to determine the value to the public at large of the massive subsidies to drug development experimentation which have been provided, we must carefully examine the industry's claim that such subsidies are critical to drug manufacturers' profits.

PROFIT HISTORY. Drug development is not merely a process of pursuit of knowledge and medical care capacity. It forms one of the critical tools in the competition between drug manufacturers for market and the prescription dollar in an industry with over 700 firms, of which only 28 had fourth quarter, 1974, sales of over $22 million. The observation made in 1970 by the Health Policy Advisory Center (Health-PAC) that, "Control is concentrated in the top fifteen (companies), who sell more than half of all drugs," appears to remain valid. This two-tiered industry, with the bulk of market shares (and profits) controlled by the houses with extensive brand-name prescription items on the market, performed remarkably in the 1960's according to the Health-PAC review:

"For the last ten years, the drug industry has held either first, second or third place among all U.S. industries in terms of profitability, outdistancing such obvious money-makers as the cosmetics, aerospace, recreation and entertainment industries."

We can turn to a more recent look at the profit picture for the drug industry in order to determine its capacity to develop therapeutic capacities in the absence of a subsidy.

CURRENT PERFORMANCE. The profitability of the major firms in the pharmaceutical industry may be compared to all-industry average performance data as a means of measuring the capacity of drug firms to adjust to denial of the implicit experimentation subsidies associated with experiments on prisoners. We use data from the quarterly survey of corporate performance prepared by *Business Week* for recent years.

As Table 1 indicates, the major companies in the industry for which *Business Week* gathered data performed at a level which almost doubled the overall profitability and returns evidenced by big business as a whole in the United States.

DENIAL OF THE SUBSIDY. Despite their outstanding performance in the past, the drug companies may be vulnerable to major profit losses if the implicit subsidy associated with experiments on prisoners is denied to them. We can examine the hypothetical impact of such a denial on the industry's 1974 profits as a means of examining this possibility. The findings of our examination, presented in Table 2, make it evident that even without the subsidy, the industry's profit performance is superior to the all industry average. Under the assumption that none of the experiment cost increases can be passed on to customers, the industry still shows average profits three percent above the national industry average.

An adjustment on these figures is, however, in order. The $229 million subsidy denial is in reality to be spread across all the pharmaceutical firms operating in the United States, but the sales and profit data in Table 2 apply only to twenty-eight large, U.S. based firms on which data were available. In addition to the small com-

From "Prison Inmates in Medical Research," U.S. House of Representatives, Committee on the Judiciary, September–October 1975, p. 16.

Table 1 *Drug Industry and All-Industry Profitability[1] (In percent)*

	Industrial group	
	DRUG INDUSTRY	ALL-INDUSTRY COMPOSITE
Profit rate (1974)	9.3	5.3
Return on common equity (1965–75 annual average)	16.0	8.0
Growth in per share earnings (1965–75 annual average)	11.0	6.0

[1] Data are all from: "Business Week," "Survey of Corporate Performance: 1st Quarter, 1975" (Mar. 24, 1975, pp. 57–91).

panies whose size led to their exclusion from the *Business Week* survey, Parke, Davis and Company (perhaps the industry leader in the number of prescription products marketed) was excluded due to the absence of data. Foreign-based enterprises such as the giant Hoffman-La Roche firm (which sold one billion Librium and three billion Valium tablets in the United States in 1974, with a retail value of $670 million and 90% of the U.S. tranquilizer market) are also excluded.[4] Thus, the profit declines attributable to loss of the subsidy derived from experiments on prisoners will, for the industry as a whole, be even smaller than Table 2 suggests.

In conclusion, we can state unequivocally that, even in the total absence of the subsidy now provided to pharmaceutical manufacturers, *and no price increases,* those firms would continue to reap profits at rates which exceed the national industry composite levels and thus would continue their new drug development at comparable levels of effort.

Table 2 *Drug Industry Profits and Subsidized Experiments, Major U.S. Firms, 1974 (All dollar figures in millions)*

		Experience excluding subsidies		
Actual [1]	CONSTANT PRICES[2]	CONSTANT INCREASE[3]	50 PERCENT COVERAGE PRICE INCREASE[3]	100 PERCENT COVERAGE PRICE INCREASE[4]
Sales	$21,634.9	$21,634.9	$21,749.4	$21,863.9
Profits	$2,013.7	$1,784.7	$1,899.2	$2,013.7
Profit rate (percent)	9.3	8.2	8.7	9.2
Wholesale price increase (percent)[5]	0	.53	.53	1.06

[1] Taken from Business Week, "Survey of Corporate Performance: 4th Quarter, 1974" (Mar. 24, 1975, pp. 57–91).

[2] Derived by elimination of $229,000,000 subsidy reflected in reduction in profits, assuming constant dollar sales.

[3] Derived by elimination of $229,000,000 subsidy, compensated for by a $114,500,000 price increase, reflected in higher sales totals and only a $114,500,000 drop in profits.

[4] Derived by increasing sales by $220,000,000 to compensate for subsidy denial, and leaving dollar profits unchanged.

[5] The hypothesized percentage increase in dollar sales volume given subsidy denial (this estimate, therefore, assumes no change in unit sales).

Conclusion

The purpose of this chapter has been to explore prison as a social institution reflecting society's rules and values. The materials in this chapter give some indication of the constant state of flux which surrounds the dominant ideology of imprisonment. This can be attributed in part to a common ambivalence toward punishment. On closer examination, however, the evolving theories of incarceration suggest something more profound about the relationship of the individual to the state. Historically, the emergence of new ideologies in this area of thought reflected a rearrangement in the balance between the freedom of individuals and state authority. As one noted author suggests:

> Prison means the rigorous regulation of space, because the guard can and must see everything. It is also the rigid regulation of the use of time, hour by hour. Finally, it involves regulation of the slightest bodily movements or change of position.*

* Michel Foucault, *New York Times,* August 5, 1975.

The technology that has developed around the ideology of imprisonment reinforces this view. A constantly increasing capacity exists to control individual movement, including at its most extreme, psychotropic drugs and electronic manipulation of the brain. And the ability to perfect techniques of surveillance is constantly improving. This expanding technological power has implications for the nature of prison and for society in general. Thus, the emerging theories of prison work as discussed in this chapter must be evaluated in light of the increasing power of the state over all individuals in society.

Restructuring of power relationships in the context of prison has implications for all people. What goes on in prison is not separate from what happens in other institutional settings. The material in this chapter should be viewed from that perspective. After all, our prisons resemble our military bases, our places of work, our hospitals, and the schools in which our children are educated.

Suggested Additional Readings

Punishment

Burkhardt, Kathryn. *Women in Prison.* Garden City, N.Y.: Doubleday, 1973.

Cleaver, Eldridge. *Soul On Ice.* New York: McGraw-Hill, 1968.

Foucault, Michel. *The Birth of the Prison.* New York: Pantheon, 1978.

Mitford, Jessica. *Kind and Usual Punishment.* New York: Alfred A. Knopf, 1973.

Rothman, David. *The Discovery of the Asylum.* Boston: Little, Brown, 1971.

Sykes, Gresham. *Society and Captives: A Study of a Maximum Security Prison.* Princeton, N.J.: Princeton University Press, 1958.

Wright, Eric Olin. *The Politics of Punishment.* New York: Harper Colophon Books, Harper & Row Publishers, 1973.

Institutionalization and Reform

Attica: The Official Report of the New York State Special Commission on Attica. New York: Bantam Books, 1972.

Blumberg, Abraham. *Criminal Justice.* Chicago: Quadrangle Books, 1967.

Goffman, Erving. *Asylums.* Chicago: Aldine Publishing Co., 1962.

Morris, Norville. *The Future of Imprisonment.* Chicago: University of Chicago Press, 1977.

Murton, Tom and Hyams, Ore. *Accomplices in Crime: The Arkansas Prison Scandal.* New York: Grove Press, 1970.

Treatment

Erikson, Kai T. *Wayward Puritans: A Study in the Sociology of Deviance.* New York: John Wiley & Sons, 1966.

Menninger, Karl. *The Crime of Punishment.* New York: Viking Press, 1968.

Szasz, Thomas. *Law, Liberty and Psychiatry.* New York: Macmillan, 1963.

Szasz, Thomas. *Psychiatric Justice.* New York: Collier Books, 1965.

Behavior Control

Delgado, José. *Physical Control of the Mind.* New York: Harper Colophon Books, Harper & Row, Publishers, 1971.

Li, Victor. *Law Without Lawyers.* Palo Alto, Calif.: The Portable Stanford, 1977.

Lifton, Robert Jay. *Thought Reform and the Psychology of Totalism.* New York: W. W. Norton, 1961.

Rickett, Adele, and Richett, Allyn. *Prisoner of Liberation.* Garden City, N.Y.: Doubleday, Anchor Books, 1973.

Photograph by Thomas H. Brooks/Stock, Boston.

But to tear down a factory or to revolt against a government...because it is a system is to attack effects rather than causes; and as long as the attack is upon effects only, no change is possible. The true system, the real system, is our present construction of systematic thought itself, rationality itself, and if a factory is torn down but the rationality that produced it is left standing, then that rationality will simply produce another factory. If a revolution destroys a systematic government, but the systematic patterns of thought that produced that government are left intact, then those patterns will repeat themselves in the succeeding government. There's so much talk about the system. And so little understanding.

Robert M. Pirsig, *Zen and the Art of Motorcycle Maintenance*

chapter six

Law in Context

Law Is a Social Creation

Law is a *created* thing, like a building. It has structure and meaning, and, like a building, it always exists in a *context*. A building exists in the context of earth and space. Law exists in the context of a society. Particular people build buildings for particular purposes in particular places. Whether they know what the purposes are or why any building is built where it is depends on the knowledge the people have about that building and its relation with society.

The same is true with law. Many people in a society may have little idea how the legal system in that society works, what its structure is, or even what purposes it serves. But this does not change the fact that the law is created out of the life of that society. Whether they understand it or not, the law is built out of the people's own lives.

The analogy between physical buildings and legal structures may be carried further. A building exists in earth and space. But a building is also *made from* earth and space. Likewise, law exists *in* society and is also *made from* society. In constructing law, people make use of people and relations among people. Relations among people can be looked at as the material of which society consists. These are the *resources* for legal construction. They are also the *context* in which the legal construction takes place. This situation presents us with the central questions about law and society: What is the relationship between the constructed legal relations and the surrounding social relations? How does the construct exist in the society? Where does it come from? How is it maintained? These and other questions go to the ideas and forces behind law and society.

Understanding the law requires understanding the society. And understanding the society requires understanding the relationships among the people who compose it. Chief among these relationships are the economic linkages: the relationships underlying the processes of production and consumption in the society. For example, the question of who "owns" the land is an issue of *legal* relations. Understanding the law on this point also requires an understanding of the *economic* issue of who "works" the land. This combination of legal and economic relations is the formal *organization* of society. It is only in terms of analyzing this

complex framework that we could begin to see the place and nature of law in the society.

This chapter allows us to analyze and question some of the ideas and economic relations that are integrated with the law, to see how these function in society. The readings and questions in the chapter are intended to provoke thoughts and feelings about the nature of law, and to develop awareness of the kinds of events in people's daily lives where legal/economic/social structures are produced and maintained.

The Importance of People's Knowledge of the Law

Legal theorists do not always admit that law exists in a context. Laws are sometimes spoken of as if they are independent of society, as if they have some basis that is "deeper" than society or outside society. In the early days of the common law, for example, laws were regarded as coming from God. Judges were said to have "found" the law, rather than to have "made" the law. Even though people's ideas on this point have changed considerably since that time, there is still a dominant tendency in American society to think that the law exists somewhere by itself, in a realm of pure thought or in books of cases.

Many people do not see that legal ideas and decisions are the product of human activity. They do not understand the relation between legal roles (judge, police, lawyer, juror, jailer, and so on) and legal rules. They also fail to see the relation between legal and economic structures in society. These people view the law as a mysterious phenomenon that is bigger than they are, as something that stands above human activity and regulates it.

If law is seen as something bigger than people, then people think they are not responsible for the law. If society is perceived as being dependent on law and law is a mysterious force, then people feel they are absolved from paying attention to and taking responsibility for their social relations with each other. In this way, the problems and conflicts of social life are passed to someone else to take care of. This is a fundamental ingredient in the alienation of people from their own lives.

When people are alienated from themselves in this way and do not take direct responsibility for the shape of their own lives, the law becomes the province of a special group of people, people who do the "law jobs." The work of the law jobs is to handle the conflicts of alienated society by making and enforcing rules. The people in these jobs are in a double bind, however, which is imposed by the conditions of alienation. On the one hand, they cannot admit that they are taking responsibility for the shape of society because that would expose them as social controllers. This would undermine the social order by revealing the foundations of law in society. Alienated society would collapse on itself. On the other hand, they cannot actually refuse to take responsibility for social conflicts because to do so would throw the problems of society back onto the masses of people, thus exposing the fact that society is more basic than law. Either way, the holders of law jobs in an alienated society are trapped into a game with the masses of people. They can neither fully acknowledge their power over others nor abdicate that power. The result is that they must exercise the power behind a set of masks. Law in an alienated society is a facade for the exercise of power.

Many masks are actually incorporated into the facade. "Neutrality," "fairness," "reasonableness," and "expertise" are some of the most basic masks. They serve to hide what is going on from the gaze of curious onlookers. They serve to rationalize the system.

The slave laws of early United States history are a flagrant example of this process. Within a general theoretical framework of freedom, justice, and equality for all people, it was nevertheless possible for the law to build and enforce a system of slavery. Indeed, some of the very same people who drew up the documents for democratic government also wrote and enforced the slave laws. This schizoid split was only possible because of the masks that the alienated society generated to cover itself.

The slave laws did not exist in a vacuum. They did exist in the context of a particular society. Slave laws were integral to the functioning of that society, but they were not the *basis* of the society. The basis of the society was in the actual relations of domination among the people. These relations were shaped by assumptions of white rule, male supremacy, and economic exploitation of earth and labor. These assumptions have roots that go back into the origins of Western European society. In other words, the slave laws were built in a slave society, and not the other way around.

It follows from this analysis that the struggle to eliminate slavery in America was fundamentally a struggle to strip away the masks of the law and to change the power relations that operated behind the masks. Legal change could occur and endure only to the extent that the actual relations among people in the society, the ways in which people thought and acted, were rearranged. That this required force and violence is an indication of how deeply ingrained such social ideas and patterns of behavior were.

Legal change is not simply a matter of writing new words in the law books. It is more profoundly a matter of people's lives changing. Looking at slavery from this perspective, we can see that slavery was eliminated from American society only to the extent that the actual relations of domination and subordination among people were eliminated. Slavery continues to exist to the extent that domination and subordination continue to characterize relationships among people. An answer to the question whether slavery exists therefore requires a detailed historical analysis. Slave laws as such no longer exist in the United States. The struggle against domination has progressed to the point where these specific laws are gone. But social relationships of domination and exploitation continue to exist, and are even expressed in other laws of various sorts. Laws protecting capital and restricting labor, laws equating corporations with human beings, laws that limit the ability of communities to exist as self-governing groups or that preserve the position of power elites within groups: these are examples of laws that reflect social relationships of domination and subordination.

In each instance, the first prerequisite to change is to understand how the laws reflect the social situation. To try to change the laws without understanding and dealing with the social relationships themselves would be futile. Such efforts are so shallow that they would just as likely result in cynicism and despair as in progressive movement. Legal change in advance of social understanding is only a mirage, which fails to cut through the alienation of people from their own lives. It strengthens the system of masks.

There are situations of social change without legal change. These too can be understood when we see law in its social context. Laws such as those against marijuana and sex are created and enforced in attempts to prevent social change, to preserve a certain social context for law. That social changes occur despite the laws shows that society is more basic than law. Social relations among people have a life of their own, which law can distort but not destroy.

Archaic laws exist despite social changes; this is not a simple matter to understand. Many people try to pass off this situation with the comment that "the laws are out of date." Although this may seem to be true, it is actually not accurate. Because law is based on society, it is not possible for there to be a law without a social foundation. The laws always reflect certain characteristics of the society in which they exist. Thus laws about morality have a social basis even when it appears that the morality of the society has changed from the time when the laws were enacted. In each case it is necessary to engage in an analysis of the society to find the current social basis of the old law.

The existence of laws that appear "out of date" reflects certain particular conditions in society. Foremost among the social conditions that support archaic laws are: arbitrariness of power, vagueness about values, uncertainty as to the significance of social change, and contradictions about the meaning of truth in social relations. These are characteristic qualities of a society caught in the situation of stagnant laws. It should be clear that these qualities are more likely to be found in alienated societies than in societies in which people have direct responsibility for the shape of the society they live in. Stagnant law presents the picture of a society in which people are alienated from the power structure that governs their lives and therefore from themselves as well, a society in which the law and real life are two different matters.

Once again, the issue of change in the law in these circumstances depends upon the people's understanding of their current social situation and the ways in which the laws reflect this situation. Alienation must be seen for what it is. Its roots must be discovered in history and in people's daily lives. Power, values, social change, and the meaning of truth must all be understood and agreed upon among the masses of people, for only when the social conditions that give rise to stagnant laws are remedied will the legal stagnation itself be eliminated.

The viewpoint that law creates society, that society is based on law rather than law being based on society, obscures the ways in which a legal system actually works. This viewpoint is often used to conceal the ways in which a legal system benefits some people in a society and not others. By pretending that the law is more basic than the people, a legal theorist can spend much time analyzing the internal processes of the law (what the powers of judges are, how appeals are taken, and so on) without ever having to discuss how these internal features relate to the society in which

the law exists. Questions of power and privilege can be bypassed with this pretense. Questions of historical development can be dealt with abstractly, as if *only* ideas, and not real people are involved.

To begin to understand law we must abandon the idea that law is a neutral, independent entity. In fact, this idea of neutrality must be seen for what it is: namely, an idea that is used to advance the interests of legal power without revealing the basis of that power in people's lives.

Law is the *official* structure of society. It is the structure that is *enforced*. The material from which this legal structure is built is the daily life of people in society, the relations among people as they are lived out every day.

The Devil Tree *Jerzy Kosinski*

"He says the car overheats. It idles bad when it's hot and doesn't accelerate right."

"Well, take a look at the radiator. If it's okay, check the belts and the pump."

"I did all that. I even put in a new gasket for the intake manifold. Now he's back and says the same thing's happening again."

The mechanic walked over to Whalen. "Well," he said, "the only other thing it could be is vapor lock. Sometimes the heat under the hood makes the gas evaporate in the fuel line. What we may have to do is install a bigger fuel pump. You know these Italian engines are temperamental; they're not built for everyday driving. You ever tried working on one?"

"That's not my job. All I want is for you to fix my car so I can get where I'm going."

"Well, that may take a while. We'll have to order the new pump. These engines are so rare we don't bother keeping parts in stock."

From Jerzy Kosinski, *The Devil Tree* (New York: Harcourt Brace Jovanovich, 1973), pp. 164–165.

"But I want it now."

"I don't think we can do it."

"You have to. Otherwise—"

"Otherwise, what?"

"Otherwise, my lawyers will pressure you, you'll overheat and your business will evaporate."

Questions

1. In this vignette from *The Devil Tree*, Jerzy Kosinski presents a situation of social conflict in which one of the people involved threatens to call in legal force. What is the effect of such threats on relations between people? Is there anything in the situation that indicates whether the threat is likely to be successful? What would success consist of?

2. Is there any element of justice or injustice in the situation?

3. Is there any way to resolve the conflict other than by force of law?

4. Whose interests are served by the availability of legal force in this situation?

1 The Structure of Legal Relations

An investigation of legal structures in a society can begin with a focus on a specific legal institution, such as prison: Who are the prisoners in the society? Who are the guards? And who are the people in command of the guards? These questions, if they are to lead us to an understanding of law in its social context, must be pursued beyond the area of legal structure itself. Thus we must determine whether there are relationships *other than* their legal relations among the prisoners, guards, and those in command. Do these groups form different classes of economic power in society just as they form different classes in the legal structure?

There are also more general questions about the shape of legal relations in society: What are the relationships between those who make the rules in a society and those who don't? How is the power to make rules structured and distributed in the society? As we deal with these questions, we must remember that a primary function of law is to regulate the appropriation and distribution of the productive power of people in society. For this reason we can ask these questions in regard to banks as well as courts. The formal organization of society consists of legal and economic structures functioning in combination with each other.

As we carry out this inquiry into legal and economic relationships, we are led still further into questions about power in the social structure: How do the holders of power explain/rationalize/justify their dominant position? What are the effects of this dominance? What kinds of relationships among people are promoted by the power structure? What kinds of social relations are excluded by the structure?

In embarking on this investigation of the power and structure of law in society, we must be very careful to distinguish between the official answers to these questions and the answers that are available from a critical perspective. The official answers come from the power structure itself, whereas a critical perspective acquires its information from a vantage point outside the framework of official theory. The materials in this section are collected to provide a critical approach.

Address to the Prisoners in the Cook County Jail *Clarence Darrow*

If I looked at jails and crimes and prisoners in the way the ordinary person does, I should not

From the 1975 edition of the 1902 speech to the prisoners. Copyright Charles H. Kerr Publishing Company. Reprinted by permission. (Abridged.)

speak on this subject to you. The reason I talk to you on the question of crime, its cause and cure, is that I really do not in the least believe in crime. There is no such thing as a crime as the word is generally understood. I do not believe there is any sort of distinction between the real moral conditions of the people in and out of jail.

One is just as good as the other. The people here can no more help being here than the people outside can avoid being outside. I do not believe that people are in jail because they deserve to be. They are in jail simply because they cannot avoid it on account of circumstances which are entirely beyond their control and for which they are in no way responsible.

I suppose a great many people on the outside would say I was doing you harm if they should hear what I say to you this afternoon, but you cannot be hurt a great deal anyway, so it will not matter. Good people outside would say that I was really teaching you things that were calculated to injure society, but it's worth while now and then to hear something different from what you ordinarily get from preachers and the like. These will tell you that you should be good and then you will get rich and be happy. Of course we know that people do not get rich by being good, and that is the reason why so many of you people try to get rich some other way, only you do not understand how to do it quite as well as the fellow outside.

There are people who think that everything in this world is an accident. But really there is no such thing as an accident. A great many folks admit that many of the people in jail ought not to be there, and many who are outside ought to be in. I think none of them ought to be here. There ought to be no jails; and if it were not for the fact that the people on the outside are so grasping and heartless in their dealings with the people on the inside, there would be no such institution as jails.

I do not want you to believe that I think all you people here are angels. I do not think that. You are people of all kinds, all of you doing the best you can—and that is evidently not very well. You are people of all kinds and conditions and under all circumstances. In one sense everybody is equally good and equally bad. We all do the best we can under the circumstances. But as to the exact things for which you are sent here, some of you are guilty and did the particular act because you needed the money. Some of you did it because you are in the habit of doing it, and some of you because you are born to it, and it

comes to be as natural as it does, for instance, for me to be good.

Most of you probably have nothing against me, and most of you would treat me the same way as any other person would, probably better than some of the people on the outside would treat me, because you think I believe in you and they know *I* do not believe in them. While you would not have the least thing against me in the world, you might pick my pockets. I do not think all of you would, but I think some of you would. You would not have anything against me, but that's your profession, a few of you. Some of the rest of you, if my doors were unlocked, might come in if you saw anything you wanted—not out of any malice to me, but because that is your trade. There is no doubt there are quite a number of people in this jail who would pick my pockets. And still I know this—that when I get outside pretty nearly everybody picks my pocket. There may be some of you who would hold up a man on the street, if you did not happen to have something else to do, and needed the money; but when I want to light my house or my office the gas company holds me up. They charge me one dollar for something that is worth twenty-five cents. Still all these people are good people; they are pillars of society and support the churches, and they are respectable.

When I ride on the streetcars I am held up—I pay five cents for a ride that is worth two and a half cents, simply because a body of men have bribed the city council and the legislature, so that all the rest of us have to pay tribute to them.

If I do not want to fall into the clutches of the gas trust and choose to burn oil instead of gas, then good Mr. Rockefeller holds me up, and he uses a certain portion of his money to build universities and support churches which are engaged in telling us how to be good.

Some of you are here for obtaining property under false pretenses—yet I pick up a great Sunday paper and read the advertisements of a merchant prince—"Shirtwaists for 39 cents, marked down from $3.00."

When I read the advertisements in the paper I see they are all lies. When I want to get out and find a place to stand anywhere on the face of the earth, I find that it has all been taken up long ago before I came here, and before you came here, and somebody says, "Get off, swim into the lake, fly into the air; go anywhere, but get off." That is because these people have the police and they have the jails and the judges and the lawyers and the soldiers and all the rest of them to take care of the earth and drive everybody off that comes in their way.

A great many people will tell you that all this is true, but that it does not excuse you. These facts do not excuse some fellow who reaches into my pocket and takes out a five-dollar bill. The fact that the gas company bribes the members of the legislature from year to year, and fixes the law, so that all you people are compelled to be "fleeced" whenever you deal with them; the fact that the streetcar companies and the gas companies have control of the streets; and the fact that the landlords own all the earth—this, they say, has nothing to do with you.

Let us see whether there is any connection between the crimes of the respectable classes and your presence in the jail. . . .

The reformers who tell you to be good and you will be happy, and the people on the outside who have property to protect—they think that the only way to do it is by building jails and locking you up in cells on weekdays and praying for you Sundays.

I think that all of this has nothing whatever to do with right conduct. I think it is very easily seen what has to do with right conduct. Some so-called criminals—and I will use this word because it is handy, it means nothing to me—I speak of the criminals who get caught as distinguished from the criminals who catch them—some of these so-called criminals are in jail for their first offenses, but nine tenths of you are in jail because you did not have a good lawyer and, of course, you did not have a good lawyer because you did not have enough money to pay a good lawyer. There is no very great danger of a rich man going to jail.

Some of you may be here for the first time. If we would open the doors and let you out, and leave the laws as they are today, some of you would be back tomorrow. This is about as good

a place as you can get anyway. There are many people here who are so in the habit of coming that they would not know where else to go. There are people who are born with the tendency to break into jail every chance they get, and they cannot avoid it. You cannot figure out your life and see why it was, but still there is a reason for it; and if we were all wise and knew all the facts, we could figure it out.

In the first place, there are a good many more people who go to jail in the wintertime than in summer. Why is this? Is it because people are more wicked in winter? No, it is because the coal trust begins to get in its grip in the winter. A few gentlemen take possession of the coal, and unless the people will pay seven or eight dollars a ton for something that is worth three dollars, they will have to freeze. Then there is nothing to do but to break into jail, and so there are many more in jail in the winter than in summer. It costs more for gas in the winter because the nights are longer, and people go to jail to save gas bills. The jails are electric-lighted. You may not know it, but these economic laws are working all the time, whether we know it or do not know it.

There are more people who go to jail in hard times than in good times—few people, comparatively, go to jail except when they are hard up. They go to jail because they have no other place to go. They may not know why, but it is true all the same. People are not more wicked in hard times. That is not the reason. The fact is true all over the world that in hard times more people go to jail than in good times, and in winter more people go to jail than in summer. Of course it is pretty hard times for people who go to jail at any time. The people who go to jail are almost always poor people—people who have no other place to live, first and last. When times are hard, then you find large numbers of people who go to jail who would not otherwise be in jail.

Long ago, Mr. Buckle, who was a great philosopher and historian, collected facts, and he showed that the number of people who are arrested increased just as the price of food increased. When they put up the price of gas ten cents a thousand, I do not know who will go to jail, but I do know that a certain number of people will go. When the meat combine raises the price of beef, I do not know who is going to jail, but I know that a large number of people are bound to go. Whenever the Standard Oil Company raises the price of oil, I know that a certain number of girls who are seamstresses, and who work night after night long hours for somebody else, will be compelled to go out on the streets and ply another trade, and I know that Mr. Rockefeller and his associates are responsible and not the poor girls in the jails.

First and last, people are sent to jail because they are poor. Sometimes, as I say, you may not need money at the particular time, but you wish to have thrifty forehanded habits, and do not always wait until you are in absolute want. Some of you people are perhaps plying the trade, the profession, which is called burglary. No man in his right senses will go into a strange house in the dead of night and prowl around with a dark lantern through unfamiliar rooms and take chances of his life, if he has plenty of the good things of the world in his own home. You would not take any such chances as that. If a man had clothes in his clothes-press and beefsteak in his pantry and money in the bank, he would not navigate around nights in houses where he knows nothing about the premises whatever. It always requires experience and education for this profession, and people who fit themselves for it are no more to blame than I am for being a lawyer. A man would not hold up another man on the street if he had plenty of money in his own pocket. He might do it if he had one dollar or two dollars, but he wouldn't if he had as much money as Mr. Rockefeller has. Mr. Rockefeller has a great deal better hold-up game than that.

The more that is taken from the poor by the rich, who have the chance to take it, the more poor people there are who are compelled to resort to these means for a livelihood. They may not understand it, they may not think so at once, but after all they are driven into that line of employment.

There is a bill before the legislature of this state to punish kidnaping children with death. We have wise members of the legislature. They know the gas trust when they see it and they always see it—they can furnish light enough to be seen; and this legislature thinks it is going to stop kidnaping children by making a law punishing kidnapers of children with death. I don't believe in kidnaping children, but the legislature is all wrong. Kidnaping children is not a crime, it is a profession. It has been developed with the times. It has been developed with our modern industrial conditions. There are many ways of making money—many new ways that our ancestors knew nothing about. Our ancestors knew nothing about a billion-dollar trust, and here comes some poor fellow who has no other trade and he discovers the profession of kidnaping children.

This crime is born, not because people are bad; people don't kidnap other people's children because they want the children or because they are devilish, but because they see a chance to get some money out of it. You cannot cure this crime by passing a law punishing by death kidnapers of children. There is one way to cure it. There is one way to cure all these offenses, and that is to give the people a chance to live. There is no other way, and there never was any other way since the world began; and the world is so blind and stupid that it will not see. If every man and woman and child in the world had a chance to make a decent, fair, honest living, there would be no jails and no lawyers and no courts. There might be some persons here or there with some peculiar formation of their brain, like Rockefeller, who would do these things simply to be doing them; but they would be very, very few, and those should be sent to a hospital and treated, and not sent to jail; and they would entirely disappear in the second generation, or at least in the third generation.

I am not talking pure theory. I will just give you two or three illustrations.

The English people once punished criminals by sending them away. They would load them on a ship and export them to Australia. England was owned by lords and nobles and rich people. They owned the whole earth over there, and the other people had to stay in the streets. They could not get a decent living. They used to take their criminals and send them to Australia—I mean the class of criminals who got caught. When these criminals got over there, and nobody else had come, they had the whole continent to run over, and so they could raise sheep and furnish their own meat, which is easier than stealing it. These criminals then became decent, respectable people because they had a chance to live. They did not commit any crimes. They were just like the English people who sent them there, only better. And in the second generation the descendants of those criminals were as good and respectable a class of people as there were on the face of the earth, and then they began building churches and jails themselves.

A portion of this country was settled in the same way, landing prisoners down on the southern coast; but when they got here and had a whole continent to run over and plenty of chances to make a living, they became respectable citizens, making their own living just like any other citizen in the world. But finally the descendants of the English aristocracy who sent the people over to Australia found out they were getting rich, and so they went over to get possession of the earth as they always do, and they organized land syndicates and got control of the land and ores, and then they had just as many criminals in Australia as they did in England. It was not because the world had grown bad; it was because the earth had been taken away from the people.

Some of you people have lived in the country. It's prettier than it is here. And if you have ever lived on a farm you understand that if you put a lot of cattle in a field, when the pasture is short they will jump over the fence; but put them in a good field where there is plenty of pasture, and they will be law-abiding cattle to the end of time. The human animal is just like the rest of the animals, only a little more so. The same thing that governs in the one governs in the other.

Everybody makes his living along the lines of least resistance. A wise man who comes into a country early sees a great undeveloped land. For instance, our rich men twenty-five years ago saw that Chicago was small and knew a lot of people would come here and settle, and they readily saw that if they had all the land around here it would be worth a good deal, so they grabbed the land. You cannot be a landlord because somebody has got it all. You must find some other calling. In England and Ireland and Scotland less than five per cent own all the land there is, and the people are bound to stay there on any kind of terms the landlords give. They must live the best they can, so they develop all these various professions—burglary, picking pockets, and the like.

Again, people find all sorts of ways of getting rich. These are diseases like everything else. You look at people getting rich, organizing trusts and making a million dollars, and somebody gets the disease and he starts out. He catches it just as a man catches the mumps or the measles; he is not to blame, it is in the air. You will find men speculating beyond their means, because the mania of money-getting is taking possession of them. It is simply a disease—nothing more, nothing less. You cannot avoid catching it; but the fellows who have control of the earth have the advantage of you. See what the law is: when these men get control of things, they make the laws. They do not make the laws to protect anybody; courts are not instruments of justice. When your case gets into court it will make little difference whether you are guilty or innocent, but it's better if you have a smart lawyer. And you cannot have a smart lawyer unless you have money. First and last it's a question of money. Those men who own the earth make the laws to protect what they have. They fix up a sort of fence or pen around what they have, and they fix the law so the fellow on the outside cannot get in. The laws are really organized for the protection of the men who rule the world. They were never organized or enforced to do justice. We have no system for doing justice, not the slightest in the world. . . .

The people who are on the outside, who are running banks and building churches and making jails, they have no time to examine 600 or 700 prisoners each year to see whether they are guilty or innocent. If the courts were organized to promote justice the people would elect somebody to defend all these criminals, somebody as smart as the prosecutor—and give him as many detectives and as many assistants to help, and pay as much money to defend you as to prosecute you. We have a very able man for state's attorney, and he has many assistants, detectives, and policemen without end, and judges to hear the cases—everything handy.

Most all of our criminal code consists in offenses against property. People are sent to jail because they have committed a crime against property. It is of very little consequence whether one hundred people more or less go to jail who ought not to go—you must protect property, because in this world property is of more importance than anything else.

How is it done? These people who have property fix it so they can protect what they have. When somebody commits a crime it does not follow that he has done something that is morally wrong. The man on the outside who has committed no crime may have done something. For instance: to take all the coal in the United States and raise the price two dollars or three dollars when there is no need of it, and thus kill thousands of babies and send thousands of people to the poorhouse and tens of thousands to jail, as is done every year in the United States—this is a greater crime than all the people in our jails ever committed; but the law does not punish it. Why? Because the fellows who control the earth make the laws. If you and I had the making of the laws, the first thing we would do would be to punish the fellow who gets control of the earth. Nature put this coal in the ground for me as well as for them and nature made the prairies up here to raise wheat for me as well as for them, and then the great railroad companies came along and fenced it up.

Most all of the crimes for which we are punished are property crimes. There are a few personal crimes, like murder—but they are very few. The crimes committed are mostly those against property. If this punishment is right the criminals must have a lot of property. How much money is there in this crowd? And yet you are all here for crimes against property. The people up and down the Lake Shore have not committed crime: still they have so much property they don't know what to do with it. It is perfectly plain why these people have not committed crimes against property: they make the laws and therefore do not need to break them. And in order for you to get some property you are obliged to break the rules of the game. I don't know but what some of you may have had a very nice chance to get rich by carrying a hod for one dollar a day, twelve hours. Instead of taking that nice, easy profession, you are a burglar. If you had been given a chance to be a banker you would rather follow that. Some of you may have had a chance to work as a switchman on a railroad where you know, according to statistics, that you cannot live and keep all your limbs more than seven years, and you can get fifty dollars or seventy-five dollars a month for taking your lives in your hands; and instead of taking that lucrative position you chose to be a sneak thief, or something like that. Some of you made that sort of choice. I don't know which I would take if I was reduced to this choice. I have an easier choice.

I will guarantee to take from this jail, or any jail in the world, five hundred men who have been the worst criminals and lawbreakers who ever got into jail, and I will go down to our lowest streets and take five hundred of the most abandoned prostitutes, and go out somewhere where there is plenty of land, and will give them a chance to make a living, and they will be as good people as the average in the community.

There is a remedy for the sort of condition we see here. The world never finds it out, or when it does find it out it does not enforce it....

And this has been the history of the world. It's easy to see how to do away with what we call crime. It is not so easy to do it. I will tell you how to do it. It can be done by giving the people a chance to live—by destroying special privileges. So long as big criminals can get the coal fields, so long as the big criminals have control of the city council and get the public streets for streetcars and gas rights—this is bound to send thousands of poor people to jail. So long as men are allowed to monopolize all the earth, and compel others to live on such terms as these men see fit to make, then you are bound to get into jail.

The only way in the world to abolish crime and criminals is to abolish the big ones and the little ones together. Make fair conditions of life. Give men a chance to live. Abolish the right of private ownership of land, abolish monopoly, make the world partners in production, partners in the good things of life. Nobody would steal if he could get something of his own some easier way. Nobody will commit burglary when he has a house full. No girl will go out on the streets when she has a comfortable place at home. The man who owns a sweatshop or a department store may not be to blame himself for the condition of his girls, but when he pays them five dollars, three dollars, and two dollars a week, I wonder where he thinks they will get the rest of their money to live. The only way to cure these conditions is by equality. There should be no jails. They do not accomplish what they pretend to accomplish. If you would wipe them out there would be no more criminals than now. They terrorize nobody. They are a blot upon any civilization, and a jail is an evidence of the lack of charity of the people on the outside who make the jails and fill them with the victims of their greed.

Notes and Questions

1. Is it appropriate for a lawyer to talk to prisoners the way Darrow did?

2. In the introduction to the lecture, which he had printed in pamphlet form and sold for 5 cents, Darrow wrote:

   Realizing the force of the suggestion that the truth should not be spoken to all people, I have caused these remarks to be printed on rather good paper and in a somewhat expensive form. In this way the truth does not become cheap and vulgar, and is only placed before those whose intelligence and affluence will prevent their being influenced by it.

   What does this indicate about his views on the class structure of society?

3. If Darrow thinks that jails are the invention of the ruling class, how can he say that some people are "born with the tendency to break into jail"?

4. Does Darrow assume that the basic motivation of all people is to get rich? Does he view the drive for wealth as a basic social problem?

5. Why do you suppose that Darrow's vision of class structure is not more widely known in America, especially because his reputation as a defense law-

yer is almost legendary? What do you imagine Darrow's answer to this question would be?

6. Does it seem reasonable to you to think of kidnapping and theft as ways of surviving in a capitalist economy?

7. What do you think people's main aim in life would be if "every man and woman and child in the world had a chance to make a decent, fair, honest living"?

8. It was said that one of the prisoners in the audience commented that the speech was "too radical." What do you think Darrow might have said that this shows about prisoners?

9. How would Darrow answer the questions at the end of this chapter about the *Akwesasne Notes* cover (p. 534)?

10. As you think about what Clarence Darrow said to the prisoners, read Emma Goldman's remarks on law, order, and crime:

    Order derived through submission and maintained by terror is not much of a safe guaranty; yet that is the only "order" that governments have ever maintained. True social harmony grows naturally out of solidarity of interests. In a society where those who always work never have anything, while those who never work enjoy everything, solidarity of interests is non-existent; hence social harmony is but a myth. The only way organized authority meets this grave situation is by extending still greater privileges to those who have already monopolized the earth, and by still further enslaving the disinherited masses. Thus the entire arsenal of government—laws, police, soldiers, the courts, legislatures, prisons —is strenuously engaged in "harmonizing" the most antagonistic elements in society. . . .

    Crime is naught but misdirected energy. So long as every institution of today, economic, political, social, and moral, conspires to misdirect human energy into wrong channels; so long as most people are out of place doing the things they hate to do, living a life they loathe to live, crime will be inevitable, and all the laws on the statutes can only increase, but never do away with, crime.*

---

* Alix Schulman, ed., *Red Emma Speaks* (New York: Vintage, 1972), p. 57.

Cracking the Safe   *Chuang Tzu*

For security against robbers who snatch purses,
rifle luggage, and crack safes,
One must fasten all property with ropes, lock it
up with locks, bolt it with bolts.
This (for property owners) is elementary good
sense,
But when a strong thief comes along he picks up
the whole lot,
Puts it on his back, and goes on his way with
only one fear;
That ropes, locks, and bolts may give way.
Thus what the world calls good business is only
a way
To gather up the loot, pack it, make it secure
In one convenient load for the more enterprising
thieves.
Who is there, among those called smart,
Who does not spend his time amassing loot
For a bigger robber than himself?

In the land of Khi, from village to village,
You could hear cocks crowing, dogs barking.
Fishermen cast their nets,
Ploughmen ploughed the wide fields,
Everything was neatly marked out
By boundary lines. For five hundred square miles
There were temples for ancestors, altars
For field-gods and corn-spirits.
Every canton, county, and district
Was run according to the laws and statutes—
Until one morning the Attorney General, Tien
Khang Tzu,
Did away with the King and took over the whole
state.
Was he content to steal the land? No,
He also took over the laws and statutes at the
same time,
And all the lawyers with them, not to mention
the police.
They all formed part of the same package.

Of course, people called Khang Tzu a robber,
But they left him alone
To live as happy as the Patriarchs.
No small state would say a word against him,
No large state would make a move in his direc-
tion,
So for twelve generations that state of Khi
Belonged to his family. No one interfered
With his inalienable rights.

The invention
Of weights and measures
Makes robbery easier.
Signing contracts, setting seals,
Makes robbery more sure.
Teaching love and duty
Provides a fitting language
With which to prove that robbery
Is really for the general good.
A poor man must swing
For stealing a belt buckle
But if a rich man steals a whole state
He is acclaimed
As statesman of the year.

Hence if you want to hear the very best speeches
On love, duty, justice, etc.,
Listen to statesmen.
But when the creek dries up
Nothing grows in the valley.
When the mound is levelled
The hollow next to it is filled.
And when the statesmen and lawyers
And preachers of duty disappear
There are no more robberies either
And the world is at peace.

Moral: the more you pile up ethical principles
And duties and obligations
To bring everyone in line
The more you gather loot
For a thief like Khang.
By ethical argument
And moral principle

The greatest crimes are eventually shown
To have been necessary, and, in fact,
A signal benefit
To mankind.

Question

1. Compare this ancient Chinese poem with Clarence Darrow's speech to the prisoners. Does the similarity between the two indicate a basic difference between Chinese and American societies?

The Poverty of the Sociology of Deviance: Nuts, Sluts, and Preverts   *Alexander Liazos*

C. Wright Mills left a rich legacy to sociology. One of his earliest, and best, contributions was "The Professional Ideology of Social Pathologists" (1943). In it, Mills argues that the small-town, middle-class background of writers of social problems textbooks blinded them to basic problems of social structure and power, and led them to emphasize melioristic, patchwork types of solutions to America's problems. They assumed as natural and orderly the structure of small-town America; anything else was pathology and disorganization. Moreover, these "problems," "ranging from rape in rural districts to public housing," were not explored systematically and theoretically; they were not placed in some larger political, historical, and social context. They were merely listed and decried.

Since Mills wrote his paper, however, the field of social problems, social disorganization, and social pathology has undergone considerable changes....

The "deviant" has been humanized; the moralistic tone is no longer ever-present (although it still lurks underneath the explicit disavowals); and theoretical perspectives have been developed. Nevertheless, all is not well with the field of "deviance." Close examination reveals that writers of this field still do not try to relate the phenomena of "deviance" to larger social, historical, political, and economic contexts. The emphasis is

From Alexander Liazos, "The Poverty of the Sociology of Deviance: Nuts, Sluts, and Preverts," *Social Problems*, Vol. 20:1 (Summer 1972), pp. 103–120. (Abridged and some footnotes omitted.)

still on the "deviant" and the "problems" *he* presents to himself and others, not on the society within which he emerges and operates.

I examined 16 textbooks in the field of "deviance," eight of them readers, to determine the state of the field.... A careful examination of these textbooks revealed a number of ideological biases. These biases became apparent as much from what these books leave unsaid and unexamined, as from what they do say. The field of the sociology of deviance, as exemplified in these books, contains three important theoretical and political biases.

1. All writers, especially those of the labelling school, either state explicitly or imply that one of their main concerns is to *humanize* and *normalize* the "deviant," to show that he is essentially no different from us. But by the very emphasis on the "deviant" and his identity problems and sub-culture, the opposite effect may have been achieved. The persisting use of the label "deviant" to refer to the people we are considering is an indication of the feeling that these people are indeed different.

2. By the overwhelming emphasis on the "dramatic" nature of the usual types of "deviance"— prostitution, homosexuality, juvenile delinquency, and others—we have neglected to examine other, more serious and harmful forms of "deviance." I refer to *covert institutional violence* (defined and discussed below) which leads to such things as poverty and exploitation, the war in Vietnam, unjust tax laws, racism and sexism, and so on, which cause psychic and material suffering for

many Americans, black and white, men and women.

3. Despite explicit statements by these authors of the importance of *power* in the designation of what is "deviant," in their substantive analyses they show a profound unconcern with power and its implications. The really powerful, the upper classes and the power elite, those Gouldner (1968) calls the "top dogs," are left essentially unexamined by these sociologists of deviance.

I

Always implicit, and frequently explicit, is the aim of the labelling school to humanize and normalize the "deviant."... Statements by Becker and Matza are representative of this sentiment.

> In the course of our work and for who knows what private reasons, we fall into deep sympathy with the people we are studying, so that while the rest of society views them as unfit in one or another respect for the deference ordinarily accorded a fellow citizen, we believe that they are at least as good as any one else, more sinned against than sinning (Becker 1967)....

For a number of reasons, however, the opposite effect may have been achieved; and "deviants" still seem different. I began to suspect this reverse effect from the many essays and papers I read while teaching the "deviance" course. The clearest example is the repeated use of the word "tolerate." Students would write that we must not persecute homosexuals, prostitutes, mental patients, and others, that we must be "tolerant" of them. But one tolerates only those one considers less than equal, morally inferior, and weak; those equal to oneself, one accepts and respects; one does not merely allow them to exist, one does not "tolerate" them.

The repeated assertion that "deviants" are "at least as good as anyone else" may raise doubts that this is in fact the case, or that we believe it. A young woman who grew up in the South in the 1940's and 1950's told Quinn (1954): " 'You know, I think from the fact that I was told so often that I must treat colored people with consideration, I got the feeling that I could mistreat them if I wanted to.' " Thus with "deviants"; if

in fact they are as good as we are, we would not need to remind everyone of this fact; we would take it for granted and proceed from there. But our assertions that "deviants" are not different may raise the very doubts we want to dispel. Moreover, why would we create a separate field of sociology for "deviants" if there were not something different about them? May it be that even we do not believe our statements and protestations?

The continued use of the word "deviant" (and its variants), despite its invidious distinctions and connotations, also belies our explicit statements on the equality of the people under consideration....

Szasz (1970) has urged that we abandon use of the term: ...

> The term "social deviants"... does not make sufficiently explicit—as the terms "scapegoat" or "victim" do—that majorities usually categorize persons or groups as "deviant" in order to set them apart as inferior beings and to justify their social control, oppression, persecution, or even complete destruction.

Terms like victimization, persecution, and oppression are more accurate descriptions of what is really happening. But even Gouldner (1968), in a masterful critique of the labelling school, while describing social conflict, calls civil-rights and anti-war protesters "political deviants." He points out clearly that these protesters are resisting openly, not slyly, conditions they abhor. Gouldner is discussing political struggles; oppression and resistance to oppression; conflicts over values, morals, interests, and power; and victimization. Naming such protesters "deviants," even if *political* deviants, is an indication of the deep penetration within our minds of certain prejudices and orientations....

The lists and discussions of "deviant" acts and persons reveal the writers' biases and sentiments. These are acts which, "like robbery, burglary or rape [are] of a simple and dramatic predatory nature..." (The President's Commission on Law Enforcement and the Administration of Justice.) ...

Simmons (1969) also informs us that in his study of stereotypes of "deviants" held by the public, these are the types he gave to people: homosexuals, beatniks, adulterers, marijuana smokers, political radicals, alcoholics, prostitutes, lesbians, ex-mental patients, atheists, ex-convicts, intellectuals, and gamblers. . . .

The omissions from these lists are staggering. The covert, institutional forms of "deviance" (part II, below) are nowhere to be found. Reading these authors, one would not know that the most destructive use of violence in the last decade has been the war in Vietnam, in which the U.S. has heaped unprecedented suffering on the people and their land; more bombs have been dropped in Vietnam than in the entire World War II. Moreover, the robbery of the corporate world—through tax breaks, fixed prices, low wages, pollution of the environment, shoddy goods, etc.—is passed over in our fascination with "dramatic and predatory" actions. . . .

Becker (1964) claims that in the labelling perspective "we focus attention on the other people involved in the process. We pay attention to the role of the non-deviant as well as that of the deviant." But we see that it is the ordinary non-deviants and the low-level agents of social control who receive attention, not the powerful ones (Gouldner, 1968).

In fact, the emphasis is more on the *subculture* and *identity* of the "deviants" themselves rather than on their oppressors and persecutors. To be sure, in varying degrees all authors discuss the agents of social control, but the fascination and emphasis are on the "deviant" himself. Studies of prisons and prisoners, for example, focus on prison subcultures and prisoner rehabilitation; there is little or no consideration of the social, political, economic, and power conditions which consign people to prisons. Only now are we beginning to realize that most prisoners are *political prisoners*—that their "criminal" actions (whether against individuals, such as robbery, or conscious political acts against the state) result largely from current social and political conditions, and are not the work of "disturbed" and "psychopathic" personalities. This realization came about largely because of the writings of political prisoners themselves: Malcolm X (1965), Eldridge Cleaver (1968), and George Jackson (1970), among others. . . .

One wonders about other types of "deviants": how do those who perpetrate the covert institutional violence in our society view themselves? Do they have identity problems? How do they justify their actions? How did the robber barons of the late 19th century steal, fix laws, and buy politicians six days of the week and go to church on Sunday? By what process can people speak of body counts and kill ratios with cool objectivity? . . . Editors seem unaware that such questions should or could be raised. . . .

Because of these biases, there is an implicit, but very clear, acceptance by these authors of the current definitions of "deviance." It comes about because they concentrate their attention on those who have been *successfully labelled as "deviant,"* and not on those who break laws, fix laws, violate ethical and moral standards, harm individuals and groups, etc., but who either are able to hide their actions, or, when known, can deflect criticism, labelling, and punishment. The following are typical statements which reveal this bias.

". . . no act committed by members of occupational groups [such as white-collar crimes], however unethical, should be considered as crime unless it is punishable by the state in some way" (Clinard, 1968). Thus, if some people can manipulate laws so that their unethical and destructive acts are not "crimes," we should cater to their power and agree that they are not criminals. . . .

The implication of these statements is that the sociologist accepts current, successful definitions of what is "deviant" as the only ones worthy of his attention. To be sure, he may argue that those labelled "deviant" are not really different from the rest of us, or that there is no act intrinsically "deviant," etc. By concentrating on cases of successful labelling, however, he will not penetrate beneath the surface to look for other forms of "deviance"—undetected stealing, violence, and destruction. When people are not powerful enough to make the "deviant" label stick on others, we overlook these cases. But is it not as much a *social fact,* even though few of us pay much attention to it, that the corporate economy kills and maims more, is more violent, than any violence committed by the poor (the usual subjects of studies of violence)? By what reasoning and necessity is the "violence" of the poor in the ghettoes more worthy of our attention than the military bootcamps which numb recruits from the horrors of killing the "enemy.". . .

But because these acts are not labelled "deviant," because they are covert, institutional, and normal, their "deviant" qualities are overlooked and they do not become part of the province of the sociology of deviance. Despite their best liberal intentions, these sociologists seem to perpetuate the very notions they think they debunk, and others of which they are unaware. . . .

II

. . . If we take the concept *violence* seriously, we see that much of our political and economic system thrives on it. In violence, a person is *violated* —there is harm done to his person, his psyche, his body, his dignity, his ability to govern himself (Garver, in Rose, 1969). Seen in this way, a person can be violated in many ways; physical force is only one of them. . . . A person can be violated by a system that denies him a decent job, or consigns him to a slum, or causes him brain damage by near-starvation during childhood, or manipulates him through the mass media, and so on endlessly.

Moreover, we must see that *covert institutional violence* is much more destructive than overt individual violence. We must recognize that people's lives are violated by the very normal and everyday workings of institutions. We do not see such events and situations as violent because they are not dramatic and predatory; they do not make for fascinating reading on the lives of perverts; but they kill, maim, and destroy many more lives than do violent individuals.

Here are some examples. Carmichael and Hamilton (1967), in distinguishing between *individual* and *institutional* racism, offer examples of each:

When white terrorists bomb a black church and kill five black children, that is an act of individual racism, widely deplored by most segments of the society. But when in that same city—Birmingham, Alabama—five hundred black babies die each year because of lack of proper food, shelter, and medical facilities, and thousands more are destroyed and maimed physically, emotionally and intellectually because of conditions of poverty and discrimination in the black community, that is a function of institutional racism.

Surely this is violence; it is caused by the normal, quiet workings of institutions run by respectable members of the community. Many whites also suffer from the institutional workings of a profit-oriented society and economy; poor health, dead-end jobs, slum housing, hunger in rural areas, and so on, are daily realities in their lives. This is surely much worse violence than any committed by the Hell's Angels or street gangs. Only these groups get stigmatized and analyzed by sociologists of deviance, however, while those good people who live in luxurious homes (fixing tax laws for their benefit) off profits derived from an exploitative economic system—they are the pillars of their community.

Violence is committed daily by the government, very often by lack of action. The same system that enriches businessmen farmers with billions of dollars through farm subsidies cannot be bothered to appropriate a few millions to deal with lead poisoning in the slums. Young children

. . . get it by eating the sweet-tasting chips of peeling tenement walls, painted a generation ago with leaded paint.

According to the Department of Health, Education, and Welfare, 400,000 children are poisoned each year, about 30,000 in New York City alone. About 3,200 suffer permanent brain damage, 800 go blind or become so mentally retarded that they require hospitalization for the rest of their lives, and approximately 200 die.

The tragedy is that lead poisoning is totally man-made and totally preventable. It is caused by slum housing. And there are now blood tests that can detect the disease, and medicines to cure it. Only a lack of purpose sentences 200 black children to die each year (Newfield, 1971).

Newfield goes on to report that on May 20, 1971, a Senate-House conference eliminated $5 million from an appropriations budget. In fact, 200 children had been sentenced to death and thousands more to maiming and suffering.

Similar actions of violence are committed daily by the government and corporations; but in these days of misplaced emphasis, ignorance, and manipulation we do not see the destruction inherent in these actions. Instead, we get fascinated, angry, and misled by the violence of the poor and the powerless. We see the violence committed during political rebellions in the ghettoes (called "riots" in order to dismiss them), but all along we ignored the daily violence committed against the ghetto residents by the institutions of the society: schools, hospitals, corporations, the government....

The bias against examining the structural conditions behind white-collar crime is further revealed in Clinard's suggestions on how to deal with it.... The only recommendation in three pages of discussion is to teach everyone more "respect" for the law. This is a purely moralistic device; it pays no attention to the structural aspects of the problem, to the fact that even deeper than white-collar crime is ingrained a whole network of laws, especially tax laws, administrative policies, and institutions which systematically favor a small minority. More generally, discussions on the prevention of "deviance" and crime do not deal with institutional violence, and what we need to do to stop it.[1]

But there is an obvious explanation for this oversight. The people committing serious white-collar crimes and executing the policies of violent institutions are respectable and responsible individuals, not "deviants"; this is the view of the President's Commission on Law Enforcement and the Administration of Justice.

> Significantly, the Antitrust Division does not feel that lengthy prison sentences are ordinarily called for [for white-collar crimes]. It "rarely recommends jail sentences greater than 6 months—recommendations of 30-day imprisonment are most frequent."
>
> Persons who have standing and roots in a community, and are prepared for and engaged in legitimate occupations, can be expected to be particularly susceptible to the threat of criminal prosecution. Criminal proceedings and the imposition of sanctions have a much sharper impact upon those who have not been hardened by previous contact with the criminal justice system....

In short, despite the supposedly central position of *social structure* in the sociological enterprise, there is general neglect of it in the field of "deviance." Larger questions, especially if they deal with political and economic issues, are either passed over briefly or overlooked completely. The focus on the actions of "nuts, sluts, and preverts" and the related slight of the criminal and destructive actions of the powerful, are instances of this avoidance.

III

Most of the authors under discussion mention the importance of *power* in labelling people "deviant." They state that those who label (the victimizers) are more powerful than those they label (the victims). Writers of the labelling school make this point explicitly. According to Becker (1963), "who can . . . force others to accept their rules and what are the causes of their success? This is, of course, a question of political and economic power." Simmons (1969) comments that historically, "those in power have used their positions largely to perpetuate and enhance their own advantages through coercing and manipulating the rest of the populace." And Lofland (1969) makes the same observation in his opening pages:

> It is in the situation of a very powerful party opposing a very weak one that the powerful

---

[1] Investigation of the causes and prevention of institutional violence would probably be biting the hand that feeds the sociologist, for we read that the government and foundations (whose money comes from corporate profits) have supported research on "deviant behavior," especially its prevention. "This has meant particularly that the application of sociological theory to research has increased markedly in such areas as delinquency, crime, mental disorder, alcoholism, drug addiction, and discrimination" (Clinard, 1968). That's where the action is, not on white-collar crime, nor on the covert institutional violence of the government and economy.

party sponsors the *idea* that the weak party is breaking the rules of society. The very concepts of "society" and its "rules" are appropriated by powerful parties and made synonymous with their interests (and, of course, believed in by the naive, e.g., the undergraduate penchant for the phrases "society says...," "society expects...," "society does...").

But this insight is not developed. In none of the 16 books is there an extensive discussion of how power operates in the designation of deviance. Instead of a study of power, of its concrete uses in modern, corporate America, we are offered rather fascinating explorations into the identities and subcultures of "deviants," and misplaced emphasis on the middle-level agents of social control. Only Szasz (1961, 1963, and notably 1970) has shown consistently the role of power in one area of "deviance," "mental illness." Through historical and contemporary studies, he has shown that those labelled "mentally ill" (crazy, insane, mad, lunatic) and institutionalized have always been the powerless: women, the poor, peasants, the aged, and others. Moreover, he has exposed repeatedly the means used by powerful individuals and institutions in employing the "mental illness" label to discredit, persecute, and eliminate opponents. In short, he has shown the political element in the "mental illness" game.

In addition, except for Szasz, none of the authors seems to realize that the stigma of prostitution, abortion, and other "deviant" acts unique to women comes about in large part from the powerlessness of women and their status in society. Moreover, to my knowledge, no one has bothered to ask why there have always been women prostitutes for men to satisfy their sexual desires, but very few men prostitutes for women to patronize. The very word *prostitute* we associate with women only, not men. Both men and women have been involved in this "immoral" act, but the stigma has been carried by the women alone.

All 16 books, some more extensively than others, discuss the ideology, modes of operation, and views of *agents of social control,* the people who designate what is to be "deviant" and those who handle the people so designated. As Gould-

ner (1968) has shown, however, these are the lower and middle level officials, not those who make basic policy and decisions. This bias becomes obvious when we look at the specific agents discussed.

For example, Simmons (1969) tells us that some of "those in charge at every level" are the following: "university administrators, patrolmen, schoolmasters, and similar public employees...." Do university administrators and teachers run the schools alone? Are they teaching and enforcing their own unique values? Do teachers alone create the horrible schools in the slums? Are the uniformity, punctuality, and conformity teachers inculcate their own psychological hang-ups, or do they represent the interests of an industrial-technological-corporate order? In another sphere, do the police enforce their own laws? ...

The only type of rule creator Becker discusses is the moral crusader, no other. The political manipulators who pass laws to defend their interests and persecute dissenters are not studied....

The basic social, political, and economic structure, and those commanding it who guide the labelling and persecution, are left untouched. We have become so accustomed to debunking these low-level agents that we do not even know how to begin to direct our attention to the ruling institutions and groups ....

In a later paper, Becker (1967) poses an apparently insoluble dilemma. He argues that, in studying agents of social control, we are always forced to study subordinates. We can never really get to the top, to those who "really" run the show, for if we study X's superior Y, we find Z above him, and so on endlessly. Everyone has somebody over him, so there is no one at the top. But this is a clever point without substance. In this hierarchy some have more power than others and some are at the top; they may disclaim their position, of course, but it is our job to show otherwise. Some people in this society do have more power than others: parents over children, men over women; some have considerable power over others: top administrators of institutions, for one; and some have a great deal of power, those Domhoff (1967) and others have shown to be the ruling class. It should be our task to explore and describe this hierarchy, its bases of strength, its uses of the "deviant" label to discredit its opponents in order to silence them, and to find ways to eliminate this hierarchy....

A historical description of the origins of police forces [shows] that they have always been used to defend the status quo, the interests of the ruling powers. When the police force was created in England in the early 1800's, it was meant to defend the propertied classes from the "dangerous classes" and the "mob." With the rise of capitalism and industrialism, there was much unrest from the suffering underclass; the professional police were meant to act as a buffer zone for the capitalist elite. Similarly, in America during the early part of this century, especially in the 1930's, police were used repeatedly to attack striking workers and break their strikes. During the Chicago "police riot" of 1968, the police were not merely acting out their aggressions and frustrations; as Hayden shows, they acted with the consent, direction, and blessing of Mayor Daley and the Democratic party (which party represents the "liberal" wing of the American upper class).

It must be stressed that the police, like all agents of social control, are doing someone else's work. Sometimes they enforce laws and prejudices of "society," the much maligned middle class (on sex, marijuana, etc.); but at other times it is not "society" which gives them their directives, but specific interested groups, even though, often, "society" is manipulated to express its approval of such actions. Above all, we must remember that *"in a fundamentally unjust society, even the most impartial, professional, efficient enforcement of the laws by the police cannot result in justice"* (Cook, 1968). More generally, in an unjust and exploitative society, no matter how "humane" agents of social control are, their actions necessarily result in repression.

Broad generalization is another device used by some of these authors to avoid concrete examination of the uses of power in the creation and labelling of "deviance." Clairborne (1971) has called such generalization *"schlock."* The following are some of the tactics he thinks are commonly used in writing popular *schlock* sociology....

The Plausible Passive:

"New scientific discoveries are being made every day.... These new ideas are being put to work more quickly..." [Toffler, in *Future Shock*, is] thereby rather neatly obscuring the fact that scientists and engineers (mostly paid by industry) are making the discoveries and industrialists (often with the aid of public funds) are putting them to work. An alternative to the Plausible Passive is the Elusive Impersonal: 'Buildings in New York literally disappear overnight.' What Toffler is trying to avoid saying is that contractors and real estate speculators *destroy* buildings overnight (Clairborne, 1971).

Rampant Reification, by which "conceptual abstractions are transformed into causal realities," also abounds. Toffler:

speaks of the "roaring current of change" as "an elemental force" and of "that great, growling engine of change—technology." Which of course completely begs the question of what fuels the engine and whose hand is on the throttle. One does not cross-examine an elemental force, let alone suggest that it may have been engendered by monopoly profits (especially in defense and aerospace) or accelerated by government incentives (e.g., open or concealed subsidies, low capital gains tax, accelerated depreciation...) (Clairborne, 1977).

There are parallels in the sociology of deviance. Clinard (1968) argues that urbanization and the slum are breeding grounds for "deviant behavior." But these conditions are reified, not examined concretely. He says about urbanization and social change:

Rapid social and cultural change, disregard for the importance of stability of generations, and untempered loyalties also generally characterize urban life. New ideas are generally welcome, inventions and mechanical gadgets are encouraged, and new styles in such arts as painting, literature, and music are often approved (1968).

But the slum, urbanization, and change are not reified entities working out their independent wills. For example, competition, capitalism, and the profit motive—all encouraged by a government controlled by the upper classes—have had something to do with the rise of slums. There is a general process of urbanization, but at given points in history it is fed by, and gives profits to, specific groups. The following are a few historical examples: the land enclosure policies and practices of the English ruling classes in the 17th and 18th centuries; the building of cheap housing in the 19th century by the owners of factory towns; and the profits derived from "urban renewal" (which has destroyed neighborhoods, created even more crowded slums, etc.) by the building of highways, luxury apartments, and stores.

Another favorite theme of *schlock* sociology is that "All Men Are Guilty." That means nothing can be done to change things. There is a variation of this theme in the sociology of deviance when we are told that a) all of us are deviant in some way, b) all of us label some others deviant, and c) "society" labels. Such statements preclude asking concrete questions: does the "deviance" of each of us have equal consequences for others? Does the labelling of each of us stick, and with what results?

For example, Simmons (1969) says:

> ...I strongly suspect that officials now further alienate more culprits than they recruit back into conventional society, and I think they imprison at least as many people in deviance as they rehabilitate. We must remember that, with a sprinkling of exceptions, officials come from, are hired by, and belong to the dominant majority.

Who is that dominant majority? Are they always the numerical majority? Do they control the labelling and correctional process all by themselves? These questions are not raised. . . .

The preceding examples typify much of what is wrong with the sociology of deviance: the lack of specific analysis of the role of power in the labelling process; the generalizations which, even when true, explain little; the fascination with "deviants"; the reluctance to study the "deviance" of the powerful. . . .

IV

. . . We should not study only, or predominantly, the popular and dramatic forms of "deviance." Indeed, we should banish the concept of "deviance" and speak of oppression, conflict, persecution, and suffering. By focusing on the dramatic forms, as we do now, we perpetuate most people's beliefs and impressions that such "deviance" is the basic cause of many of our troubles, that these people (criminals, drug addicts, political dissenters, and others) are the real "troublemakers"; and, necessarily, we neglect conditions of inequality, powerlessness, institutional violence, and so on, which lie at the bases of our tortured society.

Notes and Questions

1. Think about the concept of "deviance." Where do your ideas come from? Who are the "good people"? The "bad people"?

2. What are the connections among academics, social theorists, and other "thinkers" and the legal economic order? What theories of deviance do you see implemented by the legal order? What groups of people benefit or lose from different theories of deviance?

3. Liazos refers to the word *tolerate* as a tip-off that hierarchical views are being presented. What other words and phrases can you think of that indicate an underlying belief in a hierarchy? Evaluate news stories, speeches, books, and the like, to discover similar code words.

4. Liazos notes that the concept of "society" and "society's rules" are appropriated by the dominant class and made to serve the interests of that class. Do you think that the use of such phrases as *society says,* or *society expects,* or *society does* shows that the user's mind has been captured by the ruling class?

5. How many examples of "schlock" sociology can you find in today's newspapers, TV programs, or elsewhere? What is the effect of this type of thinking and speaking? How often do you find yourself engaging in "schlock" sociology?

6. Does Liazos's critique suggest a direction for action or change? What is it?

7. Liazos stresses the interplay between the ideas of people in power and the ideas that are put forward by sociologists as theories of deviance. As you study this relationship, note what Karl Marx wrote about the ideas of the ruling class:

> The ideas of the ruling class are in every epoch the ruling ideas: i.e., the class, which is

the ruling material force of society, is at the same time its ruling intellectual force. The class which has the means of material production at its disposal has control at the same time over the means of mental production, so that thereby, generally speaking, the ideas of those who lack the means of mental production are subject to it. The ruling ideas are nothing more than the ideal expression of the dominant material relationships, the dominant material relationships grasped as ideas; hence of the relationships which make the one class the ruling one, therefore, the ideas of its dominance. The individuals composing the ruling class possess among other things consciousness, and therefore think. In so far, therefore, as they rule as a class and determine the extent and compass of an epoch, it is self-evident that they do this in their whole range, hence among other things rule also as thinkers, as producers of ideas, and regulate the production and distribution of the ideas of their age: thus their ideas are the ruling ideas of the epoch.*

* Karl Marx, "German Ideology," (1845) in *Marx's Concept of Man,* Erich Fromm, ed. (New York: F. Ungar Pub. Co., 1966), pp. 212–213.

Virginian Liberators   *John T. Noonan, Jr.*

The Legal Structure of Pre-Revolutionary Slavery

On the eve of the Revolution, slavery in Virginia did not exist as a relationship of brute power. A social institution, it was given its shape by a hundred assumptions and omissions, intentions and neglects, customs and conventions. Law formed a part of these multiple pressures and, although far from the whole institution, was essential to it. The statutes on the control of slaves provided not a set of detailed instructions which the slaves meticulously obeyed but a message primarily directed at the white community. The statutes defining the legal status of slaves determined the dispositions to be made at a slave's birth and at a master's death. Slavery was not a transient condition: the law gave it immortality. Control statutes and status statutes together were indispensable to the creation and maintenance of the institution.

The statutes on control were designed on the model of a criminal code regulating public behavior. No slave was to leave his or her owner's plantation without a pass. No slave was to carry a club, staff, or other weapon. No slave was to own a horse, hog, or cow. No slave was to run away and lie out, hiding and lurking in swamps, woods, or other obscure places. No slave was to resist his or her owner administering correction. No slave was to lift his or her hand in opposition to a Christian, provided the Christian was not a Negro, mulatto, or Indian. No slave was to attempt to rape (the possibility of successful rape was not contemplated) a white woman. No slave was to prepare or administer medicine. No slave was to meet with four or more other slaves. No slave was to attend a religious service except with his or her "white family." The statutes were accompanied by provisions specifying punishments for their violation, ranging from whipping to castration to death. . . .

The statutes, the legislature prescribed, were to be read aloud at the door of each parish church twice a year, on the first sermon Sundays in March and September, so that the slaves could make no pretense of ignorance if they disobeyed. . . .

The pedagogy of the statutes pointed to the slaves as creatures who must be coerced, upon whom it was right to exercise force. The statutes measured the amount of violence that masters might employ. The owner's boisterous passions were to be modeled to the community's norm.

Violence on the slaves was authorized and rationalized by being put in the form of a rule. Punishments were set as though each penalty had been measured to the act prohibited. The model of this approach was an act of 1723 whose ostensible purpose was to put slave witnesses "under greater obligation to tell the truth." If their testimony was shown to be false, not by "due proof," but merely by "pregnant circumstances," then

> every such offender shall, without further trial, be ordered by said court to have one ear nailed to the pillory, and there to stand for the space of one hour, and then the said ear to be cut off; and thereafter, the other ear nailed in like manner, and cut off, at the expiration of one other hour; and moreover to order every such offender thirty-nine lashes, well laid on, on his or her bare back, at the common whipping-post.

Sadistic in its precision of detail, this statute appeared to focus on the witnesses. It was to be read to them before they gave testimony, in the only case in which they could give testimony—the trial of another black.... Directed to read it to black witnesses, the judge was reminded of their unreliability, their subjection, their amenability to physical threats. Compelled to bring these brutal threats into the actual conduct of his court, he was instructed in the act of administering justice.

The communication made by the statute to the judge in the paradigm case of a trial was the communication transmitted by other control laws to sheriffs, deputy sheriffs, constables, prosecutors, county courts, and owners. More powerful in intensity than the standards mumblingly communicated to the slaves was the clear word brought to the masters: the community is with you in your exercise of domination.

"Without force, the alienability of the title to the human capital of blacks would have been worthless," write Fogel and Engerman, stressing in their fundamental reevaluation of Southern slavery that the plantation system required a judicious blending of economic incentive with coercion. But what made it possible for slavery to continue for more than a generation? Without acceptance of the rule that the slaves could be transferred by their owners and by the testaments of their owners, neither force nor economic incentive could have maintained the system. To regulate birth and overcome death, and incidentally to determine the transmission and distribution of slaves, a special world had to be created in which rules had a force, a magic, of their own. This second function of the law of slavery depended on a mass of concepts, decisions, and statutes, whose exact application to human beings required the industry and imagination of lawyers.

"Slaves," said the index to the first laws of Virginia, "See Negroes." From the beginning of the colony, "slave" and "Negro" were terms of art indicating a special legal status. The content of these terms was largely given by the popular understanding of what a slave or Negro was. From the beginning, Africans were distinguished from Europeans by complexion, physiognomy, customs, language, and treatment. Lawyers did not single-handedly determine their definition. Yet when it came to the key questions posed by death and birth, answers could not be given by popular perception. What happened to an African when the one for whom he worked died? What happened to a child born of an African? Answers to these questions issued from the use of concepts and rules which, even before they were written up as a code, had the character of law. Africans in Virginia, having arrived by means of purchase, were viewed as *property*.

"For the better settling and preservation of estates within this dominion"—so their desire for immortality was confessed—the Burgesses in 1705 decreed that plantation slaves "shall be held, taken, and adjudged to be real estate (and not chattels)." The object of the statute was to secure the perpetuity of ownership in plantations, insuring that slaves would descend with the land they worked. Designation of plantation slaves as real estate dramatized the triumph of landed proprietorship over death. The dead owner's slave was not cast into a state of nature. The slave was to pass "to the heirs and widows of persons departing this life, according to the manner and custom of land of inheritance held in fee simple." Slaves in the possession of merchants and factors were exempted from the operation of the statute and were to be held "as personal estate in the same condition as they should have been, if this act had never been made." Whether real estate or personal estate, slaves were property, subject to all the rules by which the rights of the dead were imparted to their spouses or to their descendants.

Overcoming the death of the master, determining the status of the offspring, the legislators and courts of Virginia presented a doctrine on the morality of slavery. They taught that it was good. In the pedagogy of the law, slaves were identified with the soil—the literal foundation of prosperity in the colony—or, generically, with property. As long as the teaching of the lawgivers was accepted, slavery could not be criticized without aspersion on the goodness of wealth itself. . . .

Locke's notion that a purpose of government was to protect property could justify all measures taken to secure the stability of the slaveholder's domain. The masters' ties of commerce, marriage, and kindred, so often intertwined with the masters' property arrangements, and dependent upon them, confirmed the position of the slaves. Property was the most comprehensive and most necessary of social categories. Catalogued within it, slaves fell within a classification which announced that it was right and good to maintain their enslavement.

The concept of property performed a further function. It put the slaves at a distance from the world of men and women. "Slave" and "Negro" functioned in the same way, but neither term by itself carried a primary meaning suggesting the non-human. "Property" obliterated every anthropoid feature of the slave. Consistently inculcating this description, the statutes assured the owning class that they did not need to attend to the person of the slave in any conveyance, lease, mortgage, or devise they cared to make of their human possessions.

Addressees of the property statutes were only in an incidental way the slaves themselves. In theory, as real estate or personal estate, they could not be addressed at all. Definition as property determined their physical location, their employment, their sexual opportunities, and their familial relationships whenever they were made the object of

sale, lease, mortgage, foreclosure, gift, bequest, intestacy, or entailment. They could not, however, apply this law to themselves. If they grasped the general idea that they and their children were always at the direction of another, they had deciphered the message of the law for themselves.

The law treating slaves as property conflicted with the control statutes which treated the slaves as responsible, triable, teachable human beings. . . .

Inconsistency was not fatal to the dominant message communicated to the trustees and executors, lawyers and judges, auctioneers and sheriffs who had to manage the transfer of particular persons when ownership in them passed, and to the testators and heirs, donors and donees, buyers and sellers, mortgagors and creditors, who wanted to know the terms upon which ownership in particular persons could be conveyed. To all those interested in the disposition and distribution of slaves, the message communicated was single: individuals do not have to be looked at when a conveyance is made. . . .

Between 1705, when the definition of plantation slaves as real estate was enacted, and the Revolution, legislators and lawyers argued how far the metaphor of real estate should be pressed. Lenders wanting the largest tangible assets of the plantations as collateral wished that the slaves be as freely transmissible as other forms of personal property. Owners seeking credit had a corresponding need for slaves to be readily disposable. Against these interests ran the dynastic desire of the planters to have the slaves descend with the land to their families in perpetuity. . . .

Virginian lawyers of the eighteenth century, even when they were revolutionaries, it might be supposed, were so imprisoned by traditional legal assumptions about slavery that they had no choice but to ratify the legal institution. However universalist their proclamations of liberty, they lacked, it might be imagined, a concept which would correspond in law to what they announced as ideology. Suppositions of this sort would be mistaken. Only a dozen years old, new but already popular and prestigious, the *Commentaries on the Laws of England,* by the Professor of the Laws of England at Oxford, provided both a legal critique of slavery and a concept on which to base a law of universal liberty. . . .

In retrospect, Jefferson recalled two reasons for refusing to make the laws afresh with Blackstone as a basis. First, new laws would have to be "systematical.". . . Second, the result would be to "render property uncertain."

The first reason could not have been controlling. The old law was not systematized. Why should the new have been? . . .

The key difficulty is focused on in Jefferson's "render property uncertain." The property which would have been made most fundamentally uncertain was property in slaves. John Quincy Adams accurately described the committee's dilemma: If they had started afresh, "they must have restored slavery after having abolished it; they must have assumed to themselves all the odium of establishing it as a positive institution, directly in face of all the principles they had proclaimed."

Slavery, nonetheless, had to be dealt with. . . . Jefferson did the text on the control laws. The bill was reported to the legislature in 1779. Managed by James Madison, it was adopted without substantial alteration in 1785. . . .

Jefferson discarded the detail which had made the old control laws exact and hideous and substituted a simple scheme of elegant generality. Instead of specifically proscribing meetings of groups of slaves, the practice of medicine by slaves, hiding out by runaway slaves, and the lifting of a slave's hand in opposition to a white Christian, he prohibited "riots, routs, and unlawful assemblies, and seditious speeches." Instead of specifically designating thirty-nine lashes, castration, or death as sanction, he made each crime punishable by whipping at the discretion of a justice of the peace. The statute on false testimony of slaves disappeared. The new provision on seditious speeches was a far broader control of the use of language. Milder but more comprehensive, functionally the new statute did not differ from the colonial grotesquerie it replaced. Its message to the white community—the message of the legislature, the message drafted by Jefferson and approved by Jefferson, Pendleton, and

Wythe—was: We are with you in the use of measured force.

The opening clause of the new legislation parodied the revolutionaries' statement on the inalienable liberty of human beings. "Be it enacted by the General Assembly," the committee bill said, "that no persons shall henceforth be slaves within this commonwealth, except such as were so on the first day of this present session of the Assembly, and the descendants of the females of them." This was not unlike saying, "Be it enacted that no persons shall henceforth be convicts within this commonwealth except such as are already convicted and those subsequently found guilty by process of law." No one was born a hereditary slave in Virginia unless he was the descendant of a female slave. Still, the provision was not wholly innocuous or tautological: it banned the importation of slaves. But the ban on imports, increasing the value of slaves already within the commonwealth and to be born within it, did not touch the institution. The new statute proclaimed the lawfulness of slavery in Virginia, provided for its perpetuation, and left the slaves the option of "locking up their faculties" or providing the slaves of the next generation. . . .

The [work of] Wythe and Jefferson . . . may be measured not only against the principles of Blackstone but against the work of Edmund Burke, who in 1780 drafted and in 1792 proposed a code for the amelioration of the conditions of slavery in the British colonies. . . .

The difference between Burke's draft and the Virginians' statutes is this: accepting the slaves as human beings, Burke worked toward their enjoyment of human liberties; Jefferson and Wythe treated the slaves as human beings for the purposes of the control laws; they proposed no law by which their enjoyment of human liberties was recognized. . . .

For that decision they were responsible—that is, it must be recognized that they as human beings performed the acts by which slavery was continued as a legal institution. They chose to participate in the system. With their own hands they put on the masks of the law and imposed them on others.

The Virginia Paradox

...In 1768, in *Blackwell* v. *Wilkinson,* Wythe had argued that the real nature of a slave was "personalty." In 1770 he had won *Howell* v. *Netherland* by standing on the power of the legislature to cancel freedom. In 1792, in *Turpin* v. *Turpin,* he had ruled that slaves passed by will "as if they were chattels." In 1798, in *Fowler* v. *Saunders,* he had declared that a transfer of slaves was like a transfer of a quadruped or kitchen utensil. As a lawyer and as a judge, he had not challenged the power of legislatures and judges to suppress a birthright....

The split between the ideals of the American Revolution and the maintenance of slavery was evident to contemporaries like Tucker; it has now been comprehensively explored by David Brion Davis, who has probed with particular sensitivity Jefferson's "uncertain commitment" to universal liberty. The liberators were divided, knew they were divided, and were able to function because they entered a universe with distinctive rules.

Jefferson did not apply his reproach to Wythe. Wythe did not apply it to himself.... He took the legal universe to be self-contained. When he entered that special world, he accepted the masks of the law—they were the law's creations, not his. He did not see it as his fault that these fictions effected the distribution of slaves and the perpetuation of slavery....

The Virginia paradox was this: Wythe believed that human beings are by nature free. He believed that the legislature is not omnipotent over nature. He believed that the legislature can enslave human beings. Rule-centered, he perceived with sharpness the injustice of an unjust rule; he did not perceive the injustice of removing human beings from consideration as persons. The Virginia paradox is the legal paradox, generally.

At least half of the property cases before the Chancellor involved the disposition of slaves. He could not have compassion for each of them as a person and still be a judge. His role in a slave system necessitated the use of masks. If he acted at all in his judicial office, those he disposed of had to fall within an appropriate subdivision of property. He needed to suppress humanity in the objects he transferred. He had to impress upon them the mask of property. The operation was not wholly external.... He could not pay attention to his torment. He had to act with apathy. He had to suppress humanity in himself. He had to put on himself the mask of the court.

When one reads of the earnest efforts of young eighteenth-century lawyers to master Roman law, one could weep at their futility—what possible relevance had the learning of fifth-century Byzantium to the affairs of America? Tears would be misplaced. Learning the Roman law was far from ineffective indoctrination in the fiction-making power of a legal system. Citation of Roman law, as Wythe cited it in *Turpin* v. *Turpin,* was not mere harmless display of erudition; it was active evocation of the magic of the law. Roman law could make a horse a consul and did make a horse a priest; it could and did extinguish a person's past; and if it did these "impossible" things, it could and did unmake persons. Legal education has often been education in the making and unmaking of persons. Wythe was a superb teacher.

The essential was that no exceptions be permitted to break the spell. The control statutes, modeled on criminal law, had judges' options, sheriffs' options, prosecutors' options, owners' options. No one had options under the property concept, save the owner who had the option, following a prescribed ritual, to end the spell altogether and make his slave free. If emancipation was not granted, the property concept was absolute and all-enveloping for purposes of distribution and perpetuation....

George Wythe is the first of all the lawyers of the United States who from 1775 to 1865, North and South, kept slavery in existence. He is first not in that he caused the others to follow him, but in that, as professor of law, as legislator, as Chancellor of the Commonwealth of Virginia, he taught the others. His pupils followed in his path. Jefferson wanted to end the evil of slavery. So did Henry Clay, James Monroe, and John Marshall. Deploring the evil, they overcame their objections to it as Speaker, President, and Chief Justice, respectively, and sustained the system, accepting the power of the law to convert persons into personalty. They could believe in the natural law of freedom, and champion emancipation, and enforce slavery, so long as the legal universe was a special world with its own rules.

Like Wythe himself, they personally owned slaves. Their acceptance of the masks of the law did not blind them to the personalities of those they knew domestically. Sally Hemings, for example, his wife's half-sister and his slave, was a person Thomas Jefferson responded to when on an April day in Paris he spent two hundred francs on "clothes for Sally." Yet when he died her ownership moved under the property clauses of his will and her eventual fate had to depend on the claims of Jefferson's creditors not consuming the estate. The masks he had accepted, constructed, sustained, permitted him to distribute Sally Hemings in a fashion that would have been impossible if in the act of transmission he had to confront another living person. At the critical moments the masks of the law covered the faces of the slaves. Only an act of violence could shatter the concealing forms.

Slavery survived in Virginia after the Revolution not as an act of brute power and not as a discredited social habit, a colonial vestige repudiated by an enlightened ideology. It survived as a full-blown social institution with the control mechanisms and metaphors for transfer and distribution of the colonial regime intact. As an institution its survival was assured by the cataloguing power, the rule-making capacity, the indifference to persons of—the law? That is to depersonalize those responsible; better say—the lawyers. Without their professional craftsmanship, without their management of metaphor, without their loyalty to the system, the enslavement by words more comprehensive than any shackles could not have been forged.

Questions

1. What was the significance of the fact that the Virginia legislature required the slave laws to be read in churches?

2. Noonan says that the message of the slave laws to the masters was "the community is with you." Why would the masters need to hear this message?

3. What are the implications of Noonan's comment that the laws of property and inheritance are designed to "overcome death"? Is there a relationship between desire for immortality and private ownership of property?

4. What social institutions besides slavery can you think of as examples in which domination of some people by others is not only accepted but regarded as a beneficial practice? Does managerial control of labor fall into this category? What about teachers' control of students? Parents and children? Husbands and wives? In each of these situations, what is the relationship between the dominant person and the ruling class of society? How is the "magic" of the law involved in each of these situations? What is the underlying logic of this "magic"? Whose interests does it serve?

5. What significance do you find in the following facts? George Wythe had emancipated his mulatto slave, Michael Brown, and his housekeeper, Lydia Brodnax, and had prepared a will leaving property and stock in trust to support them. The rest of his estate was to go to his grandnephew, George Wythe Swinney. Apparently unhappy with this arrangement, Swinney poisoned both Wythe and Brown. Wythe lived long enough to disinherit Swinney, but Swinney could not be successfully prosecuted for murder. The reason: The chief witness, Lydia Brodnax, was prevented from testifying by the application of a Virginia law which permitted blacks to testify only against blacks.

When the Masks of the Law Are Stripped Away   *Peter d'Errico*

Jurisprudence has no meaning apart from the

Reprinted by permission from *Learning and the Law* (Winter, 1977). Copyright © 1977 by The American Bar Association. (Emended by the author.)

history of social struggle and the development of human consciousness. A total critique of law begins with an understanding of the dialectic of social and psychic change.

The Nature of a Total Critique

In developing a total criticism of the legal system, it is extremely helpful to look at the origins of abstraction. Always there is the interplay of psychology and politics, in which the law pretends to support basic human needs while at the same time actually removing these needs from the realm of action open to ordinary people. Early American law, concerned with protecting and advancing the rights and prerogatives of the developing ruling class, contains many examples of the process at work.

Ruling class fear of popular participation in American lawmaking took jurisprudential shape in what has been called the "instrumental conception" of law (Morton Horwitz, "The Emergence of an Instrumental Conception of American Law, 1780–1820," in *Law in American History,* 1971). The ruling class of merchants and politicians was concerned with consistency and official control in the formulation of legal rules. Control of juries by judges became a major issue. A demand arose for published reports of legal decisions, so as to relieve so-called uncertainty and contradiction. Courts for the first time began to treat some questions as "matters of law," and to reevaluate jury assessments of testimony. It is no coincidence that the governmental institutions which thus took shape in the United States were heavily weighted on the side of protecting the rights and privileges of minorities: the most powerful minority was the property owners (Baran and Sweezy, *Monopoly Capital,* 1966).

It is important to see how this early American conflict between popular democracy and the ruling class involved the co-optation and cooperation of the citizenry at both social and psychological levels. The popular demand was to open law and the legal process to democratic, local control. The ruling class response was to consolidate its control through the institutionalization of a new jurisprudence.

This institution-building occurred not simply as a matter of observable social behavior, but also, and more profoundly, as a matter of human consciousness. "The concept of institutionalization is misleading ... unless it includes the concept of internalization. At one level institutionalization can be consciously apprehended as repetitive and patterned aspects of social life. If institutionalization referred simply to this, such patterns could relatively easily be changed at any time according to the needs or wishes of particular interests. The point is that change is very difficult to achieve ... because the commitments to values are not entirely under conscious control ..." (Weinstein and Platt, *Psychoanalytic Sociology,* 1973).

It is thus the internalization of jurisprudence, not merely its institutionalization, with which we must be concerned. This is where the real power of mystification lies. The social struggle and dialectic presented in the conflict over access to the legal process in early America was a psychic and a social phenomenon, in which jurisprudence and economics played interwoven, complementary roles.

The triumph of the instrumental conception of law was built on the transition from a sacred to a secular mode of perception and explanation. It left, however, the basic patterns of power and thinking intact. (Calvin Woodard, "The Limits of Legal Realism: An Historical Perspective," in *New Directions in Legal Education,* Packer, Ehrlich and Pepper, 1972). As the common law lost its aura of ancient stability and certainty, the instrumentalists moved to fill the gap with their view of law. The goals of industrial and commercial growth upon which this view rested were portrayed by legal and political authorities as constituting the "public good." They could no longer call upon God, as in the common law, to be the ultimate source of consistency and validity for these principles. Instead, a new god—capital—was found to play the role of Guiding Hand in the formulation of legal rules. In this way, the role of the ruling class as the agents of a distant and abstract power had been preserved in the new jurisprudence.

Popular consciousness, only partially awakened from feudalistic slumber, rested again on the notion of legalism: the idea that positive legal authority exists in its own right and is for that reason to be respected. In the years to come, this jurisprudence, as the handmaiden to capitalism, would permit and defend the increasing centralization of wealth and power, the mechanization and rationalization of life, and the subordination of people and places to the abstract rule of property and profit.

A single legal concept or doctrine can cloud ordinary life, setting up the framework of a legalistic psychology for the supremacy of law. An example of such mystification is the concept of the "reasonable man," which is a major theoretical linchpin underlying the application of law to social conflict.

"Reasonable man" is that fictional character whose daily existence is lived out wholly within the bounds of rules and in accordance with the power system which creates, manipulates and enforces those rules. This obedient servant of the legal order is always ready to subordinate the situational and customary concerns of human life to the abstract admonitions articulated by legal power. He is the contrivance of a jealous legalism, used to rationalize the subjugation of real people to the claims and interests of the state. He is the idea and the essential myth of the ruling class.

A recent case decided by the Court of Appeals of the State of New Mexico is a clear example of this doctrine in action:

> The question of contributory negligence becomes one of law only when reasonable minds cannot differ on the question and readily reach the conclusion that plaintiff's conduct falls below the standard to which he should have conformed for his own protection....
>
> Given the foregoing facts we believe that plaintiff was contributorily negligent as a matter of law. The fact that plaintiff subjectively did not consider his actions dangerous is not the issue.... The issue is would a reasonable prudent person anticipate the danger of using his foot to dislodge a clog in an area where there were moving parts of the machine which would cause serious injury.
>
> ...Plaintiff asserts that there was an issue of fact as to "(w)hat effect the custom of the community had on the standard of care when all the witnesses testified it was the common custom in the community to do what plaintiff

did." Several witnesses testified by deposition that it was customary in the community to use one's foot to kick loose and unstop the machine when it became clogged.

> As stated in *Wills v. Paul* (24 Ill. App. 2d 417, 164 N.E. 2d 631 [1960]): "...In determining whether the particular acts of a plaintiff constitute negligence, the test is not the frequency with which other men commit such acts but whether the plaintiff at the time of the occurrence, used that degree of care which an ordinarily careful person would have used for his own safety under like circumstances...."
>
> "We find it difficult to accept a philosophy which asserts that negligent and careless conduct by frequent repetition in a community converts it into a non-negligent conduct..." *Ferguson v. Lounsberry*, (58 Ill. App. 2d 456, 207 N.E. 2d 309 [1965]). Custom in and of itself is not conclusive. It must meet the standard of ordinary care. (*Karl Cox, Jr. v. Karl Cox v. J.I. Case Company*, 89 N.M. 555, 555 P.2d 378 [1976]).

What we see here is a clear subordination of real people to abstract, mystical, "ordinary" persons of the law. The denial of real ordinariness in the affirmation of legal ordinariness is especially poignant in this case because the legal "masks" of "defendant" and "plaintiff" conceal a father-son relationship in which the son has worked for the father all of his adult life. The pain of a personal injury suffered in such circumstances, for which the real human beings are trying to obtain financial compensation from the artificial, corporate being, is ignored and compounded by three judges who rule from behind the mask of "the court," upholding the allied interests of law and capital.

Like every idea of the ruling class, the "reasonable man" is effective and "real" only to the extent that it is rooted in the minds of the masses of people who make up society. Every act of jurisprudence—in court opinion, scholarly text or journalist's report—aims to preserve, defend and deepen this root in the name of "respect for law." In becoming rooted, the figure of "reasonable man" is transformed into a psychological trap by which the political power of the state is brought to bear on situations of spontaneous and customary behavior. In the end, reason itself becomes perverted. What is "reasonable" is what serves the interests of power, and not what any person might be able to figure out by means of the intellect.

This, then, is the first feature of a real demystification and attack on abstraction. We must build a critique that does not fall into the trap of "partial criticism"—a critique in which one tries to hang on to political realities while attacking their psychology, or tries to maintain the psychological status quo while attacking the political order. What makes the whole enterprise of a critical study of law feel so risky is that one knows that this work is subversive of established power. Academic disciplines, like the processes of legalism itself, do not encourage such criticism. They attempt to bottle the subversive power of awareness, providing approved and pre-formulated questions and modes of questioning designed to snare the thinker and observer into the net of the discipline.

Procedure, which has been called the heart of the law, operates by similar seduction. It captures the forces of social conflict by appearing to offer personal solutions to systemic and organic problems. Since this is ultimately not possible, there is neither social resolution nor personal satisfaction.

In the meantime, those who have lost their way in the legal maze are probably grateful to escape with their skins.

Questions

1. What is the meaning of legal certainty and consistency? Do you see a conflict between legal consistency and democratic government? If so, which of the two is more valuable? Why? Is "legal consistency" used as a code phrase for preserving the position of the dominant powers in society? Is it a part of what John Noonan calls the "magic" of the law?

2. What are the means and motivation by which the masses of people in society come to believe in the values of the dominant minority?

3. How is it that economic growth could take the place of God as the basic rationalization for law?

4. How does an abstract concept become "real" to people? What is the relationship between the abstract ideas in people's minds and the actual material circumstances in which they live? Is the "magic" of law involved in this relationship?

5. What is the significance of the conflict between law and custom as alternative ways of judging people's behavior?

2   Legal Relations and Social Relations

Society consists of relations among people in the context of the natural environment. These relations are built into a structure of power with legal and economic aspects. Societies are different from one another according to the needs of people to relate to different environments, and also as a result of choices made in the history of the group's development. These social differences are reflected in the kinds of legal structures that are built in each society.

An understanding of law in context requires

that we see the ways in which societies are different. This means that we must pay attention to the kinds of relations that exist among people, and also to the kinds of relations that exist between groups of people and the environment each group occupies.

In some ways, the legal structure of a society may serve as a mask, concealing the real ways in which people live and are organized in their environment. This is especially true in societies in which a ruling class hides behind a facade of legal equality for all citizens. In other ways, a legal structure can serve as a window to the inner workings of a society, letting the watcher see what values are important to the people in the society.

In either instance, whether the law is masking or showing the real relations among people, the important point to keep in mind is that *law and society are not the same thing*. "Citizens of the state" is not the same as "people of the country." One refers to a legal category; the other refers to living beings inhabiting a geographical place. Law exists in society and has effects on it.

It may be that the people of a country are organized into a state structure in which they are citizens. The differences and similarities between their state and another will reflect and depend upon the differences and similarities between their way of life and the other

group's. These ways of life are organic and cannot be understood in terms of legalities alone. This is especially clear when the state organization is taken over by another society, as may be the case after war and·conquest. In this event, the difference between law and society will be even more apparent than where the legal structure is indigenous to the society.

The readings that follow explore the connections and gaps between legal structure and social structure. Notice as you read how these structures consist of relations among people. Notice how these relations are connected to environments, so that different places give rise to different human relations. Pay attention to the ways in which hierarchies appear and disappear, and to the ways in which people create communities. Notice how social change is reflected in legal change, and how one kind of social structure changes into another.

The Rule of Law Versus the Order of Custom   *Stanley Diamond*

The lowest police employee of the civilized state has more "authority" than all the organs of gentilism combined. But the mightiest prince and the greatest statesman or general of civilization may look with envy on the spontaneous and undisputed esteem that was the privilege of the least gentile sachem. The one stands in the middle of society, the other is forced to assume a position outside and above it.

—Engels

We must distinguish the rule of law from the authority of custom. In a recent effort to do so (which I shall critically examine because it is so typical), Paul Bohannan . . . contends that laws result from double institutionalization. He means by this no more than the lending of a specific force, a cutting edge, to the functioning of cus-

tomary institutions: marriage, the family, religion. But, he tells us, the laws so emerging assume a character and dynamic of their own. They form a structured, legal dimension of society; they do not merely reflect, but interact with, given institutions. Therefore, Bohannan is led to maintain that laws are typically out of phase with society, and it is this process that is both a symptom and cause of social change. The laws of marriage, to illustrate Bohannan's argument . . . are not synonymous with the institution of marriage. They reinforce certain rights and obligations while neglecting others. Moreover, they subject partners defined as truant to intervention by an external, impersonal agency whose decisions are sanctioned by the power of the police.

Bohannan's sociological construction does have the virtue of denying the primacy of the legal order and of implying that law is generic to unstable (or progressive) societies, but it is more or less typical of abstract efforts to define the eternal essence of the law and it begs the significant questions. Law has no such eternal essence; it has a definable historical nature. Thus, if we inquire into the structure of the contemporary institutions which, according to Bohannan, stand in a primary relation to the law, we find that their customary content has drastically diminished. . . .

We live in a law-ridden society; law has cannibalized the institutions which it presumably reinforces or with which it interacts. Accordingly, morality continues to be reduced to or confused with legality. In civil society, we are encouraged to assume that legal behavior is the measure of moral behavior. . . . Efforts to legislate conscience by an external political power are the antithesis of custom: customary behavior comprises precisely those aspects of social behavior which are traditional, moral and religious—in short, conventional and nonlegal. Put another way, custom *is* social morality. The relation between custom and law is basically one of contradiction, not continuity.

The customary and the legal orders are historically, not logically related. . . . William Seagle writes:

> The dispute whether primitive societies have law or custom, is not merely a dispute over words. Only confusion can result from treating them as interchangeable phenomena. If custom is spontaneous and automatic, law is the product of organized force. . . .

Parenthetically, one should note that students of primitive society who use the term "customary law" blur the issue semantically, but nonetheless recognize the distinction.

It is this over-all legalization of behavior in modern society which Bohannan fails to interpret. In Fascist Germany, for example, laws flourished as never before. By 1941, more edicts had been proclaimed than in all the years of the Republic and the Third Reich. At the same time, ignorance of the law inevitably increased. In a sense, the very force of the law depends upon ignorance of its specifications, which is hardly recognized as a mitigating circumstance. As Seagle states, law is not definite and certain while custom is vague and uncertain. Rather, the converse holds. Cus-

tomary rules must be clearly known; they are not sanctioned by organized political force, hence serious disputes about the nature of custom would destroy the integrity of society. But laws may always be invented and stand a good chance of being enforced: "Thus, the sanction is far more important than the rule in the legal system . . . but the tendency is to minimize the sanction and to admire the rule."

In Fascist Germany, customs did not become laws through a process of double institutionalization. Rather, repressive laws, conjured up in the interests of the Nazi Party and its supporters, cannibalized the institutions of German society. Even the residual, customary authority of the family was assaulted: children were encouraged to become police informers, upholding the laws against their kin. "The absolute reign of law has often been synonymous with the absolute reign of lawlessness."

Certainly, Germany under Hitler was a changing society, if hardly a progressive one, but it was a special case of the general process in civilization through which the organs of the state have become increasingly irresistible. It will be recalled that Bohannan takes the domination of law over custom to be symptomatic of changing societies. But the historical inadequacy of his argument lies exactly here: he does not intimate the over-all direction of that change and therefore fails to clarify the actual relation between custom and law. Accordingly, the notion that social change is a function of the law, and vice versa, implies a dialectic that is out of phase with historical reality. . . .

Laws follow social change and reflect prevailing social relationships, but are the cause of neither. . . . This view of the relationship between law and society accords with aspects of the Marxist perspective on the history of culture. Customary societies are said to precede legal societies, an idea which, semantics aside, most students of historical jurisprudence would accept. But Marxists envision the future as being without laws as we know them, as involving a return to custom, so to speak, on a higher level, since the repressive, punitive and profiteering functions of law will become superfluous. Conflicts of economic and political interest will be resolved through the equitable reordering of institutions. Law for the Marxists and most classical students of historical jurisprudence, is the cutting edge of the state—but Marxists, insisting on both a historical and normative view of man, define the state as the instrument of the ruling class, anticipating its dissolution with the abolition of classes and the common ownership of the basic means of production. Sir Henry Maine equates the history of individual property with that of civilization:

> Nobody is at liberty to attack several property and to say at the same time that he values civilization. The history of the two cannot be disentangled. Civilization is nothing more than the name for the . . . order . . . perpetually reconstituting itself under a vast variety of solvent influences, of which infinitely the most powerful have been those which have, slowly, and in some parts of the world much less perfectly than others, substituted several property for collective ownership.

In the words of Jeremy Bentham: "Property and law are born together and die together."

Thus, law is symptomatic of the emergence of the state; the legal sanction is not simply the cutting edge of institutions at all times and in all places. The double institutionalization to which Bohannan refers needs redefinition. Where it does occur, it is a historical process of unusual complexity and cannot be defined as the simple passage of custom into law. It occurs, as we shall see, in several modes. Custom—spontaneous, traditional, personal, commonly known, corporate, relatively unchanging—is the modality of primitive society; law is the instrument of civilization, of political society sanctioned by organized force, presumably above society at large and buttressing a new set of social interests. Law and custom both involve the regulation of behavior but their characters are entirely distinct. No evolutionary balance has been struck between developing law and custom, whether traditional or emergent.

Archaic Law and Local Custom

The simple dichotomy between primitive society and civilization does not illustrate the passage from the customary to the legal order. The most critical and revealing period in the evolution of law is that of archaic societies, the local segments of which are the cultures most often studied by anthropologists. More precisely, the earlier phases of these societies, which I call proto-states, represent a transition from the primitive kinship-based communities to the class-structured polity. In such polities, law and custom exist side by side; this gives us the opportunity to examine their connections, distinctions and differential relationship to the society at large. The customary behavior typical of the local groups—joint families, clans, villages—maintains most of its force; the Vietnamese, for example, still say: "The customs of the village are stronger than the law of the emperor." Simultaneously, the civil power, comprising bureaucracy and sovereign, the dominant emerging class, issues a series of edicts that have the double purpose of confiscating "surplus" goods and labor for the support of those not directly engaged in production, while attempting to deflect the loyalties of the local groups to the center.

These archaic societies are the great historical watershed; it is here that Sir Henry Maine and Paul Vinogradoff located the passage from status to contract, from the kinship to the territorial principle, from extended familial controls to public law. For our understanding of the law, we need not be concerned with the important distinctions among archaic societies, or with the precise language or emphases of those scholars who have recognized their centrality. The significant point is that they are transitional. Particularly in their early phase, they are the agencies that transmute customary forms of order into legal sanction. Here we find a form of double institutionalization functioning explicitly. We can witness, so to speak, what appears to be the emergence of a custom, in defense of the kinship principle against the assault of the state, and the subsequent shift of the customary function into its own opposite as a legal function. The following example from the archaic proto-state of Dahomey, prior to the French conquest in 1892, will make this process clear.

Traditionally in Dahomey, each person was said to have three "best" friends, in descending order of intimacy and importance. This transitional institution, . . . of the same species as blood brotherhood, reinforced the extended family structure, which continued to exist in the early state, but was being thrown into question as a result of the political and economic demands made by the emerging civil power. So for example, the best friend... of a man charged with a civil crime could be seized by the king's police in his stead. However, these traditional friendships were so socially critical, so deeply held, so symbolically significant that the person charged, whether or not he had actually committed a civil breach, would be expected to turn himself in rather than implicate a friend in his punishment. Whether or not he did so, the custom of friendship was given a legal edge and converted by the civil power into a means of enforcing its will. This example of double institutionalization has the virtue of explicitly revealing the contradiction between law and custom. But there are other examples in which the law appears as a reinforcement of customary procedure.

In eleventh-century Russia, for instance, Article 1 of the codified law states:

> If a man kills a man... the brother is to avenge his brother; the son, his father; or the father, his son; and the son of the brother (of the murdered man) or the son of his sister, their respective uncle. If there is no avenger (the murderer) pays 40 grivna wergeld....

Similarly, circa A.D. 700, the law of the Visigoths states: "Whoever shall have killed a man, whether he committed a homicide intending to or not intending to... let him be handed over into the potestas of the parents or next of kin of the deceased...." In these instances, a custom has been codified by an external agency, thus assuming legal force, with its punitive character sharpened. Such confirmation is both the intimation of legal control and the antecedent of institutional change beyond the wish or conception of the family....

Simpson and Stone explain this apparent reinforcement of custom by the civil power as follows:

> Turning then to the role of law in the emergent political society... it is true that political institutions, independent of the kin and the supernatural, had risen to power; yet these insti-

tutions were young, weak and untried. Their encroachment on the old allegiance was perforce wary and hesitating. Social cohesion still seemed based on nonpolitical elements, and these elements were therefore protected....

Ultimately, local groups have maintained their autonomy when their traditional economies were indispensable to the functioning of the entire society. They could be hedged around by restrictions, harassed by law or as we have seen, they could be "legally" confirmed in their customary usage. But so long as the central power depended on them for support, in the absence of any alternative mode or source of production, their integrity could be substantially preserved....

As the state develops, according to Maine, "the individual is steadily substituted for the family as the unit of which civil laws take account." And in Jhering's words, "The progress of law consists in the destruction of every natural tie, in a continued process of separation and isolation." That is to say, the family increasingly becomes a reflex of society at large. The legal stipulation that spouses may not testify against each other appears as one of the last formal acknowledgements of familial integrity and the exception that proves the historical case. Clearly, the nuclear family in contemporary, urban civilization, although bound by legal obligations, has minimal autonomy; obviously, the means of education, subsistence and self-defense are outside the family's competence. It is in this sense that, given the absence of mediating institutions having a clearly defined independent authority, the historical tendency of all state structures vis-à-vis the individual may be designated as totalitarian. Indeed, the state creates the disaffiliated individual whose bearings thus become bureaucratic or collective; the juridical "person," who may even be a corporation doing business, is merely the legal reflection of a social process. If "totalization" is the state process, totalitarianism cannot be confined to a particular political ideology but is, so to speak, the ideology, explicit or not, of political society.

This étatist tendency has its origins in archaic society. We can observe it with unusual clarity in the proto-states of sub-Saharan Africa. In East

Africa, pastoralists, competing for land, and in West Africa, militaristic clans, catalyzed by the Arab, and, later, the European trade, notably in slaves, conquered horticulturalists, thereby providing the major occasions for the growth of civil power. Since the basic means of exploiting the environment in these polities remained substantially unchanged, and, to some extent, survived under colonialism, we can reconstruct through chronicles extending back for centuries and by means of contemporary field work, the structure of early state controls, which evolved in the absence of writing and the systematic codification of law. . . .

In such societies, Rattray tells us, referring to Ashanti:

> the small state was ever confronted with the kindred organization which was always insidiously undermining its authority by placing certain persons outside its jurisdiction. It could only hold its own, therefore, by throwing out an ever-widening circle to embrace those loyalties which were lost to it owing to the workings of the old tribal organization which has survived everywhere. . . .

Concerning the Islamized Nupe of the Nigerian Middle Belt, Nadel saw "a much more subtle development and a deeper kind of antagonism [than interstate warfare], namely, the almost eternal antagonism of developed State versus that raw material of the Community which, always and everywhere, must form the nourishing soil from which alone the state can grow." And Engels refers to the "irreconcilable opposition of gentile society to the state."

I have documented this conflict in detail in a study of the Dahomean proto-state. There, as elsewhere, it is apparent that the contradictory transition from customs to specified laws, double institutionalization if you will, is by no means the major source of law. Whether the law arises latently in confirmation of previous usage or through the transformation of some aspect of custom which the law itself may have provoked, as in the ambiguous example of the "best friend," neither circumstance brings us to the heart of the matter. For we learn, by studying intermediate

societies, that the laws so typical of them are unprecedented; they do not emerge through a process of double institutionalization, however defined. They arise in opposition to the customary order of the antecedent kin or kin-equivalent groups; they represent a new set of social goals pursued by a new and unanticipated power in society. These goals can be reduced to a single complex imperative: the imposition of the census-tax-conscription system. The territorial thrust of the early state, along with its vertical social entrenchment, demanded conscription of labor, the mustering of an army, the levying of taxes and tribute, the maintenance of a bureaucracy and the assessment of the extent, location and numbers of the population being subjected. These were the major direct or indirect occasions for the development of civil law.

The primary purpose of a census is indicative. Census figures provide the basis on which taxes are apportioned among conquered districts and on which tribute in labor is exacted from kin units. The census is also essential for conscripting men into the army. . . .

The census figures represented the potential power of the state and were carefully guarded; perhaps they were the first state secret. The act and intent of the census turned persons into ciphers and abstractions; people did all they could to avoid being counted. Suspicion persists; even in the United States the authorities during the period of census taking find it necessary to assert that census information will not be used to tax or otherwise penalize the individual and in fact, to do so is said to be against the law.

The double meanings of certain critical terms in common English use—"custom," "duty" and "court," reveal this conflict between local usage and the census-tax-conscription system of the early state. We have been speaking of custom as traditional or conventional nonlegal behavior, but custom also refers to a tax routinely payable to the state for the transportation of goods across territorial borders. All such taxes are clearly defined legal impositions, frequently honored in the breach, and they do not have the traditional command of custom. . . .

Fiscal or legal coercion and political imposition

were not the purpose of these ancestral ceremonies which ritually reenacted reciprocal bonds. The customs of the sovereign were laws, the ceremonies of the kin groups were customs.

Similarly, the term *duty* implies a moral obligation on the one hand and a tax on the other. Naturally, we assume that it is the duty of citizens to pay taxes: the paradox inherent in the term becomes more obvious as we examine archaic civilizations.

The term *court* is analogously ambivalent. On the one hand, it refers to the residence or entourage of the sovereign; on the other, to a place where civil justice is dispensed, but at their root the functions fuse. The prototypical juridical institution was, in fact, the court of the sovereign where legislation was instituted, for which no precedent or formal analogue existed on the local level....

Clearly, the function of the court was not primarily the establishment of order. In primitive societies, as in the traditional sectors of protostates, there already existed built-in mechanisms for the resolution of conflict. Generally speaking (as Max Gluckman, among others, has shown), in such societies conflicts generated by the ordinary functioning of social institutions were resolved as part of the customary ritual cycle integral to the institutions themselves. With regard to more specific breaches, we recall Rattray's observation on the Ashanti: "Corporate responsibility for every act was an established principle which survived even the advent of...the administration of public justice." That is to say the kin unit was the juridical unit, just as it was the economic and social unit. Furthermore,

> Causes which give rise to the greater part of present "civil" actions were practically nonexistent. Inheritance, ownership of moveable and nonmoveable property, status of individuals, rules of behavior and morality were matters inevitably settled by the customary law, with which everyone was familiar from childhood, and litigation regarding such matters was... almost inconceivable. Individual contract, moreover, from the very nature of the community with which we are concerned, was also un-

known, thus removing another possible, fruitful source of litigation.

The primary purpose of the historically emerging court, the sovereign's entourage and habitation, was to govern....

In the census-tax-conscription system, every conceivable occasion was utilized for the creation of law in support of bureaucracy and sovereign. We observe no abstract principle, no impartial justice, no *precedent,* only the spontaneous opportunism of a new class designing the edifice of its power. It should be re-emphasized, however, that in certain instances formal analogues for civil imposition existed on the local level, but no formal or functional precedents. Civil taxation, for example, can be rationalized in the context of reciprocal gift-giving in the localities, but such gift-giving was not confirmed by law or specifically used by the sovereign; similarly, corvée labor is a political analogue of local cooperative work groups. But such evolutionary and dialectical relationships are most important for their distinctions.

Stubbs writes about the Norman kings that "it was mainly for the sake of the profits that early justice was administered at all." Burton relates that at Whydah in Dahomey in the event of a financial dispute, the Yevogan, the leading bureaucrat in the district, sat in judgment. For his services, he appropriated half the merchandise involved, in the name of the king and another quarter for various lesser officials. The remainder presumably went to the winning contestant in the judicial duel. Among the Ashanti, the central authority relied on the proceeds of litigation as a fruitful means for replenishing a depleted treasury. Litigation, Rattray notes, came actually to be encouraged.

Tolls were an important source of revenue. In Ashanti, the king had all the roads guarded; all traders were detained until inquiries were made about them, whereupon they were allowed to pass on payment of gold dust. W. Bosman writes that in early eighteenth century Whydah, "in proportion to his country, the king's revenue is very large, of which I believe, he hath above one thousand collectors who dispose themselves throughout the whole land in all market roads and passages, in order to gather the king's toll which amounts to an incredible sum, for there is nothing so mean sold in the whole kingdom that the king hath no toll for it. . . ."

The punishment for the theft of property designated as the king's was summary execution by kangaroo courts organized on the spot by the king's agents. . . .

In Maitland's words, "the king has a peace that devours all others." If in these proto-states, the sovereign power is not yet fully effective, it nonetheless strives to that monopoly of force which characterizes the mature state.

The purpose and abundance of laws inevitably provoked breaches. The civil authority, in fact, continually probed for breaches and frequently manufactured them. . . .

Thus, rape was invented as a civil crime. If rape had occurred in the traditional joint-family villages (and such an occurrence would have been rare, as indicated by the necessity of civil definition), the wrong could have been dealt with by composition (the ritualized giving of goods to the injured party), ritual purification, ridicule and, perhaps for repeated transgressions, banishment; the customary machinery would have gone into effect automatically, probably on the initiative of the family of the aggressor. Such examples as this only sharpen the point that in early states crimes seem to have been invented to suit the laws. The latent purpose of the law was punishment in the service and profit of the state, not prevention or the protection of persons, not the healing of the breach. As Seagle indicates, "The criminal law springs into life in every great period of class conflict," and this is most obviously the case during the initial phases of state formation. . . .

One may even state that the substantial rationale for law developed after the fact of its emergence. For example, civil protection of the market place or highway was certainly not necessary to the degree implied in the archaic edicts at the time they were issued. Joint-family markets and village trails were not ordinarily dangerous places, if we are to believe the reports of the earliest

chroniclers as well as those of more contemporary observers. More significantly if trouble had developed, the family, clan or village was capable of dealing with it. But, in an evolving state, the presence of the king's men would itself be a primary cause of disruption. Indeed, as Quénum, a descendant of Dahomean commoners, informs us the soldiers were referred to as bandits and predators who victimized many people. Sometimes their forays were confined to a compound, where someone, whether man, woman or child, resided who had spoken badly of the sovereign or whom the king suspected. . . .

As the integrity of the local groups declined, a process which . . . must have taken generations or even centuries, conditions doubtless developed which served as an ex post facto rationalization for edicts already in effect. In this sense, laws became self-fulfilling prophecies. Crime and the laws which served it were, then, co-variants of the evolving state. . . .

The intention of the civil power is epitomized in the sanctions against homicide and suicide; indeed, they were among the very first civil laws. Just as the sovereign is said to own the land, intimating the mature right of eminent domain, so the individual is ultimately conceived as the chattel of the state. In Dahomey, persons were conceived as *les choses du monarque*. Eminent domain in persons and property, even where projected as a fiction, is the cardinal prerequisite of the census-tax-conscription system. We recall that Maine designated the individual the unit of which the civil law steadily takes account. Seagle stated the matter as follows: "By undermining the kinship bond, they [the early civil authorities] made it easier to deal with individuals, and the isolation of the individual is a basic precondition for the growth of law."

Homicide, then, was regarded as an offense against the state. In Rattray's words, "The blow which struck down the dead man would thus appear to have been regarded as aimed also at the . . . central authority." In Ashanti, homicide was punishable by death in its most horrible form as customarily defined, in Dahomey, by death or conscription into the army. There is a nuance here which should not be overlooked. By making homicide, along with the theft of the king's property, a capital offence, the sovereign power discouraged violent opposition to the imposition of the civil order. . . .

Traditionally, murder in a joint-family village was a tort—a private, remediable wrong—which could stimulate a blood feud, not to be confused with the *lex talionis,* until redress, though not necessarily injury in kind, was achieved. But a breach was most often settled by composition. As Paul Radin put it: "The theory of an eye for an eye . . . never really held for primitive people. . . . Rather it was replacement for loss with damages." And this is echoed by Peristiany: "they claim restitution or private damages and not social retribution." In any case, the family was fully involved. "The family was a corporation," said Rattray, and "it is not easy to grasp what must have been the effect . . . of untold generations of thinking and acting . . . in relation to one's group. The Ashanti's idea of what we term moral responsibility for his actions must surely have been more developed than in peoples where individualism is the order of the day." This more or less typical anthropological observation makes it clear that the law against homicide was not a "progressive" step, as if some abstract right were involved which the state, the moral idea coming of age, finally understood and sought to establish. "Anti-social conduct [is] exceptional in small kinship groups," writes Margery Perham of the Igbo. Crimes of violence were rare, Richard Burton reported of Dahomey, and "murder virtually unknown."

Acts of violence, of course, must be distinguished from crimes of violence. The incidence, occasion for, and character of violence in primitive societies is a subject of the utmost importance. But the question here has to do with crimes in which violence is used as a means to an end, such as the theft of property. In contemporary societies, unpremeditated acts of personal violence that have no ulterior motive, so-called crimes of passion, may not be penalized or carry minor degrees of guilt, that is, their status as legally defined crimes is ambiguous. This would certainly seem to reflect a historically profound distinction

between crime and certain types of violence; in primitive societies violence tends to be personally structured, nondissociative and thereby self-limiting. As with other crimes defined by civil law, crimes of violence may have increased as the social autonomy, economic communalism and reciprocity of the kin units weakened. But this is much less important than Dalzel's observation that in Dahomey "many creatures have been put to death . . . without having committed any crime at all," thus exemplifying the power of the sovereign literally to command the lives of his citizens. . . .

The law against suicide, a capital offense, was the apotheosis of political absurdity. The individual, it was assumed, had no right to take his own life; that was the sole prerogative of the state, whose property he was conceived to be. The fanatical nature of the civil legislature in claiming sole prerogative to the lives of its subjects is conclusively revealed among the Ashanti, where, if the suicide was a murderer, "the central authority refused to be cheated thus and the long arm of the law followed the suicide to the grave from which, if his kinsmen should have dared to bury him, he was dragged to stand trial." This contrasts remarkably, if logically, with the behavior of the more primitively structured Igbo, as reported by Victor Uchendu, an anthropologist who is himself an Igbo:

> Homicide is an offense against *ala*—the earth deity. If a villager is involved, the murderer is expected to hang himself, after which . . . daughters of the village perform the rite of . . . sweeping away the ashes of murder. If the murderer has fled, his extended family must also flee, and the property of all is subject to raids. When the murderer is eventually caught, he is required to hang himself to enable the [daughters of the village] to perform their rites. It is important to realize that the village has no power to impose capital punishment. In fact, no social group or institution has this power. Everything affecting the life of the villager is regulated by custom. The life of the individual is highly respected; it is protected by the earth-goddess. The villagers can bring social pressure, but the murderer must hang himself.

It can hardly be argued that the purpose of the civil sanction against suicide was to diminish its incidence or to propagate a superior moral consciousness. Dare we say, as with other crimes, that attempts at suicide increased as society became more thoroughly politicized? The law against suicide reveals, in the extreme, the whole meaning and intent of civil law at its origins. In the proto-state, the quintessential struggle was over the lives and labor of the people, who, still moving in a joint family context, were nonetheless conceived to be *les choses du monarque.*

Law and Disorder

If revolutions are the acute, episodic signs of civilizational discontent, the rule of law, from Sumer or Akkad to New York or Moscow, has been the chronic symptom of the disorder of institutions. E. B. Tylor stated: "A constitutional government, whether called republic or kingdom, is an arrangement by which the nation governs itself by means of the machinery of a military despotism."

The generalization lacks nuance, but we can accept it if we bear in mind what seems to be Tylor's point of reference: "Among the lessons to be learnt from the life of rude tribes is how society can go on without the policeman to keep order." When he alludes to constitutional government, Tylor was not distinguishing its ultimate sanction from that of any other form of the state: all political society is based on repressive organized force. In this he was accurate. For pharaohs and presidents alike have always made a public claim to represent the common interest, indeed to incarnate the common good. Only a Plato or a Machiavelli in search of political harmony, or a Marx in search of political truth, has been able to penetrate this myth of the identity between ruler and ruled, of equality under the law. The tradition of Plato and Machiavelli commends the use of the "royal" or "noble lie," while that of Marx exposes and rejects the power structure (ultimately the state) that propagates so false a political consciousness. On this issue, I follow Marx....

The legal order, which Plato idealized, is as

Tylor maintained and Marx understood, synonymous with the power of the state. "The state," writes Paul Vinogradoff, "has assumed the monopoly of political co-ordination. It is the state which rules, makes laws and eventually enforces them by coercion. Such a state did not exist in ancient times. The commonwealth was not centered in one sovereign body towering immeasurably above single individuals and meting out to everyone his portion of right." And Engels, reflecting on the origins of the state, asserts: "The right of the state to existence was founded on the preservation of order in the interior and the protection against the barbarians outside, but this order was worse than the most disgusting disorder, and the barbarians against whom the state pretended to protect its citizens were hailed by them as saviors." Moreover, "The state created a public power of coercion that did no longer coincide with the old self-organized and (self) armed population." Finally, in a passage that epitomizes the West's awareness of itself, Engels writes:

> The state, then, is by no means a power forced on society at a certain stage of evolution. It is the confession that this society has become hopelessly divided against itself, has estranged itself in irreconcilable contradictions which it is powerless to banish. In order that these contradictions, these classes with conflicting economic interests may not annihilate themselves and society in a useless struggle, a power becomes necessary that stands apparently above society and has the function of keeping down the conflicts and maintaining "order." And this power, the outgrowth of society, but assuming supremacy over it and becoming more and more divorced from it, is the state....

In a word, the state is the alienated form of society....

The Response to Civil Law

I agree with Nadel that in the transition from primitive to political society the means of control and integration employed were, in a wider sense, "all...deliberately conceived and [executed]: they are agencies of an assimilation conscious of itself and of the message which it carries." Finally, we are led to ask, as did Nadel about the Nupe:

> What did the tax-paying law-abiding citizen receive in return for allegiance to king and nobility? Was extortion, bribery, brutal force, the only aspect under which the state revealed itself to the populace? The people were to receive, theoretically, on the whole, one thing: security—protection against external and internal enemies, and general security for carrying out the daily work, holding markets, using the roads. We have seen what protection and security meant in reality. At their best, they represented something very unequal and very unstable. This situation must have led to much tension and change within the system and to frequent attempts to procure better safeguards for civil rights.

The struggle for civil rights, then, is a response to the imposition of civil law. With the destruction of the primitive base of society, civil rights have been defined and redefined as a reaction to drastic changes in the socioeconomic structure— the rise of caste and class systems, imperialism, modern war, technology as a means of social exploitation, maldistribution and misuse of resources, racial hatred. The right to socially and economically fruitful work, for example, which did not come into question in a primitive society or in a traditional sector of an early state (and therefore was not conceived to be a stipulated right) becomes an issue under capitalism. The demand implies a need for profoundly changing and, if not changing, discarding the system and indicates that our sense of the appropriately human has very ancient roots indeed. However, the struggle for civil rights reminds us that legislation alone has no force beyond the potential of the social system that generates it. . . .

Procedure is the individual's last line of defense in contemporary civilization, wherein all other associations to which he may belong have become subordinate to the state. The elaboration of procedure is a unique if fragile feature of more fully evolved states, in compensation, so to speak, for the radical isolation of the individual; procedure permits the individual to hold the line, while working toward associations designed to

replace the state. In the proto-states, the harshness of rudimentary procedure was countered by the role of the kinship units which, as we recall, retained a significant measure of functional socioeconomic autonomy and, therefore, of local political cohesion. But "law has its origin in the pathology of social relations and functions only when there are frequent disturbances of the social equilibrium." Law arises in the breach of a prior customary order and increases in force with the conflicts that divide political societies internally and among themselves. Law and order is the historical illusion; law versus order is the historical reality. . . .

Questions

1. Why does Diamond say that custom is definite and known whereas law is vague and uncertain? What does this mean?

2. What are the implications of the fact that the institution of private property is linked with the growth of law and the state? Do you think that private property could exist today without the state?

3. What are the forces that bind people together in groups and societies? What are the forces that split people apart? What are the functions of law and custom in regard to these forces?

4. Can you think of modern examples of the struggle between law and custom? (Recall the New Mexico case discussed in the preceding section and in chapter one.) What does Diamond mean when he says that this is a struggle "over the lives and labor of the people"?

5. What is the significance of the fact that the etymology of certain legal words reveals a "double meaning" in contrast to the original meanings of these words ("custom," "duty," "court," and so on)? Can you think of other examples in which law takes over language and changes its meaning? What functions are served by this process of applying new meanings to old terms?

6. Diamond shows links between the historical development of law and the power and profit of a new ruling class in society. Do you think these links exist today? Can you give examples?

7. Diamond says that customary rituals serve to

"heal" situations of social trouble, while legal procedures serve only to extend the power of the state in cases of trouble between people. What does he mean? Does this seem true today? Is there any source of healing left in society if law has totally "cannibalized" custom?

8. Diamond notes that the law against suicide presumes that the state *owns* each individual person. Does this concept bear any relation to the ways in which property served as a *mask* for people under slave law?

9. What does it mean to say "the state is the alienated form of society"?

10. Diamond says that "procedure is the individual's last line of defense in contemporary civilization." How can this be, if procedure is a part of the legal system?

A Land of Giants and Pygmies   *The Duke Adolphus Frederick of Mecklenburg*

Ruanda is certainly the most interesting country in the German East African Protectorate—in fact, in all Central Africa—chiefly on account of its ethnographical and geographical position. Its interest is further increased by the fact that it is one of the last negro kingdoms governed autocratically by a sovereign sultan, for German supremacy is only recognized to a very limited extent.

Added to this, it is a land flowing with milk and honey, . . . a land which offers the brightest of prospects to the white settler. . . .

To anyone with an intimate knowledge of African affairs it seemed a sheer impossibility that so powerful a sovereign, the ruler over some one and a half million people, would voluntarily submit to the new regime and agree to enter upon no undertakings within his vast, thickly populated, and unexplored realms except by permission of the European Resident.

To compel him to do so would have meant bloody wars and an enormous sacrifice of human life as the inevitable consequence. The sudden change of existing conditions, too, would have involved a heavy pecuniary sacrifice, as the government would have found it necessary, with such a large population, to appoint a relatively large number of European officials. As such measures would have proved impracticable, complete anarchy would have followed.

So the country was therefore allowed to retain its traditional organization, and the sultan was given full jurisdiction over his fellow-people, under control of the Resident, who was to suppress cruelty as far as possible. In one word, the government does not acknowledge the Sultan as a sovereign lord, but fully recognizes his authority as chief of his clan. Kindred tribes, non-resident in Ruanda, are therefore not subject to the Sultan's jurisdiction, but are under the administration of the Resident.

The fundamental principle is the same with all Residents. It is desired to strengthen and enrich the Sultan and persons in authority, and to increase thereby their interest in the continuance of German rule, so that the desire for revolt shall die away, as the consequence of a rebellion would be a dwindling of their revenues. At the same time, by steadily controlling and directing the Sultan and using his powers, civilizing influences would be introduced. Thus by degrees, and almost imperceptibly to the people and to the Sultan himself, he eventually becomes nothing less than the executive instrument of the Resident. . . .

Similarly to their sovereign ruler, the chiefs are descended from various distinguished families or clans. These clans hold land, pay taxes to the Sultan, are keen to avenge the bloodshed of kinsmen, and possess a totem—some object of adoration, which usually takes the shape of an animal or plant. . . .

From what I have written it will easily be seen that the greater part of Ruanda is eminently

From *In the Heart of Africa* (London: Cassell & Company, 1912). (Abridged.)

adapted for colonization by white men, ... and that there is a splendid opening here for the establishment of business on a vast scale.

The entire region, however, is one which is quite unknown to the German government, and so it would be a very desirable thing if the state would decide upon sending out a commission, composed of agricultural experts, to examine into the conditions that exist. ...

The great central portion of the country is entirely bare of trees. The question of fuel being one of the most important, as regards colonization, this matter should be inquired into at once. Time should be seized by the forelock and a judicious afforestation undertaken of those parts which most require it; for there is no doubt that we should not rest content with the railway systems already established at Lake Victoria—the gleaming rails must be pushed still farther ahead, so as to insure that we are not robbed of those rich territories lying westward of the lake. ...

When we took our leave of the Sultan, at early dawn on the 12th of August, it was with a certain amount of satisfaction. We had been afforded an insight into the court life of a negro prince and favored with a display of his power such as no one had ever experienced previously or would probably ever experience again. When the illimitable power of this Sultan has receded before European influence, and when busy throngs of traders encroach upon the haughty aloofness of this most aristocratic of all negro tribes and the white man's herds graze in its pastures, then we shall be able to appreciate to the full the value of our remarkable experience.

Notes and Questions

1. Consider the relations today between dominant nations and "underdeveloped" nations, or between large multinational corporations and the "host" countries in which they operate. In what ways do these relations display an ongoing rearrangement of social structures by powerful groups competing for control over the life and labor of the people? How do these powerful groups try to capture the allegiance of the people?

2. Jane Jacobs has written about contemporary American cities, emphasizing the difference between real and artificial communities. In her analysis, it is significant whether people feel that they belong to a place and that the place belongs to them.

When people say that a city, or a part of it, is dangerous or is a jungle what they mean primarily is that they do not feel safe on the sidewalks.

The first thing to understand is that the public peace—the sidewalk and street peace—of cities is not kept primarily by the police, necessary as police are. It is kept primarily by an intricate, almost unconscious, network of voluntary controls and standards among the people themselves, and enforced by the people themselves. In some city areas—older public housing projects and streets with very high population turnover are often conspicuous examples—the keeping of public sidewalk law and order is left almost entirely to the police and special guards. Such places are jungles. No amount of police can enforce civilization where the normal, casual enforcement of it has broken down. ...

An incident at Washington Houses, a public housing project in New York, illustrates this point. A tenants' group at this project, struggling to establish itself, held some outdoor ceremonies in mid-December 1958, and put up three Christmas trees. The chief tree, so cumbersome it was a problem to transport, erect, and trim, went into the project's inner "street," a landscaped central mall and promenade. The other two trees, each less than six feet tall and easy to carry, went on two small fringe plots at the outer corners of the project where it abuts a busy avenue and lively cross streets of the old city. The first night, the large tree and all its trimmings were stolen. The two smaller trees remained intact, lights, ornaments and all, until they were taken down at New Year's. "The place where the tree was stolen, which is *theoretically* the most safe and sheltered place in the project, is the same place that is unsafe for people too, especially children," says a social worker who had been helping the tenants' group. "People are no safer in that mall than the Christmas tree. On the other hand, the place where the other trees were safe, where the project is just one corner out of four, happens to be safe for people." *

Jacobs says that city planners, architects, politicians, real estate developers, bankers, and others who make decisions about the building and rebuilding of cities often act from false ideas about how communities work. These false ideas center on making things look good rather than on making things really good as places for people to live. Jacobs believes that community life consists of people watching out for each other, and that people do this unless the environment they live in prevents or obstructs them. The basic problem, she maintains, is to understand and provide for the complexity of healthy social relations. She says, for example, that no amount of law enforcement can take the place of a living network of relations among people.

What qualities do the living relations have that law does not? Can you see how law enforcement might actually damage a living network of people's lives? What other social and economic forces might damage a network of human relations? What are the relationships between social order and legal order? Can law exist only when society is broken?

3. Farley Mowat has written about life among some of the Eskimo people in Canada. Their social order, he asserts, is based on principles that diverge widely from the legal order of the Canadian state. In a sense, one might say that the Eskimo law is not based on "principles" at all, but rather on concrete, existential experience stretching over many generations.

> This is the first great law of the land: that a man's business is sacred unto himself, and that it is no part of his neighbor's duty to interfere in any way unless the community is endangered. However, this does not mean that assistance is withheld in cases of need. In fact, the second and perhaps the most important law of the land is that while there is food, equipment, or bodily strength in any one of the tents, no man in another tent shall want for any of these....
>
> The two unwritten laws I have mentioned are loosely combined with all other laws of

---

* Condensed by permission of Random House, Inc. from *The Death and Life of Great American Cities,* by Jane Jacobs. Copyright © 1961 by Jane Jacobs.

the land into a code of behavior known as the Law of Life. All of the delicately balanced minor and major restrictions which go to make up the law are flexible, and yet they impose barriers beyond which an Ihalmio does not dream of stepping. Very probably it is the flexible nature of the laws, their openness to individual interpretation, and their capacity to adjust to individual cases, that accounts for the remarkable absence of what we know as "crime" in the camps of the Ihalmiut.

Of all the stories written about the Innuit, as a whole, the majority have dwelt with a morbid and smug satisfaction on the Eskimo deviations from the moral codes we white men have developed. Tales of cannibalism, wife-sharing, murder, infanticide, cruelty and theft appear with monotonous frequency in arctic stories, where they not only serve to supply a sensational element, but also provide the popular justification for the intrusion of the self-righteous white men who would destroy the laws and beliefs of the People in order to replace them with others which have no place in the land....

[T]here are deviations from law, and there are crimes in the land; for no race of men can be free of these things. But there are also certain forces which the People control and which in turn direct the actions of men, and these forces keep the law-breaking within narrow bounds. To understand these forces is to realize why the Ihalmiut have no need of our laws to maintain the security of their way of life.

There is absolutely no internal organization to hold authority over the People. No one man, or body of men, holds power in any other sense than the magical. There is no council of elders, no policeman. There are no assemblies of government and, in the strictest sense, the Ihalmiut may be said to live in an anarchistic state, for they do not even have an inflexible code of laws.

Yet the People exist in amity together, and the secret of this is the secret of co-operative endeavor, limited only by the powers of human will and endurance. It is not blind obedience or obedience dictated by fear. Rather it is intelligent obedience to a simple code that makes sense to those who must live by its rules....

However, methods of punishment do exist. Should a man continuously disregard the Law of Life, then little by little he finds himself isolated and shut off from the community. There can be no more powerful punishment in the lonely wastes of the Barrens, and in fact it is a punishment which can easily be fatal in a world where man must work closely with man in order to live. A small dose of ostracism usually brings the culprit to an acute awareness of his defects and he ceases to transgress the law. Thus while there is no overt act of justice or of social revenge, nevertheless the object is achieved and the wrong-doer almost invariably returns into the community once again, with no permanent stigma attached to his name. The law does not call for an eye for an eye. If possible the breaker of law is brought back to become an asset to the camps. His defection is tacitly forgotten, and to all intents and purposes it never happened at all.

Such is the punishment for most major offenses. Minor offenses are dealt with by employing the powerful weapons of ridicule, and the Ihalmiut are masters of that art. A man capable of doing his own hunting, but whose family must be fed by other hunters because he is lazy or simply indifferent, is made the subject of the drum-dance song and an object of biting laughter. Only a very callous man can face that sharp laugh for long. However, he knows that when he returns to his duties, the songs about him will disappear, and in time all memory of the incident will be washed from the minds of the People by common consent.*

Mowat traces the virtual absence of crime in Eskimo society to a strong sense of social cohesion. What are the sources of this cohesiveness? Are there sources of genuine cohesion available to people in legal society? Does social cohesiveness come at the expense of other factors, such as the generation and acquisition of material wealth? Do you think that tribal affiliation precludes individual advancement? What is the relation between the internal forces of Eskimo society and the external force of the Canadian state? Is this a good example of the split between organic, customary law and alienated law?

* Copyright 1951, 1952 by Farley Mowat. From *People of the Deer* by Farley Mowat, by permission of Little, Brown and Co., pp. 167, 169, 176–178.

The Group   *Vine DeLoria, Jr.*

Of more concern for the present situation with which we are confronted may be the community context....

It is in the conception of the community that Indian tribal religions have an edge on Christianity. Most tribal religions make no pretense as to their universality or exclusiveness. They came to the Indian community in the distant past and have always been in the community as a distinct social and cultural force. They integrate the respective communities as particular people chosen for particular religious knowledge and experiences. A substantial number of tribal names indicate the fundamental belief that the tribe is a chosen people distinct from the other peoples of mankind. *Dine,* the Navajo word for themselves, means the people. The Biloxi called themselves *taneks aya*—first people; Kiowas noted that they were the principal people. Washoes relate that *washui* means person, and Klamaths called themselves *maklaks*—the people or the community. The concern in almost every instance is to identify the community and distinguish its uniqueness from the rest of the creation....

It is with respect to the attitude displayed toward strangers that a community's psychic identity can be determined. A community that is uncertain about itself must destroy in self-defense to prevent any conceivable threat to its existence, whereas a community that has a stable identity

Reprinted from *God Is Red* by Vine DeLoria, Jr. Copyright © 1973 by Vine DeLoria, Jr. Used by permission of Grosset & Dunlap, Inc. (Abridged.)

accords to other communities the dignity of distinct existence, which it wishes to receive itself. The admonition of the early Hebrews to honor the stranger in their midst because they were once strangers in Egypt indicates the degree of community security enjoyed by the people. Their faith in the continuity of their nation precluded the destruction of others simply because they had different customs and beliefs. Logan, the Mingo chief, appealed to the Virginians for justice at the peace council following the back country war of 1774: "I appeal to any white man to say if he ever entered Logan's cabin hungry and he gave him not meat; if he ever came cold and naked and he clothed him not." Such hospitality characterized the tribal religious communities precisely because they were communities limited to specific groups, identifiable to the world in which they lived and responsible for maintaining a minimum standard of hospitality and integrity.

The obvious benefit of a tribal religion is its co-extensiveness with other functions of the community. Instead of a struggle between church and state, the two become complementary aspects of community life. The necessity of expanding the political functions of government into the social welfare field is avoided as religious duties cover the informal aspects of community concern, and the coercive side of community life as we have traditionally seen it in Western democracies is blunted by its correspondence with religious understandings of life. Yet religious wars are avoided because of the recognition that other peoples have special powers and medicines given to them, thus precluding an exclusive franchise being issued to any one group of people.

In the closing decades of the last century, the Indian tribes could not be broken politically until they had been destroyed religiously, as the two functions supported each other to an amazing degree. Some Indian agents were able to keep control of reservations because of their use of Indian police. The tribal members would not kill their own people, and those Indians still resisting the Army refused to kill the tribal policemen. When religious ceremonies were banned and the reservations turned over to missionaries and political patronage appointees, the decline of both the

traditional political leaders and the religious solidarity of the people was accomplished in a very short time. The Indian Reorganization Act made some restoration of tribal religion possible by abolishing the rules and regulations that forbade the practice of tribal religions on the reservations. By creating corporate forms of government for political and economic ends, however, the federal government created the same problems of religious confusion in the Indian tribes that existed in America at large.

Today with tribal governments severed from the tribal religious life, the integrity of the governments is dependent only on the ability of outside forces to punish wrongdoers. If the people of the reservation see no wrong in the actions of their tribal government in a political sense, they generally keep them in office in spite of constant failures of that government or council to act on behalf of the reservation community.

Even with large defections of the tribal members to Christianity and Mormonism and with the political structure of the respective tribes frozen into quasi-corporate forms of activity, Indian tribes have shown amazing resilience in meeting catastrophes visited on them by government policies and outside interference. The primary identity of the group remains and in many cases has been perpetuated by the government with its incessant concern for administration and distribution of individual and tribal trust property. The major difference between Christianity and tribal religions thus remains active. Tribal members know who they are, and for better or for worse the whole tribe is involved in its relations with the rest of the world.

The opposite is true for Christianity. Mention the failures of either the religion or Western culture as influenced by Christian thinking, and the average Christian will tell you that Christians were not really responsible. Question any outstanding evangelist, theologian, or church leader today as to the orthodoxy of his theology or practice, and people will deny that he is remotely related to Christianity. The self-critical mechanism for analyzing behavior is thus missing from Christianity, whereas it is consumed within the tribal communities. No one will reject a tribal member as not belonging to the tribe. He may be viciously attacked as corrupt, as having assimilated, or as being a stupid traditional. He is never disclaimed as a tribal member. . . .

Another phenomenon existing in tribal religions that does not exist in Christianity is the absence of a paid professional religious staff. Tribal religions do not have the massive institutions which Christianity requires to perpetuate itself. While the Indian religious leader may receive gifts for his work in conducting ceremonies, he does not have pension plans, regular working hours, vacations and the other benefits the professional Christian clergyman enjoys. The Indian religious man looks at his religious powers as partly a blessing and partly a curse of added burdens of social responsibility. The Christian clergyman looks up the church hierarchical scale and begins plotting from the time of his ordination how quickly he can reach the apex of the pyramid. The scramble for rich parishes, seats on seminary faculties, appointments to church national staff positions, and boards of directors is quite irreligious and could only take place in direct opposition to the concept of religion, not as a part of it.

Indian religions consequently do not need the massive buildings, expensive pipe organs, fundraising drives, publications, and other activities that the Christian denominations need to perpetuate themselves. The religious ceremonies of the tribal religions are carried out with a minimum of distracting activities. Many take place in sacred locations, where the people can be in contact with the spiritual powers who have always guided the tribe. Other ceremonies can be performed as the occasion arises, and wherever the need is shown. Many Indian religious ceremonies have been held in apartments within the large urban areas far from the sacred lands of the tribe. Take away the large buildings and other secular achievements of Christianity, and it would vanish within a decade. Unless the Christian God is confined within a quasi-Gothic stone structure, He cannot operate. Needless to say, He does not do very well even with His real estate.

The two concepts of community are carried over into secular life. Today the land is dotted with towns, cities, suburbs, and the like. Yet very few of these political subdivisions are in fact communities. They are rather transitory locations for the temporary existence of wage earners. People come and go as the economics of the situation demand. They join churches and change churches as their business and economic successes dictate. Lawyers and doctors climbing the ladders of affluence will eventually become Episcopalians and Presbyterians. Businessmen will gravitate to those churches in which their level of secular concern is best manifested.

Within each town and city exist many denominational branches of Christianity; each competes with the others for financial and political control over an extensive portion of community affairs. People may live side by side for years having in common only their property boundaries and their status as property taxpayers. At no point do the various denominations serve to integrate cities, suburbs, or even neighborhoods. . . .

Outside of ethnicity, no unique thing distinguishes one group of Christians from another in the same manner as tribal groups are distinguishable. In the first place, the tribes have a discernible history, both religious and political. The various Indian languages have in the past acted to bind each tribe even closer, and in this respect they have been paralleled by the Roman Catholic use of Latin and the ethnic use of European languages as liturgical languages. Latin early became artificial but the use of German, Swedish, and other languages in services meant solidification of the religious community to a real degree. In this respect some denominations of Christianity were closer to Indian tribes than they would have cared to elaborate.

Only with the use of Hebrew by the Jewish community, which in so many ways perpetuates the Indian tribal religious conceptions of community, do we find contemporary similarities. Again the conception of group identity is very strong among the Jews, and the phenomenon of having been born into a complete cultural and religious tradition is present, though many Jews, like many Indians, refuse to acknowledge their membership in an exclusive community.

Today many of the Indian tribes are undergoing profound changes with respect to their traditional solidarity. Employment opportunities away from the reservations have caused nearly half of the members of Indian communities to remove themselves from the reservations for work and educational programs leading to work. Massive economic development programs on the reservations have caused population shifts that have tended to break down traditional living groups and to cause severe strains in the old clan structure. And the tragedy of the Indian power movement is that it avoids looking realistically at this obvious change in living conditions. While Indian tribes have been able to maintain themselves in the face of sweeping technological changes, the day may be fast approaching when they too will fall before the complexity of modern life.

For that reason the future may be already a threat to Indian tribal and religious existence as it has never before appeared to be. New social, political, and religious forms must be found to enable the tribal religions to exist in a religious sense, in spite of the inroads being made by the conditions of modern life. In a few selected communities, this transition is being made. In Christian perspective the Amish and perhaps the Mormons show how successfully communities can be established and maintained, when they are restricted to ethnic communities residing in specific locations and preserving specific religious doctrines and ceremonial forms. The rest of Christendom and Indian religious and political leadership would do well to look at these groups as having made a realistic decision to perpetuate themselves as a community.

Surveying the past and looking to the future, the question of religion and its relationship to the social structures of mankind becomes more important. The universal and hardly identifiable conception of a religion for everyone as articulated by Christianity no longer appears to have validity. Where Christianity has most successfully entrenched itself into the lives of people, it has been on an ethnic or racial basis and has had to adopt the cultural and political outlook of the people of the land in which it has chosen to exist. In America it has become virtually impossible for Christianity to have positive effects on our society's movements. Lacking a specific people to which it

could relate, Christianity has simply become a captive of the novelty of American life. Then to protect itself it has had to support the political structure of secular America, for without that structure the whole content of American Christianity would be meaningless.

The conflict over tax exemption of Christian churches and church property is a point in question. Would American Christianity be able to continue without its tax exemption? If there were no deductions allowed for contributions to church programs, what would the effect be on church income and programs? How would individual Christians respond to annual taxes on their massive churches, cathedrals, and investments? The fact that the churches are not willing to risk such a tax is indication enough that without a favored position in the secular world and its political and economic structures, most of what we now know as American Christianity would not and could not exist.

The fundamental question of the nature of religion, therefore, must certainly involve a rejection of the structures Christianity has traditionally used to perpetuate itself and promulgate its message. For without the alliance with political structures that lend it credence and protection, Christianity would have vanished long since. It lives today because it has become so intimate a part of Western culture that its existence or reason for existence is rarely questioned. Is this condition necessarily a feature of religion as it has been experienced by mankind at various times and in various places? Is institutionalism necessary to religion in any sense? American society must honestly face and answer that question before it can understand the nature of the problems it faces.

Questions

1. If a real community consists of particular people living in a particular place and sharing a specific vision of the meaning of their lives, is such a group inevitably going to be in conflict with law and the state?

2. Does it seem to you that law is in the same predicament as Christianity: uncertain about itself, beset with contradictions, and undermined by its

own claim of universal validity? Would law be able to exist without the economic and military force that currently supports it?

3. Do you think there is a gap between law and justice that is parallel to the gap DeLoria sees between churches and religious experience? What other parallels and contrasts do you find between law and religion as foundations for community life?

4. What do you think are the ingredients of an organic society? Can an organic community be created by any action or inaction of the state?

3   Ideology and Organization

... [O]ur present system of economic and political dependence is maintained not so much by wealth and courts as it is by an inert mass of humanity, and ... the school today represents the most efficient medium to accomplish that end.

Emma Goldman, "The Social
Importance of the Modern School,"
in *Red Emma Speaks* (1972)

We did not think of the great open plains, the beautiful rolling hills, and winding streams with tangled growth, as "wild." Only to the white man was nature a "wilderness" and only to him was the land "infested" with "wild" animals and "savage" people. To us it was tame. Earth was bountiful and we were surrounded with the blessings of the Great Mystery. Not until the hairy man from the east came and with brutal frenzy heaped injustices upon us and the families we loved was it "wild" for us. When the very animals of the forest began fleeing from his approach, then it was that for us the "Wild West" began.

Chief Luther Standing Bear, of the
Oglala Band of Sioux in *Touch the
Earth,* T. C. McLuhan, ed.

A physical building may outlast the purposes for which it was built. When social relations change to such an extent that the building is no longer functional, the structure must be abandoned or modified. Similarly, a society may outgrow its legal system. The combined effect of ongoing social change may leave the people with no choice but to abandon or redesign that structure. As the American Declaration of Independence says: "... whenever any Form of Government becomes destructive of these ends it is the right of the people to alter or to abolish it, and to institute new Government, laying its foundation on such principles and organizing its powers in such form, as to them shall seem most likely to effect their Safety and Happiness."

The problem of conscious social change, especially revolutionary change, is that it requires a knowledge of how to build, of how to translate ideas into living human relations. It requires a knowledge of where we have come from and where we are going. As Robert Pirsig's comment at the beginning of this chapter suggests, our conceptions can trap us. The way we think about law and society has an effect on the kinds of social and legal relations we look for and attempt to build. To avoid being trapped by our ideas, we must see them clearly and understand our creative power as people. We must work on our *thoughts* and *theories* to be able to work on our *practices*. If we want to affect social organization, we must pay attention to social ideology.

The articles in this section focus on the *way we think* about what we do and how we live. The aim is to see how the logic of our social structure becomes illogic when it is viewed in a larger context, or on the basis of different assumptions about people's relations with one another and with the world. We will see that when the context changes, the elements in the context also change.

Throughout this section, the underlying questions are: What kind of law do we, must we, or may we have? By whose will and for whose interests does our law exist?

The Third Wave: A Classroom Experiment in Fascism   *Ron Jones*

For years I kept a strange secret. I shared this silence with two hundred students. Yesterday I ran into one of those students. For a brief moment it all rushed back.

Steve Coniglo had been a sophomore student in my world history class.... We were studying Nazi Germany and in the middle of the lecture I was interrupted by the question, How could the German populace claim ignorance of the slaughter of the Jewish people? How could the townspeople, railroad conductors, teachers, doctors claim they knew nothing about concentration camps and human carnage? How can people who were neighbors and maybe even friends of the Jewish citizen say they weren't there when it happened? It was a good question. I didn't know the answer.

Inasmuch as there were several months still to go in the school year and I was already at World War II, I decided to take a week and explore the question.

On Monday I introduced my sophomore history students to one of the experiences that characterized Nazi Germany, discipline. I lectured about the beauty of discipline: how an athlete feels having worked hard and regularly to be successful at a sport; how a ballet dancer or painter works hard to perfect a movement; the dedicated patience of a scientist in pursuit of an idea. It's discipline. That self-training. Control. The power of the will. The exchange of physical hardships for superior mental and physical facilities. The ultimate triumph.

Reprinted by permission of the author. (Abridged.)

To experience the power of discipline, I invited —no, I commanded—the class to exercise and use a new seating posture; I described how proper sitting posture assists concentration and strengthens the will. In fact, I instructed the class in a mandatory sitting posture. This posture started with feet flat on the floor, hands placed flat across the small of the back to force a straight alignment of the spine. "There, can't you breathe more easily? You're more alert. Don't you feel better?"

We practiced this new attention position over and over. I walked up and down the aisles of seated students, pointing out small flaws, making improvements. Proper seating became the most important aspect of learning. I would dismiss the class, allowing them to leave their desks, and then call them abruptly back to an attention sitting position. In speed drills the class learned to move from standing position to attention sitting in fifteen seconds. In focus drills I concentrated attention on the feet being parallel and flat, ankles locked, knees bent at ninety-degree angles, hands flat and crossed against the back, spine straight, chin down, head forward. We did noise drills in which talking was allowed only to be shown as a detraction. Following minutes of progressive drill assignments the class could move from standing positions outside the room to attention sitting positions at their desks without making a sound. The maneuver took five seconds.

It was strange how quickly the students took to this uniform code of behavior. I began to wonder just how far they could be pushed. Was this display of obedience a momentary game we were all playing, or was it something else? Was the desire for discipline and uniformity a natural need? A societal instinct we hide within our franchise restaurants and TV programming?

I decided to push the tolerance of the class for regimented action. In the final twenty-five minutes of the class I introduced some new rules. Students must be sitting in class at the attention position before the late bell; all students must carry pencils and paper for note taking; when asking or answering questions, a student must stand at the side of their desk; the first word given in answering or asking a question is "Mr. Jones." We practiced short "silent reading" sessions. Students who responded in a sluggish manner were reprimanded and in every case made to repeat their behavior until it was a model of punctuality and respect. The intensity of the response became more important than the content. To accentuate this, I requested answers to be given in three words or less. Students were rewarded for making an effort at answering or asking questions. They were also acknowledged for doing this in a crisp and attentive manner.

Soon everyone in the class began popping up with answers and questions. The involvement level in the class moved from the few who always dominated discussions to the entire class. Even stranger was the gradual improvement in the quality of answers. Everyone seemed to be listening more intently. New people were speaking. Answers started to stretch out as students usually hesitant to speak found support for their effort.

As for my part in this exercise, I had nothing but questions. Why hadn't I thought of this technique before? Students seemed intent on the assignment and displayed accurate recitation of facts and concepts. They even seemed to be asking better questions and treating each other with more compassion. How could this be? Here I was enacting an authoritarian learning environment, and it seemed very productive. I now began to ponder not just how far this class could be pushed, but how much I would change my basic beliefs in open classrooms and self-directed learning. Was all my belief in Carl Rogers to shrivel and die? Where was this experiment leading?

On Tuesday, the second day of the exercise, I entered the classroom to find everyone sitting in silence at the attention position. Some of their faces were relaxed with smiles that come from pleasing the teacher. But most of the students looked straight ahead in earnest concentration. Neck muscles rigid. No sign of a smile or a thought or even a question. Every fiber strained to perform the deed. To release the tension, I went to the chalk board and wrote in big letters: "Strength through discipline." Below this I wrote a second law: "Strength through community."

While the class sat in stern silence, I began to talk lecture sermonize about the value of community. At this stage of the game I was debating in my own mind whether to stop the experiment or continue. I hadn't planned on such intensity or compliance. In fact I was surprised to find the ideas on discipline enacted at all. While debating whether to stop or go on with the experiment, I talked on and on about community. I made up stories from my experiences as an athlete, coach, and historian. It was easy. Community is that bond between individuals who work and struggle together. It's raising a barn with your neighbors, it's feeling that you are a part of something beyond yourself—a movement, a team, La Raza, a cause.

It was too late to step back. I now can appreciate why the astronomer turns relentlessly to the telescope. I was probing deeper and deeper into my own perceptions and the motivations for group and individual action. There was much more to see and try to understand. Many questions haunted me. Why did the students accept the authority I was imposing? Where is their curiosity or resistance to this martial behavior? When and how will this end?

Following my description of community I once again told the class that community, like discipline, must be experienced if it is to be understood. To provide an encounter with community I had the class recite in unison "strength through discipline," "strength through community." First I would have two students stand and call back our motto. Then I would add two more until finally the whole class was standing and reciting. It was fun. The students began to look at each other and sense the power of belonging. Everyone was capable and equal. They were doing something together. We worked on this simple act for the entire class period. We would repeat the mottos in a rotating chorus, or say them with various degrees of loudness. Always we said them together, emphasizing the proper way to sit, stand, and talk.

I began to think of myself as a part of the experiment. I enjoyed the unified action demonstrated by the students. It was rewarding to see their satisfaction and excitement to do more. I found it harder and harder to extract myself from the momentum and identity that the class was developing. I was following the group dictate as much as I was directing it.

As the class period was ending, without forethought I created a class salute. It was for class members only. To make the salute you brought your right hand up toward the right shoulder in a curled position. I called it the Third Wave salute because the hand resembled a wave about to top over. The idea for the three came from beach lore that waves travel in chains, the third wave being the last and largest of each series. Since we had a salute, I made it a rule to salute all class members outside the classroom. When the bell sounded, ending the period, I asked the class for complete silence. With everyone sitting at attention I slowly raised my arm and with a cupped hand I saluted. It was a silent signal of recognition. They were something special. Without command the entire group of students returned the salute.

Throughout the next few days students in the class would exchange this greeting. You would be walking down the hall when all of a sudden three classmates would turn your way each flashing a quick salute. In the library or in gym students would be seen giving this strange hand jive. You would hear a crash of cafeteria food only to have it followed by two classmates saluting each other. The mystique of thirty individuals doing this strange gyration soon brought more attention to the class and its experiment into the German personality. Many students outside the class asked if they could join.

On Wednesday, I decided to issue membership cards to every student that wanted to continue what I now called the experiment. Not a single student elected to leave the room. In this the third day of activity there were forty-three students in the class. Thirteen students had cut class to be a part of the experiment. While the class sat at attention I gave each person a card. I marked three of the cards with a red x and informed the recipients that they had a special assignment to report any students not complying with class rules. I then proceeded to talk about the meaning of action. I explained how discipline and community were meaningless without action. I discussed the beauty of taking full responsibility for one's action. Of believing so thoroughly in yourself and your community or family that you will do anything to preserve, protect, and extend that being. I stressed how hard work and allegiance to each other would allow accelerated learning and accomplishment. I reminded students of what it felt like being in classes where competition caused pain and degradation. Situations in which students were pitted against each other in everything from gym to reading. The feeling of never acting, never being a part of something, never supporting each other.

At this point students stood without prompting and began to give what amounted to testimonials. "Mr. Jones, for the first time I'm learning lots of things." "Mr. Jones, why don't you teach like this all the time?" I was shocked! Yes, I had been pushing information at them in an extremely controlled setting but the fact that they found it comfortable and acceptable was startling. It was equally disconcerting to realize that complex and time-consuming written homework assignments on German life were being completed and even enlarged on by students. Performance in academic skill areas was significantly improving. They were learning more. And they seemed to want more. I began to think that the students might do anything I assigned. I decided to find out.

To allow students the experience of direct action I gave each individual a specific verbal assignment. "It's your task to design a Third Wave Banner. You are responsible for stopping any student that is not a Third Wave member from entering this room. I want you to remember and be able to recite by tomorrow the name and address of every Third Wave member. You're assigned the problem of training and convincing at least twenty children in the adjacent elementary school that our sitting posture is necessary for better learning. It's your job to read this pamphlet and report its entire content to the class before the period ends. I want each of you to give me the name and address of one reliable friend that you think might want to join the Third Wave...."

To conclude the session on direct action, I instructed students in a simple procedure for initiating new members. It went like this. A new member had only to be recommended by an existing member and issued a card by me. Upon receiving this card the new member had to demonstrate knowledge of our rules and pledge obedience to them. My announcement unleashed a fervor.

The school was alive with conjecture and curiosity. It affected everyone. The school cook asked what a Third Wave cookie looked like. I said chocolate chip, of course. Our principal came into an afternoon faculty meeting and gave me the Third Wave salute. I saluted back. The librarian thanked me for the 30-foot banner on learning, which she placed above the library entrance. By the end of the day over two hundred students were admitted into the order. I felt very alone and a little scared.

Most of my fear emanated from the incidence of tattletaling. Although I formally appointed only three students to report deviate behavior, approximately twenty students came to me with reports about how Allan didn't salute, or Georgene was talking critically about our experiment. This incidence of monitoring meant that half the class now considered it their duty to observe and report on members of their class. Within this avalanche of reporting one legitimate conspiracy did seem underway.

Three women in the class had told their parents all about our classroom activities. These three young women were by far the most intelligent students in the class. As friends they chummed together. They possessed a silent confidence and took pleasure in a school setting that gave them academic and leadership opportunity. During the

days of the experiment I was curious how they would respond to the equalitarian and physical reshaping of the class. The rewards they were accustomed to winning just didn't exist in the experiment. The intellectual skills of questioning and reasoning were nonexistent. In the martial atmosphere of the class they seemed stunned and pensive. Now that I look back, they appeared much like children with so-called learning disabilities. They watched the activities and participated in a mechanical fashion. Whereas others jumped in, they held back, watching.

In telling their parents of the experiment, they set up a brief chain of events. The rabbi for one of the parents called me at home. He was polite and condescending. I told him we were merely studying the German personality. He seemed delighted and told me not to worry. He would talk to the parents and calm their concern. In concluding this conversation I envisioned similar conversations throughout history in which the clergy accepted and apologized for untenable conditions. If only he would have raged in anger or simply investigated the situation, I could point the students to an example of righteous rebellion. But no. The rabbi became part of the experiment. In remaining ignorant of the oppression in the experiment, he became an accomplice and advocate.

By the end of the third day I was exhausted. I was tearing apart. The balance between role playing and directed behavior became indistinguishable. Many of the students were completely into being Third Wave members. They demanded strict obedience of the rules from other students and bullied those that took the experiment lightly. Others simply sank into the activity and took self-assigned roles. I particularly remember Robert. Robert was big for his age and displayed very few academic skills. Oh, he tried harder than anyone to be successful. He handed in elaborate weekly reports copied word for word from the reference books in the library. Robert is like so many kids in school that don't excel or cause trouble. They aren't bright, they can't make the athletic teams, they don't strike out for attention. They are lost, invisible. The only reason I came to know Robert at all is that I found him eating lunch in my classroom. He always ate lunch alone.

Well, the Third Wave gave Robert a place in school. At least he was equal to everyone. He could do something. Take part. Be meaningful. That's just what Robert did. Late Wednesday afternoon I found Robert following me. I asked what in the world was he doing. He smiled (I don't think I had ever seen him smile) and announced, "Mr. Jones, I'm your bodyguard. I'm afraid something will happen to you. Can I do it, Mr. Jones, please?" Given that assurance and smile, I couldn't say no. I had a bodyguard. All day long he opened and closed doors for me. He walked always on my right. Just smiling and saluting other class members. He followed me everywhere. In the faculty room (closed to students) he stood at silent attention while I gulped some coffee. When accosted by an English teacher for being a student in the "teachers' room," he just smiled and informed the faculty member that he wasn't a student, he was a bodyguard.

On Thursday I began to draw the experiment to a conclusion. I was exhausted and worried. Many students were over the line. The Third Wave had become the center of their existence. I was in pretty bad shape myself. I was now acting instinctively as a dictator. Oh, I was benevolent. And I daily argued to myself on the benefits of the learning experience. By this, the fourth day of the experiment, I was beginning to lose my own arguments. As I spent more time playing the role, I had less time to remember its rational origins and purpose. I found myself sliding into the role even when it wasn't necessary. I wondered if this doesn't happen to lots of people. We get or take an ascribed role and then bend our life to fit the image. Soon the image is the only identity people will accept. So we become the image. The trouble with the situation and role I had created was that I didn't have time to think where they were leading. Events were crushing around me. I worried that students might do things they would regret. I worried for myself.

Once again I faced the thoughts of closing the experiment or letting it go its own course. Both options were unworkable. If I stopped the experiment, a great number of students would be left hanging. They had committed themselves in front of their peers to radical behavior. Emotionally and psychologically they had exposed themselves. If I suddenly jolted them back to classroom reality I would face a confused student body for the remainder of the year. It would be too painful and demeaning for Robert and students like him to be twisted back into a seat and told it was just a game. They would take the ridicule from the brighter students that participated in a measured and cautious way. I couldn't let the Roberts lose again.

The other option of just letting the experiment run its course was also out of the question. Things were already getting out of control. Wednesday evening someone had broken into the room and ransacked the place. I later found out it was the father of one of the students. He was a retired air force colonel who had spent time in a German prisoner-of-war camp. Upon hearing of our activity he simply lost control. Late in the evening he broke into the room and tore it apart. I found him that morning propped up against the classroom door. He told me about his friends that had been killed in Germany. He was holding on to me and shaking. In staccato words he pleaded that I understand and help him get home. I called his wife and with the help of a neighbor walked him home. We spent hours later talking about what he felt and did, but from that moment on Thursday morning I was more concerned with what might be happening at school.

I was increasingly worried about how our activity was affecting the faculty and other students in the school. The Third Wave was disrupting normal learning. Students were cutting class to participate, and the school counselors were beginning to question every student in the class. The real Gestapo in the school was at work. Faced with this experiment exploding in one hundred directions, I decided to try an old basketball strategy. When you're playing against all the odds the best action to take is to try the unexpected. That's what I did.

By Thursday the class had swollen in size to over eighty students. The only thing that allowed them all to fit was the enforced discipline of sitting in silence at attention. A strange calm is in effect when a roomful of people sits in quiet observation and anticipation. It helped me approach them in a deliberate way. I talked about pride. "Pride is more than banners or salutes. Pride is something no one can take from you. Pride is knowing you are the best . . . It can't be destroyed. . . ."

In the midst of this crescendo I abruptly changed and lowered my voice to announce the real reason for the Third Wave. In slow methodic tones I explained what was behind the Third Wave. "The Third Wave isn't just an experiment in classroom activity. It's far more important than that. The Third Wave is a nationwide program to find students who are willing to fight for political change in this country. That's right. This activity we have been doing has been practice for the real thing. Across the country teachers like myself have been recruiting and training a youth brigade capable of showing the nation a better society through discipline, community, pride, and action. If we can change the way that school is run, we can change the way that factories, stores, universities, and all other institutions are run. You are a selected group of young people chosen to help in this cause. If you will stand up and display what you have learned in the past four days . . . we can change the destiny of this nation. We can bring it a new sense of order, community, pride and action. A new purpose. Everything rests with you and your willingness to take a stand."

To give validity to the seriousness of my words I turned to the three women in the class whom I knew had questioned the Third Wave. I demanded that they leave the room. I explained why I acted and then assigned four guards to escort the women to the library and to detain them from entering the class on Friday. Then in dramatic style I informed the class of a special noon rally to take place on Friday. This would be a rally for Third Wave members only.

It was a wild gamble. I just kept talking. Afraid that if I stopped, someone would laugh or ask a question and the grand scheme would dissolve in chaos. I explained how at noon on Friday a national candidate for president would announce the formation of a Third Wave Youth Program. Simultaneous to this announcement over 1000 youth groups from every part of the country would stand up and display their support for such a movement. I confided that they were the students selected to represent their area. I also questioned if they could make a good showing, because the press had been invited to record the event. No one laughed. There was not a murmur of resistance. Quite the contrary. A fever pitch of excitement swelled across the room. "We can do it!" "Should we wear white shirts?" "Can we bring friends?" "Mr. Jones, have you seen this advertisement in *Time* magazine?"

The clincher came quite by accident. It was a full-page color advertisement in the current issue of *Time* for some lumber products. The advertiser identified his product as the Third Wave. The advertisement proclaimed in big red, white and blue letters, "The Third Wave is coming." "Is this part of the campaign, Mr. Jones?" "Is it a code or something?" "Yes. Now listen carefully. It's all set for tomorrow. Be in the small auditorium ten minutes before 12:00. Be seated. Be ready to display the discipline, community, and pride you have learned. Don't talk to anyone about this. This rally is for members only."

On Friday, the final day of the exercise, I spent the early morning preparing the auditorium for the rally. At eleven-thirty students began to ant their way into the room; at first a few scouting the way and then more. Row after row began to fill. A hushed silence shrouded the room. Third Wave banners hung like clouds over the assembly. At twelve o'clock sharp I closed the room and placed guards at each door. Several friends of mine posing as reporters and photographers began to interact with the crowd, taking pictures and jotting frantic descriptive notes. A group photograph was taken. Over two hundred students were crammed into the room. Not a vacant seat could be found. The group seemed to be composed of students from many persuasions. There were the athletes, the social prominents, the student leaders, the loners, the group of kids that always left school early, the bikers, the pseudo-hip, a few representatives of the school's dadaist clique, and some of the students that hung out at the laundromat. The entire collection, however, looked like one force as they sat in perfect attention, every person focusing on the TV set I had in the front of the room. No one moved. The room was empty of sound. It was as if we were all witnessing a birth. The tension and anticipation were beyond belief.

"Before turning on the national press conference, which begins in five minutes, I want to demonstrate to the press the extent of our training." With that, I gave the salute, followed automatically by two hundred arms stabbing a reply. I then said the words "Strength through discipline," followed by a repetitive chorus. We did this again and again. Each time the response was louder. The photographers were circling the ritual, snapping pictures, but by now they were ignored. I reiterated the importance of this event and asked once more for a show of allegiance. It was the last time I would ask anyone to recite. The room rocked with a guttural cry: "Strength through discipline."

It was 12:05. I turned off the lights in the room and walked quickly to the television set. The air in the room seemed to be drying up. It felt hard to breathe and ever harder to talk. It was as if the climax of shouting souls had pushed everything out of the room. I switched the television set on. I was now standing next to the television, directly facing the roomful of people. The machine came to life, producing a luminous field of phosphorous light. Robert was at my side. I whispered to him to watch closely and pay attention to the next few minutes. The only light in the room was coming from the television and it played against the faces in the room. Eyes strained and pulled at the light, but the pattern didn't change. The room stayed deadly still. Waiting. There was a mental tug of war between the people in the room and the television. The television won. The white glow of the test pattern

didn't snap into the vision of a political candidate. It just whined on. Still the viewers persisted. There must be a program. It must be coming on. Where is it? The trance with the television continued for what seemed like hours. It was 12:07. Nothing. A blank field of white. It's not going to happen. Anticipation turned to anxiety and then to frustration. Someone stood up and shouted.

"There isn't any leader, is there?" Everyone turned in shock, first to the despondent student and then back to the television. Their faces held looks of disbelief.

In the confusion of the moment I moved slowly toward the television. I turned it off. I felt air rush back into the room. The room remained in fixed silence, but for the first time I could sense people breathing. Students were withdrawing their arms from behind their chairs. I expected a flood of questions, but instead got intense quietness. I began to talk. Every word seemed to be taken and absorbed.

"Listen closely. I have something important to tell you. Sit down. There is no leader! There is no such thing as a national youth movement called the Third Wave. You have been used. Manipulated. Shoved by your desires into the place you now find yourself. You are no better or worse than the German Nazi we have been studying.

"You thought that you were the elect. That you were better than those outside this room. You bargained your freedom for the comfort of discipline and superiority. You chose to accept the group's will and the big lie over your own conviction. Oh, you think to yourself that you were just going along for the fun. That you could extricate yourself at any moment. But where were you heading? How far would you have gone? Let me show you your future."

With that I switched on a rear screen projector. It quickly illuminated a white drop cloth hanging behind the television. Large numbers appeared in a countdown. The roar of the Nuremberg Rally blasted into vision. My heart was pounding. In ghostly images the history of the Third Reich paraded into the room. The discipline. The march of super race. The big lie. Arrogance, violence, terror. People being pushed into vans. The visual stench of death camps. Faces without eyes. The trials. The plea of ignorance. I was only doing my job. My job. As abruptly as it started, the film froze to a halt on a single written frame. "Everyone must accept the blame—no one can claim that they didn't in some way take part."

The room stayed dark as the final footage of film flapped against the projector. I felt sick to my stomach. The room was sweating, it smelled like a locker room. No one moved. It was as if everyone wanted to dissect the moment, figure out what had happened. As if awakening from a dream and deep sleep, the entire roomful of people took one last look back into their consciousness. I waited for several minutes to let everyone catch up. Finally questions began to emerge. All of the questions probed at imaginary situations and sought to discover the meaning of this event.

In the still darkened room I began the explanation. I confessed my feeling of sickness and remorse. I told the assembly that a full explanation would take quite a while. But to start, I sensed myself moving from an introspective participant in the event toward the role of teacher. It's easier being a teacher. In objective terms I began to describe the past events.

"Through the experience of the past week we have all tasted what it was like to live and act in Nazi Germany. We learned what it felt like to create a disciplined social environment. To build a special society. Pledge allegiance to that society. Replace reason with rules. Yes, we would all have made good Germans. We would have put on the uniform. Turned our head as friends and neighbors were cursed and then persecuted. Pulled the locks shut. Worked in the defense plants. Burned ideas. Yes, we know in a small way what it feels like to find a hero. To grab quick solutions. Feel strong and in control of destiny. We know the fear of being left out. The pleasure of doing something right and being rewarded. To be number one. To be right. Taken to an extreme, we have seen and perhaps felt what these actions will lead to. We each have

witnessed something over the past week. We have seen that fascism is not just something those other people did. No, it's right here. In this room. In our own personal habits and way of life. Scratch the surface and it appears. Something in all of us. We carry it like a disease. The belief that human beings are basically evil and therefore unable to act well toward each other. A belief that demands a strong leader and discipline to preserve social order. And there is something else. The act of apology.

"This is the final lesson to be experienced. This last lesson is perhaps the one of greatest importance. This lesson was the question that started our plunge in studying Nazi life. Do you remember the question? It concerned a bewilderment at the German populace claiming ignorance and noninvolvement in the Nazi movement. If I remember the question, it went something like this: How could the German soldier, teacher, railroad conductor, nurse, tax collector, the average citizen, claim at the end of the Third Reich that they knew nothing of what was going on? How can a people be a part of something and then claim at the demise that they were not really involved? What causes people to blank out their own history? In the next few minutes and perhaps years, you will have an opportunity to answer this question.

"If our enactment of the Fascist mentality is complete, not one of you will ever admit to being at this final Third Wave rally. Like the Germans, you will have trouble admitting to yourself that you came this far. You will not allow your friends and parents to know that you were willing to give up individual freedom and power for the dictates of order and unseen leaders. You can't admit to being manipulated. Being a follower. To accepting the Third Wave as a way of life. You won't admit to participating in this madness. You will keep this day and this rally a secret. It's a secret I shall share with you."

I took the film for the three cameras in the room and pulled the celluloid into the exposing light. The deed was concluded. The trial was over. The Third Wave had ended.

I glanced over my shoulder. Robert was crying. Students slowly rose from their chairs and without words filed into the outdoor light. I walked over to Robert and threw my arms around him. Robert was sobbing. Taking in large uncontrollable gulps of air. "It's over." "It's all right." In our consoling each other we became a rock in the stream of exiting students. Some swirled back to hold Robert and me momentarily. Others cried openly and then brushed away tears to carry on. Human beings circling and holding each other. Moving toward the door and the world outside.

For a week in the middle of a school year we had shared fully in life. And as predicted we also shared a deep secret. In the four years I taught at Cubberly High School no one ever admitted to attending the Third Wave rally. Oh, we talked and studied our actions intently. But the rally itself. No. It was something we all wanted to forget.

Questions

1. What difference is there, if any, between the self-discipline of artists, dancers, athletes, and so on, and the discipline of students, soldiers, or workers conforming to the rules of an authority figure?

2. Why do you think so many students were eager to be involved in a highly controlled organization?

3. Jones says that community is "that bond between individuals who work and struggle together." How does this compare to definitions of community in section two of this chapter? Is a group really a community if the people who work and struggle together do not know why they are doing this, or have no control over the purposes of their work and struggle? Do the inmates of a prison form a community?

4. Jones says that he was "following the group dictate" as much as he was "directing" it. Do you think this is true of authority figures in general? What are the implications ?

5. Jones says that his students were "learning more" under the new regime, and also that "the intellectual skills of questioning and reasoning were nonexistent." How can this be?

6. Does it make sense to say that everyone is equal in a totalitarian organization? Can the ruler and helpers be regarded as equal to the rest?

7. What was the nature of the oppression in the classroom experiment? How and why do people participate in their own oppression? Does oppression exist if you are not aware of it?

8. Jones says that fascism exists "in our own personal habits and way of life." Can you identify others than the ones he lists? What are the sources of fascist habits and beliefs?

The Law Is Terror Put Into Words   *Peter d'Errico*

It is my purpose in this essay to focus on that form of legal studies which is critical, humanistic and self-developmental in its educational goals. And in this context, I will explore the potential for the emergence of a fundamental restructuring of the way we think about law.

After five years of teaching and studying law within the framework of a college curriculum, I have come to regard this mode of legal studies as a form of cultural action. The barriers and

The author wishes to thank Marilyn S. Berman for her help in the writing and revision of this article. Reprinted by permission from *Learning and the Law* (Fall, 1975). Copyright © 1975 by the American Bar Association. (Abridged.)

suspicions which have isolated the study of law within law school are transcended through this action, opening the way to a reexamination of basic assumptions and thought patterns underlying our traditional views of law.

A humanistic and critical approach to legal studies, emphasizing the development of self-knowledge, begins by drawing together the ways in which the phenomena of law have been studied by various scholarly disciplines. Jurisprudential, sociological, historical, economic, psychological, anthropological and other modes of analysis are brought into an interdisciplinary focus. Building on the interpenetration of different modes of thought, this approach to legal studies becomes *transdisciplinary*. The transition from interdisciplinary to transdisciplinary inquiry is extremely important. It is the necessary effect of a serious interpenetration of disciplines.

Much of the failure of "law and society" programs in law school has been due not so much to an inability to achieve cooperation across disciplinary lines as to the refusal to move beyond the notion of separate but equal discipline structures. . . . Indeed, transdisciplinary exploration begins with the realization that any discipline functions as much to *limit* inquiry as to structure it, and then proceeds to examine the universe of questions which surround every discipline.

Legal studies, in its most significant form, involves such an exploration into the unknown.

Changing Consciousness of Law

We are living in a time of changing consciousness about the meaning and function of authority. Law, which is often taken to be the backbone of authority structures in society, has come increasingly under scrutiny, both for its role in maintaining oppressive social conditions and for the exceeding narrowness of legalism as a world-view.

In a sense, we no longer believe in our system of legal rules the way we used to. We are beginning to see through the facade of a "government of laws" to the people who animate that system. And further, we are coming to understand that legalism is as much an obscuring veil as a clarifying lens for approaching social problems. Law and legal thinking are as frequently the cause of social trouble as the means of resolving it. Thus, as Addison Mueller has noted, in our "free-enterprise" economy, "freedom of contract" is the consumer's losing card [*Contracts of Frustration,* 78 *Yale L.J.* 576 (1969)].

This growing skepticism and criticism about law is part of the decline of legalism in our culture. The decline, however, is not a simple matter. It is beset with resistance and contradiction. For example, even as the evidence becomes more and more clear that prison is a dysfunctional, self-defeating, self-perpetuating social institution, the force of the state is called again and again into action against the victims of that institution. Like-wise, even though crime is increasingly understood to be a product of social stratification, rather than a phenomenon of human nature against which society structures itself, the state spends ever more money to preserve the existing social structure and to thwart the forces of social change.

In an overall way, these contradictions are forcing us to realize that our justice system is only another social institution, subject to all the ills that befall any other institution: bureaucracy, pre-occupation with its own maintenance and expansion, depersonalization of those whom it is supposed to serve, etc. Disenchantment with law as the basis for authority in social and personal life is now so pervasive that we are at a crisis in the history of law itself. . . .

The central purpose of law school education . . . is socialization into the legal profession. This process is the antithesis of free and open-ended inquiry into the nature and function of law. That is why the contracts teacher, for example, cannot pause to consider the basic injustice of "freedom of contract" in a monopolistic economic system. To do so would not only take time away from the job of teaching how to manipulate legal doctrine, it would positively disrupt the socialization process itself. That is, criticism of basic legal forms and processes is incompatible with the inculcation of allegiance to the framework of legalism as a way of thinking and acting.

This incompatibility is especially significant in the first year of law school. It is there that so many idealistic young people, eager to "help others" and "change society," first encounter the full force of legalism and come to grapple with its peculiar and surprising ability to step aside from every question of substance and value conflict. Questions about social history, or economics, or psychology, or even of philosophy, are admitted into the classroom only to the extent that they do not distract from the main task. That task is learning how to sidestep all such questions in the parsing of doctrine and, thus, in the exercise of legal power.

Law students are taught to seek and use power, rather than truth. And as a way of persuading them to give up any persistent pursuit of the latter, they are encouraged to think of the "justice" they can accomplish when they have acquired power. The first year is complete when the students can no longer separate "justice" from "law," and when all critical consciousness has been engulfed by positivism and social relativism.

A critical, humanistic legal studies program, in contrast, does not take as its starting point an acceptance of the particular form of law which has developed in this society, nor a commitment to socialize its students into such an acceptance or allegiance. Indeed, this kind of legal studies is ... willing to start with premises that are diametrically opposed to the structure and concepts of legalism. It is not afraid to admit that legalized oppression is a reality to many people in this country. In a legal studies class, questions about the fairness of the structure of economic activity and of the legal apparatus sustaining and enforcing that structure are not only admissible, *they are central.*

A discussion about criminal law would not be complete without an examination of the social history and politics of crime control. Similarly, psychological and sociological data are scrutinized for an understanding of such phenomena as oppression and social stratification. The aim of such scrutiny, furthermore, is not the inculcation of an easy social relativism, but rather the development of a critical consciousness about what might be called the "politics of everyday life." This is an arena of activity that is not apprehended by the method or framework of legalism, due to the latter's elevation of official explanation over personal experience.

It is interesting to note that this kind of critical approach to law study occasionally meets with resistance even among undergraduates. Business school students, for example, are more likely than others to feel threatened and annoyed by a critique of legalism. It is their very professionalization and allegiance to the ideology of capital which is shaken by such criticism. Most people do not like to have basic assumptions challenged; they fear the ambiguity which is generated in this process. But for those who are building a career on the challenged assumptions, the fear of ambiguity can be paralyzing.

I have, on occasion, asked in class, "What is the difference between business and stealing?" and "What is a loophole in law?" The response to these queries is usually laughter and a quick rush of suggested answers. As the students are pressed on their answers to the first question, and it becomes clear that no logical or philosophical explanation exists to rationalize the distinction in an overall way, the atmosphere grows more serious.

An underlying feeling of confusion sets in, and the students are ready to look deeper into the ideology of legalism and at the process of legal socialization (how people come to learn and accept legal distinctions, etc.). Similarly, with the second question, students begin to ponder the significance of a concept which has meaning only within a legalistic social structure, and yet whose function is to permit escape from the structure. That the concept has no true juridic existence is a paradox which stimulates further inquiry into the nature and function of law, its value orientation, and so on.

In this mode of legal studies, as education *about* law rather than education *in* law, one is free to see legalism itself as pathology rather than enlightenment, as a manifestation of social alienation rather than a means to social unity, as dispute-masking rather than dispute-settling, and as a handmaiden to economic exploitation rather than a mechanism for equity in resource allocation.

As professional law training is distinguished by its commitment to the existing legal system, to the ideology of legalism that informs that system, and to the social order which the system and the ideology both serve, so is a critical legal studies distinguished by its freedom from these commitments and its consequent ability to provide a basis for analysis of the very thought structures which underpin the legalistic ethos.

Law school, having excluded any external vantage point from which one might gain a critical perspective, is thus unable to comprehend the actual effects of legalism on the society in which it operates. With minor exceptions, even natural law—positivism's only serious antagonist within the law school world—is no longer a viable option. The result is that professional legal education provides no basis for analyzing the psychic and social phenomenon of legalism, and no entry point through which any such critique might enter the curriculum. That such a critique can be built, however, is exceedingly clear.

We Are Authority Addicts

Daily life under legalism is permeated in all its aspects by a belief in authority, and an accompanying tension between authoritative descriptions of the world and our own individual perceptions of life. We are authority addicts, hooked on rules. As Judith Shklar has noted, the institutional and personal levels of commitment to legalism form a social continuum: "At one end of the scale of legalistic values and institutions stand its most highly articulate and refined expressions, the courts of law and the rules they follow; at the other end is the personal morality of all those men and women who think of goodness as obedience to the rules that properly define their duties and rights" [*Legalism* (1964) p. 3].

At every moment, even to the level of how and when to eat, smile, sleep, talk, touch and move, and beyond this to the level of how and what we are supposed to think, fantasy and dream, there are rules. Life for most people seems to be a project of obedience, of duty and responsibility to authority. Constantly there is the struggle to fit ourselves into someone else's dream, someone else's definition of reality. And with this struggle, as part of it and in turn perpetuating it, goes a fear of letting go of authority as well as attempts to impose our authority on others, preoccupation with what others think, feelings of isolation from others and the world, and fear that we will not exist if we do not define ourselves, label our relationships and categorize ourselves and each other.

David Cooper, studying such phenomena in *The Death of the Family* (1971), writes:

> If, then, we wish to find the most basic level of understanding of repression in society, we have to see it as a collectively reinforced and institutionally formalized panic about going mad, about the invasion of the outer by the inner and of the inner by the outer, about the loss of

the illusion of "self." The Law is terror put into words (p. 33).

Under legalism, we are constantly trying to control ourselves and each other within limits laid down by authority, all the time not seeing any alternative to this positivistic world, accepting it as necessary and inevitable. In law school, one learns to put the terror into words and to conceal its true nature. The heart of law school training is the refinement into positivism of a pre-existing allegiance to authority, the inchoate legalism acquired by the ordinary person in school and family.

The vaunted "case method" is nothing more than a frank recognition that authority is what counts; what is important to the lawyer is what has been held to be important.

The law student learns that *finding* the law regarding some particular social or economic conflict is more important than *understanding* the conflict. The student is trained to manipulate the language of a judge's opinion, and to exclude... consideration of... social, political, historical, and other factors and forces involved in the case....

The verbal framework and apparatus for the exercise of power which is thus created in law school becomes reality for the lawyer; the legal system takes primacy over the effects it has on real people in real social situations. Witness Edward H. Levi, discussing "The Nature of Judicial Reasoning":

> Perhaps it should be said that the effect of... (a legal decision) so far as the judge or lawyer is concerned is primarily on the fabric of the law. The lawyer's or the judge's function may be sufficiently self-delimited so as to exclude from the realm of their professional competence the larger social consequences... For the judge or lawyer the relevant effects are upon the web of the law, the administration of law, and the respect for law [*Law and Philosophy*, Hook, ed. (1964) p. 264].

The result of this process, as legalism continues to build on itself, is an increasing separation between the concerns of law and the concerns of justice. Law becomes preoccupied with preserving itself and the social order with which it is identified. The concern of justice, in contrast, remains the achievement of social *wholeness* rather than simple order.

Charles Silberman, in his powerful critique of the 1971 [Association of American Law Schools] curriculum study report, "Training for the Public Professions of the Law," pointed out this divergence between the concern for social order and a concern for justice. Noting that the words "justice" and "injustice" do not appear in the AALS report, Silberman called for the "depoliticalization" of law school, saying that law school is

> politicized through its commitment to the status quo.... The point is that where gross injustice exists, the pursuit of justice may involve the exacerbation of social conflict, not its resolution. It is precisely this commitment to conflict resolution rather than to justice that creates the lawyers bias for the status quo....

The concept of a person's "rights," for example, is basic to legalism. It is one of the most powerful formulations in gaining and sustaining popular support for the operation of the legal system.

The common understanding of this concept is that law takes the side of the people against governmental or other systematic injustice. This uncritical view is elaborated upon in law school and throughout the legal system. Actually, however, once one understands that the central concern of legalism is with the maintenance of its own power system, one sees that the law only *appears* to take the side of the people. In fact, the real concern of legalism in its recognition of popular claims of right (civil rights, etc.) is *to preserve the basic governmental framework in which the claims arise.*

The concept of civil rights has meaning only in the context of an over-arching system of legal power against which the civil rights are supposed to protect. Ending the system of power would also end the need for civil rights. But it is precisely here that one sees the impossibility of ending the oppression by means of civil rights law. In the end, this analysis points to the concept of personal "rights" as being a technique for depersonalizing people. We are taught to respect the rights of others, and in doing so we focus on the abstract bundle of rules and regulations which have been set up by judges and other officials to govern the behavior of people. In this focus, we miss the actual reality of the others as whole, real individuals. We end up, in short, respecting the law rather than people; and this, for legalism, is the essential aim.

Due process is another sacred cow become fair game. Legalism would have us regard this notion as the key to freedom under law, the means by which fairness and regularity are incorporated into legal decision-making. In reality, due process is the attempt of the system to insure that claim and counterclaim, freedom and grievance, both occur only within the existing legal universe and in its terms.

Every due process decision is thus only a further elaboration of the pre-existing legalist mazeway. People confront the claim of law to control social life, and the law responds; whatever the legal response to the confrontation, the law is concerned with itself first and foremost. The basic due process problem, as far as legalism is concerned, is only to preserve the apparatus of official legal control, even when the framework of that control must bend to meet the demands and needs of the people whose lives the officials govern. In a critical view, due process is essentially a technique for co-opting social change forces that threaten, or appear to threaten, official control of society.

In my own experience in practice—in an urban ghetto, on an Indian reservation, and in a middle class college community—I found again and again that people were able to see through law and legal processes in ways I had been taught to close my eyes to. When their vision was rebuffed by law, it became the basis for a deep cynicism about legal process. I saw, moreover, that even when lawyers succeeded in legalism's own game—the creation of a new rule, or the vindication of an old one—that we didn't really win anything, because legalism wasn't dealing with the roots of problems, but only with their surface appearances.

And it is not only "radical" law or legal services practice which generates such insight and skepticism. I found many traditional lawyers in conventional practices who were well aware that the law was not reaching their clients' real problems: economic, familial, psychological, and so on. These lawyers were sometimes deeply troubled by this awareness, and yet they remained unable even to articulate their experience. Locked into the mazeway of legalism in their education, and bereft of any critical viewpoint, they seemed resigned to a life of legal routine.

As my own critical consciousness has developed, I have come to regard legalism as a defunct social ideology. Capable at one time of unleashing tremendous productive social forces, legalism is now only a source of confusion and contradiction. Far from uniting America into a coherent and just society, traditional ideas of law foster division and give the stamp of approval to inequality.

One Legacy of Legal Realism

If "authority" is needed for this iconoclastic view of legalism, one need only look back to the last major jurisprudential shakeup in American history, legal realism. Karl Llewellyn, one of the most profound thinkers and observers in the realist movement, commenting on "the place and treatment of concepts," wrote [in *A Realistic Jurisprudence—The Next Step, Col. L. Rev.* 453 (1930)] "... categories and concepts, once formulated and once they have entered into thought processes, tend to take on an appearance of solidity, reality and inherent value which has no foundation in experience." In a time like the present, when belief in the central myths, or explanations of reality, around which our social life has been organized is increasingly breaking down, it becomes especially important to go beyond superficial exploration of social phenomena to an examination of concepts. The legal realist movement opened the door to new ways of thinking about the law, ways colored by non- or even anti-legalist perspectives....

A humanistic legal studies accepts this challenge.... Dealing with the central themes of human social life in a problem-oriented, question-posing way, this mode of study is free to pick up on even the most radical and far-reaching changes which are occurring in human consciousness. Le-

galism's continuous attempt to preserve old values by giving them new meaning can be replaced by an attempt to follow new meanings into a transvaluation of the central features of law and social life.

Professional legal education is an example of what Paulo Freire calls "the banking concept of education":

> Education thus becomes an act of depositing, in which the students are the depositories and the teacher is the depositor. Instead of communicating, the teacher issues communiques and makes deposits which the students patiently receive, memorize, and repeat. This is the "banking" concept of education, in which the scope of action allowed to the students extends only as far as receiving, filing, and storing the deposits. They do, it is true, have the opportunity to become collectors or cataloguers of the things they store [*Pedagogy of the Oppressed* (1974) p. 58].

At first, the law teacher "owns" the law and the students seek to possess this as a piece of property, something worth having. Later, the property having been conveyed, the students enter into the status of co-owners, taking upon themselves the role of guardian of this property which they have acquired and which will support them as a means of earning a living....

In legal studies, on the other hand, at least in its humanistic, self-developmental mode, the teacher is a student among students. Students and teachers are engaged as partners in critical thinking and a mutual quest for humanization. In this quest, the existing cultural framework of legalism is viewed not as a limit but as a challenge in an ontological and historical process of people becoming more fully human....

What will be necessary, however, in order for movement in this direction to occur, is the emergence of a radical consciousness, an awareness of life that goes beyond positivism and social relativism. And this means that the inadequacy of legalism must be admitted.

Legalism is no longer the ideology of human freedom and liberation. It is the ideology of the state and of property. When the law schools can go this far, their classrooms will become experimental laboratories in self-government, offering to the world both a new vision of human freedom and concrete proposals for social transformation.

In legal studies, our search is for a way of life and a paradigm for understanding law which do not require the acceptance of social oppression and personal repression as unalterable features of human existence. It is a search which is a praxis: reflection is merged with activity so that we are neither academics separated from the "real" world, nor "activists" cut off from the process of inquiry and education.

A transcending paradigm is not merely an idea to be imposed upon the thinking and behavior of people. It is a world-view which arises from the conscious living of people, out of our common struggle to understand and intervene in the processes by which human reality is created. Education on this scale is the objective of critical, humanistic, self-developmental legal studies.

Questions

1. What similarities and what contrasts do you find between daily life under legalism as it is described here and the fascist habits and ways of life referred to by Ron Jones in the preceding article?

2. What are the sources of people's belief and trust in rules? What are the sources of skepticism about rules?

3. Alienation and isolation are referred to as qualities of life under legalism. Compare this to the references in Stanley Diamond's article in the previous section, where these same qualities are discussed in terms of the historical development of law. What other connections do you find between the two articles?

4. David Cooper, quoted in this article, comments on "the loss of the illusion of 'self.'" Do you think this is an illusion that people in tribal society do not have? (Recall Vine DeLoria's remark that "tribal members know who they are.")

5. Compare the discussion of how lawyers are taught to exercise power with John Noonan's analysis of the slave laws in section one. Do you see how the law creates its own reality, and how respect for law supersedes respect for people?

6. Whose interests in society are served by positivist thinking, thinking that is premised on the notion that the way society *is* organized is the way it *has* to be? Whose interests are served by social relativism, thinking that society *could* be organized differently but that the differences are unimportant? By what means might people develop awareness of life that "goes beyond positivism and social relativism"?

Socialist Law and Legal Institutions *Michael E. Tigar*

American society is built upon capitalist economic institutions. The right of property is a basic element of the constitutional legal order. Property is among the things which the state is committed to protect, just as it is theoretically committed to protect "civil liberties" and "civil rights." The protection of private property by the state is justified in the writings of eighteenth-century social theorists on the basis that the relationship between a man and "his" property is not a relationship of dominance and subordination, but one between a man and an object. John Locke even adopted a labor theory of property rights to underscore this point. Locke argued that when a man mixes his labor with the earth and produces, for example, some food, his right to ownership of that which he has produced is self-evident.

Locke's theory explodes, as does the theory that private property involves only a relationship between men and things, with the coming of industrial capitalism. In this society, some men own the means of production, and others sell their

From *Law Against the People,* Robert Lefcourt, ed. (New York: Random House, 1971). © 1971 by Michael E. Tigar. Reprinted by permission. His thoughts in this essay are further developed in his book *Law and the Rise of Capitalism,* published by Monthly Review Press. (Abridged.)

labor. The men who mix their labor with the raw material of production do not own the goods they make and are not considered as "selling" these goods to the capitalist. This division, it has been remarked in the writings of contemporary scholars, is the root of alienation in industrial society. This notion aside, however, the relationship between the owner of the means of production and his employee does involve dominance of one man over another. If it is difficult to see this point in the context of a one-man shop, consider the great power of a large corporation over the quality of life in its community. Job opportunities, working conditions, living conditions—a great deal depends upon the unilateral decision of the plant owner. . . .

One cannot understand the "repression of dissent" without looking closely at the forces in the interest of which it is employed. The relationship between these forces and their tactics at this period is but a special instance of the relationship between the forms of state power and the system of social relations which these forces protect. The state is not, despite emphasis in the legal forum on the adversary system, neutral.

Too often, however, this generation of Movement activists tends to regard the response of the state to protest as a knee jerk, with the ruling class wielding the rubber hammer. This simplistic view of the process of litigation and adjudication is held because of an incomplete analysis of the relationship between the state and the interests it protects. Since the state is a structure erected upon the basis of social relationships at a given period, the set of formal legal precepts about the way in which state power is to be exercised is ideology with a kind of life of its own. That is, though the principled application of formal rules—such as the rule that freedom of speech shall not be abridged—may under some circumstances cut against the will of the holders of public and private power, these rules may nonetheless be so applied. The ideology of law and legal rules will not correspond at every moment with the wishes and demands of the wielders of power. The judges, assigned the task of interpreting and applying legal rules, are now more, now less, careful to follow out these rules to the limit of their logic

regardless of whose interest they may serve in a particular case. Too, there are rules of law acquiesced in and indeed promoted by sections of the ruling class which advance and protect the interests of the poor, the dispossessed, and the discriminated. The genesis of such legislation is usually in social struggle, and its purpose is usually to buy off more fundamental demands for change.

To the extent that there is a conflict between ruling class self-interest and legal rules, there is an opportunity for creative and innovative litigation in present-day America. But those of us who are lawyers ought not fool ourselves that we are doing more than fighting a holding action against the power of the state and on behalf of the movement for social change. We must identify with and understand our Movement clients, for through them and not through us will the changes come that insure the realization of the ideal of justice. No system worthy of the name of justice can be built upon a foundation of social relations which put the means of production in the hands of private persons and the state's instruments of terror and coercion at their service.

Although most sections of the Movement recognize these facts, many still assume that a change in fundamental social relations—the coming of a socialist order of things—will of itself assure an end to injustice. Those who believe this forget that in neither capitalist nor socialist society is there a one-to-one mechanical correspondence between the interests served by the institution of state power and each particular decision made by each agency of the state. Continual struggle goes on in socialist countries to accommodate socialist legal norms and practice to fundamental socialist principle. A socialist society—the Soviet Union, China, Cuba—is one in which the means of production have already passed from private hands, or are being gathered up into public hands.

The long-range professed socialist goal is that the state "wither away," coercion and the apparatus of state power becoming unnecessary. Adherence to rules of social conduct, the Marxist theory runs, will be secured through the voluntary acquiescence of every man in shared goals, enforced by a kind of collective community sentiment. To put it another way, the state is to be replaced by an apparatus for the administration of things.

Any thought that these changes would come automatically—and such thoughts have been expressed—is surely visionary. Repression, bureaucratization, and even terror have been used by almost every socialist regime. Too, socialist countries have determined—rightly or not—that there is need for a more or less extensive system of state organization run according to rules of order. By this means is created a superstructure analogous to that existing in capitalist countries.

The question remains: what form should socialist legal organization take? Although there is substantial room for debate, some factors can generally be agreed upon. Such a system must seek to accommodate and deal with attitudes and behavior conditioned by life under capitalism; it must command public acquiescence in the fairness of its rules and procedures; and it must be amenable to change as the experience of living in a new society changes the character of the people subject to its regime. It is an error to assume that all problems of the achievement of justice become merely administrative under a new system of social organization. . . .

Take the first of these problems, that of defining justice in a socialist society. Under capitalism, Black and Brown Americans are kept at an economic disadvantage. Given menial jobs on the fringes of the labor force, they provide a source of cheap labor which is usable in times of full employment at low wages. This subordination of Blacks and Browns is the domestic analogue of American capital's exploitation of labor in the Third World in the production of primary products and semimanufactures for shipment to this country. The existence, in this country and abroad, of a supply of cheap labor for the production of primary products and the performance of menial tasks has been a mainstay of capitalism.

The coming of a socialist society would abolish the economic necessity for superexploitation of nonwhites; it would not, however, do away automatically with racial attitudes which have been generated under capitalism. That is, the inferior position of Blacks and Browns in this country has

come about because of the needs of a capitalist system. An elaborate system of ideological, superstructural justification for this fact has been generated by these concrete conditions. This justification, in the form of theories of racial superiority or their more sophisticated variants, has by now acquired a life of its own in the consciousness of millions of people. Social change alone will not eradicate that consciousness; experience and struggle may do so.

Consider too the question of sexism. In this society, the capitalist obtains from most workers the labor of two people for the price of one. The wife stays home to cook, clean, and tend the children, without pay. Suppose for a moment we did not have the institution of marriage and that each person either had to clean and cook his own meals or pay to have these jobs done. . . . The social determination of the basic wage would be different. As with the Blacks, an elaborate ideology about the natural role of women has developed to justify their subjection. While a system of socialist production relations would end the economic foundation for such a system, it would not end the attitudes conditioned over centuries which are part of almost every man's ideological baggage. Again, experience and struggle are the determinants of whether this question will be successfully resolved.

The governors of socialist societies recognize these and other problems, but in the Soviet Union, there is evidence that struggle to achieve a new concept of justice has not occurred. In the aftermath of the Khrushchev denunciation of Stalin there was much talk of the new socialist man and where he was coming from. The Soviet Communist Party Draft Program in 1961 spoke of achieving communism—the withering of the state—within twenty years. There has, however, been remarkably little discussion, in the Soviet Union or other socialist countries, of the precise meaning of "withering away of the state."

One goal of a new socialism, nevertheless, is the eventual transfer of power from the state to the people. Within the legal sphere, this means, in part, the development of an informal judicial system administered predominantly by lay people instead of a class of trained professionals. George

Feifer's book, *Justice in Moscow,* describes the operation of people's courts, with jurisdiction over petty criminal offenses, domestic strife, and minor civil suits. These courts sit with one professional judge and two lay judges, in an atmosphere asserted to be informal. With some minor exceptions, these courts operate much like courts . . . in Western countries.

At another level are "comrades' courts," a product of the post-Stalin era. These informal bodies, each with a territorial jurisdiction extending over a few city blocks, a particular factory, or some other living or working unit, are designed to dispense informal justice in minor social disputes, and to handle petty infractions of law best summarized as "disorderly conduct." Quite similar to the comrades' courts are the assemblies of the community, established in 1961 and possessing, among other features, the rather considerable power to deal with "parasitism" and incorrigible antisocial behavior by means of banishment from the community. The comrades' courts represent a genuine effort to place Soviet citizens in the midst of administering Soviet justice. In a future communist society, the Soviet Communist Party has written, "Comradely censure of anti-social actions will gradually become the principal means of eradication of bourgeois views, customs, and habits."

And yet, if the reports of observers can be credited, the participation of lay assessors in people's courts is generally desultory and pro forma, and the atmosphere little different from that of a municipal court in the United States. The comrades' courts, while they do cause excitement and interest in their proceedings, do not appear to have a significant impact on Soviet life. Moreover, there are indications that the existence and operation of these courts have met with some opposition from the Soviet legal establishment. . . . The comrades' courts operate informally both as to procedure and as to the rules they apply to judge and regulate conduct. Using such vague terms as "antisocial" and "disorderly," they appear to devise precise rules to settle individual cases in a rather freewheeling manner. . . .

But the comrades' courts cannot overcome a fundamental defect which remains in Soviet no-

tions of law and its relationship to the level of social development. A dominant theme in Soviet thinking is that of "socialist legality," of harmony to written rules (including rules guaranteeing procedural rights) as the principal protection of "individual rights." This notion is no doubt comforting to Western observers, and even to radical lawyers in this country. So much of our time, as lawyers, is spent seeking to vindicate claims for justice founded upon written rules expressed as limits upon the state's power to punish particular acts (guarantees of free speech, for example) or to proceed in particular ways (the guarantees of procedural rights). We cherish these concessions and contradictions. But in a socialist society, there ought in theory to be a different approach. A socialist society is theoretically engaged in laying the technical basis for a new form of civilization, and in that process human consciousness is to be transformed. At bottom, Marxist theory emphasizes that there must be a unity of theory and practice, of thought and work, of rule and reality.

However, while the comrades' courts and assemblies of the community in the Soviet Union pursue this unity through the creation of forms of popular participation, there remains a vast bureaucratic institution charged with the development and elaboration of legal rules and structures. The Stalin terror is largely gone, but high valuation is still placed on formal positive law. Soviet lawyers, and some Western observers, would no doubt argue that the maintenance of such a structure is necessary to insure that state institutions follow certain basic norms of substantive and procedural law for the benefit of individuals. But the experience of other socialist countries, engaged in different experiments in developing legal institutions that maximize popular involvement, suggests that the Soviet thinkers are too firmly implanted in their European code law tradition.

Contrast the Soviet view with that of the Chinese, for example. The Chinese revolution was, it must be recalled, fought over a long period of time and over an extensive area. A far greater percentage of the people were engaged in revolutionary struggle than in the Soviet Union. Institutions of governance were developed in the course of the revolution and designed to return decision-making power to the people. More important, perhaps, the Chinese legal tradition has eschewed formal legal rules, which are regarded in Chinese philosophy dating to early Confucian thought as inherently inferior to principles of behavior derived from common consent or custom, and enforced through community pressure and community-based mediation agencies operating largely informally. Attempts made by Western imperialism beginning in the early twentieth century to impose "code law" in the tradition of the French and German experience were largely failures, serving only to regularize certain economic relations between the local bourgeois and comprador elements and the businessmen of the Occident.

René David has written, in *Les Grands systèmes de droit contemporains*:

> Marxist-Leninist philosophy contains elements which accord with this traditional philosophy: positive law has never appeared to the Chinese as being a necessary condition, or even a normal condition, of a well-ordered society; positive law is, on the contrary, a sign of an imperfect society, and a connection exists between the idea of positive law and that of coercion. Communism, presaged in Marxist thought, is nearly an ideal society as such a society is envisaged by the Chinese.

Others, including the American author Jerome Cohen, have also commented upon the connection between traditional Chinese views of law and the legal theory of the Chinese Communists.

Too, the Chinese revolution has been alert to the problem of separating mental from manual labor and to the important task of shaping institutional forms to reflect constantly changing material conditions of production and exchange. The restructuring of the universities in the Cultural Revolution is the most recent example of this process at work. The Chinese legal system reflects this systematic drive to prevent the formation of positive legal rules which acquire a life of their own, and a consistent attention to the application of principles derived from common experience and shared expectations about behavior in making legal rules. In defining criminal offenses, this process takes the following form: the single most

important theoretical underpinning of the criminal law is Mao Tse-tung's work, "On the Correct Handling of Contradictions Among the People." There, Mao underscored the importance of the concept of contradiction in Marxist thought. Marxism, he reiterated, is based upon dialectical and historical materialism. Briefly, Marxist dialectics maintain that events in the real world, including historical events, move through the resolution of contradictions which inhere in all life situations. In society, the interests of social classes and groups are contradictory. The resolution of these contradictions takes the form of a synthesis on a new and higher level. Within that new synthesis there will develop a new contradiction in the form of an antithesis, leading to a still newer synthesis, and so on. Mao distinguished between contradictions which he termed "antagonistic," "between the enemy and us," and those which he termed "nonantagonistic," "among ourselves." An example of the former is the contradiction between the large bourgeoisie and comprador class and the majority of the Chinese people—workers, peasants, small farmers, small businessmen, and so on. The power base of the large bourgeoisie and the compradors had to be destroyed in order for the Chinese revolution to succeed; there could be no compromise with those whose means of livelihood depended upon the maintenance of a system of exploitation which was at the root of poverty and famine and kept in power by terror and coercion. Once the Chinese revolution was successful, however, there was no guarantee that the interests of workers, peasants, small farmers, and small businessmen would always be identical. Indeed, there was every reason to suspect that there would be contradictory demands upon social resources by these groups. Yet these demands were consistent with the maintenance of the basic system of social organization introduced by the revolution.

Chinese criminal law rests upon this basic formulation. Offenses committed in the name of bringing back the former system of social organization, or which objectively aid the reimposition of that system, are regarded as the occasion for severe measures. However, even in this field there is extensive concern with the rehabilitative potential of various social institutions, and careful attention to the problems of rehabilitation in individual cases.

More significant, however, for purposes of this essay, are the legal rules and institutions designed to deal with contradictions among the people. In general, there is a preference for dealing with disputes at the lowest and most informal level of adjudication. The farm community, the families living on a city block, and other informal groupings are enjoined to and do intercede freely to achieve an accommodation in both civil disputes and those which involve a minor infraction of criminal law rules. (Snow reports that there are only 250 lawyers in all China.)

As some observers have reported, a traffic law violator is likely to be pulled over to the side by a foot policeman and given a long lecture about the importance of abiding by rules so that the police and courts will not have to intervene. As the lecture continues, passersby are likely to join and turn the occasion into a discussion of the preferability of not having to have formal institutions of coercion. More serious disputes are thought to require more formal treatment, but the emphasis is not upon the vindication of abstract principle but upon the accommodation of conflicting interests to ensure protection of larger social goals....

Chinese contract law, to take another example, is likely to be far less reliant upon formal rituals of contract law as conceived in Western business law contexts. In the Soviet Union, contracts between state organs and state-run enterprises have a decidedly managerial flavor, although there has been some effort to decentralize decision-making and put factory workers more directly into the process of management. In China, the making of economic contracts for production and supply involves thousands of people; these contracts are the basis of output predictions and relations between the various sectors of the economy. It is not unusual for an entire farm community, an agricultural or factory commune or similar economic unit, to have a mass meeting to decide upon the terms of a contract of production and supply. The thought, no doubt, is to integrate the managerial and production functions, and take from the "contract law" the aura of a legal rule or principle divorced from the participation of those whose labor power makes up the goods which will fulfill the contract.

In sum, the Chinese legal system is built upon a sense of community, and seeks to prevent the creation of an ideology of law and state which would be a barrier to social development and contradict the goal of eliminating the coercive aspect of state power. There are, of course, risks and disadvantages in such a system. Most obvious to Western critics is the absence of an orderly and organized system of insuring procedural fairness and respect for substantive rights. American constitutional scholars, proceeding in most cases from premises narrowly defined by the dominant assumptions of constitutional doctrine in this country, regard the absence of such a system as an incurable defect. How can one secure respect for rights unless those rights are written down in a code and unless some branch of government is given the duty to see that they are not denied? ...

However, it seems likely that in terms of Chinese tradition, a system of social organization which relies upon constant and active debate about social goals and priorities has a great chance of developing a broad consensus about minimal human rights and securing respect for them.

Consider, too, the development of legal institutions in Cuba. The available evidence suggests that the entire tone and tenor of Cuban life have been changed by the Revolution. There has been, since the Revolution left its liberal reformist phase and embarked upon a program of socialist construction, detailed and consistent attention to nonmaterial incentives to production, involving the entire population in setting social priorities, and developing informal systems of dispute resolution.

Interestingly, part of the pre-Revolutionary system of courts and judges, still staffed to a large extent with lawyers whose experience and education antedate the Revolution, continues to function. The judges in their robes still sit in large courtrooms and hear major cases, basing their decisions (at least in criminal matters) on the 1938 Cuban Code. Why this system has been permitted to continue is difficult to know. Perhaps its existence is tolerated because it is being undermined from two directions by newly developed institutions of justice.

The first of these is the revolutionary tribunals which try alleged counterrevolutionary activity. These tribunals are manned by the armed forces. It would be worthwhile to conduct an independent evaluation of their procedures, including the sort of evidence relied upon and the standards of proof required for conviction. In the absence of such a study, one can only report that the existence and functioning of the tribunals do not appear to have caused great concern, distrust, or dismay on the part of the Cuban people. Cuba is, after all, still under siege and subject to armed attack, overt and clandestine, by groups operating from the United States and elsewhere in Latin America.

The second set of institutions, undercutting the jurisdiction of traditional courts, is the popular tribunals. These bodies, run by nonlawyer judges elected by a majority of the citizens in a particular area, have extensive powers to deal with a wide range of criminal and civil matters. Their emphasis, we know from reports of those who have spent a great deal of time observing them, is upon nonpenal solutions to problems brought before them. Their powers include incarceration (in jail or under house arrest), compulsory psychiatric treatment, compulsory work in agriculture for a stated period, attendance at a school to complete one's education through the sixth grade, and a host of other corrective or compensatory sanctions. The most common minor sanction is the public admonition. The jurisdiction of these courts is defined by category of offense rather than by a code of laws. These categories include delicts, a category sharing some notions of the common law tort and crime categories, and contraventions, a category of conduct less serious than delicts and including "disorderly conduct" sorts of behavior. Delicts include conduct analogous to defamation, threats and coercion, violation of rationing regulations, cheating one's business

customers, and other kinds of conduct regarded as affecting fundamental social interests. These categories are familiar to the civil law tradition.

The basis for determining whether an individual has by his conduct committed a delict or contravention is uncertain, except that the lay judges feel a sense of obligation to reflect revolutionary consciousness in their judgments, and to find a basis of decision that reflects the community will. There is no code as such, only a very general manual for the lay judges. Since the sessions of the tribunals are held in the evenings and extremely well-attended, the educational value of the proceedings is considerable. Since the judges are not only elected, but hold regular jobs in the daytime, they are unlikely to regard themselves as separate from the communities they serve.

The crucial distinction between the Soviet and Cuban popular tribunals is in the revolutionary character and commitment of the societies of which they are a part. There appears to be an effort in Cuba to rely very little upon rigid structures and forms, a constant effort to renew institutional norms with revolutionary experience. There is a marked fear of creating a class of persons—whether they be students, lawyers, professors, or governors—who do not work but merely live from the labor of others. Evidence of this same effort appears in China, where the historical suspicion of rigid forms makes the task easier at least in the realm of law. This is not to doubt, in either the Cuban or Chinese experience, the role of a central authority in making social and economic decisions. The presence and influence of the state are felt everywhere in these societies. Clear, however, is a commitment to move away from reliance upon state power as the instrument of social cohesion and control.

What can be the lesson of this historical sketch for the Movement in this country? We have, all of us, been schooled to believe that protection of basic rights requires a quasi-independent class of lawgivers expounding a detailed set of rules....

In the courts and in political forums we have sought to create progressive legal rules to protect and extend the rights of people's movements. But we have not sought to hear the people's authentic voice in the courts and halls of justice, only to keep that voice from being stilled by the application of legal rules which are at bottom designed to protect privilege. It has been the principle that we have sought to defend, not the institution which administers it.

In considering a new system of social relations for this country, we must ask what forms are likely to protect revolutionary gains and at the same moment ensure respect for persons against the arbitrary exercise of power. The Soviet experience shows, I think, that reliance upon formal legal rules to embody fundamental social decisions about goals is an error. The creation of a class of persons whose task is thought and speculation is not merely futile but dangerous: Such a class does not work but lives off the labor of others, and has no practice with which to integrate its theory. . . .

If this is so, then the most important questions about the structure of a legal order in a new society are answered not by lawyers as technicians of the existing order, but by Movement activists in seeking to live and work together to bring about change. How does the Movement deal with sexism and racism in its midst? How are disputes settled? What respect is given the views of others? What steps are taken to prevent elitism and the separation of theory and theorists from practice and struggle? The dominant form of Movement organization today is the collective group organized in a particular area or around a particular issue or set of issues. The truly remarkable fact about Movement groups is the recognition that life together in struggle is not possible unless these interpersonal issues, which are microcosms of social conflicts in a larger arena, are raised, discussed, and dealt with.

Indeed, if the goal of a new society is the demystification of law, one must consider demystifying the Movement lawyer here and now. Certainly lawyers have skills, experience and knowledge to share. But the increased moves toward self-defense by Movement people on trial, toward breaking down barriers to real communication with juries in criminal trials, and toward making lawyers responsible to the Movement they seek to serve, are concrete steps toward understanding and building a legal system in a new order of things. This attack on "professionalism" and "elitism" by lawyers is part of a broader concern which the Movement must have with solving its own internal problems while struggling with problems outside itself, rather than deferring consideration of internal problems. . . .

The kind of society we get, as the experience of socialist countries has shown, is the kind we build for. This has been and is true of every revolutionary struggle in the past twenty years. The building of legal institutions, in the sense that procedures and rules crystallize out of struggle, is an ongoing process which involves everyone in the movement for change. There is no reason, in this process, to forget the lessons of our own history as a people and the regard traditionally paid in bourgeois rhetoric to such matters as freedom of discourse and procedural regularity. Indeed, failure to recognize a fundamental American commitment to these principles would be wrong. It would be equally mistaken, though, to regard these rights as the creatures of a state apparatus and necessarily bound up with the creation and maintenance of such an apparatus. . . .

How does the movement for change propose that America be governed? Just in the way that it creates and maintains means to govern itself.

Questions

1. What do you think Tigar means by saying that the basic changes in society will come through the *clients* of radical lawyers rather than through the lawyers themselves?

2. What is the relationship between social change and change in people's consciousness? Is this a problem of the chicken and the egg?

3. What do you think are the factors that determine whether people will struggle for change? What areas of life are open to struggle? What do you think Tigar means when he says that "interpersonal issues" and conflicts are "microcosms of social conflicts in a larger arena"?

4. What are the implications of Tigar's claim that the "people's courts" in the Soviet Union "operate much like courts in Western countries"?

5. What similarities and what differences do you find between the socialist goal of a stateless society and the stateless tribal societies described in section two of this chapter?

6. Compare Tigar's discussion of Chinese culture with the poem by Chuang Tzu in section one of this chapter. Can you find similar sources of anti-legalist feeling in American history and literature?

The Organizational Revolution   *Frederick C. Thayer*

We must sweep away the conventional baggage of what we know as "politics" and "economics." Our system of representative government is designed only to preserve *hierarchy,* and our economic system is based upon the ideal of *competition.* Yet neither hierarchy nor competition has a place in our future, for both compel us to repress ourselves and each other. The organizational revolution is an attempt to end repression, and the alienation that accompanies it. . . .

When the organizational revolution has run its course, and when societies have been transformed as they must be if we are to survive, the world of organizations will be one of innumerable small face-to-face groups characterized by openness, trust, and intensive interpersonal relations. . . .

This entire book argues for a *different* way of looking at the world in which we live, and especially at the organizations (nation-states, universities, public agencies, corporations, and whatever) which dominate the world's activity. The initial premise, which may seem extremely disorienting at first glance, is that formal organizations as we think of them either *do not exist* or are *dysfunctional.* The most useful work is accomplished only through *other* processes for which we now have no accepted explanation or theory. To put it simply, we do not yet know *how* we do useful work. When we discover an explanation or theory—and this book is an attempt to suggest how we might begin—we will apply the same organizational principles to all social structures, from families to corporations to nation-states. All distinctions between public and private, national

and international will be erased as we learn that democracy cannot exist anywhere unless it exists everywhere—though in ways we cannot yet completely understand, predict in detail, or design. The reader must be willing to assume that an intellectual leap is at least possible, and that a revised view of the world might conform more closely both to how useful things *are* done and how they *should be* done. The change we seek is, first and foremost, *a different way of seeing things as they are today.* Much of the organizational revolution is invisible because we cannot see it within the intellectual frameworks we use. Thus, change must begin in a way we usually do not think of as change, because everything remains the same except the way we look at it. Later change will follow, of course, but only after this first step. As a starting point for understanding the nature of the intellectual leap, the world of organizations provides two research and operational approaches which seldom are directly compared. . . .

Hierarchical Span of Control Versus the Small Group

In formal organizations, no principle of management remains more significant than "span of control," i.e., the number of subordinates one supervisor can effectively manage. The superior-subordinate relationship is vertical. The superior must evaluate subordinates, moreover, on a periodic basis (often through the use of "efficiency reports"), a system which gives the superior massive leverage, in that his evaluations of subordinates determine who is promoted and who is fired. The precise ratio of subordinates to superiors has never been scientifically determined, but management literature recommends spans of control between three and nine subordinates in most environments, four being considered most desirable. At lower levels of routinized work, spans of control can expand, so it is thought, to about thirty.

Turn quickly now to different research, based upon small-group processes which do not include superior-subordinate relationships. The small group is conventionally defined as one in which each member must receive an impression or perception of each other member that is distinct enough to enable the member to react or give some opinion of each of the others—and to recall later one or more impressions of each of the others. Research into the processes of "action-taking groups" (where decisions are made), subcommittees in legislative bodies which do the toughest detailed work (both in Western and non-Western cultures), experiments with various-sized groups of youngsters, and the observations, of, for example, sociologist Georg Simmel and bureaucratic commentator C. Northcote Parkinson all reach the same conclusion: *the size of effective small groups is precisely the same as that prescribed for vertical spans of control.* It is possible to be almost mystical about the problem of "numbers," in that some of our current organizational problems may be traceable to the shift from "hunting" to "agricultural" societies many centuries ago, and our social hierarchies seem to date from that shift. When people hunted together in bands, their languages seldom had words for numbers over five, which is still the most desirable size for an effective small group. While common sense would seem to dictate that there can be no "magic" number, five appears so often in so many environmental situations as to carry persuasion with it.

These results come from research shaped by two theories which, by definition, determine the researchers' interpretations of those results. Only the theories and the interpretations differ, *not the results themselves.* Which theory conforms to organizational reality? Do groups produce effective outcomes because one individual is armed with authority to direct the work of four subordinates, or because five individuals interact in a nonhierarchical process in which no individual is "boss" of the others? Even two "classical" theorists of administration, Chester Barnard and Lyndall Urwick, were reluctant to use the vertical pattern to describe their experiences. Barnard acknowledged hierarchy on grounds that it was forced upon organizations from without, thus implying it was unnatural, and Urwick surrounded his views on spans of control with explicit caveats which interpreters often overlook. Both seem to have distorted their observations to make them fit conventional wisdom.

Is it possible that the effective conduct of social business occurs *in spite of* hierarchy, not because of it? This should not be too startling a question. Theorists have admitted for years that a principal objective of any permanent organization is its own survival—a finding which holds for corporations, nation-states, and public agencies. Many organizations, in other words, spend their time exacerbating the problems they supposedly want to solve. This is why welfare agencies behave in ways which perpetuate poverty instead of removing it, and why the Federal Bureau of Investigation pours money and people into the Communist party. To ensure survival ("boundary maintenance" in the jargon of administration, "security" in that of the nation-state), hierarchical leaders direct a competitive struggle for resources (corporations for markets, universities and public agencies for funds, armies for territory). This requires that organizational members be kept under strict discipline, through the dispensing of rewards and punishments. This is why organizations use the military stereotype for selecting leaders, searching for "decisive," "hard-nosed," "tough-minded" executives who can "ruthlessly" cut away "deadwood" in the name of effectiveness. Organizations select those who excel at repressing others, place them in positions they cannot handle because reality does not correspond to the theory, and thus operationalize the "Peter Principle." The error lies not in those who select leaders, nor in the leaders themselves, but in the conventional wisdom that both use. The vertical theory, then, explains only how we create problems; in solving them, we use another theory, yet to be articulated in detail, that has the effect of eliminating the typical formal organization as an agent of social purpose. . . .

The "Withering Away" of Organizations

"Withering away" may be a frightening phrase, but no other will quite do. A reanalysis of past trends and an assessment of current ones make it possible to view all effective social interaction through horizontal, rather than vertical, lenses. Conventional organization theory concentrates on the permanent formal organization. But we have entered an era of interdependence in which autonomous organizations, including nation-states, can do little of importance alone, unless one considers the disciplining of employees an achievement. Everything useful is done in cooperation with other organizations and individuals, and in most cases these broader relationships cannot be twisted into superior-subordinate patterns....

That we do not have thousands of documented examples is due to the conventional organizational assumption that the only important actions are those of authoritative decision-makers. We condemn committees as the worst form of organization, failing to note that in so doing we imply that individuals should act only in total isolation from one another—never, never together. Yet just the opposite is true: nothing of any significance can be, or should be, done alone. Committees were one of the first responses to the need to bring people together in groups. They deserve an honored place in the history of organizations, even if we have done our best to ensure they do not work....

A [committee process which crosses organizational boundaries] is likely to be effective only when the committee chairman's role is one of facilitation—*not* one of personal responsibility for, and authority over, outcomes. This suggests a law for such processes, which turns conventional wisdom inside out: *The effectiveness of group processes is inversely proportional to the amount of formal decision authority assigned to chairmen; the less the authority assigned an individual chairman, the more likely an effective outcome.* This does not imply that chairmen cannot be or should not be responsible for outcomes; they can be, indeed, and they should be, but the same can be said for all other members. The individualistic perspective thus gives way to a collective one which assumes that each individual makes, or can make, a unique contribution to the small-group outcome.... [T]here are and can be no exceptions to this law—not for presidents, governors, generals, or university presidents. Achieving effective outcomes requires *collective responsibility,* and further requires that we pay attention to the number of individuals involved in each group—something for which the literature on span of control and small groups provides broad guidelines. If a problem requires the involvement of many individuals from many organizations, we must create enough groups to keep each one small enough to be effective. Groups can then be linked together through overlapping memberships. The skills required of chairmen, of those holding overlapping memberships, and indeed of all members are not the skills of giving and carrying out orders....

Citizen Participation and the "Charrette"

Participation disorients many of the elite managers who dominate organizational systems. It means they must face demands from lower-class citizens whose capabilities they have denigrated for years. When this occurs, the elites argue that involvement is dangerous because the outsiders are not well enough educated to deal with the expert professionals who make day-to-day decisions. For other elites who face demands from affluent suburbanites and sophisticated college students, the same arguments do not apply. In these cases, the elites insist that they are the only ones with legal authority to make decisions. Both arguments make them uncomfortable. Either they must stress their own inherent superiority or tell citizens that what happens to them or their children is none of their business, even if those citizens are, by conventional wisdom's own standards, as qualified as the professionals. Having no consistent argument to advance, the elites feel trapped within a theory from which they see no escape. Meanwhile, the trend toward involvement has advanced far beyond the "maximum feasible participation" of the 1960's, which turned into an old-fashioned power struggle; those in authority defined participation as something that would destroy them, and those on the outside did indeed seek control. Only after intense discomfort on all sides has it become clear that the issue is not a *transfer* of authority but a *sharing* of it. This shift has not been a noisy one, but it is revolutionary, and it is happening in countless organizations. Here is one black principal's description of how he manages an elementary school:

> ...The secret...is not to get upset about the power struggle. The old-line principals are fighting like mad because the parents want some power. You see, I don't care, quite frankly. I really don't.... There are certain decisions that have to be made. I can share the decision-making process with all the people who want power. I would do it anyway. I want to know what the parents feel. I feel it's essential that teachers tell me how they feel.... The PTA president recently came in and told me she had just hired someone. I said, "Fine, who did you hire?" Well, the thing is she can't hire anybody. But she had somebody she wanted me to hire, and it was a good person ...an aide...and we needed one. The old-line principals would have got uptight and started a long discussion about how you can't hire her, how dare you, and all of this kind of thing. But the new-style principal has to share all this power.... You have all these various elements to deal with, and you have to get them to cooperate with one another, and you have to share power with them. Everyone is jealous of what everyone else is doing, and you've got to move and circulate and get the whole thing working. If you're going to be uptight about power, then you're going to be in trouble....

The "charrette" is the best example we have yet. A word used to describe horse-drawn carts which carried prisoners to the guillotine, and also the carts used later to gather up the plans the Beaux Arts architectural students submitted for the annual Paris competition, "charrette" has acquired a new meaning for school and other forms of community planning. In contemporary settings, the charrette is a process vehicle (without wheels), systematically constructed to collect and sort out as many ideas as possible generated by individuals directly interested in a given project....

The only known way to begin is to assemble in one place, say a large auditorium or arena, people whose perspectives encompass the major conflicts within a community. These may include ghetto residents, policemen and police chiefs, elected and appointed public officials, professional civil servants, affluent suburbanites, businessmen, and others. All they have in common when they begin is a temporary agreement that there is a problem to be solved, that they want to explore it, and that they will bring in professional process-facilitators. If the process survives an initial period of intense hostility, subcommittees are formed, consultants are attached to each one, and interaction is continued. Each group is structured to include persons whose interests are diametrically opposed. Periodic progress is reported to the entire body, or to the steering committee, so that conflicts between subcommittees can be worked out. Individuals move back and forth between groups until they find the one of greatest concern to them, or until they decide to leave....

Regrettably, even those who shout the loudest in praise of charrettes assume that such processes are, and must remain, temporary undertakings. Once an agreed plan is developed, the assumption is that the charrette should be disbanded and the "official" government should get on with implementation. In Toronto, where the city's director of education has predicted that "never again will the Board of Education build a neighbourhood school without the active involvement and participation of the neighbourhood residents," there is no evidence that charrette supporters see the process as a quasi-official addition to the formal structure of government. Yet it seems obvious that no plan ever can be implemented precisely as written, and that changes in a plan should be "fed back" and worked out with those who developed it in the first place. Therefore the charrette which is abandoned at this early stage can become only another temporarily satisfying "experience" which, over time, leads to long-term disillusion. Once again, the problem is in the way we look at things. If we can visualize a charrette sound enough and strong enough to develop a workable plan, we ought to be able to regard it as an ongoing process which sees things through. To get to that point, however, we will first have to examine our theories of political government....

We commonly assume that participative processes would add substantially to the cost of government, if only because of the extra time required. But it can be argued that before long all of us will recognize that participative decisions can be uniquely "cost effective"—to use a favorite phrase of recent years. One of the major problems in the United States is that a great many decisions are made solely to overcome the unintended consequences of earlier decisions; i.e., only when an attempt is made to implement certain decisions is it discovered that something prevents their being implemented, something the decision-makers did not know when they decided what to do. Most of the time, the unintended consequences affect individuals and groups who were not consulted before decisions were made. There could be no better way of discovering as many such problems as possible than to include in decision processes those individuals most likely to be affected by them. Although this would slow down the processes, it would produce more effective decisions which, because hidden consequences had been discovered in advance, would become cost-effective through *cost avoidance*....

To suggest that citizenship itself consists, or should consist, of an individual's involvement in decision processes—and to add that the governance of organizations is best visualized as a series of group processes in which no individual is identified as "in charge" of any process—is to begin to come to grips with the enormity of the intellectual obstacles which inhibit the full flowering of the organizational revolution. People everywhere are trying to make organizations more attractive to those who work in them, to remove the alienation which affects all of us, and to behave in more humane fashion toward each other. That they have yet to succeed is because none of us completely understands how much change is needed in the way we look at things. The unfortunate probability is that the fundamental causes of our alienation from our work and from each other are deeply imbedded in our

theories of political government and economic activity....

There will be plenty to do in the future for those we now term leaders, but not the traditional function of issuing orders. They will feel disoriented and threatened for a time, until it is clear to them that this revolution seeks not merely to overthrow them in favor of other elites, but to transform *relationships* between individuals and groups so that none dominates others. This revolution cannot be understood as a threat, only as an opportunity. The first step toward a livable future is to understand how our conventional theories of politics and economics stand in the way of attaining it.

Notes and Questions

1. How do you think the military model of hierarchical organization came to dominate people's ideas about social structure?

2. A common rationale for hierarchy is that this is the only way to organize large groups of people. But might not the opposite be true: the more people there are, the *less likely* it is that they can all be organized into a single chain of command?

3. What are the implications for schools and education if our society moves away from vertical structures and toward horizontal organization?

4. Can you identify daily-life events and attitudes that reflect a belief in hierarchy and competition? What about attitudes that reflect a belief in cooperation?

5. What is the significance of the fact that Thayer's own work background includes years of experience in high levels of the government/military establishment?

6. As you contemplate the ideas of Frederick Thayer, read the following remarks by Frederick Engels on the true meaning of competition and community:

   The truth of the relationship of competition is the relationship of the power of consumption to the power of production. In a world worthy of mankind there will be no other competition than this. The community will have to calculate what it can produce with the means at its disposal; and in the light of the relationship of this productive power to the mass of consumers it will determine how far it has to raise or lower production, how far it has to give way to, or curtail, luxury.*

7. The following excerpts from *Don't Push the River,* by Barry Stevens, are also relevant to an understanding of vertical and horizontal social structures:

> The cross-cultural conference was run (by not running it) in what Wilfred calls the "horizontal" way. It seems to me, as I watch it, that vertical organization is resorted to as a result of a depletion or absence of communication. If you can't somehow or other have a community movement which is a spontaneous sort of urge which results in something coming about, then the only alternative you have is to build some kind of pyramid and put the toughest guy at the top, or maybe you don't put him there, he just automatically gets there. You have an organization within which there is no communication, there is simply a passing down of orders from the top to the various levels and this is no longer society—this is a machine.
>
> Horizontal organization, as I have experienced it with Hawaiians (years ago—I don't know about now), is like what Wilfred describes as the Indian way. A person arises as a leader for a particular thing at a particular time—and moves back whenever that time is over. Communication is present. I have experienced this among white folks too, in occasional places. Trust is present, too. Here at Lake Cowichan we were working toward horizontal organization. As soon as something got out of hand a little, some people were pushing for the vertical way. But we got it back to horizontal. Now, in Fritz' absence, it has become vertical. Organization. Intel-lectual organization instead of organismic organization. The white man doesn't realize that his burden is the one he puts on his own back. Then he educates everyone and they put it on their backs, too.
>
> The kitchen seems to run now with horizontal organization, for the first time. With vertical organization, everyone who wasn't working in the kitchen had to stay out. With horizontal organization, we can drift in and have tea or coffee and enjoy ourselves and each other, and get better acquainted....
>
> We're killing the Indians. America needs Indians. We're killing ourselves. Indians think we need them too. "Indian" is not skin-color. It is a way of living which does not lead to Vietnam.
>
> "Indian" is a Navajo woman who told me that when she was in school, the white woman physical education instructor taught her how to cheat, how to stumble so that it would throw off another player and seem to be an accident, how to *win.* "And now," she said, "I have to work so *hard* to get that out of me."
>
> "Some of us here are working so hard at that too. Some others of us are just now discovering the games we play, and that what we're out for is to win. Even husbands and wives and parents and children and children and parents and children and children.
>
> "At the cross-cultural conference in Saskatchewan, a white man suggested that a way to help the Indians would be to educate them about our legal system and procedures. Indians, everyone agreed, are disadvantaged with our police and in our courts because they tell the truth.
>
> "Who should switch, the Indians or us? Which world would you prefer to live in?" *

---

* Frederick Engels, "Outlines of a Critique of Political Economy," in *The Economic and Philosophical Manuscripts of 1844* (New York: International Publishers, 1964), p. 216.

* From *Don't Push the River* by Barry Stevens © 1970 Real People Press.

The Plague   *Albert Camus*

"To make things simpler, Rieux, let me begin by saying I had plague already, long before I came to this town and encountered it here. Which is tantamount to saying I'm like everybody else. Only there are some people who don't know it, or feel at ease in that condition; others know and want to get out of it. Personally, I've always wanted to get out of it.

"When I was young I lived with the idea of my innocence; that is to say, with no idea at all. I'm not the self-tormenting kind of person, and I made a suitable start in life. I brought off everything I set my hand to, I moved at ease in the field of the intellect, I got on excellently with women, and if I had occasional qualms, they passed as lightly as they came. Then one day I started thinking. And now— . . .

"When I was seventeen my father asked me to come to hear him speak in court. There was a big case on at the assizes, and probably he thought I'd see him to his best advantage. Also I suspect he hoped I'd be duly impressed by the pomp and ceremony of the law and encouraged to take up his profession. I could tell he was keen on my going, and the prospect of seeing a side of my father's character so different from that we saw at home appealed to me. Those were absolutely the only reasons I had for going to the trial. What happened in a court had always seemed to me as natural, as much in the order of things, as a military parade on the Fourteenth of July or a school speech day. My notions on the subject were purely abstract, and I'd never given it serious thought.

"The only picture I carried away with me of that day's proceedings was a picture of the criminal. I have little doubt he was guilty—of what crime is no great matter. That little man of about

thirty, with sparse, sandy hair, seemed so eager to confess everything, so genuinely horrified at what he'd done and what was going to be done with him, that after a few minutes I had eyes for nothing and nobody else. He looked like a yellow owl scared blind by too much light. His tie was slightly awry, he kept biting his nails, those of one hand only, his right. . . . I needn't go on, need I? You've understood—he was a living human being.

"As for me, it came on me suddenly, in a flash of understanding; until then I'd thought of him only under his commonplace official designation, as 'the defendant.' And though I can't say I quite forgot my father, something seem to grip my vitals at that moment and riveted all my attention on the little man in the dock. I hardly heard what was being said; I only knew that they were set on killing that living man, and an uprush of some elemental instinct, like a wave, had swept me to his side. And I did not really wake up until my father rose to address the court.

"In his red gown he was another man, no longer genial or good-natured; his mouth spewed out long, turgid phrases like an endless stream of snakes. I realized he was clamoring for the prisoner's death, telling the jury that they owed it to society to find him guilty; he went so far as to demand that the man should have his head cut off. Not exactly in those words, I admit. 'He must pay the supreme penalty,' was the formula. But the difference, really, was slight, and the result the same. He had the head he asked for. Only of course it wasn't he who did the actual job. I, who saw the whole business through to its conclusion, felt a far closer, far more terrifying intimacy with that wretched man than my father can ever have felt. Nevertheless, it fell to him, in the course of his duties, to be present at what's politely termed the prisoner's last moments, but what would be better called murder in its most despicable form.

"From that day on . . . I took a horrified interest in legal proceedings, death sentences, executions, and I realized with dismay that my father must have often witnessed those brutal murders—on the days when, as I'd noticed without guessing what it meant, he rose very early in the morning. I remembered he used to wind his alarm-clock on those occasions, to make sure. . . .

"I came to grips with poverty when I was eighteen, after an easy life till then. I tried all sorts of jobs, and I didn't do too badly. But my real interest in life was the death penalty; I wanted to square accounts with that poor blind owl in the dock. So I became an agitator, as they say. I didn't want to be pestiferous, that's all. To my mind the social order around me was based on the death sentence, and by fighting the established order I'd be fighting against murder. That was my view, others had told me so, and I still think that this belief of mine was substantially true. I joined forces with a group of people I then liked, and indeed have never ceased to like. I spent many years in close co-operation with them, and there's not a country in Europe in whose struggles I haven't played a part. But that's another story.

"Needless to say, I knew that we, too, on occasion, passed sentences of death. But I was told that these few deaths were inevitable for the building up of a new world in which murder would cease to be. That also was true up to a point—and maybe I'm not capable of standing fast where that order of truths is concerned. Whatever the explanation, I hesitated. But then I remembered that miserable owl in the dock and it enabled me to keep on. Until the day when I was present at an execution—it was in Hungary—and exactly the same dazed horror that I'd experienced as a youngster made everything reel before my eyes.

"Have you ever seen a man shot by a firing-squad? No, of course not; the spectators are hand-picked and it's like a private party, you need an invitation. The result is that you've gleaned your ideas about it from books and pictures. A post, a blindfolded man, some soldiers in the offing. But the real thing isn't a bit like that. Do you know that the firing-squad stands only a yard and a half from the condemned man? Do you know that if the victim took two steps forward his chest would touch the rifles? Do you know that, at this short range, the soldiers concentrate their fire on the region of the heart and their big bullets make a hole into which you could thrust your fist? No, you didn't know all that; those are things that are never spoken of. For the plague-stricken their peace of mind is more important than a human life. Decent folks must be allowed to sleep easy o' nights, mustn't they? Really it would be shockingly bad taste to linger on such details, that's common knowledge. But personally I've never been able to sleep well since then. The bad taste remained in my mouth and I've kept lingering on the details, brooding over them.

"And thus I came to understand that I, anyhow, had had plague through all those long years in which, paradoxically enough, I'd believed with all my soul that I was fighting it. I learned that I had had an indirect hand in the deaths of thousands of people; that I'd even brought about their deaths by approving of acts and principles which could only end that way. Others did not seem embarrassed by such thoughts, or anyhow never voiced them of their own accord. But I was different; what I'd come to know stuck in my gorge. I was with them and yet I was alone. When I spoke of these matters they told me not to be so squeamish; I should remember what great issues were at stake. And they advanced arguments, often quite impressive ones, to make me swallow what none the less I couldn't bring myself to stomach. I replied that the most eminent of the plague-stricken, the men who wear red robes, also have excellent arguments to justify what they do, and once I admitted the arguments of necessity and *force majeure* put forward by the less eminent, I couldn't reject those of the eminent. To which they retorted that the surest way of playing the game of the red robes was to leave to them the monopoly of the death penalty. My reply to this was that if you gave in once, there was no reason for not continuing to give in. It seems to me that history has borne me out; today there's a sort of competition who will kill the most. They're all mad over murder and they couldn't stop killing men even if they wanted to.

"In any case, my concern was not with arguments. It was with the poor owl; with that foul procedure whereby dirty mouths stinking of plague told a fettered man that he was going to die, and scientifically arranged things so that he should die, after nights and nights of mental torture while he waited to be murdered in cold blood. My concern was with that hole in a man's chest. And I told myself that meanwhile, so far anyhow as I was concerned, nothing in the world would induce me to accept any argument that justified such butcheries. Yes, I chose to be blindly obstinate, pending the day when I could see my way more clearly.

"I'm still of the same mind. For many years I've been ashamed, mortally ashamed, of having been, even with the best intentions, even at many removes, a murderer in my turn. As time went on I merely learned that even those who were better than the rest could not keep themselves nowadays from killing or letting others kill, because such is the logic by which they live; and that we can't stir a finger in this world without the risk of bringing death to somebody. . . .

"Yes, Rieux, it's a wearying business, being plague-stricken. But it's still more wearying to refuse to be it. That's why everybody in the world today looks so tired; everyone is more or less sick of plague. But that is also why some of us, those who want to get the plague out of their systems, feel such desperate weariness, a weariness from which nothing remains to set us free except death.

"Pending that release, I know I have no place in the world of today; once I'd definitely refused to kill, I doomed myself to an exile that can never end. I leave it to others to make history. I know, too, that I'm not qualified to pass judgment on those others. There's something lacking in my mental make-up, and its lack prevents me from being a rational murderer. So it's a deficiency, not a superiority. But as things are, I'm willing to be as I am; I've learned modesty. All

I maintain is that on this earth there are pestilences and there are victims, and it's up to us, so far as possible, not to join forces with the pestilences. That may sound simple to the point of childishness; I can't judge if it's simple, but I know it's true. You see, I'd heard such quantities of arguments, which very nearly turned my head, and turned other people's heads enough to make them approve of murder; and I'd come to realize that all our troubles spring from our failure to use plain, clean-cut language. So I resolved always to speak—and to act—quite clearly, as this was the only way of setting myself on the right track. That's why I say there are pestilences and there are victims; no more than that. If, by making that statement, I, too, become a carrier of the plague-germ, at least I don't do it willfully. I try, in short, to be an innocent murderer. You see, I've no great ambitions.

"I grant we should add a third category: that of the true healers. But it's a fact one doesn't come across many of them, and anyhow it must be a hard vocation. That's why I decided to take, in every predicament, the victims' side, so as to reduce the damage done. Among them I can at least try to discover how one attains to the third category; in other words, to peace."

Questions

1. What does Camus mean when he says that "the social order around me was based on the death sentence"?

2. What does he mean by the "plague"?

3. Do you think that Camus's experience in court could be understood as seeing through the masks of the law? (Recall John Noonan's article in section one.)

4. Why does Camus regard his refusal to kill as "a deficiency, not a superiority"?

5. What might Camus's response be to these lines from John Lennon's song, "Working Class Hero": "There's room at the top they are telling you still/But first you must learn how to smile as you kill"?

This cartoon and editorial note appeared on the cover of *Akwesasne Notes*, Vol. 6, No. 2, late spring, 1974. *Akwesasne Notes* is the official publication of the Mohawk Nation at Akwesasne and is an international journal for issues and events relating to native peoples.

WHO EATS
OUR LAND?
at
Black Mesa
Tesuque
James Bay
Bear Butte
Lame Deer
Alaska
    Pipeline
Havasupai

MEMO TO OUR
LAYOUT ARTIST
BELOW—

People: I don't think we should use this cover.↑ While it is fashionable to blame large corporations for consuming Indian land and water, and while it's true they do, we fail to realize that the European/American life-style itself is the ultimate consumer — the corporations are the harvesters. People can look at the cover, sitting in comfortable suburbs, and say "Evil Corporate Power Structure" but continue to be outraged if there is a gas shortage or if there isn't enough water for their lawns. Indians, too, need to understand that by adopting European life-styles, they place themselves at the mercy of the very corporations they condemn.

Why not show the American consumer's addiction by showing land, trees, earth, rivers, connected to a hypodermic syringe, labelled "more and more", being administered to a consumer junkie by a corporate pusher.

— Rarihokwats

Questions

1. Do the concepts "consumer junkie" and "corporate pusher" have meaning beyond the context of the struggle for Indian land?

2. Why is land important to people?

3. Why is land important to corporations?

4. Do you agree with editor Rarihokwats that the suburban American way of life is inevitably dominated by the "corporate power structure"?

5. What is the role of law in the struggle for control over land? (Recall the cases in Chapter One, Section 3.)

6. Which seems to you more basic in determining the nature of a society: the laws or the land?

Epilogue: Praxis

Once an oppressed people understand the nature of their oppression, they are in a position to begin changing the circumstances that give rise to and perpetuate their condition. This task is very difficult because it involves seeing the world in new ways, ways that require people to see themselves differently also.

When the peasants overthrow the king, they have not only changed the world, they have changed themselves. They are no longer peasants because there is no longer a king. What is their new world to be? Who are they now? The former peasants have the opportunity to construct a new order of life. This order can be as different from the old as their ideas and the environment will allow. If their minds are bound up with a vision of life under the monarchy, their new world will not look very different from the old. The first official U.S. Senate chamber resembles nothing so much as a throne room. Many of our contemporary institutions look remarkably like feudal structures, despite the years of political turmoil which have transpired since the middle ages of Western civilization. The Puritans, seeking a just society and fleeing religious persecution, proceeded to try to destroy the tribal, communal societies of the indigenous peoples of America, and built a rigid, hierarchical society of their own in the "new world." Similar examples may be found in the histories of other nations around the world. Again and again, people in revolution confront the problem of understanding who they are and who they might become.

Perhaps you can imagine the nature of such thinking and struggle for identity if you contemplate your own personal history. How did you answer when you were small and someone asked what you were going to be when you grew up? What was your vision of the world then? How did you see yourself? How is that world now? Does it still exist? Do you see it the same way? How did the changes come about? And what about now: Who are you, and why are you studying about law? What can you do in the world as it is? Your answers to these questions must always take into account that as the world is changing so, simultaneously, are you changing. The problem becomes how to recognize what is really going on, what is real change and what is superficial, what will endure and what will not. And in the midst of all this, what are you going to do today?

Karl Marx once dealt with this problem of simultaneous personal and social change. He wrote that "the coincidence of the changing of circumstances and of human activity or self-changing can only be understood as revolutionary practice." While people often assume that revolution means war, in which one "permanent" social structure is changed into a new "permanent" structure, this view actually ignores the continuous nature of social change and misses the relationship between revolutionary and ordinary change.

It is extremely difficult for people to find stable reference points to hold their lives together during the most crucial moments of this ongoing movement of social and personal change. And because of this difficulty, people will put up with oppression and the stress of injustice for long periods of time before finally coming to any action for change. As the American Declaration of Independence says: "... all experience hath shewn, that mankind are more disposed to suffer, while evils are sufferable, than to right themselves by abolishing the forms to which they are accustomed."

Oppression is measured by the lack of power people have over their lives, by the lack of clarity they have about who they are and what their place is in the world. It is not necessary to be poor to be oppressed. Many Americans who are materially well-off are nevertheless anxious, unhappy, empty of respect for themselves and others, and unable to grasp any meaning to their lives. This is oppression in its most basic sense, as it affects the spirit of a people.

In some ways it is easier for a poor person to acknowledge the existence of oppression, for there is no doubt about the lack of power. But the more subtle and manipulative the social structure is, the more likely it is that this lack of power over one's life can be masked behind an accumulation of material possessions. Tribal societies frequently looked down upon people who attempted to accumulate private wealth. This was regarded as antisocial, as taking away from the community. It would seem that when there is no real community, when the communal impulses have been suppressed from the network of social relations, that then comes the time for accumulation without end. Accumulation to mask the lack of wholeness.

The first step to understanding society today is to understand the meaning of oppression, and to see that it is not measured primarily in material terms. This is the vantage point from which one may then begin to survey the world and see what needs to be changed. From this vantage point one sees that both the guard and the prisoner are oppressed by a system of law that is built to preserve the prerogatives of private property. One sees that both the judge and the defendant are oppressed by a system of decision making that elevates rules over people. In these relationships, all parties suffer the oppression of being false to themselves, of living false lives. Indeed, it might be said that the guard suffers in this way more than the prisoner, and the judge more than the defendant. For it is the master who is truly living the false life. It is the master who lives off the energies of the slave, and who therefore is most removed from a sense of completeness and peace in the world. Perhaps peace is not so highly regarded by the master. But is it not the masters who envy the spirit of the slaves? Is it not the judge and the guard who are angered most by any show of independence from the prisoners?

Understanding law in context ultimately means understanding ourselves. We must acquire a sense of who we are and what our relations are to others. The kin and community structures which once might have provided a firm basis for this understanding have long been fragmented in Western society. The corporate and governmental structures which have been put in the place of kin and community do not provide the same kind of basis for a sense of identity and power over one's life.

Whether our existing organizations can be sufficiently re-arranged to end oppression, whether certain features may be valuable and others not—these and other questions cannot be answered in advance. What can be said at this point is that the process of social movement goes on whether everyone is aware of it or not. The advantage of awareness is that it allows people to take a conscious part in shaping society. This participation determines the nature of the society that is built in and from our lives.

Suggested Additional Readings

Bankowski, Zenon and Mungham, Geoff. *Images of Law.* London: Routledge & Kegan Paul, 1976.

Brown, Dee. *Bury My Heart at Wounded Knee.* New York: Bantam, 1970.

Cooper, David. *The Death of the Family.* New York: Random House, 1971.

DeLoria, Vine, Jr. *Custer Died for Your Sins.* New York: Avon, 1969.

Douglass, James W. *Resistance and Contemplation.* New York: Dell, 1972.

Engels, Frederick. *The Origin of the Family, Private Property, and the State.* New York: International Publishers, 1973.

Friere, Paulo. *Pedagogy of the Oppressed.* New York: Seabury Press, 1973.

Hindess, Barry and Hirst, Paul Q. *Pre-Capitalist Modes of Production.* London: Routledge & Kegan Paul, 1975.

Horwitz, Morton J. *The Transformation of American Law, 1780–1860.* Cambridge: Harvard University Press, 1977.

Kosinski, Jerzy. *Being There.* New York: Bantam, 1970.

Malcolm X and Haley, Alex. *The Autobiography of Malcolm X.* New York: Grove Press, 1965.

Pirsig, Robert. *Zen and the Art of Motorcycle Maintenance.* New York: Bantam, 1973.

Quinney, Richard. *Critique of Legal Order.* Boston: Little, Brown, 1974.

Reich, Wilhelm. *The Mass Psychology of Fascism.* New York: Farrar, Straus & Giroux, 1970.

Rowbotham, Sheila. *Woman's Consciousness, Man's World.* New York: Penguin, 1973.

Schulman, Alix Kates, ed. *Red Emma Speaks.* New York: Random House, 1972.

Shklar, Judith. *Legalism.* Cambridge: Harvard University Press, 1964.

Smedley, Agnes. *Daughter of Earth.* Old Westbury, N.Y.: The Feminist Press, 1973.

Terzani, Tiziano. *Giai Phong! The Fall and Liberation of Saigon.* New York: St. Martins' Press, 1976.

Unger, Roberto. *Knowledge and Politics.* New York: Free Press, 1975.

Waters, Frank. *The Man Who Killed the Deer.* Chicago: Swallow, 1942.

Zaretsky, Eli. *Capitalism, the Family, and Personal Life.* New York: Harper & Row, 1976.

INDEX